# YORK COUNTY, SOUTH CAROLINA

# WILL ABSTRACTS

## 1787–1862
## [1770–1862]

*Abstracted by*

Brent H. Holcomb

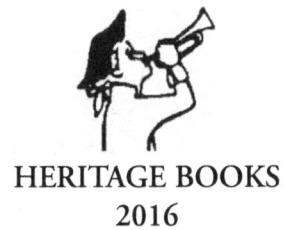

HERITAGE BOOKS
2016

# HERITAGE BOOKS
*AN IMPRINT OF HERITAGE BOOKS, INC.*

**Books, CDs, and more—Worldwide**

For our listing of thousands of titles see our website
at
www.HeritageBooks.com

Published 2016 by
HERITAGE BOOKS, INC.
Publishing Division
5810 Ruatan Street
Berwyn Heights, Md. 20740

Copyright © 2002 Brent H. Holcomb

All rights reserved. No part of this book may be reproduced or transmitted in any form or by any means, electronic or mechanical, including photocopying, recording or by any information storage and retrieval system without written permission from the author, except for the inclusion of brief quotations in a review.

International Standard Book Numbers
Paperbound: 978-0-7884-5733-3
Clothbound: 978-0-7884-5950-4

# INTRODUCTION

York County was formed in 1785 as a county of Camden District. It remained in Camden District for higher court cases until the year 1791, when it became a part of Pinckney District for such purposes. York County was under the Camden District Court of Ordinary 1781-1787. York obtained its own court of ordinary (or probate court) in 1787. In the year 1800 with the end of the county court system, York County became York District. The term county was resumed in 1868. A small corner of York County was taken, with parts of Union and Spartanburg counties, to form Cherokee County in 1897.

In the colonial period the area of York County was considered part of Craven County in South Carolina. Prior to the border surveys of 1764 and 1772, the area was included in the North Carolina counties of Anson, Mecklenburg, and Tryon. In fact, when the border survey was completed in 1772, the Tryon County Court House was found to be in South Carolina, in present-day York County. Therefore, earlier probate records, deeds, land grants, and other records for this area may be found in records of these North Carolina counties. In York County Will Book A, pages 176-177, is recorded the will of Elisabeth Lusk of Tryon County dated 7 October 1770 (see page 29). Wills from the above named North Carolina counties have been abstracted and published by Brent H. Holcomb. Because the border survey added territory to South Carolina, this area was known as the "New Acquisition." From 1772 through 1781 wills from this area were recorded, like other South Carolina wills, in Charleston. Wills of the colonial period in South Carolina (Charleston wills) were abstracted and published by Mrs. Caroline T. Moore, which abstract volumes are now available from Brent H. Holcomb. The wills and estates of Camden District have also been published. Therefore, with the publication of this volume, wills for the York County area through 1862 are now available in abstract form. Because of the close proximity of Mecklenburg County, North Carolina, to York County, the excellent publications of abstracts of deeds, wills, court minutes and other records by Herman W. Ferguson (600 Chad Dr., Rocky Mount, NC 27803) are highly recommended for further research.

The wills abstracted in this work are found in the following York County will books: A (1787-1799, LDS microfilm renumbered YK 72 at the South Carolina Archives], Will Book A-1 (1800-1813, South Carolina Archives microfilm C1695), Records Book D (1814-1820, South Carolina Archives microfilm C1690), Will Book or Estates Records Book G (1819-1837, South Carolina Archives microfilm C1691), Estates Records Book 2 (1837-1840, South Carolina Archives microfilm C1694) and Will Book 3 (1840-1862 South Carolina Archives microfilm C1695). When necessary the original wills in the estate packets have been consulted. A few wills which were not recorded in the will books are included on pages 352-359. It is possible that there are other unrecorded wills in the estates packets, available on microfilm at the South Carolina Archives. The abstracts of will books A and A-1 have appeared in issues of the *South Carolina Magazine of Ancestral Research*.

My thanks to Mr. James D. McKain for preparing the excellent indices: the testator index, personal name index, slave index, and the place index.

Brent H. Holcomb
May 1, 2002

1873 MAP COURTESY OF THE SOUTH CAROLINA
DEPARTMENT OF ARCHIVES AND HISTORY

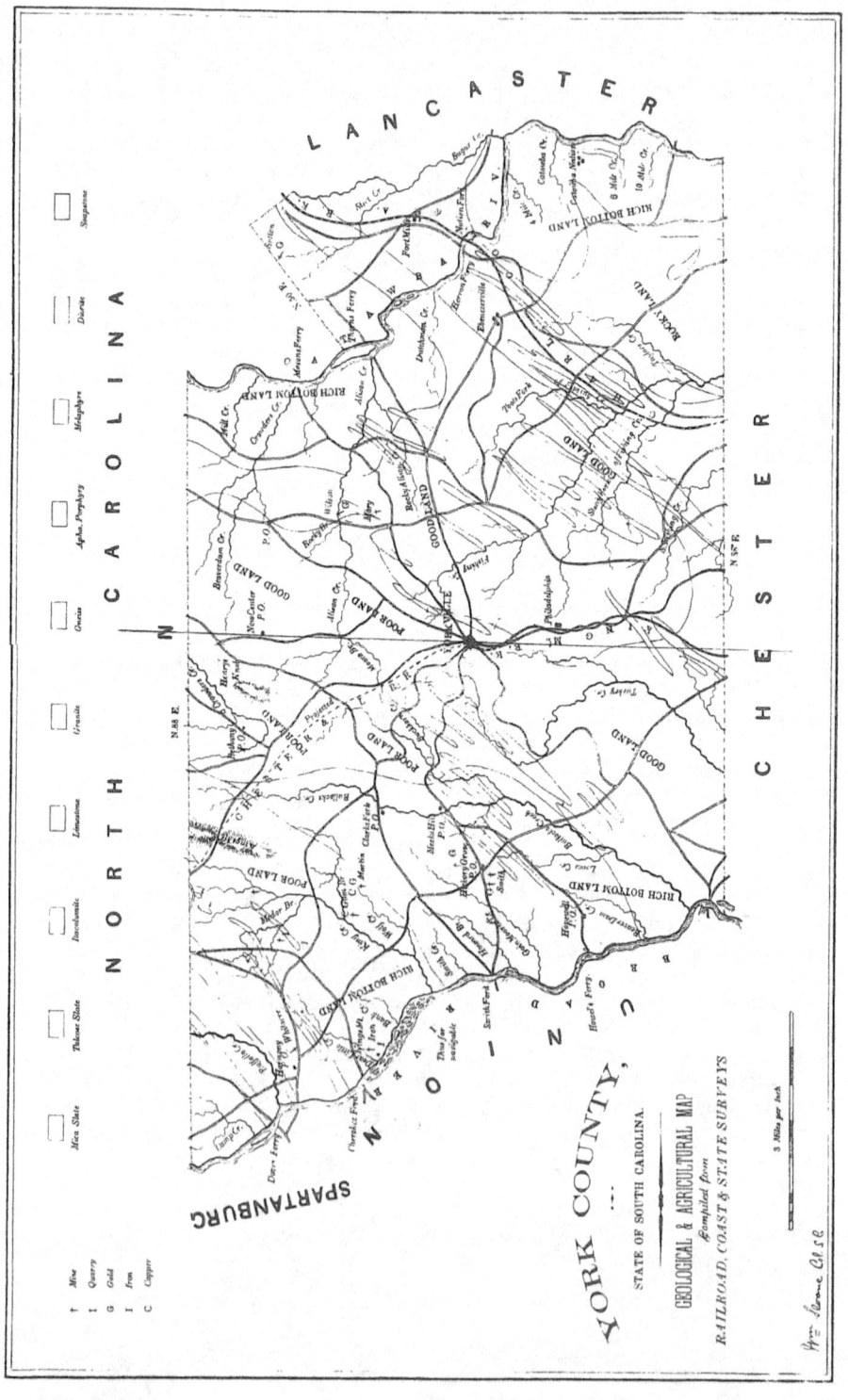

## CONTENTS

| | |
|---|---|
| Will Book A 1787-1799 | 1 |
| Will Book A-1 1800-1813 | 33 |
| Estates Records Book D 1814-1820 | 101 |
| Will Book or Estates Records Book G 1819-1837 | 128 |
| Estates Records Book 2 1837-1840 | 215 |
| Will Book 3 1840-1862 | 230 |
| Testator Index | 360 |
| Personal Name Index | 369 |
| Slave Index | 453 |
| Place Index | 464 |

## YORK COUNTY SC WILL BOOK A 1787-1799

Pages 1-2: Will of Samuel Denton of State of South Carolina and County of York... to my beloved wife Elisabeth of my personal estate after paying all my debts, the one half of the land & the stock of cattle & hoggs & houshold furniture & the stock of horse beasts, excepting the young bay mare and the little Black horse, them Sundry propertys before mentioned to remain in her custody as long as she remain a widow; at her death or if she marry the same half of the land & the profits thereof shall fall to my well beloved son John, and the remaining part of the stock to be equally divided between all my well beloved children, excepting my son Benjamin & my son Joshua them two shall have no part of it, this division before mentioned among my children shall not be before the decease of my wife Elisabeth except she marry. To my beloved son Joshua the remaining half of the land, and the young bay mare got by Joseph Leech's horse. To my well beloved son Benjamin the little black horse which he has in possession. To my son Joshua all my working tools, plows, hoes, axes & other working tools belonging to the plantation. I leave Elisabeth Denton & Joshua Denton, my executors, dated 12 April 1786. Samuel Denton (LS), Wit: Peter Aiken (T), George Hoge, James Riley (W).

Pages 2-4: 14 Feb 1783, Will of John Ash of Camden District in So Carolina... to my son Robert Ash, a negro boy named Dave; to my son William Ash, tract of 210 acres being part of tract called McNabbs tract, also a negro woman named Jill and his choice of either of the s'd negro womans two male children whose names are Micke & Joe, or if he shall choose to keep both the negro children, then he pay to my daughter Isbel Patterson's oldest son John £30 Virginia money, and £50 the same currency to be paid in equal divisions among the remaining number of my s'd daughters then surviving children; to my daughter Mary, a negro woman named Nell with a bond or obligation from William Burris (Charles Porter & Isaac Watson securities) to me for upwards of thirty pounds Pensylvania Currency; to my daughter Isbel, a negro woman named Hannah, and the sums above mentioned be paid by my son William to my said daughter Isbels children as they come to the years of maturity if he shall choose to keep both the negro children; to my daughter Elizabeth a negro girl named Rach, and the sum of £150 SC currency to be paid by my wife Isbel Ash at her decease; to my wife Isbel Ash a negro fellow named Tom, a negro woman named Philles & Negro child named Hannah; after the decease of my wife, my estate to be equally amongst my five children viz Robert, William, Mary, Isbel & Elisabeth Ash. William Ash and wife Isbel Ash, exrs. John Ash (LS). Wit: Samuel Carson & Andrew Carson, D'd Gordon.

Pages 4-6: Will of Richard Leathem of County of York, planter... to my beloved wife Catharine, all my household furniture, her wearing cloathes, my plantation tools, my gray horse, sorrel mare, her saddle & Bridle, three cows & Calves, all my sheep & hoggs, grain, wheat, crop that is in the ground, and the use of the plantation during her widowhood; the remainder of my estate to be sold at publick vendue and after debts are discharged, the remainder to be divided into five parts, three of which parts to be given to Sarah & Ruth, the other two parts to Ann & Purdey, also my lands to be given to Purdey my son; my wife and Robert Leathem, exrs. dated 20 January 1788. Ritchard Leathem (mark). Wit: Thomas Gillham, Moses Leathem, Isaac Gillham.

Pages 6-7: Will of Joseph Waddle of the County of York... to my well beloved wife Lydia, her living off my land I now live on during her remaining a widow, likewise one sorrel mare, one bed & furniture; to my son David half the land I now live on, that is the side next Matthew Biggers, and to be divided between him and my son John, Johns part to begin at the mouth of a branch above the upper field, likewise one sorrel horse, my sons David and John shall now have possession of the land until they come to the age of twenty one years; to my daughters Ann, one young sorrel mare, one bed and furniture; unto the rest of my children viz Lydia, Sarah, Susannah, Margaret & Elizabeth, five shillings apiece for each of them at this present time, but when my sons David & John shall come of age, they shall pay ten pounds to each of the girls. the remaining part of my stock of cattle not here mentioned and all other iron tools, to the discretion of my wife to be disposed towards raising of the children, and my waggon I allow to be sold in order to help school the children;. my wife & friend John Drennan, exrs.. dated 5 November 1787. Joseph Waddle (LS), Wit: John McCall, Matthew Bigger & David Turner.

Pages 8-9: Will of Joseph Bigger of York County dated 22 July 1786... to my beloved wife Sarah Bigger, the one third of my personal estate, and her living on the real estate during her lifetime; the remaining two thirds of my personal estate to be divided amongst my daughters Margaret, Agnes, Sarah, Eleanor except one horse that I will to be given to my son Robert Bigger when he comes to the age of twenty one years. at the discretion of my executors when any of the above mentioned daughters marry than I will that my personal estate be appraised and said daughter to get her equal part; my real estate, viz the land I now live on be equally divided between my two sons Robert and Joseph Bigger, and if they could not agree in the division, then the land to be valued and the one purchase from the other according to the valuation, and if my wife with the rest of my family should at any time that it most to their advantage to sell that land and purchase land in another part of the Country, and my wife and two sons Robert & Joseph have full power to sell and convey such titles; if my sons Robert & Joseph, should die before marriage that their part of the Land or valuation of it be equally divided amongst my surviving daughters mentioned. My wife & James Ramsey, exrs. Joseph Bigger (LS), Wit: John Howe, Joseph McKenzie, John Kincaid.

Pages 9-11: Will of John Dickey of the New Acquisition District, State of South Carolina... to my well beloved wife Martha all my personal estate exclusive of my plantation. utensils, also I allow that my wife shall have the full and whole right of the house I now live in during her widowhood, and I allow that my son David Dickey shall "cut and hole home forewood" and also to Mill for her and bring home her meal from the mill at all times as she stands in need of the like done during her widowhood; it is my will that my wife have the benefit of my spring and spring house during her widowhood, and my son David Dickey shall sow or case to be sowed yearly and every for my wife Martha Dickey half a Bushel of Flax seed and to find sufficient food for two cows and a horse for my said wife; if my son David Dickey does or will live in the house with his mother my wife during her widowhood and will find a sufficient maintenance for her it is well, otherwise if he should be take himself to a house of his own or otherwise to live that he is to pay or cause to be paid from the time of leaving his mother £30 Virginia currency yearly; to my daughter Susannah one crown sterling; to my daughter Jane a crown sterling; to my son John Dickey, a crown sterling; to my son George Dickey a crow sterling; to my son Robert Dickey a crown sterling; to my son David Dickey the plantation I now live on with all my plantation utensils; my son David to pay to each of his two sisters Mary and Martha Dickey five shillings sterling; my son David Dickey shall pay my funeral charges and pay off the rest of the legatees what is willed to them; to my daughter Eleanor a crown sterling; I appoint my sons John Dickey and David Dickey exrs... dated 14 January 1784. Jno Dickey (LS), Wit: Robert Kennedy, William Dickey, James Dickey.

Pages 12-13: Will of Samuel Porter of Camden District, Province of South Carolina, 28 July... to my oldest son Matthew Porter five shillings sterling; to my daughter Agnes the sum of five shillings sterling; to my son David five shillings sterling; to my daughter Violet five shillings sterling; to my son James five shillings sterling; to my son Nathaniel, the plantation or tract of land that I now live on with the improvement; my well beloved wife Sarah shall have the one third of the produce of s'd plantation or tract of land with the one third share or part of any profits arising from s'd plantation during her time of life with all my household furniture at her use to be disposed of her with an equal divided betwixt Ann my daughter and my daughter Ruth; likewise to my wife Sarah, my horse and mare with my horned cattle and hoggs excepting one to my daughter Rebecca, the young horse colt; also to Rebecca ____ lawful money to be paid by my son Nathaniel; Rebecca shall have the use of my horse or mare to ride to sermons and other necessary places. I appoint William Byers, Senior, and David Porter, executors. dated 28 July 1744. Samuel Porter (LS), Wit: William Williamson, William Byers.

Pages 13-14: Will of John McKnight of County of York, Camden District, 20 June 1785... to my beloved wife one bed and furniture, one wheel, her choice of the mares in my stock and saddle, and also unto my son Robert one mare, saddle, and his apparel, and unto my daughter Mary one cow, one bed and furniture, one spinning wheel; to my daughter Sarah one bed and furniture, one cow and shipping wheel; to my daughter Eleanor, one cow, one bed and furniture; to my daughter Isabella one cow; to my daughter Betsy one cow; and further one set of Smith tools to be appraised and the price equally divided to my daughters Mary, Sarah, Eleanor, Isabella and Betsy and my son Robert to share equal part with them; my land the which I live on, being 200 acres, to be equally divided, 10 acres to my wife and other 100 to my son Robert and his heirs, and at the expireation of her widow or natural life (that is to say my bel'd wife) the land to be equally shared to the above daughters and son; 350 acres of land situated on Serats Creek, 96 District to be sold and divided to my beloved wife, my son Robert, daughters Mary, Sarah Eleanor, Isabella and Betsy; the household and kitchen furniture with the plantation tools, hoggs, sheep, and every other moveable to be equally shared or divided as my executors shall in their judgment see convenient to the above mentions daughters and son with my belov'd wife. I appoint my wife and my son Roberts, exrs. John McKnight (LS), Wit: John Blackney, William Fowler, James Fowler.

Pages 15-16: Will of Robert Lattimore of Craven County, South Carolina, farmer... to my son George Lattimore, all that tract of land which I now live on with all the plantation tools in case he lives to have heirs of his own body, and in case of his death, my executors dispose of said property at publick venue and the monies arising from such sale to be equally divided amongst my after named grandsons s'd Robert Love and James Love, Robert Lattimore son of Arthur Lattimore, as much as both the above named Hezekiah and James McKenzie equal to the above named Loves and Arthur & James Kennedy, the same; to my wife Ann Lattimore one bay horse named Diamond, her riding saddle & Bridle, her bed and furniture, and all the household furniture; she to have one third part of all profits arising or produced from my s'd plantation during her natural life for her support. All the remainder to my son George Lattimore, and I appoint my sons-in-law, Joseph McKenzie & Andrew Love in trust for my son and wife and also for my grandson Robert Lattimore, dated 25 October 1784. N. B. I also will to each of my daughters viz Rebecca McKenzie and Ann Love and Nancey Kennedy to each one dollar. Robert Lattimore (LS), Wit: Jo's Howe, Matthew Bigger.

Page 16: Will of Mary Enlow, widow, of County Craven, Province of South Carolina, 28 August 1774.... to my younger daughter Christian Enlow all that I have at my death. Mary Enlow (mark) Wit: David Watson, Dillon Enlow (mark).

Pages 17-19: Will of Jackson Neely, Senr, of the Indian Land and District of Camden, State of South Carolina... to my beloved wife Ann, the third pat of all my moveable estate, her cloathing besides her bed and bed cloaths, a horse and saddle, the benefit of the mansion house with the children during widowhood; to my beloved son Samuel Neely, a part of my land laid out for him in Mecklinburgh County, North Carolina, 132 acres, and five shillings sterling to be levied out of my estate; to my son by law Matthew Brown, a crown sterling to be levied out of my estate; to my son David Neely a part of my land laid out for him in Mecklingburgh County, NC, 134 acres and a crown sterling to be levied out of my estate; to my son David Neely, a part of my land laid out for him in Mecklinburgh County, NC, containing 134 acres and a crown sterling to be levied out of my estate; to my son by law Henry Creswell, five shillings sterling to be levied out of my estate; to my beloved son by law James Henry, a gown pattern and five shillings sterling to be levied out of my estate; to my son Thomas Neely, all the rest of my lands and improvements lying in Mecklingburg County, NC not before devised, 250 acres with a mare and colt and saddle, a sett of plow irons and five shillings sterling; top my beloved daughter Hannah Neely her own clothing and a bed and bed cloths, a horse and saddle, a yearling heifer and a crown sterling; to my beloved daughter Jane Neely her own cloathing a bed and bed cloaths, a horse and saddle, a yearling heifer, and a crown sterling; to my beloved sons Matthew Neely and Robert Neely, two thirds of the benefits of my Indian land claim after the decease of marriage of their mother viz of the improved land; I likewise allow the wagon and hind gears to be sold for the benefit of the legates; my wife Ann Neely and son Samuel Neely, exrs., dated 21 January 1785. Jaxon Neely (X) (LS), Wit: Wm. Kerr, Thomas Bratton, Alex Brown.

Pages 19-20: Will of Michael McGarrity of the County of York and State of So Carolina, 18 October 1787... that tract of land whereon I now live to e sold that the money arising from thence to devolve to my loving wife Elizabeth. to my wife one sorrel horse and her saddle, two beds and the furniture, all my dresser furniture and her choice of two cows out of my stock. to my nephew [sic] Katrine Williams one black mare between one and two years old, and one bed and furniture, and all plantation utensils to be sold and the money arising from the sale to be divided two thirds to my wife and one third to Katrine Williams; my wife Elizabeth and Andrew Love, exrs. Michael McGarrity (mark) (LS), Wit: William Love, Matthew Smith, Mary Brown (+).

Pages 20-22: 8 July 1788, Will of Alexander Hemphill of York County, State of South Carolina... to my dear and loving wife Mary Hemphill my sorrel mare and foal branded with a P with saddle & bridle also the choices bed "& furniture together with all her wearing aparel, also two calves and cows one Moyld red & white cow, also one other Red & white cow, both unmarked with their calves; to my eldest son Robert Hemphill, my stallion now in the stable, also his saddle "& bridle; the lands where on I now live to my death children viz the said lads to be appraise by men chosen by my executors and then divided equally into five parts, one part to my son John Hemphill to be devoted to his use for his Education, one part to my daughter Janet Hemphill to be paid when the dividend to each party shall take place; to my sons Robert, James & Samuel my plantation on which I now live to be divided equally, to each one third when the youngest comes to age to be equal to John and Janets part. My executors to confirm unto the purchase my plantation of 227 acres known by the name of Megarritys place, with my new waggon and what other articles they make think necessary for the family to spare. My wife and Andrew Love to be executors. Alexdr Hemphill (mark) (LS), Wit: Robert Faries, A. Glass, Hugh Berry.

Pages 22-25: Will of James Pursley, planter... to my dearly beloved wife Jane Pursley the negro wench I now have named Dinah, also my big bay mare, also tow of her choice cows and calves, with the east end of my present dwelling house, also forty acres of land of my present plantation whereon I now live including all the cleared Land on the east side of Ellisons Creek waters and at her death to my son Robert Pursley; to my said wife Jane Pursley her choice bed and furniture also dresser & furniture; to my eldest son John the sum of £12 prock in credit in Col'n Hills Books; to my second son James Pursley, £25 prock in credit in Hill's Books; to my young son David my ball'd horse; the plantation whereon I now live to my son Robert excepting the aforesaid forty acres during my wifes life, in case he dies without an heir the lands or value thereof be equally divided between my children; to my eldest daughter Jane Ridley one cow and calf; to my second daughter Margaret Nickells, £15 prock in credit in Coln Hlils Books; to my third daughter Agnes Fitchett, £15 prock in Credit in Colo Hills Books; to my youngest daughter Elizabeth Stevenson as much as will buy her a black gown; to my grandson Daniel Nichells my little bay mare; to my daughter Mary Hemphill as much as will buy her a black gown; at the death of my wife one of the negroes aforesaid be sold and equally divided among my children; to my son Ephraim Pursley, £25 prock in Credit in Coln. Hills Books. my wife Jean Pursley and my son Robert Pursleys exrs., dated 14 August 1788. James Pursly (LS), Wit: Robert Faries, James Nickes, David Pursley. Codicil made 14 August 1788 to my son Robert Pursley my gray hose and brown horse called Jockey; to my daughter Elizabeth Stevensons nine pounds prock in Credit in Coln. Hills books.

Pages 25-27: 3 September 1778, Will of James Craig of Camden District, South Carolina... to my well beloved wife one third of my personal estate, one negro woman named Sally, one large bay mare called Phenix, one bed & furniture, her choice of three milch cows out of my flock, the pewter and furniture of the shelf and one chest, all which I give my wife to be appraised on oath by three honest men, also I allow my wife her living off my land during her life or widowhood; to each of my beloved children an equal share of my real and personal estate, except my son John whom I give one more called Doll and my rifle gun over and above his equal share, and my son Robert whom I give a filley called Pigeon over and above his equal share; my land to my sons John and Robert to be equally divided between them; to my daughter Martha a bed and furniture; to my son James McCoy one negro boy named Ben; to my daughter Jean one bed and furniture; to my son William an equal share of my real and personal estate with my other children. I allow my books to be equally divided between my wife and children, each to have an equal share. My wife Hannah, my son John Craig, and friend Thomas Neel exrs. James Craig (LS), Wit: Samuel Craig, David Howe, And'w Neel.

Pages 27-28: Will of Joseph Laney of York County, South Carolina... to my wife Elizabeth Leany the house and plantation wherein I now dwell with all benefits rising therefrom, also her bed and furniture, and what remains due to me from Thomas Griffey of three bonds after paying William Bell what I owe to him, likewise Charles Stice what I owe him, and the plantation I got from William Bell to be sold after my decease and to be divided among my wife and children, each having an equal share except Eleanor McCown that is to get five pound sterling, and after the decease of my wife, the plantation to be sold and divided among the then living children. David Leech & Moses Leathem, exrs, dated 18 July 1788. Joseph Leaney (X) (LS), Wit: Thomas Gillham, Wm. Leaney, Wm. McQuown.

Pages 28-29: January y'e 15th 1784, Will of Catharine Berry... to my daughter Violet Simril, five shillings sterling; to my son Hugh Berry, five shillings sterling, to my daughter Catharine Barron, my bed with its furniture and all my wearing body cloaths to be equally divided betwixt my daughters Violet

Simral and my daughter Catharine Barron; to my son John Berry, five shillings sterling; to my son Andrew Berry five shillings sterling; to my son William Berry, the plantation I now live on; to my son Roger Berry three grown cows and calves; to my son Richard Berry, five shillings sterling. My sons Hugh & William Barry (Berry), exrs. Keatrin Barry (O) (LS), Wit: Samuel Watson, Jean Barry (mark), John Watson.

Pages 29-31: 21 September 1788, Will of James Beard of Fishing Creek & County of York, South Carolina... to my wife Mary Beard the benefit of my plantation whereon I now live during her widowhood for the support of my daughters during the time of their being unmarried but at the expiration of her life or widowhood, my land be sold and divided into four equal parts between my wife Mary, son John and daughters Jane and Catharine; to my wife Mary Beard my roan'd horse and young colt as her right, and she to have the benefit of my horses and farming implements while they all live together; to my daughter Jane Beard my sorrel mare with her saddle and bridle; to my daughter Catharine my black horse called Tarleton with her saddle and bridle; my household furniture to be divided into three lots, my wife to have her choice of the divisions and the remainder to be divided between my daughters by lot. Robert Howie, John Murphy, Senior and my wife Mary exrs. James Beard (mark) (LS), Wit: John Murphy, Robert Howie, Mary Beard (X).

Pages 31-35: Will of Daniel Sturgis of the County of York... wife Jane, all my estate real & personal viz the land I now live on and all my personal estate such as my horses, cows, sheep, hogs, and household furniture such as beds, bed cloaths, pots, pewter, dresser and furniture and all the iron tools belonging to the plantation; my two sons Laban and John Sturgis to be guardians of my hold estate during my wifes life time and after my wifes deceased that Laban Sturgis my oldest son have all the land & improvements on the road beginning at the mouth of the spring branch & to run a straight line to the s'd waggon road; my son Laban to make his brother Daniel equal to himself on the north side of s'd road, that is in building of house & planting of fruit trees &c; my oldest son to pay unto John Sturges my third son £4 sterling a year for five years in Country produce, wheat at three shillings, corn at two, oats at two &c; all my children more especially my daughter Mary have free access to my house I now live in as their homes during their leading a single life; my fourth son Joshua shall have the one half of the profits arising from my boat as she now stands together with one acre of land on the south end of Punch's land with timber and fire wood to support the same during the running of said boat and no longer and if Joshua Sturgis should dispose of s'd Boat out of the family it shall immediately descend unto Daniel Sturgis with all the above mentioned premises; to my son Daniel, all the land lying on the north side of the Wagon road beginning at the mouth of the spring branch; David my son do pay unto Joshua the sum of £20 for the space of five years, that is at the rate of four pound per annum in country produce; to my son James Armstrong Sturgis one new chest; to my daughter Mary Sturgis, one negro wench named Rose which Mary is to have during her life time and at her death to my son Daniel Sturges and his heirs; to my daughter one feather bed &bed cloaths; to my daughter mary one mare of bay coulour and her mother's saddle at the mother;'s decease, one cow & calf at the day of her marriage alive and good, one new pewter dish & three plats; likewise over and above what I have will;d to my sons Laban one feather bed cloaths, to Daniel one ditto that I now make use of myself; likewise all the remaining part of my estate to be equally divided amongst all my children Laban, James, John, Joshua, Daniel & Mary, dated 22 October 1787. Daniel Sturgis (LS), Wit: Abraham McCorkel, Andrew Ferguson, Jno. Drennan.

Pages 34-35. State of South Carolina, York County. Will of Matthew Bigger of the state & county aforesaid... to my well beloved wife Ann Bigger all my estate I now possess real and personal, to wit the plantation I now live on, one negro man named Jack, one negro woman named Keat, one negro child named Sue with all the offspring of the s'd female negroes with all my horses, cows, hoggs, household furniture, bed, pots, pans &c, as along as she remains a widow. At her death to go to the use of James Bigger my brother Moses' son; unto Ann Drennan one young negro wench out of my estate if she continues to live with her Aunt Ann; to Matthew Bigger my brother James' son, five shillings sterling; my friend William McKee and friend John Drennan Esqr., sole exrs, dated 5 December 1788. Matthew Bigger (LS), Wit: Thos. Drennan, Wm. Kerr, Jno. Drennan.

Pages 35-36: Will of John Milom of County of York...to my wife Judith, all my horses, cattle, hogs, household & kitchen furniture; unto Hannah Basdell, one bed an d furniture and at her decease to be left to Mary Ireland my granddaughter; to my wife Judith one young negro girl named Lucey and at the decease of my beloved wife the property to be left or willed at her pleasure; to my loving children John Barklet, Benjamin, Thomas, and Nancey each of them to have paid to them one shilling sterling. my son Thomas Milom executor, dated 3 June 1789. John Milom (mark) (LS), Wit: John Leech, James Fowler, Hannah Basdill (H).

Pages 36-40: Will of Stephen Miller of York County... to my beloved wife Hannah, the use of the plantation on the Catawba Indian land whereon I live. I also give her for the term of her life two negro slaves Will and Nan, one horse called smoaker and my largest bay mare, also four cows and calves, all my sheep and hoggs and household goods and working tools. Also to my wife untill my several children hereafter named arrive to the age of 21 years, their several shares of slaves, the better to enable her to raise and school my children, tho' each child to have their share when married; to my daughter Jane, the wife of Moses White, two negro slaves, one boy Peter and girl Lisle, one bay horse, two cows and calves and one feather bed and furniture; to my daughter Anne, one negro man slave Tober, one girl child slave Beck, one grey mare that has been called hers also two cows & calves and one feather bed & furniture; to my daughter Elisabeth one tract of 300 acres of land in Mclenburg County, NC, on or near the head of twelve mile Creek, one negro woman Dinah and a molatto child slave son of said Dinah named Joe, one horse and two cows & calves, one feather bed and furniture; to my son James, 400 acres in Anson County, NC, on Lick Creek of Brown Creek, one slave named Phil and one small boy slave Ned, also one horse & two cows &

Calves, one bed and furniture, and after the death of his mother the leased plantation whereon I now live. I give to my daughter Mary the one moiety or half of tract of land on Jones Creek in Anson County, the said tract of 600 acres, one negro boy slave named Nat, and one horse & two cows & calves and one bed and furniture, to my said daughter Mary the one half of the negroes and their increased lent as aforesaid to my said wife, and the half of all the property lent as aforesaid, and the half of what specie certificates I have, and also the half of what debts is due me except as hereafter excepted. I give to the child my aforesaid wife is now pregnant with the other half of the aforesaid land on Jones Creek, Anson County, one boy slave Sam, one horse, two cows & calves and one feather bed & furniture, the one half of the slaves & their increase lent as aforesaid, and half of specie certificates & debts due me at the death of my wife except as hereafter excepted, the division of the land last mentioned to my daughter Jane and the one not yet born. My wife Hannah Miller executrix, and Theoderick Webb, James Miller & Jesse Miller executors... dated 8 May 1789. Stephen Miller (LS), Wit: Priscilla Miller, Turner Sharp, Priscilla E. Webb. Codicil: one se of black smiths tools not mentioned in my will to my son James, and if that either of my children die without lawful issue or before they come to lawful age, then their shares to be equally divided amongst the res of my children, dated __ June 1789. Wit: Charles Miller, James Webb, William Miller.

Pages 41-42: Will of Henry Wray Senior of the County of York... to my well beloved wife Agness Ray, all my household furniture, with all my plantation tools with the crop that is now in the ground with all my cattle but two cows excepted, with my old gray horse and bay more and a young black horse, and I allow that she shall have her maintenance off this plantation during her life time. I give to my daughter Isabell one cow which my wife pleases to give her. I give to my daughter Sarah one two year old heifer big with calf. to my son Henry this plantation that I now live on, also one young gray horse with all my wearing cloths. my friend Alexander Galloway and my son Henry Ray, exrs, dated 26 August 1789. Henry Ray (H) (LS), Wit: Isaac Gillham, Thomas Gillham, John Creige (mark).

Pages 42-44: ____ 1789, Will of Oliver Wallace Jun'r of York County... to my wife Judith Wallace my oldest bay mare with a woman's saddle & bridle, also a feather bed & furniture with all her wearing apparel and an equal part with my 3 daughters and my household furniture. My said wife to have as comfortable & genteel a living off of the plantation I now live on as the same will admit of, with the service of my negro boy Snow, to assist in the rasing & support my four children during my said wife's state of widowhood, and one cow & Calf for my said wife for her use and benefit forever. The remainder of my cattle stock to be equally divided between my 3 daughters and the unbequeathed part of my household furniture with my present sheep & hog stock. To my son Oliver Berry Wallace the plantation whereon I now live, estimated 100 acres of land with all my plantation utensils, one P Steel-yards and one P Spoon-moulds & young hold colt. I appoint my friend Thomas Wallace & Andrew Love Esq'r, my executors and my said with Judith Wallace, executrix... Oliver Wallace (LS), Wit: Jas. Mitchell, Jas. Wallace, Wm. Davison. 17 July 1789.

Pages 44-45: Will of Esther Henderson of York County, 7 November 1789. To my son Robert Henderson the hose that he now hath in possession from me and a red and white cow and my bed & furniture. To Mary Henderson my black gown and petticoat and apron and shift. To Robert Henderson one gown to make him a coat. After paying my lawful debts and funeral charges, the remaining part of my money in the hand sof Robert Patrick, I will to my daughter Mary Todd & Esther Henderson to be equally divided between them. To my son Samuel Henderson my Bible & Confession of Faith, also the one half of the money in his hand coming to me, the other half to be divided as aforementioned between my daughter Mary Todd and my granddaughter Esther Henderson. To my son Samuel my spinning wheel and reel & dresser furniture & Chest, pots & Crook. To my son Robert Henderson some coarse cloth and pot now at Roberts Henderson, also any thing else that is forgot of my estate except one bagg of flour to my son Samuel Henderson. I appoint Robert Patrick and Joseph Howe, my exrs. Esther Henderson (mark) (LS), Wit: John Howe, Jane Howe, Martha McCown.

Pages 46-48: Will of Thomas McAdorry, 14 November 1789. To my wife Ann McAdorry, as comfortable & genteel a living off of the plantation whereon I now lie as the same will afford without any lett, hinderance, or molestation during her naturel life, a dark bay mare named Fennix, a bed & furniture, to be her ruse & benefit for ever. To my daughter Elisabeth a young dark bay mare that has been under the character of my s'd daughters mare for some time past. To my daughter Martha a two year old horse colt. To my daughter Mary a year old mare cold. To my daughter Ann a young mare, a cow & calf, a bed furniture with such other title as have been assigned to her before the date here. The tract of land whereon I now live containing by estimation 200 acres be as equally divided between my three sons James, Robert & Thomas in quantity, quality & natural conveniences as the same will admit of & my son Thomas's part to include my present dwelling house with as much of the improvements as his division will include. To my son James a brown mare, to Robert a young bay horse & to Thomas a year old mare. My said wife do have the full power to divide my household & kitchen furniture, plantation tools and all my unbequeathed property among my six children now unmarried. My wife Ann McAddory, extx, James Mitchell and Robert Howie, both of York County, and James Williamson of Chester County, exrs. Thomas McAdory (mark) (LS), Wit: Samuel Williamson, Robert Bozel, James Gibson (mark).

Pages 48-52: Will of Alexander Love of New Acquisition District, State of South Carolina, 20 March 1781. to my son Andrew all that parcel of land (surveyed by Francis Adams) & which he is now in full possession to him for ever. Likewise to my son James al that tract which he is now in possession of and which adjoins lands of Michael McGarraties. In case of default of heirs of his body then the same to be sold and the money thence arising to be equally divided amongst my remaining sons & my daughter Elizabeth unless that my s'd son James hath before his decease made a will. To my son

Alexander, all that tract of land which he is now in possession of & which adjoins the lands devised to my son Andrew and the lands devised to my son James, likewise 100 acres of the tract I now live on to be divided off in the said adjoining Samuel Curry & Alexander Clark's land. To my son William, that tract whereon I no live. I bequeath to my sons Andrew, James, Alexander and William to be held in equal partnership by them then in case of default in any of them of such heirs then to devolve to the remaining brethren, all that tract known by the name of the Mines. To my loving wife Margaret one negro wench named Kate & at her death to my son James. To my son William. a negro slave named York & one wench named Jean. To my son Alexander one negro wench named Chloe. To my wife Margaret one large bay paceing horse with a star in his face, also a saddle & all the plenishing and furniture in the house. At her death my silver buckles to my son Alexander. My silver clasps to my son William. My oldest sorrel mare to my son Andrew. To my daughter Elizabeth three cows & three heifers also three ewes & three wathers. Alexander Love (A) (Seal), Wit: John Fergus Junr., Robert Gabbie, Mary Carnahan (mark). Codicil dated 25 March 1781. to my daughter Elizabeth one negro wench named Melie and one black paceing horse with a star in his face, one new saddle, one chest of drawers, one bed & furniture. To my daughter Margaret one negro wench Lucy, and then to devolve to Margaret's daughter Sarah.

Pages 52-53: Will of Robert Black Sen'r of New Acquisitions, Camden District, yeoman, 9 October 1779.... to my beloved wife Agnes all the moveables now in my possession except such as may be necessary to be sold to pay the following legecies; to my son George £10 current money of this state; to my son Robert £10 current money of this state; to my daughter Elisabeth £10 current money; to my daughter Agnes £10 current money of this state; to my sons John & Jacob, the whole of my lands being one half of a tract purchased by me and my son George which is divided by a ling running from Lockards Road to the River. My wife Agnes and my son George, and James Blankhead [sic], executors. Robt Black (O) (Seal), Wit: Thomas Woods, Edith Woods, Andrew Woods.

Pages 54-55: Will of Rachael Ross of the County of York, State of So Carolina... to my son James, a bed and furniture; to my son Alexander, my still also the money arising from the price of the stud horse, likewise two & cows & a bed & furniture; to my son William my case of drawers also a young born Horse & two cows, and a bed & furniture; my sheep shall be equally divided amongst my three sons James, Alexander & William. The remainder of my cattle to be sold and as much to be taken out of the price as will purchase a desk for my two sons James Ross & Alexander Ross, the remainder of the price of my cattle to be equally divided amongst my three sons. To my son James a gold broach & Ring. To my son Alexander a whole Joe & a diamond ring; to my son William my own silver shoe buckles & two gold rings. To my niece: Rachael Murphy, daughter of John Murphy, my lutestring skirt. I appoint George Ross and Andrew Love, my executors... dated 1 April 1790. Rachel Ross (O) (Seal), Wit: Jas. Ross, William Carson Sen'r., William Carson.

Pages 55-56: Will of Margret Steward of South Carolina, Camden District... to James Young's children, £20 currency; to Alexander McWhorter's children, £20 currency, which said money is in the hands of my son in law James Young; to my daughter Mary, my bed and all furniture belonging to the same. My beloved son Alexander McWhorter, exr. ...dated 6 July 1790. Margret Steward (mark) (LS), Wit: Moses Ferguson, John Young. Proved by the oath of Moses Ferguson before Jno Drennan, J. P., 6 July 1790.

Pages 56-57: Will of Andrew Leathem of State of So Carolina, County of York... to my wife Jean, my lands, stock of cattle, horses, sheep, hogs & plantation tools,m houses & household furniture & one negro woman named Pol during her natural life and at her decease my lands & what may remain of the stock in hand to be bequeathed in the following manner. My Lands, stocks & plantation utensils to be equally divided to my sons Moses, Andrew & Robert Leathem & to my grandson Purdy Leathem. To my daughter Sarah at the decease of my wife Jean, the negro Pol. Moses Leathem and Charles Gillmore, exrs... dated 6 May 1790. Andrew Leathem (mark (Seal), Wit: James Fowler, Samuel Scott, Andrew Leathem.

Pages 57-59: 25 July 1775, Will of Robert Patterson of Craven County, Farmer... my wife Sarah and my sons Robert & Peter to be my whole & sole executors; to Sarah my beloved wife, her full thirds of all my moveable affects & The homestead place till my son William comes of age & half afterwards while she lives & her horse & saddle; to my son Thomas, £50 lawful money of South Carolina to be levied out of my estate & all my cloaths except my fur hat and one gray three year old colt to his son John; to my daughter Sarah one cow & calf & what is between Joseph & me; to my son William my homestead place after his mothers death, all only from where the line crosses the road that goes to Peters old place & straight a Cross to the sold saw pitt below the muddy branch & so straight on to the outside line & from that said line down to Peter. I likewise give to my sons Peter & Robert each of them an equal part of my Land & Claims in the Province of Virginia. I likewise give to my children all & Every one of them that is now single with my daughters Elizabeth and Lydia, each of them one equal part of the remainder of my moveable affects. Robert Patterson (R) (Seal), Wit: Nathaniel Harrison, James Dickey.

Pages 59-60: 23 November 1790, Will of Walter Ashmore of York County, South Carolina.... to my wife Cleranah, all my household furniture & lands, the old sorrel mare, one old cow "& three large yearlings and three sheep & Five hogs, also a third part of money due by bonds from William Ashford & William Hall. To Margaret Ashmore, one large black horse, one cow & two yearlings, two sheep and two hogs. To my daughter Mary Ashmore one brown horse, two cows & two yearlings, two sheep & two hogs; to my son William Ashmore, one bay horse & saddle, two cows & two yearlings, two sheep & two hogs. To my son Walter Ashmore, one black mare & Saddle, also two cows & two yearlings, two sheep & two hogs. To my daughter Ellenor Ashmore, one young sorrel mare, 2 cows, 2 yearlings 2 sheep, 2 Hogs. To my sons William & Walter Ashmore, all my smith tools, and they pay to their mother the sum of £8 6/8 SC currency in hard money. The other two parts of that money in the hands of William Ashford William Hall be equally divided between my three daughters. The thirty pounds in Latcham[?] Hand & 9 pounds in Samuel & Nathaniel Greens hands, nine pounds in George Cally, to my two sons. Walter Ashmore (Seal), Wit: Walter Davies, Thomas Blankenship, Richard Blanks (+).

Pages 60-61: Will of James Lewis of York County, 27 July 1786.... to my beloved wife Margaret Lewis, her living on the part of the real estate whereon I now live as also the care, charge & Benefit of my personal estate during her life time and at her death to be sold at public vendue (except the negroes) and the money arising from such sale to be equally divided among my grandchildren then living except Jinsey Clark whom I will to have ten pounds over & above the equal part with the rest of my grand children, also to my daughter Margaret Clark, the part of my land or real estate that lyes in North Carolina making Mill Creek the division line between her part & the part whereon I now live. I also will to my daughter Margaret Clark the negroe wench named Kit at my beloved wifes death. I will to my son John Lewis the negro man named Pero & wench named Jude, also my cloathing & my books to be divided between my son John Lewis & daughter Margaret Clark. I appoint my son John Lewis & son in law, John Clark, exrs. James Lewis (Seal), Wit: John Howe, John Glen, Margaret Clark. Proved by the oath of John Howe 15 Sept 1786 before Wm Hill, J.P.

Pages 62-63: Will of John Carnahan... to my loving wife Marey Carnahan, one black mear, saddle and bridle, one feather bed, etc; to George Patterson, negro Jack; to James McCallen, negro London; to William Stevenson, negro Rorey; to James Jameson, negro Gin and her posterity at my wife Mary's deceased, my waggon and hind geers; to Frances Guttery, negro Nan and at her decease to Marey Carnahan if alive; to my wife Marey Carnahan, George Patterson, James McCallen, Wm. Stephon[sic] and Frances Gutery, and James Jamison all my plantation and crop in the ground with my working tools. I make my wife Marey Carnahan and James Jameson, sole executors. dated 12 Dec 1790. Jno Carnehen (Seal), Wit: Jno McCall, Greze McCall, Jno Keown.

Pages 63-64: Will of John Jordon of the County of York... to my beloved wife Jane Jordon, the grey mare & her side saddle & a bridle together with all my household furniture (one bed & bed cloaths excepted), four cows & five head of Sheep & her living on the plantation & in the house we now live in, and fifteen hogs; to my son James & to my daughter Margaret, my daughter Catharine, to each of them five shillings sterling; to my son John a piece of Land whereon he now lives including his House & improvements, beginning at the nearest corner to the division line of the field where my son James lives then a direct course to Johns field; to my son Robert the remainder of all my land, also all my horse creatures & cows not already disposed of, one bed &bed cloaths, all my plow irons & plantation tools, and half the waggon, the other half to my son John. My sons James Jordon & Robert Jordon, exrs, dated 10 January 1791. John Jordon (Seal), Wit: John Venables, John Venables Junr., Jno. Wilson.

Pages 65-66: Will of Henry Smith of York County... my beloved wife [not named] do hold & possess all my estate real & personal during her life or widowhood and after her death to be disposed of in the following manner. To my eldest son Abraham, my second volume of Pools Annotations. To my son David the plantation whereon I live, to hold the same in fee tale, and in case he dieth without heir of his body,to be sold & divided amongst the res of my children male 7 female. To my son John, 50 acres of land, to my son Henry 100 acres the which they are already possessed of; to my son Henry my negro fellow named Sam with one half of the fishery in his Brother John's division. To my son Jonathan, my negro wench named Rose reserving at the same time forty pounds to be paid by him to his brother William in trade & her first child if she has any to my daughter Sarah Ramsey. To my grandchild Henry Jolly, a mare worth ten pounds with two milch cows to his mother. The remainder of my estate to be divided equally amongst my daughters, married & single. My beloved wife and two sons John & Williams, exrs., dated 11 July 1790. Henry Smith (Seal), Wit: Nathan Guyton (N), Nicholas Correy.

Pages 66-68: Will of John Wilson of York County, yeoman... to my beloved wife Sarah Wilson, her wearing apparel, bed & bed cloaths, and her choice of any horse creature she will make choice of now my property and her saddle & Bridle, and the remaining part of the household furniture after the parts hereafter are taken out to the legatees. My wife shall have her living upon the plantation and benefit of the house until her death or see cause to remove,and three cows & Calves, and the use of the negro wench during her life; after her death the said negro is to be sold and her offsprings and the moneys arising from the sale of said negro to be equally divided amongst the legatees, and the remainder in the hand sof my wife to be disposed of for the use of and raising the younger children. To my daughter Elisabeth one two year old heifer and that is to be her part of my estate. To my son Joseph one yearling red heifer and twenty w't of feathers as his part of my estate; to my son Elijah one two year old Colt, saddle, and bridle, bed and bed cloaths; to my daughter Mary, one Bay filley, saddle and bridle, bed and bed cloaths, and two cows and calves, to be chosen by her after her mothers choice as above. To my son Robert a last springs colt which he now claims, a saddle & bridle, and bed and bed cloaths. To my son Hezekiah the first colt that comes of a mare known by the name of Midge, and if that should fail the first colt that comes of the bay mare. To my sons Elijah, Robert and Hezekiah, the plantation I now live on to be equally divided among them, reserving to my wife her living as above, and my son Jose the hundred acres he now lives on as long as he shall upon it, but as soon as he small move off, then the said Land is to return to the other male legatees and to be divided with the other part of the tract. My daughters Mary to have a spinning wheel. My exrs to dispose of so much of my estate as will purchase every child above one Bible and let them have them as soon as convenient. I appoint my wife Sarah Wilson extx and Joseph Steel and Elijah Wilson, exrs, dated 3 July 1791. John Wilson (Seal), Wit: Robert Patton, Arthur Starr, John Workman.

Pages 68-69: Will of William Leech, late of Pennsylvania now of York County... To my dear & loving wife Margaret Leech, my waggon & team with all my other estate both real & personal to her use & to be at her disposal with all the household furniture & all things therein (the children's cloaths that is made for them excepted). My wife Margaret Leech & Richard Sadler Sr my brother in law appointed executors, dated 1 August 1791. William Leech (LS), Wit: David Leech, Jr., Rebecca Morris.

Pages 69-70: Will of Jane Graham of York County, 16 August 1790. To my daughter Margaret Templeton, all my tract of land in the aforesaid county, containing 389 acres joining the lands of John Carnahan on Turkey Creek, likewise three pots, three pewter dishes, six plates, and one pewter tea pot, one three year old sorrel mare; to my daughter Nancy, one sermon book, also one feather bed with the furniture thereunto belonging; to my daughter Margaret all my apparel of whatsoever kind or quality with my large Bible and the remaining part of my estate. My daughter Margaret Templeton and my friend Hugh Berry, exrs. Jean Graham (X) (LS), Wit: Jas. Willson, George Templeton, William Templeton (+).

Pages 71-72: Will of Nanny Gordon of York County, State of South Carolina, 12 October 1791. To my son John Gordon my negro boy called Jerry; to my son James one young negro boy named Stephen; to my daughter Eleanor Henry my negro wench Sue and it is my will that my son Samuel Gordon be paid twenty three pounds ster. in trade by sd. Henry out of for his share of said negro; to my youngest son Hugh Gordon the young negro child now at the breast named Harry when it arrives to the age of three years and it is my will that it remains with its mother till that time; to my oldest daughter Nanny Floid my negro wench Floro; to my grand-daughter Mary Gordon, daughter of Robert Gordon, one sorrel horse 9 year old; all the rest of my unwilled property whereof I shall die seized in possession, it is my will that it be sold by public sale and distribution thereof made in manner following (viz) to my son William Gordon twenty pounds sterling in trade out of the above and the remainder to be equally divided amongst my seven Children to wit Samuel, John, James & Hugh Gordon, Nanny Floid, Eleanor Henry & Margaret Elder. My sons John & Hugh Gordon, exrs. Nanny Gordon (X) (LS), Wit: Robert Faries, John Gordon, Nelly Henry (X).

Pages 72-74: Will of James Tipping of Camden District in South Carolina... my wife Rosannah Tipping to have her living & be support off of the plantation whereon I now live as sufficient & fully as my estate will allow during her natural life, I also give her one feather bed with its furniture and an equal part of division of my moveable estate with my children that shall be living at my death together with what ready money I shall have (if any there be) I give to my said wife; to my son Henry Tipping the tract of land whereon I now live containing by estimation 270 acres and at the decease of my said son Henry to the legitimate heirs of his body; to my daughters Jane Rainey wife of William Rainey an equal part or division with the rest of my children of my chattel estate what she has already rec'd is to be included in her part; to my daughter Elizabeth Tipping, the one fourth part or an equal division of my moveable estate. my wife, son-in-law William Rainey, and David Gordon, exrs., dated 12 August 1783. Wit: D'd Gordon, Jno. Davison, Elijah Fleming.

Pages 74-77: South Carolina, York County. Will of Hugh Shearer of county aforesaid, farmer. To my beloved wife Lydia during her natural life the use & benefit of the fifty acres of Land I now live on (the which a reserve by me of a tract of Land given my son William in his life-time) with the use & benefit of all furniture, tools, also one bay mare with the use and benefit of as many of the stock of cattle as will be sufficient for her maintenance during her lifetime with the work of a certain negro named Betty & negroe Rachel; at the death of my wife Lydia, the negroes Bett & Rachel to be put under the direction of my executors and Bett at my wife's death be free from slavery yet to live with and under the care of my executors and to have the benefit of her own labour. My negroes Rachel, Tom, Solomon, Edie & Abel to serve my executors until they are thirty one years of age and my executors shall learn or use a lawful endeavour to learn the said Negroes to read the Bible; to my grandson Tho's Shearer two cows and to my grandson Hugh Shearer one cow &c and at the death of my wife my executors may as they think proper divide the property that may remain. to my trusty and beloved friend James Fowler, one bay horse known by the name of Gilbert. James Fowler and David Gordon, exrs.... dated 15 October 1789. Hugh Shearer (mark) (LS), Wit: Robert Fowler, Hezekiah Salmon, Lucy Neel.

Pages 77-80: Will of James Ferguson of York County & State of South Carolina, 7 January 1793. To my beloved wife Annaritta, full possession of the dwelling house I now live in, with what household plenishing she thinks proper to keep with two cows & calves with one plough and two pair of gears and tacklings with two work hoses and my negro man Sandy and my negro wench Rachel during her natural live (if she remains a widow), and at her death or marriage whatever of the above articles is then in being is to be valued by three neighbours consentably chosen by my sons and all but my negro man Sandy, that I allow to be given to my son Richard, and the rest of the above mentioned articles to be equally divided among my other children Thomas, James, Hamblet and Margaret; to my son Thomas two tuns of Iron endue me by George Galbreath the first due Feb 1st 1793, the 2d due Feby 1st 1794 in order to purchase him land; to Rebecca Long one young cow or heifer; to my two sons James and Hamblet, 500 acres of wood land on the south end of the plantation on which I now live; to my son Richard at his mothers death or marriage, 128 acres off land on the north end of my plantation including the buildings and clear land now in tillage; to each of my children the respective horse beasts heretofore named unto them; remainder of personal state equally divided among my four sons and my daughter Margaret. Col. Samuel Watson & my son-in-law John Smith, exrs. James Ferguson (LS), Wit: James Ferguson, Hamblet Ferguson, Richard Ferguson.

Pages 80-81: Will of Jane Moore of York County, 21 May 1791. to my beloved daughter Margaret my negroe wench named Flora; to my son Robert my negroe boy named Peet; to my beloved daughter Rosannah Bell my negro girl named Betts with my dresser furniture; to my son Jesse my negro named Rachel; to my son John my negro boy named Andy with my bed and all its furniture and my trunk; if my negro wench Flora has nay more children, it is my desire that my granddaughter Jane Moore, Samuel Moore's child, gets the first and if she has more than one, my grandson Joseph Moore, William Moore's son, to get the second with a young sorrel mare; the remainder to be equally divided betwixt my sons Robert, Jesse and John and my daughter Rosannah Bell, except my plantation or farming utensils all those I desire to remain on the plantation for the use of my sons Jesse and John. Ja's Hemphill and Samuel Moore, exrs. Jane Moore (LS) Wit: Joseph Sadler, Mary Black (mark).

Pages 81-83: Will of Eleanor Donahy, 7 January 1793. to my children William Donahy, John Donahy, Samuel Donahy, Andrew Donahy and Isabella Donahy, all the personal property that I am present possessed of, to be equally divided. My good friend William Love of Bullocks Creek & William McMorris of Little River, exrs. Elenor Donahy (X), Wit: Saml Denny, James Davison. Before the signing of this my last will and testament it is to be observed that as my daughter Mary having before got her divided, and she is now to receive one English shilling.

Pages 83-85: Will of Mary Boyls of York County. To my daughter Jane Alcorn my Silver buckles and the suit of cloaths I made for her. What I have given to my daughter Sarah Clark I allow to be her part; to my daughter Mary her bed & bedding; to my daughter Margaret her bed and bedding; to my daughter Ann my bed and beding & wheel; to my son John his school Bible and Edwards against Taylor; to my son Eleazer my house Bible; to my daughter Mary one pewter Dish and three plats; to my daughter Margaret one pewter dish and two plates; to my daughter Ann the crook and what pots there is and my tea pot; what other dresser furniture there is to be equally divided in three shares between Mary, Margaret and Ann; the horses and cows, sheep and hoggs to be sold and the boys to be schooled out of it and to be put to trades when they are fit; the plough irons, gears, and other tools to be sold also and an equal divide made of the remainder between my five children that are now at home with me; to Mary, Willison's catechism; to my daughter Margaret a book called true Christianity; to my daughter Ann, Guthrie's sermons and the Confession of Faith. My son-in-law William Clark exr.... dated 4 May 1793. Mary Boyls (LS), Wit: Andrew Carr, William Clark, Abigail Campbell, Catrin Carr.

Pages 86-88: Will of Patrick Robinson of the County of York, Pinckney District. To my dearly beloved wife Sarah the house and Land that I now live on during her life or widowhood, with all my household goods and stock; to my daughter Elizabeth Gillham whom I likewise constitute and ordain, the land on the west side of Broad River between Gilkey's Creek and Ebet's Creek; to my well beloved daughters Cetura & Sarah, land on No West side of Bullocks Creek adjoining land on which I now live; to my daughters Agnes and Jane, the land I now live on after my widows decease or marriage; to my daughter Cetura the young sorrel mare at her marriage with a fifth part of my stock and household furniture; to my daughter Sarah the bay horse at her marriage, with a fifth part of my stock and household furniture; to my daughter Jane a fifth part of my stock and household furniture at her marriage; to my daughter Agnes at her marriage a fifth part of my stock and household furniture. my wife and Samuel Robinson, exrs.... dated 12 March 1793. Patrick Robinson (LS), Wit: Joseph Robison, Samuel Nesbitt, Isaac Laney.

Pages 88-90: Will of Thomas Thompson of York County. To my Thomas and John Thompson my sons, the tract of land that I now live on; To my son John one bed with all the furniture belonging to it and a black mare and to my daughter Phanney a negroe girl named Cate and a Bed with all belonging to it and a cow & calf; my four negroes and all moveable estate not heretofore mentioned divided between my six daughters Sarah Wright, Mary Tatem, Anna Wright, Elisabeth Reeves, Rhoda Parham and Rebecca Reeves. Duncan Sinclair and William Wright, exrs.... dated 9 August 1793 Thomas Thompson (X) (LS), Wit: William Wright, David Gareson, Catherine Wright.

Pages 90-91: Will of James McCord of York County, 31 July 1793. To my beloved wife Jane McCord, all my household furniture & all the horses, cows, hoggs & sheep to be at her disposal for her use & the Children to be continued without any sale, except the youngest bay mare and the last spring colt to my son John McCord as his right and property with the plantation tools betwixt him and his mother Jane McCord, and her to have her living on the Land while she lives and where she lives; to my son William McCord, that lower end of the Land on which he is settled so far up as he has cleared; to my son John McCord, the upper end of plantation, if he dies without issue land to be divided between other children. James McCord (LS), wit: William Laughlin, David Watson, Mary Watson.

Pages 91-93: Will of Nathaniel Irwin of the County of York, 13 December 1793. to my beloved son by law and daughter Abraham and Mary Roach, thirty pounds Virg'a money, three cows, four sheep; to my beloved daughter Abigail Irwin £100 north currency; to my beloved son Alexander Irwin, one fourth part of my real estate; to my beloved son William Irwin, one fourth part of my real estate; to my beloved son Nathaniel Irwin, one fourth part of my real estate; to my beloved son James Irwin, fourth part of my real estate; to my beloved daughter Susanna Irwin, £50; to my beloved daughter Suffia Irwin, £50 prock; my beloved wife Leah Irwin to enjoy the mansion house during her life or widowhood; my wife Leah Irwin and my brother-in-law Jacob Julian, exrs. Nat Irwin (LS), wit: Wm. Kerr, Wm. Elliot, John F. Garrison, Mark Garrison, Isaac Garrison.

Pages 94-96: Will of James Murphey of Fishing Creek and York County, 18 July 1787. To my son John Murphey 200 acres of patented land where he now lives, as the same was run out for him when he settled it; the remainder of my land be divided into three divisions equally and the division including my improvement, I give unto my grandson James Murphey and at the next adjoining I give to his brother Robert Mur-phey; the remaining division to his brother Alex'r Murphey; to my daughter Susanna Sadler a note or obligation on John Miles for £17 s10 with all interest on the same, which note or money she is to have the use of untill her decease or death and then to her daughter Mary Miles; to my daughter Rachel Sadler a debt due me from her son Isaac

Sadler for £15 sterling and £5 to be paid by my executors; to my daughter Mary Sadler one dollar and no more; to my well beloved wife [not named], my two mares and all my cattle, sheep and hogs with all my household furniture and all my other goods not disposed of; my son John Murphy and Richard Sadler, exrs. James Murphey (X) (LS), Wit: John Adair, John Beard, Thos. Hale.

Pages 96-98: Will of Nathaniel Henderson Senior of York County, 8 February 1794. To my wife Ellanah Handerson, a bright bay mare about eight years old & her present horse colt one year old & a sorrel in colour, a grown cow, a feather bed, bedstead & furniture compleat and what of my household and kitchen furniture I am now in possession of and which came by her marriage to me, also the benefit of my two negroes Dick and Sall until her death of change of station; my wife to carry on the plantation with my sons Nathaniel & Robert, but if objected to by my wife than the tract on which I now live, 640 acres, be divided between my sons Nathaniel, Daniel, James, Robert, Samuel, & Thomas the most equitable way; to my daughter Elizabeth Henderson, my negro girl named Pheoba who is about 7 or 8 years old with the unbequeathed part of my household & kitchen furniture, a feather bed and furniture, two grown cows, with a small survey of land on Pacolet River which is not to include the old place; to my son Nathaniel Henderson my negro girl Lucy; to my son John Henderson five shillings sterling; my son John Henderson of Elbert County, Georgia and my son Samuel, exrs. Nathaniel Henderson (LS), wit: Joseph Carrell, James Clinton Thomas Carrell.

Pages 99-102: Will of John Smith of Bullocks Creek in York County, planter. to my wife Jane Smith, all my goods and chattles or moveable estate with one half of my plantation including my dwelling house; to my beloved nephew Robert Hartness the other half of my plantation during the lifetime of my wife and at her death all of my estate real and personal, also my negro fellow named Will, and not to give him worse usage than I myself have heretofore done and that he shall never sell my said negroe Will and to defend him from the insults of both black & white as far as in his power lieth; my wife Jane Smith and nephew Robert Hartnes, exrs... dated 13 February 1794. John Smith (mark), wit: John Scott (mark), David Scott, Robert Kennedy. Codicil: 17 February 1794 my negro slave Will to be set free. Wit: William Scott, John Miller, Robert Kennedy.

Pages 102-103: Will of William Wilie of York County. My estate real and personal to be sold at public sale for the discharged of my just debts, the remainder I order to be put on Interest for the use of my two Children untill they become & arrive to the lawful age of the state; my son John to be instructed in an art & occupation & to learn to Read the Bible & write a legible hand; my daughter Martha to be taught to read the Bible and write a legible hand; I appoint my brother John Wilie, exr... dated 25 November 1794. William Wilie (mark) (LS), Wit: John Jarrett, George Watson, Joseph Smith.

Pages 104-105: York County. Will of James Robinson... to Jephus Arnold, a back heifer; to Charleston Robinson, a black stear; to John Cook, a spotted heifer; to Thomas Torn[?] a spotted heifer; to Serah Robinson, a sorrel mare with a bleeze face. I will that Catharine have the Colt that the Roan mare is with at present (and if not with colt) the value of it to be given her out of the remaining of the estate; to Williman Robinson, my son, a bay mare colt; to Washington Robinson, my son, a roan mare colt; all the remaining part of my movable estate for the use of my beloved wife and the five unmarried children to wit John, Catharine, Sarah, William, and Washington during my wife's widowhood and if not marry during her life; all the five unmarried before mentioned when married off to have such a part as my wife and they shall think to be equal. The tract of Land that I now live on be equally divided between my three sons John, William, and Washington after my wife's decease. My wife Lucy Robinson and my son John Robinson, exrs.... dated 4 June 1794. James Robinson (X) (LS), Wit: Duncan Sinclair, John Robinson, Charles Robinson.

Pages 106-107: Will of Jonathan Whitley of the County of York. To my wife Sarah Whitley, one negro fellow named Will & a negro woman named Fanny during said Sarah's natural life and at her decease the negro fellow to my grandson Jonathan Whitley and Fanny to be free; to my grandson Jonathan Whitly one negro fellow named George & a bond due from Joseph French to me; to my son in law John Mitchell, all the remainder of my moveable property, one small bay Horse to be given to my son in law James Davis and also the tract of land whereon I now live to John Mitchell and his wife my daughter, and at their death to my grandson Johnathan Mitchel; to my grandson Jonathan Davies, a tract of land that belongs to me on the waters of Houlston River and my grandson Jonathan Mitchel when he possess the land where I now live, he is to pay his sister Lilly Mitchel, thirty pounds sterling cash or forty pounds in trade; My executors to be Henry Plaxco, John Mitchel, James Davis... dated 23 September 1793. Jonathan Whitley (X) (LS), Wit: Jane Plaxco (mark), James Plaxco, Robert Lusk.

Pages 108-109: Will of David Byers of South Carolina, County of York... 2d January 1794.. to my beloved wife Sarah the plantation I now live on and all the plantation tools I now possess for her use & to be disposed of at her death to whom she pleases... likewise I will her my gray horse, my sheep, hogs & geese with the household furniture. I will to my wife Sarah and daughter Marget to be equally divided between them. Likewise to my wife four milk cows and to my daughter Marget four cows each with their increase from this time. To my wife My negroe wench Cherry to be disposed of at her pleasure. To my daughter Marget my negro boy Prince and my riding bay mare, my negro fellow June until the death of my wife and then to be given to my son Samuel Byers. My negro Boy Sampson I allow to be appraised and the half of the appraisement is to be given to my stepson John Carson. I allow a vandue to be made of the remainder of my horses & Cattle and my clothes to be disposed of at the discretion of my friends, likewise my books. To my daughter Jeane Porter ten pounds sterling; to my son William Byers five pounds sterling; to my son Samuel Byers ten pounds sterling; to my daughter Ann Harris ten pounds sterling; my son William Byers, John McCaw and

Samuel Watson, exrs... David Byers (Seal), Wit: Jno Templeton, John Watson, Saml Watson.

Pages 110-111: Will of David Johnston of York County. To my beloved wife Sarah Johnston, a negro woman named Sukey, also a childs part of all my personal estate together with a horse and saddle, and her choice of all the horse creatures to take which ever one she pleases and that he have her living upon the tract of Land where I now live; to my dear children Jean, Mary, Elizabeth & Sarah, to each of them a childs part of my personal estate with the one half of the value of my land; to my son David, a childs part of my personal estate with the remaining half of my lands; my wife shall have the benefit of a negro boy named Virgil; my beloved brethren Robert Leeper and Robert Johnston, exrs., 15 October 1794. David Johnson (Seal), Wit: Wm. Maclean, Matthew Harper, Mary Johnston (mark).

Pages 112-113: Will of James Young of York County, 10 May 1793. To my son James, my daughter Mary, and my daughter Agness, to each a young cow; to my beloved wife [not named], all the rest of my cows and cattle, and one gray horse and the mare called Betty and her filly, one feather bed and furniture, and al the pewter and vessels belonging to the kitchen. To James, Mary, and Agnes each a fether bed and furniture; to my son the one half of Williamsons Bond and the half of all other money due me in Pennsylvania; the other half to be equally divided between my wife and two daughters. To my granddaughter Jane Stuart Fleming, ten shillings sterling; to my grandson young Elijah Fleming, ten shillings; to my son-in-law Elijah Fleming, ten shillings. My wife and son James, exrs. James Young (LS), Wit: Joseph Hamille, John Williamson.

Pages 113-117: Will of Joseph Carrel of Camden District, 2 January 1784. to my well beloved wife Jennet Caryl, the third of all my personnal Estate and her living on the plantation during her life, and in the new house, which I now live in and also a negro wench named Peg to be at her call & for her service whilst my wife lives and at her decease the said wench Peg, her offspring (if any) to my son Joseph in consideration of the land, also a negro boy named Adam and another named Cube and at her decease to be the property of my grandsons Joseph & Samuel Caryl, sons of my son Samuel deceased; the other two parts of my personnal estate I bequeath to my wife during her life (the waggon, the plantation tools & Henry's works excepted) & to be disposed of by her at her death to whom of her children or grandchildren she pleased. To my daughter Mary married to William Ratchford, the sum of five shillings sterling; to my daughter Ann married now to James Alexander, five shillings sterling; to my son Thomas Caryl, a tract of 470 acres on the north side of Little Catawba joining Robert Leepers land, also another tract in the Indian Land on which he lives; to my son Joseph Carrel to his heirs, all the piece of land I bought of William McNaught situate in indian Land with the wench Peg after his mother's death; to my daughter Hannah married to Richard Venable, a negro wench named Nann; to my grandsons Joseph Caryl & Samuel Caryl (sons of my son Samuel deceased), two tracts of land joining each other on Allison Creek & on which I live, one of them 600 acres and the other 200 acres, also fifty pounds proc. money being the contents of a note from Capt. Meek & Nathaniel Porter, also a claim on the public for cattle to help pay the land tax if needed and if not needed for that use to the two girls Mary & Elizabeth Caryl, daughters to my son Saml deceased; unto Jennet Rachford my granddaughter a negro boy named Dick; to each of my children one of Henry's volumes. I appoint David Dickson, James Ramsey and John Wilson. Wit: David Dickson, Margaret Carrel & John Wilson. Codicil: 16 February 1784. Wit: Samuel Clouney, Jane Dickson & John Wilson, exrs. Joseph Carell (LS), Wit: David Dickson, Margaret Caryl (M), John Wilson. Codicil 16 Feb 1784, signed Joseph Caryl (LS), Wit: Samuel Clouney, Jane Dickson, John Wilson.

Pages 119-121: Will of Richard Willson of York County, yeoman... my wife Mary Wilson to live on the plantation in order to raise the children on during her life or widowhood, with the assistance of my executors shall sell at public sale twelve months credit my waggon and two horses. John Willson my oldest son shall have the bay mare with a reed cow and yearling and three year old heffer and fether bed; if my son William lives that he keep the brown two year old filley and a cow his own purchase in the hands of Robert Willson with a bed and two year old heifer called his own. Mathew Wilson, Thomas willson, Elijah Willson, nancy Willson and Milley Willson shall receive at their or either of them coming of age or getting married the sum of £18 sterling. I think that I have given heretofore Rachel Mooney, John Willson and William Willson the value of said sum. Mary Willson, John Willson and Jonathan Mooney, exrs. dated 28 November 1794. Richard Willson (mark) (LS), wit: Thomas Jenkins, Mary Jenkins (X), James Willson.

Pages 121-124: Will of George King of York County, Pinckney District, planter.... to my eldest son George two pounds in lieu of an equal share of my real estate with my other sons as I did once give a plantation to him, and I likewise gave him a deed of gift of personal estate, which I also hereby confirm. My real estate be divided into three equal parts and my three sons Samuel, Benjamin and John shall each of them have one of those equal shares; my personal estate be divided into four shaves that my beloved wife Mary and my said sons shall have them. My three younger sons Samuel, Benjamin, and John, exrs... dated 26 November 1792. Geo King Sr (LS), wit: John Morris, Margaret Robinson, Wm. Robinson.

Pages 124-126: Will of Labon Sturgis of the County of York... to my sister Mary Sturgis one bed, bedstead and furniture, one chest, one hat which I now wear, one pair of silver buckels, one six galon pott; unto Jean Sturgis the daughter of James Sturgis, the sum of twelve pounds sterling to be paid her at the age of eighteen by my executor; unto Jean Bratton Sturgis, daughter of John Sturgis, twelve pounds sterling to be paid her at the age of eighteen years by my executors; to Nancy Sturgis daughter to Joshua Sturgis, twelve pounds sterling to be paid her at the age of eighteen years. To my nephew George Sturgis, my saddle, curb bridle, car shear plough, one set of drawing chains with hems and hangings; to my brother Daniel Sturgis, all the residue of my estate, plantation horses, half of the waggon and geers which is betwixt us in copartnership, cows, corn fodder, flour & hay, him paying the thirty six pounds to the three former mentioned legatees. My brother Daniel Sturgis, exr... dated 17 October 1793. Laban Sturgis (LS), wit: Joseph Moore, Fredrick Reeves, Allen Reeves (X).

Pages 126-128: Will of Patrick McFadden of the "state of York in South Carolina"... to William Clinton one young horse, saddle, and bridle with one red heiffer three years old, also a big coat and one months schooling; to Agnes White my daughter the third of my movable property and also to John McFadden and James Ouneil & William ouneil my daughter's three oldest sons, my land on White Oak Creek; to Patrick Anderson £20 sterling of money of the State of South Carolina each and paid to David Chambers for William Anderson the child's father; to Youttaraih Currie my granddaughter £10 sterling money of South Carolina. The negroe Nancy is to be sold with the rest of my property and this to be conveyed to the use of my daughters children and Agnes White and Catharine Anderson except Patrick to not share. John Hamby and George Montgomery, exrs... dated 27 December 1795. Patrick McFaden (mark) (LS), wit: William Veich, Charles Cleighton.

Pages 128-129: 10 September 1795, will of James Nickles... do leave my afairs in the hands of William Amberson, to put my property to sale and the children schooled out of it and to be divided between my wife Jane and the children, only my gun and shot bag that to my son Matthew and the property that is in John Nickels's' hands to be divided with the rest. James Nickles (mark), wit: John Henderson, Matthew Amberson, William Amberson. Proved by the oath of William Amberson and Matthew Amberson 30 September 1795 before Alex'r Moore, J. P.

Pages 129-131: Will of Robert Adams of York County, State of South Carolina... to my wife Elizabeth Adams, one gray mare and her yearling foal, saddle and bridle with all the household furniture she brought with her when we were joined in the marriage state, and also the furniture and property she hath since claimed as her own special earning and by her named called without infringeing on any of my property; to all my married daughters five pounds sterling to each of them; to my son Robert Adams his roan horse and my riding saddle with all my body clothes or wearing apparel and also my negroes shall be sold & also that each of my married daughters to hold and enjoy all their clothing and other property which they call their own; the remainder of my estate real and personal to be appraised and sold & an equal dividend and distribution made between my loving wife Elizabeth Adams and my son Robert Adams and all my unmarried daughters namely Sarah, Anna and Martha. The sum of ten pounds sterling for the use of Bethel Congregation; Adam Beard, Arthur Armstrong, exrs... dated 14 April 1795. Robert Adams (LS), wit: Arthur Faries, James Campbell.

Pages 131-133: Will of James Smith of York County & State of South Carolina... to my wife Lillus Smith, two beds and furniture & the half of all the dresser furniture, two pots and an oven, one big plough and a fluke, an ax & hoe, two pair of drawing chains and any two horses or mares which she shall choose out of my stock, three cows and calves of her own choosing, her saddle & wearing apparel, four head of sheep; likewise to my said wife the plantation on which I now live during her widowhood provided she chooses to live on it, but if she chooses to have it then the said Land is to be sold & my said wife is to have one third of the purchase price of said land to enable her to purchase land in whatever part of the world she shall chose to move to, and the land so purchased by her on her marriage or death to descend to my youngest child; also during her widowhood my negro man named Peter & my negro woman named Nann & on her marriage or death they are to be sold and equally divided among my children; My wife Lillus Smith, John McClenahan, exrs., dated 25 March 1794. James Smith (LS), wit: Wm. Smith, George Dantaff, Robert Neely. Codicil dated 21 November 1795, negro wench I have purchased and child, if my wife should choose to keep the said negrow woman in the room of the one mentioned to her she shall be at liberty as to and one the same terms. James Smith (mark) (LS), wit: Elizabeth Simpson, Robert Crocket.

Pages 134-136: Will of John Patterson of the County of York and State of South Carolina... unto my wife Rebecca Patterson, all and singular my household furniture and also sixty pounds, dollars at eight shillings of which there is thirty seven pounds in the hands of John Currence to be paid in such trade as he can give, and also three pounds in the hands of James Tate, and the remainder from me John Patterson; to Rebecca Currence the sum of five pounds cash dollars at eight shillings to be put out at interested until she comes of age; to Hugh Brevard my great grandson, the sum of five pounds cash dollars at eight shillings to be put out at interest until he comes of age; to William Patterson my son, one suit of my wearing apparel; to my grandson William Patterson, the remaining part of my estate. William Patterson, Col. Samuel Watson, exrs.... dated 18 February 1795. John Patteson, Wit: William Choat, John Currence, William Currence. Codicil dated 30 June 1795.

Pages 137-138: Will of Joseph Steel... to my beloved wife Rebecca one Road horse, one sorrel mare, four cows and calves, one bed and furniture, and to keep possession of my mansion house during her widowhood, having her sustenance of the Land, with the use of the Plantation tool during the term of her s'd widowhood; I likewise give one negro woman named Phebe to my wife during her widowhood; to my son John one negro man named George, he taking possession of him at the decease of my father Archibald Steel, also one black mare and my silver watch; to my son William, one negro boy named Jim; to my son Archibald, one negro boy named Peter; to my daughter Jenny, £50 sterling to be paid her when she comes of age; to my son Samuel one half of the plantation of land whereon I now reside; to my son Alexander, the other half of my said land; the remainder of my property to be sold and the money arising from the same to go to the schooling and educating my children and the remained if any there be to be equally divided amongst my children. My wife Rebecca, Samuel Anderson, and William Steel, exrs.... dated 24 August 1795. Joseph Steel (LS), Wit: Alex'r Moore, Samuel Williamson, Arthur Starr.

YORK COUNTY SC WILL BOOK A 1787-1799

Pages 139-143: Will of William Patton of the County of York in the State of South Carolina, black smith... to my wife Elizabeth the full and free possession of the Land I now live on including my improvement from the lower end of the survey up to where the Indian paths intersects my path and so on to Forrester's line; likewise a negroe woman named Rose with her bed and furniture and one walnut chest, and the half of the kitchen furniture, for the education and maintenance of my children and the rents that may be coming due to the Indians for all my Land until such time as the other heirs get the land in their own possession; to my son John the premises above described in the first clause at his mothers decease or marriage with my body clothing and Shoe & Knee buckles; to my son William the whole of the lands within my claim joining to the above; to my son Thomas all that part of my old plantation on Neeley's Creek. to my daughters Margaret, a mulatto girl named Jude; to my daughter Jane a negro girl named Mall; to my daughter Elizabeth, the remainder of my land on Neeley's Creek to a line between Alex Campbell and myself, with the half of my kitchen furniture. Elizabeth Patton, James Patton, exrs... dated 30 May 1795. William Patton (LS), wit: James Whiteside, Thomas Whiteside, Margaret Whiteside. Codicil dated 11 June 1795 leaving black smith tools to be sold for the payment of dents, and to daughters Margaret and Jane a bed and furniture when they arrive to the age of 18 years. William Patton (LS), wit: James Whiteside, Thomas Whiteside.

Pages 144-146: Will of Jeannett Carrel, wife of Joseph Carrel Senior, deceased, dated 25 January 1796... to my five surviving children Mary Ratchford, Ann Alexander, Thomas Carrel, Joseph Carrel and Hannah Wenable [Venable], be equal shearers in the bonded debts due to my deceased husband's estate by whose will I am empowered to make these bonded debts in such bequeathments as I shall choose. To my granddaughter Elizabeth Carrel, Daughter of Thomas Carrel, my feather bed and furniture & my chest. I allow my son Thomas to receive no more from my son Joseph and my grandson Joseph Carrel than five pounds. Son Thomas Carrell, exr. Jenneat Carrel (X) (LS), wit: Moses Carrell, Moses McWhorter, David Gordon.

Pages 146-148: Will of Thomas Walker... my land in Rutherford County, North Carolina be rented out by my executors until my son James shall attain the age of 21 years; one third part to my wife, one third part to my daughter Peggie, one third part to my son James. My negro boy Ben to my son James. To my wife my negro girl Luce. I appoint my wife Mary Walker, Felix Walker and Wm. Smith, exrs.... dated 14 June 1795. Tho's Walker (LS), wit: James Simpson, Wm Smith, A. Wilkinson.

Pages 149-152: Will of Hugh McCleland of the state of So Carolina and York County, taylor... to my wife Elizabeth the third part of my estate both real and personal; to my beloved son James McCleland, the one half of the plantation I now live on including the improvement, this not to take place during his mothers life time, but after her decease to be by him personally enjoyed for the term of the lease; to my beloved son Robert McCleland the other half of the premises above mentioned; to my sons Hugh McCleland and William

McClelland, a horse creature and saddle to the value of £17 sterling, and each a fourth part of any personal property after my beloved wife's part is taken off; my friend Samuel Lusk Senior and my son James McCleland, exrs... dated 19 August 1795. Hugh McCleland (Seal), wit: Hugh Whiteside, Abram Whiteside, Samuel Whiteside. Codicil dated 30 March 1796. Since my beloved wife Elizabeth is deceased, I bequeath unto my three beloved daughters Jane, Agness and Elizabeth, three eighth parts of the personal estate before willed to my wife Elizabeth, and I appoint my executors to delivered unto William Potts of the State of North Carolina a sufficient title for 350 acres which he bargained with me for. Hugh McClelland (mark), wit: Hugh Whiteside, Margaret Neal (O).

Pages 152-155: Will of Robert Leeper of York County, State of South Carolina... I appoint my daughter Blanch Leeper and William Maclean of Lincoln County, North Carolina, exrs. To my son Robert Leeper my silver watch which I have long worn, as a memorial of me; to my granddaughter Catherine Leeper, oldest Daughter of Robert Leeper, a negro girl named Fanny; to my son James Leeper, the sum of five shillings; to my daughter Blanch Leeper my stock of horses, cows, sheep and hogs, and my household furniture with three negroes Sam, Doll & Phebe, and two others named Dick and Frank be kept together as equally belonging to Blanch and my son John Leeper. To my son John Leeper, £60 in money and in case he enters into the estate of matrimoney and finds it not consistent with his interest to live with his sister Blanch or her with him, two of the negroes named Dick and Frank to be for his sole use... dated 13 April 1795. Robert Leeper (Seal), wit: Wm. MacLean, Robert Johnston, Joseph Beaty.

Pages 155-156: 2 September 1795. Will of Francis Birk of the County of York & State of South Carolina... to my wife Frances, my whole estate to be sold and the money to be kept and delivered to her or laid out for such necessaries as she stands in need of during her lifetime, after her decease to George Riddle and his heirs. My wife Francis, extx... Francis Burke (Seal), wit: Jos. McKenzie, Henry Craig, John Fearis.

Pages 156-158: Will of Hugh McWhorter of York County, State of South Carolina, 6 September 1795... to my brother in law John Richey the Plantation I now live on with the houses, building and improvements, a six pound note upon Sherid Thompson, my part of the crop of corn which is at Moses McWhorter's place and a yearling heifer, and all my clothes (save a coat and jacoat which I do leave to your son Alexander); to my brother in law Shadrach Rawls a sum of money which is part of the price of my negro boy which he has in his own possession; to my sister Sally my mare and a cow, my bed and bedstead, twenty bushels of corn due from Thomas Whitaker. Samuel Watson, James B. Fulton, exrs. Hugh McWhorter (mark), wit: David Watson, Thomas Drennon, Matthew Stevenson.

Pages 158-160: Will of Richard Champion of Bullock Creek in the County of York & state of South Carolina... to my wife Margaret the plantation or track of land I now live on during her natural life and after her deceased to be equally divided between my three sons John, George and Richard Champion. To my son John Champion one negro woman named Su; to my son George Champion one negro woman named Luce; to my son Richard Champion one negro girl named Hannah. My wife shall have during the minority of my within mentioned children John, George and Richard, my horses and cattle, hogs and plantation tools for the purpose of raising and schooling my children; Three sons to have an equal share in any monies or other property that shall be had from the will, deed, or legasy that may accrue from an estate said to be left to me by my uncle Richard Goodall. Wife Margaret and beloved friends William Champion & John McSwain, exrs.... dated 22 April 1796. Richard Champion (R) (Seal), wit: Will Minter, John Martin, Wm. Cavanah, Jean Stevenson (mark).

Pages 161-162: Will of Joseph Boggs of York County in the State of South Carolina... to my beloved wife Jean, one third part of my personal estate and the priviledge of living in her choice of the mansion houses where I now live, also the benefits of said plantation untill my youngest surviving child arrives to the age of sixteen years; to my son Aaron Boggs ten shillings; to my daughter Jean Wisher ten shillings, the remainder of my estate to be sold for the rest of my children viz. James Boggs, Polly Boggs, Joseph Boggs, William Wallace Boggs, Agness Boggs, Elizabeth Boggs, John Renicks Boggs and Thomas Gilleland Boggs when my youngest surviving child arrives to six years of age, then I left my wife the privilege of said mansion house during her life or widowhood and a fifth part of the benefits of said plantation. Thos. Boggs, David Neely and Eliga Flemming, my trust and beloved friends, exrs.... dated 24 August 1795. Jos Boggs (Seal), wit: Francis Adams, William Eakin, Mary Renix.

Pages 162-164: Will of Abraham McCorkle of the County of York, State of South Carolina.... to my wife Margaret, the plantation where I now live during her widdow-hood and a bed & furniture and my black mare & her saddle and such things as is necessary for carrying on the plantation. To my son Joseph five shillings; to my daughter Mary five shillings; to my daughter Elizabeth one feather bed & furniture, one young bay mare and one saddle as soon as it can be got from Jesse Dougless & one brindled heifer, six sheep and six geese; to my son James land Northwest side of Saluda Road at his mother decease or marriage and to work the land for his mother and to have his living off the land during her widowhood; to my son Abraham when he comes of age, the lower part of the land; to my son Stephen land South side of Saluda Road when of age; to my daughter Betsy out of the benefits of the saw mill, ten pounds at the expiration of two years and at the expiration of four years, ten pounds. John Baxter & my son James, exrs. Abraham McCorkle (LS), wit: John Hart, Fredrick Reeves, Andrew Baxter.

Pages 164-165: Will of James Richardson of the County of York and State of South Carolina... all my estate both real & personal (except beds & furniture, the dresser & all the furniture, one spinning wheel, one table & chairs) to be exposed to public sale at the discretion of the executors. To my wife Margaret Richardson $250 with all the above excepted articles & her third of the whole estate. To Jane Richardson $125; The remainder of my estate to be equally divided between Thomas & James Richardson & Jane Richardson. Joseph Robb & Robert Harris, exrs... dated 6 November 1796. James Richardson (LS), wit: Robert Young, Robert Clark Tecerd[?] (X), Plannes Winget.

Pages 165-166: Will of Robert Love of Clark's Fork, York County, State of South Carolina... unto my eldest son John one shilling sterling. I leave all the lands I am ow possessed of with my still & vessels to be equally divided between my two sons william & Robert but allow them to pay all my debts & to give my wife Elenor the quantity of fifty bushels of good sound Indian Corn yearly during her life. I leave all my moveable property to be equally divided between my wife Eleanor and my three daughters Janet, Francis & Elizabeth. My wife Elenor & cousin William Love, exrs... dated 4 October 1796. Robert Love (mark) (Seal), wit: Will. Love, Peter Patterson, Sarah Patterson (S).

Pages 166-168: Will of James Hanna of the State of South Carolina in the County of York... to my beloved wife Jane a negro wench named Diana, one horse & saddle, dour cows & the whole of my household furniture to be equally divided between her and my daughter Elizabeth, my desk & Clock excepted. To my daughter Elisabeth one negro girl named Sarah and one horse & Saddle & two cows; to my grandson James Hanna (son of William Hanna) a negro man named Samson & my clock; to my grandson James Hanna (son of Rob't Hanna) a negro boy named Sam; to my granddaughter Rosanah Berry Hanna, daughter of Robert Hanna, a negro girl named Dovve; to my daughter Martha a negro boy named James; to my daughter Deborah, at the decease of my wife, a negro woman named Kitty; I bequeath a negro man named joseph to be sold and the price equally divided amoungst my children, William Berry excepted. To my son James Hanna, the plantation whereon I now live and my desk at the decease of my wife; Remained of estate to be sold. William Hanna, Robert Hanna & my wife Jane Hanna, exrs... dated 13 February 1797. James Hanna (Seal), wit: Nathan Cooper, Sarah Hanna, James Hanna.

Pages 168-169: Will of Arthur Starr of the County of York, State of South Carolina...   to my wife Hannah Starr, the plantation I now possess until Pamela Williams Starr becomes of age, then to be equally divided between them, and if Pamela W. Starr does not live till the age of sixteen, I appoint her share to Doctr. William Morrisons eldest daughter Hannah. The negro wench named Dian to my wife Hannah, also the wench named Jamima and at her death or marriage to belong to Pamela. Alexander Moore, Esq., William Morrison and Alex Morrison, exrs... dated 28 March 1797. Arthur Starr (Seal), wit: Wm. McKee, David Houston, James Morrison.

Pages 169-173: Will of Jane Meek of Bullocks Creek, York County, State of South Carolina... 22 May 1794. The plantation on the waters of Bullocks Creek wherein I now live containing 175 acres to be equally divided between my two sons James & Adam Meek. To my son Moses Meek my negroe boy named Geoffry, also my negro wench named Sall and my negro boy named January. To my said son James Meek one feather bed & underbed & bedstead (on which I formerly lay) with the white curtains hanging there on also with Bolster & pillows, also three sheets& one blanket also one desk, one large pott, one brass candlestick and one coverlid or rug, also one pewter dish, etc. To my son Adam Meek one negro boy named Morris. To my daughters Rebecca Scott one feather bed & bedstead with bolster & pillows & one pair of cotton sheets, one coverled, one cotton blanket, one suit of blue & white striped curtains, one table cloth, four pewter dishes, ten plates, etc. To my daughter Jane Hope my negro girl named Jude. To my granddaughter Jane Kilpatrick one feather bed striped with small stripes, also with bolster & pillow & one coverlet or rug; My clothes may be equally divided between my two daughters Rebecca Scott & Jane Hope. To my grandson James Hope, son of Samuel Hope, when he arrives to the age of 21, one note which amounteth to seven pounds sterling. To my granddaughter Margaret Meek, daughter of my son Adam Meek, in case Moses Meek and Jane hope have nothing to pay. My three sons Moses, James, & Adam Meek, exrs. Jane Meek (mark) wit: John Henderson, John McNabb, William Smith.

Pages 173-175: Will of William Calley of South Carolina & County of York... to my wife Mary Calley, one third part of the land I now live on including the buildings and what part of the Cleared land she may chuse during her natural life & then to descend to my youngest son Pelick, likewise my two negroes one named Derryman & the other Tirie and my mares known by the name of Currey mare & Titlemon as also my cows, hoggs, sheep and remainder of my stock of horses and ready monies and what other of my debts that can be collected from my debts; to my beloved son James Calley, 100 acres of land that he now lives on adj. John Brattons line; to my son John Calley, one third part of the tract of land I now live on; to my son Wm Calley, one third part of the tract & now live on; to my son Jacob Calley, all my hatting tools to his use and to live on the plantation as long as he pleased; my wife Mary Calley & Capt. James Mitchell, exrs.... dated 7 September 1797. Wm Calley (Seal), wit: John Martin, David Gordon, Reuben McConnell.

Pages 176-177: 7 October 1770. Will of Elisabeth Lusk of Tryon County [North Carolina], widow... to my beloved son Robert Lusk one young grey horse; to my beloved son Samuel Lusk twenty bushels of corn now in the hands of Hugh McClelan; to my son in law Hugh McClelan twenty bushels of corn; to my beloved daughter Elisabeth McClelan a black gown & mantle; to my son in law Hugh Whiteside a roan colt; to my daughter Margaret Whiteside one woman's saddle; to my son James Lusk all the remainder of my estate real & personal . My son Robert Lusk and son in law Hugh Whiteside, exrs. Elisabeth Lusk (mark), wit: Samuel Neeley, Dorcas Wharey (mark), Martha Workman (mark).

Pages 177-178: Will of John Hart of the County of York and State of South Carolina... To my sons Samuel, Joseph, James, William, & John the sum of thirty five dollars each to be paid three years after my decease; to my daughter Elizabeth one negro woman named Philis, one black mare& colt, half of all my cattle and household furniture & $300 in cash; to my son Ebenezer my plantation whereon I now live, one negro man named Bob, the remainder of my cattle and household furniture; my sons John and Ebenezer, exrs.... dated 24 July 1798. John Hart (Seal), wit: Chas. Brumfield, James McCorkle.

Pages 178-179: Will of Margaret Baxter.. to my dear mother Jean Baxter my negro wench named Ester; to my beloved brother John Baxter, a dark bay colt that goes by my name; to my sister Janet Baxter my saddle; my bed & cloathing to be divided amongst my sisters and my chest to be left for the use of the family. To Jenny Baxter Turner the price of a cow that is in my mothers hands. John Baxter and James Baxter, exrs.... dated 19 March 1798. Margaret Baxter (X), wit: Jesse Hill, James Baxter.

Pages 179-181: Will of William Watson Sen'r of Fishing Creek, 20 August 1798... to my beloved wife Violet Watson during life & to be disposed of by her at her death so that she leaves the same to some of her sisters children, one third part of my plantation where on I now live, also one third part of all the debts due to me & ready money in the house; I allow Hugh Berry to keep or retain as much more of my moveable estate in his hands as will make the one third; to my two sisters Elizabeth Walker & Alice Alexander each the sum of $200. My old negro woman Rose be sett free and forever absolved from slavery & to get her a spinning wheel, bed cloaths, etc, and Isaac, Philip & Frederick, three male children, sons of my negro wench Amy to be bound out to good farmers or tradesmen until they come to the age of 31 years and then to be free. The remainder of my negroes to choose their masters; the remainder of my estate to my two sisters Elizabeth Walker and Alice Alexander and my cousin Watson Walker (son of Felix Walker). My wife Violet, Hugh Berry, Col. William Bratton & John McCraw, exrs. William Watson (mark) (LS), wit: Jos. Gabie, John Gabie, Roger Barry.

Pages 181-182: Will of Andrew Baxter of the County of York & of South Carolina... I appoint John Baxter & James Baxter, my lawful executor. I bequeath to my honoured mother one mare & my bridle mare named Calley and next to my Honoured Father one coult & my rifle Gun & shot pouch and four hoggs, and to my brother John Baxter one mare named Dandy and my saddle & Bridle and my little ax and to Miss Polly McCall one heifer & ten bushels of corn and the remainder of my corn to be left to the use of the family and to my uncle James Baxter one ax... dated 29 December 1798. Andrew Baxter (X), wit: Samuel McCall, William Potts, John Potts, James Baxter.

Pages 182-183: Will of Robert Hartness of Bullocks Creek & York County & State of South Carolina... to my loving wife Jane her bed & bed clothes, saddle & bridle with one cow being her choice; remainder of my cows with my horses and hoggs and farming tools with my two negroes shall remain on my plantation for the use and purpose of raising my children so long as my wife Jane remains a widow and at her marriage my plantation on Bullocks Creek be sold and equally divided between my wife and children; the price of my plantation near Yorkville after my children is schooled be equally divided between my wife and children. My wife Jane and James Martin, exrs... dated

1 April 1799. Rob't Hartness (Seal), wit: Samuel Scott, John Scott, David Scott.

Pages 183-184: State of South Carolina, York County. Will of William Thompson of the county & state aforesaid... To my grandson Hugh Brevard twenty dollars then the residue of all my estate real & personal to be divided between my wife Youpheme Thompson and my son in law John Brevard. My wife Youpheme Thompson and John Barron, exrs... dated 16 October 1798. William Thompson (LS), wit: John Barron, Hugh Simpson.

Pages 184-185: Will of William Dale of State of South Carolina and York County... To my wife Anne Dale the tract of land on which I ow live containing about 235 acres and my negro wench Nan and all my household furniture. To my sons George Dale and James Dale, 100 acres in the Black Jack Grounds and joining the lands of my two sons aforesaid; to my son Robert Dale a tract of land on the stoney fork of Fishing Creek. which I bought of John Beaird, 200 acres. To my daughter Anne, one small negroe child named Hannah; my negro wench to my wife during her life. My five negroes Ned, Sara, Joe, Harry & Will to my children Elizabeth Henry, Mary Dennis, George Dale, James Dale, Frances Brown, & Robert Dale. My wife Anna and Alexander Moore, Esq., exrs.... dated 26 May 1798. William Dale (Seal), Wit: John Bates, Rebekeh Bates, Mary Bates, John Bates, Jr.

Pages 186-187: Will of Joseph How of York County and State of South Carolina, 8 July 1799. To my wife Isabella Howe, a good sufficient living on the plantation I now live on, also free possession of my dwelling house particularly her bed room and all the furniture belonging thereto with the cupboard furniture and a negro woman named Rose, then the said Rose to be William howe my son's property; to my son John Howe, 150 acres including the 50 acres purchased from James Bigger (after lifting the fifty dollar note due to Moses Neely), also negro woman name Feab, a negro called Suf; to my son Joseph Howe, tract of land on Crowders Creek known by the name of Joshua Patrick's old place if he pleases to live on it, if he does not then to be equally divided between my two sons Jno & Thomas; to my son Thomas the land he now lives on or occupies near the waggon road also a negro boy called Harry; The land I now live on with waggon, also a negro man named Munday with the old negroes to remain on the place to work for the benefit of the whole; to my daughter Isabella Howe, one negro girl named Nell, one good horse and saddle with a bed & furniture, also two cows & calves; to my daughter Mary Dunlap Howe, one negro girl named Suf, also my big riding mare. My friends John Allison, John Howe, William Howe, exrs. Jo's Howe (LS), wit: Jas. B. Fulton, Rob't Patrick, Isaac Price.

Pages 187-188: Will of William Kennedy of the county of York & state of South Carolina... my beloved wife [not named] to keep the property together i her own lands so long as she remains my widow, my son Andrew being married and receive his full part, therefore I allow my son William to have the plantation on which I now live when he comes of age. The rest of my property to be divided amongst my wife and seven children that are yet single. My son

Andrew and David Hutcheson, exrs.... dated 24 August 1796. William Kennedy (Seal), Wit: Joseph McCorkle, James McCorkle, Wm. Kerr.

Pages 189-190: 19 January 1799. Will of Hugh Allison of the County of york and State of So Carolina. I am old and infirm in body... To my son Robert Allison my dwelling plantation also my right of all horses, cattle, sheep & hogs & Negroes by giving sums as I shall mention hereafter to the rest of my family. To my daughter Margaret £10 sterling & her mother blue cubbert; to my daughter Rosana £10 sterling and my bed & furniture; to my daughter Martha one shilling, likewise her son Robert Johnston I allow £10 sterling; to my daughter Catharine one shilling; to my son Alex'r one shilling; to my son Hugh one shilling. My son Robert Allison, sole executor. Hugh Allison (Seal), wit: Isaac Hope, Robert Love, Catren Hope.

Pages 190-191: Will of William Beatty of Yorkville of York County, State of South Carolina... to my wife Elizabeth all my estate both real & personal during her natural life and at her death to my son William the one half of the house and lot which I now possess in Yorkvillle and the other half to my two daughters Agnes & Sarah. If my three unmarried children should get married during the life of my widow, whatever marriage patrimony she may see meet to give them shall be counted as so much of their dividend at her death. My wife Elizabeth & son Jonathan, exrs.... dated 3 February 1799. Wit: Daniel McNeel, Jo's Kerr, Jon'a Beatty.

Pages 191-193: 24 September 1799. Will of Samuel Gay of York County & state of South Carolina... To my beloved daughter Mary Gay, her maintainance off of this my old plantation whereon I now live during her unmarried state. I also give one negro child Nell[?] & my old plantation known as Aunt Jane's place containing 150 acres to be sold and the price be equally divided between my said daughter & my grandson William Gay; To my two grandsons Samuel G. McConnell & James Hall Gay, all the plantation whereon I now live on the left side of the orad leading Jane Bratton's old place, Samuel McConnell to have the house & that part that joins Thomas Carson on the west and James H. Gay that joins Widow Dale on the east; to my granddaughter Esther Hemphill, one feather bed & furniture. My kitchen & dresser furniture to be equally divided between my daughters Jane & Mary. To my daughter Rebecca Walker the sum of five shillings. To my two sons in law the sums of five shillings each vizt James Hemphill & John McConnell. My daughter Mary Gay & Col. William Bratton, exrs. Saml Gay (mark), Wit: Robert Howe, Thos. Carson, Robert Murphy, Geo. Dale.

This ends the Records of the County Court Clerks-- Oct'r Term 1799.

# YORK COUNTY SC WILL BOOK A-1 1800-1813

**Pages 1-5**: April 6th 1800. James Powell Junior to me Alexander Moore, Ordinary of York District an Instrument of writing containing the last Will and Testament of James Powell upon which Robert Kenedy and Ann Thomson were subscribing witnesses to the same.

Will of James Powell of the State of South Carolina, York County, planter... to my beloved wife Sarah, a negro wench named Beck the wench that formerly belonged to her before I married her, one Bed and furniture, one mare named Keat which I purchased of Ned Gallimore and her saddle to her and my present Room in the north East corner of my house and her maintainance with the rest of my family during her Widowhood and one good Cow and Calf and one pot that she had in possession when I married her; to my son James Powell, one mulatto Boy named Ned and the young stud horse and one bed and furniture and a writing Desk and one new Saddle and Bridle and as much money as will buy a new suit of cloaths and my rifle gun and one half of a three Hundred Acre Tract of Land on Cherokee Creek, Spartanburgh County, the lower part of the tract; to my daughter Nancy one negro girl named Milley and negro boy named Daniel, one bed and furniture, two cows, the same being all now in her possession except the negro boy; to my son Thomas a wench named Feeb the younger, the upper half of a tract of which my son James gets the lower half and a mare named Creeping Keat & my still and Eighteen vessels & my smooth bore gun, a new saddle & bridle, one bed and furniture; to my son John one negro named Abram, one horse named Clearout, one bed & furniture, one tract of land on Kings Creek of 445 acres including a shoal on said creek; to my daughter Patsey a negro boy named Ephraim, one Bed and furniture, one horse of $100 value and a new saddle and bridle; to my daughter Jennet a negro boy named Elias, one horse of $100 value, and a new Saddle and Bridle, a Bed and furniture; to my daughter Betsey one negro girl named Rachel, one horse of $100 value and a new saddle and bridle, one bed and furniture; to my daughter Sarah, one negro Girl named Hesse, one horse of $100 value and a new saddle and bridle, and a Bed and furniture; to my son Volhonorous, one negro Boy named Ben, one horse of $100 value and a new saddle and bridle and a Bed and furniture, 500 acres of Land to be run of the lower end of a tract of Land belonging to me on Guyen Moores Creek in York District; to my son James Caps one tract of Land that I purchased at the sale of Gardners estate and one cow and calf and a mare called Big gut; the further part of my land on Guyen Moors Creek to be sold by my Executors and the money arising therefrom to be applying in discharging my Just debts and legacies; my children under age to have the whole benefit of the aforementioned property for their support and for the education of my children; my friends William Love Esqr., Mager Adam Meek, Edward Bears and my well beloved wife and son Sarah Powell and James Powell, executors; 17 March 1800. James Powell (LS), Wit: Joseph Kerr, Ann Thomson, Robert Kenedy. Sarah Powell and James Powell qualified.

**Pages 6-7**: April 11th 1800. James Scott produced before me an Instrument of Writing containing the last Will of David Scott Deceas'd upon which Robert Kenedy came before me Alexr Moore Ordinary for the District of

# YORK COUNTY SC WILL BOOK A-1 1800-1813

York and made oath as the Law directs... William Kenedy and John Seahorn were subscribing witnesses.

March 6th 1800. Will of David Scott of Bullocks Creek in York District.... unto my brother James Scott my Still and all the Still vessels including the Kegs &c; all my estate Real and Personal to be sold (excepting what I have bequeathed to Brother James) and to be divided as follows: to my well beloved wife Margaret one fifth part thereof and the remainder to be equally divided between my daughter Mary and the children with which my wife is now pregnant and if either of my Children dies before they come of age, I allow the survivor to be the others heir and if both dies before they come of age, I allow both their shares to be divided between my brother James Scotts children; my well beloved Brother James Scott and Samuel Scott and my wife Margaret Scott, executors... David Scott (LS), Margaret Scott (C), Wit: William Kenedy, John Seahorn, Robert Kenedy. James Scott, Samuel Scott and Margaret Scott qualified.

**Pages 7-8:** York District, So Carolina. Ralp Smith came before me and being duly sworn as the law directs saith that he saw William Wilson sign seal and deliver the within instrument of writing as his last Will and Testament and that Nicholas Curry, John Ramsey and William Smith were subscribing Witnesses to the same. Sworn before me this 11th April 1800.

Will of William Wilson of York County.... to my grandchild William Kirkpatrick, all my estate Real and personal to be enjoyed by him as his natural right for ever, excepting 100 dollar to be paid to Saley Seismore... my grand son William Kirkpatrick, executor. 2 March 1800. William Wilson (C) (LS), Wit: Nicholas Corry, Ralph Smith, John Ramsey, William Smith. William Kirkpatrick qualified.

**Pages 8-11:** William Hill produced an Instrument of Writing containing the last Will of William Hill Senior Deceas'd upon which Joseph Swan came before me and being first duly sworn said he saw William Hill Senior Sign Seal and delivered the sd instrument of Writing as his last Will and Testament and that John Swan and John Porter were subscribing witnesses, May 2d 1800.

1 January 1799. Will of William Hill of County of York & State of So Carolina.... to my well beloved wife Elizebeth, one fourth part of my personal estate and also an honorable & Comfortable maintainence off the Land I now live on & in the House I now live in as formerly enjoyed during her widowhood; to my son William all that part of my Land within the following boundaries, on Wt side of Stoney fork adj. David Porters Land... between my house and where David Porter formerly lived; to my daughter Agness, one fourth part of my personal property; to my daughter Kezia, one fourth part of my personal Estate; to my son Hugh all the remainder of my Lands for his use; to my daughter Elizabeth, one fourth part of my personal Estate; my negro fellow Simon to be kept on the plantation to help to raise my family together with my farming implements during my wifes widowhood to be under

her direction; if my widow should marry or be called away by death before my Daughter Elizabeth arives to the Year of 18, sd negro shall continue as aforesaid untill sd time and then shall be sold & the money arising therefrom equally divided amongst all my children; after my decease my personal property to be valued by John Swan, James Carothers, Jos. Swan and Saml Dinsmore or any two of them, but if when any of my Daughters marry & my personal property should either be augmented or diminished it is my will that my Executors look into the state of sd property, and at that time give her or them an equal share of what the amount may be; if any of my children should by misconduct forfeit any part of their property my Executors having knowledge thereof, they are hereby authorised to take from such that part thereof as they in the Judgment may think proper; my sons William & Hugh that no one of them dispose of their lands without the consent of the other; my wife Elizabeth and my trusty friend Brother Samuel Dinsmore & my son William exrs... William Hill (LS), Wit: John Swan, Jos Swan, John Porter. Elizabeth Hill, Wm Hill & Samuel Dinsmore qualified.

**Pages 11-14:** 20 August 1779 [sic]. Will of John Brandon, Sr., of York County, South Carolina; to my daughter now Elizabeth Mathews one feather bed and furniture (which she is now in possession of) and at the time my son George Brandon should or shall arrive to 25 yrs of age, then my daughter Elizabeth be paid of my estate £20 Virginia money (my s'd son George now being in his seventh year of age) which bequeathed substance is to be to the use and benefit of her my said daughter and her present husband and at her deceased to be equally divided amongst her then surviving children by her present husband John Mathews; to my daughter now Sarah Kendrick, one feather bed and furniture (which she is now in possession of) one cow and calf, one soral horse colt came of a mare called Poll and at the time my son George Brandon should or shall arrive to 25 yrs of age £20 Virginia money... her present husband Anthony Kendrick; to my son John Brandon a Bay mare called Strainer with a saddle and bridle; to my son James Brandon a bay colt called Liberty and a saddle and bridle; to my daughter Pressillar one feather bed and furniture, one cow and calf & a horse creature, saddle, and bridle; to my daughter Sussey one feather bed & furniture and at the time my son George Brandon should or shall arrive to 25 yrs of age to my last two mentioned daughters £25 a piece; my beloved wife Mary Brandon do have as plentifull sufficient & comfortable a living out of my unbequeathed property as the same will admit of during her natural life, 247 acres of land in Halifax County in Virginia on the north side of Dan River which was bequeathed by my s'd wife's father John Lawson Senior to her and myself; also eight negroes whose names are Harry, Ned, Fann, Patt, Daniel, Fabby, Dico & Hannah; my six sons John, James, Irvine, Joseph, Francis & George Brandon; my wife and surviving sons allowing it optional with her and them to either continue living in South Carolina or return to Virginia; my wife Mary, my sons John & James Brandon, Robert Johnston & David Gordon, all of York County, SC, my executors. John Brandon (LS), Wit: Zadok Darby, Richard Horsely (R), John Farley, Thomas Brandon. 5 May 1800 proved the will of John Brandon, late of the District of York deceased, by the oath of Zadock Darby and Richard

Hornly and qualified Mary Brandon, John Brandon, James Brandon, executors before Alexr Moore, Ordinary Y. D.

**Pages 14-16:** Will of William Adams of York County, State of South Carolina... to my loving wife Margret Adams, my negro wench named Ame and her choice of any of the Horse creatures on my plantation and her choice of three cows and calves, her bed and furniture and the one half of the dresser and a good comfortable sustenance on my place during her widowhood; to my loving daughter Cathrine Carrigan, £2 sterling and to Jean Campbell, £2 sterling;to my loving son Robert Adams £2 sterling; to my loving son James Adams, £2 like money; to my loving daughter Rachel Barnett, £2 sterling; to my loving daughter Margret Watson, £2 sterling; to my loving sons Joseph and William Adams my plantation on which I now dwell to be divided equally between them both also the remainder or what is left from a straight line from the corner at the Cross Roads to the Rocks; my negro Sam to the aforesaid Joseph and William; all the stock not mentioned and the waggon and still and all farming tools to said Joseph and William; to my loving daughter Elizabeth Adams my negro boy Curry and the rest of the land adjoining my son Roberts and £20 sterling to be taken off or deducting out of my two sons estate that is Joseph & William if she lives to come to age; my loving son Robert Adams and my friend James Hill, executors... 1 March 1799. William Adams (LS), Wit: James Ramsey ,Hugh Gordon. 5 May 1800 proved the will of William Adams by the oath of Hugh Gorden and qualified Robert Adams, exr., before Alex'r Moore, Ordinary Y. D.

**Pages 16-17:** Will of Edward Bland of the County of York, farmer... to Frankey my dearly beloved wife, the whole of my estate as long as she doth live except a soral mare which I allow my beloved son William Bland to have provided he make a true indever to find two young cretors that is now strays which I allow for my two daughters Dosha & Elizabeth; after my wife's death the estate be equally divided among my children including all that may or shall be received during her life; my wife Franky my executrix and my son in law George Plaxco executor... 12 October 1797. Edward Bland (LS), Wit: William Bland, James Plaxco. 9th day of June 1800 the will of Edwd Bland was proven before me by the oath of James Plexco and qualified George Plexco executor before Alex'r Moore, Esqr. Ordinary Y. D.

**Pages 16-17:** Will of John Venable Junior... to my beloved wife Agness all my household furniture of every kind, one of the horse creatures which ever she chooses, three cows, her choice of the cattle, all my sheep and geese & her side saddle also that she have the use & benefit of my plantation during her widowhood and that at her death or marriage it shall be sold at publick sale; also the remainder of my personal estate be sold and the money arising from the sales be equally divided between my wife Agness and my four sons viz John, Bryson, Andrew & Francis Venable; I appoint John Venable Senior, James Venable and Agness Venable, executors... dated 25 June 1800. John Venable (LS), Wit: Francis Adams, John Venable, James Venable, James Henderson.

YORK COUNTY SC WILL BOOK A-1 1800-1813

**Page 19:** Will of George Mellon... to my wife Jane the choice of my horses and the other be sold to school my child, the land for the use of my wife while she keeps single and should she marry then in such case the child's guardian or executor shall take possession of it for the use of sd. child; all the stock of cattle is to be given to my wife for her disposal for sever; my regimental clothes for my brother John; my brother Jonathen is to have a suit of Nanken; the remainder of my clothes to be divided among my family &c; the hogs & sheep to be sold and the money appropriated to the purpose of schooling my son Zanzas; Col. William Moore and Robert Johnston, executors... dated 18 August 1799 at the Eutaw Springs. George Mellon, Wit: John Millwee, John Patterson.

**Pages 20-25:** Will of Samuel Knox of the County of Mecklenburg and State of North Carolina... to my well beloved wife Mary I bequeath one bed and furniture which she commonly called her own also two horses named Jean and Fox; also two negroes named January and Nan, six cows of her own choosing, hogs, for her maintenance, also four sheep with a new saddle and bridle, one walnut chest, one mahogany table, with all the pots, pails, and dresser furniture except the floor handled knives and forks which are to be equally divided between my widow and three daughters and for her my widow to remain and enjoy this may mansion house and farm during her widdowhood; the negroes and them to be equally divided among my three daughters Jean, Sarah, and Mary; to my daughter Jean, one roan horse named Flint with three cows and four hogs; to my daughter Sarah, one soral mare named Dawson with six head of neat cattle, five hogs and two sheep and in case she does not come for said legacy in the space of five years after my decease then to be divided between my daughters Jean and Mary; to my daughter Mary, a soral horse named Ball and six cattle, six young hogs, four shall, negro named Eve; to my grandson John Pettes, one negro man name Jack and one gold watch;to my grandson Stephen Pettes, one negro woman Bet; to my grand daughter Agness Pettes, one negro man Frank and four head of neat cattle; to my granddaughter Mary Pettis, daughter of George Pettis, one mullato boy named Duff and one philly a colt of Dawson; to my granddaughter Mary Candlesh, three negroes Tom, Will, and Pheb, and one plantation whereon Alexander Candlesh lived in York County on waters of Steel Creek joining Geo Pettis, William Pettis, Jos Jackson, and Jesse Horn, and one plantation in Mecklenburg county, No. Carolina, joining John Neely, Charles Calhoun, Walter Davis and Robert Barnett on the waters of Steel Creek about 300 acres, and one plantation near Biggars Ferry on the Cataba joining lands of David McMican, Samuel Neely, and Martin West, 300 acres, also one plantation joining the Indian line and the lands that was formerly Jackson Neely and another tract of my own and David Knoxes all that the patent contains also a lease of land in South Carolina joining the last mentioned tract and a small tract of land joining Martin Wests and Standerds lines and if Alexander Candlish returns to these parts to live, he is to occupy and possess any tract willed to sd. Mary Candlesh and two of said negroes for 25 years after my decease and not sell, barter, or trade said land or negroes; and in case sd. Mary Candlish dies before she arrives to the age of 18 years then sd. land and negroes to descend to her brothers or sister; to my granddaughter Rebecca Pettis, a negro girl named Poll and five head of neat cattle; to my grandson Samuel Knox Pettis son of William Pettis, the plantation whereon I now live and as much in the south state joining this tract as will make this tract 800 acres with all the improvements and one negro woman Dinah, one man called Step and one negro boy called Moss and his father to have the use of s'd negroes till sd heir is 21 years of age; to William Pettis, I bequeath all the remainder of land in South Carolina except the tract my Brother Robert Knox lives on which he is to hold during his life and then to descend to Wm Pettis except a tract joining Richard Springs on the Millstone branch and Clems branch and that tract I bequeath o my grandson Stephen Pettis, one half of said tract is John Knox and the lease i his name and mine and John Pettis son of George Pettis, tract of land joining the lines of Richard Robison, John Price, Mr. McRea, Jas Blackwood, Wm. Ferguson, Robt McCormick, about 128 acres and one piece of land that Gorden lived on & a small tract joining Widow Neels, Jas Porters and Capt. Harts and two warrents in the hand of the County Surveyor and these last mentioned lands I bequeath to my executors herein after named to be sold and the money arising from the sale to be equally divided among my grandchildren above named and my two stills, my stallon, my two waggons, my guns, my sword and all horses and cattle not mentioned to be sold and the money arising from the sale, the brick house that is now begun to be completed and done off according to what Thomson Hargrove and Charles Wright has agreed to do it for s'd house to be 20 feet high about the stone work and chimneys; to my brother John's son Samuel Knox, one young bay horse and to Sa'l Knox Pettis my grandson, one tract of land joining Samuel Calhoone and my own and Samuel Neelys lines about 30 acres; the grain in the ground after a sufficient quantity laid off for the maintenance of my widow to be sold; my wearing apparel to be divided between my brothers Mathew Knox and David Knox and the plantation that is between David Knox and me I bequeath him my half of it and I bequeath Jas Tagert my best Hatt; I appoint my wife Mary Knox my executrix and William Pettis and Jas Tagert my exrs... dated 5 May 1794. Samuel Knox (LS), Wit: James J. Gordon, Joseph Knox (mark), George Pettus.

**Pages 25-27:** Will of Jacob Julian of the County of York... to my beloved wife Rachel Julian, my dun horse, two cows, one feather bed & furniture, one reel, one loom, two spinning wheels, & saddle & bridle, two iron potts, one skillet; all the rest of my perishable property be sold at publick sale on twelve months credit and the money thence arising be equally divided among my five daughters Mary, Margeret, Martha, Hannah, & Susanna; to my beloved wife during her widowhood the pat of my land beginning at a corner on Sugar at or near the Fish Dam... to the North Carolina line to Sugar Creek and after her widowhood to my beloved son Jacob; to my beloved son George, the part of my land that lies in the bounds adj. James Glovers line, on the Road that leads over to said Glovers field along my son Jacob's line to the North Carolina line thence to Hugh Harris's Indian Land line, on John Rookers line, Thomas Barnett's line during the term of the lease of s'd land; to my beloved son James the residue of my land between Glovers line & Isaac Weathers during the term of the lease of s'd land; my friend Jonas Rodgers have the priviledge of occupying the house he now lives in & that pat of uncultivated land allotted for my son James for the term of three years rent free; my friends Thomas Barnett, William Alexander & my son George Julian, executors... dated 21 October 1799. Jacob Julian (mark), Wit: J. Rooker, Thos Barnett, George Julian Senior. Before assigned I Jacob Julian, do give to my beloved daughter Mary a certain sorel colt the foal of my soral young mare[?] over & above her before mentioned legacy.

**Pages 28-29:** State of South Carolina, York County, October 7th 1799. Will of John Garvin of the aforesaid state & county now in a low condition and on my sick bed... to my lawful and trusted wife Margaret Garvin, the one third of all my moveable property also the one third of my land, she taking the same where she pleases; the rest of my family I wish to let them have an equal divide of the remaining property of my real and personal property except my daughter Mary whom I bequeath to her five shillings sterling and no more; to my son William I bequeath a gun barrel which Mr. Alex'r Clark is to make for me to him provided he furnishes [finishes?] a Waggon now on hand; I bequeath to whoever stays on the premises with my wife all my Carpenter Tools and when they remove off, to be disposed of and distributed among the rest, Mary exempted; the plantation tools to be kept on the plantation for their use; also to my son William a pair of wagon wheels now finished to him and he may finish and have the same; all this property except the waggon and wheels to William shall be left on the plantation until my youngest son Robin is of age who with my son James I desire should be schooled there being a three years old heiffer whom my daughter Violet always claimd, I wish to let her have the same clear of all dispute; my lawful and trusty friends Mr. John Cooper and Mr. Andrew Love my executors. John Garvin (X), Wit: Jno Sale, Benjamin Garvin.

**Pages 30-31:** Will of Alexander Black of the State of South Carolina and York County... to my well beloved son Joseph Black the loom & beden & four sheep; to my well beloved son Alexander Black the plantation lying on the waters of Cataba River and Moores Branch in York County, 150 acres & my bed and furniture; to my well beloved son David Chambers, ten shillings & ten pence; to my well beloved daughter Ann Black, one Bay mare and a colt of four years old and seven head o cows and bed and furniture and the household furniture and the remainder of the sheep and the remainder of my money; David Chambers, Bosten on the Covenant; Alexander Black, Blackwall; and my indent between Joseph and Ann Black; and the remainder of the books between Joseph and Ann Black whom I make the sole executrix of my will... dated 2 January 1794. likewise I make Joseph and Alexander Black my two sons, executors. Alexander Black (+) (LS), Wit: Joseph Johnston, Hugh Rogers, Alexander Johnston.

**Pages 32-33:** State of South Carolina, York County. Will of James Bigger of state & county aforesaid... to my well beloved wife Eddy Bigger, a bay mare with a blais in her forehead named Pleasure with her sadle, a bed and furniture & to have the dwelling house that it not yet finished and her living on the plantation during her widowhood and the children to be raised and schooled off the plantation; I allow the plantation I now live on to be equally divided betwixt my two eldest sons Moses and Mathew, each of them paying $200 to James & William McKee their brother Moses to have the part that the improvements is on; my negroes to be divided equally betwixt my wife and children at the time that my son Mathew comes of age if required; my aunt Ann Bigger to have her living on the plantation during her life; my wagon & geers and all the farming tools to be kept for the use of the plantation likewise my house & cattle and all my other moveable property to be equally divided betwixt my wife and children at the time that Mathew comes of age if required; I appoint my friend William McKee and my friend Robert Johnston, my executors, dated 24 March 1800. James Bigger (LS), Wit: Jos McKinzie, Jas Ramsey, William Davis.

**Pages 34-36:** David Hutchison produced to me the will of William Craig deceas'd when John Hart & Agness Hutchison came before me and being duly sworn proved the will of William Craig.

William Craig of the county of York & State of South Carolina, being in a sick & low condition... my beloved wife to keep the Land & as much stock as her & my other executor may think for the benefit of the estate in her own hands as long sa she remains my widow & when my youngest son comes of age, I allow the land to be equally divided either by partition or sale as them and my executors may think best; my shop tools, waggon & my horse, my rifle gun & watch and whatever other property my executors may find not of us, I allow to be sold and the money arising therefrom to be equally divided amongst sons & daughters allowing my beloved wife her third of all except the land which I allow to my sons only my beloved wife to have her maintenance of it as long as she remains my widow & my children to receive their part as they come to full age; the children to be schooled & all debts paid out of the money arising from the sale; I appoint my wife Mary Craig and David Hutchison my sole executors... dated 24 Feb 1801... my still not above mentioned I allow to be sold & managed as the other property & my negro wench Minta I allow to my wife as long as she remains my widow. William Craig (LS), Wit: James Redmond, John Hart, Agness Hutchison (X). Proved before Alex'r Moore, Esquire, Ordinary, 7 March 1801. Qualified Mary Craig and David Hutchison executors at the same time.

**Pages 36-37:** March 18th 1801. The last will and testament of John Milan deceas'd was proven before me by James Martin evidence thereto.

Will of John Milan of York County or District, State of South Carolina... to my son James Millan $10 and to my son William Milan $10 and to my daughter Ann Millan, her bed and furniture, her chest, and her clothing and saddle and $130, and three year old horse colt and two cows, her wheel and reel; to my son Archibald Milan, the southwest side of my plantation, he is to have the half of it laid off by the executors; to my son Robert Milan, the northeast side with the "mention house." My smith tools to remain undivided for the use of my four sons and my waggon to remain here for the use of my four sons on their plantations if any of them wants to go to town there are to be equal shares in the use of the waggon; my smallest still to my son Robert Milan; my son Archibald Millan is to have two cows and all the remainder of my moveable estate is to be equally divided between Archibald and Robert Millan after my debts is paid and James, William, and Robert, my three sons is to assist their brother Archibald each of them ten days in building an house; I appoint Henry Rea, William Kenedy, and Alex'r Galloway to be my executors. John Milan (O), Wit: James Martin, Wm. McClain, James Moore. March 18th 1801. Quallified Henry Rea, William Kenedy & Alex'r Galway executors.

**Pages 38-40:** James Dickey produced the will of John Dickey Senior deceased when John King came before me and proved the will, 6 April 1801. Alex'r Moore, Ordinary, Y. D.

State of South Carolina, York District. Will of John Dickey, 22 March 1801... to my son John Dickey, all my land lying on the east side of Turkey Creek in the state and district aforesaid and what it lacks of 100 acres to be made up off the head of the bottom; to my son Mathew Dickey, 100 acres, the lower end of the tract on which I now live including part of the cleared ground, and the remainder of the land I bequeath unto my [son] David Dickey, except 190 acres of barred land which is joining said land which is to be divided between John, Mathew, and David; one tract of 88 acres joining with Joseph Jemison, McKinney, and Turner with all my other goods and chattles is to be sold except one mare known by the name Fly which I bequeath to my daughter Rebeckah also one young bay horse which I bequeath to my daughter Sarah and each of them a saddle; to my son William Dickey, $20; the remainder of my estate to be equally divided between Martha, Rebecca, John, Mathew, Sarah, and David, by each of my sons viz john, Mathew, and David allowing £75 each for the land to go in their part of the divide; John and James Dickey to be my executors. John Dickey (LS), Wit: S. Fowler, John King, David Leech Junior. Qualified John & James Dickey executors, April 6th 1801.

**Pages 41-42:** So Carolina, York District. Robert Faris, Esq'r, came before me & proved the will of Robert Adams, 8 April 1801.

South Carolina, York District. Will of Robert Adams of district and state aforesaid... at my death my bar mare, saddle & bridle be delivered to Robert Patrick Junior, Capt. Will'm Patricks son, also my smooth gun; my other saddle be given to Adam Beard Junior, son of Adam Beard; my clothes to be equally divided between the male children of Adam Beard, William Patrick, Christopher McCarter, & John Berry; all the remainder of my estate in cash or otherwise shall be equally divided amongst my seven sisters to wit, Mary, Sarah, Ann, Izabella, Martha, Elizabeth, & Hannah; my brother in laws William Patrick & Adam Beard, executors, dated 27 May 1800. Robert Adams

(Seal), Wit: Arthur Faris, Hanna Faris, Rob't Faris. April 6th 1801 qualified William Patrick executor.

**Pages 43-45:** South Carolina, York District. June the 13th 1801. David Daniel produced the will of David Muldoon decd, whereupon James Cathey made oath to prove the will.

Will of David Muldoon of the State of South Carolina and York District, farmer, being very sick and weak in body... to Mary my beloved wife the one third of my real and personal estate as the law directs; to my wifes daughter Elizabeth $5; my daughter Elinor, my son Elias, Sarah, Rebecca and Lucinda, my daughters, be coequal of the remaining part of my estate; John Downing Senior and David Daniel, my sole executors.. dated 5 June 1801. David Muldoon (LS), Wit: Mary Neely (X), James Cathey (I). June 13th 1801 Qualified David Daniel executor.

**Pages 46-48:** 26th June 1801. Proved the will of Margret McNight late of the District of York deceased by the oaths of Col. Joseph Brown, Andrew Egger & Elizabeth Lee and at the same time qualified Isabella McNight & Elizabeth McNight, executors.

Will of Margret McNight, widow, of the District of York & State of South Carolina, being sick & weak in body.... to my three daughters Mary, Issabella, & Elizabeth, all my plantation on which I now live during the time that they shall respectively live single & unmarried & at the time of the death of marriage of any or either of them, the survivor or survivors of them which shall remain unmarried shall enjoy the whole until the whole of them shall either die or marry & at the death or marriage of all my three daughters, I believed unto my grandson John McNight one moiety of my said tract; the other moiety to remain to my three daughters; to my daughter Mary McNight, my bed and furniture and at her death then to go to my granddaughter Margret McLelan Freeman & my grandson John McNight Lindsey, jointly; to my two daughters Issabella and Elizabeth each of them a bed & furniture which is now called theirs; to my grandson Moses McLeaven a bed & furniture which is now called his & also one young cow; to my son Robert McNight my large looking glass to be delivered to him at the death or marriage of all my three daughters; the remainder of my estate to my three daughters; my two daughters Isabella McNight & Elizabeth McNight, executors... dated 20 Dec 1800. Margret McNight (X) (LS), Wit: Jo Brown, A. Egger, Elizabeth Lee (X).

**Pages 49-52:** 6 July 1801. Proved the will of David Porter Deceas'd by the oath of Samuel Curry, William Hamilton, and Francis Curry. At the same time qualified William Porter, Col. Andrew Love, and John Wilie, executors.

State of South Carolina, York District. Will of David Porter Senior of the District and State aforesaid... my wife Isabel Porter do occupy and enjoy the Improvements of the Land whereon I now live, that is the part thereof which lies on the west side of the Road leading from John Wilsons to the Reverand George G. McWhorters with timber to keep the same in repair and liberty to have three acres more cleared with all the profits arising therefrom for her comfortable support during her widowhood also one mare called Brown and horse called Buck with plows and working tools, two cows, two beds and furniture, etc., also the use of my negroes during her widowhood and at the end of which or her natural life to be divided amongst my children it the following manner; my son James to have an equal share with the other children provided he pays off a note of mine of $70 and interest which was given to widow Bishop of Chester District but if he does not pay off or take up said note the amount thereof is to be counted in his share; my son William have free boarding for himself and William Hamilton in order to work at his trade (in consideration of his having work with me on the plantation after he came of age) over and above his equal share for the space of one year; my son John for the same reason I allow to have $100 over and above his equal share; the amount of $60 be deducted from my daughter Peggy's equal share which I allow her to have and be added to the share of my son John as part of the $100; $70 be deducted from an equal share which I allow my son David $40 of which is to make up the $100 extraordinary bequeathed to my son John, and the remaining $30 to be laid out in repairing the houses, fencing and meadow on that pat of the improvement bequeathed to the use of my wife; to my son Francis $25 to be laid out in schooling for him, my shot gun, my large House Bible, and a Book lent to the Rev. Mr. Walker over and above his equal share; no part of my property be exposed to publick sale unless my executors may deem it necessary and unavoidable but that when my executors may think a division ought to take place that they have an appraisement made by three or more honest and disinterested neighbours and the division be made according to said appraise- ment; my son William Porter, Col. Andrew Love, and John Wilie, executors... David Porter (LS), Wit: Francis Curry, Samuel Curry, William Hambleton (mark). [Codicil] It is hereby declared that the part of my land not mentioned in the foregoing will may be occupied by any of my sons that lives on the plantation, dated 16 May 1801.

**Page 53:** August 10th 1801. Proved the will of William Brown deceas'd by the oath of Hugh Drenan.

Will of William Brown of the County of York and State of South Carolina... 16 April 1794. to my son Charles Brown, all the property or worldly effects that I am possessed of; I do bind my said son Charles Brown to find my wife Jean Brown sufficient vittles, apparal, and lodging in his own house during her life; to my son Archibald Brown, five shillings sterling to be paid in cash or effects to that amount; to my son in law William Tom, five shillings sterling to be paid in cash or effects to that amount. William Brown (mark) (LS), Wit: Robert Lusk, Hugh Drenan.

**Pages 54-55:** August 18th 1801. Proved the will of Neal McKinney deceasd late of york District by the oaths of James Jemison & Jeph Jemison.

YORK COUNTY SC WILL BOOK A-1 1800-1813

28 February 1801, Will of Neal McKiney of the State of South Carolina and York District being sick of body... to my wife Jean McKinney, one mare and colt and all and singular my stock of cows and hogs, all household furniture and plantation tools and book accompts to be at her disposing while she remains unmarried and after to be equally divided; I appoint my wife Jean McKinney and James McKinney, executors. Neal McKinney (LS), Wit: James Jemison, William Scott, Joseph Jemison. August 18th 1801-- Qualified Jean McKiney Executrix.

**Pages 56-57:** Will of Thomas Gilham of the district of York & State of South Carolina.... to my well beloved wife Jane Gilham, the one half of my land with the improvement, house, and household furniture during her natural life or widowhood & after that time expires I allow the same land to my son William Gillham; to my son Charles Gillham, the other half of my land when he arrives at the full age of 21 years and in case he should die before he arrives to the age of 21, then the land shall be divided equally between my daughters; I allow my executors full power to make use of my land to the best advantage for the schooling and raising of my children & all the profits arising from my plantation to be equally divided amongst my children at the discretion of my executors; I appoint my wife Jane Gilham & Ezekial Gilham to be executors.... dated 25 August 1801. Thomas Gilham (Seal), Wit: Ralph Rodgers, Chas. Gillham, Adam Meek. November 10th 1801 proved the will of Thomas Gillham deceas'd by the oath of Adam Meek. November 20th 1801 Qualified Jane Gillham & Ezekial Gillham, exrs.

**Pages 58-61:** Whereas a Dedimus Issued from the Ordinaries Office for the District of York dated the fifth day of Octbr 1801 Directed to Joseph Winningham, a justice of the peace appointed for the District of Orangeburgh in the State of South Carolina, said Joseph Winningham Esq'r made on the dedimus the return following.

South Carolina, Orangeburgh. Agreeable to the power invested in my by Alexander Moore, Esq'r, Ordinary for the District of York, I have examined George Crawford & Uriah Gilbert subscribing witnesses of the will of Robert Millar deceas'd, they have declared on their oaths as pr affidavits on the back of said will... 22 Oct 1801. Joseph Winningham, J.P.

State of South Carolina, Orangeburgh District. Personally appeared before me Joseph Winningham George Crawford a witness to the will of Robert Millar... 22d Oct 1801. George Crawford. Also appeared Uriah Gilbert who also proved the will, 22 Oct 1801. Joseph Winningham, J.P.

Will of Robert Miller of York County... after my lawful debts and funeral expenses are satisfied, $6 to be paid to my land lady as a small compensation for her kindness shewn me, as also one dark gown pattern to Mrs. Woods & of the same piece a gown pattern to be taken off for my mother, the piece being of dark purple that those two patterns to be taken from Mrs. Woods has an Inventory of Butter that I will discount in Sugar; Robert Faris, Esqr., will receive $10 in goods exclusive of what I owe him in the trade of a horse; Mr. Arthur is to have $5 in goods; Robert's wife Hannah, she shall take choice of one of the shalls; as to the remainder of my stock of goods on hand, I leave it to my father & Robert Faris to manage as they may see most expedient; my advice is to advertise my goods at Dunkins Creek for sale & to give a credit, the present load I would have carried up to my father & to sell it out for butter or cash in the spring or to carry the load to Mrs. Woods as I think it would be more advantageous, will she or he except the said load between the old people & my sisters, one obligation I lay upon my sisters that they shall maintain the old people should they be incapable of maintaining themselves; as to all my out standing debts at both places, I desire to be collected further I desire to go to Dunkins Creek to take a full inventory of my goods there; Capt. Lattimore he will be able to prove my books as there kept regular & straight & he acted as Clerk; also has Mrs. Woods which veracity is established in York, Lincoln, Rutherford... dated 31 Oct 1800. Robt Miller (LS), Wit: George Crawford, Uriah Gilbert.

**Pages 62-64:** Will of David Hamilton of the State of South Carolina and County of York... to my well beloved wife Jean, the one third of all my personal property to be at her own disposal at her death; to all my children hereinafter mentioned, to each of them five shillings lawful money: to my son James Hamilton, to David Hamilton, to Alexander Hamilton, to my daughter Catharine Hamilton wife of James Hamilton, to John Hamilton, to my daughter Elizabeth Bogs wife of Aaron Bogs, to Thomas Hamilton; to my daughter Jean I bequeath three feather beds with their now furniture, a loom and tacklings and £25 sterling to be paid in horse of the value of between fifteen and twenty pounds and the remainder in cattle or other good trade; to my son William, all my real estate, the land on which I now live and all the remainder of my personal estate after the above mentioned legacies are paid and I do hereby revoke and compleately render null and void all formerly wills, deeds of gift or any other things touching or concerning my property above mentioned; my two sons John and William Hamilton, joint executors... dated 24 April 1797. David Hamilton (Seal), Wit: Samuel Davidson, John Bunkhead, John McCullock. November 10th 1801. Proved the will of David Hamilton by the oaths of Saml Davidson and Saml McCulloch. Qualified William Hamilton exrs. at the same time.

**Pages 65-66:** South Carolina York District. Will of James Crow... unto Jenney Crow my little negro boy by the name of Squire & likewise to be schooled to common English Scholler & said negro to be put out to hire for the use of s'd child & I allow the sum of $40 to be laid out by my executors if they see that there is occasion for cloathing for Jinney Crow; to my Stepson James Irwin when he arrives to the age of 21 years, $50; the remainder of my negroes to be sold at publick sale & my land likewise and the money arising from the same & my whole estate not already willed to be delivered to any one of my brothers (viz) Thomas, Robert, Jason, of John Crow & for that one to divide the same into four equal divisions for him to take one division and give the other three division to three brothers above mentioned; I appoint my faithful friends Hugh White Esq,r Capt. Thomas McNeal, & Andrew Elliott, exrs... dated 1 Dec 1800. James Crow (LS), Wit: Jesse Betty, William White. Proved the will of James Brow by the oaths of Jesse Bettey & William White 23 Oct 1801. At same time qualified Hugh White, Thomas McNeal & Andrew Elliott exrs.

**Pages 67-71:** January 19th 1802. Samuel McCleland & Thomas McCleland produced the will of Robert McCleland deceased upon which John Bates & Michael Stedman proved the will and pronounced that at the time he was of a sound & disposing mind & memory.

Will of Robert McCleland of York District and State of South Carolina, being sick and weak in body... to my beloved wife Anne McCleland one third part of all my estate and particularly to have my old negro wench named Darcus and to have that part of my land on which I now live during her life time and to have the power of disposing of the said one third part as she pleaseth, in which is included one third of my cattle, she to have her first choice; to my daughter Mary Anne McClelan my negro girl named Sabina also a mare named Kate with her colt, likewise one third part of my cattle, two beds and furniture and to have such other part of my estate as will make her full share equal to one fourth part of what is remaining after the share of my wife is taken off but the mare and colt, two beds and furniture to not be reckoned in the calculation of her share as they belong to her already but it must be remembered that said share of daughter Mary Anne is to stand charged with two years schooling to my grandson John McCleland and a suit of clothes to my grand daughter Anne McClelan when my said grand daughter comes of age; to my son Samuel McCleland one fourth part of the residue of my estate after my beloved wifes share is taken off which is to include my negro girl Ruth; to my son Thomas McCleland one fourth part of the residue of my estate after my beloved wifes share is taken off which is to include my negro girl Cynthia, but let it be remembered that there is one black stud horse, one black gelding and a mare colt with a bed and furniture is not to be reckoned in the calculation as they belong to Thomas already; to my son Elias Baxter McClelan one fourth part of the residue of my estate after my beloved wifes share is taken off which is to include my negro boy Moses, but one soral mare and colt with a bed not to be reckoned in the calculation as they belong to him already; to my grandson John McClelan 150 acres of land in my Indian Lease in which land is to be included the dwelling house and improvements where my son Robt decd. formerly lived, the said land to stand charged with its proportion of rent payable to the Indian Nation when said rent becomes due; my said grandson to be invested in the said land at the age of 21 and said land to be in the possession and in the care and management of Priscilla McClelan during her widowhood who is the mother of my said grandson John McClelan; It is my will that Thomas Carrol Senior, John Berry, and James Risk do divide my Indian Land, one third laid off to my wife, and the residue shall remain after my wifes share and the 250 acres herein before left to my grand children John McCleland shall be laid off to be equally divided between my three sons Samuel, Thomas, and Elias Baxter and my daughter Mary Anne

YORK COUNTY SC WILL BOOK A-1 1800-1813

McCleland according to their Judgments and good discretion; I appoint my sons Thomas and Samuel McClelan, exrs... dated 10 Dec 1801. Robert McClelan (mark), Wit: John Bates, Wm. Davis, M. Stedman. Jan 19th 1802 Qualified Saml McClelan, Thos McCleland, exrs.

**Pages 72-74:** Janry 9th 1802, Daniel Sturges produced the will of Jane Sturges alias Bratton whereupon the Rev. Wm. Blacstock, James Turner Junior & James Turner Senior made oath to prove the will.

18 June 1798. Will of Jane Sturges alias Bratton of Indian Land, York County, State of South Carolina... to my daughter Mary Wilson alias Sturges five shillings sterling and to her son and my grandson Daniel Sturges wilson my two negroe children Bob and Abraham only if my said daughter Mary should have any more children, whether one or more, he, she, or they shall be equal sharers in the above two negroes with Daniel Sturges Wilson; if he and they should die without heirs, in such case said negro boys shall be given to my son Daniel Sturges; to my sons John, Joshua and Daniel Sturges, five shillings sterling each; and sons Joshua and Daniel are to be my executors; to my daughter Mary all my clothes and the remainder of my effects. Jane Sturges alias Bratton (+), Wit: William Blackstock, James Turner Junior, James Turner Senior (mark). Janry 9th 1801 qualified Daniel Sturges exr.

**Pages 75-76:** January 8th 1802. The Rev. John Rooker produced the will of Michael Rodgers decd upon which John Smith came and proved the said will.

Will of Michael Rodgers of the District of York & state of So Carolina... to my beloved wife Alice Rodgers, the one half of my estate and grant her the loan of the other half; to my beloved brother Jonas Rodgers, the one half of my estate at the decease of my wife; my beloved Brother Jonas Rodgers & friend John Rooker, exrs, and my wife Alice Rodgers executrix... dated 1 Dec 1801. Michael Rodgers (X), Wit: John Smith, Elizabeth Withers (X). Qualified Exr. at the same time.

**Pages 77-80:** January 21st 1802. John Hutchison Esq'r produced the will of Samuel Atkins whereupon Lewis Croxton and Benjamin Croxton proved it by their oaths.

State of South Carolina, York District. Will of Samuel Atkins of four Mills Creek near the Old Nation ford in the state and district aforesaid, planter.... to my beloved wife Sarah who made her elopement from my bed, five shillings sterling for her part, and that her son John do receive one shilling and no farther divide of my estate; to my beloved wife Rebeccah, during her widowhood, the use and benefit of the plantation whereon I now live when at home, also six negroes by name Jack, Joe, Nance, Luce, Furrow, and Grace with all other moveable goods to the end that she may be comfortably provided for befitting a person of her years and circumstance; if my wife Rebecca should marry again or at her decease the above mentioned property to be sold except two negroes Joe and Nance, and the moneys arising from the sale to be divided: to my wife Rebecca;s son Robert willis, one negro called Joe; also to her daughter Mary Willis, one negro called Nance and no farther divided of my estate; the remainder to be equally divided between my sister Mary Fosters three children Henry Foster, Catharine Foster & John Foster; I appoint John Hutchison, Esqr., and Mr. Read schoolmaster, executors... dated 5 Dec 1801. Saml Atkins (Seal), Wit: Robert McElwain, Lewis Croxton, Benjamin Croxton. Janry 21st 1802 qualified John Hutchinson Esq'r ex'r.

**Pages 80-81:** Febry 26th 1802. James Mitchell produced the will of James Benoist deceased. March 5th 1802 was proved by the oath of Moses Ratchford.

Will of James Benoist of York County and State of So Carolina, being weak in body.... to my beloved cousin Henry Palmer of the State of Kentucky the whole of my estate real and personal & my will is that the said Henry Palmer shall pay all just debts & collect all monies due to me and I empower said Henry Palmer to sell and dispose of my lands and make titles thereto; I appoint said Henry Palmer and my beloved friend James Mitchel of York County, So Carolina, executors... dated 19 September 1801. James Benoist (Seal), Wit: Wm. McLean, Mary Ratchford (O), Moses Ratchford. Qualified James Mitchel Ex'r at the same time.

**Pages 82-84:** March 1st 1802. Ralph Rodgers produced the will of Charles Gilham dec'd upon which James Wilson proved the will.

Will of Charles Gilham of the District of York and State of So Carolina, being weak in body... unto my wife the sum of five shillings; to my beloved daughter Elizabeth Gilham 100 acres of my new survey on the west side of Bullocks Creek with 50 acres added to it on the same side of the Creek of the land I purchased of Delap including a part of the Bottom with her bed and furniture; to my daughter Sarah Gilham 100 acres of land on the west side of Bullocks Creek known by the name of the Duck pon plantation or place, also her bed and furniture; to my son John Gilham, the remainder of my land with my mansion house & my bed and furniture & one chest of drawers, my grey horse and bay mare, one set of plow irons & two pair of gears, 1 big pot, etc; unto John Mongomery £15 to be paid out of the unbequeathed property; unto Hampton Wade £10; the remainder of my estate I allow to be appraised & sold & equally divided between my three youngest children; I appoint my eldest son Thomas Gilham, Ralph Rodgers & Adam Meek to be executors... dated 25 Oct 1800. Chas Gillham (LS), Wit: James Wilson, Jonas Bayles, Sarah Davidson. March 1st 1802 Qualified Ralph Rodgers named exr.

**Pages 85-87:** March 5th 1802. James Faris produced the will of James Faris deceased, whereupon Richard Faris proved the will by his oath.

Will of James Faris of York county and State of South Carolina, being in my ordinary state of health... 5 January 1802... to my beloved wife Jean two negroes, Graes and Dine and two mares Poll and Sorral and the third of the cattle with her bed and bedding and to live to the plantation as long as she pleases; to my son James Faris, two negroes Dan and Dun with half of the plantation and the third of the cattle; to my son Richard Faris the other half of the plantation with two negroes named Rody and Sank with the third of the cattle;to my grandson Elias Faris one black horse coalt; to my son William Faris the soral mares colt; to my son Alexander Faris $5; to my daughter Margret married to David Strain $5; to my daughter Agnes married to Benjamin Garrison $5; to my daughter Jean married to John Adare as much as will pay the Doctors bill or bills; to my daughter Susanna married to John Faris $5; to my daughter Ann married to James Faris $5; my wife Jean Faris and my son James Faris, executors. James Faris (LS), Wit: James Faris, Richard Faris, John Kerr. March 5th 1802 qualified James Faris, exr.

**Pages 88-90:** May 3d 1802. Elizabeth Miller produced the will of John Miller deceas'd upon which John Faris proved the will upon oath. Josiah Moore, clerk for Alex'r Moore, Ordinary.

Will of John Miller... to my son James Miller five shillings sterling as his full share; to my daughter Esther McPeke five shillings sterling as her full share; I desire that all my Rail and perishable estate by praised and sold if occasion requires it at the discretion of the executors except the two negroes; I give to my son John Miller, that negro man Rody; to bequeath to my son Hendy Miller the negro man named Daniel; the rest of my daughters married and unmarried be made up their shares in proportion with what they have got already equal with what Ester McPeke has got as her dowry; my daughters Jean Hope, Mary Lowry, Shusanah Hutton, Elizabeth Miller, Margaret Drinnin; I give the remaining part to my dearly beloved wife Elizabeth Miller if anything of consequence remains and to be at her discretion to divided at her decease whom I constitute one of my executors with her two sons John Miller and Hendry Miller; my two sons John Miller and Hendry Miller to take care and provide for their mother a comfortable menteanence... dated 31 January 1801. John Miller (Seal), Wit: Bennit Highfill, Thomas Barnet, John Fearis. At the same time qualified Elizabeth Miller & Henry Miller executors.

**Pages 90-92:** July 19th 1802. Robert Fowler exhibits the will of James Fowler deceas'd whereupon William Robertson proved it upon oath.

Will of James Fowler of the District of york and State of South Carolina made this 18th day of December 1801... my bed and furniture to Mary Fowler my grand daughter daughter of my son Robert Fowler and my watch to James Hinds Fowler my Grand son, and my horse, saddle, and bridle to my son Robert. At the end of one year after my decease I will that Robert pay $25 to my son William also at the end of two years to pay $20 to my son Stephenson; also my gun and shot pouch to my son Robert also my wearing apperal to be equally divided between William and Robert except one suit of black Casimire viz coat, waistcoat and small clothes I will to Stephenson; also an equal divide of books between William and Robert; I appoint my sons William and Robert

# YORK COUNTY SC WILL BOOK A-1 1800-1813

as executors. James fowler (LS), Wit: Wm. Roberson, Mary Stephenson. July 19th 1801 Qualified Robert Fowler Ex'r.

**Pages 93-95:** November 1st 1801. Delphy Arnold & William Arnold exhibited the will of Josephus Arnold dec'd upon which John Drenan Esq'r and William Arnold proved it upon oath.

Will of Josephus Arnold of the State of South Carolina & York District, being weake and sicke in body.... to my beloved wife Delphy Arnold, one sorral mare, 1 bed & furniture, 1 spinning wheel, one loom & tacklings, one chest, two Ewe sheep, one cow called Willey & the half of the dresser furniture, one pot, one chair; to my son William one black filey, one bed & furniture, one peace of land leased from the Catawba Indians of 74 acres he paying my son John the half of the purchase money I gave for the same which was $3.50 per acre, one barr shear & coulter, one pair of drawing chains, one cow and Whitleys yearling, one Iron tooth harrow, one bull & yearling heffer, two Ewe sheep, one mattock, one chair, one falling ax; to my son I bequeath one gray mare, one black cow & calf, 1 pair of drawing chains and the half of the price of the land aforementioned to be paid by my son William unto John when he arrives to the age of eighteen years, 1 shovel plough, two sheep, 1 chair, one broad ax; to my daughter Polly one bed & furniture & the half of the remaining half of the dresser furniture, one cow called white face & her yearling, one dutch oven, one cotton wheel, the gray mares colt she has now, one walnut table, two sheep, one chair; to my step daughter Rebeccah Lovens, the sorral mares colt, one cow called Brindle, one bed & furniture to be made new & the remainder of the dresser furniture, one Dutch oven, two sheep, one chair; my young bar horse I allow to be sold by my exrs in order to pay my just debt; my wife Delphy Arnold & my son William Arnold, executors.. 7th May 1802. Josephus Arnold (X) (Seal), Wit: William Arnold, Thos Drenan, Jno Drenan. November 1st 1802 Qualified Delphy Arnold & William Arnold exrs.

**Pages 96-98:** Octbr 4th 1802. Edward Byers and Adam Meek exhibited the will of John Gorden deceased upon which John Harbeson proved it upon oath.

Will of Jno Gorden of Clarks Fork of Bullocks Creek, York District and State of So Carolina, being weak of body.... to Margret my loving wife her bed & furniture with her saddle & a black filley two years old also her wheel with the little dresser & furniture also the big table & her pick of two cows and calves & her choice of two pots & a Dutch oven & her choice of two pails & her choice of three of the Hogs & A Bushel of Salt & fifty bushels of Corn & two stacks of blades; I allow the bed I lye on my wife Margret to keep it in her possession for my son Jonathen till he comes of age all the said property to her excepting said Filley in case she marries & then to fall to my sons part; the rest of my estate excepting a looking glass I leave to my wife to be put to publick sale & to go to the maintenance & benefit of my son Jonathen & if my son Jonathen dies before he comes of age his share of the estate to be divided betwixt my wife Margret & my brothers Jonathen & Forbes Gorden equally; Edward Byers & Adam Meek, my executors... dated 21 Sept 1802. John Gorden (LS), Wit: Jno Harbison, James Gorden, Samuel Thomson. Qualified Edward Byers & Adam Meek ex'rs at the same time.

Account of the afore mentioned Wills & Estate sent to the Secretary in Columbia.

**Pages 99-101:** Novbr 23d 1802. Samuel Robertson exhibited the will of Hugh wilson Deceas'd upon which Mary Ann Dickey proved it upon oath. John Dickey appeared and proved the will of Hugh Wilson 23 Nov 1802.

8 June 1802. Will of Hugh Wilson of South Carolina, York District, planter, being weak in body... to my true and well beloved wife Martha Wilson all my estate real and personal during her life or widowhood except as herein after excepted; to Elizabeth Broadwill her freedoms; to John Lockhart his freedoms these freedoms with the payment of all my just debts to come out of my personal property the above freedoms to be paid when the above mentioned Elizabeth and John comes of age; the plantation whereon I now live with the appurtenances thereunto belonging I allow to be sold at the death of marriage of my wife Martha and the money to be for the use of the above mentioned Elizabeth Broadwill and the heirs of her body but if she should die without issue, I allow the said money to be divided equally among the children male and female of my brother James Wilson; my wife Martha and Samuel Robertson Senior, my executors. Hugh Wilson, Wit: Thomas Woods, Mary Ann Dickey, John Dickey. Qualified Martha Wilson and Samuel Robertson Senior named ex'rs in the above will Novbr 23d 1802.

**Pages 102-103:** Will of James Glover of the State of South Carolina and County of York, farmer... I will and ordain that my beloved wife Polly for to have free possession of the premises where I now live and the use of the negroes and household furniture and farming utensils during her life time or widowhood at the expiration of s'd life time or widowhood the whole of the land to be equally divided among four of my sons namely William Glover, James Barns Glover, Mortler[?] Glover and John Glover and at the same time all the other property to be put unto publick sale namely Negroes and stock of all kinds with household furniture and unto my three younger sons viz Benjamin Glover, Joseph Glover and Berry Glover for to have $100 each and an equal share of what remains of the amount of the sale; my wife Polly and Natty Marable to be executors... dated 30 Dec 1797. James Glover (X) (Seal), Wit: Jemima Marable (X), Nathaniel Weathers, James Barr. Qualified Polly Glover and Natty Marable executors Dec 31st 1802.

**Pages 104-106:** Will of James Watson of the State of South Carolina & District of York... 5 September 1802.... to my son David Watson $200; to my son John Watson $200; to my son William Watson, the plantation on the buckhorn fork of Bullocks Creek containing 200 acres with him the said William paying $20 to the executors of my estate to be converted to the use aftermentioned; to my son Samuel Watson my negro boy named March, said

Samuel paying Elizabeth Findley $50; to my son Aron Watson the plantation I now live on with two plows and tacklings and a bay filley with a white in her face two years old; to my daughter Jeane one bed and furniture; one spinning wheel & a horse creatur and saddle and bridle to be valued to be as good as the creature that my daughter Ann got from me when she was married & Two cows and calves and the third of the coset furniture; to my beloved wife Jeane two horse creatures her bed and furniture and all the remainder of the household furniture that is not mentioned above and all the plantation tools for her use and benefit while she lives on the premises and if disposed to remove off said premises said tools to remain unmoved for the use of my son Aron; to my wife two negroes Easther and joe as long as she lives single and remains on the premises; to my wife at my decease $50 -in money; to my daughters Elizabeth Finely and Ann Hemphill one cow and calf for each of them and the remainder of my cattle, sheep, hogs, geese &c I leave at the whole disposal of my wife; I allow my executors to purchase four Bibles and give one to Samuel my son and one to each of my daughters; to my son David my old Bible with Cains notes contained in it; likewise my House Bible I leave to my wife; the remainder of my books to be equally divided amongst my children; the whole of my wearing apperal to my son Samuel;' i appoint my sons David, John, & Saml Watson exrs. James Watson (LS), Wit: Katharine Watson (X), David Watson, Saml Watson.

**Pages 106-107:** Will of Robert Bell of the district of York and State of South Carolina, being weak of body... the plantation whereon I now live be divided between my two sons John & Robert agreeable to quantity & quality my son John taking that part or end of that tract on which he has improved; to my on Robert Bell all the remainder of my personal property, he paying all my just debts & delivering to Jenny Crow or her guardian one father bed with its furniture, likewise one Calico bedquilt & one dun heifer; my son Robert deliver to my son in law James Davis one two year old bay filley or mare; my two sons Jo'n Bell and Robert Bell ex'rs.. dated 12 Oct 1802. Robert Bell (X) (Seal), Wit: John L. Davies, John Bell, Elizabeth Davis (mark).

**Pages 107-109:** Will of Robert McCurdry of the state of South Carolina and District of York being in a very low state of health... to my beloved granddaughters Hannah and Elizabeth Guyton $50 each; to my beloved grandson Robert McCurday Guyton a negro boy named Isaac and $50; to my beloved granddaughter Betsy Bankhead $50; to my beloved grandson Robert McCurdry Bankhead a negro girl named Amy and $50; to my beloved granddaughter Jean Bankhead a certain mare named lyd; to my beloved wife Mary five bushels of wheat and one fat hog; to my two beloved daughters Margaret Guyton and Jean Bankhead $17 each; to my beloved wife and three daughters Mary Bankhead, Margaret guyton and Jean Bankhead the remainder of my estate both real and persona to be sold and equally divided amongst them at my death by my trusty friends my beloved wife Mary, John Bankhead Snr., Aaron Guyton and John Bankhead Junr, which I leave as executors... dated 18 January 1803. Robert McCurdry (Seal), Mary McCurdry (X) (Seal), Wit: Floyd Bostick, Edward Summerford, Jno Smitty.

**Pages 109-110:** Will of William Barry of York District in the State of South Carolina, 9 October 1802... to my well beloved wife Jane Barry two negroes named Seaser & Sarah & the use of the plantation as long as single & wagon, two horses, one mare & filley & all farming utentials, cows, sheep & hogs, and al the household furniture except so much as may be named to John or Jane Berry hereafter and if she marreys the one third of all and the other two thirds to the legatees but the two negroes I make her right and title; to my eldest son John Henderson Barry a piece of land lying on a branch of Wild Catt in the Indian Boundrey which I & my friend John Barry purchased from Samuel Creswell; I do obligate sd John Barry to make a just & lawfull title to his cousin John Barry; also I bequeath to John Barry a horse, saddle & bridle & one three year old filly and negro boy named Joseph, bed & furniture; to my oldest daughter Jane Barry a negro girl named Dianah and horse named Bald, saddle & bridle, one feather bed & furniture; to my daughter Catty[?] Porter Barry a negro girl named Aney; to my daughter Peggy a negro girl named Mary; to my daughter Kate Bearry [sic] a negro girl named Malindah; to my daughter Elizabeth Barry a negro girl named Luecy; to my son James Hannah Barry a negro boy named Sampson; also to James H. Barry a piece of land lying between me and Col. Watson near to Mr. Ekins field; to my son William Andres Barry a negro boy named Antoney & also the tract I now live on; if any of the legates should die the negroes willd to them should be equally divided amongst the legatees & if any of the negroes shoed die the other of the legatees should pay that legatee to the amount of sd Negro if died before the legatee is of age; if the above named Sarah has now more children to give to the legatee in lue of the deceased; John Barry, John H. Barry and Jane Berry my wife, my executors. William Barry (LS), Wit: John Henderson, Jenney Berrey, Catharine Barry.

**Pages 111-114:** Will of David Beard of the District of york in the State of South Carolina... to the children of Mary Adair of Denegor near the town of Antrim in the County of Antrim, Ireland, to wit, the children of said Mary Adair begotten by me of her body, to each of them £50 lawful money of this state, the one a boy, the other a girl (the boy sis said to be dead) in the case the girl is to inherit the boys share as well as her own and in case the boy is living and the girl dead, the boy to inherit the girls share as well as his own; unto David Beard Martin (son of James Martin of Bullocks Creek) £100 sterling for the express purpose os a liberal education; to my niece Jane Hartness £40 sterling; unto the Rev. Mr. Walker, our present minister in Bethesda Congregation £5 sterling provided he be living & the actual minister of the Gospel in said Congregation at the time of my deceased; to my niece Catharine Martin, wife of James Martin, one negro boy named Jim; to the aforesaid daughter to Mary Adair, one half of my plantation that I now live on to be equally divided according to quantity and quality, provided she may be living and shall come to possess the same within the term of three years after my decease; unto David Beard Martin, the other half of my said plantation; in case the said daughter of Mary Adair shall to come posses her part within the time above described, I devise the same unto David Beard Martin; my negro fellow Tony do have $15 in case also one horse, his choice of my stock; to my negro Peter, $10 and one horse also his choice of my stock; to my negroes Harmon, Arma, Silva & Nani, $8 each; all my negroes (except Jim) be sold to master of their own choosing in the following manner (viz) each to choose three purchasers and the highest bidder of the three to be the buyer so as not to part Peter & his wife Sylva nor to sold under their appraisement; also all the residue of my estate to be sold at publick sale by my executors and after my debts are paid & the aforesaid legacies are paid, the remainder to James Martin of Bullocks Creek; in case neither of the children of Mary Adair should come to inherit, then the same to be equally divided between the children of Jane Hartness and Catharine Martin; Capt. James Mitchell & James Martin, Esqr., executors... dated 26 June 1802. David Beard (Seal), Wit: Jonathan Sutten, John Graham, Mary Graham (X). March 11th 1803 qualified James Mitchell & James Martin Esqr.

**Pages 115-118:** May 2d 1803 Saml Carol & William Love produced the will of Joseph Carol deceased whereupon Robert Faris proved it upon oath.

7 Feb 1803. Will of Joseph Carol of York District and State of South Carolina, am sick and weak in body... to my three oldest children viz Samuel, Elizabeth, and Jennet, the sum of one dollar each; to my daughter Sarah one bay mare, saddle and bridle, two cows and $50 out of negro Wills price with her bed and furniture; to my son Joseph the smith tools and the sorral horse, saddle and bridle, also 150 acres of land the new entry over the creek with 60 acres of the old place including the Creek; to my son John one brown colt, saddle and bridle, also my 200 acres of land lying on the Beaver Dam; to my daughter Hannah, my gray mare the colt now with excepted with saddle and bridle; to my son Henry the colt the gray mare is now with, saddle and bridle, also my old plantation exclusive of the mill dam and the other legacies otherwise disposed of; to my three youngest children viz Elias, Martha, and Isbell, Will's Price when sold to be equally divided amongst them except the above named $50; to my beloved wife Martha Carol my negro boy Peat and two horses, the bay and the black with all my farming utensils and all the stock of every kind not disposed of and the benefit of the mill with 100 acres of land during her lifetime and at her death to return to my son Elias; my wife Martha Carrol to assist in executing this will with my son Saml Carrol and my friend Wm. Love. Joseph Carol (LS), Wit: Robert Love, Robert Faris, Saml Hemphill. May 3d 1803 qualified Martha Carol, Saml Carol & Wm. Love, exrs.

"See 118 after 177 page error there in pageing."

**Pages 119-120:** April 10th 1803. John Polk produced to me the will of John Polk Senior deceased, whereupon John Fairs proved it.

Will of John Polk of York County in the State of South Carolina... to my beloved wife Eleanor Polk all my personal estate consisting of a negro woman slave called Amy, a horse, horned cattle, household furniture, kitchen furniture & tools for agriculture; my son John, exrs., dated 25 Aug 1803. John

Polk (Jo) (LS), Wit: John Farrels, John Holt. April 10th 1803 qualified John Polk executor.

**Pages 121-122:** July 4th 1803. Benjamin & Edmond Chambers produced the will of James Chambers deceased whereupon Elizabeth Chambers & Benjamin Chambers proved it.

Will of James Chambers of York District in the State of South Carolina... to my well beloved wife Polly all my household furniture, my negro girl Pate, also two of the horse beasts her choice, also six head of cattle her choice, also farming utensils and half of my lands, hogs and sheep; to my son Edmund Rutter the remaining pat of my estate to be sold and put out to interest for him land excepted. N. B. the debts to be settled first out of the estate and also my wife to raise and school my son Edmond and which ever of them departs this life first the other to be the heir of the estate; my wife Polly and Edmond Chambers, exrs., dated 24 June 1803. Jas Chambers. Wit: Elizabeth Chambers (mark), Benjamin Chambers, Jno Chambers. July 4th 1803 qualified Polly Chambers & Edmond Chambers exrs.

**Pages 123-124:** July 18th 1803. Col. Andrew Love produced the will of Jean Miskelly deceased whereupon William Robertson proved it.

31st July 1802. Will of Jean Miskelly, widow woman, in York District and State of So Carolina, being weak in body... to my young relation Jack Clark, one two year old heifer which is intended for the purpose of schooling s'd boy; to my daughter Jean Garvin[?], part of my wearing apperal consisting of 3 gowns, 2 petticoats, one quilted the other flower flannel, all my head cap, one set of neat china ware, one fine bed sheet, one coarser do &one pillow, one bed, ruff, one tea pot & cream jugg which the said daughter may dispose of as she pleases after my deceased with a womans cloak & fine shift; to my son William Miskelly five shillings sterling; to my son James Miskelly fifteen head of cattle of different ages, with my dresser, two common cupboards with my part of the furniture belonging to both of the same with all my other unbequeathed kitchen & chattle property; my friend Col. Andrew Love & David Gorden, both of the District aforesaid, exrs. Jean Miskelly (X) (LS), Wit: William Robertson, John Hill.

**Pages 125-126:** June twenty eighth 1803. Will of James Powell of Sate of South Carolina, York District, being weak in body.... to my dear and beloved wife the gray mare, one bed and furniture and her saddle & Dresser and furniture, half dozen chares, one writing desk; to my beloved daughter Sarah my part of the unbequeathed part of my fathers estate, my part of a tract of land on Cherokee Creek, Spartanburgh District, also my negro boy named Ned and my part of my brother Thomas Powells estate and if my dear daughter dies before it come to age, her part to devolve to my beloved wife. My friends my beloved wife and her father John Smith to be executors, my part of the land on Cherokee Creek. James Powell (mark), Wit: Joseph Kerr, Alex'r Thompson, Nancy Akins. August 1st 1803 Qualified John Smith & Powell Exrs.

YORK COUNTY SC WILL BOOK A-1 1800-1813

**Pages 127-128:** 26th day of August 1786, will of Frances Miskelly of York County in the State of South Carolina (single woman) being weak in body... I give to my mother Jean Miskelly 100 acres of land which was bequeathed to me by my father which land I allow to be to the use & benefit of my said mother during her natural life and after her decease my will is that the said land be equally divided amongst my brother in law Thomas Garvins then surviving children; to my mother one feather bed with the furniture thereunto belonging, also a dark brown horse, also eight head of cattle which is the remainder of my stock after my brother James Miskellys number is taken out, one third or my bequeathed part of the dresser furniture and after her decease to be given to my sister Jean Garvin, also my part of the flax and cotten to my said mother; to my brother James Miskelly one Dun colored cow & calf, three head of year old cattle, and the sums specified in James Morrows note of hand being for £70 s5, also the sum ascertained in Joseph Wallaces obligation which is for £31 s1 both being payable in November 1779 with the sum that my mare sold for which is now in the hands of Mr. Andrew Love; after my mothers decease the part of the negroes bequeathed to me by my father to my sister Jean Garvins then surviving children; to my sister a petticoat pattern of black colemanco and the remainder of my wearing apparel to my sd sisters female children; to my brother William Miskelly, the sum of five shillings sterling money of SC; James Tipping, William Rainey, my executors. Frances Miskelly (LS), Wit: John Garvin, Benjamin Garvin, Dd. Gordon. Nov 26th 1803 proved by the oath of Benjamin Garvin. Sept 5th 1803 qualified William Rainey Exr.

**Page 129:** Oct 31st 1803. Robert Harris produced the will of Eleanor Polk whereupon Taylor Polk made oath that he was present.

Will of Eleanor Polk of York County in the State of South Carolina... to my daughter Eleanor Polk, all my personal property devised to me by the will of late husband consisting of a negro woman slave called Ame, a sorral horse, horned cattle, household and kitchen furniture and tolls for agriculture; my friend Robert Harris, exrs, 6 May 1803. Elanor Polk (X), Wit: Taylor Polk, Wily Sanders, Eleanor Polk (X). October 31st 1801 qualified Robert Harris exr.

**Pages 130-132:** December 5th 1803. Hannah Farris produced the will of Robert Faris deceased whereupon Joseph [sic] proved the will.

16 June 1803. Will of Robert Faris of York District and Sate of South Carolina am sick and weak in body... to my son Moses $20; to my son David a saddle and bridle and a cow and calf; to my daughter Sarah $5; to my daughter Anne her bed and furniture, her wheel, one cow and calf; to my daughter Harriet[?], a bed and furniture, a sorrel filley, cow and calf, her wheel; to my son Robt Arthur my plantation known by the name of Bethel; to my daughter Mary a bed and furniture and my sorrel mares last spring colt; to my daughter Isabella Gordon a bed and furniture and cow and calf; to my son John McWhorter the plantation I now live on to be his at the death or

marriage of his mother; to my beloved wife Hannah the plantation, two work horses, sufficient ploughs, hoes and other implements for farming to carry on said plantation for the purpose of raising my children to her death or marriage; to James Bigger when he has fully complyed with his indenture a horse and saddle worth $70; I appoint my wife Hannah and her brother John and my son Moses to execute this will. Robt Faries (LS), Wit: Robert Love, Samuel Hemphill, Joseph Carrel. Quallified Hannah Faries, John Faries & Moses Faries exrs, Dec 5th 1803.

**Pages 133-134:** January 2d 1804. Robert Harris produced the will of Clark Ticer whereupon Spill Kimble, Alex'r Hynes & Richard Spears proved the will.

Will of Clark Ticer of South Carolina, York District, dated 26th Novr 1803... to my son Henry Ticer $5; to my daughter Mary $100, her bed and furniture and side saddle. I will that my son Hugh be made a good English Schollor out of my estate. I will my daughter Jaen three months schooling and her bed and furniture; my son Samuel to be schooled out of my estate; my daughter Sarah to be schooled and $35 in cash; the remainder of my estate to be equally divided between my above named children Henry Ticer excepted. All my property to be sold by publick sale except the above named-- my plantation, three negroes and stud horse at two years credit. Robt Harris, exrs. Clark Ticer (X) (Seal), Wit: Spell Kimble, Alex'r Hynes, Richard Spears. Qualified Robt Harris exr Jany 2d 1804.

**Pages 135-137:** Jany 6th 1804. John Gillon produced the will of Andrew Sprott deceased whereupon Jeremiah Alderson and William Weathers proved the will.

Will of Andrew Sprott of the State of South Carolina and District of York, being verry sick and weak in body.... to Elizabeth my beloved wife a black three years old mare and a new saddle to be got for her and bridle, also a bed and furniture and two cows such as she chuses and also to have a children part namely a sixth part of all the remaining estate; unto each of my five children viz Polly Sprott, James Sprott, Susannah Spott, David Sprott, and Charity Sprott, one fifth part of my whole estate that is not before bequeathed; James Sprott shall have a negro man named Jordan by paying the rest of the heirs their share of his value; David Sprott shall have a negro woman Milly by paying the rest of the heirs their equal shares of her value; said negroes are to remain unsold but kept for the use of the family until the heirs come to age; the land also is to remain not sold until the heirs come to age; my children to be schooled at the expence of my estate; John Gillon and Alexander Scott shall be executors... dated 26 Dec 1803. Andrew Sprott (O) (LS), Wit: Jeremiah Alderson, William Weathers. Qualified John Gillon and Alex'r Scott exrs, Jany 6th 1804.

**Pages 138-140:** February 25th 1804. John Spencer produced the will of James Kenmure whereupon David Roddy proved the will.

## YORK COUNTY SC WILL BOOK A-1 1800-1813

Will of James Kenmure of South Carolina and York District... to my wife Elizabeth Kenmure part of the plantation I now live upon containing 150 acres including all the improvements thereunto belonging to be laid off beginning at David Roddy's line by the creek and taking in all my houses and clear land, and to fall to my daughter Elinor at my wifes decease; also to my wife all my money, notes, horses, cattle, hogs, goods and chattles as a support during her life and what of this property remains at her death to be equally divided amongst my children; to my daughter Margrets children vis Elizabeth and William Meglamery 100 acres of land to be laid off along the Indian line and if they die without issue or before they come to maturity, said land to return to my children as their property; to my son John Kenmure, 320 acres off the west end of the plantation on which I now live taking in the house and spring where he now lives with all his improvements; to my son John Kenmure all the land I am possessed of in Chester District; the remainder of the last purchased tract of land to be equally divided among my children; to my son in law John Spencer 20 acres off the old tract to be laid off between John Kenmure and him; John Kenmure and John Spencer exrs., dated 29 Oct 1803. James Kenmure (mark), Wit: David Roddey, Margret Gray, Elizabeth Campbell. Febry 2th 1804 quallified John Kenmure & John Spencer exrs.

**Pages 140-142:** March 6th 1802 The will of William Wilkie deceas'd was produced and John Elmore proved the will.

Will of William Wilkie of the State of South Carolina, York District... to my wife Elizabeth all my household goods in general that shall be in her possession at my decease & also my bay mare and saddle that she now rides and two cows, half of the hogs and the remainder of the stock; to my son George Wilkie all my farming utentils of every kind, also 160 acres which is all my home tract and all the McColloch tract the lies on the south east side of the branch coming down from the mountain through my land, by estimation 60 acres but his mother shall have peaceable possession on the land and one third part of all that is made on the land during her widowhood; the remainder of the McCollock tract on the south west side of the branch, 140 acres, shall be sold to the highest bidder and the money divided amongst my six daughters Sabra, Sarah, Deborah, Elizabeth, Rebecca & Ann... my so George Wilkie and Jacob Green, exrs., dated 14 Dec 1802. William Wilkie, Wit: William Martin, John Elmore (X), Thomas Martin (X). Qualified George Wilkie & Jacob Green exrs. March 6th 1804.

**Pages 143-145:** March 6th 1804 was produced the will of Mary Renicks deceased and Doctor Jonas Moore proved the will.

__ October 1800, Will of Mary Renicks (widow woman) in York County & State of South Carolina... to my daughter now Mary Fleming my negro girl Nance and at her decease the said negro girl and her increase (if any) be equally divided amongst my said daughters then surviving children by her present husband Elijah Fleming; to my daughter Elizabeth Ekin £5 sterling; to my daughter Jean Bogs (widow woman) £10 sterling; to my two grand

YORK COUNTY SC WILL BOOK A-1 1800-1813

daughters Agness Wisher & Mary Moore forty shillings each; to my grandson James Wisher five shillings; to my son James Renicks now living in Canetuckey £5 sterling; to my daughter Jean Bogs my riding horse, stock of cattle & hogs, household furniture & kitchen furniture; to her daughter Elizabeth Bogs one feather bed & Furniture and to my other grand daughter Mary B. Fleming another feather Bed & Furniture; to my grandson James Wisher 50 acres of land to be laid off joining the survey Jonathan Kuykendal now lives on; remainder of my survey of land now occupied by John Wish, 100 acres, to my grandson John Renicks Bogs; my wearing apperal to the discretion of my three daughters Elizabeth, Jean & Mary; my son in law Elijah Fleming and my daughter Jean Bogs, exrs. Mary Renicks (M) (LS), Wit: Alex'r Moore, J. Moore, James Moore. Quallified Jean Bogs, exrs., 1804.

**Pages 146-147:** April 1804. Pheby Galimore a woman of colour presented the will of Edward Gallemore deceased whereupon John Thomson proved the will.

Will of Edward Gallimore of the County of York & State of South Carolina being very weak & sick in body... to my beloved wife Pheby Gallimore all and entirely my estate at her disposal during her life and at her death should she not survive the children, I desire that she may leave each of the children an equal part... dated 21 Feb 1801. Edward Gallimore (X), Wit: John Thompson, Matthew Gibson, James Powell.

**Pages 148-153:** August 6th 1804. Proved the will of Doctor John Alison late of York District deceas'd by the oaths of Joseph McKinzie and John McCall. At the same time qualified Elizabeth Alison executr'x & James Mitchell & William Smith Esq'r exrs.

Will of John Alison of the State of South Carolina & District of York, being low in health... to my son Albert Alison the whole of the tract of land whereon I now live and so much of my plantation known by the name of Lattimores place as is herein after mentioned, to begin where the said last plantation joins the one I now live on, at the corner farthest from the River, to the Beaverdam Creek where is crosses the Waggon Road which leads from the ferry to the Iron Works... which joins land formerly the property of Col. Joseph How, but that my wife Elizabeth Alison do have the use and occupation of the houses and land for the purpose of supporting herself and raising the rest of my children during the minority of my said son and for four years afterwards and one third part of the above devised lands during her natural live should she remain a widow; my executrix and executors to sell and execute titles for the remaining part of my Lattimore plantation not herein before disposed of and to sell and execute titles for all that plantation on which I formerly lived lying near to the Aera Iron Works and known by the name of my old place; my household furniture to be kept by my wife for the use of the family until my children shall arrive at such ages as my executors may thing proper to give each of them respectively their equal share together with my wife; my executors do sell all my cattle, hogs, and horses in their discretion; my negroes remain on the plantation to work the same for the benefit of my wife and children until my executors think it prudent to divide the same; my executors to have my children educated; my executrix to sell a tract of land willed by my father to me in the state of Tenessee; my executors to adjust my disputes with Col. William Hill respecting several tracts of land in the state of North Carolina... bonds between Traddle and myself; my wife Elizabeth Alison my executrix and Richard Alison & James Mitchell and William Smith, my executors... dated 5 June 1804. J. Alison (LS), Wit: C. Hagin, John McCall (X), Jos McKenzie. Codicil makes a further disposition of certain negroes... Sam and Jude now in the possession of Col. William Hill be kept by the said Col. William hill and Mrs. Hill his wife and that they be intitled to the benefits of their labour for their support and after the deaths of said Col. William Hill and Mrs. Hill the same negroes be sold and the monies be divided among my wife and children.. dated 5 June 1804. J. Allison (LS) [same witnesses.

**Pages 154-157:** July 30th 1804. Proved the will of Joseph White by the oath of William Eliot. At the same qualified Martha White executrix & Hugh White ex'r.

State So Carolina, York District. Will of Joseph White of the state and district aforesaid, being sick & weake in body... my land in Lancaster District So Carolina to be sold at publick sale by my executors and two negroes Dinah and Jack to be sold for the express purpose of paying off all my lawful debts; to my beloved wife Martha White her choice of my beds and choice of furniture to be put to that bed without any valuation of the same, one skin trunk to be valued and she to take it at its valuation if she sees proper, and my cupboard furniture to be appraised and if she thinks proper to take it at the appraisement and if not to be put to sale, and her saddle and bridle and mare by the name of Nell I freely give. All my negroes the remain I allow to be made into two lots by two men to be chosen by my execrs. for that purpose and to appraise said lots, one lot is to be made up of Lucy and her family and the other that my wife Martha shall have that lot; all my perishable property to be put to sale with all my farming utensils and carpenters tools with house and kitchen furniture except the cupboard furniture all to be sold; my wife the one half of my Indian land totally at her own disposal after the said land is appraised; my wearing apperal to be made up in three lots and appraised and that my brother Hugh White and my brother in law Wm. Barnett and Wm. Eliot Senior my father in law take the sd. lotts from casting lotts for choice and being accountable to my son Wm. Eliot White for the amount when said child comes to the age of twenty one years; my friend James Harris Esq;'r and my wife Martha and my brother Hugh White, exrs.... dated 27 June 1804. Joseph White, Wit: wm. Elliott, John Springs, Wm. B. Eliott. Proved July 30th 1804.

**Page 158:** Will of Thomas Harp... to my daughter Cherybim Harp the sorral mare with a bed and bedding; likewise a feather bed & Bedding to Elizabeth daughter of Bawley Harp; my just debts to be paid by my heirs that is if the land which I now hold as my situation my not be disturbed but the place whereon the Carters now dwell & a piece of land adjoining my plantation of 121 acres if this land does not discharge my debts, my heirs must stand culpable to discharge s'd debts; my wife Elizabeth Harp the plantation whereon I now dwell & at her death to be equally divided to my children & Cherubim Harp; to my wife Elizabeth Harp six head of horned cattle with the remainder of my household property... 14 May 1804, Wit: Wm. Stanton, James Keinan, William Hall. Proved in York District by the oath of James Keenan 3 Sept 1804.

**Pages 159-160:** Octbr 1st 1804. Peggy Burns produced the will of Lauglin Burns whereupon Luke Burns proved the will.

Will of Laughlin Burns of York District, finding myself in a bad state of health... to my son Henry $40 to be paid out of Reuben Hills note of hand; to my wife Peggy the whole of the property except the land now in my possession while she lives and remains a widow; at her decease the property is to be sold by vandue and equally divided among my children except one feather bed which I will to my daughter Patsey Fewell besides her share of the above division, the part of my sold [sic] to Henry Burns and James Keenan being take out of the full tract the ballance of the land to be side or otherwise equally divided between my sons James, Robert, Daniel, and Luke. There is a young bay mare I made a present of to my son Luke some time ago that does not belong to the above mentioned property. My wife Peggy and my good neighbour William Hall executors, 10 July 1804. Laughlin Burns (X) (LS), Wit: Paul Flanagen, Luke Burns (mark), John Flynn. Qualified Peggy Burns extx & William Hall exr. Octbr 1st 1804. Codicil... notes to the amount of $186, $100 of which to be given to my son Malichi if he should come to this country as is expected, if he should not come to be sent to him the first good oppourtunity; the balance of notes to my wife Peggy to defray the expences of my funeral and her own. 10 July 1804.

**Pages 161-162:** Will of John Spence of the State of South Carolina and York District... 25 May 1801. To my beloved wife Elizabeth Spence, the money arising from the sale of my plantation and whatever of my personal estate my beloved wife Elizabeth may give up to my executors to be sold and they to make lawful titles to the purchasers for the same; to my son in law William Davis five shillings sterling; to my son in law Joseph Forbis five shillings sterling; to my daughter Elizabeth Spence my Loume with all the Reads and geares belonging thereunto; to my son in law William Stewart five shillings sterling; to my two grandsons John Davis son of William Davis and John Forbis son of Joseph Forbis all my wearing apperal to be equally divided; John Watson and Samuel Watson Junior, exrs. John Spence (Seal), Wit: Hugh Watson, Samuel Watson, Robert Watson. Octr 24th 1804 the above will was proved by the oath of Robert Watson. 24 Oct 1804 Quallified Samuel Watson Junior and John Watson nov 1 1804.

## YORK COUNTY SC WILL BOOK A-1 1800-1813

**Pages 162-164:** Novbr 5th 1804. Proved the will of Alex'r Ekin deceas'd by the oaths of James B. Fulton, William Ekin & Thomas Ekin.

Will of Allexander Eakin Jun'r of the State of South Carolina, York District, 26 Sept 1804. to my beloved wife Jean Eakin, one bay horse and one cow to her disposal and my negro girl Mimay to her use, at her death said negro girl and her issue to be equally divided between my four daughters Nancy, Elvey, Peggy & Elizabeth and my household furniture to my wife to her disposal; the amount of Samuel Crafts & Thomas Carrols note of $300 and my father Alex'r Eakins note of $100 & David Strains and Daniel Jones note of $65 & Wm. Eakins note of $13 be collected as soon as possible and that sum with $140 in cash to be laid out in land in the State of Tenasee except what of it may be necessary to lay out for the support of the family and move them to said state and the land so purchased to my son William Eakin reserving my wifes possession of the same during her life; my rifle gun be sold for the support of the family; my wife Jean Eakin and my friends John Arnold and Charles Robertson my executors s'd Robertson to assist my wife in the collection of the above sums and when collected to be acquitted as to any further trouble. Alexander Eakin (LS), Wit: Jas B. Fulton, Wm. Akin, Thomas Eakin. Novr 5th 1804 Qualified Jean Eakin and Charles Robertson. Jany 7th 1805 Qualified John Arnold.

**Pages 165-167:** Novbr 6th 1804. Proved the will of Jesse Beaty deceas'd by the oaths of William Partlow and Thomas Hudson.

Will of Jesse Beaty of York District and State of South Carolina... to my dear and loving wife Rebekah Beatey the land and plantation I bought of John Bell untill William Jackson Beatey comes of age if she remains a widow; if she marrys she is to have land and house no longer, but to be rented out for the use of John Beaty and Will Jackson Beaty my two sons; to my two sons John Beaty and William Jackson Beaty the land I bought of John Bell to be divided equally between them, John B. is to have the half that lies next to Isaac Garresons and William Jackson Beaty the house and if either dies without heir land descends to the other; to my daughter Betsy Beaty one bed and furniture; Will Jackson my exrs, 14 Sept 1804. Jesse Beaty (LS), Wit: Wm. Partlow, Thomas Hudson (mark).

**Pages 167-171:** January 7th proved the will of William Ratchford Senior deceas'd by the oaths of Joseph Wallace and Benjamin Chambers.

20 Feb 1801, Will of William Ratchford Senior of York Co'ty in the State of South Carolina, being in my common health... to my following names children whose names are now Margret Tate, Moses Ratchford, Joseph Ratchford, Jean Jewell, Elizabeth Henderson, John Ratchford, Mary Hetherington & Abigal Henderson the sum of five shillings sterling each; to my two sons Samuel & George Ratchford, the survey of land I now live on which contains between 600 and 700 acres; if my son William will agree and allow an adjacent part he holds by patent to the inclusive survey I now live on to come under

equal divided with my two sons Saml & George, then the whole of my own part with that of my sd son William be equally divided between my three sons William, Samuel & George; if William does not consent to this mode of division then Samuel & George to hold my part of land; my wife Mary Ratchford is to have as full comfortable & plentifull a living off my sd part of land as the same will admit of during her life, with the benefit of my negro woman named Mender; my daughter Ann McCarra do have an uninterrupted enjoyment with my sd wife in her part of my mansion house and should sd. daughter survive my wife she is to be continue in the enjoyment of my wifes part of her house while on the premises or in widowhood; my sons Moses & Samuel Ratchford with my wife said, exrs. Wm Ratchford (O) (LS), Wit: Jo Wallace, Williamson Byers, Benj Chambers, Wm. McClain. Janry 7th 1805. Qualified Moses Ratchford and Saml Ratchford.

**Page 172:** Jas Morrow's settlement of the estate of John Morrow deceas'd for the years 1804 & 1805 as administrator. Widows third $77.80, subject to division divided amongst 7 legatees $22.25 each.

Thos Barnett's settlement of the estate of Jacob Julian decd in 1805 as exrs. produced vouchers for paying on this and former settlements to legatees and creditors by self & wm. Alexander & George Julia exrs. Janry 21st 1805.

**Page 173:** Daniel Peeler's settlement of the estate of Anthony Peeler as administrator 1805. Feby 16th 1805.

Littlebury Patterson & Benjm Patterson's settlement of the estate of George Patterson decs'd as admrs... Spell Kimble's act. Widow and seven heirs Feb 18th 1805.

Jno Scott's Settlement of the estate of David Scott decs'd for the year 1805 as exr. Febry 4th 1805.

**Pages 174-176:** Will of Thomas Manion was proved March 4th 1805 by the oath of Littleton Sandiland.

Will of Thomas Manion of the State of So Carolina and District of York... to my beloved wife Elizabeth three negroes viz Charles, Beck & Phebe as also 100 acres of land the upper part & half of the tract of land I live on & includes my plantation for her to enjoy during her natural life; to my daughter Catey Manion a tract of 150 acres in Union District on Quintons Branch; to my son William Manion three negroes viz Bob, Winne & Rhode; to Elizabeth Davis my daughter two negroes Anthony and Ruth; to my daughter Polley Davis two negroes Sam and Amey; to my son Thomas Manion 100 acres it being half the land I live on & the lower part also three negroes Dick, Jenney, and Little Charles; to my son Robert Manion at the death of his mother 100 acres it being the land first mentioned also five negroes Sal, Eliza, her child sucking, Jim & Lewis; Charles shall be given to my so Robert, Phebe & her increase to my daughter Catey Manion & Beck and her increase to my daughter Elizabeth Davis; I appoint Randolph Sandaland & my son Robert Marion, exrs... 29 July 1802. Thomas Manion, Wit: John Ramsey, Littleton Sandaland, Randolph Sandlin. March 4th 1805 Qualified Robert Manion, exr.

**Page 177:** April 8th 1805. Proved the will of William Kerr deceas'd by the oaths of James Stewart & James Harris.

Will of William Kerr of the State of South Carolina and District of york being sick and weake in body... to Mary Jean Whiteside, one third of all my estate; to Dorcas Whiteside daughter of Mary Jean Whiteside the two parts of all my estate to be given to her at the discretion of Mary Jean Whiteside & my executors to order a division of my estate... my faithful friend John Harris as executor... dated 25 March 1805. Wm. Ker (LS), Wit: James Stewart, William McKinney, James Harris. April 8th 1805 qualified John Harris exr.

**Pages 118-119:** The will of Joseph Feemster deceas'd was proved before me May 6th 1805 by the oath of Richard Ingram witness thereto.

Will of Joseph Feemster of York District and State of South Carolina... to my wife Elizabeth the following negroes Rorey, Hannah, Tom and Sue, and the horse kind Scot, Ben and her colt and old Bett likewise all her cattle and their increase, the household furniture she brought with her and also one bed and furniture of her own choosing and also my house and the old 150 acres of land to her behoof whilst she remains my widow, also my chest of drawers during her widowhood and afterward to be the property of my daughter Martha and the plantation tools I leave for the use of the plantation and my son James; to my son John, the following negroes Jacob, Sall, and her child Harry, and Sam, likewise my old Blassingame horse; to my son James all the rest of my lands the forementioned excepted 150 acres which is to be his when the term above mentioned shall expire, likewise my waggon and geers and young Bett, Dick & Cagle, also negroes Jack, Venice, and her children George, Hannah, and Jacke, my clock and desk; to my daughter Martha negroes Phillis and Serena, and to her daughter Clarinda my negro boy named Sye; to my granddaughter Jenny Feemsters my negro wench called Pheb, and all my pewter and other shelf furniture to be equally divided between her and my granddaughter Agnes Feemster, daughter of John Feemster; my negro wench Maria to be the property of my wife or any of my children as s'd negro shall choose; all my other property not bequeathed shall be equally divided in four shares and be given to my wife and my three children; my two sons John and James Feemster to be executors of my will, dated 27 Oct 1804. Jos. Feemster (LS), Wit: Richard Ingram, Archibald Scott, Jno Love.

**Pages 120-123:** The will of Andrew Love deceas'd was proved before me May 6th 1805 by William Love, Exrs., witness thereto.

10 Sept 1803. Will of Andrew Love of York District and State of South Carolina... to my beloved wife $100 in cash paid as hereafter mentioned, also her choice of bed, bedstead and furniture with two cows her choice, also her

YORK COUNTY SC WILL BOOK A-1 1800-1813

wheel and chair, one pit with the half of the dresser furniture with the priviledge of my room and press with 40 bushels of corn per year, two cows, feed, fire wood cut and hauled during their stay here; to my daughter Mary $1; to my son James $50; to my son Robert $100; to my son William $100; to my son Andrew $100; to my son John $100; to my daughter Sarrah $50; to my daughter Elizabeth $145 and two cows, one bedstead and furniture, the second choice; to my sisters son Andrew Donaghy $60; to my two sons Mathew and Saml the interest of $400 to be paid yearly; to my son Andrew three tracts of land containing 800 acres with all the improvements thereunto belonging except such reserved as is above disposed of with all my horses, cattle and hogs, waggon and hind geers, still and tubs, farming utensils, household kitchen and dresser furniture not above disposed of provided he pay the above bequeathed legacies to be above named legatees as follows viz the one half at the end of one year after my deceased, the other two years after that also to pay my son Mathew and my son Saml the interest of $400, also to find them in sufficient cloathing, boarding, washing, and lodging and they to work in moderation if they do not like to live with him they may choose to go to any of my family they may think best, and always to draw the aforesaid interest to keep them in decent cloathing fit to appear abroad the principle still to continue with him. If my son Andrew does not see fit to undertake the above property and pay the above legacies then I allow my son William to fall into the place in every respect. If he will not take it then my will and pleasure is that the named property be sold by my exrs and distributed amongst my legatees agreeable to the above proportion. If the above property be sold, the exr is to keep the above named $400 nominated to Mathew and Saml at interest; if my wife sees cause to move from here, I allow her 20 bushels of corn yearly during her life; my wife Sarrah and my sons James & Andw to execute my will. Andw Love (LS), Wit: Robt Love, Samuel Ewing, Wm. Love. Qualified William Love exr May 6th 1805.

**Pages 124-125:** The will of Hugh Ticer deceas'd was proven July 11, 1805, by the oath of Thomas Webb.

Will of Hugh Ticer of State of South Carolina, York District... to my wife Ann Ticer 100 acres, the part whereon the dwelling houses now stand as long as she remains single for the support of my children, after marriage or death the s'd 100 acres to be sold for to support the surviving heirs, being the children of my lawful wife; the remainder of the land to be sold for 12 months credit... dated 23 June 1805. Hugh Ticer (H) (Seal), Wit: Thomas Webb, John Jackson. Qualified Robert Harris ex'r July 12th 1805.

**Pages 126-129:** The will of Alexander Ekin Deceas'd was proven August 5th 1805 by the oaths of John Hall and James Wilson.

Will of Alexander Eakin being low in body... to my beloved wife Nancey Eakin all my household furniture, all my stock of horned cattle and my gray mare and a free possession of her room and fire place and a sufficient support for her off my plantation during her life; to my son Joseph Eakin all my plantation I live on both pattent and Indian Clame subject to the reserve made for my wife; to my son joseph my negro woman Vilet, my new waggon and team of horses, one soral, one black, one gray and one other soril colt, my still, smith tools, rifle gun and farming utensils with the condition that said son Joseph give unto my grandson Hiram Howe at his arriving to the years of 18 one good horse, saddle and bridle valued at $100 and a good compleat suit of clothes from the hat to the shoe all of a superfine quality with a second shirt and stockings of the same quality; to my beloved wife Nancy my negro woman Lid during her life and to be the property of my son Joseph on condition that he pays to my grandchildren the children of Alex'r Eakin deceased viz unto each one of them $40 William, Nancey, and Elphy, Pegey and Betcy five in all; if my said negro woman should have any children previous to my wife's death s'd children to be divided between my son Thos and William Eakin; to my son Thomas Eakin my negro boy Sam; to my son William Eakin my negro woman Horah and my negro boy Isaac; to my son Joseph Eakin my riding chair and harness and s'd son Joseph is out of his legacy to pay all my lawful debts and he is to have all the produce made for sale on my plantation this year to help defray s'd debts; to my grandchildren Eakins Alex'r and Ephrum Lackey my negro girl Mary and for s'd girl to remain with my daughter Ester Lackey during her s'd Ester's life; to my granddaughter Jemimey Willson, daughter of Jean Willson, my negro girl Miley; my wife Nancey Eakin my executrix and William Barron and my son Joseph Eakin, exrs., 17 April 1805. Alex'r Eakin (Seal), Wit: William Hall, John B. Hall, James Willson (mark). August 5th 1805. Qualified Nancy Ekin, Wm. Barren & Joseph Ekin exrs.

**Pages 130-132:** South Carolina. Will of Samuel McKee of York District.... unto Arthur Stafford & Samuel McKee Stafford sons of James Stafford Junior $50 to each to be paid them in one and two years from the day of my decease; it is my intention to emancipate and manumit my two negro slaves now in Charleston named Chisshire & Sylvia, I will and desire that if I should die before the execution of this my intention that my nephew James McKee shall emancipate and manumit the said two negroes in one year after my decease or otherwise I revoke all parts of this my will made in his favour; to my brother William McKee my silver watch as a token of remembrance; all the rest of my estate to my nephew James Mckee; I apoint my beloved brother William McKee and my nephew James Mckee, exrs., 9 Jan 1805. Samuel McKee (LS), Wit: Wm Ed Hayne, Aron Wood, Robert Patrick. Qualified James McKee exr. August 5th 1805.

**Pages 133-137:** The will of Francis Rea deceas'd was proven August 5th 1805 by the oath of David Jackson witness thereto.

2 Febry 1804, will of Francis Rea residing on the waters of Crowders Creek in York District, State of South Carolina, in an infirm state of health... to my dear and loving wife Seah Rea (if sue survives me) her support during life off that part of the land belonging to the mansion house, viz 250 acres off which she is to have a sufficiency of grain, two cows, the use of the dwelling house, household furniture and all farming utensils her bedding, cloathing and what

pertains thereto, also the benefit of the hoggs and the loom for the use of the family while living together; the waggon to be kept on this plantation whereon I now live for the use of said plantation and of my sons William, Alexander, and Francis if they reside on this plantation; plantation to be sold at the decease of my wife and the price thereof to be divided amongst my daughters if their parts and portions cannot be made up otherwise, but if it can then the price of the waggon is to be equally divided amongst the legatees; to my son William Rea providing he comes and lives upon the place on the following terms, to give a reasonable quantity of grain off it yearly for the support of my wife and daughters, he is to have at my wifes decease 100 acres as a free gift and the remaining 150 belonging to the mansion house at the valuation of men and the price to be divided as shall afterwards be specified; to my daughters Mary Rea, Elizabeth Rea, and Sarah Rea, to each of them one horse worth $100, saddle, bed and furniture, two cows and calves to each of them, also three wheels; to my son Alexander Rea 200 acres off the south east end of the plantation the Meadow ground equally divided between said 100 acres and the 250 acres belonging to the mansion house and said Alexander not be sold to a stranger, if any of the family is willing to give a reasonable price; to my son Francis Rea 50 acres off the west end of the plantation; to my grand daughter Rachel Jamison one cow at my wife's decease; my wife Sarah Rea, extx, and my son William Rea and John Henry exrs. Francis Rea (mark) (Seal), Wit: Robert Adams, David Jackson, James Montgomery. Qualified Sarah Rea, Wm. Read & John Henry, August 5th 1805.

**Pages 137-138:** The will of Samuel Lesly deceas'd was proven before me September 1805 by the oath of Gilbert Enloe.

August 10th 1805. Will of Samuel Lesly of State of South Carolina and York District... my body to be buried in a desent Christian manner at the discretion of Samuel Lesly Capt and Benjamin enloe, whom I appoint executors; I allow my plantation to be rented for the term of Eight years the rent to be yearly collected for the use of schooling and supporting my children then to be sold at publick sale the price kept at intrust and equally divided to them as they come of age; my moveable property to be sold and bequeath to my wife Elenor 3 Dollars, my children five times about through the amount of my moveable property after my debts are all paid. Samuel Lesly (Seal), Wit: Gilbert Enloe, Mary S. Lesly. Qualified Samuel Lesley and Benjamin Enloe exrs. Septr 2th 1804.

**Pages 139-142:** The will of Duncan Sinclair deceas'd was proven before me September 20th 1805 by the oaths of Elizabeth Ferguson and Charles Hamill witnesses thereto.

Will of Duncan Sinclair of the District of York and State of South Carolina & on the 22d day of June 1805, being in a low and languishing state of health.... to my dear & loving wife Mary Sinclair her living off the plantation where of I am now possess'd & the disposal of the stock of cattle for the use of the family as long as she lives or continues a widow; to my son James

Sinclair $5 in cash to be paid by my executors whenever called on & this is to be his share of my estate; to my daughter Ann $50 cash; to my daughter Preshus $50 cash; to my son John a horse to be valued at $70; to my son Robert a horse to be valued at $70; to my daughter Katharin $50; to my three youngest sons viz Jesse, Elias & Elijah Sinclair when the youngest is of age each an equal divided of my land & my wife to have the disposal of it for the benefit of the family as long as they live on it nevertheless if the family should find it convenient to remove to the western waters, I do order that my executors be vested with full powers & authority to sell & make sufficient titles to the same; the money acquired by the sale of said land be laid out for land & equally divided amongst my three youngest boys or otherwise laid out to interest so that they can have it as they come of age; I do likewise will that out of the present crop there be as much disposed of it at the fall as will be sufficient to pay all just debts and if there should not be enough the remaining part to be paid out of the next crop; I recommend my children to live with their mother until they get Homes & ways of living of their own & equally divide what they may acquire by their industry; nevertheless if they do not see cause so to do but call for their share as soon as of age then they quit all claim to anything more; I appoint my wife Mary Sinclair & Charley Robertson executors. Duncan Sinclair (Seal), Wit: Jona Ferguson, Elizabeth Ferguson (mark), Charles Hamill. Qualified Mary Sinclair & Charley Robertson exrs. Sept 20th 1805.

**Pages 143-145:** Will of Mathew Gibson of the State of South Carolina, York District... to my beloved wife Elisabeth a young mare named Tansey, a new saddle & her bed & furniture; to my son Thomas my rifle; to my son William the smallest chest; to my daughter Catharine one side saddle to be repaired, all the rest and residue of my estate to be in the possession of my beloved wife for to support, raise & school my children; when my oldest son Thomas comes of age or in case my wife should marry before that period, than I allow all the estate then remains to be appraised and sold by my executors and the money arising therefrom to be equally divided between my beloved wife and children to wit Thomas, William, Catharine, Matthew, Ramsey & John; I also appoint my wife Elizabeth & my brother Hugh Cain as executors... dated 4 May 1805. Mathew Gibson (Seal), Wit: John Cain, Margret Gibson (X), Joseph Kerr.

The will of Mathew Gibson deceas'd was proven before me September 2d 1805 by the oath of John Cain a subscribing witness thereto.

**Pages 146-147:** The will of James McPhilimey deceas'd was proven before me August 15th 1805 by the oaths of Robert Wallace, Gilbreath Caldwell and Margaret Caldwell subscribing witnesses thereto.

November the 19th 1804. The will of James McPhilimey being very sick and weak in body.... to my mother five shillings sterling and likewise to my brother John five shillings and sixpence to be raised and levied out of my estate; I allow my land to be valued or sold and devided among my three aunts viz

Agness Caldwell, Margaret Wallace & eleanor Caldwell; I ordain William Caldwell & James Wallace the sole executors. James McPhilimey (mark), Wit: Robt Wallace, Gilbreath Caldwell, Margaret Caldwell (mark). Qualified Wm. Caldwell & Jas Wallace at the same time exrs viz August 5th 1805.

**Pages 147-150:** The will of Archibald Steel deceas'd was proven before me Novemb'r 4th 1805 by the oaths of John Starr and James Young subscribing witnesses thereto.

30th April 1796. Will of Archibald Steel of York County in the State of South Carolina... to my wife Agness Steel all my household & kitchen furniture, two cows and calves, with the full enjoyment of my dwelling house and as sufficient and comfortable a living off of the plantation I now live on as the same will admit and the full use of a negroe boy named George, and at her decease the s'd negro boy I bequeath him to my grandson John Steel (son of Joseph) and remainder of what is bequeathed to my said wife I allow at her decease to be equally divided amongst my present surviving children John, William, James & Robert Steel or their heirs; to my son John Steel nine pounds sterling money of SC; to my son James Steel one feather bed and furniture & thirteen pounds ten shillings sterling money of SC; I make my two sons William & Robert Steel equal shearers in the survey of land I now live on which contains 350 acres; my sons John & James Steel's part be made out of my unbequeathed part of chattle substance; my two sons John & William Steel my executors. Archibald Steel (LS), Wit: John Starr, James Young, Saml Johnson.

**Pages 151-153:** The will of Jacob Randall deceas'd was proven before me February 3d 1806 by the oath of David Watson and that Sarah Ranncipher and Hanna Randall were subscribing witnesses to the same.

Will of Jacob Randall of York District, State of South Carolina... to my well beloved wife Phebe Randall the house I now live in & 25 acres of land joining said house also 14 acres of land I bought of Nicholas Whisonant joining the same for her use during her life then to my son John Randall also all the household furniture to be at her disposal, also two cows and calves, one young horse, one mare & saddle to be at her disposal; to my son Levi one sorrel mare, two cows & Calves, one work bull cattle now being in his possession; to my son John Randall one young horse he has now in possession & all of my husbandry utensils; to my daughter Hannah Randall one bay mare, four cows & calves, & $10 in money; to my granddaughter Sarah Rounscifer one cow & Calf & one heifer; to my daughter Sarah Rouncival $1 also my daughter Ruipheny Peeler $1 also Elizabeth Wilson $1 & Susanna Whisonant $1; to my son Silas Randall $9 he has in possession; the remainder of my property to my beloved wife Phebe Randall & my son John Randall, dated 12 October 1805. Jacob Randall (LS), Wit: David Watson, Sarah Rouncipher (mark), Hannah Randall (X). Feby 3d 1806 qualified John Randal executor.

## YORK COUNTY SC WILL BOOK A-1 1800-1813

**Page 154:** Will of Thomas Parker of State of South Carolina & District of York... to Elizabeth Morgan and Robert Morgan and Caty Morgan all my estate both real and personal to be equally divided betwixt Elizabeth Morgan, Robert Morgan, and Caty Morgan, the said Elizabeth Morgan's son and daughter; my brother Robert Parker, my sole executor, dated 19 Oct 1805. Thomas Parker (R) (LS), Wit: Abraham Green, Thomas Bridges, John Moreland (X), Nancy Bridges. Qualified Robert Parker exr. December 1st 1805.

**Pages 155-156:** The will of William Farris dec'd was proven by the oaths of John Cooper and Enoch Doster, November 14th 1805.

Will of William Farris of York District, dated 18th April 1805... to my son David Farris one smooth bored gun or what is commonly called a french musket which is the whole of what I mean to bequeath him at this time; to my daughter Margarett Farris a two year old female horse created a bay in color with saddle, bridle, feather Bed & Furniture; to my daughter Mary Farris a feather bed & furniture & a two year old heifer; to my son John Farris who is now absent to the western country & is now in possession of a horse, briddle & Saddle, the same I allow to him; if my son James Farris lives and gives his aid in supporting my present family till he arrives to the age of maturity, I allow him the right of putting my mare to my studd horse & he shall have the colt (if any) as his sole right, but if this endeavor should not succeed, then $50; to my son Joshua Farris, a two year old steer which I allow to have the common support from the plantation till the steer arrives to a suitable age for fatning for markett; to my son Isaac Farris another two year old steer; to my daughter Sarah Farris a year old heifer calf; the right of claim to my rifle gun I do not give a specifick claim to none of my children but allow the use of said gun to the benefit of whatever plantation my family live upon; in confidence of my wife's discretionary abilities, I authorize & empower her to have the final disposal of my landed property and allot her my unbequeathed chattel property; my friend & my beloved wife nancy Farris & William Dorster my executors. William Faries (LS), Wit: John Cooper, Enoch Doster, David Gordon. Qualified Nancy Faries extx & William Dorster Exr to the above will Nov'br 15th 1805.

**Pages 157-158:** December 7th 1805. The will of John Hall deceas'd was proven by the oaths of Thomas Bogs & Henry Greer.

Will of John Hall of York County, 30th October 1796... to my son William Hall the survey of land whereon I now live containing 130 acres, if he dies in the age of minority, I allow said land to be sold and the money arising from the said sale to be equally divided between my three youngest children whose names are Betsy, Nancy, and Ann Hall; to each of my three daughters a feather bed, bedstead & furniture & an equal divide of my kitchen furniture; all of my unbequeathed chattel substances to be sold to the best advantage and after paying the sum of five shillings to each of my other daughters Martha, Sarah, Margaret & Jean, the clear ballance of the same to be equally divided between my three first mentioned daughters; as I am in possession of information that my deceased father has left me a legacy in Ireland to an amt that I am yet not able to a certain but be the am't what it will when justly made I allow the whole of that bequeathment to be equally divided between my four said children William, Betsy, Nancy & Ann Hall; I appoint John Poag and Samuel Poag both of York Co'ty my executors. John Hall (LS), Wit: David Gordon, Thomas Bogs, Henry Greer. Qualified Patrick Higgens admr. with the will annexed Decemb'r 20th 1805.

**Pages 158-160:** June 2d 1806. The last Will & testament of Walter Crawford Deceas'd was proven before me by the oath of George Knox.

Will of Walter Crawford now living on the waters of Clarks Fork in York District State of South Carolina, being in an infirm state of health... to my brother James Crawford, one dollar; to William Crawford, one dollar; to my sister Letty Crawford, all the worldly property whereof I am now possessed except one year old colt which I will and bequeath to my nephew Walter Quin to be managed for the most advantage to the Child and also my plantation of land containing about 286 acres whereon I now live at the decease of my sister Letty Crawford, said land to be the property of my sister Letty Crawford during her life-- all chattles, household furniture, farming utensils &c. I lave to her own disposal; to my brother James Quin one Dollar; to my nephew Walter Quin the year old colt at my decease and my plantation at the decease of my sister Letty Crawford as is specified above. I appoint James Quin, exr., and Letty Crawford extx., dated 11 April 1806. William Crawford (X) (LS), Wit: William Dixon, James Mtgomery, George Knox. June 2d. qualified James Quin, exr.

**Pages 160-161:** June 2d 1806. The last Will & testament of John Harbison was proven before me by the oath of John Brown witness.

Will of John Harbison of Clarks fork of Bullocks Creek, York District, State of South Carolina, being weak of body... to my daughter Esther, all my estate personal and real as follows: I allow the plantation I live on to be rented till she comes of age or is married, not stilling to be done on it nor none cleared only within the fences the rent of it to go to the benefit of her for cloathing & a bed and six months schooling; what ready money is I allow to be put to interest & I allow the place of min on Moores Creek to be sold with all and every other thing belonging to me except thirty bushels of corn I allow to uncle James Harbison; all to be sold a years credit & all my just debts paid the remainder to be put to interest for the benefit of her & I allow her to live either at John Browns or Wm Loves & if she dies before she comes of age I allow the whole of it to my brother James Harbison in Ireland if he comes after it in five years; if not I allow the land to be sold & all to be divided equally betwixt Patrick Spences children now living in Chester (only I allow Esther my Bible her wheel & Bed & Clothes & the suit of Clothes & told her to Patk Spence). I ordain John Brown of Clarks fork & Wm Love Esqr of

Bullocks Creek, my exrs, dated 30 Jan 1806. Jno Harbison (LS), Wit: John Brown, James McKee.

**Pages 162-163:** October the 6th 1806. The last Will & testament of Sarah Byers was proven before me by the oaths of Jacob Peters, Robert Black, and William Byers, witnesses.

Will of Sarah Byers of South Carolina & district of York, 21st August 1806... to my well beloved son John Carson, the plantation I now live on with all the plantation tools I now possess, and one feather bed & Furniture, two cows; to my daughter Sarah Jackson five shillings sterling; to my second daughter Elizabeth Jordon my negro wench named Cherry; to my third daughter Grizzle Jordon one feather bed and furniture; also four head of growing cattle; to my fourth daughter Margaret Henry, forty silver dollars to be paid by John Carson her half-brother out of the ballance of my property; my son Joseph Carson, John Jordon and Robert Jordon, exrs. Sarah Byers (X) (LS), Wit: Jacob Peters, Robert Black, Williamson Byers. Qualified John Carson, John Jorden & Robert Jorden, exrs., 6 Oct 1806.

**Pages 163-164:** Oct'r 28th 1806. The last Will & testament of Abraham Thrift was proven before me by the oaths of Ezekiel Gilham & Adam Meek, witnesses thereto.

Will of Abraham Thrift being in a sick and low condition... to my beloved wife one mare, one cow & heifer & my stock of hogs, two feather beds & their furniture & all the rest of my household furniture together with my Crop & the remainder of my property to her; after her death whatever may remain of said estate unto Spencer Thrift. I appoint my wife and the aforesaid Spencer executors... dated 19 Sept 1806. Abraham Thrift (X), Wit: A. Meek, Ezekiel Gilham, Shadrock Thrift (X). Octr 18th 1806 Qualified Spencer Thrift & Widow Thrift exrs.

**Pages 165-167:** Jan'y 24th 1807. The last Will & testament of Benjamin Ellis was proven before me by the oaths of John Bates Esq'r and John Bates, Mary Ellis & Sachariah Bates witnesses to the same.

Will of Benjamin Ellis of the State of South Carolina, York District, planter... to my beloved wife Elizabeth Ellis, my whole estate real and personal during her widowhood for the purpose of raising my four children named as followeth: Tom Sumner Ellis, Priscilla Ellis, Elizabeth Hall Ellis and Robert Ellis; if my negroe wench named Daphne should have any child or children my will is that her first child shall be the property of my son Tom Sumner Ellis as soon as he attains the age of 21 years; her second child shall be the property of my daughter Priscilla Ellis when she attains the age of eighteen years or be married; her third child shall be the property of my daughter Elizabeth Hall Ellis when she attains the age of eighteen years or be married; her fourth child shall be the property of my son Robert Ellis as soon as he attains the age of 21 years. I appoint my brother Robert Ellis to be the guardian of my children, and I appoint him my sole executor [not dated]. Benjamin Ellis (LS), Wit: John Bates Sen'r, Mary Ellis (X), Sachariah Bates.

**Pages 167-168:** April 19th 1806. Will of Margaret Love of South Carolina and District of York, the widow of Alexander Love deceas'd, finding myself very sick and weak of body... to my daughter Jean Murphy wife of John Murphy, then shillings; to my son Andrew Love ten shillings; to my son Alexander Love a bay horse, a dark bay mare, and a bay mare likewise my whole stock of black cattle and sheep, also three beds and clothing and all my household furniture; to my son William Love, ten shillings; to my daughter Elizabeth Miles wife of Charles Miles ten shillings; I appoint my son Alexander Love my sold executor. Margaret Love (mark (Seal), Wit: Joshua Akin, Alexander Akin, George Akin (X). Febry 19th 1807 the will of Margret Love was proved by the oaths of Joshua Eakin and Alex'r Eakin.

**Pages 169-171:** Will of Adam Meek of the District of York... to my beloved wife Ann Meek, the one sixth part of all my lands lying on Bullocks Creek and adjoining thereto together with the sixth part of the movable property except that part taken out for my daughter Margaret Meek for the advantage of remaining in the house she now lives in; to my son James Meek the one half of all the above mentions lands with one sixth part of the moveable property; to my [daughter] Margaret Meek, my tract lying on Clarks fork known by the name of Gordons old place with two negroes Juna & Sam, one horse and saddle to be worth $150 with one bed and furniture; to my daughter Jean Meek four likely negroes between the age of ten and twelve years or there about with a horse and saddle worth $150 with one bed and furniture; to my son William Meek, one half of all the above mentioned land with one sixth part of the moveable property excepting that tract willed to Margaret Meek; I appoint my eldest son James Meek & Edward Byers to be my executors, dated 23 Jan 1807. Adam Meek (Seal), Wit: Moses Meek, David Byers, Jess Roberts. Febry 18th 1807. The will of Adam Meek was proven by the oaths of Moses Meek and David Byers. Febry 18th 1807. Qualified James Meek Exr. N. B. The sixth bequeath being left out I have inserted it at the last; Sixthly, I bequeath to my daughter Agness Meek four likely negroes between the age of ten and twelve years or there about with a horse and saddle worth $150 with one bed and furniture.

**Pages 172-175:** March 9th 1807. The last Will & testament of James Gibson Senior deceas'd was proven before me by the oaths of Robert McAdory and William Ash witnesses to the same.

Will of James Gibson of the District of York and State of South Carolina... to my well beloved wife Martha Gibson, her maintainance off the plantation whereon I now live during her life or widowhood, also her wearing apparel and bed and bedding with all my household & kitchen furniture except such as shell be hereafter mentioned, also a negro child named Charlett, and at her death the said negroe to be sold & the money arising therefrom be equally divided amongst my children, also two cows; to my beloved son James Gibson the third part of the tract of land whereon I now live, 250 acres, joining John Denis and my son William Gibson; also I give him one bay horse with his wearing apparel; to my son Joseph Gibson, the third part of the same tract, to the east end, and a brown yearling colt; to my son Thomas Gibson, the third part of the said tract of land, a three year old brown horse, & one years schooling to be paid from the plantation; to my daughter Margret Gibson her bed & bedding & Wearing appeal; also her one white faced heifer; to my daughter Jean Gibson, her bed & bedding & wearing apparel; to my daughter Martha Gibson her bed & bedding & wearing apparel, one spotted heifer; my money be collected, my debts be paid & the ballance be equally divided between my three sons James, Joseph & Thomas and my three daughters Margret, Jean, and Martha; my wife Martha Gibson & my trusty friend Col. William Bratton, my executors, dated 2 Dec 1803. James Gibson (mark) (LS). [witnesses names not recorded]

**Pages 175-177:** March 14th 1807. The last Will & testament of Henery Craig deceas'd was proven before me by the oath of James Ramsey Senior and James Ramsey Junr & James McCully subscribing witnesses to the same.

12 December 1805, will of Henry Craig of State of South Carolina and County of York, being weak in body.... my wife Mary to have and enjoy all the profits arising from the plantation I now live on during life and at her deceased, to fall to my son John Craig; I also allow my wife all my horses, black cattle, sheep, and hogs, all my household furniture and farming utensils, also my negro woman Dinah and my negro boy Sam and to be at her disposal at her death; my son Robert is to enjoy the sole benefit of Dinah during my wife's lifetime; also to my wife my negro man Ben and my negro woman Rose, and at her decease Ben I allow to my son Robert and Rose to my daughter Martha Glenn; to my son James, my negro man named Bobb; to my daughter Jean Nesmith, $100; to my daughter Polly Duff, my negro man Primas; to my daughter Elizabeth Brison, my negro woman Silvy; to my daughter Margaret Anderson my negro girl Rachel; I appoint my son James Craig and my friend James Glenn, my executors. Henry Craig (Seal), Wit: James Ramsey Senr, James Ramsey Junr, James McCully. March 23rd 1807 qualified James Glenn exr.

**Pages 178-179:** Will of John Good Senior of York District & State of South Carolina, being weak of Body... to my loving wife her maintenance out of the land while she lives, her bed and furniture for the same, and one chest of drawers to her own disposal. My land I leave to be divided between my two sons John Good Junr and James B. Good to be divided beginning at the foot of the long Bottom (as it is called) to a post oak on William Nelsons line, the upper part of James Good except the half of the fishery. I allow the said James B. Good when he comes possessor of his part the land to pay his mother $15 per year which shall be as part of her maintainance. I also allow s'd James G. Good a bay mare that he calls his own and my silver shoe buckle. The land where on I now live I allow it for John Good also one half of the fishery which was excepted from James Good. I allow my daughter

YORK COUNTY SC WILL BOOK A-1 1800-1813

Anne Good out of the goods and chattels when she wants them as much as any one of her sisters that is married and s'd Anne good is to have the Loom also to dwell as usual while she is single. I also allow Mary Bratton $2 per each person and the remainders part when the debts are paid I allow it to be divided equally between my wife and John Good. I appoint my wife and John Good for executors, 19 Oct 1805. John Good (mark) (LS), Wit: Henry Good, George Hood, John McKenney. April 18th 1807 the will of John Good deas'd was proved by the oath of Henry Good and George Hood and John McKinney. At the same time qualified Martha Good extx and John Good extr.

**Pages 180-181:** April 22nd 1807. The last Will & testament of Samuel Forman was proven before me by the oath of Capt. Joseph Davie and that John Crockett and Jesse Crosby were subscribing witnesses to the same.

Will of Samuel Foreman of State of South Carolina and District of York, Farmer... to my beloved son James Foreman, one negro boy called Lewey; to my son Benjamin Foreman, one negro boy called Arnold; to my son William Foreman, one negro boy called Lewis; to my son Elligah Foreman, all my real estate of which I am possessed, also one negro boy called tom, two horses, two feather beds, two cows and calves, one large chest, one large pewter bason and the Bofatt; to my daughter Lidea Starling, one negro girl called Annica; to my daughter Sarrah Edwards, one negro girl called Pinny; to my daughter Mary Night one negro wench called Lovey; the residue of my property not herein bequeathed to be equally divided between my children both male and female taking or drawing alike; my sons James Foreman and Elijah Foreman, exrs, dated 16 Sept 1806. Samuel Forman (LS), Wit: joseph Davie, John Crockett, Jesse Crosbay (X).

**Pages 182-185:** June 1st 1807. The last Will & testament of James Kolb Deceas'd was proven before me by the oath of David Gordon and said David Gordon, Ezekiel Morris and Elenor Leech were subscribing witnesses to the same.

13 December 1802, the will of James Kolb Sen'r of York Co'ty, South Carolina... after my decease my four children whose names are Mary Love, Margaret Feemster, Ruth Love & Silas Kolb be paid three dollars each by my executors; to my daughter Jean Kolb, one feather bed and furniture and I allow her her full right of claim in a small stock of cattle which is the issue of a certain cow given by D. Gordon, with a saddle & Briddle; further to s'd daughter Jean a negro girl now in her first year of age named Surrenna; to my daughter Catharine Kolb, one feather bed & furniture, a womans saddle & briddle, one cow & calf, also a negro girl Fanny now in her fifth year of age; to my daughter Elisabeth Louisa Kolb one feather bed & furniture, a woman saddle & Briddle, a cow & calf, a negro girl named Milley in her third year of age; to my son Joseph Kolb, the tract of land whereon I now live which is an inclusive survey of 319 acres but to remain during the life of my present wife Elizabeth Kolb; to my son Joseph a sorrell mare, a featherbed, furniture, a cow & calf, saddle & Briddle, and if my negro woman Rachel should have

75

another child, to be his; if my daughters Jeanny, Catty or Betsey should die without issue, I allow the deceased daughters female negro & increase (if any) to by my present wife distributed to any of my then surviving children; to my present wife Elisabeth Kolb the negro woman Rachel. I appoint my wife Elisabeth Kolb and my son in law William Feemster of Chester Co'ty my executors. James Kolb (LS), Wit: David Gordon, Ezekiel Morris, Eleanor Leech (X). June 1st 1807. Qualified Elizabeth Kolb extx.

**Pages 185-187:** August 3rd 1807. The last Will & testament of Thomas Drennan Deceas'd was proven before me by the oaths of John Brumfield and Daniel Jones and said John Brumfield, Daniel Jones, and James Lewis were subscribing witnesses to the same.

Will of Thomas Drennan.. my son Thomas Drennan otherwise called Thomas Farris son of Isbel Farris should have half of the tract on which I now live at the lower end of the tract; to my son William Drennan otherwise called William Harverson son of Marget Harverson, the other half of said tract at the upper end; my stock of cattle & hogs & mare & Saddle (which I desire to be sold at public sale) to be equally divided between my two sons above named. To my son William above mentioned a certain bay horse colt known by the name of Samson; the land belonging to my son William be rented out & that the cattle which I have given to him be fed out of the rents & that William have a tolerable english education; my cousin Mary Drennan have a reasonable support of corn given to her; my brother John Drennan have me morning gown and red waistcoat; to my nephew David Drennan, my watch. I appoint Charles Robertson & David Collins my executors, dated 21 May 1807. Thomas Drennan (Seal), Wit: John Brumfield, James Lewis, Danl Jones.

**Pages 188-189:** August 3rd 1807. The last Will & testament of Sarah Kuykendall was proven before me by the oath of Peter Harris and said Peter Harris Dupont and Sammy Harris were subscribing witnesses to the same.

South Carolina, York District, Febry 8th 1806. Will of Sarah Kuykendal, being weak in body.... to my beloved and eldest son Samuel Kuykendal $11 and one feather bed and one strand of home made thin curtains, and two white sheets and one blue one, and one rose blanket and the one half of my cattle; to my aforesaid son Samuel Kuykendal's second son James the half price of one negro man named David, and one large pewter dish and one basin, and one iron hatrack; to my second son Jonathan Kuykendal, the rest or remainder of my money and all the debts I have coming to me by notes of hand in the country, and the other half of the aforesaid negro, the said negro to be sold and the price to be equally divided between my grandson and my son Jonathan Kuykendal; to my said son Jonathan Kuykendal, all the remainder of my personal property and household furniture except my wearing cloathing; to my well beloved and eldest daughter Elizabeth Armstrong one new callico frock and new home made frock, and one old fashioned home made own and one riding coat and two petty coats; to my second daughter Mary Carrol, one callico gown, one new home made habbit, and three petticoats. I ordain my two sons Samuel Kuykendal and Jonathan Kuykendal, executors. Sarah Kuykendal (X) (Seal), Wit: Dupont Peter Harris, Sammy Harris. The date above qualified Saml Kuykendal and Jonathan Kuykendal exrs.

**Pages 190-191:** August 3rd 1807. The last Will & testament of John McSwain was proven before me by the oaths of Moses Lathem and Edward Graham who were subscribing witnesses to the same.

Will of John McSwain, being weak in body.... to my loving wife Sarah one bed and furniture and one mare and colt and saddle and the dresser and furniture until some of the children become of age, then to be equally divided, likewise two cows and calves and 50 acres of land on first Broad and as for my negro wench I give to my wife Sarah during her widowhood and the remainder of my estate to be equally divided among my children viz Hanor, Catharine, Elisabeth, and John, and the place I now live on to be rented out yearly untill the youngest of my children comes of age, and in case my wife is pregnant and has a child it is to have an equal share. I appoint William McSwain and my wife Sarah, executors, dated 19 May 1807. Jon Mc--- (LS), Wit: Moses Leathem, Edward Graham. August 3d 1807. Qualified Sarah McSwain an executor to the above will.

**Pages 191-192:** South Carolina, York District. Will of Jean Simeral, being low in body... all my property consisting of a bed and furniture, a wheel and dresser, and my wearing apparel be sold to the best advantage and the money arising from the sale to be put to interest until my daughter Sinthey Simeral comes of age and for it to be given to her at that time. I appoint Jas B. Fulton, my lawful executor, dated 17 March 1807. Jean Simeral (mark) (Seal), Wit: John Brumfield, James Brumfield. August 3d 1807. The last will and testament of Jean Simeral was proved by the oaths of John Brumfield and James Brumfield. August 3d 1807 qualified James B. Fullton executor.

**Pages 193-195:** Will of Thomas Spratt of the district of York and State of South Carolina... to my son in law Hugh White my negro man Harry & to his eldest son Viz Thomas Spratt White I give a young negro child called Simeon; to my son in law Isaac Garrison's second son viz Thomas Spratt Garrison, my negro woman Luse, the mother of the above named Simeon which she is to keep with her and raise without expence until he is five years old; to my son in law Arthur Ervin's oldest son called Thomas Spratt Ervin, ny negro man called Charles & unto his s'd Ervins youngest daughter now called Elizabeth, my negro girl called Milly; to my son James Spratt my bed & furniture & his son Thomas Spratt, my part of the ferry with 36 acres of land adjoining the same and the remainder of said tract I allow to be equally divided betwixt Isaac Garrison, Hugh White, Arthur Ervin either by partition or sale as they may think best... my sorrel horse & notes I allow to Hugh White my son in law; my bay mare to Isaac Garrison; my stud colt to my son James & out of the crop of corn now in the ground I allow Mrs. Nelson six bushels the one fourth of the remainder I allow to my daughter Susannah with six hogs, her choice of my stock, two cows, my two year old stear, my sheep; to my son

James with all of my plantation tools and my two sons in law Isaac Garrison & Arthur Ervin at the recovering of their part to pay into the hands of my executor each of them $25 and by them to be given to my granddaughter Patsy McNeal[?]; the negroes I allow to stay on the plantation until the crop is finished and then to my grandchildren. I appoint David Hutchison my sole executor, dated 3 July 1807. Thomas Spratt (Seal), Wit: Eli Wiggins (X), Martha White. Whereas in this my will I have mentioned to Arthur Ervins youngest daughter a negro girl Milley and to Hugh White a negro fellow Harry and after considering of the same, I have thought property to change it. I give said negro Milly to my daughter Elizabeth White and negro harry to Arthur Ervin, 11 July 1807. Thomas Spratt (mark), Wit: Sam Elliott, Hugh White, James Spratt. Proven by Sam Elliott.

**Page 196:** Jean Ramsey's settlement on the estate of Alex'r Ramsey deceas'd for the year 1805, 1806, and 1807 as administratrix. Accts on William Clain[?], John McCaw, John C. Gibson, Carson, Doctor Moore, Benjamin Chambers, Doctor Simpson, Wright, Neely, McNight, Lesly. October 5, 1807.

**Pages 197-198:** South Carolina, York District. Will of John Barnett Senior... to my son John the plantation ne now lives on, being the place I purchased of William Arnold, and also the negro boy Neptune now in his possession; to my daughter Polly Carter one negroe girl named Jenny[?] also the gray filly and her saddle' to my daughter Fanny one horse called Nimrod and her saddle; to my wife Elizabeth, all the residence of my negroes, household furniture, and stock not otherwise disposed, during her widowhood or life, but if she chooses to marry then to take a child's part. I will that the plantation whereon I now live be sold and the money applied for the purchase of another plantation for the family to live on; unto all my children except my son John, an equal proportion of the residue of my estate. My executors to sell the negro fellow Siah and the money appropriated in the most useful manner for my family, also two fillies to be sold. I appoint my wife Elizabeth, my son John and my friend Charles Robertson, exrs. John Barnett (LS), Wit: Pa. Hill, John Brumfield, James Faires.

**Pages 198-199:** Will of Robert Black of York District and State of south Carolina, being weak in body.... to my wife Elizabeth my rooned mare, three cows, one bed and furniture with the dresser and furniture, and the use of the plantation I now live on with my negro girl Sucky during her life or widowhood for the raising and schooling of my children and then to return to the use of my two sons Joseph and John, also plows and farming utensils; to my two sons William and Samuel all that tract of land on Packlot River in Spartan-burg District to be equally divided between them and my grey mares colt to my son William and my black mares colt to my son Samuel, also a piece of land on Long Creek in Lincoln County, North Carolina. The remaining part of my estate to be divided between my two daughters Martha & Mary and my two sons Joseph and John; the issue of the above negro girl Sucky if any to be divided between the whole of my children. My wife Elizabeth &my friends Samuel Carrel and William Love Senr, exrs., dated 24

## YORK COUNTY SC WILL BOOK A-1 1800-1813

Oct 1807. Robert Black (Seal), Wit: Nathaniel Givens, Agnes Givens, Saml Carrel. Nov 2d 1807. The last will and testament of Robert Black was proved by the oath of Nathaniel Givens and Agnes Givens who were subscribing witnesses.

**Pages 200-201:** January 9th 1808. The last Will & testament of Robert Patton Deceas'd was proven before me by the oath of John Hutchison, Esqr., who was a subscribing witness to the same.

Will of Robert Patton of York District and State of South Carolina... to my wife Sarah Patton during her life the plantation on which I now live which I purchased from James Baxter and her negroes viz Jane, Ben, Tom, Luce, Betty, Mary, Sarah, Tilda, Fanny & Catto, my plantation tools & household & kitchen furniture, stock of creatures of all kind, and at my wife's death to be sold except such part as shall be hereafter named and the money arising therefrom to be equally divided among all my children. I give to my son Thomas the negro girl which he has in possession; to my son James's oldest son my negro girl Betty at my wife's death; to my son John's son Robert, my negro girl Selline which my said son has now in possession; to my daughter Elizabeth Bratton my negro Nelly and at her death to be the property of the daughter Mary; to my son Joseph my negro girl Fanney at my wife's death; to my son David my negro woman Sarah and that child Sam at my wife's death. I appoint John McClenahan & John Hutchison Sen'r executors, dated 20 May 1807. Robert Patton (LS), Wit: Jno Hutchison, James McCorkel.

**Page 201:** December 7th 1807. Was proven before me by the oaths of John Barnett and Gazaway Wilson who were subscribing witnesses to Jean Farris's will.

November 5th 1807. Will of Jean Farris.. unto my daughter Ann Farris one negro girl named Diner; to my daughter Jean Adair my bed & bedstead also bed furniture; to my granddaughter Poly Adair one pewter dish; to my granddaughter Polly Brown one pewter dish. James Faris & Alexander Faris, exrs. Jean Faris (X), Wit: John Barnett, Gazaway Wilson.

**Page 202:** January 15th 1808. Was proven before me the last will and testament of Mary Haggins by the oath of Hugh Whiteside and that James Hamilton was a subscribing witness to the same.

Will of Mary Haggins of York District and State of South Carolina... to my grandson William esq. $31; to my granddaughters Mary Cry, $31; to my grandson William Hagins (son of Joseph), $31; to my granddaughters Mary Patten Haggins (Joseph's daughter), $31; to my grandson William Hagins (son of William); to my granddaughter Elizabeth Hagins, Williams daughter, $31; to my granddaughter Sarah Baxter[?], $31; to my granddaughter Mary Baxter, $31 and a cow called White face & her calf, and also my household furniture and wearing apparel. All my property not above mentioned to be divided among my children as my executors may think proper. I appoint John

McClenahan Sen'r, exr., dated 9 Aug 1807. Mary Haggins (mark) (LS), Wit: James Hamilton, Hugh Whiteside.

**Pages 203-205:** The last will and testament of Elijah Bayley Senior was proven before me May 20th by the oaths of Robert Davidson, John Ratchford, and John Mills witnesses to the said will.

21 March 1808, the will of Elijah Bailey Senior, now of York District in the State of South Carolina, being under a long and lingering indisposition of body.... my three sons Bagwell, Elijah, and William Bailey, each of them five shillings sterling money of this state which is the whole of what I mean to bequeath them at this time; the negroes whose names are Will, Moses, Melinda and Wiltha, formerly under the direction and care of Joseph Tiller in Richland District, the said negroes with all the increase of the female number of them, I allow to be equally divided amongst my daughter Margaret Tiller's children which children she had by Joseph Tiller her husband. I bequeath to my granddaughter Mary Bailey, daughter of Caleb, all my household and kitchen furniture, which I now possess on the plantation I now live on, also all my stock of cattle; one sorrel horse to be sold; to my three daughters whose names are Mary Dillet, Leah Dupont, and Scarborough Ward, each of them five shillings sterling; my unbequeathed chattle property which consists chiefly in provisions say corn, meat, sock of fowls, with my plantation utensils shall be continued on the plantation of my present residence under the care of Jean Bailey (widow woman) for the sole purpose of supporting her and her family. I appoint Robert Davidson of said district, my executor. Elijah Bayly Sener (LS), Wit: Robert Davidson, John Ratchford, John Mills. May 30th 1808 qualified Robert Davidson Ex;'r to the above will of Elijah Bayly deceas'd.

**Pages 205-208:** June 7th 1808. The last will and testament of John Smith was proven by the testimony of John Clark and Adam McCrevan subscribing witnesses to the said will.

26th November 1807, Will of John Smith of South Carolina in York District... to my dearly beloved mother Sarah Smith, living in the State of Maryland in the city of Baltimore, the one half of the moneys arising from my stock in trade in merchandize in the Carolinas in company with Andrew Harth which suppose will amount to $850 perhaps more or perhaps left, one lot with a brick house three story high in Bank Street and one lot with a brick house thereon two story high in Water Street, both in Baltimore, also my two shares int he water company in Baltimore, to be at her disposal for the raising and cloathing my sister Sarah Cantwell's two children Katherine Gough Cantwell and James Smith Cantwell. My sister Sarah Cantwell shall have the management of the houses and lots already named. To my two cousins Katherine Gough Cantwell and James Smith Cantwell the two brick houses and lots when my cousin James Smith shall arrive at the age of 21. To my sister Sarah Cantwell the one half of my monies arising from my stock and trade in company with Andrew Hart. To my uncle Thomas White and my cousin

Thomas White Junior what they stand indebted to me. To Miss Polly Clark daughter to John Clark where I kept my store my saddle horse called Joe and my gold watch to be kept by her as a remembrance of me. To my friend and comrade in trade Robert Clendining my riding chair and harness that I left in the city of Charleston, South Carolina. I appoint my friends Doctor William MaClean and William Smith of South Carolina, attorney at law, my executors. John Smith (LS), Wit: Joseph Neele, John Clark. A. McCraven. June 7th 1808 Qualified Doctor William McClean exr.

**Page 209:** State of South Carolina, York District. To Alexander Moore, Esquire, judge of the Court of Ordinary... I find by a copy of the last will and testament of John Smith of the District and state aforesaid deceas'd that he hath nominated Doctor William McClean & myself as is Executors. I cannot make it convenient the burthen thereof. I am therefore obliged to withold my name.... William Smith. June 6th 1808.

September 24th. The last will and testament of Michael Stewart was proved by the testimony of James Neel and Robert McCullough and that Mary Carson was a subscribing witness to the same.

**Pages 210-211:** Will of Michael Stewart, being sick & weak in body... to my beloved wife Rosanna Stewart one third part of my land and the use of the whole land during her widowhood & while she continues to keep the Children & School them clear of any expense to estate, also one third part of the amount of the sale of my personal estate, viz houses, cows, sheep, hogs, also plantation utensals & household furniture, the present crop both on the ground & in the barn, I give her for the support of herself & children for the present year. I bequeath to my daughter Sarah one third part of the amount of sale of all my personal estate; to my son Alexander Stewart, my plantation whereon I now live to be enjoyed & possessed by him after he arrives to the age of 21 years; I appoint James Stewart my trust & well beloved friend and brother in law Francis Adams, exrs. [not dated]. Michael Stewart (X) (LS), Wit: John Hill, Robert McCullough (R), Mary Carson (X). Septr 24th 1808, Qualified James Stewart and Francis Adams, exrs.

**Pages 211-212:** December 16th 1808. The last will and testament of John Venable deceas'd was proven by the oaths of James Venable & Robert Jorden witnesses thereto.

Will of John Venables Senior of the State of South Carolina and District of York... to my beloved wife Jane all my household furniture, my mare and three cows, her choice of my stock and $60 in cash, also allow her to live in my house and to be upheld in every necessary means for her subsistence in a decent manner. At her decease I allow the plantation to be sold at publick vandue and the price to be equally divided between my two sons William and Archibald. I allow my wife to have the benefit of my negro wench untill her decease then my wench to be the property of my son James; the remaining part of my property I allow to be publickly disposed of after my decease and from the amount of that property I allow my son Richard to get $10, my son in law William Watson one dollar, also my son in law Andrew Lesley one dollar; then whatever remains to be equally divided between my wife and other three sons (viz) James, William, and Archibald. I appoint my wife and my son James and Robert Jorden executors, dated 31 August 1808. John Venables (LS), Wit: Asahel Enloe, James Venables, Robert Jorden. December 18th 1808. Qualified Jane Venables, James Venables & Robert Jorden executors.

**Page 213:** South Carolina, York District. Will of Lucy Nash of York District, being sick of body.... to my beloved son Travis Myrick Nash, one horse, bridle, and saddle, one years schooling, bed & furniture, also $100 to be raised and levied out of my estate after my debts are discharged; to my beloved daughter Polley Turner Nash one bed and furniture, side saddle and clothes, my part of what may be recovered of the estate of Mathew Myrick, late deceased of St. John Parish, and the money arising from my estate after it's sold for twelve months to be kept at interest untill she is married or eighteen years of age (namely one negro man Dick, one negro Thomas, mare and colt, cattle, hogs, household and kitchen furniture). I appoint John Adams and Samuel Neely, my executors, dated 5 Feb 1809. Lucy Nash (X) (Seal), Wit: D. Boyers, Thos Barron. Feby 20th 1809, Qualified John Adams and Saml Neely, exrs.

**Pages 214-215:** South Carolina, York District. Will of James Foreman, being in a low state of health... to my beloved wife Sarrah Foreman, the use and free enjoyment of the place whereon I now live her natural life time or widowhood and also the negroes which is my right and also three horses, five head of cows, also two thirds of all the household furniture, harth, and kitchen furniture, two thirds of the corn, oats & furrage, fifteen head of hogs, also her bed and furniture; all my real estate be equally divided between my sons James Thomas Foreman and William Foreman. My personal property shall be sold and equally divided among my children both male and female that is to Nancy Foreman, Mary Foreman, James Thomas Foreman, Sally Foreman, and William Foreman. I appoint my friends Benjamin Rowel and John Black, exrs., dated 11 Feb 1809. James Foreman (X) (Seal), Wit: Rob B. Walker, William Hill, John Crockett. Qualified Benjamin Rowel and John Black exrs.

**Pages 215-217:** July 3d 1809. The last will and testament of William Minter deceas'd was proven by the oath of John Blair subscribing witness thereto and further saith that Robert Wilson, Elizabeth Wilson, William Jamieson and James Gill were subscribing witness thereto in this deponants presence and that the sd William Minter was in his right mind when he signed & executed s'd will.

Will of William Minter of the State of So Carolina and district of York... to my beloved wife Martha Minter, the plantation whereon I now live during her life or while she remains a widow, one feather bed and its furniture that is in the dwelling house and kitchen. To my son John Minter of Chester District, the tract of land whereon he now lives, 200 acres; to my son William Minter,

100 acres of land to be taken off the tract I now live on and also whatever quantity of land may be included by continuing the line that runs off the said 100 acres in a straight direction untill it strikes Thomas Wilsons line which will be of another survey bearing date 7 Dec 1791, but the said Wm Minter pay unto is brother Joseph Minter $50; to my two sons Josiah and Jacob Minter, my tract of land in Chester District whereon my grist mills are. I also give unto them my cotton machine and still with their appurtenances; to my daughter Mary Moor five pounds; to my son Joseph Minter five pounds; to my daughter Sarah Minter $100 and one horse & saddle; to my son Jonathan Minter at the death or marriage of his mother the plantation whereon I now live; the residue of my estate to be equally divided among all my children. I appoint my wife Martha Minter executrix and my sons John and Josiah Minter executors, dated 26 Sept 1807. Will Minter (LS), Wit: Jno Blair, Robt Wilson (mark), Elizabeth Wilson (mark), William Jamieson, James Gill. July 3d Qualified Margaret Minter extx and Josiah Minter extrs.

**Pages 218-219:** 30th September 1808, Will of George Watson of York District, State of So Carolina, being very sick & weak in body.... to my well beloved wife Mary Watson, one bay mare with my cows, hogs, household furniture, & plantation implements with my loom & tacklings, and at her death the loom & tacklings to go to my step daughter Ruthey Bratton; and the rest of the property willed her to be at her disposal; my friend Hugh Bratton, sole executor. George Watson (LS), Wit: Robert Bratton Senr, Ja Simpson Junr. June 24th. Qualified Hugh Bratton ex'r to the above will.

**Pages 219-222:** Will of Joseph Alexander, minister of the Gospel... to Baldwin & Joseph Byers, the succeeding issue of my daughter Martha, the sum of £5 to each; to my daughter Sarah Barnett, Evans Sermons 2 Vol and all the money which can be raised by the sale of Havels in addition to what she has already received; to my son Samuel David Alexander, 200 acres on which he now liveth according to the platt of survey made by William Gaston, Esquire, together with my Duke Steuarts philosophy of the human mind. but as my son Samuel has occasionally administered medicine & attended on me & family & seeing I am conscientiously satisfied in my own mind that he has been fully paid for the same & ought to be satisfied & contented, seeing also that no kind of settlement between him & me has or probably could ever be had, In justice therefore to the rest of my children it is my will & desire that if my son will at any time after my deceased set up & prosecute a demand or account for his medicinal services or on any other account or demand, that the gift of all & every article & thing so as before given & devised of the said land as to him devised be refunded & revoke. I give to my daughter Editha Walker Turretine opera Guyses Paraphrase in addition to what she has received; to Joseph Alexander King the youngest child of my daughter Esther, $25. Considering that the old plantation was worn out I give & bequeath unto my son George Baldwin Alexander all the remainder of my lands, two oxen, one cart, one bed & bedding, one negro boy named Dave, Pickins works, Dodriges works, chiefly in his possession. To my daughter Judah Bankhead $10 in addition to the $120 she has received in the room & place of the last divided of my estate & this last being attested by her receipt & given her in an hour of distress when her husband durst not be seen. I further will to her Walkers sermons. I give to my daughter Ann Garrison, Edwards on original sin & edwards on the religious effectives. To my daughter Margret McJunkin, $125 or in their room a negro girl added to $125 given her in wench named Diana & John Newtons works. All property of which I shall die possessed except what is herein disposed be sold & equally divided among such of my surviving children as have not receive their divided. I appoint my friend Joseph McJunkin Senr & Col. Joseph Hughs, exrs., 19 July 1809. Joseph Alexander, V. D. M., D. D. (Seal), Wit: John Black, Jacob Black, John B. Black. August the 10th 1809. The last will & testament of Doctor Joseph Alexander Deceas'd was proved by the oaths of John Black and Jacob Black witnesses thereto. Qualified the exrs at the same time.

**Pages 222-224:** August 7th 1809. The last will and testament of Jenny Ramsey was proven on the oath of William Adams witness thereto.

Will of Jane Ramsey of York District in the State of South Carolina, being sick and weak in body... to my son William Ramsey, $30; to my daughter Jenny Davidson, $30; to my daughter Martha Ramsey, $30 in money and the value of $10 in cloathing; to my son James Ramsey, my bed & furniture; to my two sons William & James, all the remainder of my estate to be equally divided between them. I appoint my friend John Brown, Esqr., and my son William Ramsey, executors, dated 15 Jan 1809. Jenny Ramsey (LS), Wit: Francis Adams, Mary Adams (M), William Adams. August 7th 1809. Qualified Wm Ramsey exr.

**Pages 225-227:** August 14th 1809. The last will and testament of James Young was proven by the oath of David Gordon witness thereto.

3rd August 1809, Will of James Young of York District in the State of South Carolina... I impower my executors to sell to the best advantage 100 acres of land off the upper end of the survey I now live on, joining lands now owned & occupied by Capt. Ro. Hanna, myself, and the Cuttawba Indian boundry or line. My wife Margaret Young being in a pregnant situation and (it not being) for me to know whether the babe will arrived to the years of maturity or not, therefore I think it advisable to distribute my property in the following manner... after all my wifes right of dower is taken out of my estate, the remainder of the same I allow to be divided a nears a possible in quantity and quality the one half of said neat estate, which consists in land, negroes, stock of different kinds, household & kitchen furniture & plantation utensils all to be to the use of my wife during her pleasure... the baby (yet not born) if it arrives to the years of maturity, I allow it the other half of my neat estate, but if said babe should die in the years of maturity, then I allow all its part to be equally divided between my two sisters now Mary Cooper & Nancy Wallace & my nephew Young Fleming & niece Jean Fleming, each of said four legatees to enjoy their parts of the same. I allow the babe to have all the future increase (if any) of my negroe woman named Winny, but if death takes place with this babe, then I allow such increase to be the sole property of my wife; in case death takes place with boy my wife & the babe, I allow the childs part of the future increase of s'd negro woman to be equally divided between the then surviving children of Elias Wallace & Rob't Cooper. I appoint Elias Wallace, Robert Cooper & my said wife Margaret Young, exrs. James Young (LS), Wit: John McConnel, John Starr, David Gordon.

**Page 228:** May 9th 1809. The last will and testament of Mary Drennon was proven by the oath of John Soward witness thereto.

So Carolina, York County. Will of Mary Drennon... to James ___, five shillings; to George Camble, five shillings; to Joseph Strain, five shillings, and the remainder of my property to Synthy Simril. [not dated] Mary Drennon, Wit: James Simril, Samuel Carrothers, John Soward.

**Pages 228-229:** January 6th 1810. The last will and testament of Richard Sadler Senior was proven by the oath of David Leech Senior and that George Reed and Jos Feemster were subscribing witnesses thereto.

State of South Carolina, York District. Will of Richard Sadler, Senior of the District and state aforesaid, planter.... to my dear and loving wife Jane Sadler, my whole estate real & personal, including the land on which I now live, and the negroes now in my possession, named Peter, Rachel, Abraham, Cynthia, Prince, and Tony, with all the horses, cattle, hogs and sheep; to my oldest son David Sadler, $20; to my second son Richard Sadler, $20; to my third son Joseph Sadler, $20; to my daughter Eleanor Black, $20. My wife Jane Sadler and my son David Sadler, be executors. Richard Sadler (LS), Wit: Geo Reed, Jos Feemster, David Leech Sr.

**Pages 230-231:** May 8th 1810. The last will and testament of James Thomson deceas'd was proven by the oath of Edward Byers one of the witnesses thereto.

Will of James Thomson of the District of York & State of South Carolina, being sick & weak in body... to my brother Nathaniel Thomson, my claim of a certain tract of land in the State of North Carolina, Bunkham County, Butree[?] Creek, commonly known by the name of the cove, 50 acres, likewise $50 deducting whatever he may have against my estate out of the $50. To my sister Mary Ann Edmiston, $5; to my brother Moses Thomson, $100; to my brother Samuel Thomson, $200; to my sister Betsey Hann Greer, $100 at the expiration of two years. If she should die without issue before the money becomes due from my estate, to my brother Samuel Thomson; to my two brothers Alexander & John Thomson the remainder of my estate to be equally divided between them. I appoint Alexander Thomson & John Thomson, my executors, 11 June 1808. J. Thomson (LS), Wit: Edward Byers, John Cain, John Leech (X). May 7th 1810 qualified Alexander Thomson and John Thomson exrs.

**Page 232:** May 21st 1810. The last will and testament of John McCanc was proven on the oath of Samuel McCullough witness thereto, who on oath says that Sarah and Mary McCullough were subscribing witnesses with himself.

State of South Carolina, In the District of York. Will of John McCance... my brother David McCance should have my plantation whereon he now lives; the ballance of my estate should be equally divided amongst my brothers & sisters allowing David an equal share in the dividend of said ballance. I nominate Samuel McCullough, Thomas Neely, John Chambers & Joseph Davie, exrs., 28 Aug 1809. John McCance, Wit: Saml McCullough, Sarah McCullough, Mary McCullough. May 31st 1810 qualified Joseph Davie executor.

**Pages 233-235:** August 6th 1810. The last will and testament of William Nelson Senr was proven by the oaths of William Hamilton and John Good witnesses thereto.

3 August 1805. Will of William Nelson of York District, State of South Carolina, farmer... to my well beloved wife Margaret, two negroes viz January and Peg with all their increase and one black mare, saddle and bridle, and one choice cow, one bed and furniture, one walnut chest, with the use of the plantation until my eldest son William comes of age; to my eldest son William, two negroes, one large house Bible and shot gun; to my son Robert two negroes Daniel and Nell; to my son Andrew, negroes Rachel and Judy; to my daughter Anne, two negroes Hanah and Feb; if my wife should bring another child into the world as I suppose she will, it shall have the first two children of Amy or Hanah. The negroes left to my children to be hired out yearly and the money arising therefrom to be laid out to the use of my children. I appoint my wife and Charles Lockert, executors. William Nelson (Seal), Wit: J. Rogers, Wm. Hamilton, John Good. August 6th 1810 qualified Margett extx in the above will.

**Pages 235-236:** August 6th 1810. The last will and testament of Jane Kerr dec'd was proven by the oath of James Glass witness thereto.

State of South Carolina, York District. April 26th 1810. Will of Jane Kerr in a low state of health... to my cousin Robert Kerr, son of my uncle Andrew Kerr, the one half of my tract of land which is on the headwaters of Alison Creek to be divided according to quantity and quality my cousin Robert his choice or his father my uncle may choose for him; to my cousin William Kerr my s'd uncles son, the other half of my aforesaid tract of land with this exception that he will pay to my two half sisters Peggy and Polly Finly $100 to each of them when they come to eighteen years of age, and if one of them dies while a minor the surviving one shall have the $200, if both die while minors s'd money shall be divided equally between my four cousins Andrew, James, Zenas & Joseph E., sons of my uncle Andrew Kerr; to my cousin John Kerr, son of my uncle Andrew Kerr, my roan mare; to my cousin Polly Kerr, daughter of my s'd uncle, my riding saddle and also my bed and furniture; to my three cousins Isabella, Margret and Mary daughters of my s'd uncle, an equal division of all the moneys due to me on notes bonds, with this exception that what is due from my said uncle shall not be received with interest neither shall he pay any thereon; to my two half sisters aforesaid an equal division of all my wearing clothes except such as I wear at home at my work such is I call my every day clothes which I give my three aforesaid cousins Isabella, Margret, and Mary; I ordain my uncle Andrew Kerr and George Davis, exrs. Jean Kerr (X). Wit: J. Hemphill, James Glass, Mary Glass. August 6th 1810, Qualified Andrew Kerr and George Davis exrs.

[the original will (York County Estates, Case 58, File 2624) has two lines stricken: "And lastly I ordain and apoint my two uncles John and Andrew Kerr executors of this my last will and testament."

**Pages 237-238:** August 6th 1810. The last will and testament of Joseph Clark dec'd was proven on the oath of Nicholas Curry witness thereto.

Will of Joseph Clark of York District, St. of So Carolina, being in a sick and low state of body.... to my five daughters viz Margret, Elizabeth, Suzan, Mary and Sarah, a tract of 500 acres lying above and adjoining the land where my son Thomas Clark now liveth, to be equally divided by them in any manner that they or any three of them pleaseth; to my son Thomas clark, 100 acres of my last survey to be laid off to him below the mouth of the creek adj. James Dicksons land; the rest of my estate consisting of lands, goose, and chattles, be sold and equally divided amongst my children male and female. I appoint William Love Senr of District afores'd and my son James Clark to be my executors, dated 10 July 1810. Joseph Clark (LS), Wit: Nicholas Corry, Joseph Dawson, Jess Parker (X). August 6th 1810 qualified James Clark named exr.

**Pages 238-239:** South Carolina, York District. Will of Dorcas Wherry.... to my daughter Peggy Strait my negro man James & $20 cash to her son Samuel & my chest, saddle & Wheel to her daughter Dorcas & Mary & Dorcas a good suit of clothing & cloak each out of the moneys arising from the vendue; to my daughter Polly McClintock my negro woman Aim; to my daughter Hannah my negro girl Rachel & two beds & furniture & all household furniture except one bed which I allow for Wm. Wherrys son Samuel; my land to be sold & the remainder of my personal property & the moneys arising from these sales to be equally divided between my sons William, Andrew, Samuel, Thomas & John & daughters Peggy & Polly. I nominate Samuel Wherry & Andrew Sherry exrs., dated 17 Oct 1810. Dorcas Wherry (mark) (Seal), Wit: Leonard Strait, Peter Boyd, Peggy Boyd (X). November 1st. The last will and testament of Dorcas Wherry dec'd was proven on the oaths of Leonard Strait & Peter Boyd witnesses thereto and that she was in her right mind when she executed the same.

**Pages 239-240:** 4th March 1810. Will of James Deen of York District & State of South Carolina, being weak in body... to my loving neass Hannah Kilpatrick, all my negroes Billy, Cate & Ginny; to said Hannah Kilpatrick, the remainder of my lands, goods & Chattles that remains after my lawful debts are paid. I appoint Robert Kilpatrick & Jonathan Beatie my exrs. Jas Deen (Seal), Wit: W. Beatty, Robert Lusk. The last will and testament of James Deen Deceas'd was proven on the oaths of William Beaty witness thereto and that the said deceas'd was in his right mind when he executed the same.

**Pages 240-241:** Will of Rebecca Montgomery of South Carolina & York District, being sick & afflicted in body... to my daughter Lucressey her bed & furniture, a horse, and what sheep, hogs & geese are in my possession at my decease, also a chest, a dozen plates, a dish, two pots & a skillet, the half of the cotton and the corn belonging to me; to my son Hillery one bed & furniture; to my son Benjamin one Bed & Furniture, also one cow & half of the farming utensils; also I will to my daughter lucressey a pair of smoothing irons, my cotton cards, a cotton wheel, a reel and her choice of the flax wheels & half of the wheat; my mare, two young cattle, the ballance of the kitchen ware & the ballance of the farming utensils to be sold; a third of what may remain I will to my daughter Ann Yarborough; the ballance to be equally divided between the other legatees; whatever may be coming to me out of the John Carrenton's estate, Lamuel Carrentons one years schooling. I appoint John Watson & William Stewart my executors, dated 8 Sept 1810. Rebecca Montgomery (mark) (Seal), Wit: Benjamin Montgomery, James Tate.

**Pages 241-243:** November 24th 1810. The last will and testament of Samuel Kuykendall was proven by the oaths of Jacob Davison and Elizabeth Davison witnesses thereto.

State of South Carolina, York District. Novemb'r 16th 1810. Will of Samuel Kuykendal, being weak in body.... to my beloved wife Susannah Kuykendall, one negri girl named Mille during her life or widowhood & my plantation of land I now live on during life or widowhood, one sorrel mare and young sorrel colt and all my stock of cattle; to my oldest son Jonathan Kuykendall a negro man named Stephen and the said negro I allow to remain on the plantation to the use of his mother & family untill my said son Jonathan arrives to the age of 21 and also one sorrel mare that oldest mare I have and a rifle gun and a debt coming to me from Hance McWhorter by note of hand for $100 and if the negro girl Mille should have increase the first child to go to my aforesaid son Jonathan, also if another negro girl named Hannah should have increase, I allow the first child to my said son Jonathan; to my second son James Kuykendal, the negro girl named Hannah if he sees fit when he comes of age to take her for a sum of money, the half price of a negro willed to him by his grandmother which I received and became his guardian for and if he does not see fit to take her, I allow the said negro to be sold to pay him up the said legacy and I allow the said negro girl Hannah to remain on the plantation to the use of my executors until said James arrives at the age of 21 years; to my two sons John Coburn Kuykendal and Jesse Kuykendal my plantation of land I now live on, to be equally divided between them and also a young sorrel mare I give to my said son John C. Kuykendal; to my youngest son Samuel Kuykendal, said negro girl Mille to come to him at the expiration of the time willed to his mother except the first child to his brother Jonathan;

it is also my will that my wife Susannah should give my children schooling out of what I have left her. I appoint my wife Susannah and my son Jonathan my executors. Saml Kuykendal (LS), Wit: Jonathan Kuykendal, Jacob Davison, Elizabeth Davison, John Hartgrove.

**Pages 244-246:** November 27th 1810. The last will and testament of Col. Samuel Watson was proven by the oath of Hugh Watson witness thereto who on his oath said that Robert Watson and Catherine Watson were subscribing witnesses to said will at the same time.

Will of Samuel Watson of State of South Carolina and York District, 1 March 1809.... to my beloved wife Elizabeth Watson her living in the house we now live in with a liberty of working a Sufficient quantity of the clear land to raise a sufficient support for her & family & stock during her widowhood, for which term I leave to my wife my negro man Tom and my negro woman Leethe with half of the farming utensils, etc; to my son in law John Eakin, five shillings sterling; to my son James, my watch; to my son Robert Watson ,my negro man Tom at the death of his mother or at her removal off the place, also my little negro boy named Tomson; as the said plantation is part of three old plantations, it is my will that it be surveyed and a plat made, and to make a deed for the same & son Robert is to have the other half of the farming utensils; my property to be appraised and my son John to have two thirds of the appraisement and my son Samuel the other third; my negro boy named Ben to my son Hugh; my negro boy Isac to my son William; to negro girl Linday to my son David; to my son in law John Berry, a note of $100 that I lent him; to Betsy McWhorter, a negro child named Addaline; to each of my grandsons Samuel Watson son of Jas Watson, Saml Watson son of John Watson, Sam Watson son of David Watson, Saml Watson son of John Berry, James Watson son of Saml Watson, Sarah & Saml Watson, son & daughter of Hugh Watson; Saml Watson son of Robert Watson, $20 each; my wife $60; whatever may be due upon Hills & Capt Haynes bond at my death, be equally divided between my son in law John Berry and my seven sons and each of them to collect their own part if they can get it without sueing. I appoint my sons John & Saml Watson, exrs. Samuel Watson (Seal), Wit: Hugh Watson, Robert Watson, Catherine Watson. Novbr 17th 1818, Qualified John Watson. March 4th Qualified Saml Watson.

**Pages 247-248:** Will of James Campbell of York District, South Carolina... to my wife Ann Campbell her riding mare & saddle, her bed & furniture; the dresser & furniture to be divided between my wife and my two youngest daughters; the nine dollars in possession of Robert Latimore shall be paid to my wife; my son Robert Campbell shall have one large moild cow; my daughter Ann Campbell shall have one black and white moild cow & steer calf & one sorrel horse, saddle & bridle, her own bed & furniture; to my daughter Rachel one red cow, & heifer calf, with one bed & furniture; my son William shall have a sorrel horse, one bay steers colt & black cow & one heifer calf, and the remainder of my cattle with the hogs to remain for the use & support of my family, and the sheep to be at the disposal of my wife; my grandson

James D. Campbell in Kentucky have my saddle & one furr hat; the $10 in possession of Christopher Turner to be equally divided between my daughters Margaret & Sarah & the $10 in the hands of Samuel Waller to assist in purchasing a saddle for Rachel J. Campbell; to my son William Campbell the plantation whereon I now live; my wife Ann Campbell shall have a comfortable maintenance from said plantation during life or widowhood; my son Robert shall have the privilege to live on said plantation by assisting in raising grain for the support of himself and the family while he shall have a single life; my two sons Robert & William my executors, dated 20 Aug 1810. James Campbell (X) (LS), Wit: Thomas Davis, Saml Waller.

**Pages 248-249:** Will of William McCleland of State of South Carolina & District of York, being at this time weak of body.... to my beloved wife Margret one black mare & two cows, one bed and furniture, one spinning wheel & all the affairs belonging to the dresser & to have a decent support of the plantation while she lives; to my oldest daughter Margaret five shillings; to my second daughter Susanna five shillings; to my third daughter Polly, her bed and furniture; to my fourth daughter Sidney, her bed & furniture, one cow & spinning wheel; to my youngest daughter Ruthey, one bed & furniture, one cow & spinning wheel when she comes of age; the plantation whereon I now live to be divided in four shares, a share to each of my four oldest sons Jno, William, Saml & Jordan, only they paying to their youngest brother James his fifth part of said plantation. My present wife Margaret McCleland, Robert Allison Esqr & Andrew McWhorter, my executors, dated 3 Nov 1810. William McClelan (LS), Wit: Hugh McWHorter, John Carson, William Watson.

**Pages 249-251:** The last will and testament of Francis Gilmore deceas'd was proven April 23d 1811 upon the oath of Robert Kenedy subscribing witness thereto.

Will of Francis Gilmore Sn'r of Clarks Fork of Bullocks Creek in the District of York, being weak in body.... unto my daughter Elizabeth Swan five shillings; to my son James Gilmore five shillings; to my daughter Sarah Swan five shillings; to my son Enoch Gilmore five shillings; to my son Francis Gilmore five shillings; to my daughter Jean monks five shillings; to my youngest Joshua Gilmore, the remainder of my estate both real and personal excepting my negro woman Fann whom I allow to be set free at the expiration of four years after my decease and I allow my son Joshua to exercise a guardianship over her all the rest of her life. I appoint my son Joshua Gilmore, exr., dated 26 March 1811. Francis Gilmore (LS), Wit: Nathaniel P. Kenedy, Robert Kennedy.

**Pages 252-253:** Will of William Jackson being low in body... to my wife Elizabeth the plantation I live on, one feather bed & furniture, one bay mare called Teana & colt called White Foot with her saddle & bridle, two cows & calves, ten head of hogs; to my son Lewis Elbert one negro man called Sampson, one colt called Ceiler; to my daughter Becky Maria, one negro woman called Nance & her child called Arter, one bed and furniture. Provided my wife Elizabeth should bring forth, as she I believe to be pregnant & the child should live be it male or female, I will it one negro called Sam; the remainder of my property to be sold and the money arising from the sale with what notes and money are on hand that all my lawful debts to be paid excepting my old negro woman Fab & for her to live with any of my relations she pleases & for them to pay her for her services. I appoint Zebulon Jackson & William Pettus, exrs., 28 March 1811. William Jackson (LS), Wit: Wm. Partton, Mathew West, John Smith. Proved upon the oaths of Wm Patton, Mathew West and John Smith. At same time viz May 3d 1811 qualified Zebulon Jackson exr.

**Pages 254-256:** Will of William Carson of the County of York, South Carolina... to my wife Shusanna Carson, a free and peasible possession in my dwelling house with a comfortable mentainance from the land during life if continuing a widow, likewise my horse called Dick with her saddle and bridle, bed and furniture, four cows with some young cattle, sheep, hogs, and geese; to my old son Samuel Carson, 100 acres of land whereon he lives, from side to side of the land with a right maid out of the original patons; to my son William Carson, 100 acres where he lives agreeable to the lines we have marked; to my daughter Mary Carson, $10 to be paid by Francis; to my daughter Jean Carson, a saddle horse or mare with her saddle and bridle, with her chest, bed and furniture, two cows; to my son Robert Carson, all my plains; to my daughter Shusanna Martin, $10; to my son Francis Carson, my plantation where I now live with all the farming utensils, wagon and gears, his bed and furniture; to daughter Marthew Carsen, her young mare with saddle and bridle, bed and furniture; my guns to be sold to pay the legacies as far as they go; the loom and tacklings for the use of the family; my wife Susan Carsen and James Cambel, my exrs., 13 June 1808. William Carson (Seal), Wit: William Byers, Samuel Carson.

**Pages 257-259:** South Carolina, York District. Will of Thomas Black Senior of state and district aforesaid... to my beloved wife Mary Black, one half of the survey of land I now live on containing 200 acres including my buildings and one half of the cleared land, with three milk cows and hogs sufficient for her next years meat, with the use of my three negroes Peter, Jin & Lucy during her life, and at her death Peter and Jim to John Starr and the other to be divided among my children; to my daughter Meribah Black, the other half of my household and kitchen furniture (except such as shall be hereafter mentioned), my sorrel mare, and $400 in cash, a young mare four years old, a colt of her mates, two cows & calves; to my son Thomas Black, $400 to be paid him out of my estate to my daughter Jane Neely, my bureau. The remainder of my property to be disposed of in the following manner: my land in partnership with the Rev. Mr. McCall to be sold and to be equally divided among my now living children; the balance of property to be sold after the decease of my beloved wife and among to be equally distributed among my then living children; to my wife, half of my household and kitchen furniture;

my sons John & James Black, exrs., 14 June 1811. Thos Black, Wit: Jo Simpson, Jno Miller, Richard Sadler.

**Pages 260-261:** 28 November 1807, Will of John Morris of York District, South Carolina, planter, being weak in body... to Rebecah my dearly beloved wife the bed and furniture she now lieth on and a necessary supply of all the comforts of this life; to my granddaughter Ann Saile the bed and furniture she now calls hers, one cow & Calf; to Catharine Vicalson the run of the house she now lives in as long as she chuseth, ten bushels of Indian corn every year; to my beloved son Ezekiel Morris all my lands & tenements, horses cattle, sheep and hogs, my loom and tackellen; he and my wife Rebecca to be executors. John Morris (Seal), Wit: Joseph Kolb, Catherine Kolb.

**Page 262:** South Carolina, York District. May 8th 1811. Will of Mary Dunken, being weak in body... to my niece Ann Kidd, all that tract of land on which I now live (which was wil'd to me by my beloved Husband Thomas Dunkin to dispose of at my pleasure), for her use her lifetime and after her death to her heirs forever; also to my s;d niece Ann Kidd, all my stock of every description and all my household goods of all kinds. I appoint Charles Browmfield, Henry Kerr and George Davis, exrs.. Mary Dunkin (mark), Wit: Roger Barry, George Kidd, Mary Mcfordsany (mark).

**Pages 263-264:** Will of Samuel Thompson of the State of So Carolina and district of York, being low in body... to my brother Nathaniel Thompson, $250 to be paid by Moses Thompson eighteen months after the date of this; to my brother Moses Thompson, one negro man due me from my brother Alexander & John Thompson to be worth $500; to my sister Mary Ann Edmiston[?], $250 to be paid her by Robert Grier, two years after the death of this; to my sister Betsy Hannah Grier, one negro man named Peter which I have now in my possession; to my venerable mother one negro boy named Ned with my new fir hat; to my two brothers Alexander Thompson & John Thompson, all the balance of my property with $400 due me from the estate of James Thompson now in their hands. I appoint Alexander Thompson and John Thompson, exrs., 3 March 1811. Samuel Thompson. Wit: Thomas Brown, Robert Grier. The above will was proven August 5th 1811 upon the oath of Thomas Brown witness thereto.

**Pages 264-266:** The last will and testament of William Burris deceas'd was proven on the oath of Capt James Mitchell witness thereto who on oath saith that John Wright and Andrew Wright were subscribing witnesses at the same time, 3 Oct 1811. Qualified Mary Burris extx the date above.

Will of William Burris Senior of State of South Carolina and District of York being sick and weak in body... the negroes and the other property give to all my children before the date of this my last will and testament to be their property; a certain negro girl named Tally to my daughter Easther Buris; to my daughter Esther Burris her bed and furnature and a sorrel mare; to my son John Burris a negro by named Archey though to remain with my beloved wife Mary Burris and for her use during her natural life; unto my wife Mary Burris the whole of the remaining part of my property real and personal and that one third of my estate real and personal be at her disposal at her death. The other thirds of my estate real and personal at the death of my wife Mary Burris be equally divided among all my children or their heirs. I appoint my wife Mary Burris sole executor, dated 30 April 1811. William Burris (mark (LS), Wit: Jas Mitchell, John Wright, Andrew Wright.

**Pages 266-267:** The last will and testament of Nancy McMurry was proven on the oath of William Neely witness Febry 3d 1813.

South Carolina, York District. Will of Nancey McMurry, being in a low state of health... to my nees[?] Mary Tippens, my bed and its common furniture; to Elizabeth Ekins for her respect to me & kindness, one large earthen dish and fore blew soape plates say the plates edged with blue; to my neise Mary White McMurry, my best and all my bodily apparel, also one pewter dish or large plate or bason; all the remainder of my property as to my land and everything be sold and my debts paid out of the same and the remainder to be given to my nephew William Simpson McMurry; my brother William McMurry, exr., dated 18 Jan 1812. Nancy McMurry (mark), Wit: Joseph Davis, William Neely, Wm. Akins. Qualified Wm McMurry exrs., Feb. 3, 1818.

**Pages 268-270:** Will of James Henry of the District of York and State of South Carolina, being in a low state of health.... to Mary my beloved wife the plantation I now live on to be equally divided between her & my daughter Mary Erwin & likewise the household furniture; to my wife Mary a certain bay mare the one I formerly rode on myself & her colt, and I will that an equal divide be made of my stock of cattle between my wife & daughter Mary Erwin; to my wife Mary, one negro fellow named Prince & the old wench named Peg to be hers while she lives & at her decease for the negro Prince to fall into the hands of my grandson James Henry McGill; the two horse creatures with sheep & hogs & farming tools for the use & support of the family; the two remaining negro fellows George & Peter with the young wench named Pru be my daughter Mary Erwins; my daughter Martha McGill shall have the property that she has already received of my estate & $10 & the half of my books; my daughter Mary Erwins part of my estate be put under her lawful trustee & guardian; if my daughter Mary Erwin should decease before her mother the young wench named Pru shall be the property of my wife Mary & at the death of both said wench & her children shall be the property of my granddaughter Betsy Bell McGill and George & Peter at the decease of my daughter Mary shall be the property of my daughter Martha's heirs equally; a certain bay filley now four years old be the property of my niece Mary Erwin otherwise shall be marriage if she comes within the space of two years otherwise William McGill is hereby authorized to make sale of the mare; I appoint my wife Mary and my son in law Wm. McGill be my executrix & executor, 1 June 1811. James Henry (Seal), Wit: Gilbert Enloe, Henry Wright, James Crawford.

# YORK COUNTY SC WILL BOOK A-1 1800-1813

**Pages 270-271:** The last will and testament of William Watson was proven on the oath of Archibald Steel & that William Peters & Saml Smith were subscribing witnesses thereto April 6th 1812.

Will of William Watson of York District, South Carolina... to my beloved wife Mary Watson, all my property during her life or widowhood, after her death of marriage in the manner following: to my son James Watson, $10; to my grandson son of James Watson, one heifer calf one year old; the remainder of my property to be equally divided between my two sons David & Robert whom I appoint executors, 23 August 1809. William Watson (mark) (Seal), Wit: Will Pettus [Peters?], Saml Smith, Archibald Steel.

**Pages 271-272:** The last will and testament of John McElmoile was proven on the oath of Isaac McFaddin witness thereto who on his oath says that Thomas Faris & Mary Polk were subscribing witnesses at the same time April 22d 1812.

Will of John McElmoile Sen'r of York District... to my wife Mary McElmoile & my two sons James & John McElmoile the plantation which I live containing 200 acres to be held by them jointly & no part of it to be sold during my son James lifetime & at my wifes death the whole of said plantation to be my son Johns; to my son Daniel McElmoile a tract of 154 acres on the waters of Turkey Creek which I purchased from Abraham Livingston; to my daughter Margret McElmoile a lease for 70 acres of land in the Indian Claim which I purchased from James White; to my son my negro boy Bob to assist him in the maintenance of his mother;to my said wife my sorrel mair Gin; to my son Danl my sorrel mare call'd Dolly; to my son James my gray mare call'd Duck' to my son John my sorrel mare called Silver heels & sorrel mare called lightfoot; to my daughter Margaret my black mare called Venus' my stock of cattle, hogs & sheep to be equally divided among my legatees; to my wife, my walnut table, cooking & big pot, all the rest of my household & kitchen furniture to be equally divided among all my legatees; to my son Daniel a barshear plow and a shovel plow; to my daughter Margaret $10 out of the money coming from Wm. McCreight; I appoint John McClenahan executor, dated 11 Dec 1811. John McElmoile (LS), Wit: Isaac McFadden, Thos Faris, Mary Polk.

**Pages 273-275:** Will of Alexander Black of the State of South Carolina & District of York, 26 February 1812... to my loving wife Isabel her living in my dwelling house, her maintenance off the produce of my land, with one third part of the personal property I may die possessed of except what is hereafter named to my children to be at her disposal, also my cupboard & what furniture belongs to it, also my grew horse & shirk filley, saddle & Bridle, her bed & bedstead & furniture, also my books, hogs & sheep & Cattle, plantation tools & kitchen furniture to be at her disposal; to my son William the plantation he now lives on about 150 acres, also a bay horse & colt, one bed & furniture, one rifle gun got of Chambers, also one cow & Calf, one breeding sow & three head of sheep; to my daughter Mary, one bay mare four years old, a colt of sorrel mare Chambers got, one bed & Furniture, her saddle, one cow & calf & two head of sheep; to my daughter Elizabeth, one bed & Furniture, one roan mare called Blaze, one cow & calf when needed; to my daughter Jane, one bed & Furniture, one cow & Calf, also one horse creature if can be spared when needed; to my son Templeton, the third part of this plantation whereon I now live at the end and next to William McCorkle in the other side of Watsons branch, one bed & furniture, one two year old horse colt, one cow & Calf; to my daughter Sarah Anne, one bed & furniture, also one cow & calf, one horse creature if can be spared when comes to need one; to my daughter Isabel, one & furniture, one cow & Calf, one horse creature if can be spared when she comes of age; to my son James the third of my plantation where I now live beginning at the head of Watsons branch along that upper part, one bed & furniture, one last spring colt, one cow & calf; to my son Joseph, the part of that plantation whereon my brother Joseph & Sister Anne Black now lives at their decease, one bed & furniture, one co w& Calf, one horse creature if to be spared when he comes of age; to my son Hamilton Wilson, the third part of this plantation where the house now is and next to Mathew Ambersons, one cow & Calf, one bed & furniture, also one horse creature if to spare; to my son Isabel two notes of hand I have on William Chambers, also that plantation in York District whereon my father Alex'r Black formerly lived on the waters of Moores branch also her legacy left her from her father; also my smith tools and all belong to shop for the use of my sons equally; my waggon & furniture for the use of the plantation. My wife Isabel & my son William exrs. Alex'r Black (Seal), Wit: Robert Miller, Joseph Black, Mathew Amberson. May the 12th 1812. The will of Alex'r Black deceas'd was proven on the oath of Robert Miller witness thereto.

**Pages 275-276**: June 11th 1812. The last will and testament of Joseph Sadler deceas'd was proven by the oaths of Samuel McNeel and David Sadler witness thereto.

Will of Joseph Sadler of the District of York in the state of South Carolina... my wife Elizabeth Sadler shall inherit & forever possess all my real estate that is to say a plantation containing 100 acres of land where I formerly lived on joining land with Richard Sadler Senior deceased on Fishing Creek in york District; to my wife Elizabeth Sadler, all my personal property that is the following negroes Lond, Peter, Charlotte, Silvey, Sabina, & Henry & their issue, & all other moveable property such as horses, cows, hogs, sheep, plantation tools, household & kitchen furniture; my wife Elizabeth Sadler, executrix, dated 9 May 1812. Jo Sadler, Wit: Saml McNeel, John Bratten, David Sadler.

**Pages 277-279:** Will of Andrew Allen of York District & State of South Carolina, planter... to Jenny Allen my well beloved wife, one third of the plantation whereon I now live & one half of all the household furniture, one black horse colt, & one sorrel colt, two milk cows, her wheels & reels & loom & tacklings also her own saddle, waggon & Farming tools to remain on the plantation for the use of the family in general; my three oldest boys has already received their parts that I allot for them (namely James, Jno & Thomas). The forementioned Jno Allen remaining sole proprietor of the plantation whereon he now lives. To my son Andrew Allen one young sorrel mare and saddle; to my son Willm, Jewel's young colt & Saddle; to my two youngest sons Wilson & Samuel each of them $70; the plantation whereon I now live the whole of it to be divided equally between my four youngest sons at the death of their mother & whatever more property remains I allow to be equally divided among my four youngest sons namely Andrew, William, Wilson & Samuel. I make Jenny Allein my wife executrix & Andrew Allen my son, executor, dated 3 July 1811. Andrew Alein (X) (Seal), Wit: Jas Wilson, Alex'r Faris. N. B. I bequeath to my beloved wife my best furr hat & body clothes & also all my books the one half of the household furniture mentioned above with the last mentioned articles is at her own disposal. I bequeath to Andrew Allen my nephew & Betsy Allen my niece $50 a piece as they come of age providing there is not suit raised against any of my legatees by them or any other person, 10 October 1811. Andrew Allen (mark), Wit: Stewart Ferguson, Hiram Hutchison. June 30th 1812. The will of Andrew Allen deceas'd was proved before me on the oath of Alex'r Faris witness thereto. June 30th 1812. The codicil to the above will was proved on the oath of Stewart Ferguson. At the same time, viz June 30th 1812, qualified Jenny Allen executrix & Andrew Allen executor.

**Pages 280-282**: August 3d 1812. The last will of Robert Patrick deceas'd was proven on the oaths of Saml Henderson & Christiana Henderson witness thereto who on their oath say that William McClean was witness at the same time.

Will of Robert Patrick, blacksmith, of the District of York & State of South Carolina, being very weak in body, 5 June 1812... to my beloved wife Rosannah Patrick, her living clear on my real estate in the house wherein I now live or on such other part of my land as she may think more eligible during her life time together with the beds & their furniture, dresser & furniture, kitchen furniture, also the use of one negro woman named Suff, and at her death the said negro woman Suff shall belong to my son Robert Patrick; to my daughter Sarah Patrick, one half of the land whereon I now live; also to my daughter Esther Patrick alias Esther Bigger & Mary Patrick, 200 acres on Mill Creek whereon my daughter Esther now lives to be equally divided between said Esther & Mary Patrick; also to my son Robert Patrick, one half of the tract of land whereon I now live & for his taking care of & supporting my daughter Isabella Patrick the above named negro woman Suff at my wife Rosannah's decease, with my blacksmith tools, my waggon, still & still vessels, and all my farming tools & implements of husbandry; my horses, horned cattle, sheep & hoggs be continued on the premises whereon I now live for the use of my children, and at my wife's death to be equally divided among my children; sa to the division of my negro slaves I bequeath Jesse to my daughter Sarah, my negro slave Walker to my daughter Mary, my negro slave Amos & Jenny, I will that they shall remain with my family and at the death of my wife, said slaves to become the property of my son Robert; my negro slave Pegg to my daughter Sarah with whom she now lives; the negro child which has not received a name to my daughter Margrett; my wife Rosannah Patrick executrix and my son Robert Patrick executor. Robert Patrick (LS), Wit: Samuel Henderson, Christiana Henderson, Wm. McClean.

**Pages 283-284**: October 19th 1812. The last will of Ralph Vicars was proven on the oath of Thomas Davis evidence thereto who on his oath says that James McCamon and Thomas McCants was witness at the same time. At the same time qualified John Vicars, executor.

Will of Ralph Vicars, being weak of body... to my daughter Charity Ross, five dollars; to my son Theofillus Vicars, five dollars; to Mary Berry my daughter, five dollars; to my son John Vicars, $100; to my well beloved wife Ann Vicars, all the remaining part of my estate. Ann Vicars & John Vicars, exrs., 22 August 1810. Ralph Vicars (LS), Wit: Thomas Davis, James McCannon, Thomas McCants.

**Pages 284-285**: County of Antrim. Whereas it appears by a letter received here from James Mitchel & James Martin of the District of York & State of South Carolina stating that David Beard who left the county of Antrim in Ireland & settled in the said District of York in American died there on the fourth of March 1803 and by his will bequeathed unto his children David Beard & Jane Beard begotten by him on the body of Mary Adair of Dunagon in the Kingdom of Ireland, certain legacies which are mentioned in said will and of which will the said James Mitchel & James Martin are said to be executors, now I, Mary Adair, of Rathvey Parish of Dunagon in the County of Antrim, and who is mother to David Beard & Jane Beard do swear that David Beard who left the Parish of Antrim & settled in the District of York in the state of South Carolina & is reported by the above to have died some time ago is father to my above named children... that her son David Beard went from hence to go to Scotland about nine years ago & has not returned nor has been since heard of, and that her daughter Jane Beard the bearer hereof is daughter to above late David Beard of York in South Carolina... 10 October 1804. Before Thos Benjn. Adair. Mary Adair (X). Wit: John Steele, William Kirk. I do hereby certify that the afore named Jane Beard was born & is resident in this parish at present, dated at Ballysavage 2 September 1805. Bern'd Lyndon of Dunagon & Kilbride.

**Pages 286-287**: Jan'y 4th 1813. The last will & testament of William Miller deceased was proven on the oaths of John Currence, Isaac Campbell and Wm. Love witnesses thereto. At the same time qualified John Currence, executor.

14th November 1812. Will of William Miller of York District & State of South Carolina, being very weak & sick of body... at my death the plantation I now live on to be sold at publick sale & after my just debts are all paid the remainder to be equally divided among my three children viz Mary, Elizabeth & Sarah, Elizabeth's share I allow the executors to keep in their hands till her children come of age &then to be equally divided among them, also the one third of the pewter. My desire is also that Mary have one bed & furniture, also one half of all the household furniture (pewter as before excepted), also one cow she calls her own. Sarah to have all the cattle on the plantation (one cow excepted as before) with my black horse & mare, also all the farming utensils she should think proper to leave the place of, also two beds & furniture & one chest & loom, my hogs also for the use of the plantation. William Miller (S) (Seal), Wit: John Currence, Isaac Campbell, Wm. Love.

**Pages 288-289**: Jan'y 1st 1813. The last will & testament of James Campbell deceased was proven on the oaths of Samuel Campbell and John Fearis witnesses thereto.

Will of James Campbell... to my daughter Francis Dunwoody, one blanket of my bed as her full share of dowry; to my son John Campbell, the large Bible as his full share; to my son Samuel Campbell, my ____ chair as his full share of dowry; to my son Andrew Campbell, all my wearing apparel at my deceased as his full share; to my daughter Janet Campbell, all my household furniture of every king not otherwise disposed of, viz one walnut table, one cupboard & all the dresser furniture, bedding & household furniture the dresser excepted which I allow to remain in the house for the use of my son Samuel which he is to have & possess the house & the lands belonging thereunto agreeable to a former contract & bargain made with him; my son John Campbell and my daughter Jannet Campbell, executors, 31 Jan 1805. Jas Campbell (Seal), Wit: John Campbell, Samuel Campbell, John Fearis.

**Pages 289-290**: North Carolina, Halifax County. Feby the 5th day 1813. will of Isles Cooper of the County & state above mentioned... all of my property to my beloved wife Nancy Cooper during her natural life or widowhood for the support of all my children (mention the property of two negroes follows their names Simeon and Edmund, two waggon loads of property of the several descriptions, one waggon & four horses). My wife Nancy do pursue her journey if she thinks proper to the South State & for her to comply with several contracts that I have made relative to my agreements; my wife Nancy Cooper & my trusty friend brother in law Thomas Willey my executors. Hesl Cooper (Seal), Wit: H. Perkins, Stourton Edwards. May 21st 1813. The last will & testament of Hesl Cooper deceas'd was proven on the oath of Stourton Edwards witness thereto, who on his oath says that H. Perkins was a witness at the same time.

**Pages 291**: York County, August 1st 1812. Will of William Smith in my full senses... my wench Lucy with what other property belongs to me, I give to my friend Captain William Fair, it is my desire that he will not sell the wench against her inclination. William Smith (LS). James Farley being duly sworn saith that he is well acquainted with the hand writing of the above named William Smith having frequently seen him sign his name.... James Farley, 6 July 1813, before T. S. Neilson.

# YORK COUNTY SC WILL BOOK A-1 1800-1813

**Pages 292-293**: Will of William Wright Senr of the District of York... to my beloved daughter Rachel Talbert, five shillings; to my Robert Ferguson, five shillings; to my beloved son John Wright, five shillings, to my beloved daughter Mary McAdory, five shillings; to my beloved son George Wright, five shillings; to my beloved daughter Martha Thompson, five shillings; to my beloved son William Wright, five shillings; to my beloved daughter Margaret Murphy, five shillings; to my beloved daughter Catherine Wilson, five shillings; to my granddaughter Betsy B. W. Porter, five shillings; to my beloved granddaughter Jane Ferguson, a horse, saddle & Bridle with $80, two beds with their furniture, two cows & calves & other household furniture to the amount of $20, and if my negro wench Sylla has any more offspring, the first child she may have before my death I will also to my granddaughter, and if said granddaughter shall die without issue, the above shall be given to my granddaughter Betsy B. W. Porter, daughter of my beloved daughter Elizabeth Porter, deceased; to my well beloved son Andrew Wright, the plantation I now own & live upon, also my negroes Sylla, Ned & Anthony; my sons George Wright & Andrew Wright, exrs., 8 Sept 1810. Willm Wright (LS), Wit: Jno King, Jno Blair, Agness Blair.

**Pages 294-295**: Will of William Crawford of the State of South Carolina and District of... to my beloved wife Mary, all my household furniture her living in the dwelling house where I now live also her dower of my lands; to my son James, the note of hand I have on him for $40 on condition he pays Polley Cavenny $25 two years after the probit of this will; to my daughter Agness I give her mare, saddle and bridle, bed and furniture, her chest and spinning wheel, also all my stock of horses, cattle, and hogs, also all moneys and notes not otherwise disposed of, also her living on the plantation in the house with her mother while she lives single, also all my kitchen furniture and other lumber not claimed by her mother; to my daughter Mary, five shillings; the representative of my daughter Issabella, 38 dollars; to my daughter Margret, the tract of land I bought of John Henry on both sides the south line, also one horse; to my son William all the remainder of my land now heretofore devised with the grist mill and all other appurtenances thereunto belonging, also all my plantation tools and implements of husbandry. I appoint my son William exr., 16 August 1813. Wm Crawford (O), Wit: Jno Wilson, A. B. Wilson, Robert Wilson.

**Pages 295-297**: Oct'r 26th 1813. The last will & testament of John Smith was proven on the oaths of Benjn Parson & Wm Pettis witness thereto. At the same time qualified Wm. H. Smith, one of the executors.

Will of John Smith of the District of York & State of South Carolina, being weak of body... to my beloved wife one feather bed, bedstead & furniture, one horse creature the black mare, the bed she claims as hers; to my daughter Elizabeth Smith, one feather bed & bedstead, the bed that is called hers with all the bed clothes that is said to belong to her bed, with table cloths, towels, napkins & any other cloathing generally called hers; to my daughter Jane Smith, one feather bed & bed stead, the best that is called hers, with all the bed cloaths, etc; to my son Robert Smith, one feather bed, bedstead & furniture; to my son Joseph Smith, one feather bed, bedstead & furniture; to my granddaughter Jane Harris, daughter of Phebe Harris, one feather bed, bedstead & furniture, the bed generally call'd mine; I leave or rather lend to my beloved wife Mary Smith, during her life or widowhood, the following property: the plantation I now live on, with two negroes Cambridge & Sam, also one horse creature called Buck, four milk cows, ten head of sheep, ten geese & all my stock of hogs, with farming utensils necessary to carry on the farm. After her death or marriage the above property to be sold & the money arising from such sale to be equally divided among my children & John Cheek Smith or their lawful heirs. The remainder of my negroes with the residue of my property to be equally divided or sold & the money arising from such sale to be equally divided between all my children & John Cheek Smith. I appoint Wm. H. Smith, Robert Smith & Joseph Smith, exrs., 21 Aug 1813. John Smith (X) (LS), Wit: Sam Henderson, B. Person, Will Pettis. Codicil: my wife Mary Smith shall have an equal divide of all my negroes except Cambridge & Sam during her natural life & then to be equally divided among all my children & grandson John Cheek Smith.

**Pages 298-299:** Will of William Wright of the State of South Carolina and District of York, being sick and weak in body... I allow my wife her living off my land her lifetime if she chuses it and a negro woman called Dinah to work for her and her own two beds and furniture not to destroy the land or timber and if she moves off the land the woman to be given up to the estate. I likewise allow her a bay horse while she lives on the plantation, the remainder of all my property I allow to be sold and equally divided betwixt all my children John, William, Polly, and Sally, allowing the heirs of Allen Reeves deceased, one third of share to be equally divided amongst them. I allow William Lytle to keep which property he has already got and a note that I have upon him. My two sons John and William shall pay my estate on intrust for what money he owes me. I appoint my sons John and William Wright executors, 11 Oct 1813. William Wright (X), Wit: Joseph Moore, Nathaniel Thomason, Dudley Bishop. November 29th 1813. The last will and Testament of William Wright Deceas'd was proven on the oath of Nathaniel Thomasson and Dudley Bishop who say he was in his right mind when he executed it. At the same time qualified Wm Wright executor.

[End of Will Book A-1.]

## YORK COUNTY SC WILL BOOK D 1814-1820

Pages 1-2: South Carolina, York District. Will of Alexander Moore of district aforesaid... To my well beloved wife Catherine Moore, one negro woman named Lucinda, one bed and furniture, also her support off my plantation and to live in my mansion house so long as she continues my widow, her horse, saddle and bridle worth $60. My plantation formerly called Wateres plantation to my son William Moore. The plantation whereon I now live to be equally divided according to quantity and quality between my two sons Alfred and Maurice A. Moore. To my daughter Rachel Moore one negro woman named Sarah. To my daughter Darchus A. Moore one negro woman named Delilah. To my son James Moore one negro man named Sam. To my son William Moore one negro man named Moses. My negro boy named Tony to my son Alfred. To my son Maurice one negro boy named Bob. The balance of my property to be sold and after payment of debts, to be equally divided among all my legatees. The negro girl named Ealse now in possession of E. J. Adicks I allow to my daughter Sarah Adicks. I appoint my two sons James and William Moore, exrs., 8 Dec 1813. Alex'r Moore (Seal), Wit: Mary Irwin, John Moore, And'w Sprigs. February 18th 1814. Proved the will of Alexander Moore, late of York District, Ordinary deceased, by the oath of John Moore. Qualified James Moore and William Moore executors. Benj. Chambers, O. Y. D.

Pages 2-4: South Carolina, York District. Will of John Patterson... to my loving wife Mary the tract of land on which I now live during the term of her natural life and at her death to devolve to my son Andrew, also to my wife one negro woman named Dianna, also one negro man named Petre. At the death of my wife the negro woman Dianna to go to my daughter Sarah Venable & my negro man Petre be set free & that he get one currying knife & one set of shoemaker tools. To my wife Mary my cupboard and furniture & all the bedding and the household furniture. My wife to have such number of my stock of horses & cattle as she may choose and at her death to be equally divided between all my children. My negro boy Joseph to my daughter Mary Ferguson. My negro boy Larkin to my daughter Hannah Venable. To my daughter Anny Beard my negro woman Sarah & negro child a boy Allison by name. To my son John's widow and children $100. To my daughter Elizabeth Eaking $200. To my daughter Jenny Turner one negro boy named Lewis. One loom & tacklings to my son Andrew. The use of my wagon jointly to my wife and my son Andrew and at her death the wagon to go to my said son Andrew. I appoint John Currence, my son Andrew & James Duff Junior, exrs., 12 Nov 1813. John Patterson (Seal), Wit: William Patrick, David Patrick, Mary Thompson.

Pages 4-5: Will of Martha Neely of York District, widow... To my daughter Clarinda my new calico ___. To my daughter Clarissa my nedle wrought counterpaine. To my son Amzi my silver watch leaving said watch to the care of my brother James Feemster till my son Amzi arrives at the age of 20 years. The remainder of my property to equally divided among my three children. I desire that the property be kept and not sold except as may be unprofitable to be kept and I desire that James Feemster & John Minter may be the judges. I appoint John Minter executor, 19 Feb 1814. Martha Neely (LS), Wit: Margaret Fair, Nancy Egger (mark).

Pages 5-6: South Carolina, York District. Will of James Webb... To my son Stephen Webb and my son Thomas Webb my mill & the land belonging to said mill. Top my wife Peggy Webb, one horse and saddle worth $100 & one negro fellow named Warren and 100 acres of land adj. my plantation on Cataba River with the houses on said land. To my son Samuel Webb 100 acres of the said tract of land. To my daughters Hannah Webb and Nancy Webb my negro fellow named Jack. To my daughters Kesiah Webb and Elender Webb my negro fellow Edom, and Kesiah Webb one horse worth $100. Likewise two tracts of land in Anson County, North Carolina, to be sold to discharge my debts with such other artickles as my executors shall think proper and a negro wench Betty. I give to my five daughters the remainder part of my land on Cataba River. I give to my sons Stephen Webb and Thomas Webb my still & cotton machine. I appoint my wife Peggy Webb and my son Stephen Webb, exrs., 11 April 1803. James Webb (Seal), Wit: Nath Harris, Jos. Robb.

Pages 6-7: Will of Thomas Barnet... To my son William Barnet all my lands & tenements not otherwise disposed of, both the plantations that I now live on and the part of the land that the said William Barnet now lives on. I also give to my son William Barnet my roaned mare Fenix as his property. To my son Alexander Barnet my negro man named Will. To my daughter Mary Clinton & her husband Joseph Clinton my negro or yellow coloured girl named Lavina. To Scintha McCarter & her husband Robert McCarter my negro woman named Ann, and the negro woman Ann is to get the best bed and furniture. After payment of debts remainder to be divided equally amongst my four children Alexander Barnet, Mary Clinton, William Barnet & Scintha McCarter. I constitute my son Alexander Barnet & my son in law Robert McCarter, exrs., 15 Nov 1813. Thomas Barnet (X) (Seal), Wit: James Bigger, Alexander Barnet, John Fearis.

Pages 7-9: Will of Nicholas Smith of York District... To my beloved wife all my personal estate consisting of horses, horned cattle, implements of Husbandry & household furniture. To my wife Mary all my plantation during her natural life and after her death to my son George Smith with paying the following legacies. To my son Thomas Smith $40; to my son James Smith $40; to my son William Smith $40; to my daughter Jenney Coward $40; to my son Neamiah $1; To my son John Smith $1. I ordain my wife Mary & my son George, exrs., 1 March 1815. Nicholas Smith (Seal), Wit: Richard Ingram, James Scott. Proved 15 April 1814. Letter testamentary to Mary Smith & George Smith, 25 April 1814. Warrant of appraisement directed to James Scott, John Mosley, Richard Jackson, Jno'a Huff & Jno'a Sutton or any three or four of them, to be returned by 15 May 1814.

Pages 10-12: South Carolina, York District. On 18 Feb 1814 the will of Alexander Moore late of York District was proved... letters testamentary to James Moore and William Moore, 18 Feb 1814. Warrant of appraisement directed to James Williamson, Benjn Rowel, John Moore, and John Black or any three of four of them, to be returned by 24 Feb 1814.

Pages 12-14: South Carolina, York District. On 21 Feb 1815 the will of John Patterson late of York District was proved... letters testamentary to John Currence and John [sic, for Andrew] Patterson, 21 Feb 1814. Warrant of appraisement directed to William Pattrick, James Briant, Isaac Campbell, and Alexander Barnett or any three of four of them, to be returned by 26 Feb 1814. James Duff, one of the executors named in the will, refused to qualify, 21 Feb 1814.

Pages 14-15: South Carolina, York District. On 28 Feb 1814 the will of Martha Neely, late of York District, was proved... letters testamentary to John Minter, 28 Feb 1814. Warrant of appraisement directed to John King, James Scott, Allen Dowdle, and John Couch, or any three of four of them, to be returned by 20 March 1814.

Pages 15-17: South Carolina, York District. On ____ 1815 the will of James Webb, late of York District, was proved... letters of administration to Stephen Webb. Warrant of appraisement directed to Robert Watson, John Springs, Andrew Herrin, James Spratt, and Honory Talley, or any three of four of them, to be returned by 12 March 1814. Margaret Webb being unwilling to take the burden & execution of said will, refused to qualify, 12 March 1812.

Pages 17-21: Will of Daniel Harshaw of District of York... To my beloved wife Catherine during her natural life my plantation on Turkey Creek whereon we now live with the appertenaces thereunto belonging. After her death to my oldest son James now living int he state of "Luisianna" the sum of $100,and in case he does not apply for said legacy before his decease the said sum I do hereby bequeath to his reputed illegitimate son Jephtha Harshaw and to John Peter's son Hugh Simpson alias Harshaw (born shortly after my son James's marriage with her), five shillings. To my second son Hugh the plantation whereon we now live. To my son Hugh's oldest daughter Cinthia my negro girl Agge about 6 years old. To son Hugh's second daughter Catherine my negro girl Sarah about 3 years old. To my son Hugh's son Daniel my plantation on York road called Harshaw's old place & also my negro boy David about 5 years old. I appoint my wife Catherine and my son Hugh exrs., 26 Nov 1812. Daniel Harshaw (mark) (LS), Wit: Richard Ingraham, John Blair, Wm. Jameson, Thomas Hogg. Catherine Horshaw being unwilling to take the burden & execution of said will refused to qualify, 6 May 1814. Catherine Horshaw (mark). Proved by the oath of Capt. John Blair 6 May 1814. Letters testamentary to Hugh Harshaw 6 May 1814. Warrant of appraisement directed to Capt. John Blair, Henry Ray, James Scott, and Richard Ingram, or any three of four of them, to be returned by 1 June 1814.

Pages 21-23: South Carolina, York District. On 20 March 1815, the will of Thomas Barnett, late of York District, was proved... letters testamentary to Alexander Barnet & Robert McCarter, 29 March 1814. Warrant of appraisement directed to William Patrick, John Faries, Robert Patrick, and Edward Moore, or any three of four of them, to be returned by 10 April 1814.

Pages 23-26: South Carolina, York District. Will of William Erwin Senr of district aforesaid... To my beloved wife Sarah Erwin my lease of Indian land with my negroes Simon & Lydia, with all my household & kitchen furniture & plantation tools. My son William at the decease of my wife I allow to receive my lease of Indian land & negro man Simon with the plantation tools. To my daughter Catherine my negro woman Lydia & a sufficient of the crop in hand for the support of herself and negro and horses. My stock of cattle & household furniture to be equally divided between my son & daughter. The moneys I have on hand amounting to $600 and upwards, I order to be applied to such purposes as my son William may judge to be most advantageous to the comfort & support of my family. I appoint my son William executor, 23 Jan 1814. William Erwin (mark (LS), Wit: Archy Miller, Mary Miller. Letters testamentary: will proved 8 June 1814, granted to William Erwin Junr, named executor. Warrant of appraisement directed to Joseph Carrel, Isaac Harris, Wm. Fewel, John Carrel or any three or four of them, returnable by 1 August next.

Pages 26-28: Will of Ealeanor Moore, widow of James Moore deceased... To my daughter Betsey Patrick one large pewter bason, one large pewter dish & a pewter _____ & half pint tankard. To my daughter Frances Davis' children or her daughter Amy Davis my chest. To the rest of the children one small pewter dish & a small pewter Bason. To my son Edward Moore whom I live with, the rest of my goods & chattels. As for my other four sons John Moore, Thomas Moore, James Moore and William Moore, their full share in the dividing of their father's estate & I have nothing left to divide amongst them. My son James Moore & my son Edward Moore, exrs., 17 Nov 1813. Ealeanor Moore (X) (LS), Wit: Joseph Clinton, Mary Clinton (mark), John Fearis. James Moore refused to qualify, 2 June 1814. Proved by the oath of John Fearies 2 June 1814. Letters testamentary to Edward Moore 2 June 1814. Warrant of appraisement directed to John Faries, Abr'm Barnett, James Clinton, Saml McCully or any three or four of them, returnable by 15 June inst.

Pages 30-31: Will of Alexander Allison of the District of York, being advanced in life.... To my son Hugh Alison one tract of land of 320 acres on the waters of Clarks fork. To my son James Alison one negroe child named Jincey, he paying the taxes of said negro at my decease. To my son Thomas Alison one negro girl named Hannah and one bay horse. To my son Alexander Allison one negro man named Levi. To my daughter Agnes Lassley one negro woman named Dinah & two beds & furniture, one chest of drawer, also all my horned cattle, sheep & hogs, timber wheels & kitchen furniture, also one tract of and of 284 acres on the head branch of Bullocks Creek in consideration whereof my said daughter Agness shall pay to my two grandchildren Robert Alexander Allison & Eliza allison $100 each as son as they come of age. To my son Thomas one negro girl named Runy[?] which I allow him to and my daughter Margaret during her lifetime. To my granddaughter Margaret Lessley one negro girl named Ann. I appoint Robert Alison and Samuel Lessley my executors, 6 July 1814. Alexander Allison (Seal), Wit: Saml Turner, Hugh Allison, Winslow Wright (X). Proved by the oath of Samuel Turner and Hugh Allison 25 Oct 1814.

Pages 32-36: Will of Ann Dale of York District, widow... to my daughter Elizabeth Henry my negro woman named Nan and at her death the said woman with her issue to be equally divided amongst her three children William Henry, James, and Palmer Henry. To my daughter Mary Downes my bed and furniture, one little spinning wheel & saddle now in her possession, also one cow, walnut chest, and small looking glass. To my son James Dale my negro fellow named Jack, and my negro boy named Ned. To my daughter Frances Brown my negro girl named Sarah, and at her deceased to be divided amongst her children. To my granddaughter Charlott Brown daughter to Samuel Brown one negro girl Lidia. To my grand daughter Marian Dale, daughter of James Dale, one negro girl named Rachel. To my son Robert Dale the land whereon I now live & also a small tract adj. purchased of Alexander Moore Esqr., which includes all my real estate, and at his death to my grandson James Dale, oldest son of Robert Dale. To my son Robert Dale one negro boy named Abb & all my farming utensils, one table & one third part of my hogs, one cow & heifer & one horse called Snif, and at his death to my grandson James Dale, oldest son of Robert Dale. The residue of my estate to be sold and the money to be equally divided amongst my three children George, Frances & Ann Cheshire. I appoint Alfred Moore & Robert Lynn, exrs., 18 Oct 1815. Anna Dale (mark) (LS), Wit: Hugh Wells, Robert Lynn, John Moore. Robert Lynn refused to qualify as executor, ___ Oct 1814. Proved by the affirmation of Robert Lynn 28 Oct 1814. Warrant of appraisement directed to John Moore, Hugh Wells, Robt Murphey, Fra's Erwin, or any three of four of them. Letters testamentary to Alfred Moore.

Pages 36-38: Will of James Mitchell, being in a sick & low condition... my wife Rachel Mitchell shall have the one third part of all my property real and personal during her life. It is my will that my beloved grandson James M. Love shall have one third part of all my property real and personal. My beloved grandson Robert M. Love shall have one third part of all my property real and personal. The property willed to my beloved wife Rachel be at her death equally divided between my grandsons James M. Love and Robert M. Love. I appoint my wife Rachel Mitchell, and my two grandsons James M. Love and Robert M. Love, exrs., 28 Sept 1814. James Mitchel (LS), Wit: Samuel Givins, John Patton, Robert Ash. Proved by the affirmation of Samuel Givins Esqr 12 Nov 1814. Warrant of appraisement directed to Frances Irwin, John Black, Saml McKeal, Robt Love, and David Sadler, or any three or four of them.

Pages 38-41: Will of Daniel Givins Senior of York District... To my daughter Eleanor Givins one cow and calf with the cow that is now called hers and was bestowed to her by James Tims, one sow, one spinning wheel, one feather bed, bolster and pillows, two sheets, one blanket & bed quilt or coverlid & six pewter plates, to be delivered to her at the age of 18 years or when she marries. To my wife Lucy Givins for her land, all my lands and personal estate, after the payment of the above legacy to my said daughter Eleanor, and after her decease to my son Edward Givins. I appoint my wife Lucy Givins, executor, 18 March 1809. Danl Givens (D) (LS), Wit: James A. Whyte, Mary C. Whyte, E. Bayless. Proved by the oath of James A. Whyte 2 Jan 1815. At same time qualified Lucy Givins executor. Warrant of appraisement directed to James Feemster, J. A. White, Wm. ONeal, Jno Leech, or any three or four of them.

Pages 41-42: Major Joseph McJunkin executor to the last will and testament of Rev. Joseph Alexander deceased, final settlement Jany 6th 1815. Includes cash received from John Blair merchant, exrs of Joseph Alexander vs Saml D. Alexander, John Davidson, John Enes, Saml. B. Byers & Joseph Byers specified legacies, Jos A. King specified legacy, Judith Bankhead specified legacy, Margaret McJunkin specified legacy. Amount in the hands of Joseph Gist.

Pages 42-46: Will of John Anderson Senior of York District... To my son William Henry Anderson one half of all my land in trust for my son Samuel Anderson, and also two negroes Toby and Tann in trust for said Samuel, and at the death of my said son Samuel, to my son John Anderson subject to the life estate of my beloved wife Jane Anderson. The said negroes Tobey and Tann to vest immediately in my son William and subject to be kept by my wife on my plantation during her life. To my son William Henry Anderson the other half of all my land. To my daughter Rebecka Steel widow of Capt. Joseph Steel deceased, a negro wench Kate. To my daughter Elizabeth Wherry, wife of William Wherry, one negro wench Patts and her child. To my daughter Sarah Starr the widow of Stewart Starr decd, two negro children named Pink and Briena[?]. To my daughter Nancy Anderson, two negroes Rachel & Lidia. My old negro wench named Phebe be taken care of upon the premises where I now live. To my son John Anderson my two negroes named George & Ned. To my wife Jane Anderson the use of all my land, stock, furniture, during her life. My two daughters Sarah Starr and Nancy Anderson who are living with me, to live on my plantation as long as they remain unmarried. I appoint my two sons William Henry Anderson and John Anderson, exrs., 8 Nov 1813. John Anderson (LS), Wit John Bates Senr, William Neely, Richard Sadler. Proved by the oath of William Neely 11 Jan 1815. At same time qualified William Henry Anderson and John Anderson, exrs. Warrant of appraisement returned by 1 February next directed to Richard Sadler Esqr., John McConnel, William Neely, Thomas Robinson Esqr. & Robert Steel. Letters testamentary to William Henry Anderson and John Anderson.

Pages 47-50: 22d November 1807. Will of Jean Hamilton of York District... I leave all my worldly property to Clouder Hamilton my grandchild & William Hamilton, executor, 22 Nov 1807. Jean Hamilton (X), Wit: John Hemphill, John Good, James Good. Proved by the oath of John Good, at same time qualified William Hamilton executor, 6 March 1815. Warrant of appraisement directed to John Good, George Plexco, James Good, Jacob Black, John B. Black.

Pages 51-56: Will of William Bratton of York District... To my wife Martha Bratton the following negroes June, Lydia, Peter, Betty, Nelson, July, Cloe, Ben, Kitty, Harry, Watt, Polly, Harriet, Butler, Primus, Jack, Winney, Jim, Lucy, Araby, Patt, Icey[?], all my beds and furniture, horses, cattle, sheep, and hogs, during her life, and the use of my plantation with the tract of 200 acres I purchased of Henry Good. After the decease of my wife, I give the said tract of 200 acres to my daughter Mary Bratton with my bed and furniture, etc. The tract where I now live with stock (except the choice of one horse which I give to my daughter Mary Bratton), to my son John S. Bratton. To my said daughter Mary Bratton the following negroes Jack, Winney, Isey, Linus, Harriet, and her increase, and she is to have her support on the plantation as long as she remains single. To my son John S. Bratton the following negroes Watt, Polly, Jim Nelson, my rifle gun, my sword and pistols and cotton machine & smith tools. To my daughter Jean Simpson two negroes June and Lydia. To my daughter Mary Foster give negroes Patt, July, Cloe, Bin & Kitty. To my daughter Ealis Sadler two negroes Peter and Betty. To my daughter Agness McCaw two negroes Archy & Luce. to my daughter Elizabeth Irwin two negroes Butler & Moses. To my son William Bratton my negro boy Harry. I appoint my wife Martha Bratton executrix, Doctor William Bratton and Doctor James Simpson executors, 27 Dec 1813. Wm Bratton (LS), Wit: Nathan Moore, Thos Moore, Eli Moore.

Proved by the affirmation of Nathaniel Moore 13 Feb 1815. Warrant of appraisement directed to David Sadler, William Moore, Robert Love, Francis Erwin and John Black, returnable 4 July next. Letters testamentary to William Bratton and Martha Bratton.

Pages 56-61: Will of Allen Dowdle of the District of York... To Nancy my wife all that plantation where I now live which I purchased of Samuel McBrier and after her death to go to my son Allen Dowdle. To my son David Dowdle the remainder of my land and other personal property, and bequeath one third of the amount to my well beloved wife and the remaining two thirds to be equally divided between my daughters Mary Dowdle and Editha Dowdle, and the land willed to my sons David and Allen Dowdle and the two thirds of my other property to my daughters Mary and Editha be appraised that the whole amount to be equally divided between my above sons and daughters, David Dowdle to pay to my daughter Mary and Editha Dowdle whatever the land may be appraised to above an equal share and Allen to pay also. My sons Joseph and David Dowdle, executors, 12 Jan 1815. Allen Dowdle. Wit: Wm. Robinson, Saml King, Archibald Roberson.

Proved by the oath of Samuel King 20 Feb 1815. At same time qualified Joseph Dowdle and David Dowdle, exrs. Warrant of appraisement directed to John Martin, James Scott, John King and James Feemster, returnable 20 June next. Letters testamentary to Joseph Dowdle and David Dowdle.

Pages 61-64: South Carolina, York District. Will of Ann Thompson... To my son Nathaniel Thompson my negro boy named Ned. To my son Moses Thompson a negro woman named Beck. I leave to my daughter Mary Ann

Edmiston $6. I leave to my son Alexander Thompson one fourth part of $475 due the first of Feb 1807 which is in the hands of the said Alexander & John Thompson. To my son John Thompson 159 acres of land whereon I now live. To my daughter Betsy Hannah Greer $6. To my son John Thompson two beds and furniture. To my granddaughter Ann Ewing Thompson one bed and some furniture. To my two grandchildren Maryan Edmiston and Samuel Edmiston two beds with some furniture. I leave to my grandson John Brown Thompson my mare. To my negro girl Beck two shifts, two cots, two franks. To my negro boy ned one suit of clothes and the rest of my estate to be equally divided between Nathaniel, Moses, Alexander & John Thompson, and they are appointed as executors, 2 Dec 1814. Ann Thompson (mark) (LS), Wit: Wm. Logan, Jno Leech (mark), Jane Leech (mark). Proved by the oath of William Logan 8 April 1815. At same time qualified John Thompson executor. Warrant of appraisement directed to Edward Byers, David Byers, William Byers, John Powel & Samuel Wiley, returnable 24 Oct next.

Pages 64-69: Will of Isaac Weathers of the District of York... To my son Edmund Weathers one young sorrel horse and one bed and furniture. To my son William Weathers one horse and saddle and one bed and furniture. To my daughter Polly Blankenship one dollar. I desire that my land and plantation be equally divided between my two sons Edmund Weathers and William Weathers, and the remainder of my estate should be divided into six equal parts which I give to my son Benjamin Weathers, to my son Edmund Weathers, to my son William Weathers; to the three children of my daughter Lucy Edwards deceased namely Sarah Edwards, Isaac Parsons, Edward and Jesse Edwards; to my daughter Susanna Blankenship, and to Isaac Blankenship son of my daughter Polly Blankenship. I appoint my three sons Benjamin, Edmund, and William Weathers, exrs., 31 Oct 1805. Isaac Weathers (LS), Wit: Jeremiah Alderman, Mary Alderson, Isaac Parish (mark). Benjamin & Edmund Weathers refused to qualify as executors, 15 Aug 1816. Proved by the oath of Jeremiah Alderson and Isaac Parish. Warrant of appraisement directed to Benjamin Persons, John Springs, Junr., Thomas Barnett, William Alderson, returnable 1 November next, Letters testamentary to William Weathers.

Pages 69-71: Will of Joseph Patton of York District... To my sister Elizabeth Bratton the whole of my estate. I appoint John McClenaghan Senr, exr., 29 Sept 1814. Joseph Patton (LS), Wit: Tenney McClanaghan, Mary Whitesides, Jane McClenaghan. Proved by the oath of Tenney McClenaghan 21 Aug 1815. Letters testamentary to John McClenaghan, 20 Jan 1816.

Pages 71-75: Will of Robert Bratton Senr of York District... To my beloved son William Bratton $5. To my beloved daughter Ann Smidday[?] $2. To my son in law William Robinson $2. To my daughter in law Mary Wallace formerly Mary Bratton $2. To my beloved son Robert Bratton the plantation whereon I now live with my negro man May also my waggon & two horses my whole estate of cattle and hoggs, my two beds and furniture. I appoint my son Robert Bratton and my friend James Simpson, exrs., 23 Aug 1814. Robert Bratton (mark) (LS), Wit: Samuel Givins, Robert Love, David Sadler. Proved by the oath of Samuel Givens Esqr. At same time qualified Robert Bratton executor. Warrant of appraisement directed to David Sadler, Robert Love, Francis Erwin, James Martin, Thomas Gibson, 17 Dec 1815, returnable 1st of February next. On 17 Dec 1815 the will of Robert Bratton Senr was proved, letters testamentary to Robert Bratton 20 Dec 1815.

Pages 75-79: Will of Mary Ratchford of York District... To my loving daughter Ann McCarra all my cattle, horses, household furniture. To Margaret Tate five shillings. To my son Moses five shillings. To my son John five shillings. To my son Joseph five shillings. To my daughter Jane Jewel five shillings. To Elizabeth Henderson five shillings. To my son William five shillings. To Mary Hetherington five shillings. To Abigail Henderson five shillings. To my son Samuel five shillings. To my son George five shillings. Dated 13 Nov 1814. Mary Ratchford (mark) (LS), Wit: Andw Boyd, Margaret Boyd (mark), John Veale. Proved by the oath of John Veale 16 Sept 1815. Warrant of appraisement directed to George Ratchford, Moses Ratchford, Robert Dunkin, Robert Davidson, and James Wood [Ward?] returnable 1 March next. Letters testamentary to Ann McCarra 2 Jan 1816.

Pages 79-82: Will of John Gebbie of York District... It is my will that my brother Joseph Gebbie and his son John A. Gebbie be left to be executors. To my brother Joseph two of my negroes viz Balaam and Ned. To my brother's oldest son John A. Gebbie three negroes viz Sue, Pen & Sue's youngest child. To Robert M. Gebbie two negroes viz Saley & Adam. To my brother Joseph's son Joseph Gebbie one negro named Elijah. To my brother Joseph's six daughters viz Rachel, Mary, Narcilla, Lisa, Selena, and Matilda, all my land to be sold and equally divided among them. To my brother Robert's son Moses Gabbie my young bay mare and all the ballance of my live stock I allow to be sold at public auction, with all my money-- to my brother Robert's daughter Elizabeth $15 to my brother Robert's son Robert $15, and the ballance to be equally divided amongst my brother Joseph's children above mentioned, 15 Jan 1816. John Gebbie (mark), Wit: John Feemster, Geo Davis, John Berry. Warrant of appraisement directed to John Feemster, George Davis, John Berry, Rodger Berry and Samuel Neely. Letters testamentary to Joseph Gebbie and John Gebbie, Junr, 22 Jan 1816.

Pages 82-86: Nov. 24th 1816. Will of John Davidson Senr of York District... To my son Robert Davidson 100 acres of land which is to include the present improvement he moved from and the said Davidson to begin on Rennicks line opposite to the square of land, Robert Davidson's field, Tipping's line... if said boundary contains more land than 100 acres the overplus to be paid at the rest of $4 an acre. To my son William Davidson the surplus and 100 acres near the meeting house road, near the long branch... a corner that Hugh Davidson made. To my two sons Isaac and Charles Davidson all the remainder of the tract I now live on to be divided by the main road that runs through it. Also to William Davidson $100 to be paid by my sons Isaac, Jacob and Charles Davidson in equal divisions, and they shall have three years from my decease to pay it. To my son Elias Davidson and my daughter now Catherine Shannon and my son John Davidson and my son Hugh Davidson, each of them five shillings sterling. All my property including an aged negro woman I enjoin and all my wife Margaret Davidson to have the sole and full power to distribute the whole except for the payment of what debts I owe, as she may think best amongst my three sons and three daughters whose names are Isaac, Jacob and Charles Davidson and my three daughters now named Mary Doster, Margaret Boyd and Anna Windsor. I appoint Elias Davidson my son and Isaac Davidson my son and Jonathan Kuykendall, my executors. John Davidson (LS), wit: Henry Tipping, Isaac Kuykendall, Sally Kuykendall. Warrant of appraisement directed to Jonathan Kuykendall, Elias Davidson, William Davidson, Jacob Buffington, and Henry Tipping, returnable 1 April next. On 13 January 1816 the will of John Davidson Senr was proved, letters testamentary to Isaac Davidson Senr 20 Jan 1816.

Pages 87-89: Will of James Leech... A humble headstone may be procured for my mother's grave, that the ground where my father is intered shall be cleared and a brick wall be made to enclose his grave with any others that my executors may think propper. It is my wish that John Leech and my dear sister Catherine be fully remunerated for their trouble, care, and kind attention to me, as my property is too small to extend a division to my dear brother and sister in New York, and as I think my brothers and sisters here in South Carolina to be more necessitory[?], I think it proper to divide the remainder equally amongst them, that is between David, Eleanor, William and Joseph. John Leech and William Leech I appoint executors, 29 June 1814. James Leech (LS). Warrant of appraisement returned by 1 May next, dated 3 Feb 1816, to John King, James Scott, William Robinson, James Feemster and William Givins. On 3 Feb 1816 the will of James Leech was proved, letters testamentary to William Leech and John Leech, 3 Feb 1816.

Pages 89-94: Will of Moses Meek of the District of York... To my son Adam Meek $114. To my son Andrew Meek that plantation I now live on 116 acres and the mill with my negro fellow Lincoln with a deduction of $500. To my son John Meek $178. To my son Robert $214. To my son Moses Meek $226. To my son William Meek $314. To my son Thomas Meek $314. I appoint Andrew Meek and James Meek, exrs., 24 July 1816. Moses Meek (LS), Wit: Edward Byers, James Hope, Nancy Black. Codicil revoking bequest to Andrew Meek and giving the plantation, mill, and negro Lincoln to sons Andrew Meek, William Meek and Thomas Meek; Andrew Meek receives one half of said land, mill and negro, and the other half to William and Thomas Meek between them. Surplus to be divided among other sons Adam, James, John, Robert, & Moses Meek, 22 Dec 1815. Moses Meek (LS), Wit: James Hope, Wm. Jameson. Warrant of appraisement returnable 1 March next directed to John Thompson, Robert Wilson, John Pilcher, David Byers & William Byers, 16 Feb 1816. Letters testamentary Andrew Meek 16 Feb 1816.

Pages 94-95: Will of William Hart of York District... To my wife Priscilla my mansion house and a genteel maintainace of my land during her life or widdowhood. To my two sons Charles and John the plantation on which I now live containing 700 acres to be equally divided between them but if the child with which my wife is now pregnant should be a boy, I allow it to share the land equal with its two brothers. I give to my wife Priscilla my negro man Joe & my negro woman Nancy and all my stock of horses, cattle, etc., and at her death to be disposed of as she may think proper among my children. This bequest is intended to enable my wife to school and raise my children and give to them as they come of age a horse, saddle and bridle. To my daughter Janey my negro woman Juda. To my daughter Margaret my negro girl Beck. To my daughter Sally my negro man Jeff. These negroes to remain on my plantation for the support of my family untill my said daughters shall severally come of age or be married. To my daughter Priscilla my negro man Toney. To my daughter Elizabeth my negro boy Sampson. To my daughter Nancy Harriet $300. I appoint my wife Priscilla and my brother John Hart, exrs., 17 Aug 1815. Wm Hart (Seal), Wit: John McClenahan, H. W. Miller. "The Warrant of appraisement & Letters Testamentary not Returned."

Pages 95-96: South Carolina, York District. John McClenahan swears that Sarah Patton a widow of Col. Robt Patton late of York District deceased is the mother of Joseph Patton who enlisted in the United States Service under Captain Campbell in the third rifle Regiment commanded by Lieut. Col. Hamilton & died in the service at or near Washington & that the Joseph left neither father, widow or child at his death. John McClenahan.

I certify that I was personally acquainted with the said Joseph Patton & with his mother Sarah Patton & believe the above statement to be Correct. Thos Robertson.

Pages 96-100: Will of John Feemster of the district of York... To my son Samuel Feemster the tract of land that he now lives on and also my new survey of land taken up in the black fork with one half of my piece of meaddow now in cultivation and a negroe boy Isom. My three daughters Agnes, Martha & Anna Feemster remain and live on the plantation that I now live on until they are severally married and at that time I allow the full possession of all my other lands not before divided to fall to my son Edward to whom I do hereby bequeath all my remaining land that is not divided to my son Samuel, and to my son Edward Feemster my negroe boy Harry with my bay mare Fance. To my daughter Agnes Feemster my negroe girl Harriot with a deduction of $#125 which she is to pay to my son Samuel Feemster when she shall receive her dividend of my estate. To my daughter Margaret Bryan one horse to be valued at $60 at trading rate, and I give to my three daughters Agnes, Martha and Anna Feemster each as much household and other property to be paid them at their marriage as my daughters Mary and Margaret Bryant got at their marriage. To my son Edward one bed and furniture known by the name of my son Joseph deceased. I allow my other remaining negroes not before divised viz Jacob, Sam, Sale, and Margaret with all my undivided property to fall into the hands of my executors to be in trust for the use of my family who are single until my daughter Anne becomes of age, then to be equally divided among all my children then living and one equal share to the issue of those who may be dead. I appoint my son Samuel Feemster and Edward Feemster, exrs., 25 Jan 1816. John Feemster (Seal), Wit: William Jamieson, James Feemster, Thomas Sheerer. Warrant of appraisement to Thomas Sheerer, Wm. Jamieson, Jos Jamieson, James Roberts & William Galloway, returnable 1 March next, dated 17 Feb 1816. Letters testamentary to Samuel Feemster and Edward Feemster, 17 Feb 1816.

Pages 101-104: Will of David Neely of the district of York... It is my desire that there be 100 acres of my plantation run out on that side of my land joining to Obadiah Alexander land and Joseph Hart's old land, and that 100 acres be sold and the price when collected be equally divided among my son Jackson Neely, my daughter Mary McMean wife of James McMean, my daughter Cotesy Henry wife of John Henry and Alexander Brown the son of my beloved wife. As my son Thomas Neely is already provided for as will make him equal with the rest of my children, I allow the remainder of my land and all other property to remain in the possession of my wife and my son William Neely until my wife's death. After her death, then the remaining land to be sold and the amount divided amongst my son Jackson Neely, mu daughter McMeen, my daughter Cotesy Henry, my wife's son Alexander Brown, my son William Neely. I appoint Obadiah Alexander executor, 24 Jan 1816. David Neely (X) (LS), Wit: Lemuel Thomason, Thomas Neely, David Hutcheson. Warrant of appraisement to Jesse Brumfield, Jesse Miller, John Ewart, Wm. McCorckle, and John Hart, dated 5 Feb 1816, returnable before 1 May next. Letters testamentary to Obadiah Alexander, 5 Feb 1816.

Pages 105-108: Citation. Polly Smith hath applied for letters of admn. with a nuncupative will annexed, 26 March 1816. Published April 15, 1816 at Ebenezar church by Robert B. Walker.

Nuncupative will of John Smith deceased. South Carolina, York District. Personally came before me the subscribing justice James Adair, Jane Adair & Ann Adair & on their oath depose that on 26 Feb Mr. John Smith prior to his death made a verbal will.. to Ann Adair, 100 acres of land the same where she now resides, Rebeckah Polly and Rettie Roper Lainey the remainder of the land of which he died possessed to be equally divided between each of them. Mrs. Smith the widow to have her maintenance off the land during her continuance as widdow. To his son Thomas a rifle gun. James Adair, Jane Adair (mark), Ann Adair (mark). Warrant of appraisement to M. T. Haco, James Pressley, Samuel Hutcheson, John Hemphill and Joseph West, returnable before 15 June next, dated 19 April 1816. Letters testamentary to Polly Smith admx. with the will annexed.

Pages 108-112: Will of Ann Clark of the District of York... my bureau with the principal part of what it contains to my niece Nancy Robertson; $100 it being part of a note due me from John Gilespie to my nephew Archibald Robison; $15 to my niece Hannah Moris' son Cyrus for his education also to his brother Clarke Washington $15 for the purpose above mentioned; $20 to my nephew William Robertson's son Clark Robison; my joint claim with William Robertson of Scott's commentary of the old and New testament to my nieces Cathrine Leathem and Nancy Robertson; what household furniture I am possessed of I give to my niece Nancy Robison, my bed furniture and wearing apparel I dispose of in private manner; the balance of a note due from John

Gillespie and a note due me from William Robeson, I desire to be equally divided between my nephews and nieces Catherine Leathem, Ann Sherer, Nancy Robeson, Hannah Moore and Rebeckah Willson, William Robinson, Arthur Robinson, and Archibald Robinson; James Scott and William Robison executors, 13 November 1815. Ann Clark (mark), Wit: Martha Robison (mark), Mary Catherine Robison. Warrant of appraisement returnable 15 June next to John King, Joseph Doudle, Joseph Kell, William B. Ash, and Samuel King, 19 April 1816. Letters testamentary to William Robison and James Scott, 19 April 1816.

Pages 112-114: 22 March 1816. Will of Sarah Rea, widow, of district of York... To my granddaughter Rachel Jamison my bed and furniture, my chest, a cow and yearling, a pot and oven or a small pot in plaugron[?] oven, a pewter dish and an equal divide of the rest of the plates, an equal divide in the rest of the dresser furniture, also an equal divide of all the ___, also a coffee box. I leave to my daughter Elizabeth Rea a table, a pot and an oven, an equal divide of the bowls[?], two sheep, an equal divide of the dresser furniture. To my daughter Sarah Rea a pot and over, a pewter dish, and an equal divide of the dresser furniture which will be a third part of it, also a third part of the bowls[?]. My books shall be equally divided between my daughters Elizabeth & Sarah and my granddaughter Rachel Jamison. My loom and tackle shall remain on the plantation whereon I now live for the use of my two daughters and granddaughter. I will to my granddaughter Charlotte Rea my spinning wheel. My friend James Hill, exr. Sarah Rea (X) (Seal), Wit: James S. Adams, John Henry.

Pages 114-117: Will of William Akin of York District... To my son Alexander Akin all that tract of land whereon I now live with this consideration that Elizabeth Akin my wife and Nancy Wisher my stepdaughter to have their necessary sustenance off said plantation during their single state. To my son Alexr Akin one feather bed and furniture. To my son George Akin one feather bed and furniture. All my household furniture, cattle, sheep, to be equally divided betwixt my wife Elizabeth Akin and Nancy Wisher my stepdaughter. To my granddaughter Ealconer[?] Leech $10. I appoint George David and Alexander Akin, exrs., 4 Dec 1814. Wm Eakin (LS), Wit: Geo Davis, Rt. Davidson, Wm. Erwin. Warrant of appraisement directed to George David, Robert Dunkin, Robert Davidson, George Ratchford, and John Chambers, 12 July 1816, returnable by 15 August. Letters testamentary to Alexander Akin 12 July 1816.

Pages 117-121: Will of Charles Curry of District of York... To my beloved wife Prudence Curry all my tract of land that is whereon I now live, 500 acres, during her widdowhood, at her death or marriage to be equally divided betwixt my two sons McConnel Curry and Robert Curry. All my stock of cows, hoggs, & sheep and furniture to my wife Prudence during her widdowhood, at her death or marriage to be equally divided between my four children McConnel Curry, Robert Curry, Margaret H. M. Curry, and Elizabeth Curry. John Curry and William Guy, exrs., 6 July 1811. Charles Curry (LS), Wit: John Kidd Sr., Robert Porter, Mrs. Tabby Morris (mark). Letters testamentary to

John Curry and William Guy 10 July 1816. Warrant of appraisement directed to John Murphy Senr, John Kidd Senr, Thomas Carson, Robert Green & Alexander Murphy, 13 July 1816 returnable 1 September.

Pages 121-127: Will of David Miller of District of York... 19 Feb 1815. To my loving wife Ruth her living in my dwelling house & off the produce of my land during her life. To my son Robert the one half of the tract of land which I now live to include my dwelling house, the other half to my son James, and each of my daughters Mary, Anna, and Isabella have the privilege of living in my dwelling house during their single life. To my son Robert the horse[?] commonly called his & the black mare to my son James. To my daughter Mary my sorrel mare. To Anna a three year old bay colt. To isabella a three year old bay filly. My negro girl Nance be for the use of my wife. If she should have any issue, the first live born child to be the property of my daughter Mary, the second to be Anna's and the third Isabella's. I appoint my sons Robert and James, Exrs. David Miller (Seal), Wit: Mary Finley (X), John Barns, Robt B. Walker. Letters testamentary to Robert Miller and James Miller, 26 July 1816. Warrant of appraisement directed to Wm McCorckle, Wm Thomason, Thos Neely Senr, John Hurst & Lamuel Stewart 26 July 1816 returnable 20 Sept.

Pages 127-130: South Carolina, York District. Will of Powel Hoff of district aforesaid... 21 March 1816. To my daughter Jane Hoff one feather bed and bedstead, one trunk and woman's saddle & a bridle, one loom & tackling. To my wife Prudence Hoff the remainder of my estate. I appoint my said wife executrix and my son in law Thomas Elison executor. Powel Hoff (mark) (Seal), Wit: Francis Adams, Wm. Adams, Mary Adams. Warrant of appraisment directed to William Adams, Francis Adams, John Sutton 1 Aug 1816 returnable 25 Sept. Letters testamentary to Prudence Hoff 1 Aug 1816.

Pages 130-133: Will of William Champion of York District... To my sons Richard and William Champion my tract of land on Kings Creek. To my son John Champion $400 to be paid by my sons Richard & William Champion. To my sons John, Richard, and William, all my carpenter tools. To my daughters Lucretia Allen, Sarah Scott, Kery Arnderd[?], Faith Mcintire, Delilah Champion, and Fanny Heflin, an equal part of my household furniture, horses, cattle, sheep & hoggs. I appoint my sons Richard & William Champion, exrs., 10 Feb 1816. William Champion (mark) (Seal), Wit: Charles W. Henry, Saml Lanos[?], Peggy Henry. Warrant of appraisement to Charles Henry, John James, James Sanlin, Wm. Caldwell & Wm. Sandlin 5 Aug 1816, returnable 1 September. Letters testamentary to Richard Champion 5 Aug 1816.

Pages 133-137: Will of Andrew Patterson of York District, 13 May 1816... To my beloved wife Elizabeth one negro girl named Miney & all the household & kitchen furniture also one young mare and colt & two cows and calves, one third of my stock of sheep and hoggs, also the moyty of money coming from my father's estate to me be left to my wife and that my negroe man Asburn be sold for cash as much as need requires. It is my desire that my son John Green Patterson have all my lands that I now possess & that my wife

Elizabeth have her living off said land. Andrew Patterson (LS), Wit: John Currance, Mary Thompson. Warrant of appraisement to William Patrick, Alexander Barnett, Isaac Campbell, Robert Patrick & Wm Currance, 26 Aug 1816, returnable 1 November. Letters of administration with the will annexed to John Currance and Elizabeth Patterson 21 Aug 1816.

Pages 137-140: Will of John Workman of the District of York... To my eldest son Robert Workman the one equal half of the plantation whereon I now live, reserving the house & improvements to my beloved wife Margaret Workman during her natural life. To my beloved wife Margaret Workman the one equal half of the tract of land including the house whereon I now live to be divided when my eldest son Robert comes of age. To my second son John Workman the one equal half of the land whereon I now live including the house, but not to receive it during the life of my wife Margaret or until he comes of age. The remainder of my property vizt negroes, horses, cattle, and other stock when my eldest son Robert when he comes of age to be divided equally between all my children vizt Robert, John, Sarah, Martha & Elizabeth. My tract of land on Taylors Creek to be sold and the money divided among my wife and children. I appoint Margaret Workman my wife to be executrix and my brother James Workman executor. Nov. 4th 1816. John Workman (LS), Wit: Haliot[?] Evans, Thos Robertson. Warrant of appraisement directed to Richard Sadler, John McConnel, Wm. Little, Wm. Reeves[?] Senr, & Thomas Roach, 19 Nov 1816 returnable 1st of January. Letters Testamentary to Margaret Workman and James Workman, 19 Nov 1816.

Pages 140-142: Will of Maddox Dyson of York District... My beloved wife Elizabeth Dyson and my three children I have by her shall have all my real and personal estate to be equally divided among them. My four children that I had by a former wife shall have no part of what I leave behind. If my wife should marry again that my land shall be sold and the money be for the three aforesaid children. I appoint my wife Elizabeth executrix and Charles Robertson executor, 16 July 1814. Maddox Dyson (LS), Wit: Hugh Riddle, A. Hill. Wm. Howe. Warrant of appraisement directed to Aaron Wood, Hugh Riddle, Reuben Gibson, Matthew Harper & Reuben Gibson 20 Sept 1816 returnable 1 November. Letters testamentary to Elizabeth Dyson 30 Sept 1816. Appraisement. The amount of the appraisement bill of Maddox Dyson decd as certified by us $1431.12½, by Aaron Wood, Reuben Gibson, Matthew Harper.

Pages 142-146: South Carolina, York District. Will of Robert Ellis of the district aforesaid... To my well beloved wife Mary Ellis all that property particularized in our marriage contract which is recorded in Yorkville. To my daughter Sally Sumner Ellis the following negroes Stephen, Austin, one feather bed & furniture, one shipping wheel, one woman's saddle, one chest which belonged to her mother & also her mother's apparel, to be delivered to her at the age of 18 or marriage. To my Benjamin Ellis negroes Luke & child named Esther, to be delivered to him at age 21. To my daughter Rebeckah Ellis negroes Any & Milly to be hers at the age of 18. AS to my lands which

I hold by Indian lease not herein disposed of by marriage contract as above, to my daughter Sally Sumner Ellis with that part of land conveyed by marriage contract to be hers at the death or marriage of my said wife. My tract of land lying on the stony fork of Fishing Creek 197½ acres, to my son Benjamin Ellis at the age of 21. The negro fellow George to my daughter Sally Sumner Ellis. I appoint John Workman and David Hutcheson, my exrs., 3 Oct 1815. Robert Ellis (LS), Wit: Thos Robertson, Wm Reeves, Robt Workman. Warrant of appraisement directed to Thos Robertson, Richard Sadler, Robert Workman, James Workman & Wm. Davis 26 Dec 1816, returnable 15 February. Letters testamentary to David Hutcheson, surviving executor, 26 Dec 1816.

Pages 146-156: South Carolina, York District. Will of William Hill of district aforesaid... TO my son Solomon Hill all that plantation held by Robert hill & Andrew Hill in trust for me during my life adj. Andrew Hill, William Edward Hayne esquire, Robert Hill, John Currance, Hugh Currance, by land purchased by Matthew Stephenson from John White, John Akins, Widow Hall, Edmund Fewell, Robert McCaw formerly Moses Ferguson's old plantation adjoining the Indian Boundary, Charles Robertson, Big Allisons Creek, John Robertson Junr, Samuel Bratton[?], late John Barnett now in possession of the widow of said John Barnett, James Fares, Joseph Waddle deceased, lands late of Robert Lattamer deceased, Joseph Woods, land formerly Thomas Pattons, to the road leading from Bigger's ferry to Hills Iron Works. To my son Andrew Hill 500 acres of land where he now lives including his improvements adj. Joseph Wood, on the great road leading from Biggers' ferry to Hills Iron Works; also a negro slave named Darky & her four children Sam, John, Madison & Francis Drake. To my well beloved wife Jane Hill two negro slaves being the two which she may make choice of from all the negroes in my possession namely Cubit, Ned, Festus, Gosia Miller, Tony Miller, Sam, Anna, Charles & Dorcus, and a ____ of 300 acres every year during her life to be paid by Solomon Hill. To my granddaughters Margaret Malvina Alison and Betsey Adaline Avalina Allison $500 in cash each. To my grandson Francis Ross son of Alexander Ross $1000 in cash.... heirs of the late Doctor John Allison deceased. To my son William hill in addition to what he has already received all my rights to those negro slaves somewhere in the western country which I have already given him a power of attorney to recover. To my son Robert Hill in addition to what he has already received two negroes slaves lately purchased named George & Abraham now in his possession. To my son Solomon all the rest and residue of my estate. My trusty friends Solomon Hill & Robert Clendenan executors, 21 May 1814. Wm. Hill (LS), Wit: Samuel Melton, Hillary McCall, Robert McElwain. Codicil made 20 Nov 1816 mentions grandsons Frank Ross & William Hill. Wit: Alexander Stewart, Robert Sinclair. Warrant of appraisement to Charles Robertson, John Barnett, Hugh Currance, David Waddle, & John Durham 25 April 1817, returnable 1 June. Letters testamentary not returned to be recorded. The amount of the appraisement of Col. Wm. Hill deceased estate 20 May 1817 $59.10.75 by Charles Robertson, John Barnett, Hugh Currance, David Waddle, John Durham.

YORK COUNTY SC WILL BOOK D 1814-1820

Pages 156-159: Will of Frederick Hambright Senr of District of York... To my wife Mary the sole & free use & possession of my dwelling house and the land on which I now live to be disposed of at her discretion, with all my utensils of husbandry, stock of cattle, hoggs & sheep, also the three mares that now belong to me, also a negro boy named Jacob, one negro girl named Eve, also two tracts of land lately purchased of my son Henry Hambright, 215 acres. To my daughter Elizabeth Jenkins $2.50. To my son John Hambright $2.50. To my son Frederick Hambright $2.50. To my son Benjamin Hambright $2.50. To my son James Hambright $2.50. To my daughter Sarah Aker $2.50. To my son Henry Hambright $2.50. To my daughter Mary Price $2.50. To my daughter Sophia Quin $2.50. To my son David Hambright $2.50. To my son Josiah Hambright one tract of land called Bogan's plan, 236 acres, also a tract of land called the Back Hill, 500 acres, one horse which he now has in possession, saddle & Bridle. To my daughter Charlotte one negro boy named Prince, one bed and furniture, saddle and wearing apparel. One negro named Isaac, my still and vessals be sold with my old wagon to pay the legatees and contingent expenses. I appoint my wife Mary, William Quinn & Josiah Hambright, exrs., 30 Jan 1817. Frederick Hambright (Seal), Wit: John Randall, Charlotte Hambright, Susannah Hambright. Warrant of appraisement directed to William Caldwell, Henry Howser, John Ellis, John Randle & John McKlewee Senr 19 March 1817, returnable 15 March. Letters testamentary to Mary Hambright, William Quin & Joseph Hambright 19 March 1817.

Pages 159-162: Will of Richard Sadler Senr of York District being aged and in a declining state of health... To my sons in law James Black & Joseph Steel my plantation whereon I now live adj. James Greer and others in trust for the lawful [heirs?] of my beloved son James Sadler, and also my negroes Pan[?] and Dan. I order that my slave Moses be sold and that the amount of his sale be divided among my following named vizt among Polly Flemming, Nancy Black, William Sadler and Rachel Steel and James Sadler allowing William Sadler two shores. I appoint James Williamson executor, 20 Aug 1815. Richard Sadler (Seal), Wit: John Gray, William Barnet Poag, R. Sadler. Warrant of appraisement to Frances Irwin, Robert Love, James Moore, Edw'd Burres, John Black 24 March 1817 returnable 20 May. Letters testamentary to James Williamson 24 March 1817.

Pages 162-166: Will of George Pettus... To my lawful & well beloved wife Jean Pettus eight negroes vizt Frank, Cate, Sall, June, Dave, Bartlet, Jake, and Harry, and at her death the said negroes becomes the property of my children vizt five of them George Pettus, Rebeckah W. Pettus, Sarah Pettus, Sinthay Pettus, Susanna Pettus. My son George Pettus is to have $600 more in the division that than four girls mentioned. I leave to my said wife all my household furniture & movables with the half of the cattle, hoggs, horses & sheep, & all the geese. To my son John D. O. K. Pettus $100. To my daughter Ann D. Pettus now Clawson, Jule & Rose her child, one head covering, one gray mare. To my son Stephen Pettus $100, one bed & covering. To my daughter Mary Pettus now called Burton a negro girl named Jude. To my daughter now called Jane Gutridge, a negro girl called Luce & mare named Suck, saddle & Bed & covering. To my daughter Elizabeth Pettus a negro girl named Sup & horse, saddle & bed & covering. To my daughter Rebeckah W. Pettus a negro boy named Elleck & horse, saddle & Bride. To my daughter Sarah Pettus a negro boy named Bob, a horse, saddle & Bridle. To my son George Pettus two negroes named Jag & Mose, horse, saddle & bridle, & the home house the land belonging to it as far as the branch that leads down this side of where Unckle Dillard lived by the spring. To my daughter Sintha Pettus a negro girl named Lile, horse, saddle & Bride. To my daughter Susanna Pettus a negro girl named Dianna, horse, saddle & bridle. I leave all lands & Tenements, waggon & team & machine to my beloved wife during her widowhood that after her death to be left to my sons. I leave Ben to be sold and divided between my four daughters Ann Clawson, Mary Burton, Jane Gutridge, and Elizabeth Harris. I appoint my wife & Stephen Pettus my son, exrs., 26 July 1816. George Pettus (Seal), Wit: Samuel B. Hill, William Brown (X), Jas Tagart. Warrant of appraisement directed to John Springs, Benjamin Persons, William Pettus, Thomas Barnett & John Harris 21 March 1817, returnable 20 May. Letters testamentary 21 March 1817 to Jean Pettus & Stephen Pettus.

Pages 166-169: Will of John Feemster of York District... All just debts be paid that there be a just & true inventory made of all my goods and chattels & that there be no part thereof sold except such things as are not necessary for the use of the farm & Clockmakeshops. The negroe stock & all to remain as they are untill my son Samuel Warren arrives at the age of 21 years for the purpose of raising & Educating my children Ely, Adaline, Minos, Melissa, John Malinda, Samuel and Eliza. The balance of my legacy out of my father's estate which I have not yet received be collected and appropriated to the purchasing of books and such things as are necessary for my sons going through their education. When my son Samuel Warren arrives at the age of 21 years, the whole estate be equally divided amongst my children except the plantation on which I now live and my two negroes, my dear wife Margaret Feemster may choose well a sufficient portion of stock & furniture while she remains a widow and at her death or marriage an equal division to be made of it among my children. I will that if my son Eli learn the clockmaking business so as to be a master workman, I allow him to have the tools over and above his divide. I appoint my wife Margaret Feemster and my son Minos B. Feemster, exrs., 29 March 1817. John Feemster (Seal), Wit: Wm. Coker, Danl Kerr, Silas Feemster. Warrant of appraisement directed to Wm Coker, James Dickey, Ezekial Morris, Wm. Feemster, Benjamin Garvin & Daniel Kerr 8 May 1817 returnable 1 July. Letters testamentary to Margaret Feemster 8 May 1817.

Pages 169-174: South Carolina, York District. Will of Thomas Clendennan of district aforesaid... To my wife Margaret Clendenan one third of the tract of land whereon I now reside and one of the rooms of my mansion house, my strawberry horse, one third of all the balance of all my stock, during her natural life and at her death to my son James Clendenan. To my son James Clendenan all that tract of land whereon I now reside on the waters of Fishing Creek adj. the lands of Doctor John Bratton, the heirs of Joseph Sadler deceased, Hugh Mills, Robert Love, heirs of Thomas Bratton deceased, and the widow Watson except such life estate to my wife Margaret and the payment of $200 to be devised to my son Alexander Clendenan, also to my son James Clendenan one half acre of land in the town of Columbia being part of a square adj. upper and Lumber, Marion decd, Bull Street, to which I have authorised my son Robert to make titles to the said James. To my son Robert Clendenan one acre of land in the town of Columbia being part of a square bounded by Upper and Sumter, Marion decd, and $100 in cash. To my son William Hasler Clendenan of Baltimore half an acre of land in the town of Columbia. To my son Alexnader Clendenan of Baltimore half an acre of land in the town of Columbia. To my daughter Elizabeth Hart[?] half an acre of land in Columbia. To my daughter Jane Black half an acre of land in the town of Columbia, bounded by Upper, Sumter, Marrion and Bull Streets. To my daughter Martha Stevenson half an acre in the town of Columbia. I appoint my sons Robert Clendenan and James Clendenan my executors, 20 Jan 1817. Robert Clendenan (Seal), Wit: Saml Moore, Saml Moore Junr, Robert J. Moore. Codicil: in the event that a suit which was commenced by John Kenedy against George Ross Esqr late Sheriff of York District for a negro woman and child which he levied on and sold as the property of Robert Dale to satisfy a judgment in my behalf and for which levy and sale I have given the said George Ross my bond, should he finally decide against the said George Ross, my son Robert is then to pay so much of the said monies as above bequeathed as may be sufficient to discharge the said bond, 10 Feb 1817. Thomas Clendenan (Seal), Wit: Eli Moore. Warrant of appraisement directed to Robert Love, James Williamson, Samuel Moore, Thomas Irwin & John Black 12 May 1817 returnable 1 July. Letters testamentary to Robert Clendenan and James Clendenan 12 May 1817.

Pages 175-178: Will of John Lindsey of York District... To my father and mother Isaac and Rachel Lindsey my best feather bed & furniture, one pided cow with her young calf, my pewter and shelf furniture, also two small potts, fraying pan & baking pan, and one large wash pot, one set of fire doggs, one pair of tongs, and one walnut chest. To Edy Parker my second feather bed & furniture, also a woman's saddle, also a five gallon pot. To my brother Thomas Putman one brown bay mare, also my riding saddle. To my nephew John Lindsey Parker one brindle & pided heifer yearling. To my sister Eda Parker $20 of my vandue notes. To Archibald Lindsay $10. To Eleanor Lindsay $10. To my brothers Elijah and Jacob Lindsay $50 each out of the notes due me from Archibald Lindsay. To my sister Drusilla Wilson $20. all the rest of my estate after my debts are paid to be divided between my father Isaac Lindsay & Elisha Lindsay & Jacob Lindsay & Eda Parker & Hannah Putman & Drusilla Wilson. I nominate Elisha Lindsay & Thomas Putman, exrs., 31 July 1817. John Lindsey (S), Wit: John Ellis, Betsy Kiser (mark), Betsey Ellis (mark). Warrant of appraisement directed to John Ellis, William Caldwell, John James, Robert Lany & Thomas Martin, 27 Aug 1817 returnable 1 October. Letters testamentary to Elisha Lindsey & Thomas Putman 27 Aug 1817.

Pages 178-182: South Carolina, York District. Will of Philip Sandefur of district aforesaid... To my beloved wife Elizabeth Sandefur my negroes Pat, Tom, Tony, Moses, Jack,Sarah and her child Harriet, also stock of horses, half of my stock of cattle, sheep and hoggs, plantation tools and furniture, also all the stock of money I have either in bank, paper, or specie. To my wife Elizabeth the plantation I now live on and at her death I dispose of it as hereafter directed. To my daughter Mary Lacey $10. To my son William Sandefur my negro man Ben and $300. The above named negro man Ben to be applied to the use of my son William for the advantage of his family. To my daughter Elizabeth Sandefur my negroes Sal, Nonie[?] & Jane. To my son Green Sandefur my negroes Wilson & Dick. To my son Lowrie Sandefur $500. To my son Philip my negroes Brook & Ralph and my plantation at the death of my wife. To my daughter Catharine Gordan my negroes Alice & Winney. My negroes Peter and Belinda to be sold to pay the legacies above. I appoint Henry Carter & my wife Elizabeth, exrs., 10 June 1817. Philip Sandefur (Seal), Wit: R. Sadler, Larkin Davis, Allen Davis. Warrant of appraisement directed to Elias Wallace, Saml Lowrie, William Little and James Johnson, Major Thos Roach 9 Aug 1817 returnable 11 December. Letters testamentary to Elizabeth Sandefur 29 Aug 1817.

Pages 182-185: December the 18th, 1816. 18 April 1814 will of Robert Howie of York District... To my eldest daughter Margaret Howie a negro woman named Pat, a horse and saddle. To my son William Howie a tract of land that I bought from Saml Corsin & Andrew Carson which I now occupy, 150 acres. To my daughter Mary McConnel $50 to be paid in horse or cattle. To my daughter Sarah Howie a negro girl named Hannah, horse & saddle. To my son Alexander Howie the tract of land I now live upon with the tract joining it formerly known by the name of Rollins place, also a negro boy named Dave & also Fir & Paddy. I appoint my only and sole executors William Howie & Alexander Howie. Robert Howie (LS), Wit: John Dennis Junr, Sarah Howie, Alexander Howie. Warrant of appraisement directed to Robt Love, John Murphy Senr, Alexr Murphy, Thos Corsin & Jacob Coonrad 15 Sept 1817 returnable 15 Nov. Letters testamentary to Alexander Howie 15 Sept 1817.

Pages 185-189: Will of Barbara Kindsey of District of York... To my daughter Sarah McCord my bedding, body clothes & household furniture. To my grandsons Daniel McCord and Daniel McKenzie[?] whom I make executor, my lands and tenements. To my granddaughter Scinthy Bridges my side saddle with its furniture. I allow my daughter Sarah McCord all the money I hold except what may be needed to pay my just debts. 21 April 1815. Barbara Kindsey (mark) (LS), Wit: William Ferguson, James Galloway, Jas Galloway. Warrant of appraisement directed to John McCord, Isaac Dawson, James Wallace, Daniel Galloway, David House 6 Jan 1818 returnable 1 March. Letters testamentary to Daniel McCord of the State of Tennessee 6 Jan 1818.

Pages 189-192: Will of William Stephenson Senr of York District... There is two notes given by me to Rebeckah Patterson one of $16 the other of $41 which my son Matthew Stephenson has received in his own name, I allow to be settled. I desire that David, Hugh, & Robert Watson value the plantation on which I now live. I allow my son William Stephenson to have a line continued from the corner of the 16 acres I let him have to my line by the York Road and whatever the land comes to more than his share, I allow him to settle up with the other legatees. I allow my daughters Polly & Barbara to have the house in which I now live also the wheat that is in the ground, I allow them what meat we have, I allow each of them to have $50 in land round about the house in which we now live also an equal share with the rest of the legatees. I allow my son Matthew Stephenson to have the remainder of my land & he is to settle up with the other legatees. I appoint my son Matthew Stephenson & John Wallace executors, 20 Dec 1817. William Stephenson (LS), Wit: John Currance, Sol. Hill, Hugh Currance. Warrant of appraisement directed to David Watson, Robert Watson, & Hugh Watson agreeable to will 17 Jan 1818 returnable 1 March. Letters testamentary to Matthew Stephenson & John Watson 7 Jan 1818.

Pages 192-196: South Carolina, York District. Will of George Wagner of district aforesaid, 9 September 1811... My negro woman named Jenny at my death be emancipated & set free. All my other negroes be set free as they shall severally arrive to the age of 30 years old. That my aid negroes for what time they may have to serve until they severally to the age of 30 years together with all my other estate be sold at publick sale, and the money arising from the sale to be equally divided amongst the following legatees vizt, John Beam, Mary Wagoner (daughter of John decd), Elizabeth Hill, Margaret Holsey, Catherine Delashmeet, Mary Mobley, Susannah Camp, Anne McClain (wife of Andrew), Isaac Wagner, Louse McClain, Margaret Watts, John Wagner, Mary Sutton (wife of James), each one equal share & Messina & Rachel McClain one share between them. I appoint Isaac Wagoner, George Hill & Andw McClain, exrs. George Wagner (mark) (Seal), Wit: Jon'a Sutton, James Scott, James Smith. Warrant of appraisement directed to Edward Byers, Saml B. Byers, Wm. Kenedy, Jno Mosley & Hugh Harshaw 12 Jan 1818 returnable 10 March. Letters testamentary to Isaac Wagoner, George Hill, and Andrew McClain 12 Jan 1818.

Pages 196-198: Will of James Roberts of District of York... To my wife Sarah Roberts one moiety of all my personal estate, debts due to me, & of my ready money, also my house, land & hereditaments in the district aforesaid on which I now reside for the support & maintenance of my said wife & my daughter Celinda. To my daughter Celinda the remaining moiety of my personal estate, etc., but should my daughter Celinda not arrive to the years of maturity, then to my brother John Roberts. I appoint John Hemphill my executor, 27 Oct 1817. James Roberts (Seal), Wit: Milton Jamieson, Saml Feemster, William Jamieson. Warrant of appraisement directed to Samuel Feemster, Jos. Jamieson, Wm. Brown, James Meek & John Good 27 Jan 1818 returnable 20 March. Letters Testamentary not returned to be recorded.

Pages 198-202: Will of William Pettus of York District... To my beloved wife during her natural life or widowhood the following negroes Jack, Arthur, Moses, Frank, Billy, Charlotte, Aggy & Pricilla, with my household and kitchen furniture, with all implements of husbandry & half of my live stock. To my son Saml K. Pettus all that tract of land left him by his grandfather for which I after obtained a lease in my own name & since which have had run off to him by Jno Fairis, after the death of my wife. My library be equally divided between my five sons viz Samuel K., George, Stephen B., William W. & Thomas N. To my son George one fourth part of all my land inclusive of that dividend to my son Saml K. according to quality including the improvement whereon Allen Felts at present lives. To my son George the following negroes viz Willis, Milly & her child George and my negro boy Joe. All my negroes not herein before disposed of remain in the possession of my wife for the maintenance & education of my six younger children viz Rebecca W. Pettus, Stephen R. Pettus, Marria Pettus, William W. Pettus and Thomas N. Pettus and that the said negroes with their increase divided equally between them as they severally arrive of age or marry. The residue of my land be divided equally according to quality between my two sons Stephen Bullock & William Wadkins[?]. At the death of my wife or her intermarriage the land divided or loaned to her belong to my youngest son Thomas Newton. I appoint John Springs Jr & John Kendrick my executors, 18 July 1817. Will Pettus (LS), Wit: J. Booker, ___ Fox, Ben. W. Thompson. Warrant of appraisement directed to Benjamin Persons, John Harris, Robert Bell, John Jackson & James Harris 24 March 1818 returnable 1 May. Letters testamentary not returned in order to be recorded. Inventory certified March 27, 1818 at $20,216.20 by Benj Persons, John Harris, John Jackson, and Robert Bell.

Pages 202-205: Will of Tenny McClenaghan of York District... To my wife Margaret McClenaghan the whole of my estate both real & personal during her life & at her death to dispose of my personal estate as she may think proper, but as to my real estate at my wife's death to be equally divided between my two sons James & John McClenaghan. And whereas no division of the real estate which descended to me & my brother John McClenaghan from our father Robert McClenaghan has yet taken place, I do authorise my said wife to make the said division and to execute such titles to my said brother. I also authorise my said wife to convey to my said Brother all the lands I have leased from the Cattawba Indians upon east side of ten mile creek & bounding on the Catawba River. I appoint my brother John McClenaghan executor, 16 Feb 1818. Tenny McClenaghan (LS), Wit: John Dunlap, Wm. Dunlap, Jonathan Whitesides. Warrant of appraisement directed to William Dunlap, John Dunlap, Jas Harris, James Harper & John Polk 24 March returnable 1 July. Letters testamentary to John McClenaghan 24 March 1818.

Pages 205-210: Citation. James C. Denham hath applied for letters of administration with the will annexed on the estate of John Shane, 24 April 1818.

Will of John Shane of the District of Fairfield... To my granddaughter Peggy Denham 50 acres of land to be laid out square from Abraham Wheelan's line strait across on the tract to compose said 50 acres. I also leave unto my grandson John Shane 100 acres of land to containing the houses &c whereon I now live to be laid off joining the above mentioned 50 acres. To my grandson Robert Shane 100 acres of land to be laid off joining the above 100 acres let to his brother John. To my son Robert 100 acres to be laid off next & is to containing the land formerly belonging to John Rea. To my son in law

William Adams 100 acres of land to his daughter Neatey 100 acres being a tract laid off lately by Robert G. Barber & should my land turn out on being surveyed as directed & leave any surplus, I allow James Denam or his wife Peggy to get it to make his up 100 acres & is there still should remain any land above what is mentioned, I allow it for my grandson John Shane to be added to his 100 acres. To Matty Adams one cow and calf and my bed and bed clothes & my large pott. To John Adams my grandson my sorrel mare with a star in her face, also my saddle & bridle. My boos & wearing apparel be equally divided between my son Robert, son in law William Adams & James Denam, and if any or either of my brothers Samuel & Frances Shane arrives in this country in ten years from this date, they jointly or separately are to get and receive a tract of land belonging to me on Linches Creek, 100 acres, & if they do not come to this country in that time, I leave it to my son Robert Shane. All other things to be sold to pay my debts, and if there should be any left, to my grandson John Adams. I ordain my son in law William Adams and James Barber, exrs., 8 Feb 1813. John Shane (mark) (LS), Wit: Samuel C. Sulivan, Robert Pane[?] (X), John C. Denham. Warrant of appraisement directed to James Quin, John Falls, Hugh McWhorter, Samuel Lessley & James Harris 15 May 1818 returnable 4 July. Letters testamentary with the will annexed to James C. Denham 15 May 1818.

Pages 210-213: Will of David Jackson Senr of District of York, 31 March 1818... To my beloved wife Mary Jackson all my estate both real & personal during her life with the exceptions hereinafter named. I allow my son William Jackson the plantation whereon he now lies, 100 acres. I allow my son Hugh Jackson the land laid off for him on the lower part of my plantation, 100 acres. I allow each of my sons nine in number $100 a piece. My son Elias Jackson shall have all my estate both real & personal at the decease for my wife if he can make up $100 to each of my sons as above mentioned without selling property. I allow him to sell Pero but none of the negroes that I have raised do I allow to be sold. I desire that my sons John Jackson and William Jackson shall have a certain tract of land that I am possessed of in Union District adj. Samuel Davidson, if they will take it in lieu of the $100 allotted to each of them. My wife shall live with my son Elias Jackson after my decease. I ordain my sons David Jackson and Elias Jackson, exrs. David Jackson (mark) (Seal), Wit: Robert Adams, John Henry, Thomas Bankhead. Warrant of appraisement directed to John Henry, Robert Adams, Joseph Adams, Thomas Davis, and John Smith 15 May 1818 returnable 4 July. Letters testamentary to Elias Jackson and David Jackson Jnr., 15 May 1818.

Pages 214-219: Will of James Crawford of District of York being of a good old age and troubled with infirmities... I allow my beloved wife Martha to have a third of the land I now own, likewise what household & kitchen furniture in my possession to belonging to my two daughters Ann & Jean as they have furniture in the house of their own. To my wife Martha a negro boy named Isaac during life and at her death to be the property of my two daughters Ann & Jean. To my wife Martha the stock of cattle, horses, sheep & hoggs. The third of my land to my wife Martha to belong to my daughters Ann & Jean at her death. The remainder of my land to belong to my son James, likewise my farming utensils to be divided between my son James & my daughters Ann & Jean. To my daughter Mary Henry one book entitled William's Sacramental Meditations. To my daughter Martha Neely one book entitled Pike's cases of Conscience. To my daughter Margaret McKelwee one book entitled Fisher & Erskine on the Shorter Catechism. Also my daughter Elizabeth one book entitled Marshall's Gospel Mistry of Sanctification. Also my son James the Confession of faith and my other books to my wife & two first mentioned daughters as a family. I make my wife Martha & my son James, exrs., 13 March 1818. James Crawford (LS), Wit: Gilbert Enloe, Benjn Jenkins Senr (X), Benjn Jenkins Junr. Warrant of appraisement directed to Wm McGill, John McKelwee, William Crawford, John Bostic & Benjn Jenkins 25 May 1818 returnable 20 July. Letters testamentary to James Crawford 25 May 1818.

South Carolina, York District. May 23, 1818. Martha Crawford (X) declines to act as executrix.

Pages 219-222: South Carolina, York District. April 17th 1818. Will of Patrick Hamilton of district aforesaid being in a low state of health... I will that my negro woman named Charlotte and her three children, the oldest black girl named Fan, the two youngest mulatto children the girl named Rachel the youngest a boy named George, to be set free as follows. Immediately at my decease I allow Charlotte to be liberated from her servitude. Fan I allow to be set at liberty as soon as she arrives to the age of 21 years to be under the care and direction of John Brown and Benjamin Chambers. The mulatto girl named Rachel & the boy George to be under the care of John Brown & Benjamin Chambers until they severally arrive to the age of 21 years, at which time I allow them to be liberated from servitude. The young mulatto boy I wish him put to some personal capable to learn the shoe and boot making trade when he arrives to the age of fifteen years. My negro boy Richardson to be under the care of John Brown & Benjamin Chambers. I appoint John Brown & Benjamin Chambers, exrs. Patrick Hamilton (LS), Wit: Wm. Chambers, John Jackson, John Brown. Warrant of appraisement directed to Andw McWhorter, William Watson, John Jackson, Jon'a Betty & Saml Chambers 3 Sept 1818 returnable 1 November. Letters of administration to John Brown 3 Sept 1818.

Pages 222-225: Will of Ann Meek of the District of York... To my son James one twelfth part left me by Adam Meek decd will. To my daughter Margaret one twelfth part. To my daughter Jean Mitchell one third part left me. To my daughter Agness one third part left me. To my son William one sixth part left me. I appoint Edward Byers & Saml B. Byers, exrs., 27 Sept 1815. Ann Meek (LS), Wit: Ezekial Gillham, John Pilcher, Robert Pilcher (R). Warrant of appraisement directed to John Thompson, John Pilcher, Wm. Thompson, David Byers & Alexr Thompson 20 June 1818 returnable 15 August. Letters testamentary to Saml Baldwin Byers 20 June 1818.

Pages 225-230: Will of Josiah Smith of the District of York... My plantation on which I now live to my two sons Miles & Rodah to be divided between them. The whole of the profits of the plantation I now attend & the use of my house & negroes to my wife during her life time. My negroes named Jimmy, adam, Moses, Lewis, Pheby, Betsy, Granby & Alison shall from the time of my death be set free. My daughter in law Jane Smith shall take Betsy in care until the age of 21 at which age & time she shall be set free. My son Miles shall take Granby in care until the age of 21 at which age & time he shall be set free. My son Rodah shall take Alison in care until the age of 21 at which age & time he shall be set free. All the rest of my personal estate shall be equally divided between Wm. Smith, Isaac Smith, Susanah Norwood, Judey French, Elisabeth Hamton, Lucy Howel, and Jacob Stalings, Isaac Sumerford & Jemima Smith my grandchildren. My two sons Miles & Rodah Smith, exrs., 9 Oct 1815. Josiah Smith (LS), Wit: James Plaxco, Abraham Sumerford, Saml Burns. Warrant of appraisement to John Plexco, Gordon Moore, George Plaxco, Wm. Thompson, James Meek 15 Oct 1818 returnable 10 December. James Plexco, James Meek & Geo Plexco sworn before Daniel Smith, J.P. Letters testamentary to Mihill Smith & Rhoda Smith 14 Oct 1818.

Pages 230-231: Will of William McGowen of the District of York... To my two sons Joseph & James McGowen the tract of land on which I now live, my horses & all my cattle to be equally divided between them & unto my two daughters Mary & Jane, all my household & kitchen furniture. I appoint Joseph Forbus to be executor, 25 April 1817. Wm.McGowen (X) (LS), Wit: Elias Robertson, Chas Robertson, Davis Robertson, Hartwell Adkins.

Pages 232-235: 15 January 1819. Will of James Persley of the District of York... My wife Sarah Persley & James McCord Persley my only son, exrs. To my wife Sarah Persley the third of my land during life & to have her due suport off the same during her time here in this life & at her deceased the whole of my lands to be my son James McCord Presley's. To my daughter Jane Persley one cow & Calf, side saddle & bridle, $100 in money. To my daughter Rachael M. Persley one gray filly & $25 in cash. To my grand daughter Louisa Persley $25 when she comes of age. My household furniture to be divided between my wife & my two daughters. Also my rifle gun to my son J. M. Persley. James Persley (LS), Wit: Jas Peters, John Fitchet, Jacob Peters. Warrant of appraisement to Robert Persley, John fitchet, Daniel Meshew, Wm. Sorn[?], & Thos McMahan 6 March 1819 returnable 4 June. Letters testamentary to Sarah Persley and James McCord Persley 6 March 1819.

Pages 236-241: Will of Isaac Enlow of District of York, being of a good old age & afflicted with divers infirmities... To my wife Vilet all the lands I am now possessed of during her life, likewise all my negroes her lifetime, all my stock of horses, cattle, sheep & hoggs, etc. To my son Asahil my rifle guy & the apparatus & $3. To my granddaughter Louisa Ann Enloe daughter of Nathaniel Enloe my negro boy named Hicks to be hers at her grandmother's death. To Nathaniel Enloe all the borrowed money he owes me & all the notes I have upon him at my wife's death. To my son Gilbert Enloe the money he borrowed of me to buy Jerry amounting to $275 and my negro wench named Silt at his mother's death. To my daughter Elisabeth McWhorter $3. To my daughter Christiana Givens $3 & all the notes & accounts I have upon her husband William Givins. To my daughter Jane Ewing $50 and all the notes I have upon her husband William Ewing. To my daughter Hannah Ewing $200 and all the notes I have upon her husband John Ewing. To my daughter Ruth Givens or rather her daughter Elisa Given my negro girl named Rose. To my grandson Russle Washington Black my negro girl named Narcissa when he comes of age. To my sons Nathaniel & Gilbert Enloe the following negroes (viz) Aaron, Cato, Phebe & Charles. I appoint my sons Nathaniel & Gilbert Enloe, exrs., 31 Sept 1818. Isaac Enloe (E) (LS), Wit: Williamson Byers, William Black, George Gill (X). Codicil stating that the land at wife Vilet's death to be sold and vanduw and my sons Nathaniel & Gilbert to receive the price thereof. June 29th 1819. Proved the will of Isaac Enloe by the oath of Williamson Byers. At same time qualifying Nathaniel Enloe & Gilbert Enloe, exrs. Warrant of appraisement directed to Hugh Cain, Williamson Byers, James Henry B. S., George Knox & Saml Lewis[?] 4 July 1819 returnable 1 Sept. Letters testamentary to Nathaniel Enloe & Gilbert Enloe 5 July 1819.

Pages 241-244A: South Carolina, York District. Will of Patrick Conly of district aforesaid... I allow the third of my estate real & personal [to my wife] during her natura life and after her death to be equally divided amongst my children except the real estate viz the land which i allow my son Robt. The rest of my estate I allow to be equally divided among all my children viz William, Rachel, Alexander, Robt, James & Elisabeth. I appoint Thomas Reid Esqr & Saml McCullough exrs., 4 June 1813. Patrick Conly (LS), Wit: John Montgomery, Mary McCullough, Thomas McCullough. August 2, 1819, proved the will of Patrick Conly by the oath of Thomas McCullough. Warrant of appraisement directed to Robt McClellan, John Wherry, Stanton Edwards, Thos McCullough, & Wm. Armstrong 20 Dec 1819 returnable 1 Feb next. On 6 Jan 1820 Robt McClelland, John Wherry & Thos McCullough were sworn before Thomas Reid, J.P. Letters testamentary to Saml McCullough 20 Dec 1819.

Pages 244B-247: Will of Benjn Jenkins of York District... To mary my loving wife all my estate both real & personal not otherwise hereafter willed during her widowhood and at her death or marriage to be equally divided amongst her children that she has before my death. To my son John Jenkins $5. To my daughter Martha Hamilton $18. To my son Benjn Jenkins 100 acres of land off the upper end of my plantation above the waggon road if he chooses to settle on it. To my son David Mitchel Jenkins $50 & have six months schooling and then be put to a trade. To my daughter Margaret Jenkins one bed & furniture & four head of cow beasts & the colt that the sorrel mare is with now. I appoint my wife Mary Jenkins extx, Jno McElwee Senr & Wm McGill exrs., 9 Nov 1819. Benja Jenkins (LS), Wit: John McElwee, James McElwee, Thomas Faulkner. Proved by the oath of John McElwee Senr 11 Feb 1820. Warrant of appraisement directed to John McElwee, James Crawford, Wm. Quin, Francis Henry & Britton Bolen 11 Feb 1820 returnable 10 April. Letters testamentary to Mary Jenkins 11 Feb 1820.

Pages 248-254: Will of David Waddel of York District... to my wife Elisabeth Waddel that plantation whereon I now reside during her natural life & then to my stepson Richard Barnett, on his paying to my lawfull heirs the sum of $108 to be equally divided amongst them and the sum of $360 to my brother John Waddel twelve months after my decease which said sum is the equal share of the said John and the ballance due to be paid at the decease of the said Elizabeth Waddel. To my wife Elisabeth three negroe slaves to wit Aggy, Silva & Peter during her natural life and at her death to my stepson Richard Barnett & to Joel Barnett as joint tenants of said negroes. To my step daughter Elizabeth West a negro girl slave named Tildah. To Richard Barnett two negro boys slaves called Frank & Jim. To my stepson Joel Barnett two negro boy slaves called Antony & Isaac. I appoint Solomon Hill & Richard Barnett executors, 16 Dec 1819. David Waddel (XO) (LS), Wit: Wm. R. Hill, John Johnston, R. Hill. Warrant of appraisement to John Johnston, John Barnet, Wm Mason, Hugh Riddle & James Faires 18 March 1820 returnable 10 May. On 8 April 1820 personally appeared before Solomon Hill, J. P., John Johnston, Hugh Riddle & James Faires, and were sworn as appraisers on the estate. Letters testamentary 18 March 1820 to Solomon Hill & Richard Barnett.

"Here is the finish of the Book containing Wills &c entitled book D then commences the Book E by John J. Chambers."

Pages 1-3: Will of Albert Allison... to my sister Margaret Smith one negro boy called Sam. To John Latta my silver watch. To William A. Latta my gold watch. To sister Adaline Allison my undivided part of a tract of land in the state of Tennessee on Duck River, one negro boy called Anson, and all my other property, money in hand, or any monies due to me. I appoint George Ross, exr., 12 Apr 1820. Albert Allison (LS), Wit: Wm. D. Henry, Joshua Goore, T. W. McNeal. Proved by the oath of T. W. McNeal 22 May 1820. At same time qualified George Ross executor.

Warrant of appraisement directed to T. W. McNeal, Wm. D. Henry, Saml Chambers, Wm. Moore, and Robert Clendinin 22 May 1820 returnable 15 July. Letters testamentary to George Ross 22 May 1822.

Pages 3-5: South Carolina, York District. Will of Gean Neely of district aforesaid... I will that the two thirds of the land which I was entitled to & has heretofore been sold to James McMeans be conveyed to him as I consented to that sale & approved of the same, the other third of my land I give to my daughter Elizabeth McNair & at her death I allow the benefits of the same land to my grandchildren Jean McNair, Rachel McNair, & Saml McNair. My mare to my granddaughter Jean McNair for her kindness to me and for the same reason my cow to Rachael McNair my other granddaughter & what other property I have to be to the said two grandchildren. I appoint James McNair, exr., 12 May 1819. Jean Neely (mark) (LS), Wit: Jackson N. Henry, William Henry. Proved by the oath of Jackson Henry 6 May 1820. At same time qualified James McMean executor.

Warrant of appraisement directed to John Hart, James Reeve, Daniel Sturgis, Jacob Clawson & Edmund Acock 6 May 1820 returnable 4 July. Letters testamentary to James McMeen 6 May 1820.

Pages 6-9: Will of William Henry Senior of District of york, being aged & infirm... to my son James Henry my negroe man slave named Aaron, my mulatto woman slave named Rose & my negroe boy slave named Charles. To my grandson Francis Henry son of my son James Henry my negro boy slave named Primus or Prime & my saddle. To my granddaughter Elisabeth McKeam Henry daughter of my son James Henry my negro boy slave named Toney, my bed & furniture, two potts, a spinning wheel, a chest & a large pewter dish, a large pewter bason & four pewter plates. To my son Francis Henry one large pewter dish, one large pewter bason & four pewter plats. For my old negro woman slave named Sarah, I give her to such one of my children as she shall within ten days after my decease signify to my executors to be her choice of them. My negro boy slave named Cyrus be sold to the best advantage and apply the monies arising form such sale to the payment of such of my sons James Henry's debts as I am security for. To my son James Henry four head of cattle, a reel, a table, a looking glass, all my farming utensils. To each & every of my children all the real & personal estates which I have heretofore given into the possession of them. I appoint my son James Henry & my friend William McGill, exrs., __ April 1816. To my daughter Mary $4. To my son Alexander $4. To my son Malcom $5. To my daughter Isabella $5.

To my son John $3. To my son Francis Henry $4. To my daughter Jane $5. To my son Josiah $3. William Henry (LS), Wit: Hugh McWhorter, John Craft, Daniel Turner Junr.

Warrant of appraisement directed to Hugh McWhorter, Wm. McGill, Robt Allison, John McElwee Senr 22 June 1820 returnable 15 August. On 29 July 1820 Robert Allison, Hugh McWhorter & John McElwee were sworn as appraisers. Letters testamentary to James Henry 22 June 1820.

Pages 9-10: Will of John Workman Senr of District of York... To my son John Workman all that tract lying south of Taylors Creek adj. John Chandler, David Mcldree, James Mc--, which he the said John lives on. To my son James Workman all the tract on which I now do live. My tract of land on both sides of Taylors Creek, one fourth part to my daughter Mary Steel, one fourth part of my daughter Margaret Workman, one forth part to Marthew Johnston, one forth part to my three grandchildren of my daughter Elizabeth McClelland whose names are Martha McClelland, Ann McClelland & Jinny McClelland. Should all die under age, then to revert back to my own children. To my granddaughter Ellendor Chambers, the eldest daughter of my daughter Marget $150. To Thos McClelland five shillings sterling. To my son James Workman, all the farming implements 7 plantation tools. I appoint my son John Workman & Joseph Davie, esqr., 12 Sept 1808. John Workman (LS), Wit: John Crocket, James Whyte, Henry Lee. Proved 24 July 1819 by the oath of Henry Lee. At same time qualified James Workman exr.

Pages 11-14: Citation. Thomas B. Smith applied for letters of admn on the estate of William H. Smith decd, & whereas it appears that there was a last will & testament in the hands of Henry Meacham & will be contested by said Thos B. Smith, 6 Sept 1819.

Will of Wm. H. Smith. South Carolina, York District. Sept 6th 1818. The ballance of my property to go to Henry Banks Meacham to remain with his father Henry Meacham till he becomes 16 years of age. Wm. Smith (LS), Wit: Joseph Smith, Randolph C. Harris.

Warrant of appraisement directed to Benjn Persons, John Springs, Jeremiah Alderson, Wm. Goodrich & Wm. Alderson 20 Oct 1819 returnable 25 Dec.

On 3 November 1819 personally appeared before James McKee John Springs, Wm. Alderson, Wm. Goodrich, & Jeremiah Alderson, being sworn as appraisers.

Administration granted to Thos B. Smith 20 Oct 1819.

Page 14: Will of Thomas Turner of York District... to my beloved wife Mary Turner all my household & kitchen furniture excepting one bed & furniture to My daughter Isabella Turner, also one bed & furniture to my daughter Martha Turner. To my son Daniel Turner one half of my lands, the other half to my daughters Isabella and Martha after the deceased of my wife. I appoint

Robt Allison & Saml Turner, exrs., 23 July 1818. Thos. Turner (LS), Wit: Wm. Low, Malcolm Henry, Wm. Henry.

Pages 15-18: Will of Abraham Green of District of York... To my beloved wife Hannah Green one third part of all my lands including the plantation & dwelling house where I now live during her natural life time, also one third of my personal estate. To my two daughters Elizabeth Green & Lewisa Green all the remainder of my estate both real and personal. I also bequeath unto Daniel Smith & George Caruth $300 to be equally divided between them as compensation to them for serving as executors, 9 Nov 1818. Abraham Green (X) (Seal), Wit: John Caruth Senr, Peter Morgan senr (X), Robert Bridges, Ann Mary Morgan, Abraham Kolb, Anderson Quinn. Proved in common form by the oath of Robt Bridges 30 June 1820. At same time qualified Daniel Smith exr. George Caruth relinquished his right to executorship 26 June 1820.

Warrant of appraisement directed to George Caruth, Geo Plexco, John Caruth, Robt Bridges, and Henry Smith 20 June 1820 returnable 25 Aug. Letters testamentary to Daniel Smith 20 June 1820.

Pages 18-20: South Carolina, York District. Will of Saml Moore.. to my wife Mary Moore, Kate & two children Richmond & Agner, & chair & harness. To my son Saml negroes James, Jacob, Herriot & John, one bed & furniture, farming tools, waggon & Beaureau. To my daughter Elizabeth, negroes Charlotte & children June & Hannah, two beds & furniture, bureau, horse, saddle & bridle to the value of $150. The remaining personal property to be divided between my wife and son Saml. My real estate to my wife during her life then to my son Saml Moore. I will that my old negro man & woman June & Will & child Will to whomsoever they may choose to live with. My sons John S. Moore & Saml Moore Junr, exrs., 22 May 1820. Saml Moore (LS), Wit: Thos Moore, John Moore, Eli Moore. Proved by the oath of Thos Moore 4 July 1820. At same time qualified John Starr Moore & Saml Moore Junr, exrs.

Warrant of appraisement directed to Saml Rainey, Dr. John Bratton, John Starr, James Williamson Senr, & James Williamson Junr., 4 July 1820 returnable 1 Sept. Letters testamentary to John S. Moore and Saml Moore Junr 4 July 1820.

Pages 20-23: Will of John Peters Senr of York District... To my beloved wife Martha Peters for her maintenance & support the use & benefit of my plantation during her life time, my stock of cattle, sheep & bees, etc. To my son James Peters 400 acres of land including my dwelling house & improvements at the decease of my widow. To my sons John Peters, Wm. Peters, daughter Mary Givens, my son Jacob Peters, my daughter Jean Smith & my daughter Margaret Huff, each of them five shillings sterling. To my daughter Martha Peters 200 acres of land being a tract adj. Mrs. Huff & Francis Adams & my old tract. I appoint my trusty friend Wm. Love & my beloved son James Peters, exrs. [not dated] John Peters (LS), Wit: Fra's Adams, Williamson

Byers, Wm. Adams. Proved July 24th 1820 by the oath of Williamson Byers & William Adams. At same time qualified James Peters exr.

Warrant of appraisement to Galbraith Caldwell, Nathaniel Givens & Daniel Seehorn 24 July 1820 returnable 20 Sept. Letters testamentary to James Peters 24 July 1820.

Pages 23-28: Will of Jonathan Beatty of the District of York.... to my honored mother the house & lot wherein she now lives during her natural life and the sum of $50 annually during her life. To my wife Sarah the plantation which was conveyed to me by Thomas Boggs, also my clock. To my son William my plantation on the northeast side of Langrams branch of Fishing Creek known by the name of Wrights place & conveyed to me by deed by James Ward, and a tract adjoining the same conveyed to me by Roderick Wright, and a classical or liberal English education, also one ninth part of all my other real & personal property not herein otherwise disposed of. To my son Robt R. I give my plantation on the SW side of Langhams branch of Fishing Creek conveyed to me by James Ward, and when he becomes 21 years of age the house & lot where my mother now lives and $200. To my daughters Isabella, Eliza Ann, Margaret, Jane, Sarah L. & Nancy, one ninth part of my other real & personal estate, when the youngest marries or comes of age. To my uncle James Arnold the sum of $150 and the one half of my wearing apparel. To my brother Wm Beatty the one half of my wearing apparel, and to lend him upon sufficient security $1000 for three years. The following negroes for the use & support of my family viz Peter & Sylvia his wife, Friday & Sally his wife & children Joe, Jack, Tom, Manaway & Sarah. To my nephew Jonathan Beatty Wilson my silver watch. I appoint my wife Sarah Beatty, John Blair, Thos Robison, & Wm. Beatty, exrs., 1 Nov 184. Jon'a Beatty (LS), Wit: Patrick Hamilton, Joseph Boggs, John C. Kuykendall. Codicil made by Jonathan Beatty, merchant, to will made 1 Nov 1814, authorizing his executors to lay out $1000 to the best advantage on the building of a house on the property conveyed to me by Ward & known by the name of Wrights place for the use of my wife & children until the youngest marries or comes of age. I have given to my uncle James Arnold $150; therefore, I leave to him $50. The bequest to brother Wm Beatty is revoked & make void his being an executor. I gave $1000 to be deducted now from my daughter Isabella's legacy, dated 10 Dec 18165. Jon'a Beatty (LS), Wit: Saml Blair, David Scott, John S. Hopkins.

Warrant of appraisement directed to Jno Hopkins, Dr. E. Jennings, Jno Bailey, Robt Latta, Saml Chambers, Andrew Giles, T. M. Nash, Wyley L. Harris, Robert Cooper, Saml Lowrie, John Jackson & Andrew McWhorter, 21 Dec 1819, returnable 15 Feb. Letters testamentary to Sarah Beatty, John Blair & Thos Robinson, 21 Dec 1819.

Pages 28-30: Will of James Donally of District of York... to my wife Martha Donally all my real & personal estate. To James Kincaid Senr of Buncombe County, North Carolina, $200. To Sarah Mulinax $2. I appoint Wm. McElwee Senr & Wm Caldwell, exrs., 10 July 1818. James Donally (mark) (LS), Wit: Robt Caldwell, Sarah Smith (X), Wm. Caldwell. Warrant of appraisement directed to Sherod James, Wm. Champion, Jeremiah Blalock, John James & James McElwee, 11 Aug 1820, returnable 10 oct. Letters testamentary to Wm Caldwell & Wm. McEllwee, 11 Aug 1820.

Pages 30-32: Will of Wm Molinax, diseased in boddy but sound in mind... I appoint James Donally & Thos Molinax as my exrs. I allow the estate to remain on the place for the use of my wife & children until the youngest comes of age, 9 Aug 1802. Wm Molinax (mark), Wit: Wm Caldwell, James Kincaid.

Citation. Isaac Mulinax applied for letters of administration on the estate of Wm Mullinax 20 Oct 1820. Warrant of appraisement directed to John Stewart, Henry Whistenant, Henry Hood, Jas Caldwell & Jesse Ponder, 6 Nov 1820 returnable 25 Dec. Letters of administration: the will of Wm Mulinax was proved in open court and letters of administration granted to Isaac Mulinax as admr with the will annexed, 1 Nov 1820.

Pages 32-34: Will of William Davis Senr of York District... To my wife Martha Davis her bed & furniture & one milk cow & her maintenance off the plantation as long as she lives. To my son Francis C. Davis $20, also my daughter Ana Scott & my son John Davis $20 to each. To my son Wm Davis one cow & the rest of my personal property to be equally divided amongst the rest of my children younger than William either by appraisement or by sale. Thos Davis is to maintain his mother. To my grand daughter Martha E. Davis that cow she has of mine. I appoint my son Francis & J. McKenzie Junr, exrs., 23 Nov 1820. Wm Davis (X), Wit: Jas McKenzie Junr, Edward McKenzie, John A. McCaw.

Warrant of appraisement directed to Wm Kindrick, Saml McColloch, James Duff B. S., James McCulloch, & Edward C. Pugh, 1 Dec 1820 returnable 1 Feb. Letters testamentary to Joseph McKenzie & Francis Davis, 1 Dec 1820.

Pages 35-37: South Carolina, York District. Will of Martha Wallis of district aforesaid... My beloved husband the Rev. James Wallis having by a deed of trust made to David Hutcheson dated 9 May 1818 authorised me to dispose of the property therein contained agreeable to my own will & pleasure. To my husband James Wallis $500 for the great care & attention to me since our marriage. My brother Saml Elliott being in possession of a cotton gin which I paid for, I allow him to keep said gin by paying to my son Wm. E. Whyte when he comes to full age the same price it cost me without interest, also the hire of a negro man called Dick which he had in the year 1818. To my sister Dorcas one good bed with curtains & all furniture, also all my wearing apparel that I may have at my death. My negro man Ben named in the deed of trust before mentioned be sold and what stock of horses, cattle, etc., to be sold or kept or sold as my executors may thing most for the benefit of my estate. I appoint my brother Saml Elliott & David Hutcheson, exrs., 21 Oct 1819. Martha Wallis (LS), Wit: John Cathey, George Cathey, James Perry.

Citation. David Hutcheson & Martha Saml Elliott appointed executors, cite James Wallis to appear at my office in Yorkville on Monday 22 instant at eleven o'clock to shew cause why probate & letters testamentary should not be granted, 12 Nov 1819.

Page 37: South Carolina, York District. Letters of guardianship. Whereas Margaret Lowrie Martin an orphan with the age of 21 years has chosen her father James Martin for her guardian, 13 Dec 1819.

Pages 38-40: South Carolina, York District. Citation. Elizabeth Chambers applied for letters of administration with the will annexed of William Chambers, late of district aforesaid, deceased, 2 May 1820.

Will of Wm Chambers of York District. to my beloved mother Elizabeth Chambers the land whereon I now live and all my estate & effects, bonds, notes, book of accounts, my stock of horses, cattle, sheep, my negroes Tom, Sall, Isabella, Davy, Isam, Peggy & her children Rachel & Cornelious & Lavenia. At her death or before if she can to set Peggy & her two children Rachel & Cornelious & Lavenia free, and to bind Rachel & Cornelious to some industrious person or persons until they reach 21 years. I appoint James A. Whyte, exr. 9 Aug 1818. Wm. Chambers (LS), Wit: Wm. Moore, H. Ming, A. H. Chambers.

Warrant of appraisement directed to John Brown, Saml Chambers, Andrew Giles, F. M. Nash & Wm Hogge 8 May 1820, returnable 4 July. Letters of administration with the will annexed to Elizabeth Chambers 8 May 1820.

Page 40: South Carolina, York District. Will of Mary Craig, widow, of district aforesaid... to my son James Craig my loom & tackling, also to my daughter in law Mary Craig wife to James Craig my riding side saddle. Also to my son James Craig all my stock, horses, cattle, sheep, etc. To my son John Craig $2. To my daughter Jenny Nesmith $2. To my son Robt Craig $2. To my son in law James Glenn my negro boy Gilly. To my daughters Martha Glenn, Polly Duff, Elizabeth Bryson, & Margaret Anderson an equal division of all my household & kitchen furniture, and a like share to my daughter in law Polly Craig. All grain growing or collection with forrage at the time of my deceased to be equally divided between my son James Craig & my daughters Polly Duff, Martha Glenn, Elizabeth Bryson & Margaret Anderson. My son James Craig & my son in law James Glenn, exrs., 16 April 1818. Mary Craig (mark) (LS), Wit: Mary Duff (mark), Margaret Riddle, James Duff.

Pages 41-43: South Carolina, York District. Thos Reid applied for letters of administration win the will annexed of Jane Lusk, late of the district aforesaid, decd, 19 May 1821.

Will of Jane Luck of York District... To my two daughters Margaret & Martha to each of them 50 acres of land, my daughter Margaret's 50 acres to be laid off out of my own part, to each of them & to each of their children. If one or both of my two aid daughters should die without issue, then her or their shares to vest in my three sons hereinafter named. To my daughter Margaret the young sorrel mare. To my daughter Martha my big sorrel mare. To my three sons James, Robt & Andrew, all the remainder of my land. I appoint Leonard Streight of Chester District, my sole executor, 27 March 1820. Jane Lusk (LS), Wit: Jno Bates Senr, Charles Neely, Jane Latta.

Warrant of appraisement to Robt G. Mills, John Boyd, Wm. Downey, Wm Gilmore & Wm Drennan, 27 Jan 1821 27 Jan 1821 returnable 25 March. Letters of administration to Thos Reid, 27 Jan 1821.

Pages 44-46: Will of Wm Robinson Senr being sick & in a low state of boddy... to my beloved daughter Martha Robinson a negro woman named Jude & her eight negro children with all my lands & grist mill & saw mill. I also will that a negro man named Marry & a negro man named Yogue at the discretion of my executor be sold or hired & the money arising therefrom to my daughter Martha Robinson. If my daughter Martha should die without any lawful heirs, my property should be divided amongst Brother Robt Robinson's family. I appoint Saml Givens, exr., 24 Feb 1821. Wm. Robinson (mark) (LS), Wit: Geo Wright, Robt Robinson, Jane Robinson.

Warrant of appraisement directed to Robt Robertson, George Wright, Arthur Erwin, Thos Williams & Philip Williams, 7 March 1821 returnable 1 May. Letters testamentary to Saml Givens, Esq., 7 March 1821.

Pages 46-47: Will of Joseph McKenzie of York District growing old... To my loving wife Rebeckah $80 to be levied off my estate, also the one half of my household furniture & her living off my land whilst she lives on it, and the use of my negroes. To my son James McKenzie two of my negroes named Abner & Sela. To my son Robt McKenzie one negro girl Betty. To my daughter Martha Boggs my negro girl Sabrina. To my daughter Grizzel McCall my negro girl Sinda. Also to my son James $200. To my son in law Thos Howe a lease of a tract of land that I have lying in the flat rocks for ten years or longer for his share. To my son Joseph McKenzie all my carpenter tools & the remainder of my property to be equally divided between my sons Joseph, Hezekiah & Saml McKenzie & my daughters Ann Howe, Margaret Bryson & Martha Boggs. I appoint my sons Joseph & James, exrs., 27 Jan 1821. Joseph McKenzie, Wit: John Riddle, Wm. Davis, Josiah Davis.

Warrant of appraisement to John Riddle, Jos Clinton, Jas McCullock, Wm Kindrick and Henry Smith 18 March 1821 returnable 15 May. Letters testamentary to Jos McKenzie 18 March 1821.

Pages 48-51: Citation. John Berry near Yorkville applied for letters of administration with the will annexed of Violet Watson widow, 12 Feb 1821.

Will of Violet Watson widow of Wm Watson Senior of Fishing Creek, York County... Being directed by the will of my husband Wm Watson aforesaid to leave the property real & personal left me by his said will to my sister's children or some of them... Whereas John Berry the son of Rodger Berry &

Mary Berry the daughter of my sister Jane Elliott has been particularly kind & obliging to me in my old age, I bequeath to the said John Berry the tract of land whereon I now live & have since the death of my said husband lived to him & I do hereby enjoin it on the children of my two sisters as legatees. To Jane Dunn daughter of my sister Jane Elliott & Charles Moore & Rosannah Berry & Margaret Berry three of the children of my sister Mary Moore, all my negro slaves Jacob, Anny, Judy, Phillips, Pompey, Julia, Violet, Watson & Rosy that they may not be separated at a distance from each other or carried out of York District from their relatives & connections. The remainder of my estate to be sold and the money divided equally amongst the children of my aforesaid two sisters. I appoint James A. Whyte, exr., 8 Oct 1815. Violet Watson (mark), Wit: Joseph Gebbie, Rodger Barry, Robt Harper.

Warrant of appraisement directed to Joseph Gebbie Senr, George Davis, Andrew McWhorter, John Yarborough & Benjn Chambers, 28 Feb 1821 returnable 25 May. Letters of administration to John Berry son of Rodger Berry 28 Feb 1821.

Pages 51-53: Will of Robt Bozwell of District of York, being far advanced in life... To my beloved wife Margaret Bozwell her living during her natural life out of my estate. To my nephew Robt Wilson which I have raised from a child six negroes, one negro woman Suck, one girl Miriah, one girl Elvy, one girl Isbel, one girl Violet, one girl named Harriot with my plantation that I now live on, 100 acres with all my household & kitchen furniture, stock, etc. I appoint my nephew Robt Wilson & Thos Gibson exrs., 23 May 1820. Robt Bozwell (mark) (LS), Wit: Wm Kenedy, James Ash, Thomas Gibson.

Warrant of appraisement directed to Saml Givins Esqr., Reuben McConnel, Wm. Gibson, James Ash & Wm Burris 1 March 1821 returnable 25 April. Letters testamentary to Robt Wilson 1 March 1821.

Pages 53-54: Warrant of appraisement on the estate of Mary Craig decd directed to Saml McCullough, James McCullough, Wm. Kindrick, Robt Johnston & George Johnston 2 Dec 1820 returnable 1 Feb. Letters testamentary to James Craig & James Glenn, exrs., 2 Dec 1820.

Pages 54-56: Will of Saml Buchanan Senr of District of York... to my beloved wife Barbara Buchanan the free use of my plantation with all the houses, out houses, & improvements, excepting 30 acres to be laid off the upper part of said plantation for my son Samuel including the improvements which my son Saml hath made thereon, and at the decease of my said with the said plantation to my beloved son William Buchanan excepting the 30 acres spoken of above. My son William have & possess three head or horses, one bed & furniture, which he at this time claims & my silver watch. To my daughter Margaret Buchanan one mare & four head of cattle, one bed & furniture, which she at this time claims. To my beloved son James Buchanan five shillings. Whereas my son John Buchanan is dead & has left a widow & two children, five shillings each. I appoint my wife Barbara Buchanan & my son

William Buchanan, exrs. [not dated] Saml Buchanan (LS), Wit: John Bates Senr, Wm. Little.

Warrant of appraisement directed to Wm little, Richard Sadler, John Carroll, Isaac Harris, James Johnston, 26 March 1821 returnable 20 May. Letters testamentary to Wm. Buchanan 26 March 1821.

Pages 56-59: Will of James Smith of the District of York, planter, being of a good old age & somewhat infirm... To Mary my beloved wife the plantation I now live on during her life or widowhood with all the household & kitchen furniture, likewise one negro woman named Letty, one negro man Sambo, and at the end of either Sambo to become the property of my son Mijamin & letty to be disposed of at her own discretion, choice of my horses, one plow & tackling, three milk cows & a beef steer, with all my hogs & poultry. To my son Mijamin the Bullocks Creek plantation he now lives on, one negro man named Belfast, and the plantation I now live on. At the death of my wife the plantation I now live on to be sold and the price equally divided between my son John & my five daughters Elizabeth, Margaret, Isabella, Nancy & Polly, except the part of said plantation Hughy Smith now lives on, 96 acres, which I allow to be the property of my daughter Polly. I bequeath the property now in my hands of my daughter Polly's which I gave her when she was married to be hers. My sons Wm., Robt, & Hugh do receive one dollar. I appoint my wife Mary & my son Mijamin, exrs. [not dated]. James Smith (LS), Wit: Gilbert Enloe, Saml Turner, Nathaniel P. Kenady.

Warrant of appraisement directed to Hugh Cain, Wm Ferguson, Saml Burnes, Saml Turner Esqr., & Wm. Love 31 Aug 1821 returnable 25 October. Letters testamentary to Mijamin Smith 31 Aug 1821.

Pages 59-60: Will of Mial Pair of York District... to my wife Sally Pair all the rest of my property during her widowhood & for her children while they are with her & at her death or the end of her widowhood, all property be equally divided amongst the children. I appoint my wife Sally Pair & James McKorkle, exrs., 30 Nov 1820. Mial Pair (LS), Wit: Wm Shurling, John Shurling.

Warrant of appraisement directed to Wm Shirling, Wm. White, Robt Watson, Littleberry Patterson & Henry Talley 1 Sept 1821 returnable 18 Sept. Letters testamentary to Sarah Pair & James McKorkle, 1 Sept 1821.

Page 61: South Carolina, York District. Will of Samuel Hemphill Senr.... I allow my son Alexander Hemphill to have a part of the tract of land I now live on, on a corner of my son William's land, adj. Mr. Shew's line, 60 acres. The ballance of my land to my son David Hemphill, my wife to have her support off said land her life time. To my daughter Margaret Hemphill $50. All my stock of horses, cows, etc., to my son David by his paying $300 to each of the rest of my children viz Elizabeth Graham, Martha Patton, Robert Hemphill, Samuel Hemphill and William Hemphill. I appoint my wife Sarah Hemphill and my son David, exrs, 27 Dec 1820. Sml Hemphill (LS), Wit: Daniel Misheal, John Jackson.

Pages 61-63: Warrant of appraisement directed to Daniel Grimes, David Patton, Robert Pursley, James Hemphill, Thomas McKee, 1 Oct 1821 returnable 10 Nov. Daniel Graham, Robert Pursley, James Hemphill sworn before John Henry, Q.U., 29 Oct 1821. Letters testamentary to Sarah Hemphill and David Hemphill 1 Oct 1821.

Pages 63-65: Will of John Moore Senr of the District of York... To my beloved daughter Nancy Moore 100 acres of land next John Gill's land, with a young bay mare, spotted cow, clothes, wheel and chest. To my daughter Elizabeth 100 acres of land on the NW side of my plantation one cow with her bed and clothes. To my granddaughter Casindare one cow. To my son Henry all that tract of land that he has now in possession with his bed and clothes, carpenter and blacksmith tools, one gray horse. To my son John the remainder of my land that I now live on with the house and improvements, one bay horse, also stud colt. My hoggs, sheep & cattle be equally divided among my children Nancy, Elizabeth, John, and Henry. I appoint John Wright, exr., 25 July 1821. John Moore (mark) (LS), Wit: Wm. Wright, John English, Andw Wright.

Warrant of appraisement directed to John King, Archibald Robison, Andw Wright, Saml King & Arthur Robeson 7 Jan 1822 returnable 1 March. Letters testamentary to John Wright 7 Jan 1822.

Pages 65-67: South Carolina, York District. Will of Thomas Davis of district aforesaid... To my son David Davis land on both sides of the Beaver Dam Creek, on the upper end of the tract I now live on, opposite to his smith shopp and running nearly south with the path from his shop to Elias Jackson's crossing the Creek. The remainder of my tract between my two sons James Davis & Josiah Davis to be divided between them according to quantity and quality, my son James to have the first choice. To my son David Davis one heifer calf. To my daughter Anny Patrick one heifer calf. The remainder of my personal property to be divided between my single or unmarried children. I appoint my sons David Davis and James Davis, exrs., 4 Nov 1821. Thomas Davis (LS), Wit: Robt Patrick, James Moore, James Duff.

Warrant of appraisement directed to Robt Adams, Jos Adams, Elias Jackson, John Tigleman[?] & Col. Jas Duff 31 Nov 1821 returnable 30 Jan. Letters testamentary to David Davis & James Davis 31 Nov 1821.

Pages 67-69: Will of Robert Bates of York District... All my worldly estate to my beloved wife Catharine Bates during her widowhood... should she marry again, estate to my brothers and sisters share and share alike. I appoint my brother John Bates Senr, exr. [not dated] Robt Bates (LS), Wit: James P. Sandifer, Milat Sturgis, Jno Bates Senr.

Letters testamentary to John Bates Senr 3 Dec 1821. Warrant of appraisement directed to Benjn Rowel, Wm. Rowel, Archibald Steele, Thos Robertson, Saml McHood & Thos Bates 3 Dec 1821 returnable 1 February.

Pages 69-71: South Carolina, York District. Will of John D. O. K. Pettus... March 24, 1819... to be buried in a decent pine cofen with my son Samuel at Hopewell. To my beloved wife during her lifetime a negro fellow named Tom, a negro fellow named Eleck. To my son Stephen Pettus the plantation and fellow Eleck. To my daughter hannah Mary Amandah two girls Rach & Mary, a bed and furniture, horse and saddle. Mill and Ealse to be sold and the money divided between the two children. My uper plantation to be sold to pay debts. My wife to be executrix. John D. Pettus. [no witnesses]. Stephen Pettus applied for letters of administration with the will annexed 14 November 1821. Violet Pettus declined to qualify as executrix 14 Nov 1821.

Warrant of appraisement directed to Benjn Persons, Robt Bell, John Springs, Wm. Goodrich & John Goodrich 21 Dec 1821 returnable 20 February.

Pages 71-72: Repeat of the will of Thomas Davis (see pages 65-67 of this will book, on page 137)

Pages 72-75: Citation. John Baxter Junr with the will annexed has applied for letters of administration on the estate of William Baxter 3 Dec 1821.

Will of Wm Baxter, planter, of the District of York... To my mother Jane Baxter one bed and furniture, also $50. To my brother John Baxter my big sorrel horse, my waggon and harness, also he is not to be accountable to my legatees for the sum of $40 which he justly owes me. I allow him to have the crop of corn and cotton now planted he paying the hire of a negro woman that I have now and all other expenses in growing and gathering the said crop. To my brother James Baxter's son Wm Baxter, my sartorius Pilly [?]. To my sister Mary Wilson's son Henry Baxter $10 which I allow to be deposited with my brother John Baxter as guardian. My lands and mill, stock of every kind, furniture, etc., to be sue and the money arising from the sale to be divided equally between my brothers and sisters viz James Baxter, John Baxter, Mary Wilson, Margt Coram. I appoint James Moor, exr., 1 May 1821. Wm. Baxter (LS), Wit: David Hutcheson, Starling Collen.

Warrant of appraisement to Danl Sturgis Senr, John Hart, David Hutcheson, James McKee Esqr., Zadock Sturgis 10 Dec 1821 returnable 1 February.

Letters testamentary to John Baxter admr. with the will annexed 10 Dec 1821.

Pages 75-77: South Carolina, York District. Will of Jonathan Neely of district aforesaid... To my beloved wife Mary Neely herr maintainance off of the plantation whereon I now live as long as she remains my widow, also one negroe girl named Dim & if she should marry then to be divided equally among all my children all the household furniture, one bald horse & saddle, two milk cows & one loom, my children namely Peggy Eliz. Neely, Thos M. Neely, Jonathan M. Neely, Nancy Emaline[?] Neely, and James C. Neely, as it appears at present that my said wife is pregnant & if the child live, to share an equal part with my above named children except my said plantation which I give to my said three sons, to be divided when this youngest son shall become of age. I appoint James Carothers my sole executor, 26 Dec 1821. Jonathan Neely (LS), Wit: Chas Robeson, Levin Benton.

Warrant of appraisement directed to Charles Robertson, James Thom, Saml Caruthers, John Soward, Wm Caruthers 31 May 1822 returnable 1 Aug. Letters testamentary to James Caruthers Jnr 31 May 1822.

Page 78: Settlement. John Soward's settlement on Mary Drennan's estate, admr., from Aug 7th 1809. Proven accounts on Richard Timberlake, Wm Hall, Robt McCaw. Received of John Soward, admr. with the will annexed of Mary Drennan decd., $35.25 in full of the part of said estate I am entitled to by my wife who was named Legatee in said will, May 17th 1822. Wm. M. Hill.

Pages 78-81: South Carolina, York District. Will of Henry Howser late of the district aforesaid... To my wife Cristina Houser the following property: her walnut chest & wearing apparel with her bed and furniture and a four legged walnut table, two cows & $100 cash. To my son John Houser $200 that I have paid him out of my estate. To my son David Houser the tract of land on Cain Creek, Rutherford, No Carolina, purchased of John Patterson, one half of which divided according to value I will bequeath to him at $500 value. To my son in law Jacob Saphe $250 paid to him out of my estate. To my son in law Henry Houser[?] $200 paid to him out of my estate. To my son in law John Wistenant $200 paid to him out of my estate. To my son in law Joshua Moss $91.50 paid to him out of my estate. To my son in law Gilbreth Dixon $80 paid to him out of my estate. The tract of land whereon I now live with houses I purchased to Robt Black adj. said tract also 3 & 4/10 acres purchased of Nicholas Wistenant Senr adj. said tract, likewise two tracts being surveys I made adj. said land, 249 acres, the other 460 acres all to be sold on a credit of 12 months to the highest bidder at public sale. My 1000 acres on branches of Clarks fork adj. McElwee, Hambright, in York District, to be sold separately at the same time to the highest bidder. My negro man Ned be sold at publick sale to the highest bidder, also my negro name Ben, and negro woman Franky with her two children. My stock of hoses & cattle, with waggon and harness, all be sold, one still & vessels with smith tools. I will that one equal divide be made among my heirs after deducting what has already been received by each. I appoint Henry Houser and John Whistenant, exrs., 2 March 1822. Henry Houser, Wit: John Ellis, Edward Boid, George Whistenant.

Warrant of appraisement directed to John Ellis Esqr., Geo Wistenant, John Randal Esqr., Frederick Hambright & Edmund Boid 6 March 1822 returnable 1 June. Letters testamentary to Henry Houser and John Whistenant 6 March 1822.

Pages 81-83: South Carolina, York District. Will of Joseph Boyd of district aforesaid... To my wife Sary Boyd the plantation on which I now live, also three negroes Jim, Poll & Dinah. To daughter Mary Ann Mannon $20. To my son James Lee Boyd two negro boys Jep & Sambo, also $150 in cash. To my four youngest daughters Sally Jinny Clarke, Eliza, Levin, and Peggy, all the remaining part of my real and personal estate to be equally divided between them, to be in the hands of the executors until they marry & then one negro to b given each one. To my wife Sary Boyd one third part of all my house & kitchen furniture, also one third part of my stock & farming utensils. I appoint my son James Lee Boyd & Robt Mammon, exrs., 23 Jan 1822. Jos Boyd (LS), Wit: John Ellis, Thos Clark, Willis Moss.

Warrant of appraisement directed to Thos Clark, Thos Mulinax, Jacob Stroup, Middleton Sanlin & Isaac Guyton 4 June 1821 [sic] returnable 1 August. Letters testamentary to Robt Mannon and James Lee Boyd, 4 June 1822.

Page 84: North Carolina. Will of John Sitgreaves... To my wife Martha Sitgreaves all my estate both real and personal during her natural life and after her death it may be divided among such of my children as may then be living or if they all should die before my wife, I give the whole of my estate both real and personal to my said wife. I appoint my wife executrix & request the favor of Genl Jones to act as executor, 24 Oct 1795. Jno Sitgreaves.

Hallifax County, May 1802. Proved in open court by Robt Pinner and Samfort Long who testified to the handwriting of John Sitgreaves. Copy certified by Richard Eppis, Clerk of Court for Halifax County, North Carolina, 26 Nov 1821.

Page 85: South Carolina, York District. Will of Thomas Hogg of district above mentioned... To my wife Elizabeth Hogg the whole of the tract I now possess (having lately conveyed to my daughters Elizabeth Anne & Martha each 100 acres), also my negro man named Ellick. I also give to my wife all of my personal property consisting of hoggs, cows, hoses, sheep, household furniture, 25 Feb 1820. Thos Hogg (mark) (LS), Wit: John Minter, Eli Hogg, Anne Kelough.

Pages 85-87: Will of Mary Robinson... It is my will that my son John J. Abernathy who has been my most attentive, tender, and affectionate child to have all my real and personal estate consisting of John J. Jones' note indorsed by Norman and Jones dated 15th March 1819 with a mortgage on said note, also my one half of the bond and mortgage given by Jacob Davis dated 1st June 1817 for the purchase of a house and lot No. 40,Queen Street to Mary Robeson & John J. Abernathie sold to said Jacob Davis by consent of parties to make a division amongst the heirs with all the interest accruing thereon amounting to $1340, also all my bedding and bed clothes, plates, household & kitchen furniture, etc. In consequence of the disobedience of my daughter Mary Davis, I only bequeath to her $25 to purchase her a mourning suit. I appoint my son John J. Abernathie and my friend James Sweeney, exrs., 25 June 1819. Mary Robinson (LS), Wit: Eliza Swinny, Francis Sweeney, Mary Kilkelly.

Warrant of appraisement 23 April 1822 [names not included]. Letters testamentary to John Abernathy and James Sweeny 23 April 1822.

Page 87: Decree of the Court of Ordinary, May 30th 1822. John Ewing & others vs Nathaniel Enloe & Gilbert Enloe, exrs., of the will of Isaac Enloe decd. By citation to be reviewed. After hearing the witnesses in the within touching the last will of Isaac Enloe decd, I am of opinion without any hesitation to decree in favour of & do believe the instrument of writing to be the last will of the within named Isaac Enloe decd. 30 May 1822. Benj Chambers, O. Y. D.

Page 88: South Carolina, York District. Will of Jane Sadler, widow of Richard Sadler Senr, decd., being old & infirm... the plantation whereon I live & which was willed to me by my decd husband Richard Sadler, I leave to my daughter in law Elizabeth Sadler widow of Joseph Sadler decd., also my bed & bed clothes & wearing apparel with all my household & kitchen furniture. To my son David Sadler all my money which may be due to me from Wm. Sadler his son. To my daughter Ellen Black what may be due me at my death from John Black her husband. To my grandchild Jean Sadler, my horse & saddle & my negro boy Sam. To my son Richard Sadler my loom if he thinks proper to pay ten dollars to my daughter in law Elizabeth Sadler for the same. I appoint my son Richard Sadler my executor, 7 Aug 1820. Jane Sadler (X) (LS), Wit: Ed Jennings, Minor Sadler, Ethelwin Sadler.

Pages 88-90: South Carolina, York District. Citation. Samuel McCullough of Chester District has applied for letters of administration on the estate of Elias Mildoon, late of the District aforesaid decd, 23 Sept 1822 returnable 1 Dec.

Warrant of appraisement directed to John Latta, Hugh Drennon, Wm. Drennon, Wm. Downing and Wm. Neely, 4 Oct 1822. Letters of administration to Samuel McCulloch 4 Oct 1822.

Pages 90-92: South Carolina, York District. Will of William Ash of district aforesaid... To my wife Mary Ash all my household and kitchen furniture, one bay mare with seven head of cattle and four head of hoggs, two notes $40 each, the one upon my beloved son Robert Ash and the other upon my beloved son William Ash with $22 in silver, and farming tools of every kind. To my granddaughter Polly B. Ash one bed and furniture, one walnut chest, one wheel and reel, and $80 in cash or a note of the same amount that my son in law James Ash owe me, to be paid to her at the year of 21 or at the years of marriage. To my beloved daughter Margaret Ash the remainder of the above named property at the death of my beloved wife Mary Also. My wife Mary Ash shall have her living on the plantation whereon I now live if so that she continues to live out on it, if not she shall have neither claim nor title to it. To my beloved son William Ash the plantation whereon I now live, 176 acres. To my son Robert Ash my shot gun, $5. I nominate William Ash and James Ash as executors, 7 Sept 1822. William Ash (mark) (LS), Wit: Saml Ash, Robert Ash, Geo Wright.

Warrant of appraisement to Wm Gibson, Thos Gibson, Geo Wright, Wm. England, Saml Ash or Robert Wilson returnable 2 Nov 1822. Letters testamentary to William Ash and James Ash, 2 Nov 1822.

Pages 92-94: Will of John Ramsey of York District... My beloved wife Sarah Ramsey to enjoy the right of all my moveable property including my waggon with all household furniture, and she is to pay to my two daughters Leny[?] and Jenny $10 each. The plantation whereon I now live of 150 acres to be left to my wife during her life or widowhood and then to my son Thomas. My son David shall have 50 acres of land adj. where he now lives on the right hand side towards his brother Henery & my son Henry have for his part 50 acres adj. his brother David. My sons Alexander, Abraham, and John Ramsey have the balance of my land, which is 150 acres to be surveyed and divided into three parts, 50 acres each. I appoint my two sons Harvey & Alexander Ramsey, exrs., 4 July 1822. John Ramsey (LS), Wit: Saml Davidson, Jacob Childers (mark), Sarah Davidson (mark).

Warrant of appraisement directed to Abraham Smith, Henry Smith, Jos Smith, Littleton Sanlin and Thomas Whitesides 4 March 1823 returnable 1 May. Letters testamentary to Harvey Ramsey and Alexander Ramsay 4 March 1823.

Pages 94-98: South Carolina, York District. Will of Joseph Miller Senior of district aforesaid, being of weak body from my advanced age in life... My executors purchase a head & foot stone for my aged wife & self and they are to retain so much money as may be required to make such purchase out of the portions willed to my sons Joseph & John. If my said wife should survive me, she be supported from my estate, and supply 200 weight of good flower, 50 weight of good sugar, ten weight of good coffee, 40 bushels of corn, and as much fodder as may be necessary for her per year. To my son Joseph Miller the plantation whereon I now live composed of there tracts of parts of tracts one of which I bought of John Aiken, another of the son of Philip Walker, and the other of James Rush, in the whole about 200 acres. To my said son Joseph a negro woman named Lett & her children now in his possession. To my son John Miller 214 acres of land being the tract I bought of James Rush on the waters of Fishing Creek, also negroes Bob, Courey & her children now in his possession and at his death to my three grandchildren Joseph, Drusilla, & Jane Miller, children of said son John by his first wife. To my daughter Rachel the wife of Oliver McClain $150 in cash, and then to her children. To my daughter Mary the wife of Hugh Simpson $150 collars on the same terms. My executors do pay the Revd. Mr. Dixon $12 for preaching four sermons one week days two at my house and two at my son John's. I appoint my friends Capt. John Blair and Thomas Williams Junr, exrs., 7 July 1821. Joseph Miller (mark) (Seal), Wit: John Bailey, Saml Wright, James Galloway.

Warrant of appraisement directed to Matthew Carrel, Jno Burrow, David Watson, Wm. Berry and Captain G. Durham 3 Feb 1823 returnable 1 May. Letters not returned to be recorded.

Pages 98-101: South Carolina, York District. Citation. Henry Hood applied for letters of administration on George Hood 18 March 1823.

Will of George Hood of York District... to my beloved wife Mary Hood all my lands & tenements, stock & furniture for the support of her and my children and after her decease to be equally divided among my heirs. I appoint my two friends William Caldwell and John James, exrs., 20 April 1816. George Hood (X), Wit: Saml Turner, John F. Hopkins, Catherine Trimer.

Warrant of appraisement directed to Wm Caldwell, Jeremiah Blalock, Nat Henderson, Charles Henry & Jno Cavany 19 May 1823 returnable 15 July. Letters of administration with the will annexed to Henry Hood 7 May 1823.

Pages 101-102: Will of Randal Sandlin Senior of York District... to my daughter Polly, one young brown horse called Buck, one feather bed and furniture, one cow & calf. To my daughter [no name indicated] one two year old blazed face filley with a feather bed & furniture, a cow & calf. To my beloved & lawful wife Mourning, all the other of my personal estate, stock, etc., and at her decease whatever shall be let to be divided amongst my three daughters; and likewise to my beloved wife the full possession of my plantation during her life and at her decease to be divided between my two sons Littleton the eldest to have the lower part as he is now in possession of it, & Randal the upper part as he is now possessed with it. To my son in law Sherard James, full power to see this my will fully and amply executed as my lawful executor, 28 Feb 1804. Randolph Sandlin (Seal), Wit: Joseph Leach, Joseph Reed. Articles of agreement between the heirs of Randal Sandlin, 20 Aug 1806, we agree to abide by the contents of the within will of Randall Sandlin deceased: Shared James (Seal), littleton Sd. (X) (Seal), Randolph Sandlin (Seal), Joseph Reed (Seal), Morning Sandler (mark) (Seal), Jinny Sandlin (mark), Wit: William James, Jno Ellis.

Pages 102-103: Will of Daniel Bartlett the District of York... To my beloved wife Sophia Bartlett the full and entire use of the whole plantation whereon I now live during her life and after her death to my son William Bartlett during the term of my lease. To my wife all of my stock, etc. I appoint my friend Benjamin Person executor, 22 Fe 1822. Daniel Bartlett (Seal), Wit: George G. Barnett, Sarah Barnett, Thos Barnett.

Pages 103-105: 6 July 1823. Will of William Patrick of York District... My plantation to be divided equally to my three sons Josius, Davey, & Jesse Patrick. My son David Patrick to have my new rifle gun & all my farming utensils and wagon and gears. My daughter Elizabeth Patrick have her bed and furniture. My daughter Sarah to have my brown mare & her bed & furniture. My son Josiah to have my sorrel mare and my son Jesse to have my two year old colt. My horned cattle to be equally divided between my son David & Elizabeth & Sarah Patrick. My son James Duf Patrick to have $2, and my son Robert my old rifle gun, my son William Patrick $2; to my son Elias Patrick $2 & to my daughter Mary Turner $2, and to my daughter Hannah Currence $2, and to my daughter Martha Riddle, $2, and to my daughter Permilla Beard $2. My son David Patrick and William Currence, exrs. William Patrick (LS), Wit: John Currence, Christopher Turner, Hugh Riddle.

Warrant of appraisement to Isack Campbell, Alexander Barnett, John Currence, Robert Patrick Senr, Danl Currence 19 July 1823 returnable 15 September. Letters testamentary to William Currence & David Patrick 19 July 1823.

Pages 105-107: South Carolina, York District. Will of Hester Alexander... To my granddaughter Sarah Alexander Moore my bed, bestead & furniture & to my son in law John Moore the balance of my property, books of account, notes of hand & every other species of property. I appoint the said John Moore, sole executor, 28 Feb 1823. Hester Alexander (X). Wit: Ezekiel Morris, Anne Morris (X).

Warrant of appraisement directed to Ezekiel Morris, John Marley, Jno Ingram, William Jamieson Esqr. & Robert Hays, 1 Sept 1823 returnable 1 November. Letters testamentary to John Moore 1 Sept 1823.

Pages 107-110: Will of Margaret Gillespie of the District of York... To my son Jonathan Gillespie that part of my land laid off to him by William Robeson & others, being the lower part of the plantation on which I at present reside, not including my improvement farther the upper corner of my face on the waggon road below my dwelling house. To my son Johnston Gillespie that part of my land divided to him by said William Robeson & others, being the upper part and other improvements not including the improved land within the bounds of my son Jonathan Gillespie's part. To my daughter Rachel Hill & to my daughter Mary Falkener & to my daughter Margaret Falkener & to my daughter Nancy Wiley & to my son Jonathan Gillespie & to my son Johnston Gillespie, each one sixth part of my personal estate. I appoint my said sons Jonathan & Johnston Gillespie, exrs., 11 Dec 1819. Margaret Gillespie (mark) (Seal), Wit: William Jamieson, Helena Jamieson, James Lee Boyd.

Letters testamentary to Johnathan Gillespie & Johnston Gillespie 30 Aug 1823. Warrant of appraisement directed to William Robinson, Jno King, Joseph Doudle, Thomas Queen & Alexander Galloway 30 Aug 1823 returnable 1 November.

Pages 110-112: South Carolina, York District. Will of Rosannah/Rosy Hannah... My negro boy Minor I give to my brother Archibald to continue on the place for the use of the family now living together to wit Jane, Ann, Margaret, Sarah, but if either of my before named sisters or all of them should marry or by any means quit the family, then Archibald is to pay each of them so quitting the family one fifth part of the value of said negro. My interest in the land and premises whereon we now live to my before named Brother and sisters. Also to them my bay horse. To my sisters Sarah my bureau and one bed. To my brothers James Hannah & William Hannah five shillings each. I appoint my brother Archibald sole executor, 2 May 1822. Rosannah Hannah, Wit: Robert Cooper, Mansfield Gordon, Catherine Gordon.

Warrant of appraisement directed to Robert Cooper, Samuel Lowrie, Mansfield Gordon, Francis Irwin & Jonathan Kuykendall 15 Sept 1823 returnable 15 November. Letters testamentary to Archibald Hannah 15 Sept 1823.

Pages 112-114: Will of Robert L. Armstrong of York District... To my dear & loving wife Martha Armstrong one third of all my lands during her natural life or widowhood & also one young bay horse, saddle and bridle, with all the household furniture she brought with her when we were joined in the marriage state, as he own special carding[?]. To my daughter Mary Lalearin[?] Armstrong, the balance of all my lands with the price of my horse, saddle, saddle baggs, bridle & two cows & calves, the price of my books, medicine & stock of hogs be equally divided between my wife and child. To my daughter Mary Lalearin my bed & furniture. I appoint Joseph Clinton and John Henry Esqr., exrs., 10 Sept 1823. Robert L. Armstrong (LS), Wit: Robert G. Allison, Jesse K. Armstrong, Isaac C. Campbell.

Warrant of appraisement directed to Capt. Isaac Campbell, John Currance, Wm. Currance, Wm. Moore, M. A. Moore, Rt. Allison & Robt Patrick 29 Sept 1823 returnable 25 Nov. Letters testamentary to Joseph Clinton and John Henry 29 Sept 1823.

Pages 114-120: Will of William Thomson of York District... to my son Richard Thomson all my lands called the beauty spot and all my lands adj. the same whereon I now live in York District & two other tracts of land near the same lying over the river in Union District that I purchased of Joshua Petty decd, the widow Good & her children, and two other tracts in York District on the waters of Beaver dam Creek that I purchased from a Mr. Bankhead about 354 acres and three other tracts in York District at & near the mouth of Buffalo Creek, that I purchased from Richard Quin, John Dill and James Gardiner, containing in the several above described tracts 3414 acres during his natural life for the sum of one dollar per year to be paid to my executors when they call for it. At his death I bequeath all the lands whereon I now live called the beauty spot and others to his three sons William Hatten Thomson, Henry Hopson Thomson and James Maddison Thomson to be laid off to them in his life time equally as to quality & quantity, and the three tracts lying at the mouth of Buffalo Creek that I purchased from Richard Quinn, John Dill and James Gardiner, about 1100 acres to James Washington Thomson & Joseph Waddy Thompson at the death of their father Richard Thomson. To my daughter Margaret McKee all my lands on Thicketty Creek in Spartanburgh District where she now lives, 2000 acres during her life and at her death, one half to William Nicholes my grandson including the land bought of Philip Walker, the house and plantation and the out land up main Thicketty around by the race paths, & the other hand to Barlow Thomson Collins including Hainsworth and part of the Moores tracts to be made equal with the out lands to quantity & qualify by his paying his sister Caroline Collins $400. To my daughter Nancy Collins that tract of land on the north side of Pacolet River in Union District called Bullocks old field, about 600 acres, and at her death to William Nickoles her son. To Richard Franklin Thomson son of Richard Thomson that tract of land & mills on Lawsons fork that I purchased by a decree in the court of equity, 300 acres. My will is that the following lands be sold, the tract on the beaverdam creek near Gafney's & the land in partnership with William Lipscomb decd that he willed to me with lime on it, both tracts in Spartanburgh District, & one tract of land in the State of Virginia in Amherst County, and the money arising from the sale to be equally divided between all of my grandchildren at the death of my son Richard Thomson. My will is that I leave all my negroes & their increase (excepting four) to my son Richard Thomson for paying the taxes of them, and at my son's death the hold of the negroes to be equally divided among all my grandchildren namely Sarah Moore, Narcissa Otterson, Nancy McKee, Melissa Norris, William Nicholes, William H. Thomson, Henry H. Thomson, Nancy Ragland Thomson, James M. Thomson, Junius W. Thomson, Joseph W. Thomson Perry, Susan Ann Thomson & Richard Franklin Thomson, Barlow Thomson Collins & Caroline Collins. My will is that I hire two negroes worth $3000 each unto Margarett McKee during her life for paying the taxes of them, also a horse, mare & small dioned[?] stud and at her death to be equally divided between her three daughters. I also have $2000 in my executors hands to be put at interest for the support of my daughter Margaret. I also have $2000 in my executors hands to be put at interest for the support of my daughter Nancy Collins, and at her death to be equally divided between Melissa Norris & William Nicholes her children & Barlow Thomson Collins & Caroline Collins her children. I hire two negroes worth $300 each to my daughter Nancy Collins, and at her death to her four children. I leave four negroes worth $300 a piece to all my grandchildren whenever they become of age or should marry: Sally Moore, Narcissa Otterson, Nancy McKee, Melissa Norris, William Nicholes, William H. Thomson, Henry H. Thomson, Nancy R. Thomson, James M. Thomson, Junius W. Thomson, Joseph W. Thomson, Polly ___ Thomson, Richard S. Thomson & Caroline Collins. I appoint my son Richard Thomson, Smith Lipscomb & Elijah Dawkins, exrs., 26 Oct 1822. William Thomson (LS), Wit: John Hemphill, James B. Good, James S. Hemphill.

Citation Richard Thomson has applied for letters testamentary 22 Sept 1823. Warrant of appraisement directed to James Meek, Alexander Thomson Esq., John Hemphill Esq., John LittleJohn & Samuel Davidson 6 Oct 1823 returnable 1 December. Letters testamentary on the will of William Thomson of Broad River 6 Oct 1823.

Pages 120-122: April 3d 1821. Will of Christopher McCarter of York District... To my sons Elias and George Alexander McCarter, all the land I am possessed of to be divided between them in such a manner that each one's share will take part of the cleared land and of the wood land. I allow George A. McCarter's lott to include the house and other buildings where I now live, and to each of my said sons Elias and George A. McCarter $35 to each one in specie. To my daughter Mesinah $30 in specie and two cows and calves and all the dresser and kitchen furniture, two feather beds and furniture, one bay mare and saddle, bridle, and spinning wheel. To my son George A. McCarter a negro man named Joe and I allow my said son George to pay to my son Elias $100, also to my son Robt McCarter $10. I give to my son George A. McCarter a sorrel horse in place of his mare given to Misenah. To my sons James, John, and William each of them $50 and I allow James all my smith tools at their value in part of his $50 appraised. To my daughters Elizabeth, Rosanah and Mary, each of them $5. The residue of my property of whatsoever value and kind to be sold and the money arising from said sale to be equally divided between my sons James, John, and Wm McCarter, and also to my sons Elias and George A. McCarter each one feather bed and furniture. To my son George A. McCarter my clock and table. I appoint my sons Robt and Wm. McCarter, exrs. Christopher McCarter (X) (LS), Wit: John Currance, Isaac A. Campbell, Danl Currance.

Warrant of appraisement to Isaac Campbell, John Currance, Wm Currance, Robt Patrick & John Barnet 1 Nov 1823 returnable 1 January. Letters testamentary to Robt McCarter and Wm McCarter 1 Nov 1823. Order for sale.

Pages 123-125: South Carolina, York District. Will of William Little of district aforesaid... To my wife Elizabeth Little one negro man named Dave, one negro boy named Sam & one negro woman named Winy during her lifetime or widowhood, also one sorrel mare Rosetta and her offspring. Also to said Elizabeth Little during her lifetime or widowhood until my son Wiley Little becomes of age for the maintainance & support of the children, all the plantation or tract of land whereon I now live, at which time it is to be equally divided between my two sons Wm Little & Wiley Little, but my wife E. Little is to have during her lifetime a part of the plantation to cultivate with the house & all the outbuildings and furniture except one bed to each of my female children when they become of age or marry. To my daughter Sarah Sadler one negro girl named Ruth, one girl named Matilda, one bay mare Polina and one sorrel colt one year old, two beds & furniture. To my daughter Elizabeth Little one negro girl named Ann, one negro girl named Vilet, one bay horse & Norher, & one bed and furniture. To my daughter Polly Little, one negro girl named Lavina, one negro child named Harriet ,also one sorrel mare named Mariah, one bed and furniture. To my daughter Jane Little, one negro girl named Eliza, one negro girl named Sophia, also one bed and furniture, one horse, saddle & bridle of a good quality. To my daughter Margaret Little, one negro girl named Mariah, one negro woman named Phebe, one bed & furniture, one good horse, saddle & Bridle. To my son William Little, one negro boy named Absolem, also one half of the land whereon I now live and the west side of said land when divided. To my son Wylie L. Little one negro boy named Tom, also one half of the land whereon I now live and the east side when divided. My young horse Pantaloon remain int he family & be disposed of as my executors feel proper. i express my desire for the small tract of land lying on the north side of Tools Fork adj. Thos Rouches land to be sold at public auction and the money appropriated to the payment of my debts, and the remainder if any to be equally divided among each female legatee except $100 to my daughter Sarah's oldest child when he arrives at the age of 21 years. I appoint Elizabeth Little my wife and the ordinary of York District and herself to appoint an other executor, 9 Aug 1823. Wm Little (LS), Wit: P. Sandefur, James Reeves, James Johnson.

YORK COUNTY SC WILL BOOK G 1820-1837

Pages 125-126: Warrant of appraisement on the estate of William Little directed to Mathew Carrel, Joseph Carrel, Ed Jennings, Wm. Thomson & Major Thos Roach & Samuel Roach 4 Nov 1823 returnable 20 January. Letters testamentary to Elizabeth Little 24 Nov 1823.

Pages 126-129: South Carolina, York District. Will of John Hart of district aforesaid... My beloved wife Rebecah Hart & my children should live & remain on the present premises whereon I now live as long as she remains my widow and she be comfortable supported, my children schooled & maintained from the land & negroes. To my five sons William, James, John, Harry & Aloes & other heirs, all that tract whereon I now live with other pieces which I have purchased & is now attached to the same, be equally divided according to quantity and quality. The remainder of my property, my wills & land attached, my negroes, stock, etc., be divided into two equal parts, the one part to be equally divided amongst my five sons and the other equally divided to my wife and two daughters Elizabeth & Polly. I appoint my wife Rebecka Hart, executrix, & John Hart, son of my brother William Hart decd, executor, 23 Nov 1823. John Hart (LS), Wit: Wiley Reeves, C. M. Hart.

Warrant of appraisement directed to John Gallard Esq., Jesse Miller, Danl Surges, John Cohran, Andrew Herren 6 Dec 1823 returnable 1 February. Letters testamentary to Rebeckah Hart and John Hart 6 Dec 1823.

Page 129: South Carolina, York District. Will of Robert Harris Junr.... After payment of debts, all my real and personal estate to my wife Matilda R. S. Harris. I appoint Robert Harris Senr and Richard Sadler, Esqrs., executors, 18 Oct 1823. Robert Harris (LS), Wit: Eleanor Harris, Josiah Harris.

Pages 129-131: 17 July 1817. Will of Margaret Adams of York District... To my daughter Catherine Carrigon one negro boy named Sam. To my daughter Jane Campbell $20. To my son Robert Adams my negro boy named Enos. To my son James S. Adams one cow. To my daughter Rachal Barnet one negro girl named Phillis, also my bed & furniture. To my daughter Margaret Watson my negro woman named Eme, also her child called Dinah. To my son Joseph Adams my horse named Dick. To my son William the balance of my cattle. My household furniture to be equally divided between my two daughters Rachel Barnet and Margaret Watson. I appoint Joseph & William Adams, exrs. Margaret Adams (Seal), Wit: Margaret Adams, Jas. S. Adams.

Warrant of appraisement directed to John Fuglenwyden, David Davis, Elias Jackson, James Davis and Josiah Davis 28 April 1824 returnable 25 June.

Pages 131-132: Warrant of appraisement on the estate of Daniel Bartlett, Benjamin Persons administrator, directed to John Springs, John Goodrich, Bartlet Meacham, John Jackson & Henry Meacham 8 July 1823 returnable 1 September. Letters testamentary to Benjn Person 8 July 1823.

Pages 132-133: Will of William Polk of York District... to my wife Elizabeth Polk all the land I have rented from the Catabaw Indians during her life and at her death to be equally divided among my three sons John, Charles & William. I appoint my wife Elizabeth executrix, 1 ___ 1824. Wm Polk, Wit: John S. Melvaten, John Huston, James Gettys.

Warrant of appraisement directed to Wm. Dunlap, James Harper, John Polk, Jesse Simmons, John McClellan 15 March 1824 returnable 15 May. Letters testamentary to Elizabeth Polk 15 March 1824.

Pages 134-136: Will of William Kendrick of York District... My wife Priscilla to live on my plantation & have her living off the same as long as she doth live & that she doth keep my children with her & all my other property. As my children grow up or marry and leave her, she may give them such help as she is able so that what they get shall be valued that at her death there may be an equal division made among them. As for my daughter Cinthia Berry, I have gave her one cow & calf, her bed & furniture, and one side saddle. I ordain my brother Joseph Kindrick and Joseph McKinzie, esqr., exrs., 4 June 1824. William Kindrick, Wit: Joseph McKenzie, Joseph Kendrick, James R. Reeves.

Warrant of appraisement directed to Samuel McCulloch, Joseph Clinton, James Duff, James McCulloch & John Riddle 8 July 1824 returnable 1 September. Letters testamentary to Joseph Kendrick and Joseph McKenzie 8 July 1824.

Pages 136-137: Will of Elizabeth Campbell, widow of Alexander Campbell, formerly of York District, deceased, being advanced in years... to my well beloved son John 325 acres of my land to be laid off to him in the lower end of the plantation including my dwelling house and all my occupied improvements, all the livestock of horses, cows, hoggs, sheep &c. I leave to the use of the Neelies Creek Associate Reformed Congregation ten acres of land to be laid off about the old meeting house including the graveyard, study house and spring. To the rest of my beloved children, my beloved sons Thomas, Alexander, William, and Samuel, and my beloved daughters Rosannah Brown & Mary Silleman and Elizabeth Campbell and Gincey Campbell, all the remainder of my land to be divided among them equally. To my daughter Rosannah a good woman's saddle which I allow my son John to purchase for her out of the property of stock &c I have left him. To my two beloved daughters Elizabeth & Gincey Campbell each their living in the dwelling house with their boarding & priviledge to work for themselves until they either marry or wish to be removed, at which time I give them their bedding and other furniture in the house and a good cow & Calf. I constitute my beloved sons John Campbell and William Campbell, my executors, 1 August 1821. Elizabeth Campbell (mark) (LS), Wit: Thos Reid, Elizabeth Campbell, Jane Campbell.

Pages 137-140: South Carolina, York District. Will of Alexander Faires... To my son Jess, Sampson a negro man slave and Bid and Mariah negro girl slave and their increase. To my son Thomas my negro man slave Levi. To my sons Thomas, William & Samuel and Alexander and my daughter Jennet wife of

William Wallis, the following negroes to be divided equally between them viz Mary a negro woman, Joe a negro man, and Cintha & Lavenia negro girls and their increase. The above negroes remain with my son Jesse during the natural life of my wife Jennet Faires to assist to support her except Levi who is at this time with my son Thomas and I allow him to remain with him. I wish it to be understood by all my other children not mentioned in the above will that I have given them what I thought to be their just shares of my property. I appoint my son Jesse Faires executor, 16 Feb 1824. Alex'r Faires (Seal), Wit: James Carothers, Alsey Fuller.

Warrant of appraisement directed to James Carothers, James McKee, Alsey Fuller, William Carothers & Samuel Carothers 10 Aug 1824 returnable 1 October. Letters testamentary to Jesse Faires 10 Aug 1824.

Pages 140-142: Will of John Chambers Senr of York District, farmer... To my daughter Sarah Wherry's children and their heirs a negro woman named Hal & her negro girl child named Rose. To my son William Chambers all my tract of land in the Indian boundry whereon I now reside and a negro man named George and a negro boy named Andrew. To my daughter Mary a negro woman named Easther and a negro boy named Leonard & a negro girl named Zenah. To my daughter Elizabeth a negro boy named Jack & a negro girl named Mary & a negro girl named Nance. All my household & kitchen furniture to my two daughters Mary & Elizabeth, and each of them two cows & calves. Also to my daughter Mary a sorrel mare named Sally and to my daughter Elizabeth a bay horse named Isaac. The remainder of any property to be divided equally amongst my children. I appoint my son William Chambers and John Latta, exrs., 2 May 1824. John Chambers Senr (LS), Wit: W. M. Dixon, Saml Wherry.

Warrant of appraisement directed to Halcot Evans, James Workman, William Davis, Joseph Steel and William Johnson 18 Oct 1824 returnable 15 December. Letters testamentary to William Chambers and John Latta 18 Oct 1824.

Pages 142-144: Will of James Armstrong of District of York, being far advanced in years... All my just debts to be paid. To my beloved children William and James & Thomas with their marriage dividend which I have divided off to them at the time of their marriage, to each of them $1. To my beloved son John the plantation whereon I now live and my waggon and the one half of all my other personal property except my brown bay horse. To my beloved daughter Elizabeth my brown bay horse and the other half of my personal property. I appoint my son John and Thomas Reid, exrs., 25 March 1816. James Armstrong (LS), Wit: Thomas Reid, Nancy Wright (X), Mary Reid (X).

Warrant of appraisement directed to Hugh Drennan, William Drennan, Thomas Wright, Matthew Ferrell and William Gilmore 18 Oct 1824 returnable 15 December. Letters testamentary to John Armstrong and Thomas Reid 18 Oct 1824.

## YORK COUNTY SC WILL BOOK G 1820-1837

Pages 145-146: January 19th, 1822. South Carolina, York District. Will of Thomas Barron of district aforesaid... To my wife Elizabeth a sufficient and comfortable support during her life or widowhood of any part of my land on which Samuel has to the south side of the road leading straight to my brother William. I leave to his heirs Samuel Barron in consideration of his trade to pay cash of his sisters $50 the remaining part of my land to be for my other four sons, the dividing line to start at the mouth of the second draft below the ford on Kenan's line, up to Joseph Laney's, each of my boys paying to each of their sisters $100 or the value thereon in horse and saddle. My executors John Berry son of Roger, John Soward, and David Watson. Thos Barron, Wit: Zenos Milan, William Barron.

Warrant of appraisement directed to Wm Barron, John Barron, Harman[?] Alexander, Wm Cathcart & Wm. Shaw 19 Oct 1824 returnable 20 December. Letters testamentary to John Berry son of Roger Berry & John Soward, 19 Oct 1824.

Pages 146-148: Will of John Cooper, 17 September 1812, of York District... To my beloved wife Elizabeth Cooper and my daughter Margaret Cooper the tract of land on which I now live with 100 acres adjoining it on the north side bought of Livingston & 56 acres on the south west side bought of William Cooper, to be divided agreeable to quantity & quality into three equal shares: one part to my beloved wife to occupy and possessed and to dispose of as she thinks proper, the other two shares to my daughter Margaret. To my wife one negro woman named Isbel and at her death to my daughter Margaret Cooper. To my wife one half of all my stock of horses, cows & hogs, the other half to my daughter Margaret. To my son James Cooper all my claim or legacy on my father's estate in York County, Pennsylvania. To my son Robert Cooper five shillings. To my son John Cooper five shillings. To my daughter Elizabeth Davidson five shillings. To my daughter Mary Wallace five shillings. To my son William Cooper five shillings. I appoint Robert Cooper, exr. John Cooper (LS), Wit: Elias Mellon, Benjamin Garvin, James Y. Wallace.

Pages 148-150: Will of Elizabeth Gault of York District... To my oldest son John Gault the one half of his father's clothing with the whole of his father's shirts also the books that was bought for him and an equal divide of the remainder of my books with the rest of my children, also two silver tea spoons. To my second son James Gault the remaining half of his father's clothes and an equal share in my books with the rest of my children & two silver tea spoons. To my oldest daughter Barborough Gault an equal share of my books with the rest of my children and half of my furniture & half of my wearing apparel and the largest trunk & largest looking glass, one brass candlestick &one flax iron, my shovel & fire tongs. To my second daughter Eleanor Eliza Gault the remaining half of my furniture and wearing apparel, my smallest trunk & smaller looking glass & my spinning wheel & hand irons, one brass candlestick & waiter and one flat iron, and an equal share of my books. To my third son Joseph Gault my bigg house bible & an equal share of my books. To my fourth son George William Gault a silver watch and an equal share of my books. I appoint Robert Love Senr exr., 23 May 1823. Elizabeth Gault, Wit: D. Lacey, Saml Givins.

Warrant of appraisement directed to Francis Irwin, James M. Love, Mitchel Love, John Hope & Samuel Ash 17 Nov 1824 returnable 15 January.

Pages 150-152: Will of Zadock Darby of York District... To my wife Mary Darby the one half of the plantation whereon I now live including the dwelling house & spring during her life time & at her death to my grandson Zadock D. Smith.. Also to my wife Mary my negro man Lemon, his wife Fanny & her two children Garland & Sarah & my negro boy Jim, also my stock including horses, black cattle, hogs, sheep, etc. To my daughter Delilah Darby alias Delilah Jingles the plantation whereon she now lives during her life & at her death to be equally divided between her children. To my daughter Jane Darby alias Jane Smith the other half of the plantation I now live on and at her death to my grandson Zadock D. Smith. I appoint my wife Mary Darby, William Campbell of York District, Isaac Price of Macklenburgh, North Carolina, exrs., 27 July 1824. Zadock Darby, Wit: David Johnston, John Glenn, Franklin Glenn.

Warrant of appraisement directed to James Glenn, Robert Campbell, David Johnston, Robert Johnston & Richard Horsley 6 Nov 1824 returnable 1 January. Letters testamentary to Mary Darby 6 Nov 1824.

Pages 153-154: Will of David Johnston of York District... I desire that a vandew be made by my executors after my decease and all of my property to be sold. To my two beloved sisters Eliza & Evaline Johnston & my sister Nancy Woods children and brothers are better provided for all my monies arising from my estate to be kept on interest until they are married or become 30 years of age, & then to be equally divided between them two Eliza & Evaline Johnston. I appoint my brothers John & Robt Johnston executors, 5 Dec 1824.

Warrant of appraisement directed to Richard Barnet, Wm. Mayson, Thos McKee Eqr., Hugh Riddle & Andrew Hill, 1 Jan 1825 returnable 20 March. Letters testamentary to John Johnston 21 Jan 1825.

Pages 154-156: Will of James Mason of Mecklinburgh County, North Carolina... To my wife Nancy Mason during her life or widowhood the whole of the plantation I now reside on with the plantation between the river & Crowders Creek, also that part of the plantation my son Wm Mason now resides on except the part willed to him, the said Wm also the use & sold property of my ferry with all my stock, furniture, etc. To my son Wm. Mason the tract of land he now resides on in the following order adj. Resin Woods, Dr. Alison's old spring, Lid Alison's old house, along the publick road to the meadow branch, that I purchased of Allison. To my son John Mason the tract of land he is now living on & a negro boy named Jack which property shall not be subject to pay any debt of said John Mason. To my son Thompson Mason, all the two tracts of land purchased of Wm. Reeves decd estate & Wm

Reeves, also a negro boy named Isaac. To my four sons viz James Mason, David M. Mason, Richard Mason & Clayborn Mason, all the land left to my wife after her decease or future marriage, the ferry to be exclusively the joint property of my two youngest sons Richard & Clayborn. I lend to my daughter Sally Smith three negroes viz a woman named Nancy and two girls named Celia & Paulina. To my daughter Polly Bailey four negroes, viz Bridget, Joan, Elvira & Caroline. At the decease or marriage of my wife my three oldest sons have each a negro of the three then youngest to be chosen by seniority. I bequeath to my son Wm the negro boy George he has now in his possession. I appoint my wife Nancy Mason & my two sons Wm. Mason & James Mason, exrs., 18 Jan 1822. James Mason (LS), Wit: J. Rooker, Jno D. McClean, Jas Carothers. A true copy. Test Isaac Alexander, C. M. C.

Pages 156-159: Will of Priscilla Heart of York District, being sorely afflicted... To my son Charles half of the benefit of my machine and what property he has received it being understood that he is to pay the girls for the plantation on which he now lives as his note does more fully declare. I also wish 100 acres of my plantation on Morrisons Creek to be divided equally with my sons Charles & John. To my daughter Jane's children an equal part with my daughters of the ballance of my plantation on Morrisons Creek. To my son John half of the benefit of my machine & as before expressed an equal share with Charles of 100 acres of my plantation & I also give him my sorrel horse Figure. To my daughter Margaret my negro boy Jefferson & my sorrel horse Hector & also a beaurow which is called her own. I also give her an equal part with my other daughters Sarah, Priscilla, Elizabeth & Harriet of the price of the plantation on which my son Charles now lives, and an equal share of the ballance of my plantation. I give my daughter Sarah one negro woman Sinthey & an equal share with my daughters Margaret, Priscilla, Elizabeth & Harriet of the price of the plantation on which Charles now lives. I give my daughter Elizabeth my negro boy Dick, and an equal share with my others daughters of the price of the plantation. To my daughter Harriet a negro girl Lessey which said girl I have bought with the $400 left to Harriet by her father's will and an equal share in the price of the plantation. I also give her a negro woman Nancy. I allow my daughter Sarah to give $200 of the money that is due from Charles to my daughter Priscilla. I give my daughter Elizabeth my half round tables & to my daughter Harriet my silver spoons large & Small and my riding chair. I appoint my son John Hart & my brother John L. Miller, exrs., 16 Sept 1824. Priscilla Heart (LS), Wit: Jas M. Harris, Robt Miller, Margt M. Harris.

Warrant of appraisement directed to John Gallan, Jessee Miller, John Anderson, Saml Roach & Robt Miller 25 March 1825 returnable 25 May. Letters testamentary to John Hart 25 March 1825.

Pages 159-160: Decr 6th 1824. Will of Wm Hemingway of York District... To my wife one fourth part of my whole estate, both real & personal. The remainder to my three sons John Hemingway, Albert Hemingway and Wm. Hemingway in equal proportion. The proceeds of the crops be divided in equal proportion between my wife *& my sons John & Albert and they pay my son Wm $275 per annum for 6 years in lieu of his share of the crops to complete his education. I will that among my just debt John Hemingway be paid a note he has on me amounting to $650 & Albert Hemingway a note he has on me amounting to $150. I ordain John Hemingway & Albert Hemingway, exrs., 6 Dec 1824. William Hemingway (LS), Wit: Wm. Wallace, James H. Cooper, John Murphy, James Porter.

Warrant of appraisement directed to Robert Love, Wm. Grey, John Hope, J. M. Love & Alfred Moore Esqr., 7 March 1824 returnable 1 May.

Page 161: March 30th 1821. Will of Robert Turner of the district of York... to my beloved wife Rosanah Turner all my household furniture and one cow. To my son George Turner the plantation I now live on at my wife's death, and it is my will that he neither sell nor make away with any part of it during her natural life. My son George Turner to have all my smith tools and farming utensils. My son Robert Turner have a tract of land in the barrens, and to my son John Turner $2 and to my son Christopher Turner $2 and to Elizabeth Cresswell $2. To my son Wm Turner $2. To my daughter Sarah Henderson $2. and to Ann Campbell $2. Robert Turner (X), Wit: John Currens, Robt Patrick B. S., Daniel Currence.

Pages 161-162: The will of Sarah Sumner Ellis of the State of South Carolina, and District of York, single woman... to my beloved cousin Priscilla Fox, my negro girl Esther with her future increase with my bureau and two gold rings. To my beloved cousin Robert Ellis, my negro boy Austin. To my cousin Thomas Sumner Ellis, my negro man Stephen. To my beloved cousin Elizabeth Montgomery, $500 to be lived out of any monies belonging to my estate. My feather bed and furniture to my beloved aunt Elizabeth Ellis. What monies may be due to me by virtue of the will of my deceased Grandfather Robert Ellis of Northampton County, State of North Carolina, to be divided between my four within named cousins by my executors. My lands lying in York District on Tools fork of Fishing Creek be sold and the nett proceeds to be equally divided between my four within named cousins. I appoint my worthy friend Thomas Sumner Ellis and Jacob Fox Junior executors, dated 28 May 1822. Sally S. Ellis (LS), Wit: Tho Robertson, John Robertson.

Pages 163-165: South Carolina, York District. Will of Roger Berry of district of York... To my two sons James D. Berry and William Berry all the lands that I own or possess in my own right to be equally divided between them. If either die without issue, then the share to the deceased to my son Andrew L. Barry in full as was his deceased brothers. To my son Andrew L. Berry a bauld two years old colt with white legs, also a new saddle. I appoint my son John Barry and my aforesaid James D. Barry, exrs., 25 June 1825. Roger Barry, Wit: G. Davis, George Kidd, Cordelia Pierce.

Warrant of appraisement directed to George Davis, James Briant Senr, Jas Briant Junr, John Yarborough, and Cordelia Pierce 19 Sept 1825 returnable 15 November. Appraisers sworn 1 October 1825: Jas Brian, John Yarborough,

## YORK COUNTY SC WILL BOOK G 1820-1837

Cordelia Pierce before Benj. Chambers, Q.U. Letters testamentary to John Berry and James D. Berry 19 Sept 1824.

Pages 166-167: South Carolina, York District. Warrant of appraisement on the estate of Sarah Sumner Ellis directed to Thomas Robinson Esq., Hawket Evans, James Workman, Richard Sadler & Benjn Rowel 2 May 1825 returnable 1 July. Letters testamentary to Thos S. Ellis 2 May 1825.

Pages 167-168: Will of Jane Venable of District of York... To my granddaughter Mary Watson one feather bed and furniture. To my beloved son William Venable all the property I am possessed of at my death and I appoint William Watson as his guardian while my son William Venable does live to dispose of the property and put the money to my son William's use. I appoint John Peters Esquire & Francis Henry, esqrs., 15 Oct 1824. Jane Venable (X) (Seal), Wit: Robert Wallace, Mathew Watson, Wm. Love.

Warrant of appraisement directed to Robt Ellison Esq., Hugh McWhorter, James Quinn Sen, 19 July 1825 returnable 20 Sept. William Watson with a will annexed applied for administration, 12 July 1825.

Pages 169-172: Will of John Boyd of the District of York... To my beloved wife Jane Boyd one negro woman named Patsy, the plantation I now live on, my negroes Baccus, Primus, Phebe, Peggy & Henry, household and kitchen furniture. To my daughter Eliza Glen all such property as she has received viz one bay mare, bridle & saddle, one cow and calf, one bed and furniture, one spinning wheel and cards, one negro girl named Violet. To my daughter Sally Boyd one bed & furniture, bed, spinning wheel and cards, one sorrel mare, bridle & saddle, one cow & calf, negro girl named Jane. To my son Thomas Boyd one roan colt, bridle and saddle, one shot gun. To my two sons David Boyd & Thomas Boyd the plantation whereon I now live after the death or marriage of my wife, then to suffer their then unmarried sisters to remain in the mansion house. To my grandson John F. Glen $100 in cash when he arrives to the age of 21. To my five youngest daughters Jency, Pemely, Mary, Clarissa and Margaret, the negroes exception the two already willed to my sons after the death or marriage of my wife. My son David Boyd should cultivate ten acres of land adj. the land he now cultivates on the river. I appoint my wife and my friends Jno Glen & David Boyd, exrs., 27 April 1825. John Boyd (LS), Wit: William Mason, David Johnston, J. E. McKenzie.

Warrant of appraisement directed to Wm Mason, Mathew Harper Sen, Aaron Wood, Robert Campbell Sen., James Glen, 16 July 1825 returnable 15 September. Letters testamentary to David Boyd and John Glen 16 July 1825.

Pages 172-174: Will of Richard Venable of the District of York... To my mother Jane Venable all my property, 159 acres of land, my two horses, cattle, hogs and gun, $150 of notes on William Love, one on James Hemphill $10, one harrow and $10 left me by my father John Venable. I appoint my mother Jane Venable and William Watson, exrs., 2 Sept 1811. Richard Venable (X), Wit: John Carson, David M. Davis, John Falls.

Warrant of appraisement directed to James Quinn, Hugh McWhorter, 19 July 1825 returnable 20 Sept. Letters testamentary to William Watson 19 July 1825.

Pages 174-176: South Carolina, York District. Will of Francis Adams of district aforesaid... To my daughter Martha Byers my negro woman Milly with all my cupboard and kitchen furniture, also my Bible and looking glass. To my son Wm. Adams, all the remainder of my property consisting of notes & household furniture. My wearing apparel I allow to be divided in the following manner: to my son Wm Adams my suit of black broad cloth, also to my son Francis my suit of homespun, to my grandson Simpson Adams my great coat and as many of my small clothes as he thinks property to choose. Also my son John Adams my hat if he should never come to this country, I allow it to Williamson Byers, also to Martha Byers my stock of hogs and sheep. I appoint Thos Williams Esqr., William Brown and Williamson Byers, exr., 2 Sept 1824. Francis Adams (LS), Wit: Nancy McLaw, Wm. B. Erwin.

Pages 174-175: Warrant of appraisement on the estate of Elizabeth Campbell directed to John Spencer, Thos Wylie, Thos Patton, Holloway Simmons and James Ross, 21 July 1825. Letters testamentary to John Campbell 21 July 1825.

Pages 176-178: South Carolina, York District. Will of Samuel Berry late of district aforesaid deceased declared by him by word of mouth 22 July 1825. My desire is that my daughter Mary Barry shall have my negro boy Jess which I consider she is entitled to for her services as she is my eldest child and has been a good girl and always with me and as to the little black horse he is her own given to her by her brother Samuel. The balance of my property I wish to be sold and equally divided amongst my children. Wm. Barry, Hugh Hartness, James Meek. Proved by the oath of Wm. Barry, Hugh Hartness, James Meek 15 July 1825 before W. Jamison, Q.U.

Citation. Whereas Wm Barry with the nuncupative will of Saml Barry deceased annext applied for letters of adm, 3 Sept 1825. Warrant of appraisement directed to Wm Jamison Esq., John Thompson Esq., John Pilcher, Robt Hays & Alexr Thompson 25 Sept 1825 returnable 20 November.

Pages 178-181: South Carolina, York District. Will of Joseph Gebbie Senior of York District... to my wife Mary Gebbie one third part of my estate for the term of her natural life and after her decease the same to my five daughters Mary Perce, Urcilla Garvin, Saline Givens, Eliza Gebbie & Matilda Gebbie, to be equally divided among them. To my daughter Mary Perce 100 acres of land whereon she now lives, also 100 acres of land around what we call the still house to my daughter Urcilla. To my two granddaughters Elizabeth B. and Marget one seventh part of all the remainder of my estate real or personal, and also one sixth part of what I have before divided to my wife at her decease, they both shall share with their five aunts before name at the death of my wife. To my son Joseph Gebbie the tract of land that I usually call my saw mill place being north of east from my mansion house, the seat on which I first built my cotton gin. All my personal estate be sold at publick auction and after my wife shall have her third divided, I give to my grandson Robert W. the son of my daughter Rachel who is deceased $600. I appoint my said wife executrix and my son in law James H. Owens exr., 23 Sept 1825. Joseph Gebbie (X), Wit: James Kerr, William Kerr, Thos D. Kidd.

Warrant of appraisement directed to George Davis, Wm. Fewell, John Miller, Walker Benson & James D. Berry 26 Oct 1825 returnable 20 December. Letters testamentary to James H. Owens 20 Oct 1825.

Pages 181-183: Will of John Muldoon of York District being in an advanced stage of life... I leave all my property to be equally divided between my beloved sister Sarah Johnston & my beloved nephew George Straight. I appoint James Poag, exr., 15 Oct 1825. John Muldoon (X) (LS), Wit: Thos Reid, John Blalock (X), James Poag.

Warrant of appraisement directed to Wm Chambers, Saml McCulloch, Wm. Drenan, Hugh Drenan & Thos Bates 18 Oct 1825 returnable 15 December. Letters testamentary to James Poag 8 Oct 1825.

Pages 183-185: South Carolina, York District. Will of Solomon Hill of district aforesaid... I will that my executors do sell all my real estate consisting of the plantation on which I now live and also a tract of land on beaver dam creek known as a part of the Latimore tract which I bought from Isaac Suggs, and out of the proceeds my executors pay all my debts and with the balance of the money to purchase some plantation which may be suitable for the family. To my wife Nancy Hill all my personal estate of every description except as hereafter excepted and to her the tract of land which shall be purchased. My son Albert Potts[?] Hill shall receive a classical and colegiate education. I appoint my wife Nancy and my son W. R. Hill, exrs., 5 Oct 1825. Solomon Hill (LS), Wit: Samuel W. Berry, H. J. Cathcart M. D., R. Hill.

Warrant of appraisement directed to Wm Mason, William D. Henry, Isaac Campbell and John Jackson 26 Oct 1825 returnable 20 January. Letters testamentary to Wm. R. Hill 24 Oct 1825.

Pages 185-187: Will of John McCaw Senr.... to my beloved wife Mary McCaw during her life the use of the property of which I may die possessed. To my three sons Robert, William & John, one dollar to each. To Mary Byers wife of David Byers a negro woman Rose and her increase. To Ann Smith wife of Robert Smith, Peggy Will, and Melitia with her increase. To Robert McCaw & John McCaw Junr for the use of Elizabeth Meek, Pamelia Gunning and Sarah Sims, all the money which shall remain at my death or the death of Mary McCaw aforesaid. I appoint Robert McCaw and Robert Smith, John McCaw Junr, exrs., 10 March 1821. John McCaw Senr (LS), Wit: Clement Byers, Saml McCulloch, James Smith Junr.

Warrant of appraisement directed to Mijamin Smith, Hugh Cain, David Byers, Eli Meek & Galbraith Caldwell 15 Nov 1825 returnable 15 November [sic]. Letters testamentary to Robert Smith 17 Nov 1825.

Pages 187-190: Will of Hugh Miller of the District of York... To my son John Miller the one half of what is denominated my Gill tract of land on which he now lives, by original grant 340 acres. To the legal heirs & representatives of Hughey Miller my son the remaining half of said Gill tract with this reserve that my son Hugh Miller shall & may occupy said land during his life not to sell said land to any person. All my stock of negroes to be equally divided among my children. To my granddaughter Hannah Hogge a bed and furniture and $400. My stock of horses, cattle, hogs, plantation tools & household furniture to be sold & the proceeds equally divided among my children. I leave my wife Jane Miller to the care of my heirs. I appoint my son John Miller, John King, William Jameson Esqr., exrs., 23 Jan 1824. Hugh Miller (LS), Wit: Jas Anderson, Hugh Miller Junr, John Miller.

Warrant of appraisement directed to John King, John Gill, Samuel Givens Esqr., Robert Wilson & Samuel King 24 Nov 1825 returnable 20 Jan. Letters testamentary to John Miller and William Jamieson 24 Nov 1825.

Page 190: Will of Eliza Ann Anderson... to my grandmother Mary Clerk all my estate of every king in the hands of Charles Stone of Barnwell District... I appoint Mansfield Gordan, Green Sandefer, Thomas Simpson and Robert Cooper, exrs., 12 Dec 1825. Eliza Ann Anderson (seal), Wit: John C. Tipping, Philip C. Sandefer, Sarah L. Sadler.

Page 191: Will of John McFarlan of District of York... My estate real be sold to the higher bidder and the money arising therefrom to be divided equally among nine of my children to wit Wm. McFarlan, Rebecka Harris, Josiah McFarlan, Wylie McFarlin, Seala McFarlin, Paletha McFarlin, Peter McFarlin, Richard McFarlin & Martha Liles, to be paid to them on the day of their marriage or when they arrive to the age of 21. My personal estate be sold in manner above after giving to Rebeckah Harris a cow or the value thereof. 9 Dec 18__. John McFarlin (LS), Wit; Danl Gilmore, Zadock Packard, James Wylie.

Pages 191-194: Will of Hugh Wells... to my beloved wife Mary, all the property which I now possess except such as I do hereafter dispose of otherwise. My daughter Isabel to be maintained while she stays with my wife as one of my family. I give to my negro Will Blacksmith provided he behaves himself orderly to my wife and uses diligence in his business $200 to be paid in 3 years from my decease out of his labor in the shop. At my wife's decease the whole of my property divided equally among my six children viz Cintha, Thomas, Margaret, Ibby, William & Larence[?]. I appoint Doctor John S. Bratton, William Guy & my wife Mary Wells, exrs., 3 Dec 1825. Hugh Wells (LS), Wit: Robert Ash, Duncan Wyley, James Dale, Geo Dale.

Warrant of appraisement directed to Nathan Moore, Samuel Moore, Samuel Rainey, Alfred Moore & George Dale 20 Dec 1825 returnable 20 Feb. Letters testamentary to John S. Bratton, William Guy, and Mary Wells 20 Dec 1825.

YORK COUNTY SC WILL BOOK G 1820-1837

Pages 194-195: Warrant of appraisement on the estate of Eliza Ann Anderson directed to Samuel Lowrie, Minor Sadler, James Johnston, Jonathan Kuykendall and Archibald Hannah & Peter Harris, 10 Jan 1826 returnable 30 March. Letters testamentary to Robert Cooper 10 Jan 1826.

Pages 195-196: 29 March 1800. Will of Alexander Stewart of County of York... To my daughter Mary five shillings sterling. To my son James 200 acres of land whereon I now live deeded to me by John Martin with all the improvements on the same, my wearing clothes, my armed chair and the remainder of a piece of thick cloth after my daughters Rosannah and Elizabeth gets what they need of it. TO my daughter Catherine five shillings sterling. To my daughter Rosannah my 100 acres of land next William Carson with the full half of my stock and household furniture, bay mare, armed chair excepted. To my daughter Elizabeth my 100 acres of land next to Thomas Wallace with the other half of stock & household furniture. My bar horse to be equally divided between my son James & my two daughters Rosannah & Elizabeth. I appoint my friend William Love Esquire and Thomas Wallace, exrs. Alexander Stewart (mark) (LS), Wit: William Love, Michael Stewart (mark), Thomas Wallace.

Pages 196-197: South Carolina, York District. Will of Thomas Turner of the district aforesaid... To my beloved daughter Keziah Turner all my money, securities for money, goods, chattles, estate & effects. I appoint William Jamison sole executor, 20 Feb 1823. Thomas Turner (X) (LS), Wit: Helena Garrison, Milton Garrison.

Pages 197-200: South Carolina, York District. Will of Thomas McDaniel... I desire that the present crop of cotton now on hand may be immediately sold after my decease and out of the monies all my just debts and funeral expense be paid. To my wife Mary McDaniel the use of my land or plantation whereon I now live until my youngest daughter Anna Sims McDaniel marries or comes of age, then this land to be sold to the highest bidder. After the sale $1100 arising out of the sale to be given to my wife Mary for her to purchase land which land shall be hers as long as she lives or remains my widow, after which this land shall be sold and the money evenly divided between my three daughters Catherine, Sarah and Anna, or their heirs; also my four negroes Will, Anna, Scicilly and William, and my horse Snips and a mule Jack, and my riding gig, also my whole stock of cattle, hoggs, and sheep and household furniture for her to divide among my three daughters. I give to my daughter Catherine Christmas McDaniel my give negroes Winna, Jerry, Moriah, Jude and Milla. To my daughter Sarah Gist McDaniel my six negroes Silva, Caroline, Sally, Nelson, Washington and Abram. To my daughter Anna Sims McDaniel my five negroes Bill, Scylla, Harriet, Eliza & Pelina, also a mule called Buck and $220. All the rest of my estate may be equally divided among my several children herein before named. I appoint my friends Joseph Gist and William Sims Senr and John Gist, exrs., 4 Oct 1825. Thomas McDaniel (LS), Wit: James A. McCool, John black (mark), Jacob Black.

Letters testamentary to William Sims Senr 19 Jan 1825. Warrant of appraisement directed to James McCool, Joseph Reed Esqr., William Thompson, Jacob Black and Thomas Walker 19 Jan 1826 returnable 15 March.

Pages 200-202: South Carolina, York District. Will of Isabella [Barnhill] Barronhill... To my son Robert Barnhill, five shillings. To my daughter Hannah Glass five shillings. To my daughter Isabella Barronhill $25 and one cow. To my son William Barnhill five shillings. To my daughter Samuel Barnhill my stilyard. To my son John Barnhill all that parcel of land that I live on, farming tools, horses, hogs, sheep and cattle, with household furniture after Ibby gets hers. To my daughter Sarah Armstrong five shillings. To my daughter Mary McGinis five shillings. John Barnhill and Samuel Barnhill, exrs., 26 May 1815. Isabella Barnhill (mark), Wit: Andrew Kerr, Morison Whitaker, Catherine Kerr.

Letters testamentary to John Barnhill 20 Feb 1826. Warrant of appraisement directed to Saml Carrell, Henry Carrell, Joseph Wood, Saml Hemphill and David Jackson 20 Feb 1826 returnable 20 Feb next.

Pages 203-206: Will of Charles Brumfield of District of York... To my beloved wife Elizabeth Brumfield all that tract of land whereon I now live on Fishing Creek in the district aforesaid, with all the appurtenances, and a negro slave named Roary and a slave named Tom, a negro woman slave named Hannah and a negro woman slave named Sue, which said slaves belonged to her before our intermarriage, also my two mares old Bet, young Bet and young Bet's two colts. A plantation on Fishing Creek adj. the land whereon I now reside and James Briant, George Davis, being the tract which I lately purchased from William Martin, 330 acres, to be sold at publick sale to the highest bidder. To my son James Brumfield of the state of Georgia $300, from the sales of the land, etc. To my granddaughter the daughter of my late son Isaac Brumfield deceased, the Christian name of which said child I understand to be Caroline, $600 when she arrives at the age of 21 or marries. All the rest of my estate to be divided amongst my children Elizabeth McCorkle, John Brumfield, Charity Neely, James Brumfield, Mary Massey, and Jesse Brumfield. I appoint my son Jessee Brumfield and my son in law Thomas Neely, exrs., 26 Sept 1815. Charles Brumfield (LS), Wit: Robert Clendinen, John Feemster, Hugh B. Davidson.

Letters testamentary to Jesse Brumfield 29 April 1826. Warrant of appraisement directed to James Briant Senr, James Briant Junr, John Berry, Wm. Wallace and James D. Berry 20 April 1826 returnable 20 June.

Pages 206-209: Will of Josiah Hambright of the District of York... To my wife Elizabeth all my lands willed to me by my father known by the name of the Regin place and BuckHill place, with all utensils of husbandry, stock of cattle, hogs & sheep, during her life or widowhood and at her death of marriage the same to be sold and equally divided among my 4 children viz Elise, Terry, Gilley and Martain. My wife Elizabeth and Gilly Moss my father in law, exrs.,

21 May 1826. Josiah Hambright (LS), Wit: Frederick Hambright, John Hambright, Wm. Quin.

Letters testamentary on the will of Josiah Hambright to Elizabeth Hambright and Gilly Moss 15 June 1826. Warrant of appraisement directed to Wm Quin, Geo Whistenant, Frederick Hambright, Henry Howser and John Hambright 15 June 1826 returnable 15 August.

Pages 209-212: South Carolina, York District. Will of James Ross Senior of district aforesaid... To my beloved daughter Catherine Miller my silver spectackles and Bible. To my beloved daughter Catherine Miller and Harriet A. Chambers, al my beds and bed clothing. to my beloved son Arthur Ross all my wearing apparel and in case he should die before me, to my beloved grandson Franklin Miller. The rest of my property real and personal including my lands, negroes, debts due, etc., to be appraised and exposed to sale and the proceeds be divided into seven equal shares to Arthur Ross, my daughter Catherine Miller, my beloved daughter Dorcus Gordan, my beloved daughter Messina Adams, my beloved daughter Harriet A. Chambers and I wish her to take the house & lot formerly occupied by myself and at present occupied by James H. Owens on the Main Street in Yorkville is she wishes to take her share in this way then the little house on that lot by Jos G. Martin Esq., and by him sold to Benjamin Chambers and by him sold to me is appraised and to go to her. To my granddaughter Amelia Bass and Ann M. Sitgreaves and to their children one seventh part of the sale of my property. To my beloved daughter in law Margaret Ross and to my grandsons and granddaughters James Y. Ross, Andrew Ross, Dorcas Ann Ross and Abigail T. Ross, one seventh part. I appoint my friends George Ross and Benjamin Chambers, exrs., 4 Sept 1825. James Ross (Seal), Wit: K. Clendenin, T. W. L. M. Neel, James Rogers.

Citation to cite the heirs of James Ross 22 June instant to shew case why the said will should not be established as valid, 10 June 1826. June 22d 1826. The last will of James Ross Sen was proven in solemn form. Letters testamentary to Col. Geo Ross 22 June 1826. Warrant of appraisement 23 June 1826 returnable 20 August [names not included].

Pages 213-214: 19 June 1826. Will of William Love of York District... To my beloved wife Isabella during her life my house & plantation, also my stock of every kind, negroes, waggon, farming utensils, except those things hereafter disposed of, viz., to my daughter Jenny two beds and furniture, one colt; to my daughter Isabella, two beds & furniture. To my son Hugh the remainder of my estate, my plantation house and furniture, stock, negro boy Frank, waggon & farming utensils & blacksmith tools provided he pay in one year after his mother's death ten dollars to each of my five children viz Robert, William, Martha, John and Andrew, if they demand in two years after their mother's death. I appoint my wife Isabella and my son Hugh exrs. William Love (Seal), Wit: Robt Love, Mijamin Smith, Katherine G. Cain. Proved by the oath of Mijamin Smith 28 Aug 1826 and at same time qualified Isabella Love and Hugh Love executors.

Warrant of appraisement on the estate of William Love Esquire 28 Aug 1826 returnable 1 November [names not included].

Pages 214-215: Will of Sarah Hannah, widow of Col. Wm Hannah decd... To my five children now living with me Archibald, Jane, Ann, Margaret & Sarah Hannah, my real and personal estate as long as they live in a family capacity. If any of the above named children should marry then it shall be the duty of my executor to pay such child or children one fifth part of the value of my personal estate except two negroes Ned & Lucy (which two negroes I wish to continue with the remainder of my unmarried children as long as any two of them lives in a family together). It is my will that these negroes shall serve which of my children they pledge their fidelity and zeal in my service inclining me to give them choice. To my son William Hannah one bed and furniture known by the name of William's bed. To my grandchildren by my son James five shillings their father having rec'd his full proportion of my estate. I appoint my son Archibald sole executor, 3 March 1824. Sarah Hanna (LS), Wit: Mansfield Gordon, Catherin Gordon, Robert cooper.

Pages 215-218: Will of Hermon Alexander of York District, South Carolina... to my wife the negro woman Minta to be for use so long as she liveth and then to be equally divided among the surviving heirs at my wife's death. To my daughter Emeline a negro girl called Melia. To my daughter Elizabeth a negro girl called Eva. Also unto Emeline Moore a little girl now living in my family if she continues to live with my wife or until said Emeline marries, I allow her a bed and bedding, cow & calf, and $100 clear of interest any time within the space of seven years. to my wife a bed & bedding, a cow and calf. The balance of my property to be exposed to sale and enough of it sold to pay my debts and then a just estimate to be made of the neat amount, each of my sons Alfred, Oliver, Albert & Hasting to have an equal division of the same. I appoint my sons Eli, Oliver & Albert Gallatin, exrs., 5 Oct 1826. hermon Alexander (LS), Wit: James Wilson, Wm. Barron, ____ Carrol.

Letters testamentary to Eli, Oliver & Albert Gallatin Alexander, 16 Oct 1826. Warrant of appraisement 7 Oct 1826 returnable 15 Sept next.

Pages 218-219: Will of Hugh Whiteside of York District, planter... To my beloved wife Margaret my dwelling house & her living & maintenance on my land during her life, also one half of my house furniture & kitchen utensils during her life and at her death I allow her to have the disposal of the one half of my kitchen utensils and one bed and furniture, tow cows. To my two sons James and Robert my plantation whereon I now live, my son James who is nor married I allow the divide highest on the river to have immediately possession and my son Robert to have the lower divide to have possession at the death of my wife. My said two sons to pay over unto my three daughters $200 each, at my death, my three daughters Margaret, Susannah, and Betsy. I appoint my said two sons James & Robert, exrs., 2 April 1825. Hugh Whiteside (LS), Wit: Thos Reid, Wm. Love (X).

## YORK COUNTY SC WILL BOOK G 1820-1837

Pages 219-222: Will of Abraham Miller of York District, being somewhat in an advanced stage of life... To my beloved wife Elva one negro woman named Poll & a negro man named Ben, also a negro girl named Minta, all my household & kitchen furniture and utensils expect my house clock, my side board & writing desk, which I allow to be disposed of after ____. Alto to my beloved wife of my stock four cows & calves of her choice, my old horse Ball & young mare Chance, my riding chair & harness, with 200 acres of land of the tract I now live on to be laid off on the upper end including my dwelling house & improvements. To my beloved son Jonathan that plantation known by McWoods old place that I bo't of John Dunlap reserving the privilege of cutting timber to keep up the improvements on my wife's premises. To my beloved son Wm the one half of my plantation whereon he now lives including his improvements he has made on the side adj. E. Watson's land, and if he should have two heirs born to him that should live, I allow him to have the whole of said tract. If he does not have two heirs, the other half to be sold and divided equally among the others of my children. To my two sons Jerome & Abraham all the rest of my lands on the side of Taylors Creek, excepting so much at the saw mill as will be a competency for a mill yard. I appoint my son William & my sons in law Wm. Steel & Joseph Lewis in making an equal divide of the same. I allow my son Abraham to have the use of the saw mill for one year after my decease, and after that the said saw mill and other lands adjoining it equally to be between my said two sons Jerome & Abraham. To my son said Ab'm a negro boy named Rawley, and to my son Jerome a negro boy named Zacheriah, and to my son Abraham a negro boy child named Daniel. To my beloved daughter Margaret McElwee a negro girl named Chancy & a negro girl named Patience. To my daughter Betsy Steel a negro boy named David and to my daughter Jane Lewis a negro girl named Dilsey. My other property to be sold and the money arising therefrom equally divided between all my children Jonathan, Martha McElwee, Jane Lewis, Betsey Steel, Wm & Jerome & Abraham, and at the death of my wife the land I left to her and two negroes Polly & Pen to be sold & equally to be divided between my children. I appoint my son William and my two sons in law William Steel & Joseph Lewis, exrs., 13 Sept 1826. Abraham Miller (LS), Wit: Thos Reed, John Crisp (X), Wm. Miller.

Pages 222-224: Will of Alexander Thompson of District of York... All my real estate and personal estate to be appraised in the month of January after my decease which lies in the state of South Carolina and in as few days after said appraisement as practicable all my negroes shall be hired at public outcry except my negro man Sam, negro women Dilla & Silla & sam son of Isaac & one of my small negro girls for a nurse. The above named negroes I allow to be kept upon the plantation to make a support for my family. Secondly, my executors to keep my long legged mule and my old puny mule on the plantation with my black horse, my sorrel, I direct to be sold one of less value. I order six milk cows & calves, six young steers & heifers with my whole stock of hogs to be kept for the use of my family & likewise my wagon and harness, my cotton gin, threshing machine & Dutch fan. I give all my household property to my wife Elizabeth Thompson at her disposal so that it be equally divided between her and her six children. I order all my cleared lands above what is necessary to support the family to be rented from year to year for cash or a share of the crop. I wish the proceeds of my land rent & negro hie to be appropriate from year to year for the education of my children. Whatever surplus funds there are to my son John B. Thompson in compensation for a legacy left him by his grandmother Ann Thompson, to be paid when my son Joseph W. Thompson comes of age, and the other two to my sons John & Joseph Thompson, that is $200 to each. On the first of January 1834 the whole of my estate be again appraised and an equal divided to all my heirs then living who have arrived to the age of 21, and the shares of the minor children kept at hire & interest. I will that no charge be made by my executors against my children for food & clothing until 1 January 1834. I appoint my son Elizabeth Thompson executrix & John Hemphill, James H. Foster of Alabama, my sons John B. Thompson and Joseph Thompson when they arrive at 21 years, to act as executors, dated 7 May 1827. A. Thompson (Seal), Wit: A. Williams, Alexdr Stroup, _____ Grier.

Pages 224-226: Will of Robert Allison of the District of York, being considerable advanced in years... To my beloved wife Sarah during her natural life the plantation whereon I live with all my personal estate consisting of negroes, stock, wagon, still & farming utensils, household furniture &c., and after her decease to my son Robert the aforesaid plantation. To my two sons Hugh & Robert all the negroes that may be living to be equally divided between them. My son Robert should live with his mother & see that she is furnished with the necessary comforts of life and I allow him the one half of the profits arising from the farm & his mother the other half each paying an equal part of all expenses. I reserve of the aforesaid plantation above 100 acres as will be hereafter mentioned. I also give to my son Robert at his mother's decease all the household furniture, stock, etc., excepting one bed & furniture, case of drawers and wearing apparel which I allow my wife to dispose of as she may think proper. I give to my daughter Martha Cain $100 which I allow my son Robert to pay her out of his part, also a negro girl named Amy which she got when she was married. To my daughter Margaret Henry 140 acres of land on the waters of Clerks fork of Bullocks creek adj. lands of Jas Crawford & Hugh Find, also a negro boy named Len which I let her have when she was married. Also to my daughter Catherine Henry a tract of land, being apart of my aforesaid plantation adj. Samuel Lesley, to Malcolm Henry's spring branch, Isaac Hope's spring branch, to a beech corner standing on a bluff on which is cut the two first letters of my name, which should be 100 acres, also a negro girl named Sintha. To my two grandsons Albert & Thos H. Allison sons of Thos Allison decd, a tract on waters of Bullocks Creek adj. Lessley, Catherine Henry's line. The profits of the saw mill be equally divided between my two sons Hugh & Robert. I also reserved for the rest of the said mill the timber that is suitable on the tract of land named to Catherine & my grandchildren. I also bequeath o my three grand daughters Mary A. Allison, Eliza & Caroline Allison, being daughters of Thos Allison decd, $100 to be let to interest & be equally divided among them when they become of age. I also allow my son Robert to give each of my three grand sons which was named for me to wit Robert A. Cain, Robert A. Henry & Robert Allison, each a pocket Bible. I appoint my two sons Hugh & Robert, exrs., 10 June 1827. Robert Allison (LS), Wit: Jane Neely, Saml Turner, Saml Smith.

Page 227: Will of Nathaniel Harris of York District... to my daughter Martha Wilson five shillings. To my son Henry G. Harris a tract of Indian Land running as the instrument of writing I gave him. To my daughter Polly Savall five shillings. To my son John Harris $200. To my daughter Precillah Ward one horse. To my daughter Nancy Harris one horse with all her own bed clothes, on bureau & candlestand. To my son Nathl Harris the plantation I now live on, 163 acres, all my cattle, sheep, hoggs, household furniture. I appoint my son Nathl Harris, exr., 27 Dec 1816. Nathl Harris (Seal), Wit: C. Elms Junr, Thos Masunan[?].

Pages 227-228: South Carolina, York District. Will of James Tate of said district... To my beloved wife Catherine Tate the one half of the plantation I now live on, 120 acres, her half to include the house & barn during her natural lifetime and at her death to go to my son Luther Tate. Also to my wife one bed & furniture, al my kitchen & dresser furniture & my three single daughters I allow them to live with their mother & have their living while they are single. My daughter Sarah Iles to have $5 to be paid to her one year after my decease. To my son Samuel Tate the sum of $10 to be paid to him one year after my decease. To my daughter Rebeckah Wallace $5. To my son John Tate $15. To my son Hugh Tate $5. to my son Andrew $5. To my son Luther Tate the balance of the plantation I now life on by his paying to my daughter Nancy $25 at her mother's death, also to pay to my daughter Eleanor $25 and also to pay to my youngest daughter $100. My stock of horses, cattle, hogs & sheep & my road wagon to be sold at publick sale to raise money to pay off my debts. I appoint my son John Tate & John Jackson, exrs., 10 April 1827. James Tate (mark), Wit: Samuel Tate, Hugh Tate, John Jackson.

Pages 229-230: 4 Aug 1825. Will of Robert Greer of York District... I my beloved wife, two negro women Milly & Lucy & my gray mare and all of my stock of cattle, hogs, household furniture, kitchen furniture and all my upper plantation where I now live in lieu of dower, and at the day of my wife's death or marriage, this property to be equally divided among my children. To my son William T. Greer two negro boys James & Isaac and a horse & saddle worth $110 when of age. to my daughter Polly Malise one negro girl named Jane, one bed & furniture & one sorrel colt, saddle worth $15. To my daughter Anna Nercissa one negro girl named Hannah, one bed & furniture, one horse & saddle worth $110 when of age. To my daughter Rebeka Clarissa one negro girl named Tildey, one bed & furniture, one horse & saddle worth $110 when of age. To my daughter Catherine Malinda one bed & furniture, one horse & saddle worth $110 when of age. To my son John E. Greer one negro boy named Washington, one horse & saddle worth $110 when of age. To my son Joseph R. Green one negro boy named Richard, one horse & saddle worth $110 when he comes of age. To my daughter Emily Elmenah one negro girl child the first girl child that lives to be eight years old of Milly or Lucey that I left to my wife, one bed & furniture, one horse & saddle worth $110 when of age. My will is that my lower plantation on the creek that it be rented out till my youngest son comes of age, and then to be equally divided between my three sons William John & Joseph and at the day of my wife's death or marriage, the upper plantation to be equally divided between my three sons. My will is for my negroes Jacob & Pete and all above mentioned to my children to be hired out until they come of age. I appoint my brother Alexander & my brother James G. Robinson my son John E. Greer, exrs. Robert Greer (LS), Wit: John Hemphill, John Pilcher, William Logan.

Pages 231-233: South Carolina, York District. Will of Robert Love of York District... To my daughter Rachel Love a negro woman named Caty & her children & a negro boy named Ned, my sorrel horse with a bald face, a saddle & bridle, also her bed or beds & furniture. To my daughter Mary Meek, a negro boy named Henry & a negro girl named Caty who is now with her. To my daughter Nancy Love, a negro girl named Eliza and a boy named Isom, a horse worth $70 or $75, a saddle & Bridle, two beds & furniture, household & kitchen furniture equal to what my daughter Mary got. To my daughter Margaret Love I give three negroes Ben, Lyda & Ritta, a horse, saddle & bridle & household furniture, two beds & furniture equal to Nancy's. To my daughter Elizabeth Wallace, two negroes Cenia & Charlotte, a two year old sorrel mare, saddle & Bridle, two beds and furniture, household & kitchen furniture equal to Nancy's. To my daughter Eleanor three negroes Harriot, Elvy & Young Adam, a horse, saddle & bridle, household & kitchen furniture, two beds & furniture equal to Nancy's. To my son Arthur Love two negro boys Tholly and Peter, a horse & Saddle & bridle, household & kitchen furniture equal to Nancy's. To my son Andrew Franklin Love, three negroes Simon, Lewis & old Adam, a horse & Saddle & bridle, a bed and furniture, household & kitchen furniture equal to Nancy's. To my daughters Rachel, Nancy, Margaret, Elizabeth, Eleanor, & my two sons Arthur and Andrew Franklin Love, a cow & calf, to my two sons my lands to be equally divided between them, to give each of them a portion of meadow ground & also according to the quantity and quality of the said lands and improvements & should either of my unmarried children die without an heir or will, then their part of my estate to be equally divided between my six youngest daughters, my daughter Rachel & my two youngest sons. I will that 200 acres of land which I owned in Livingston County, Kentucky, be sold whenever my executors this proper and the money be equally divided amongst all my children. Also $150 to my nephew Bass, Methodist Preacher. I appoint my son James M. Love & Dr. J. S. Bratton, exrs., 29 Nov 1827. Robert Love (LS), Wit: Sam Givens, John S. Bratton, Jas Duncan.

Pages 233-234: June 29th 1826. Will of William Hall... To my beloved wife a nero girl named Mime & $400, at her death Mime & her increase is to be equally divided between my three children and their heirs. N.B. My wife is to have her bed & furniture & her clothes. The balance of my property to be equally divided between my three children by valuation, that is my land, negroes, all but Mime, that is Polly, John & William A. Hall. John is to have the 200 acres of land that he lives on. Wm. A. Hall the 200 acres that he lives on and Polly Garetson is to have her share out of the negroes so as to make her an equal divide. I allow Major T. Hall to be my executor. William Hall (LS), Wit: Major T. Hall, William A. Hall, William Garetson.

Page 234: Will of Margaret Lambeth of York District, now far advanced in age... To my son John K. Benson one third part of my wearing apparel, also of my bed clothing and one feather bed and $5 in cash. To my son Grover B. Duffy, all the balance of my estate real and personal. I appoint my son George B. Duff exr., 3 June 1823. Margaret Lambeth (X) (Seal), Wit: J. Rooker, Jacob Rooker, Joseph D. Rooker.

Pages 234-235: 4 May 1827. Will of Martha Bratton of York District... To my only daughter Betsey Adaline all my personal and real estate consisting of my bed and furniture, my stand of drawers, my wheel and cards, my wearing apparel, and all my cash in hand. I appoint my uncle James B. Good my sole executor, 4 May 1827. Martha Bratton (LS), Wit: John T. Plexico, Jno Hemphill, John Good.

Pages 235-236: South Carolina, York District. Will of Mary Patterson... To my granddaughter Ann Alvira Baird one feather bed and coverlid, three blankets, two sheets, one boulster, two pillows and slips. The remainder of the property to be sold and the proceeds equally divided amongst my four living children Richard, James, Elizabeth and Hannah, 23 Jan 1828. Mary Patterson (X) (LS), Wit: J. A. Campbell, Hugh Currance, William Currance. J. A. Campbell, exr.

Page 236: Will of Xerxes H. Cushman of the Village of York... My whole estate both real and personal to my wife Jane B. Cushman. I appoint my said wife Jane B. Cushman, sole executrix, __ Nov 1827. Xerxes H. Cushman (LS), Wit: S. Melton, A. H. Dismukes, Wm. R. Hill.

Pages 237-239: South Carolina, York District. Will of John McElwain of district aforesaid... To my beloved wife Jane McElwain my plantation & all my stock of every kind, also my household furniture & house during my natural life, her support & maintenance, and after her death to my son Charles McElwain & his son John McElwain to be equally divided. To my son in law & daughter Robertson & Sarah Kerr the sum of $10. To my son David McElwain $30. I appoint my sons Charles & David exrs., 2 Oct 1821. John McElwain (LS), Wit: James Johnston, Phil Sandefer, John Corrie.

Letters testamentary to Charles McElwain & David McElwain 26 May 1828. Warrant of appraisement directed to Saml Chambers, Alexr Moore, Jas Wright, James McCain, & Andrew McConnel 26 May 1828 returnable 25 July next.

Pages 239-241: Will of Thomas Barnett of the District of York & State of North Carolina... To my daughter Nancy Price the two negroes she has now in possession that I let her have since she married to wit Mary Ann & Matilda & also the beds, bedding, & furniture & other things that I let her have at & since her marriage. To my daughter Sarah Elsom one negro woman & her child Rachel that is now in her possession, for the purpose of nursing, raising

& supporting her children, and after said daughters death, I give the said two negroes Maria & Rachel to be equally divided among all the children she may then have. To my daughter Ann Barnett one negro girl named Sandy, one bureau, one table. To my daughter Elizabeth Meacham the negro girl Eliza that is now in her possession & all the beds & furniture & other things that she has had at & during her marriage. To my son Thomas Barnett one bed & furniture. To my son George G. Barnett one sorrel mare called his, the rifle Gun also called his & my waggon. To my wife Ann Barnett the plantation whereon I now live during her life or widowhood. To my son George G. Barnett the plantation whereon I now live after my wife's death or marriage, provided my son will pay to my son Thomas Barnett $400 in twelve months after my wife's death or marriage. To my wife Ann Barnett all the rest of my negroes that is now above willed, 16 in number. I appoint my friend Benjamin Parson & my son George G. Barnett, exrs., 15 Jan 1828. Thos Barnett (LS), Wit: Jos R. Darnall, H. McGill, Jos. Y. Darnall.

Warrant of appraisement directed to John Springs, Edm'd Weathers, Alexr Scott, James Harris & Henry Meacham 5 May 1828.

Pages 241-244: 27 May 1825. Will of Mary Harris of York District... To my beloved son Henry G. Harris three of my negroes Chaney, Mary, Dilcy, and he may at any time before or at his death give said negroes to his children. To my son John Harris three of my negroes Isham, Allison & Sarah, and he may at any time before or at his death give said negroes to his children. To my daughter Prisclla Ward seven of my negroes Sarah the elder, Mariah, Adeline, Caroline, Harriot, Sam & Eliza, and she may at any time before or at her death give said negroes to her children. To my daughter Polly Savill two of my negroes Silas & Betty, and she may at any time before or at her death give said negroes to her children. To my son Nathaniel Harris ten shillings or $2.13 3/4. I appoint my son Henry G. Harris sole executor. Mary Harris (LS), Wit: Mary Jacks, Hugh M. White, Hugh White.

Letters testamentary to Henry G. Harris 5 May 1827. Warrant of appraisement directed to Thos Webb, Stephen Smith, David Haynes, Geo Cathy & Robt Watson 5 May 1827 returnable 5 June next.

Pages 244-246: Will of John Carruth Senr of the district of York... To my four daughters Fanny Quinn, Elizabeth Henderson, Jane Allison & Polly Grayham, each the sum of $50 to be paid them by my son John Carruth out of the property herein after bequeathed to him one year after my decease. To my son George Carruth the lands & negroes which I put him in possession of & for which I have given him deeds & bills of sale. To my son John Carruth the tract of land whereon I now dwell containing 268 acres which I bought of Peter Quinn on the south east of Buffaloe Creek including the house & improvements where I now live & the remainder of the land which i purchased of James Bridges decd & which I have not conveyed to my son George Carruth, about 20 acres including the grist mill, miller's house, spring & mill pond, also 100 acres which I purchased of Thomas Dare adj. the land whereon I dwell & the lands which I conveyed to my son George Carruth. To my son George Carruth in trust for my grandson Rufus K. Carruth son of my son Adam Carruth decd four negroes, children of my negro woman named Dorcas (to wit) Charles, Moses, Lidia & Viney, to be delivered when said Rufus K. Carruth becomes 21 years of age. The estate which is coming to me by the death of my son Walter Carruth to be divided between my other children equally. To my son John Carruth all the remainder of my estate real and personal. I appoint my sons George Carruth & John Carruth exrs. John Carruth (Seal), Wit: Geo Plexco, Saml Green, Capt. Thos Logan, Capt. Saml Starns. On 16 Sept 1827 clause revoked concerning the estate of Walter Carruth "as I have otherwise disposed of the said estate." John Carruth, Wit: Geo Plexco, S. M. Caldwell, David H. Porter.

Pages 246-250: Will of Hugh White, citizen of the State of South Carolina & York District... I will that my Indian lease whereon I now live be kept & divided so that my three sons Jos F. White, George P. White and Hugh M. White will each get an equal part of the low grounds on the river & a part of the highlands on the hill in equal value, allowing the dwelling house to lie in the middle part & that my beloved wife Sarah White do remain in my dwelling house during her widowhood or natural life & I do leave to her three of my negroes viz Milley, John, and Creasy & if she removes from my dwelling house the negroes are not to be taken by her or any other person for her out of this state and district and at her death or other ways, the said negroes are all to be returned with the natural increase & to be equally divided between my three sons already named. My daughter Elizabeth Russell Campbell to have Jacob, Robb or Bob, Anna & Patty, and all the furniture that I have given her. If she dies without any live issue to return to my children or their lawful issue. My 5th part of the Indian lease called the green pons to be sold & the proceeds of it applied to the maintenance of my son James & my 5th part of Simon is to be sold & applied to the same use to be as much more as will make up $100 each and every year. The remainder of my negroes not herebefore named to my three sons (already named) in family Lotts by appraisement of the same. I appoint my sons George P. White, Joseph F. White & Hugh M. White, exrs., 25 July 1825. Hugh White (LS), Wit: Andrew Heron, James Sprott, Margaret Sprott.

Letters testamentary to Joseph F. White & Hugh M. White 29 Sept 1828. Warrant of appraisement directed to James Spratt, James McKee, Robert H. Fulwood, John Springs & John F. Kendrick 27 Sept 1828 returnable 30 November.

Pages 250-252: Will of Jane Beard of the District of York... I leave my man Tony to the care of my executors that he be kept during his life at my plantation & that he have given him one cow &calf of my stock of cattle. Whereas my father David Beard did by his will leave to me & my brother certain lands to be interested by the one which should be living & fell my lot to come & only inherited the one half of said land, the other half being kept back by fraud, my will is that the said lands be conveyed to William Kirk & Mary Bread daughter of David Beard, if each should come to America to possess the same. I ordain that James Porter & William Ash be my executors,

12 March 1824. Jane Beard (mark) (LS), Wit: Robt Dale, Elizabeth Dale (mark), Geo Dale.

Letters testamentary to James Porter 15 Oct 1828. Warrant of appraisement directed to James Brown, John Murphey, Wm. Guy, James Moore & George Dale 15 Oct 1828 returnable 15 December.

Pages 253-255: Will of Jesse Roberts of York District... To my daughter Nancy Bowans five dollars in cash. To my daughter Elizabeth Jameson five dollars in cash. To my granddaughter Rachel Jamison, one horse to be worth $40 and ten dollars in cash when she arrives to 16 years of age, and it she should not live to be 16 years old, my sons John Roberts & Andrew Roberts is to have the horse & money. To my granddaughter Salinda Roberts five dollars in cash. To my two sons John Roberts and Andrew Roberts all my negroes to be equally divided between them. My son John to have my youngest bedford colt. My son Andrew to have all the rest of my horses. My two sons John & Andrew to have my still between them, my land to be divided between John Roberts & Andrew Roberts. My sons John Roberts and Andrew Roberts to be exrs., 29 Oct 1828. Jessee Roberts (LS), Wit: John Hemphill, Wm. Jameson, Jon'a McSwain.

Letters testamentary to John Roberts and Andrew Roberts 1 Dec 1828. Warrant of appraisement directed to Jno Hemphill esqr., Gordon Moore, James Meek, Saml Feemster & Edwd Feemster 1 Dec 1828 returnable 1 February.

Pages 256-259: Letters testamentary on the will of Arthur Armstrong to Jesse Armstrong 3 Nov 1828. Warrant of appraisement directed to Capt Isaac Campbell, Wm. Currance, Jos Lawrance, Robert Jackson & Hugh Jackson, 3 Nov 1828 returnable 1 ____.

Will of Arthur Armstrong of the District of York... To my beloved wife Mary the room wherein we lodge with the cupboard, bed, chest & tea table, also one half of the furniture on the dresser, one negro woman Lin, and a little negro girl Hannah with Burl on the New Testament. To my son William $66 and 2/3 cents to be paid him by my son Jesse with the space of two years after my death. To my son William the cross cut saw, Morses Geography & Hartwells History of the Bible. To my son William $33.33 1/3 to be paid him by my son Frances within two years after he becomes possessed of the property. To my grandchildren Barronhills $66.33 1/3 to be paid them by my son Frances within two years after he becomes possessed of the property. To my son Frances one negro man named Jo at the death of my wife Mary, my family Bible, my rifle gun. To my daughter Sarah one negro girl named Mida and the first child of said negro girl to my son Jesse named Mingo on the condition that my son Jesse at my death either pays my granddaughter Nancy Malissa the value of said negro give her the use of the same value of Mingo. to my daughter Sarah one half of the furniture on the dresser with what is known to be hers being made by her own industry with the loom & that appertains thereunto, spinning wheel, bed & stead, one young sorrel mare and bridle. I allow her the use of the house with her mother also the use of the kitchen fire, one Bible known by the name of James Bible, one chest, all my bedding. To my son Jesse the tract of land on which I live, one negro man named Harry & one negro boy named Gilbert, all my farming utensils, coopers tools, augers, chissels, wagon & geers, one sorrel mare, one black horse, with the clock and Confession of Faith. All my cattle, hogs, and sheep be equally divided between my wife Mary and my son Jesse and daughter Sarah. I appoint John Jackson and Jesse K. Armstrong, exrs., 2 April 1828. Arthur Armstrong (mark) (LS), Wit: J. A. Campbell, Thomas Barnett, Robt. T. Allison.

Pages 259-260: In the Court of Ordinary Decr 1, 1828. The will of Jesse Roberts late of district of York decd was presented to me to be proved in solemn form by the executors therein name being John and Andrew Roberts and citation having been made & the heirs at law that were of age in this District being cited which was Samuel and Nancy Bowen his wife formerly Nancy Roberts, John M. Ross, at the same time being counsel for said Bowen objected to the proceedings as being illegal as the whole of the heirs at law were not cited to be present at the probate of the will, the other heirs at law being without the limits of this District. Whereupon I produced to the probate of the will in solemn form and after examining the subscribers witness to the will & no other offered in opposite thereto, although there appeared some ___ in the testator not requesting the witness to sign it as his will which appeared to be the case... decreed it to be a good & valid will. Dec 1, 1828.

Citation. Whereas John Roberts & andrew Roberts named executors of the will of Jesse Roberts decd being desirous to have the same proven in solemn form of law to prevent disputes, cite the rest of the kin or heirs at law, 24 Nov 1828.

Pages 261-263: Will of John Miller of the County of Craven and Province of South Carolina... 10 September 1779. I make my wife Jane sole executrix of all my whole estate and have the whole management of the sale both real and personal whilst she remains a widow, but if she marries then to have choice of all the negroes to take one, but at her decease the said negro is to return to my former estate and at the marriage or death of my wife my estate is to be equally divided among my sons &daughters, but if my said daughters gets any of the negroes of this my estate, they marrying the said negroes to go to their heirs. John Miller (Seal), Wit: John Bryson, Stafford Curry, Deborah Ross. Proved in **Pendleton District,** South Carolina, by the oath of John Bryson 26 Sept 1828 before James Houston.

To Jas Houston & Jacob Cosper, John Callahan, Pendleton District. Dedimus to examine the alone surviving witness to the last will of John Miller deceased, 15 Jan 1820.

Pages 263-265: South Carolina, York District. Will of William Rainey of district aforesaid... If Robert Rainey should after my decease fail or decline to perform any part of the requisites mentioned in a deed of gift made by me to my daughter Rosanna Rainey dated 12 July 1826 in that case the said Robert Rainey is altogether barred from having any right or title in any wise to the land mentioned in the deed of gift made to my daughter Rosannah Rainey. If any of my other two sons William or John Rainey on failure of Robert Rainey performing the request to the deed of gift, I will them to enjoy the lands mentioned. My grandson William G. Rainey may hold & occupy the said land during his natural life time also along with his ___ if he should think property so to do. If my son Robert Rainey at my decease do undertake to comply with the requisites contained, I bequeath my negro man Jack unto him during his lifetime & also to the heirs of him, that the said Robert Rainey will humanely treat the said negro by keeping him warm & comfortable, clothed & fed, and pay yearly the said negro Jack $5. To my son William Rainey my negro fellow April that he will humanely treat the said negro by keeping him warm & comfortable, clothed & fed, and pay yearly the said negro April $2. My negro man named Ned to my three single daughters to wit Rosanna, Lilley Ann & Rebecka Rainey and at the decease of the longest liver of the three daughters said negro be the property of Janet Kirkpatrick my granddaughter under the same restrictions and that he be paid $2 yearly. To my three single daughters a sufficient quantity of my farming utensils to carry on their farms. I appoint my son John Rainey & Samuel Wiley my trusty friends, exrs., 10 Nov 1828. William Rainey (LS), Wit: Jas Anderson, Jane Anderson (X), Andrew W. Kirkpatrick. Proved in common form by the oath of Andrew Kirkpatricck and qualified John Rainey exr., 9 Feb 1829. Samuel Wylie declined to act 9 Feb 1829.

Warrant of appraisement directed to Sam Wylie, And Kirkpatrick, Jas & Wm. Feemster & Jno Galloway 9 Feb 1829 returnable 9 May.

Pages 266-269: Will of Mary Gill, widow, of York District... To my daughter Elizabeth Taylor wife of Thomas C. Taylor of Pinckneyville, SC, my negro girl Sarah and my negro girl Betsy; to my son William G. Gill of Alabama my negro man Peter & my negro boy Absalom; to my son Thomas W. Gill my negro woman Winney and my negro girl Mariah and my negro boy Sam & my negro girl Nancy & my negro boy Moses, children of my negro man Peter & his wife Winney and it is my fervent desire that my two last mentioned sons William G. and Thomas W. Gill will endeavour never to separate Peter and Winney so as to prevent them from seeing each other at least in a week. I further bequeath to my son Thomas my colt and young ___ now in Alabama and all my other property which is in Alabama to my sons William G. and Thomas W. Gill. To my grandson James Gill son of John and Nancy Gill my share and interest to the plantation on Turkey Creek on which I now reside and to my son Gill [sic] all my share and interest in any other land and property which share is not covered by the previous bequeath. To my said son John Gill my clock & bureau. To my granddaughters Mary & Eliza Gill daughters of John & nancy Gill each one of my feather beds and furniture and to my grandson Washington Gill son of my son James Gill of Illinois by his first marriage, my negro boy Samuel. To my granddaughter Elvira Gill daughter of James Gill by his said first marriage my negro girl Rebecca. To my said grandchildren my negro man Dick. To my aforesaid granddaughter

Mary gill my negro boy Ned. I appoint my son John Gill & William Jamison Esqr., exrs., 20 Aug 1825. Mary Gill (X) (LS), Wit: Robert Wilson, Helena Jamison, Jane Purdy.

John Gill renounced any intention to qualify as executor 14 Feb 1829. Proved the will by the oath of Robert Wilson and qualified Wm Jamison, esqr., exrs., 14 Feb 1829. Letters testamentary to William Jamison 14 Feb 1829. Warrant of appraisement directed to Robt Wilson, John King, Samuel King, Jas Jamison & Robert Hays 14 Feb 1829 returnable 10 April.

Pages 269-273: York District, South Carolina. Will of John Barry... To my wife Issabella at my decease the plantation whereon I now live with all stock, furniture, etc, so that she may have a comfortable maintenance and support, and none of the negroes hereinafter mentioned be removed from the premises during her life, and at her decease I allow my property to be disposed of in the manner following. My land to my two sons Robert & John Barry. To my daughter Sarah Barry my negro girl named Sall. To my sons Robert and John each a child. To my daughter Martha Nesbit a negro girl named Jude. My negro boy named Ralph to John & Robert to belong to them in common and to work for each and they are to support and board & clothe my son Wm Barry during his life. The old negro woman named Kate I allow my sons Robert and John to keep on the plantation. To Christopher Bell $6. To my grandson Samuel Bell $60. To my granddaughter Rebecca Bell a negro child out of Juda's increase. I appoint my sons Robert & John, exrs., 10 Nov 1828. John Barry (LS), Wit: Joseph Carrel, Samuel Carrel, James Wilson. Proved the will of John Barry Sen. of Fishing Creek by the oath of Joseph Carrel 16 Feb 1829.

Letters testamentary to Robert & John Barry 14 Feb 1829. Warrant of appraisement to Jos. Carrol, ___ Harris, Robt Cooper, Minor Sadler & James M. Cain.

Pages 273-274: Will of William Dunlap of York District... To my son John Dunlap a tract of 3 and 74 acres which is lease to me by the Catawba Indians byu a lease dated 18 Aug 1815, also a negro boy named Steven & negro girl named Missy. To my youngest son William N. Dunlap 100 acres on which he now lives and which formerly belonged to my brother David Dunlap for which I have a sheriff's title, a negro boy Toney and a negro girl Salley. To my son James Dunlap 100 acres of land adj. Allen J. Green & the land bequeathed to my son William, also two negro boys named Isem & Allen & a negro girl Else. To Mary Dunlap & Susannah Dunlap my son George's two daughters 450 acres of land which I purchased from Thomas Gray. To my two sons William & James above named to be held by them jointly 477 acres lease to me by the Catawba Indians by lease dated 8 Aug 1815. To my wife Susannah Dunlap the whole of my estate not named above. I appoint my wife Susannah Dunlap extx., 27 April 1824. William Dunlap (X) (LS), Wit: John McClenahan, James McClenahan, John L. McClenahan.

Pages 274-276: South Carolina, York District. Will of William Steel of district aforesaid... To my son Jonathan Steel the plantation whereon I now live, also bed and furniture when he arrives to the age of 21 years. To my son Abraham Steel my two tracts of land on Taylors Creek, one feather bed & furniture when he arrives at the age of 21. My executors to rent out my lands by the year and hire out all my negroes in the same manner and expose all my property not herein disposed of to publick sale except a feather bed to each of my little daughters Martha & Ammaline Steel and when collected the money arising from such sale to be put to interest till my children respectively come to the age of 21 or marry. I appoint my brother John Steel and my brother in law William Miller, exrs., 15 Jan 1829. Wm. Steel (LS), Wit: Tho Robertson, A. Miller, Jane Steel. Proved by the oath of Samuel Steel and qualified John Steel Sen and William Miller, exrs 6 April 1829.

Page 276: Letters testamentary on the will of John Carruth proved 7 July 1828 to John Carruth.

Pages 276-278: Will of William Venable of District of York... To Melissa Watson daughter of Wm Watson one book called Burkett notes on the Sept[?]. I allow Clark Watson my great coat, also the above named Melissa my chest. My horse, saddle and bridle with my gear and farming utensils to be sold and the money divided between Melissa Watson & Jane Watson daughters of William Watson and my bed to Margaret Watson and Elizabeth Watson. Whatever my share of land that is coming to me is worth to William Watson, and whatever share I may have in a negro called Jerry to Clark Watson son of William Watson. I appoint Hugh McWhorter, Thomas McWhorter and Solomon Quinn, exrs., 20 July 1829. William Venable (mark) (LS), Wit: Daniel Turner (X), Robert M. Faris, Thomas Falls[?].

Citation to prove the will 6 April 1829. Declared to be valid April 13, 1829.

Pages 278-280: Will of Robert McRight of York District... To my eldest daughter Eleanor McRight alias Graham 420. To my second eldest daughter Peggy McRight alias Williams, $200 and to her son Robert M. Williams $50. to my two youngest daughters Nancy & Martha McRight to each of them one negro girl: to Nancy a negro girl named Cloe and to Martha a girl named Rachael, and to each two cows and one horse & saddle or $75 in lieu of a horse and saddle, and a spining wheel, chest, bed and furniture, the loom and tacklings. To my grandson Robert McRight $50. To my eldest son James McRight the one half of my plantation that is the south side the still house branch to be the dividing line, leaving the spring in James's side. To my son James my writing desk and my wearing apparel. To my beloved wife Nancy during her life the other half of my plantation being the part whereon I now live, three negroes Lewis, Violet & Henry, one bay mare and one brown mare, three cows and calves, the cupboard and lock, household and kitchen furniture, and at her death the part of the plantation willed to her and the negro man Lewis to my youngest son Robert McRight. The remainder sold at her death and the money arising from the sale to be equally divided between five of my children that is Peggy, James, Nancy, Martha, and Robert Mc-

Creight. I appoint my wife Nancy McRight and my son James McRight, exrs., 5 Aug 1828. Robert McCreight (LS), Wit: D. Daniel, J. Davis, Joel Ashcraft.

Warrant of appraisement directed to Thos McCullock, Saml Ashcraft, John Rimmon, Wm. Dixon and John Davis, 24 July 1829 returnable 28 Sept. Letters testamentary to Nancy McReight and James McReight 27 July 1829.

Pages 280-282: Will of Alexander Henry Senr... To my daughter Mary my negro woman slave named Clarissa, her bed and cloathing, also to be decently supported from my plantation. To my daughter Isabella my negro girl slave named Martha. To my daughter Elizabeth my negro girl slave named Lucinda. To my son Josiah all my land lying above the road To my son Alexander all my land below the road, also my negro girl slave Dovee[?], one bed and furniture. To my daughter in law Ann Henry $20. To my son Charles $20[?] to be levied out of my estate. To my grandchildren Andrew Henry, Esther Henry and Alexander, children of Charles W. Henry my son, one woman Sook and her two children Hannah and Silah provided they pay Isabella Dickson $68. Personal property to be divided among my legatees Isabella, Elizabeth, Josiah, Alexander, and Melinda. I appoint my brother Francis Henry and my son Josiah Henry, exrs., 23 Feb 1827. Alex'r Henry (LS), Wit: J. S. Logan, Martha Scoggans (mark), Jane Wishart (mark). Proved 17 Aug 1829.

Citation to the heirs to appear 3 Aug 1829. Letters testamentary to Francis Henry & Josiah Henry 15 Nov 1829.

Pages 282-284: Will of John Swan of the District of York, 25 May 1816... To Ann my well beloved wife a comfortable maintenance of all my land and in the house I now live in, my sorrel mare, saddle and bridle, her spinning wheel, and two milk cows, kitchen and household furniture. To my daughter Jane Vickers the third division of my land as laid of in a plat by Joseph Swan Senr. To my son John B. the second division of my land, remainder of my stock and farming implements. To my daughter Polly F. the first division of my land in said plat. I appoint my sons John B. Swan and John Vickers, exrs. John Swan (Seal), Wit: Samuel Lowry, Thomas Bratton (mark), Jesse Fondren. Proved by the oath of Thomas Bratton 21 Sept 1829.

Warrant of appraisement directed to Richd Streight, Robt McClaren, Mansfield Jordan, Fra's Irwin, and Jas Wallace 21 Sept 1829 returnable 20 Nov. Letters testamentary to John B. Swan & John Vickers 21 Sept 1829.

Pages 285-286: South Carolina, York District. Will of John Dunwoody of said district... To my wife Fanny Dunwoody all my estate after debts are paid, and at her death I bequeath to Thomas Ramsy & each of his children by Easter Kennedy my grandchildren $2 apiece. To James McCully & wife Jennet $2 each. To William McCreedy my son in law & wife $2 each. The ballance to be disposed of by my wife at her death to whom she pleases. My son in law James McCully & William McCreedy, exrs., 19 Dec 1825. John Dunwoody (LS), Wit: John Jackson, Henry Smith, Samuel McCully. Proved by the oath of John Jackson Esqr., 5 Oct 1829 and at same time qualified James McCully, exr.

Warrant of appraisement directed to Saml McCully, Eli Smith, Henry Smith, John Jackson & Jos. Adams 5 May 1829 returnable 5 December. Letters testamentary to James McCully 5 Oct 1829.

Pages 286-288: South Carolina, York District. Will of Francis Nisbitt, 3 Sept 1828... To my daughters Nancy & Cathy five dollars each. To my sons William and Robert I have already made right to that portion of my land which I assign for them. To my granddaughter Nancy Nisbett daughter of my son James deceased, $40 to be paid her when she comes of age or at the time of marriage. to my son Francis all that land which I am now in possession of and that he pay the sum also specified. To my wife Jane the mare called Brandy also two cows and she is to have her support from my land and remain on the plantation. I appoint David Watson and my son William Nisbett, exrs.. Francis Nisbett (mark) (LS), Wit: Samuel Watson, Wm. A. Watson, Jane S. H. Watson.

Warrant of appraisement directed to Samuel Watson, James Watson, Wm. A. Berry & Duncan McColum[?] 5 Oct 1829 returnable 5 December. Letters testamentary to David Watson and William Nisbitt 5 Oct 1829.

Pages 288-289: Will of Mary McNeil of District of York... To my two daughters Elizabeth Sadler and Margaret Lowry my two negroes Sophia and Rebecca her child, all my beds and clothing of every description, my household and kitchen furniture and all personal property. I appoint Elizabeth Sadler and Margaret Lowry, exrs., 3 May 1829. Mary McNeel (mark), Wit: T. B. Collers, S. W. Hamilton, Nathan Moore.

Pages 289-296: Will of William McLean of Lincoln County and State of North Carolina... To my beloved wife Mary D. McLean her maintenance on the tract of land whereupon we now live to include for her use the surplus if any which may arise from the production of the farm, all of which she is to hold in her own right, also a negro Dapheny and at her decease to dispose of them as she thinks proper to our children. Also to my wife Mary D. McLean, the family Bible, and other books [listed], the Confession of Faith adopted by the Presbyterian Church to dispose of as she sees fit, also all our kitchen furniture. Disposal of my western land amongst my daughters: to my beloved daughter Elizabeth Jackson McLane alias Eliza J. Campbell, to my beloved daughter Violet W. Maclean for some time formerly Violet W. Linsey, to my beloved daughter Rebecca Isabella Maclean & to my beloved daughter Mary Margaret McLean, to each 200 acres of ny land in Robinson County, West Tennessee, on waters of Buzzard Creek. To my son John D. Maclean 300 acres of the above mentioned tract on the north side of Buzzard Creek so as to include the small improvement whereon Asa Mason now lives. To my son Richard Dobbs Spaight Maclean 300 acres of the above mentioned tract. To my son Wm Mayne Maclean 300 acres of the above mentioned tract ad. the above legacies of his brothers. to my son Alexander Augustus Maclean 200 acres of the above mentioned tract. To my son Thomas Brevard Maclean 250 acres of the above mentioned western tract. Disposal of my land in Lincoln County, North Carolina: To my son Alexander Augustus Maclean all that part of the tract of land which I bought of William Youngblood to include land on each side of Little Catawba Creek with the buildings and improvements thereon. To my son Thomas Brevard Maclean, all the remaining tract of the above mentioned adj. to his brother Augustus. To the said Thomas B. Maclean the privilege of cutting timber for rails & other necessary improvements off the contiguous part of the tract of land on which I now live. To my son Robert Hamilton Graham Maclean all that tract whereon I now live after the death of his mother. My negro boy Simon to my son Alexander Augustus Maclean. A negro boy Peter to my son John Davidson Maclean. My negro boy Peter to my son John Davidson maclean. My negro boy Cyrus to my son William Hayne Maclean. My negro boy Julius to my daughter Elizabeth Jackson Maclean alias Eliza J. Campbell in trust of her brothers Richard B. S. Maclean and John D. McLean agreeable to a written contract hereafter made in like manner as the negro Catia which she has now in possession. A negro girl named Selina willed to her by her grandmother Violet Wilson Davidson & conveyed to her in trust by her grandfather John Davidson. To my daughter Rebecca Isabellah Maclean a negro girl Leane & a beaurow, with a horse or mare, saddle & bridle. To my daughter Mary Margaret Maclean my negro girl Boze with a beauro which I have had made for her. As I now have pointed out for her sister Rebecca my negro girl Milly & my negro girl Phillips with the increase of my negroes, I bequeath to my wife to be at her disposal amongst our children as she may think fit. to my son Richard D. S. Maclean books [listed]. To my son Alexander Augustus Maclean books [listed]. To my son Thomas B. Maclean books [listed]. To my son Robert Hamilton Graham Maclean books [listed]. To my daughter Eliza J. Campbell my much esteemed set of Spectators. To my daughter Violet W. Maclean all the works of Couper, etc. To my daughter Rebecca J. Maclean my Thompson's works complete. To my daughter Mary M. Maclean books [listed]. I will that I shall be buried near to my father and mother that a small monumental stone be placed at their heads, and another of the same description placed at mine. January 4th 1828, since the date of the above will I have acquired some property in consequence of which I find it necessary to make a codicil. In lieu of the lands in Tennessee which I gave to my son Richard Dobbs Spaight Maclean, I bequeath to him the tract of land lately occupied by Joseph Hartt called the Mil tract, about 200 acres, with one half of the interest in the grist '& saw mills now nearly complete, and the other half of the grist & saw mills to my son Thomas Brevard Maclean. In consequence of the death of my beloved daughter Eliza, to each of her children (viz) Violet, George & William, that land that is willed to her with 100 acres of the same tract, making 100 acres to each children and the books intended for her as the children could not for many years make any use of them, the same to be equally divided between my daughters Rebecca & Mary. To my sons John, Augusta & William the residue of my lands in the state of Tennessee. Wm Maclean (LS), Wit: Henry Cauble, Phillip Canseller Junr (jurat), W. M. Alexander. Certified to be a true copy by Vardry McBee, clerk of the court of quarter sessions in Lincoln County, North Carolina, 30 April 1829.

Pages 296-297: Will of Elizabeth Walker, widow of Col. John Walker deceased, made 1825... To my son Jacob Walker a negro woman named Sarah which I purchased from my sister Alice Alexander in her life time with all my live stock, household furniture and the residue of my legacy left me by my brother William Watson decd of York District, South Carolina, to my son Jacob Walker in Rutherford County, North Carolina. My son Jacob to collect any monies due me. Elizabeth Walker (mark) (Seal), Wit: F. Walker, Jas. Scott. Copy certified from Rutherford County, North Carolina, 5 Oct 1829.

Pages 297-298: South Carolina, York District. Will of George Riddel of district aforesaid... To my loving wife Margaret Riddle the use and occupation of my dwelling house with the half of the profits of the land & mill during her natural life. To my daughters Genny Riddel & Peggy Riddel half of the profits of the land and mill during my wife's life and at her decease to my daughter Genny and my daughter Peggy each $200 with one horse and saddle & one feather bed and furniture. To my son John Riddel $100. To my son Hugh Riddel $250. To my daughter Rosanna Bryson $50. To my son Benjamin Riddel my hands and mill with all my other goods after paying the before mentioned legacies. I appoint my son John Riddle and my son Benjamin Riddle, exrs., 29 April 1817. George Riddel (LS), Wit: James Duff Senr, Wm McKee Bigger, James Duff Junr. Proved by the oath of James Duff Senr. 7 Dec 1829. At same time qualified Benjamin Peter[?] Riddle, exrs., 17 Dec 1829.

Pages 298-300: South Carolina, York District, Indian Land. Will of John Forbes Senr. of state and district aforesaid... To my beloved wife Rebecca Forbes Senr the following property, viz., her support and maintenance off my plantation and also one bay mare named Fly. I allow my land to be equally divided between my four sons viz John, Archibald, Thomas and Arthur, agreeable to quality and quantity. To my daughter that are left Elizabeth, Margaret, Sarah and Rachel, $50 each to be paid by my sons at my death. To my daughters now with me Rebecca, Ann, and Tobitha $100 to be paid to them by my sons after my death. To my son Thomas the mare called Nance. To my son Arthur my colt. The whole of the ballance of my property to be equally divided between my wife and three daughters Rebecca, Ann, and Tobitha. I appoint my wife Rebecca executrix, Thomas & Arthur Forbes and David McElwain, exrs., Decr 24th 1828. John Forbes (LS), Wit: Wm Fairis, Jesse Bromfield, Stephen McCorkle. Proved by the oath of three subscribing witnesses 4 Dec 1829. At same time Thomas Forbes, Arthur Forbes and David McElwain qualified executors.

We do hereby certify that we are satisfied with the last will and testament of John Forbes deceased, 5 Dec 1829. Rebecca Forbes (X) (Seal), Ann Forbes (X) (Seal), Tobitha Forbes (X) (Seal), Rebecka Forbes (X) (Seal). Citation to prove will 30 Nov 1829.

Pages 300-301: South Carolina, York District. Will of Thomas Carrell of district aforesaid, being far advanced in years... To my son Joseph Carrell my negro male Silas and the money he received as the price of Bolen. To my son

John Carrell my granddaughter Esther Carrell, the daughter of my son Joseph, a young negro woman named Betty. To my grandson Thomas Carrell, son of Joseph Carrell, the negro man Lewis who he has now in his possession. To my son John Carrell my negro woman Judy and her two sons Sias & Gran[?], also my negro woman Perlinda. To my son Mathew Carrell my nero African Abel and my negro woman Pinky. To my grandson Thomas Carrell son of Mathew Carrell, my negro boy Adam. To my grandson Moses Carrell, son of Mathew Carrell, my negro child Sarah, daughter Anny. To my grandson Moses Carrell $50 in money. To my daughter Jincey Gallaher my two negroes Jim and Judy after the death of her husband John Gallaher if she should survive him. To my daughter Elizabeth Crafts and Samuel Crafts her husband the negro woman Esther and her children that are now living, dated 5 March 1824. Thomas Carrell Sen (mark), Wit: Wm. Smith, John Blair.

Pages 302-303: Letters testamentary on the will of Nathan Moore, whose will was proved 4 Jan 1830, to Zenus L. Moore, 4 Jan 1830. Warrant of appraisement directed to Sam Rainey, Sam Moore, Alfred Moore Esq., John Latta & Thomas Collins, 4 Jan 1830.

Pages 303-304: Will of Michael Martin of York District, planter... to my beloved wife Mourning Martin, the sole management of all my estate real & personal, viz discretionary to be divided among my three sons, Michael, Mannon, and Morgan. To my two daughters Martha & Mary 350 acres on Wolf Creek. I appoint my wife Mourning Martin my sole exr. Michael Martin (mark (LS), Wit: Jas Davidson, William Manning, David Barr. Heirs consented 30 Aug 1830, including Martha Ramsey and Mary Martin. James Davidson, son of James Davidson witness, proved the will 30 Jan 1830.

Page 304: Citation. John Pilcher applied for letters of administration on the estate of Robert Pilcher, 22 Jan 1830.

Pages 304-305: Settlement. Wm L. Wallace & wife, heirs at law of Robert Gill and Mary Gill admr. of the estate of Robert Gill decd. Includes hire of negro Pat 8 years, and hire of negro Winney 8 years. 13 March 1825. Mary Gill admx. of the estate of Robert Gill decd was cited to account to Wm. L. Wallace & wife for her administration on the estate.

Page 305: John Spencer in right of his wife Malinda formerly Malinda Blanton daughter of Richard & Sarah Blanton decd. John Morgan Senr who purchased the interest of the heirs at law of sd Richd & Sarah Blanton decd viz Wm Ross, Obadiah Trimmier[?], James Funches[?] and his wife, Polly Trimmier, Jas Herrald in right of his wife Susannah, one of the heirs at law of Richard & Sarah Blanton decd, Hester Blanton & Sarah Blanton both under 15 years old, heirs at law of said Richd & Sarah Blanton. Feb 10, 1830.

Pages 305-306: South Carolina, York District. Feby 18, 1828. BE it known that we James & Robert Whitesides Exrs., of the last will & testament of Hugh Whitesides decd do agree with Wm Albernon the Brother of Margaret Whitesides widow of said Hugh Whitesides decd who will make provision for her support during her life, that we will agree to & stand to whatever the three following persons may say that she will be entitled to, settled by said persons at the house of Daniel Brown on Friday 29th inst., viz Sterling Howell, Major John Sitgreaves, & Elias McLellan. James Whitesides, Robert Whitesides, Wm. Amberson. Wit: R. B. W. Fleming.

Pages 306-307: The will of Thomas Carrell was proved 8 Dec 1829, letters testamentary to Joseph Carrell and John Carrell, exrs., 8 Dec 1829. Warrant of appraisement directed to Minor Sadler, Philip Sandefur, John Barron, Thomas Simpson & Thomas Simpson Junr 8 Dec 1829, returnable 8 Dec [sic] next.

Pages 308-309: The will of Mary McNeal was proved 20 Oct 1829, letters testamentary to Elizabeth Sadler, 15 Dec 1829. Warrant of appraisement directed to Saml Moore, Geo Dale, John Black, Samuel Rainey & James Rainey 15 Dec 1829 returnable 15 Feb next.

Pages 309-310: The will of George Riddle was proved 7 Dec 1829, letters testamentary to Benjamin P. Riddle, 7 Dec 1829. Warrant of appraisement directed to James Duff Senr, Jos Clinton, John McGill, Thos Davis & An'd Patrick 7 Dec 1829 returnable 7 Feb next.

Pages 311-312: Will of Mary Latham of York District, 8 Jan 1822... To my daughter Rachel Simmons my dwelling house & all the old clear land & woodland that lies between my clear land and his line from the upper corner next to Robert Latham's down to the lower corner, excepting five acres. To my son Andrew Latham the one half of all the rest of my wood land adj. him and the strip along the west to Simmons & John Wilson's line. To my son To my son Robert Latham all the other half of my woodland joining to himself with the cotton field, my cow and my brass sifter. To my daughter Sally French $5. To my daughter Agness Wilson $5. I allow my negro girl Luce for to make her choice of my children for to live with. I appoint my son Andrew Latham & my son Robert Latham, exrs., 8 Jan 1822. Mary Latham (X) (LS), Wit: John Hemphill, Andrew Latham, Jesse Roberts.

Pages 312-314: Will of Nathan Moore of York District... To my son Thomas 100 acres of land it being the land on which he now resides and for which I have made him a title, also a negro man named Isaac which he has now in possession. To my son Zenus 100 acres of land adj. tract formerly owned by John Hartness, for which I have executed a deed dated 7 Feb 1828, also a negro boy named Lewis. To my son Robert 100 acres of land adj. Zenas Moore's corner, and a negro girl named Isabella, youngest child of Pettey's. To my son Eli 100 acres of land adj. Robert Moore, Williamson, Walker, and my own lands, according to a survey lately made by Hanna. To my three sons Jesse, John & Stanhope, the remainder of all my lands. To my son Jesse a negro man named Bob. To my son John a negro boy named Bill. To my son Stanhope a negro boy named Laray. To my daughter Eliza a negro woman named Ritta. My said daughter is to be paid annually $20 out of the proceeds of the property given to Jesse, John & Stanhope until Stanhope attains the age of 20. To my daughter Peggy a negro girl named Mima and $200. My two daughters Peggy & Jincy each have a horse, saddle & Bridle, household furniture equal to my daughter Eliza when she married. To my grandchild Daniel son of Elis a negroe girl named Rosetta. All my negroes and other personal property remain undivided until my youngest child is 21 years of age. My son Stanhope is to be sent to school until he acquires a good education. I appoint my friends Samuel Rainy, Allison Hope and My son Zenos, exrs., 2 Oct 1829. Nathan Moore (LS), Wit: George Streight, John Latta, Samuel Moore.

Pages 315-319: South Carolina, York District. Will of John Durham of district aforesaid... To my son George G. Durham my dwelling house and the appurtenances with 300 acres of land surrounding & adjacent thereto. To my daughter Elizabeth Durham the tract of land purchased by me from Alexander Eakin about 65 acres. To Hugh Currance 100 acres of land adj. the line of his land. I appoint my friends David Watson, Duncan McColm & Wm Berry to make such divisions into lots, and sell that land. The money to be divided into four shares and one share to the children of my deceased daughter Jane Stevenson, one fourth part to Hugh Currance, one fourth part to George Durham & the remaining fourth part to Elizabeth Durham. All my negro slaves not hereafter specified shall be divided by my aforesaid friends into three lots to my son George G. Durham, my daughter Elizabeth Durham and Hugh Currance. To my daughter Mary Stevenson a negro girl Milly & her daughter Mary. To my daughter Frances Dulen a negro man Lewis and a negro man Abram. To my son William Durham $300. To my daughter Elizabeth Durham two head of horses & ten head of cattle. To my son George G. Durham one gun. To my daughter Margaret Wallace $200. I appoint my daughter Elizabeth executrix and George G. Durham & Hugh Currance, exrs., 19 Feb 1829. John Durham (LS), Wit: Wm. Pressley, Hugh Stevenson, W. R. Hill.

Warrant of appraisement directed to Wm. Pressley, Richard M. Pressley, David Watson, Wm. Berry & Duncan McColm, 27 April 1829 returnable 25 June. Letters testamentary to Capt. George G. Durham and Hugh Currance, 27 April 1829.

Pages 320-323: Robert Lipscomb one of the executors of the will of Wyatt Lipscomb deceased being desirous to have the same proved in solemn form, citation to next of kin or heirs at law to appear, 21 May 1830.

South Carolina, York District. Will of Wyatt Lipscomb of district aforesaid, planter... To my beloved wife Hannah Lipscomb the following negroes during her life viz Bob, George, Peter, Joseph, Sophia, Sarah Julia, Mariah, Peggy, Clarissa & Phebia, and after her death to be divided into lots and divided among her children Eliza Jeffreys late Eliza Green and Louisa Jefferys late Louisa Green born before or after the death of my wife Hannah Lipscomb, Hannah to discharge a certain bond given by me to Daniel Smith Esquire as trustee for Elisa Green now Eliza Jeffreys and Louisa Green now Louisa Jeffreys for $1500, dated 15 Jan 1821, recorded in York District, Book K page

9013. But if my wife Hannah shall refuse to accept this legacy, then the negroes to my brother Waddy Lipscomb. To my wife Hannah all my household & kitchen furniture on the condition that she relinquishes to my brother Robert Lipscomb all claim of dower to my land. To my brother Robert Lipscomb all my land in Spartanburg District including the mill tract adj. the plantation where he now lives. To my brother Robert four negroes Daniel, Dolly, Washington & Harry. To my brother Waddy the remainder of my negroes. I appoint Col. James Jefferies of Union District trustee and guardian for the children of Eliza Jefferies late Eliza Green and Mr. Wm. Jefferies of Union District trustee for Louisa Jefferies late Louisa Green. My negro Nelson is hereby liberated from being a lave and my executors will procure suitable papers for that purpose so that he may go to Virginia or elsewhere unmolested. I appoint Daniel Smith Esq., of York District, Smith Lipscomb Senr of Spartanburg District, and my brother Robert Lipscomb, exrs., 3 Feb 1830. Wyatt Lipscomb (LS), Wit: Jas Wood, Thos Bridges, Polly Wood. Citation for heirs to attend 7 June 1830.

Pages 324-325: South Carolina, York District. Will of James McMeans of district aforesaid... My daughter Ameline shall have her bed, bedsted & furniture. My land & all the remaining property that I may die possessed of I put into the hands of my executors authorising them to sell the whole or a part as they may think most beneficial for my family. My wife shall be secured in a comfortable support during her life and then to be equally divided among my three children viz Ameline, Neely, and Eliza, as they come of age. I appoint Eli Bigger & Hiram Reeves, exrs., 19 March 1830. James McMean (LS), Wit: Wm. Campbell, E'd Kendrick, Robt M. Dunlap.

Pages 325-327: Will of Henry Smith... To my son John 100 acres of land to include the dwelling house and farm where he now lives and one negro. To my son Abraham 100 acres of land to include his new house and farm and also one negro named Phill. To my daughter Rachel Nogan $5. To my wife, one third part of all my estate both real and personal during her life except what I have given off to my sons John and Abraham. The remaining part both real and personal to be kept together for the purpose of raising and educating my children and paying them of the same proportion as my sons John and Abraham when they arrive to the age of 21. My children viz Henry, Nathaniel, James, Sarah, Netty, Scynthia. My beloved Abraham, my brother in law David Smith, Esq., James Jefferies and William Jefferies, exrs., 26 June 1830.

Warrant of appraisement directed to James McKinney, Joh'a McKinney, Jos. G. Smith, Abraham G. Smith & Josiah Henry 16 August 1830 returnable 16 October. Letters testamentary to Abraham Smith 16 Nov 1830.

Pages 327-329: South Carolina, York District. Will of Lillis Smith of district aforesaid... To my well beloved son Ebenezer Walker Smith all my estate both real and personal, and I appoint him sole exr. I authorize my old neighbour James Bates Senr to sign my seal. Lillis Smith (LS), Wit: John Bates Senr, E. Turner, Lucinea Davie.

Warrant of appraisement on the estate of Lillis Smith directed to Tennenas[?] Bates, Eaton Turner, Thomas Bates, Robert Ellis, Arch'd Steele 9 Aug 1830 returnable 9 October. Letters testamentary to Ebenezer Walker Smith 9 Aug 1830.

Page 329: South Carolina, York District. Letters testamentary on the will of William Rainey deceased to John Rainey 9 Feb 1829.

Pages 330-331: Will of Margaret White of York District... To Margaret White, Margaret Robinson, Margaret Bell, Margaret Gaston, Jane Brown, Molsey Dunlap, Jane Blair, Dorcas Blair, Benjamin Massey, George D. Blair, $30 each. To Wm White my negro man Antony and $250. To my nephew John Blair of Camden, $200. To Margaret Cherry $200. To Margaret McKorkle $20 and also to John and James Stewart $20 each. To James and Cooper Blair $50. To Eliza Harper and he heir two feather beds, bureau, my sorrel horse, my negro woman Tena and her five children namely Ritta, Katena, Jack, Fib, and William, and in the even of her death without issue then to be equally divided between James Harper Blair's heirs and William White. To John J. White all my land bounded by said White, Big Sugar Creek & Doctor Lawrence's land. My negro man Will have the privilege of choosing his master and that be appraised by two good men which shall be the price for which he is to be sold, also that all my other property be sold and the proceeds applied to the legacies mentioned & the remainder paid by Elisa Harper or her heirs if any or it reverts to James H. Blair's children and William White. I appoint William White and John Blair, exrs., 23 Aug 1830. Margaret White (LS), Wit: Buckner Lanier, Wm Glover, Susanna Lanier. Proved 22 Jan 1831 by the oath of Wm. Glover and at same time qualified Wm. White and John Blair, exrs.

Pages 331-332: Will of Jacob Benson of South Carolina, Darlington District but now in the district of York... My corn, pork, and all provisions be delivered to my wife Harriet Benson and her children. My seed cotton that I had on hand or that was in my house to sell for the purpose of getting her some groceries. My land that I purchased of Moss Jonston be reserved for my wife and children to live on till the youngest becomes of age, and then divided equally among my wife Harriet and my three [children] one by my first wife Nancy by name Briget, Jacob [not clear]. I wish Wm. Dewit to be executor, 3 Jan 1830. Jacob Benson (Seal), Wit: Wm. White, Joseph Rodgers, Dorcas White. Proved in York District 22 Jan 1831 by the oath of Wm White.

Pages 332-333: Will of Henry Harrison of the District of York... To my daughter Mary Latham the sum of $300. To my daughter Sarah Latham in addition to the sum of $300 which I have already given her, $100. To my son William E. Harrison in addition to what I have at various times given him, $100. I nominate my friend David Watson and my son Wm Harrison, exrs., 22 Jan 1831. Henry Harrison (X), Wit: Saml. Watson, Albert Watson, Jane Wilson (X). March 7th 1831, proved by the oath of Albert Watson. AT same time qualified David Watson and William Harrison, exrs.

Pages 333-334: South Carolina, York District. Will of Wm Ardary of district aforesaid... To my beloved wife Jean Ardary the house in which I now live, her maintenance off the plantation, her choice of horses, and household and kitchen furniture. To my son Alexander Ardary my negro girl named Meriah. I leave to my son Joseph Ardary the price of my negro Washington in cash, the boy to be sold. TO my daughter Nancy Ardary my negro girl Sarah, also my clock and cupboard, her bed and furniture, my panskin mare and her colt, also that piece of land on which Jeremiah Tommasson now lives to begin where the road from Samuel Chambers to Ebenezar croseth Mr. Wright's line, to James Fewel. To my sons Wm Ardary, John Ardary & Robert Ardary, the balance of my land equally divided amongst them. To John Ardary the place on which he now lives. To my daughter Jane Fewel and son in law James Fewel my loom and tackling, also a note on said James Fewel. To my daughter Polly Thomason a woman's saddle or price thereof. The balance of my property to be sold and equally divided betwixt Peggy McElwaine, Betsey Priestly, Lety Alexander, Jean Fewel, and Polly Thomasson. I appoint Alexander Moore & Joseph McCuen, exrs., 26 June 1829. Wm Ardary (mark), Wit: Alexander Moore, James Wright, Joseph McCain.

Pages 334-337: South Carolina, York District. Will of Samuel Lowry of district aforesaid... To my wife Susan Lowry during her natural life or widowhood that part of my plantation whereon I now live known by the name of the McWhorter tract with its improvements, and eight negroes Anny, Salley, Lancaster, Delpha, Joe, Edmond, Chany & Dick, they being the negroes she inherited of her father, also four horses, etc. My furniture I enforce on her to divided equally between herself and my daughters as they marry or arrive at the age of 21 years. All the remainder of my lands do remain undivided and be worked by my negroes until my youngest child arrives at full age, and then to be equally divided between all my children unless my son Samuel should wish to settle on a part of it when he arrives at full age. I wish that my son John do continue at school until he attains the age of 21 years and then to receive one seventh part of my personal estate, however, to deduct the monies expended for his schooling, etc. To my sons Samuel, James, and William each one seventh part of my personal estate not above willed when they arrive at the age of 21 years. I give to my son Samuel a negro boy called Little Joe exclusive of his share. To my three daughters Mary, Susan & Minerva each one seventh part of my personal estate when they arrive to 21 or marry. I appoint Minor Sadler and Andrew M. Hanna exrs., 1 Dec 1830. Samuel Lowry (LS), Wit: S. W. Melton, Larken Davis, Robert Carr.

Page 337: Will of Elizabeth Neeley, 19 Jan 1831. All the property I old to my son Tollotson S. Neely, and he is executor. Elizabeth Neeley (X), Wit: Joseph W. McCorkle, William Neely, Elizabeth Steel (X).

Pages 337-338: Will of Elizabeth Chambers Senr, Oct. 12th 1825.... To Emd R. Chambers son of my beloved Jas Chambers decd, $100 to be paid to him two years after my decease. To my son John Chambers, Benjamin Chambers, and Samuel Chambers an equal share of the whole of my estate which is principally in notes on themselves,and they pay to the children of Jane Adams decd, and the children of Edmd Chambers decd, $2000 in the following manner. To Francis Adams son of John Adams of Alabama, John Adams Junr & Jane C. McWhorter each $275, and to Drusilla McWhorter widow $325. To my son Edmund Chambers decd four children John J. Chambers, William Chambers, Elizabeth & Mary Chambers each $250. To my son Benjamin Chambers my negro woman slave Lavina to be kept by said Benjn or Harriet Chambers as long as they [live?] and to have a choice of who he may live with after their death. I allow $109 to be kept in reserve for my three grandchildren as a remembrance of the name Jane[?] Chambers daughter of Ben Chambers $10, John Chambers daughter Jane $10 & Samuel Chambers daughter $10, and to Benjamin Chambers daughter Elizabeth $10. My faithful negro woman Sill be maintenance and clothed by my three sons and inform it on my exrs to emancipate and set at liberty if they possible can the two mollato children which I have bound to Robert Wilson of Pendleton District, SC (Rebecca & Cornelius until they are 12 years old). I appoint my sons John Chambers & Samuel Chambers., exrs. Elizabeth Chambers (X), Wit: Wm. D. Henry, Hugh Drenan, William Gilmore.

Pages 339-340: Warrant of appraisement on the estate of Elizabeth Neely directed to Jos McCorckle, Alexr Steel, John Starr, John Anderson & John Starr Junr 28 March 1831 returnable 25 May. Letters testamentary to Tollotson Neely 28 March 1831.

Pages 340-341: South Carolina, York District. Will of James Dannal of district aforesaid... To my daughter Susan Sturges a negro girl which she has now in possession. To my son Wm Dannal my man named Kiney. To my daughter Hannah my negro boy Joe, one bed, 3 coverlids, one white cow. To my daughter Cinthey one negro girl named Harriet. To my daughter Elizabeth one negro boy Si. My land, my negro woman Ann, my stock of every kind, household furniture, plantation tools, etc. to be sold to pay debts. To my son Franklin one third of the price of what my land may sell for. The other two thirds of the price of the land with other property directed to be sold to be equally divided amongst my three youngest children Sinthey, John, Elizabeth, for their support. I appoint William Sturges my son in law, exr., 11 Jan 1831. Jas Danal (LS), Wit: John Cauthen, James Hutcheson, Leroy Hutcheson, David Hutcheson.

Pages 341-342: Will of William Bridges of the district of York... To my son Thomas Bridges half of my real estate including the improvements. The other half to my other two sons Edmond and Robert Bridges. To my said son Thomas one half of the stock and half of the money and debts, also five head of neat cattle. To my daughter Dicy White one bed and furniture. All the remaining part of my estate to be sold and one third of the amount of said sale to my daughter Dicy White, and other two thirds to my three sons Edmund, Robert and Thomas Bridges equally. I ordain said Thomas Bridges, exr., 19 April 1831. Thomas Bridges (LS), Wit: George Plexco, William Bridges, James Moreland.

# YORK COUNTY SC WILL BOOK G 1820-1837

Pages 342-343: Will of John Ellis of the district of York... To my beloved wife Elizabeth the land on which I now live with all buildings, household furniture,, her negroes Jane and Mary. To my daughter Mary Guin my negro women named Dise and her three children Elon, Tame[?], and Ned. To my sons Edmond and Stanford three negroes Rube, Bonapart and Bob, also a tract of land known by the name of the Mill Tract, 164 acres. To my daughter Huldah Dobson one negro woman named Isabella. To my daughter Louisa one negro girl Rachel. To my son Albird a negro boy named Brison. To my son William the negro woman Mary which I have given to my wife after her death. To my daughter Neomy one negro girl named Hannah. To my daughter Dulcina one negro girl name Lousana. I appoint my wife Elizabeth and my son Edmond, exrs., 1 April 1831. John Ellis (LS), Wit: John Smith, John James, Nancy Smith.

Pages 343-344: Warrant of appraisement on the estate of Mary Min directed to James Biggers, Robert Carlisle, Andrew McCarter, Archd Rhea & Wm Countryman 11 April 1831 returnable 5 June. Letters of administration to Jane Carlisle 11 April 1831.

Pages 344-345: Warrant of appraisement on the estate of Edmond Ellis directed to Sherid James Esq., John Smith, Elizabeth Wilson, Hugh Borders, and Nicholas Moss 23 May 1831 returnable 20 July. Letters testamentary to Elizabeth Ellis 23 May 1831.

Pages 345-346: Warrant of appraisement on the estate of James Darnall directed to Wm Schooley, Zaddock Sturges, John Cathy, Wm Campbell & Wm Neely 4 April 1831 returnable 4 July.

Pages 346-347: Warrant of appraisement on the estate of Thomas Bridges directed to Wm. Bridges, Jno Carruth, Alex Moreland, George Plexco, Zadock Packherd 23 May 1831 returnable 20 July. Letters testamentary to Thomas Bridges (Jr.) 23 May 1831.

Pages 347-349: Letters of administration on the estate of Wm Burns to Amos Burns 25 April 1831. Warrant of appraisement directed to Gilbert Enloe, Samuel Turner, Hugh Cain, Robert Brown and Robt Smith 25 April 1831 returnable 25 April [sic].

Pages 349-350: Letters testamentary on the estate of James Darnall to William Sturges 4 May 1831.

Pages 350-351: Will of Isaac Enloe of the District of York... To my wife Vilet all the lands I am now possessed of during her life, all my negroes, stock, cattle, etc. To my son Asahel my Rifle Gun and $3. To my granddaughter Louisa Ann Enloe daughter of Nathaniel Enloe my negro boy named Hicks at her grandmother's death. To Nathaniel Enloe all the borrowed money he owes me & all the notes I have on him at my wife's death. To my son Gilbert Enloe the money he borrowed of me to buy Jerry amounting to $275 and all the notes I have upon him except a $100 note to be given to him, my negro wench Sil at his mother's death. To my daughter Elizabeth McWhorter $3. To my daughter Christiana Givens $3 and all the notes & accounts I have on her husband William Givens at her mother's death. To my daughter Jane Ewing $50 and all the notes I have on her husband William Ewing at her mother's death. To my daughter Hannah Ewing $200 and all the notes I have upon her husband John Ewing at her mother's death. To my daughter Ruth Givens or rather her daughter Eliza Givens my negro girl Rose. To my grandson Rusel Washington Black my negro girl named Necessa at his grandmother's death and as soon as he is of age to be his property. To my sons Nathaniel & Gilbert the following negroes Aaron, Cato, Phebe, & Charles. I appoint my sons Nathaniel and Gilbert Enloe, exrs., 31 Dec 1818. Isaac Enloe (IE) (LS), Wit: Williamson Byers, William Black, George Gull (X).

Pages 351-353: Warrant of appraisement on the estate of Daniel McElmoyle directed to Geo Ross, James Lohridge, Saml Lohridge, McCaslan Wallace & Francis Miller 15 June 1829 returnable 15 August. Letters of administration to William Wright 15 June 1829.

Pages 353-354: South Carolina, York District. Will of John Moore... To Rachel Coulter & to her children, 50 acres of land, it being the upper part of the land I now live on which must include the house and spring. I also give Rachel Coulter & to her children the rent which I am to get of James McConnel, and a negro boy named More. To my brother James Moore my sorrel horse, my present crop: corn, cotton, wheat & oats, the wheat I got from McConnel for rent I allow for Rachel Coulter. My negro boy Sam must attend to the crop until it is gathered. To John Alex Moore, my boy Sam, when he arrives at the age of 21. To John Alexr Moore the balance or lower part of my land which is supposed to be about 80 acres. I allow my brother James Moore to pay my funeral expences. I constitute James Moore Junr, exr., 7 May 1831. John Moore (Seal), Wit: M. A. Moore.

Letters testamentary to James Moore junior 15 Aug 1831.

Pages 354-356: Letters of administration to Edmund Ellis on the estate of John Esqr who died intestate, dated 7 June 1831. Warrant of appraisement directed to Sherud James, Hugh Borders, John Smith, Elijah Wilson & Edwd Bird, 7 June 1831 returnable 7 August.

Pages 356-357: Letters testamentary on the estate of Elisabeth Chambers to John Chambers and Samuel Chambers, exrs., 10 Sept 1831. Warrant of appraisement directed to Wm. R. Gill, J. D. Witherspoon, Stanhope Sadler & Sylvanus Chambers 10 Sept 1831 returnable 10 November.

Pages 357-358: South Carolina, York District. Will of Margaret Cooper... to my dear brother Robt Cooper two negroes named Thomas and Isabella to descend to his heirs or if none to my brother William Cooper. To my brother Robt Cooper one bed and furniture with the present crop on the plantation, the plantation whereon I now reside to sell and divide the proceeds between my brothers William and James Cooper. To my brother John Cooper one negro boy named Ceasar. To my sisters Elizabeth Davison one negro boy named Montony and then to descend to her daughter Eliza Mary, or if no heirs to my niece Ann Galbreath. To my sister Mary Wallace one negro girl named Susan, one bed and furniture, with a stand of curtains. To my sister Elizabeth Davidson one bed and furniture & a stand of curtains. To my brother James Cooper one negro girl named Buenecid[?]. To Margaret Cooper the daughter of my brother John Cooper, all my books. It is my will that my negro woman named Isabel in consequence of her fidelity and grate assistance to my father, mother and myself, shall be at liberty to live with any one of my brothers or sisters that she may make choice of. I constitute my brother Robt Cooper sole exr., 10 July 1824. Margaret Cooper (LS), Wit: James Kuykendal, Mary S. Chambers, Serena L. Chambers.

Pages 358-359: Will of Archibald Stuart of York District... To my eldest son William Stuart 100 acres of land to be laid off where he now lives upon the condition that said Wm Stuart pay to my four youngest daughters Jane, Ann, Margaret and Sarah Stuart $200 to be equally divided among them. To my youngest son Jos. B. Stuart the remainder of my tracts of land on Crowders Creek in the District of York, my waggon, farming utensils, my patent clock. To my grandson James M. Stuart (instead of his mother Agness Stuart) $20 or a young horse of the same value when he shall arrive at the age of 21. The remainder to be equally divided between Joseph, Jane, Ann, Margaret & Sarah Stuart. I appoint Jos. B. Stuart and John A. Laney, exrs., 2 Feb 1828. Archibald Stuart (X). Wit: John Davis, Thomas Davis, Samuel D. Howe.

Pages 359-360: Warrant of appraisement on the estate of John Moore directed to Saml Rainey, Alfred Moore, Jno Brown, Thos Collins and Saml Moore 15 Aug 1831 returnable 15 October.

Page 360: Will of Robert Patrick... The plantation whereon I now reside to be divided between my two youngest sons Wm and David, William to have the upper part and David the improved part, and my wife to have her maintenance off said plantation during her life. My son John A. Patrick have the plantation whereon he now lives. My personal property to be divided according to law between my wife and children. I appoint my beloved friend John A. Patrick and my trusty friend Myles Smith, exrs., 4 Oct 1831. Robert Patrick, Wit: David Currance, William Currance, Jas Bigger.

Pages 361-362: Will of Thomas Carrel of York District... As I have sold my landed estate unto A. W. Thompson not yet executed the deeds that my executors will convey these and two small tracts of land to said A. W. Thompson. To my wife Rebecca Carrel all my real and personal estate (the lands now to be conveyed excepted) to be disposed of as she may think fit. At her death or marriage or when all my children shall arrive at full age, the property be equally divided amongst my wife and children. My executors do defend a fraudulent suit commenced against me by N. N. Coal. I appoint Joseph Whisenant and Abraham Hardin, exrs., 8 Oct 1831. Thomas Carroll (LS), Wit: Eliza Whisenant, Nasa Whisenant, David S. Catey.

Pages 362-363: Will of Robert Love of the District of York... To my daughter Jane $2. To my daughter Mary $2. To my son in law Daniel Turner $2. To my daughter Martha a part of the plantation whereon I now live adj. on a little white oak a little above the mouth of the spring branch adj. James Pursley's Creek. Also to said Martha one mare and two cows, furniture, etc. To my son William all my plantation whereon I now live with the improvements (except what is above willed), books. I appoint my sons William and Henry Carrell, exrs., 5 Oct 1831. Robt Lowe (LS), Wit: Augustus Bryant (X), James M. Pursley, William Love.

Pages 363-364: Warrant of appraisement on the estate of Margaret Cooper directed to John Chambers, Geo Ratchford, Henry Alexander, James Kuykendall, and John Dennis 5 Nov 1831 returnable 5 January. Letters testamentary to Robert Cooper 5 Nov 1831.

Pages 364-365: Letters testamentary on the estate of Robert Patrick to John A. Patrick and Miles Smith 22 Oct 1831. Warrant of appraisement directed to Daniel Currance, Wm. Currance, James Biggers, Wm Youngblood & Capt. Isaac Campbell 22 Oct 1831 returnable 20 December.

Pages 365-366: Warrant of appraisement on the estate of Robt Love directed to John Peters, James M. Pursley, Wm. Love, James Pursley, and Augustus Briant 5 December 1831 returnable 5 January.

Pages 366-367: Warrant of appraisement on the estate of Thomas Carrell Esqr. directed to Joseph Brown, Geo. Whistenant, John Stewart, Abm Hullender & Ewd. Reed 29 October 1831 returnable 19 December. Letters testamentary to Abraham Harden Esqr. & Joseph Whistenant 29 Oct 1831.

Pages 367-370: South Carolina, Fairfield District. In the Court of Ordinary, 17 Jan 1832. John R. Buchanan administered the oath to A. H. Chambers by reference to the will of Massey Mannon. Benjamin Chambers, Ordinary of York District, gave authority to the ordinary of Fairfield District to examine the witness A. H. Chambers to the will of Massey Mannon deceased, 16 Jan 1832.

South Carolina, York District. Will of Massey Mannon.... My son Rodick Mannon appointed executor, and to take into his possession the plantation whereon I now live being the one third of the plantation laid off to me originally the property of my first husband William Sanlin Senr deceased, and all my horses, cows, sheep, hoggs, household furniture. Massey Mannon (mark) (LS), Wit: John J. Chambers, Mary A. Chambers, A. H. Chambers.

Letters testamentary to Rodeck Mannon 19 Jan 1832. Warrant of appraisement directed to John White, John Whistenant, Robert Mannon, Wm. McGill and Thos Mannon 30 Jan 1832 returnable 30 April.

Pages 370-373: Will of William Dickson living on the waters of Crowders Creek, York District.... To my wife Martha Dickson all the estates and property both real and personal in her own possession and power during her life or widowhood (excepted as is hereby excepted). That at my decease of the case cash, notes of hand, and book accounts,to my wife Martha Dickson. To my granddaughter Eliza A. R. Beatty and her heirs a negro girl named Fanny and also all the property once claimed by her mother and deposited in my hands by her father Wm. Beatty for her use. To Isabella Dickson, relict of my son James Dickson decd, $50 provided that she does not insist for the payment of her dower of 100 acres of land sold by James Dickson decd to me, and in that case her recovering her dower, I allow her five shillings sterling. to the three sons of my son Wm. M. Dickson viz James Steel Dickson, Wm. Warrant Washington Dickson and Virgil Fernandes Erasmus Dickson, the plantation whereon I now live, about 354 acres to be equally divided amongst them. I will to the six children of my son Wm. M. Dickson viz Martha Jane, James Steele, Mary Levina, Amanda Emeline, William Warren Washington, and Virgil Fernandes Erasmus Dickson, all my right and claim to a mortgage of sundry articles securing to me the payment of two notes of hand signed W. M. Dickson and payable to me amounting to $62. Also to the said six children of my son W. M. Dickson the one equal fourth of the value or amount of sale of my negro man Esra. To my son William M. Dickson my silver watch. To my daughter Margaret Henry a negro boy named Joseph and one equal fourth of the valuation of my negro man Esra. To my daughter Nancy Corry $300. To my daughter Martha H. McGilliard my negro woman Chloe and any younger children of hers that may be born more than the two that is already willed and bequeathed. Also to Martha H. McGilliard the one equal fourth of the value of my man Ezra. I also allow my books to be divided amongst my four children or their heirs. I appoint Wm. McGill Esqr. and my son Wm. M. Dickson, exrs., 21 Sept 1830. Wm. Dickson (LS), Wit: John Mcgill, wm.Mcgill, Thomas McGill.

Warrant of appraisement directed to Capt. I. Campbell, Wm. Currance, Alexr Barnett, Joseph Barnett, Wm. Moore & Joseph Clinton 13 Dec 1831 returnable 10 February.

Pages 373-374: Letters of administration on the estate of Priscilla McClellan to Robert Douglas, 5 December 1831.

Pages 374-375: Letters testamentary on the estate of Archibald Stewart to Joseph B. Stewart, exr., 30 Dec 1831.

Pages 375-377: Letters of administration on the estate of Jonathan Gallespie, late of Tennessee, late of York District, deceased, intestate, to William Jamieson, Esqr., 2 January 1832. Warrant of appraisement directed to John Campbell, Esqr., Wm. Grey and Cornelius O. Daniel returnable 5 March 1832.

Pages 377-378: Warrant of appraisement on the estate of Rev. Wm Dixon directed to Wm McGill, Esqr., And. Floyd, John McElwee Senr., James Crawford, Clerk Jones & Thos C. Henry 4 Feb 1832 returnable 4 April. Letters testamentary to William M. Dixon 4 Feb 1832.

Pages 378-379: Letters of administration on the estate of Revd. James K. Kerr who died intestate to Zenos D. Kerr 6 Feb 1832. Warrant of appraisement directed to Cordelud [?], Wm Watson, Lelan Suggs, Joseph Feemster & Wm. Clerk Senr 6 Feb 1832 returnable 6 April.

Pages 379-380: Letters of administration on the estate of Edmund Clerk who lately died intestate to George R. Clerk, 9 December 1831. Warrant of appraisement directed to Joseph S. Higgins, Saml Robinson, Saml T. Higgins, John Polk, & D. W. Faires 9 Dec 1831 returnable 9 December [sic].

Pages 380-381: South Carolina, York District. Will of Jane Gallagher of district aforesaid... To my daughter Martha Gallagher my negro man Aude provided that my daughter Esther shall have half the proceeds of his labor. To my daughter Martha one bed and furniture, all my cooking utensils. To my daughter Esther Gallagher a bed and furniture. The balance of my property consisting of my negro man Jim and other pieces of property to be sold and the money arising from the sale to be equally divided between my daughters Esther and Matilda. I appoint Joseph Carroll executor, 8 March 1832. Jane Gallagher (X) (LS), Wit: O. Sandefer, Jas Johnson, Minor Sadler.

Pages 381-382: Warrant of appraisement on the estate of Margaret White, William White executor, directed to Robt Wallace, John J. Kendrick and Wm. Lier[?] 20 March 1832 returnable 1 May.

Pages 382-384: Whereas Wm Hagins has lately departed this life leaving a paper purporting to be a will dated 28 March 1832 witnessed by Dr. A. Barron, Wm. B. Dunlap and the same being witnessed only by two persons it cannot be valid in law as a will. Yet all the heirs at law being of full age and willing and desiring that the intentions of the said Wm. Hagins as expressed in the said instrument shall be carried into effect... 2 April 1832. Mary Hagins (X) (LS), James Haney (LS), D. S. Catton (LS), William J. Hagins (LS), Wit: R. A. Springs, Jno Crocket, J. Burns.

Will of William Hagins... to my wife Mary Hagins a negro woman named Rose, a negro girl named Dark, and a negro boy named London, also I allow her a bed and the house & kitchen furniture. After her deceased to my son in law David Patten the negro girl Rose & her increase and to my son William P. Hagins after the decease of my wife the negro girl Dark, and the negro boy London. To my son James Hagins the negro woman Jean and her two children Charlotte & Gace[?]. I give to my son James a claim I have against him of $100 which I am bound to Wm. Moffit for. I given him $100 out of the price of negro boy Isack to be hereafter willed. Also a claim against my son James of $50 for corn. To my son in law David Patten two negroes a girl named Anica and a malotta boy named Isack. To my Wm P. Hagins a negro boy named Jackeah, the horse, saddle and bridle which he claims. To my Mary Hagins a sorrel mare saddle, bridle, and at the death of my wife the same to belong to my daughter the wife of David Patten. I appoint my son in law David Patten, exr., 28 March 1832. Wm. Hagins, Wit: A. Barron,Wm. B. Dunlap.

Pages 384-386: Letters of administration to Dr. H. I. Cathcart on the estate of James F. Wallace who died intestate, dated 9 Jan 1832. Warrant of appraisement directed to John Fewel, Minor Sadler, Philip Sandefer Esqr., McCasland Wallace, and Alex Fewell, 9 Jan 1832 returnable 9 March.

Pages 386-387: South Carolina, York District. Warrant of appraisement on the estate of Dr. Wm. H. Clawson, George Pettus admr., directed to John Springs, John Jackson, \_\_\_\_ Meacheam, John Bennett & Wm. Bartlett 19 March 1832 returnable 15 May. Letters of administration to George Pettus Junr 19 March 1832.

Pages 387-389: South Carolina, York District. Letters of administration on the estate of Abraham Miller who died intestate to Sarah M. Miller 19 March 1832. Warrant of appraisement directed to Dr. J. T. Miller, John Hart, Edward Avery, Thomas Johnson[?], and George Morgan 19 March 1832 returnable 20 May.

Pages 389-391: South Carolina, York District. Warrant of appraisement on the estate of William S. Higgins, David S. Patton admr., directed to Wm Dunlap, John McClenachan, James Dunlap, Isaac McFadden & Thomas Massey 9 April 1832 returnable 9 June. Letters of administration to David S. Patton 9 April 1832.

Page 391: Will of Zadoc Packard... The whole of my estate to my beloved wife Mary Packard during her natural life or widowhood, and then to be equally divided between my four children Leander, Marthay, William & Margaret. My wife Margaret Packard, exr., 10 Dec 1831. Zedoc Packard, Wit: George Plexco, Wm. Plexco, G. W. Plexco.

Pages 392-393: South Carolina, York District. Warrant of appraisement on the estate of Wm Alderson, John Weeks admr., directed to John Springs, Jerry Alderson, Edmund Weathers, Henry Meacham and Bartlett Meacham 15 Feb 1832 returnable 5 April. Letters of administration to John Weeks 15 Feb 1832.

Pages 393-394: Warrant of appraisement on the estate of Zaddock Palkard [Packard], Mary Polkard executrix, directed to Wm Plexco, Smith Wilkins, Geo Plexco Esqr., Henry Moss & Wm. Moore 2 May 1832 returnable 4 July. Letters testamentary to Mary Palkard 7 May 1832.

Page 395: Will of Nathaniel Henderson in the county of York, 14 Feb 1832... To my wife Sarah one half of my lands, my negro woman named Lucy, my negro man named Harry so long as she remains my widow. To my son John the other half of my lands, my negro girl named Nancy, my negro boy Andrew. If my son John should die without issue, then this property to go to the disposal of Elizabeth Carrol and Thomas Henderson. I appoint my said wife Sarah and my son John, exrs. Nathaniel Henderson (LS), wit: Thomas Falkner, William Love, Saml Bradley.

Pages 395-397: Letters testamentary on the will of Jane Gallegher to Joseph Carrel 21 March 1832. Warrant of appraisement directed to Minor Saddler, Philip Sandifer, Charles McElwain, John Barron, John Carrel & James Johnston 21 March 1832 returnable 20 August.

Pages 397-398: Will of John Thompson of District of York... My wife Cynthia shall receive two negroes viz Absalom and Sophia his wife, two beds and furniture, and a set of china ware. To my daughter Malinda Ann three negroes viz Caty and her two daughters Rosinda and Hannah, a bed and furniture and $75 in cash. To my son Thomas Dabney two negroes viz Jane and Walker, a young bay horse and a bed and furniture. To my two granddaughters Nancy M. and Cynthia Jane Wright one negro to each viz Lond and Jim. To my three youngest children one negro to each of them, viz to Sarah L. I give Ben, to John L. I give Primas, to Cynthia E. I give Simon. The residue of my property be sold and after payment of debts, the balance shall be divided into seven equal parts: one part to my wife Cynthia, one part to Malinda Ann, Nancy M. and Cynthia Jane Wright, Thomas D., Sarah L., John L. and Cynthia E. I appoint my brother in law James M. Harris, exr., 2 June 1832. John Thomson (Seal), Wit: James Carrothers, Samuel D. Carrothers, Austin Garison.

Pages 399-401: Will of Alexander Holloway Sen of York District... To my beloved wife Mary a good feather bed, bedstead and furniture, a cow, and my riding chair, and a full support from the lands hereinafter divided and given to my sons James, Hugh A. and Peter W., and she is to live in my present dwelling during her life or widowhood. To my son James that tract of land that he now occupies adj. lands of James Feemster and others as laid off by platt of survey made by John Minter, 230 acres, one cow and calif, and a feather bed and furniture. To my son Robert Alexander, books and one volume of Christian Magazine, feather bed and furniture. To my daughter Margaret a tract of land on Quins Road, 197 acres per plat dated 9 April 1822. To my son Hugh a tract on Quins Road, 307 acres, also part of the tract laid off for my son Jonathan to adjoin the above tract adj. William Galloway, John Galloway. To my son Peter W. a tract of 352 acres and the residue of the tract laid off for my son Jonathan. My son Jonathan at the proper expence of my sons Hugh A. and Peter W. be put through a collegiate education and to be furnished in necessary books and clothing and boarding during his studies at Grammar School and college, to study divinity. To my granddaughter Elizabeth daughter of my son Samuel deceased a tract of land 103 acres adj. Leroy Givens, but if she died without issue, then to my daughter Nancy the wife of William W. Galloway. To my sons William, John, and Alexander and my daughter Nancy, one dollar, as I have heretofore given them a full share of my estate. I appoint my sons Hugh A. and Peter W., exrs., 2 July 1824. Alex'r Galloway (LS), Wit: J. A. Wylie, T. Brown, Saml Wylie. Resigned, sealed and acknowledged 10 Sept 1828 before Joseph Dowdle, Samuel Wylie, Allen Dowdle.

Pages 402-404: South Carolina, York District. Will of Elvy Miller of district aforesaid... To my son Jonathan Miller my negro girl Minta. To my daughter

Jean Sears a half dozen silver tea spoons and half dozen silver table spoons. The residue of my estate-- horses, cattle, hogs, household and kitchen furniture, to be sold by my executor and the proceeds divided amongst my surviving children. I appoint Joseph Lewis, my son in law, exr., 14 Jan 1833. Elvy Miller (her mark) (LS), Wit: John A. Wherry, Wm. C. Wherry, Thomas Robertson.

Warrant of appraisement directed to Allen Robinson, Stratton Edwards, Gray Morgan, Grey Westbrooks & Wm. Wherry 28 Jan 1833 returnable 20 March. Letters testamentary to Joseph Davis 26 Jan 1833.

Pages 404-409: Will of Joshua Tilghman of the district of York... To my beloved wife Margaret one bed & furniture, her wheels & cards. I also loan unto her a negro boy named daniel during the term of her natural life, and after her decease to my son Stephen until his second son Jackson Tilghman arrives to the age of 21. I then give the same to Jackson Tilghman or his heirs. To my wife one horse, saddle, and bridle, and at her death to my daughter Elizabeth. I also give her two cows & Calves and at her death to my son Ivy. To my son John one tract of land in North Carolina, Mecklenburgh County on the Catabaw River, 290 acres, also one negro boy named Charles until his oldest son Sherwood Tilghman arrives tot he age of 21, then to said Sherwood Tilghman or his heirs. Also to my son John one negro boy named Sam until his daughter Margaret arrives to the age of 18 years, then to her. To my son Stephen one piece of land in North Carolina, Mecklenburg County, 40 acres and one situate in York District with a good grist mill on it, 100 acres. To my son Robert a family of negroes Nelson & June his wife, & Charlotte their daughter, until the younger of my sons Robert's two daughters Mary & Nancy Tilghman arrives to the age of 18, then to them. To my daughter Scintha one negro woman named Linda with one negro girl named Jinney, and then to her heirs. If no such heirs my son in law Elijah Robinson should survive my daughter then to him during his lifetime, and then to my son John's two children John Newton and Nancy Tilghman. To my daughter Elizabeth one negro woman named Sinar with her son Sampson, daughter Mary & son Jack. To my son Ivy one tract of land whereon my mansion house is situation in York District, 250 acres with one tract in North Carolina, Mecklenburgh County adj. the above, 100 acres, also two negroes Isaac & George. The rest to be sold and divided between my wife Margaret & daughter Elizabeth and my son Stephen's oldest son Eli Tilghman. I appoint my son Stephen sole executor, 8 Oct 1832. Joshua Tilghman (mark) (LS), Wit: Stephen Pettus, Hugh Harris, James Thorn.

Warrant of appraisement directed to Alsey Fuller, Jno Viven, Saul Pettus, Stephen Pettus, Jesse Faires & James Thorn 4 March 1833 returnable 4 May. Letters testamentary to Stephen H. Tilghman 4 March 1833.

Pages 409-414: Will of John Howser of the district of York... To my wife Nancy the choice of my two plantations either the one on Kings Creek of 70 acres or the plantation where I now live, 340 acres. The one not chosen to be rented out to the highest bidder annually and the rents applied to the support and education of the family until my youngest child shall arrive to the age of 21 years. Then the plantation rented out to be sold and the money divided equally among my children after making them equal with those that have received part of their divided before hand & as I purchased all that tract of land of my father's estate sold as the McCarter tract on the south side of Kings Mountain & there remains a part of said tract viz 333 1/3 acres that I have not yet received any title for as such, I will that my executors obtain from the executors of my father's estate the title for said land if it can be obtained and sell to the highest bidder and the money divided among my children. Also to my wife Nancy one negro man named Washington, all the stock of hogs, cattle, etc. The still & vessals be sold, also a small wagon, the surplus of neat cattle. I appoint my wife Nancy and Thomas N. Martin, exrs. The negro Bill that has been omitted to be hired out annually as the negro woman until the children all comes to full age, 29 Nov 1832. John Houser (LS), Wit: Shared James, Lucy James (X), Abraham Hardin.

Warrant of appraisement directed to Sharid James Esqr., Col. Ed. Byrd, Abm Hardin, Jos Whistenant, Henry Howser, 25 March 1833 returnable 20 May. Letters testamentary to Nancy Howser and Thomas N. Martin, 25 March 1833.

Pages 413-415: South Carolina, York District. Will of Joseph Brown of district aforesaid. To my daughter Mary Ware all my whole estate, that is to say one tract whereon I now live, 337 acres on Kings Creek adj. land of Aaron Inman & Jonathan Stewart & others, cattle, hogs, furniture. I appoint my friends Abraham Hardin & Joseph Whistenant exrs., 21 Jan 1826. Jos Brown (mark), Wit: Saml Kernon, Aaron Whistenant, Nicholas Whistenant, Geo Whistenant (X) (LS).

Warrant of appraisement directed to Nicholas Whistenant, Wm. Griffin, Hezekiah Inman, Jon'a Stewart & Aaron Whistenant 29 April 1833 returnable 29 June. Letters testamentary to Joseph Whistenant 29 April 1833.

Pages 415-416: Will of John Henderson of the district of York... To Mary Henderson, my wife, the plantation I now live on during her lifetime and at her deceased my grandson Franklin Davidson shall fall heir to it. To my wife my secretary & cupboard and at her deceased to my grandson Franklin Davidson. Also to my grandson Franklin Davidson a mare by the name of Pegion. To my grandson Franklin Davidson, a negro boy named Jack. My negro woman named Feab & my negro boy Allen be kept on the plantation for the use and benefit of Mary Henderson my wife & Franklin Davidson my grandson, and be sold at the death of my wife and the amount equally divided between Violet Neely, Wm. Henderson, John Henderson, James P. Henderson & Rebeckah Pressley. I appoint my son James P. Henderson and my son John Henderson, exrs., 23 Sept 1823. John Henderson, Wit: Thos H. Douglass, Jas Simeral, Elias Garison. The executors unwilling to qualify 31 Dec 1832.

Pages 417-419: South Carolina, York District. Will of John Johnston of district aforesaid... To my wife Margaret Johnston all my household & kitchen furniture & one years provisions, my old gray mare. The remainder of my personal property be sold at publick auction and the monies used to pay my debts. When my land shall be sold that a small farm be purchased for my family to live on which farm at the death of my wife shall be sold & the proceeds equally divided between my children. I appoint my wife executrix and my friend Andrew McConnell, exr., 5 April 1833. John Johnston (LS), Wit: John A. Laney, R. Barnett, E. Johnston.

Warrant of appraisement directed to Richard Barnett, Wm Campbell, W. L. Harris, Robt Johnston & Wm. M. Bigger 22 July 1833 returnable 3 August. Letters testamentary to Andrew McConnell & Margaret Johnston 22 July 1833.

Pages 419-422: South Carolina, York District. John Roberts, executor of the will of Andrew Roberts deceased, desires to have the will proven in solemn form or form of law... cite the next or kin or heirs at law to appear, 20 May 1833. Nancy Roberts accepted the legal service of this citation, Wit: Jas Rogers.

Will of Andrew Roberts of York District... My wife to have any such property as he & my executors shall think property for the support of her & my child without it being put to sale and Robert Smith to have $200 in place of the one half of the negro girl that me & my brother John was to buy. My son John J. Roberts to have at the death of my wife all my whole estate. I appoint my brother John Roberts, exr., 4 March 1833. And. Roberts, Wit: Edwd Feemster, And Leatham, Jas. B. Good.

Warrant of appraisement directed to Jno Hemphill Esqr, Jas B. Good, Edward Feemster, James Meek & Andrew Lathan Junr 3 June 1833 returnable 3 August. Letters testamentary to John Roberts 3 June 1833.

Pages 422-423: Will of Nancy Wylie of the district of York... To my daughter Polly one black horse & chest. To my son Samuel two cows & calves, one bed & furniture, one cupboard, one folding table, all the kitchen furniture, two chests, & all the sitting chairs. I appoint my son James Wylie, exr., 21 June 1833. Nancy Wylie (LS), Wit: Jacob Randall, Peter Morris, Jas McCosh.

Warrant of appraisement directed to Wm Plexco, Wm. Moore., Jno Starns, James Wood and James Randall 8 July 1833 returnable 8 September.

Pages 423-429: South Carolina, York District. Will of Joseph Miller of district aforesaid... To my wife Nancy Miller the negro woman Pamela, the mare, saddle, bridle & blanket she now claims, two cows, the bureau, bed. My property to be kept together untill the youngest surviving child arrives at the age of 14 years before any permanent division be made except some of the children hereinafter named marries before that time, then I allow my executors to give off what I hereafter mention. My wife to have her maintenance from the plantation whereon I now reside composed of the plantation I got from Mathew Carrell & Thomas Simpson Senr, the land and negroes. My lands composed of the plantation I got from Thomas Simpson Senr,

Matthew Carrell, John Barron & what was willed to me by my father, that they be equally divided as to quantity & quality among my four sons (viz) Samuel Neely Miller, Joseph Miller, James M. Miller, Benjamin R. Miller. With regard to my son John Miller is that he receive a liberal education. All the negroes that I now have & their increase except Pamela to be equally divided among my children boys and girls. To each of my daughters I give above their share of my negroes a horse, saddle & Bridle, bureau, bed, a bible, a set of knives and forks, a set of cups &saucers & plats. My daughter Rachel's son Saml N. have their saddle & bridle this fall. I appoint my wife Nancy executrix & my friend Minor Carroll, exr., 17 July 1833. Jos Miller (LS), Wit: Jos Carrell, H. J. Cathcart, Samuel Carrell.

Warrant of appraisement directed to Jos Carrell, Jno Carrell, Wm. Barry, David Walton & John Barron 9 Sept 1833 returnable 9 November. Letters testamentary to Nancy Miller 9 Sept 1833.

Pages 429-431: South Carolina, York District. Will of Rev. William Gassaway Senr.... My estate to be divided into seven equal shares: to my son William one seventh, to my daughter Rachel Kenan one seventh, to my daughter Sarah Pressley one seventh, to my daughter Mary Fewell one seventh, to my daughter Rebeckah Robinson one seventh, to my son Caleb one seventh, and to the children of my son James one seventh among them. I appoint my sons Wm. Gasaway & Caleb Gasaway, exrs., 4 Sept 1832. Wm Gassaway (Seal), Wit: Thos Williams Jr[?], M. T. Hall, Jno R. Hall.

Warrant of appraisement directed to M. T. Hall, Jno Fewell Senr, Wm Henderson Senr, Wm. Barron Senr, & Wm Barron 7 Oct 1833 returnable 7 December. Letters testamentary to Caleb Gassaway 7 Oct 1833.

Pages 431-433: Will of William F. Rowell of York District... To my beloved wife Betsey Rowell my plantation whereon I now live, two negro men Randall and Isom, two horses Jack and Ribbon, three feather beds and their furniture, plantation tools for two hands to work with. My books to be divided among all my children except my margin Bible which I give to my wife. I give my large Bible to my daughter Mary A. Rowell, and one young mare called Pigeon. To all my seven daughters two feather beds each, Betsy Foreman has received hers already. I give $12 to each of my daughters living with me to purchase a bureau apiece. Mary A. Rowell and Nancy A. Rowell has got theirs already. I have given to my son Benjamin Rowell one horse which I rated to him at $50 as part of his share of my estate. To my wife two notes one on D. Edmond[?] Jennings and one on Carson's estate. I also give $20 to the manger of the Methodist fund of special relief. Also to my three sons Benj D. Rowell, William A. Rowell and Thos C. H. Rowell one feather bed to each. The remainder of my estate put into seven equal parts: to my daughter Mary A. Rowell, Nancy W. Rowell, Sally C. Rowell, Betsey F. Foreman, Benjamin D. Rowell, Milley E. Rowell, Hannah J. Rowell, Peggy C. Rowell, Wm. A. Rowell, Thomas E. H. Rowell. James L. Foreman and his wife Betsey Foreman has had $107 as part of their part of my estate. At the death of my wife, my land to be divided among my ten children. I appoint my son

Benjamin D. Rowell and my daughter Mary A. Rowell, exrs., 1 Aug 1833. Wm. Rowell (LS), Wit: Benj Rowell, Henry Clerk, Catherine Rowell.

Pages 433-437: York District, South Carolina. Will of John Jackson... To my five oldest children viz Henry, Sally, Cresy, Jane, & Keziah, the six hereafter named negroes Sam, Aimy, Mary, Ned, Hulday & Tom to be equally divided among them, and let it be understood that the negroes formerly given to them that is one apiece they are to have & hold as formerly given. Sampson was named two much & i have stricken out his name from the first five children. To my wife, so long as she shall live a widow, all my lands in Alabama, all the rest of my negroes vizt Fan, Peter, Isaac, Bill, Ben, Aaron, Silvy, Sampson, Jim, Mingo, Wiley, Stephen & Bachany, all my stock of horses, etc., to enable my wife and her children that are not married to move to Alabama, and when her boys comes of age, they are to have one negro a piece and the privilege of occupying a part of the land in Alabama. The girls as they come of age are to have a negro. My four sons to divide all my lands in Alabama vizt Ephraim, James Greenlee, John Newton & Isaac, and the rest of the property at the marriage or death of my wife to be equally divided among her seven children viz, Barbary, Elizabeth, Ephraim, James Greenlee, John Newton, Isaac, and Louisa. The tract I now live on to be sold. Son Henry and friend Bartlet Meacham, exrs., 18 Sept 1833. John Jackson (LS), Wit: Edward Smith, Mary Crenshaw, S. Graham.

Warrant of appraisement directed to Edward Smith, Jno Barnett, W. E. White, John Springs, Henry Meacham 21 Oct 1833 returnable 20 Dec. Letters testamentary to Bartlett Meacham 21 Oct 1833.

Pages 437-440: The widow consenting in writing... South Carolina, York District. Whereas under the will of Jeremiah Blalock executed 24 January 1829... All the property that remains at the death of my wife be sold & equally divided between the legatees, only my son William Blalock not to have a share." Now for the purpose of preventing the property (not specifically devised by name) from waste of diminution of value, I, the said Lucy Blalock, widow & relict of Jeremiah Blalock do consent that all the property not devised to me under the said will except what is herein excepted be ordered by the Judge of the Court of Ordinary to be sold, the property excepted Two horses, four head of cattle, eight head of sheep, five hoggs for present use, furniture, 200 bushels of corn and a sufficiency of roughness for the support or the stock. 13 Nov 1822. Lucy Blalock (LS), Wit: Benjn Chambers.

South Carolina, York District. Will of Jeremiah Blalock of the district aforesaid... To Mary Whistenant my daughter & heirs two negro girls Nancy & Nancy. To my daughter Anna Whistenant & heirs two negro girls Pat & Mariah. To my daughter Elizabeth Fulton & heirs two negro girls Suckey & Maida. To my son William Blalock the tract of land on which I now live. To my son John Blalock & heirs one negro girl Elisa & $200 in money or property at cash prices. To my son Edmond Blalock two negro girls Aggy [sic]. To my son Jeremiah Blalock Junr, one negro boy named Daniel, $240 in money. My wife Lucy Blalock do have her support of my tract of land that I now live on during her life or widowhood & that my negro man Russ & my negro woman Penny[?] do remain on said land during the life of my wife for her support. All the property that remains at the death of my wife be sold and equally divided between the legatees only my son William Blalock not to have a share. I appoint Wm. Blalock and Daniel A. Fulton, exrs., 24 Jan 1829. Jeremiah Blalock (X) (LS), Wit: Robt Caldwell, Thos Falkner, James Caldwell.

Warrant of appraisement directed to Robt Caldwell, Thos Falkner, Jno Whistenant, Charles Henry & Theodore Fulton 4 Nov 1833 returnable 4 January.

Pages 440-442: South Carolina, York District. Will of Elizabeth Sandefer... to my daughter Mary, wife of Wm. Lacy, $50. To my son William Sandefer's children $250 to be equally divided among them. To my daughter Elizabeth, wife of Thomas Simpson, a negro girl named Malinda during her life and at her death to go to Margaret Elizabeth, daughter of my daughter Elizabeth. To my son Lowry $100. TO my son Green a negro man named Moses. To my son Philip a negro man named Law[?]. To my daughter Catherine, wife of Mansfield Gordon, two negro girls named Harriot & Mary, and the girl may go to Elizabeth Ann, daughter of my daughter Catherine. To my daughter Caroline a negro woman named Sarah & a negro girl named Margaret. To my grandson Calvin, son of my son Green, a negro man named Jack. To my granddaughter Elvira a negro girl named Jean. To my three daughters Elizabeth, Catherine & Caroline, all my household furniture, except such bedding & Furniture as I have given to my granddaughter Elvira. The balance of my property viz one negro man named Tony, a wagon, a riding chair, the cattle, hogs, sheep, farming utensils, to be sold to pay debts and the cash legacies, any balance to be equally divided between my two sons Green & Philip, 17 Oct 1832. Green Sandefer and Philip Sandefer, exrs. Elizabeth Sandefer (LS), Wit: Wylie L. Harris, Samuel Croft, C. H. Harris, Cervantas Harris.

Pages 442-445: South Carolina, York District. Will of James Harris of district aforesaid... To my well beloved wife Jane, a negro girl named Kesiah with all her offspring and all the female offspring of Jude, also one horse, saddle & bridle, with all the household furniture that she brought with her, and I allow her the full & free possession of my dwelling house for her comfortable support & providing for my children by her. To my son Eleazer a part of the tract known by the name of the Carter tract on the south side of the Thorn ferry road, and I consider him to have received all that legacy that was due to him by his uncle John Hunter due out of my estate. To my son Henry the one half of the tract of land whereon I now live at my wife's death or marriage, 1 1st and 6th choice of my negroes, and a saddle & Bridle when he arrives at the age of 21 years, with my secretary & book case, and half of my plantation which I bought from Eleazer, also my surveying instruments. To my son Robert Harvey the one half of the land of land whereon I now live at my wife's death or marriage, a 2nd and fifth choice of my negroes, a horse and saddle when he arrives at the age of 20 years, with my clock & walnut beau book case, and half of the tract purchased from Eleazer. To my daughter Martha Jane a 3rd & 4th choice of my negroes not otherwise named, a horse and saddle when she arrives at the age of 20 years. My books to be equally divided between my wife and my children except Eleazer who has received his part, also that my son John's children receive one share. To my granddaughter Nancy Harrison one negro girl named Phebe. At my wife's decease or marriage all my negroes not taken by choice or sold be equally divided between my sons Eleazer if he has legal offspring John Hunter's sons one share, Henry & Robert Harvey & Martha Jane. I appoint my son Henry & Hugh Harris exrs., 25 Dec 1832. James Harris (LS), Wit: John M. Harris, Nancy Strong, John D. Harris, John R[?[ Strong.

Warrant of appraisement directed to Alex'r Scott, John M. Harris, Stephen Pettus, Bartlet Meacheam & Edmund Weathers 30 Jan 1834 returnable 1 April. Letters testamentary to Henry & Hugh Harris 30 Jan 1834.

Page 446: South Carolina, York District. Will of Samuel Blair of district aforesaid... To my beloved wife Mary Blair, one third of all my real & personal estate to her own use & entirely at her disposal at her death To my son Samuel Blair, two thirds of my plantation on the waters of Bullocks Creek of Broad River. To my children Isabella Blair, Nancy Blair, Elva Blair, Mary Blair & Samuel Blair, all the balance of my estate. I appoint Wm. Jameson, Robert Hays & James H. Alexander, exrs., 5 Sept 1833. Saml Blair (LS), Wit: Robt McNeely, Jno T. McNelly, Henry G. Plexco.

Page 447: South Carolina, York District. Will of Richard Sadler of district aforesaid... all my estate real and personal including lands, negroes, stock, money on hand or debts due me to my wife Mary Robertson Sadler. I appoint my son Minor Sadler, exr., 5 Nov 1833. Richard Sadler (LS), Wit: Benjn Rowell, J. H. McKorkle, Jas Williamson.

Pages 447-449: Will of Elizabeth Brumfield of the district of York... My executors to expose to publick sale the whole of my estate both real & personal except my slaves which I allow the liberty of choosing their own masters & sold by my executor at private sale for whatever he can obtain for them. I also allow my slaves to have all their little property. To my brother John Patton $100, also to my brother David Patton $100. To my beloved grand [son] James Feemster $100, also to my niece Easther Wallace daughter of John & Easther Wallace $30 when she marries or comes of age. To my niece Elizabeth daughter of Henry and Eave Carrell to be paid when she marries or comes of age $30. Also to my niece Isabella Wallace daughter of Wm Wallace & Isabella Wallace $30 when she marries or comes of age. Also to my sister Sarah James $20, also to my sister Jane James $5, also to my sister Margaret Robertson $5. Should my estate amount to more than is before bequeathed, it is my will that it be divided in property amongst the legatees herein mentioned except the last three to wit Sarah James, Jane James & Margaret Robertson which is only to receive the amount specified. I appoint my friend Andrew McWhorter my executor, 2 Dec 1830. Elizabeth Brumfield (X), Wit: James Wood, Jas. D. Barry, Hillariah Garvin.

Pages 449-452: Will of Aaron Wood of the district of York... To my beloved wife Matilda & my three children Achsah, Martha & Matilda my plantation known by the Locust Ridge place about 168 acres according to the boundaries designated in a survey made & platted by William Campbell 14 Dec 1833, which plat is now in my possession. Also ten negroes viz Ephraim & his wife Patience, Adeson, Andy, Minty, George, Sam, Amanda & Cinthy, three feather beds and furniture such as my wife may choose, $300 in cash, all my stock of hoggs & horned cattle. I do request my son in law John Greer to assist my wife in the management of the affairs of hers and the above named children. To my son Joseph Wood the plantation he lives on lying south of the Locust ridge place, also a negro girl named Sinak & her children. I will nothing to the heirs of my son Resin Wood decd, he having received al the part of my estate I intend. To my son in law Derrel White of the state of Alabama in trust for my daughter Rebeckah Rooker for her sold use & her children, one bond or sealed note on James Mason dated 15 Feb 1834 for $700 payable five years after date. To my daughter Mary Mason wife of James Mason four negroes viz Perlina and her child, Albert & Green with their increase. To my daughter Amelia Greer wife of John Greer four negroes Eliza & her children, Stephen & Frank. To the two children of my son Isaac decd of Tennessee in the care of John K. Wood $300. The remainder of my estate to be divided as follows, one to my daughter Nancy widow of Robert White one fourth part, to my daughter Elizabeth wife of Derrill White one fourth part, to my daughter Candace wife of Francis Bostick one fourth part, and to my daughter wife of ____ Boswell one fourth part. I appoint my friends Richard Barnett & William McBiggers, exrs., 19 June 1834. Aaron Wood (LS), Wit: Matthew Harper, James Harper, John T. Harper.

Pages 452-454: South Carolina, York District. Will of George McSwain of the district aforesaid... After the crop that is growing at the time of my death is gathered that all both my real & personal estate shall be sold on a credit of 12 months and the money collected, it shall be divided int he following manner: to my wife Polly one third, and the remaining two thirds of my daughter Catherine to be put at interest untill she arrives at the age of 18 years, and she is to be educated. I appoint my friends David J. McSwain Jr. & Elizabeth Hambrick, exrs., 16 June 1834. Geo McSwain (LS), Wit: Gordon Moore, David McSwain, James McSwain.

Letters testamentary to David McSwain & Elijah Hambrick 25 Aug 1834.

Pages 454-456: Will of John Kidd Senr of York District... To my beloved wife Elizabeth one bed & furniture, one cow & pot. To my son James his maintenance off the plantation also one bed & covering. To my daughter Jane an equal portion with my son James. To my daughter Martha Kidd one dollar, to my daughter in law Editha Kidd and Easther Kidd an equal portion of the kitchen furniture. To my son John Kidd one dollar. To my sons William & Robert the plantation on which I live to be equally divided between them at the death of their mother. I appoint John McKnight & Wm Guy, exrs., 16 Dec 1833. John Kidd (mark) (LS), Wit: John McKnight, John Wright, Thos J. McElhany. Codicil... having made an equal distribution of my property between my two sons Robert & William Kidd finding that all the trouble & expense is devolving on Wm. Kidd, it is my will that Robert Kidd does make to his brother a remuneration which shall be by two judicious men deemed sufficient out of his part bequeath to Robert Kidd, 9 Feb 1834. John Kidd (mark) (LS), Wit: Jas R. Morrow, Saml Snoddy, Joseph Black.

Pages 456-459: South Carolina, York District. Will of Archibald C. Hanna of the district aforesaid... All property belonging to me except my silver watch which I give to my sister Margaret to be exposed to public sale. After payment of debts, the balance of the money arising from the sale to be equally divided between my two sisters Margaret Hanna & Jane Hanna. The said Jane's part to be kept at interest for her during her life and at her death her part to be divided between my two sisters Anna Black & Sarah E. Kerr. I appoint Dudley Jones & Elijah Kerr my executors, 21 March 1834. Archibald C. Hanna (LS), Wit: Dudley Jones, Jas Jameson, Jno C. Tiping, M. Gordon.

Warrant of appraisement directed to M. Gordon, Jas Moore, Wylie L. Harris, Dudley Jones & Robt Cooper 10 Sept 1834 returnable 16 Nov. Letters testamentary to Elijah Kerr 10 Sept 1834.

Pages 459-463: Will of Walter McCarter of York District... To my daughter Hannah $50. To my two daughters Sarah & Asenath one dollar each. To my four sons Ebenezar, Eleazer, John, and David one dollar each. To my son Joel & Four daughters Isabella, Ina[?], Anna & Kizziah all that tract of land whereon I now live adj. lands of Wm. Brown, Francis Armstrong, Eleazer McCarter, Samuel Wright & others, to be divided amongst them when the youngest marries or becomes of age. All the rest of my estate to be equally divided among my five last children. I appoint my friend Nathaniel P. Kenedy & Alamath Byers, exrs., 15 Jan 1830. Walter McCarter (LS), Wit: Wm. Hasket, Jno M. Lowrie, B. T. Benson.

Warrant of appraisement directed to Wm Brown, Jno Floyd, James Turner, Francis Armstrong & Jas Wood 6 Oct 1834 returnable 6 December. Letters of administration with the will annexed to William Barronwell 6 Oct 1834.

Pages 463-467: Will of James Feemster of the district of York... To my three sons William, Joseph & James B. Feemster, the plantation whereon I now live divided among them to make the share of each when added to the plantation or parcel of land which I have previously deed to each of them of equal value. To my two single daughters Mary & Nancy Feemster in kind as much as will be equal to what my two married daughters Prudence Brown and Latitia Gaston received at their marriage. To my daughter Jane Leeth $300. To my daughters Prudence Brown, Latitia Gaston, Mary Feemster & Nancy Feemster, each $700 after their legacies are paid over. The balance of my property to be divided among my children Prudence Brown, Latitia Gaston, Wm. Feemster, Joseph Feemster, James B. Feemster & Mary & Nancy Feemster. That part of my property which consists of black persons that old Moriah be comfortable maintained out of my estate and it has been the understanding with me & my family that the little motherless child Caroline which has been ___ by my daughter Mary Feemster, I do confirm the aforesaid understanding. As the black persons belonging to me have been long in the family & it would appear harshness to force them contrary to their desire to leave the family, I will that when any of all of them wish and make choice to live with any of my children that the said negro or negroes so choosing shall be appraised and shall be given to the child or children whom they make choice of at the appraisement. I appoint my three sons William Joseph & James B. Feemster, exrs., 23 Sept 1834. James Feemster (LS), Wit: Wm. James[?], Thos. K. McKnight, J. J. Foster.

Warrant of appraisement directed to Thos K. McKnight, John Rainey, Jos Kirkpatrick, John Galloway & Hugh A. Galloway 22 Oct 1834 returnable 22 December. Letters testamentary to Wm, Joseph & James. B. Feemster, 22 Oct 1834.

Pages 467-469: Will of Richard Barnett... The whole of my estate shall be in the possession & at the disposal of my wife Frances Durham Barnett during her life or widowhood. At her death or marriage my land shall be equally divided between my two sons Jno Allen Barnett & Joseph Josiah Barnett by valuation so that they shall not have actually more of my property than an equal dividend with the rest of my children & my wife if living. My children shall have an equal and proportional share of my estate and that each one shall take possession of his or her legacy as soon as he or she shall attain the age of 21 years or be married. I appoint my wife Frances D. Barnett executrix, and Joel S. Barnett exr., 29 Oct 1834. R. Barnett (LS), Wit: A. G. Lawrence, H. J. Cathcart, J. J. Barnett.

Warrant of appraisement directed to James Wallace, Alexr Barnett, Samuel Patillow, Wm. Bigger & An'd McConnell 15 Nov 1834 returnable in sixty days. December 1st 1834 Mrs. Frances P. Barnett qualified as an executrix.

Page 469: Warrant of appraisement on the estate of George McSwain deceased, David J. McSwain & Elijah Hambrick, exrs., directed to James Meek, John Pilcher, Andrew Latham Jr., and David McSwain 25 Aug 1834 returnable 25 October.

Pages 470-471: Will of John Smith of the district of York... To my son Daniel Smith four negroes Bill, Dave, Tom & Hampton & a deed of gift previously given to be his title. To my son Abraham G. Smith five negroes Jack, Jude, Isaac, Dorcus & little Bob, all of said five negroes he now has in his possession & a deed of gift previously given. To my son Joseph G. Smith six negroes Bob, Charles, Bet, Lindy, Elmiry[?], and Agg and a deed of gift previously given, with one large folding left table, one clock & the case, and half of my stock of horse beasts, cattle, & hoggs. To my daughter Hannah Lipscomb $10. To my daughter Polly Gafney $20. To my daughter Any [Amy?] Moore $20. To my daughter in law Margaret Smith $1. To Elizabeth Stevens one sorrel filley now about three years old. I appoint Daniel Smith, Abrm G. Smith & Joseph G. Smith, exrs., 3 May 1831. John Smith (LS), Wit: Josiah Henry, Major Whitesides Jr., Jno. J. Smith Junr.

Pages 471-473: Will of James Hogge of the district of York... to my son Alexander Hogg my bay mare & my gold broach & to my son John hogge my black mare & my silver spurs & to my said sons Alexander & John Hogge my cross cut saw, and all tools. To my wife Isabella Hogge all the remaining property. I appoint my said wife and William Jamison, Esqr., exr., 26 Oct 1831. James Hogge (LS), Wit: Cornelius Daniel, S. Feemster, William Young.

Warrant of appraisement directed to Robert Wilson, Robert McNelly, Benjn Dowdle, Isaac Minter & John Hays 9 Feb 1835 returnable in 60 days. Letters testamentary to Isabella Hogge 9 Feb 1835.

Pages 473-474: Will of Samuel Hutcheson of the district of York... To my son James P. a young negro girl named Jiney about 14 years of age, a sorrel coult about 2 years old, a bed & furniture, a harrow plough & harniss, & one half of the plantation on which I now reside. To my son Samuel B. the other half of the plantation on which I now reside. To my daughter Rhoda $100; to my daughter Polly $100, to my daughter Margaret C. $100, and to my son John $100. To my granddaughter Isabella Kirkpatrick $50 and to my grandson John L. Thompson $20, to be kept at interest by my executor untill the said John comes of age. The balance of my property be sold and after payment of debts any balance to be equally divided among my children Rhoda, Polly, Margaret C., John, Samuel B. & James P. Also to my son James P. all my household furniture & I enjoin it upon him to take good care of my old female servant Ligal. I appoint my brother David Hutcheson, exr., 24 Jan 1835. Samuel Hutcheson (LS), Wit: Samuel Faires, Miles A. Faires, James M. McKee.

Page 474: South Carolina, York District. Will of Rebeckah Currance... I direct my brother Daniel to pay my mother a one hundred dollar note which I hold on him, also the one half of my hoggs. I give my woman estate to my brother William Currence & Peter his son that he pay the Doctor Lawrence's bill. I give to my nephew Hugh Ellas Davidson Currance my boy Henry. I give to my niece Eleanor Stephenson Currance my chest of drawers. My wearing apparel I give to my brother Daniel's daughter equally divided & a note that I hold on my brother Daniel of $129 to be given up to him. The remainder of my estate to be divided between my brother Daniel & my sister Elizabeth Patrick & Margaret Wood. I request my brother William Currance to execute this my will, 12 Jan 1835. Rebecka Currance (mark), Wit: Isaac A. Campbell, Robert Turner, George Turner.

Page 475: South Carolina, York District. Will of William A. Stanton of district aforesaid... To my beloved mother Eleanor Stanton my negro girl called Puff. I give unto my only brother Isom G. Stanton the whole of my land property & my negro boy called Cyrus, also my two horses & wagon. To my sister Eliza C. Stanton my small negro girl Harriet. My negro girl Selina to be sold for cash either at publick or private sale as my executor thinks proper to pay my debts. I appoint my brother Isom G. Stanton exr., 15 March 1835. W. A. Stanton (LS), Wit: John A. Laney, T. M. Boyd, Arthur A. McKenzie.

Pages 475-476: Will of Martha Donnally of the District of York, 5 April 1831... To Nancy Falkner of the district aforesaid my negro woman named Jane. To Isabella Falkner a negro girl named Mary. To John Kincaid & Isabella Kincaid my negro man named Pad[?], with all my house & kitchen furniture, one mare & cattle to be equally divided between John & Isabella Kincaid. Martha Donnally (mark) (LS), Wit: Robert Neeland, James Caldwell, Robert Caldwell.

Pages 476-478: South Carolina, York District. Will of Moses Bigger of district aforesaid... To my brother James Bigger the tract of land I now live on with the exception of 50 acres I purchased from William Moore, also my cotton ginn and thrasher, my young horse named Wellington. To my sister Mary Magh the following negroes not subject to her husband William Magh, my negro woman Mariah about 25 years of age and her children Sarah about 7 or 8, Green six or seven, Darcus five, Minerva one year old, also a note I have on William Magh for $90 with the interest, $100 worth of cotton, also all of the household and kitchen furniture which she has in her possession, cattle, hogs, etc. To my sister Elizabeth Patterson my negro girl named Carolina about 12 years old, also a note I hold on William Bigger of $400. To my brother William M. Bigger my negro man named Buff about 35 years old, also a note I hold on himself to $600. to my nephew James Neagle son of William Neagle my silver watch. To my nephew Alexander B. Bigger & James McKee Bigger, sons of Mathew Bigger, 40 acres of land which I purchased from William Moore. Also to my nieces Ann E. Bigger & Martha E. Bigger and my nephew Andrew Bigger, $50 cash. To my niece Amelia Nagle daughter of William Nagle a roan mare coult 6 or 8 months old. My brother James Bigger, exr., 16 Nov 1834. Moses Bigger (LS), Wit: Jno D. McClellan, Lawrance Cullender, Wm. A. Barnett.

Pages 478-480: South Carolina, York District. Will of Michael Steedman... To my son William Steedman $5. To my daughter Susannah wife of Elias McClellan, a negro boy slave named Nelson. To my daughter Mary wife of Wm Creswell a negro boy named Morris which negro boy I allow to be sold & the money arising from the sale of said negro to be equally divided amongst the children of my said daughter Mary Creswell. To my daughter Margaret wife of Alexander Aikin a negro girl named Sarah. For the consideration of $1 and natural love to my daughter Elizabeth Kuykendall & her children I convey to Robert M. Williams in trust for the use of my said daughter a negro woman named Jemima[?], a tract of land whereon I now live, with the exception that my wife Mary is to have her support or use of the land in common with my daughter Elizabeth. To my son James $5. To my wife Mary a negro woman named Loosy, all stock of cattle, etc. I appoint Robert McClellan Williams, exr., July 24th 1835. Michael Steedman (X) (LS), Wit: Robert McClellan, C. H. Horry.

Pages 480-481: Warrant of appraisement on the estate of John Smith B. R. decd, Joseph G. Smith, executor, directed to Jona McKenzie, Jno Smith, Henry Smith, Jas McKenzie, and Jos Leech 19 Jan 1835. Letters testamentary on the will of John Smith of Broad River deceased to Joseph G. Smith 19 Jan 1835.

Page 481: Warrant of appraisement on the estate of Samuel Hutcheson decd, David Hutcheson, exr., directed to Wm. Carothers, James Carothers, Josiah Garetson[?], James Perry & Samuel Faires, 23 Feb 1835.

Pages 481-483: Warrant of appraisement on the estate of Rebeckah Currance directed to Isaac A. Campbell, Jos Lowrance, Jesse K. Armstrong, Jas Patrick, Gassaway Wilson 30 July 1835 returnable 30 September. Letters testamentary to William Currance 30 July 1835.

Pages 483-484: Warrant of appraisement on the estate of Aaron Wood directed to Jno Harper, Lessley Wright, James McElwee, David Boyd & Jno Glenn 21 July 1834 returnable 23 September. Letters testamentary to Richard Barnett and Wm. Mc. Biggers 21 July 1834.

Pages 484-486: Warrant of appraisement on the estate of Wm. H. Stanton directed to Jno A. Laney, Alexr Barnett, Jos Clinton, Jos McKenzie, and Thomas J. Clinton, 3 August 1835 returnable 3 October. Letters testamentary to Isom G. Stanton 3 August 1835.

Pages 486-487: Warrant of appraisement on the estate of Moses Bigger, James Bigger, executor, directed to Alexander Barnett Senr, Jos Wallace, James Wallace, Wm Currance & Lessley Wright 26 Oct 1835 returnable 26 December. Letters testamentary to James Bigger 26 Oct 1835.

Pages 487-490: Will of Robert Brown... To my beloved wife Mary ne half of the land I now live on & all my negroes during her life & at her decease the land to belong to my youngest son Robert Jackson Brown. My wife to have all the furniture of the house & kitchen. My son John to have an equal share of the balance of my estate after the rest have all got their shares equal to what he has already received. My daughter Jane Jamison have the negro woman she has already received from me & as she is of more value than the one Emily Alexander has received by $50, I allow her to pay the $50 to my executor in order to be divided by them among my heirs to make them all equal. I will that my daughter Mary Love have as much out of my estate as will purchase her a negro woman equal in value to the one that my daughter & Jane & Emily has received. My son William C. Brown have an equal share of the balance after the others have all got a share equal to what he has already received. My daughter Emily Alexander to have an equal share of the balance as laid off to her brothers John &U Wm. C. Brown and to keep the negro woman she has already received. My daughter Hannah B. Brown have as much of my estate as will make her an equal share with the rest of my daughters who are married. My son Robert Jackson have the half of the plantation I now live on at his mother's death. My wife Mary and my son John C. Brown, exrs., 3 Dec 1835. Robert Brown (LS), Wit: G. Enloe, Hugh Cain, Robt T. Allison.

Warrant of appraisement on the estate of Robert Brown directed to Gilbert Enloe, Hugh Cain, Galbraith Caldwell, N. McElwee and Wm. Brown, 1 February 1836 returnable 1 April. Letters testamentary to John G. Brown 1 Feb 1836.

Pages 490-493: Will of James B. W. Simeral of the District of York... to my sister Selena Simeral my two beds & bedsteads & the bed clothing, also a small walnut table. My brother Andrew B. J. Simeral shall have all my wearing apparel. It is my will that my father shall have my horse, saddle & Bridle, and my tract of land on the waters of Dutchmans Creek adj. Austin Garison & others, all my book accounts. I appoint my brother Francis H. Simeral my executor, 16 Feb 1836. J. B. W. Simeral (LS), Wit: Jesse Brumfield, Stephen McCorkle, Miles G. Simeral.

Warrant of appraisement directed to Wm Carothers, Austin Garison, Thos Douglass, James Hutcheson & Thos Thomason 12 March 1836 returnable 10 May. Letters testamentary to Francis H. Simeral 12 March 1836.

Pages 493-494: Will of John Bates Senr living on Fishing Creek in York District & state of South Carolina am grown very old & frail... To my youngest daughter Isis[?] Bates who is now living with me & hath kept my house a number of years since all the rest of my daughters have left me, the tract of land which we both live on. To my said daughter my mare Philips & her coult named Punch, furniture, farming tools, etc., my weaving loom, shuttles & cards. I appoint my said daughter executrix, 9 Oct 1833. John Bates Senior (LS), Wit: Benjn Rowell, Catherine Rowell, Mary Rowell.

Pages 494-495: Will of John King of the District of York... to my three sons Legrand W. King, Inglesby King & Joseph A. King, my negro boy Tom, my negro girl Nancy and my negro boy Andrew to be sold in this country and the amount of sales to be equally divided among them. To my said son Joseph A. King 50 acres of land to be so run out that he may have the est send of the tract which I purchased of James Scott including the dwelling house where he now resides. To my daughter Sarah L. King my negro woman Sarah & to my daughter Easter C. Burns my negro boy Harry. To my wife Elizabeth King all and every king of property both real & personal not herein before devised with the full expectation that she will make an equal distribution according to circumstances of her estate among her four sons viz Evander C. King, James P. King, Alfred J. King, Elzaphan King. I appoint my wife aforesaid & Wm. Jamison, Esqr., exrs., 17 Dec 1831. John King (LS), Wit: Jas L. Wright, Joshua Palmer, Helena Jameson.

Pages 495-498: Will of John Robertson... To my beloved wife Charity Robertson one choice bed with furniture, also one choice cow. To my daughter Sally Minerva Robertson the 2nd choice bed & 2nd choice cow. To my daughter Rachel Dutathy Robertson the 3rd choice bed & 3rd choice cow. To my son John H. Robertson one young gray mare. My sorrel mare called Match be reserved for the use of the family that may choose to stay on the land. To my beloved wife Charity Robertson the land whereon I now live together who shall keep my said daughter Sally Minerva & Rachel Dutathy thereon. My son Benjamin shall have a decent support on the land above mentioned during the life of his mother. My property heretofore not mentioned be put to sale and the money arising from the sale shall be collected and one ninth to the following: my beloved wife Charity Robertson, my son Thos Robertson, my son Jos O. Robertson, my son James Robertson, my son Elihu Robertson, my son Wm Robertson, my son Jon H. Robertson, my daughter Sally Minerva, my daughter Rachel Dutathy. I appoint my wife Charity Robertson & my son Thos Robertson, exrs., 11 July 1835. John Robertson (mark) (LS), Wit: Wm. Anderson, W. Hill Senr, Rezin Tolbert.

Pages 498-500: Will of Laban Suggs of the District of York... Unto George W. Suggest my eldest son a certain tract of land on the waters of Allisons Creek which he has had in possession adj. Hemphill, the Lincoln Road. The balance of my land & farm whereon I now live with my possessions both real & personal, negroes, stock, etc., remain in the possession of my widow and family for the support of said family untill my youngest son Isaiah Leroy arrives at the full of age 21 years, at which time the property is to be equally divided by my executor by exposing to sale or otherwise between my beloved widow Jane Suggs if she be living in manner & form viz. To my wife Jane Suggs, one third, and the balance to be equally divided between all my children except my son Isaac F. Suggs (viz), Geo W. Suggs, Mary E. Kerr, John W. Suggs, Catherine L. Suggs, Andrew J. Suggs, Martha J. Suggs, Green M. Suggs, Wm. G. Suggs, Margaret E. T. Suggs, Laban Suggs, Jane C. Suggs & Josiah L. Suggs. I give to my son Isaac T. Suggs our family Bible at my deceased of the value of $3. My desire is that my executors give unto each legatee as they become of age or marry one horse, bridle & Saddle, one bed. I appoint my wife Jane Suggs & my son George W. Suggs, exrs., 8 Aug 1836. Laban Suggs (LS), Wit: James C. Thomasson, Josiah A. Lawrance, Moses T. Farres.

Pages 500-501: Will of Jameson Marley of the district of York... I want my land to be rented out from year to year & the proceeds of the same to be kept in the hands of an executor whom I shall appoint for the benefit of my old negro woman Lucy during her life, but if any cash remains after the death of old Lucy, I bequeath it to my neighbors in the following manner (viz) to Hugh Horshaw $50, Robert McLure $20, Col. George Ross $20, Mary Sutton widow $20. I also leave old Lucy her entire freedom to remain on the plantation or do otherwise. I appoint Hugh Horshaw exr., 17 Dec 1833. Jameson Marley (mark), Wit: Wm B. Ash, Isaac Kuykendall, Elijah Carrell.

Pages 501-502: Warrant of appraisement on the estate of Elizabeth Brumfield, Andrew McWhorter, exr., directed to J. D. Barry, Aaron Briant, James Briant Jnr., Wm Wallace & Wm Youngblood 2 July 1834 returnable 2 Sept.

Pages 502-503: Letters testamentary to Andrew Baxter on the estate of Mary Baxter 28 Dec 1835.

YORK COUNTY SC WILL BOOK G 1820-1837

Pages 503-505: Will of John Hogge of York District... All of my estate namely household & kitchen furniture to my beloved wife Elizabeth Hogge, all of the cattle & hoggs marked two smooth crops and two nicks in the left ear, and other cattle. At her deceased to be equally divided between my three sons Daniel M. Hoggs, James K. Hogge and Alexander C. Hogge. To my son Wm. G. Hogge fifty cents. I appoint my friend Wm Pressley and my wife Elizabeth Hoggs, exrs., 26 March 1830. J. Hogge (LS), Wit: Hugh Simeral, Henry J. Hogge, James Simeral.

Pages 505-506: South Carolina, York District. Will of Jane Barry... To my son John Barry $20. To my daughter Jane Moore $20. My daughter Catherine P. Jackson has rec'd a bed & furniture. To my daughter Margaret Steele the furniture of one bed. My daughter Elizabeth Jackson has rec'd her bed & furniture. To my son William A. Barry: Sally, Dovey & Richard. To my granddaughter Margaret A. Barry the chest. To my granddaughter Jane A. Barry the bedsted. My sons John & William exrs., 18 June 1836. Jane Barry (X), Wit: David Watson, Robert Stearn, Daniel M. Watson.

Pages 506-508: South Carolina, York District. Will of Aaron Boggs... To my lawful wife Martha all the household & kitchen furniture during her lifetime or her widowhood, and so soon as either Nancy or Mary marries or comes of age, my wife Martha gives to each one of them a bed & furniture, and also my youngest daughter Martha Mason comes of age that said wife do give her a bed & furniture. I will that all my stock of hogs unto my wife and two of my choice cows & the 2 horses a sorrel and a gray to remain on the plantation. Also my two sons Aaron and Thomas to continued on the plantation to aid & assist in making a support for themselves & the rest of the family until they come of age. The boy Charles & all the rest of my property to be sold &the contents of the sale to be equally divided among my children Aaron, Thomas, Nancy, Mary, and Martha Mason. I appoint Joseph Boggs, Eli McElhany & James Poag son of Nancy Poag, executors, 3 Nov 1836. Aaron Boggs (X) (LS), Wit: James McElhany, Henry Hudson, Arthur S. Williamson.

Pages 508-509: Will of Agness Greer of York District... Whereas no regular division of the property heired by law by my sister Mary Greer & Susannah Greer & myself of the estate of my unckle Robert Greer deceased, I do give to the said Mary Greer and Susannah Greer my whole estate both personal & real to be equally divided between them. I appoint my friend John Kelsey Sr., exr., 24 Aug 1835. Agnes Greer (mark), (LS), Wit: M. C. Connell [McConnell?] Curry, Thos. J. McElhaney, James Lamar Kelsey.

Pages 509-511: South Carolina, York District. Will of Smith Wilkins of said district... To my wife Sarah Wilkins the tract of land whereon I now live during her life with the two negro girls Polly & Celia, all stock, farming utensils, household and kitchen furniture, in order to enable her to raise & educate her children, and as the children arrive to mature age or may marry, that my executrix give to them such portion as she may think she will be able to give to all. I bequeath to my children Peter P. Wilkins, Dan Quinn Wilkins, Eliza Wilkins, John Wilkins, Martha Wilkins, Robert Wilkins, Drury S.

Wilkins & Franklin Wilkins, such estate as their mother with the advice of her & their most judicious friends may think she can afford. I constitute my beloved wife Sarah Wilkins, extx., 27 Aug 1836. Smith Wilkins (LS), Wit: W.T. Miller, William Camp, N. S. Wilkins.

Pages 511-512: Will of Sarah Johnston of York District... To my granddaughter Sarah E. Johnston one bed & furniture. To my granddaughter Eliza C. Wood, my bed & furniture I sleep on. To my daughter Sarah Glenn my two negroes Susanna & Mary provided she & her husband John Glenn will keep them & pay to my four granddaughters Sarah Craig, Sarah Wood, Sarah McGill & Sarah E. Johnston their valuation or worth at auction. To my four granddaughters all the remainder of my personal property to be equally divided between them. I appoint my beloved son in law John Glenn and my beloved grandson David J. Boyd, exrs., 31 Oct 1828. Sarah Johnston (LS), Wit: Milton Glenn, Nancy Price, Isaac Price.

Pages 512-513: Will of John Barronhill of York District... I desire that my wife Mary Ann Barronhill shall have the tract of land on which I now reside, between 70 and 80 acres, also bon bay mare, six head of cattle, six head of sheep, nine head of hoggs, with all household furniture, and she may dispose of the same as she may deem proper and at her deceased to divide equally between each of my children. I appoint my said wife Mary Ann Barronhill, extx., 30 March 1836. John Barronhill (LS), Wit: J. E. Davis, Jno. C. Jackson, Jno R. Logan.

Pages 514-518: South Carolina, York District. Will of Joseph Lawrance of district aforesaid, planter... To my son Allen the tract of land I bought of John Turner, about 100 acres, also one bed & furniture, & one cow & calf, and my negro girl named Dianna. To my son Allen in special trust for the separate use, support and maintenance of my daughter Frances during the term of her life the following property to wit Anaka, her daughter Sarah & her child now at the breast being female and the day after the death of my daughter the slaves to be equally divided among such child or children as said Frances may leave living. To my wife Martha her support & maintenance out of the plantation I now live on during her widowhood & at her death of marriage the same to be equally divided between my son Allen & William, and the said last mentioned tract containing 230 acres being the same I bought of Samuel Waller[?]. To my said wife a negro girl named Liza. To my son William in special trust for the separate use, support and maintenance of my daughter Clementine during the term of her life three negroes of the same [value?] as those willed my daughter Frances and under the same regulations. All of the negroes of which I may die possessed except those willed to Allen & my daughter Frances to remain on the plantation where I now live with my stock of horses, cattle, sheep & hogs, which property I charge with the education of my sons Robert & Josiah. I wish my son William to remain on the plantation with his mother during her life. At the death of my wife all the negroes & other personal property shall be equally divided among all my children. I allow my son Allen the benefit of the part of the meadow land on the Waller[?] tract & I allow so much of my stock to be sold as they may think proper to educate my sons Robert & Josiah. I appoint my wife, my son Allen, exrs., 29 July 1824. Joseph Lawrance (mark) (LS), Wit: John Currance, Isaac A. Campbell, Daniel Currance.

Pages 518-520: South Carolina, York District. Will of Mary Baxter of the district aforesaid... To my daughters Fanny & Elizabeth the mansion house in which I now live with all the improvements connected with it, provided those improvements are embraced by 50 acres of the south end of the tract, also the negro man called April about 36 years old. In the event of the death of either of them, the interest in said land an d negro to my son Andrew and daughter Matilda. To my son Andrew the remainder of the tract of land on which I now live and the negro named Leroy about 7 or 8 years old. To my grandchild Thomas Simpson one bed and furniture and I require my daughters Fanny and Elizabeth to pay him $100. To my daughter in law Violet one sorrel horse. The remainder of my property at my death not disposed of to be divided among my children Margaret Garrison, Cynthia Reeves, Mary Webb, Sarah Param, Matilda Kerr[?], and my grandson Thos Simpson. I appoint Andrew Baxter, exr., 5 Nov 1835. Mary Baxter (mark) (Seal), Wit: Wm. Faris, Jona'n Ham, James P. Simril.

Warrant of appraisement directed to E. Avery, Jesse Brumfield, Wm. Barron, Wm. Faires & Randall Weathers 27 Dec 1835 returnable 27 Feb.

Pages 520-521: Warrant of appraisement on the estate of Michael Steedman, Robert McWilliams executor, directed to W. L. Harris, E. W. Smith, Jos Kuykendall, Robt Cooper & Walker Benson 2 Nov 1835 returnable 2 January. Letters testamentary to Robt McWilliams 2 Nov 1835.

Pages 522-523: Warrant of appraisement on the estate of John King directed to Wm. Meek, John Lockhart, John Burns, Moses McClean & John Miller 9 Aug 1835 returnable 9 October. Letters testamentary to Wm. Jamison 9 Aug 1835.

Pages 523-525: Warrant of appraisement on the estate of Jane Barry directed to H. J. Cathcart, Jas Strain, Alexander Barry & M. T. Hall 6 Jan 1837 returnable 6 March. Letters testamentary to William A. Barry 6 Jan 1837.

Pages 525-526: Warrant of appraisement on the estate of Sarah Johnston directed to James L. Wright, James Harper, John Harper, Richard Morow, James McElwee 16 Jan 1837 returnable 16 March. Letters testamentary to John Glenn & David J. Boyd 16 Jan 1837.

Pages 526-527: Warrant of appraisement on the estate of Agnes Greer, John Kelsey Senr exr., directed to J. A. Love, Jno McKnight, R. M. Love, Alexr Howie, & Jno McNeal 1 Feb 1837 returnable 1 April. Letters testamentary to John Kelsey Senr 1 Feb 1837.

Pages 527-529: Warrant of appraisement on the estate of Smith Wilkins directed to Wm. Camp, Wm. Moore, Jno Carruth, John Stern[?] & John

Young 6 Feb 1837 returnable 6 April. Letters testamentary to Sarah Wilkins 6 Feb 1837.

Pages 529-530: Warrant of appraisement on the estate of John Barronhill directed to David Jackson, Henry Carroll Esqr., Fra's Armstrong, and James Hemphill 9 March 1837 returnable 9 May. Letters testamentary to Mary Ann Barronhill 9 March 1837.

Pages 530-533: Will of Robert Pursley of York District, planter... To Polly Pursley my dearly beloved wife the dwelling house I now live in & all other buildings on the premises with the land south of the road leading to Henry Wright's taking my other field north of Wright's in. It begins where the road crosses P. McCarter's line beyond my barn. To my beloved wife cattle, hoggs, farming utensils, all the grain in the ground or gathered & the half of the household & kitchen furniture, my negro girl Silvey. To my daughter Margaret Rite [Wright] $10. To my son James $10. To my daughter Catherine Pursley, Silvey at her mother's death and furniture, etc. To my daughter Delilah McWhorter $10. To my daughter Polly Patrick $10. To my son William B. Pursley my negro Cyrus & the balance of my plantation at his mother's death I will to him the whole of it, 200 acres. I order all my unwilled property to be sold to pay debts. I make my son James Pursley & James Falkner, exrs., 1 Dec 1835. Robert Purley. Test: John Felchet, James Felchett.

Whereas Robert Pursley late of York District deceased left a will which instrument of writing has been adjudged null & of no form, now we Mary Pursley, James Pursley, William B. Pursley, Henry Wright & Margaret his wife, Catherine Pursley, Thomas McWhorter & Delilah his wife, John A. Patrick & Mary his wife, the heirs at law of the said Robert Pursley, all of the age of 21, being desirous that the intentions of the said Robert should be carried into effect, for $1 do will to the said Mary Pursley that tract of land mentioned in the said instrument, and at her death to go to William B. Pursley, and we quit claim to it. likewise our claim to the negro girl Silvey, 16 March 1837. Wit: Myles Smith, A. H. Neel, Wm. B. Sweazy.

Pages 534-535: Will of John Falls of York District... to my beloved wife Elizabeth all the plantation whereon I now live (except so much as was formerly run out for my son J. C. Falls amounting to seventy acres), with all stock, except what is below willed, a negro girl named Esther, a bureau and cupboard. I give to my son Thomas $150 and a saddle and bridle worth $10. To my son John C. Fall $5, likewise to my daughter Polly Farris one cow & calf, one bureau & cupboard, not to exceed $32. To my son James the plantation which I purchased by Benjn Neely whereon McWhorter's family lived together with two thirds of the profits from the tan yard. The balance of the profits of the tan yard I give to my wife Elizabeth. To my son James $50, and a saddle worth $10. To my son Andrew a bay horse named Dick with a saddle and bridle. To my son Elam 70 acres of land that was formerly laid off for my son J. C. Falls, being a new survey taken up by Jordan with $50 in cash. To my daughter Drusilla a bed and furniture, bureau & cupboard. To my son the land whereon I now live at my wife's death. A piece of land taken up by me between Venable's old tract and James Ferry's[?] land on which Saml Faris now lives be sold for the payment of my debts. I appoint my wife Elizabeth and my son James Falls, exrs., 7 March 1837. John Falls (LS), Wit: Wm Love, Robt T. Allison, Jno Quin. Proved 21 April 1837 by the oath of John Quin.

Pages 536-537: South Carolina, York District. Will of Alexander Scott of district aforesaid... To my son John Scott a negro boy named Sam and to his children as deed of gift sheweth Cinda & her three children. To my son James G. Scott a negro boy named Tony and a negro boy named Willis, and a negro girl named Patty. To my daughter Margaret Nesbit three negro girls named Lucy, Lavina, and Matilda and a negro boy named Bill. To my daughter Nancy Boyes negroes Sarah, Nelly, Joe, Adeline and Peter. The following negroes Isom, Jordan, Dizey and her five children, and Joshua be valued and that if my son John Scott takes from at the valuation and James G. Scott takes Joshua at valuation, that my daughters Margaret Nesbit & Nancy Boyes take Dizey and her five children and Jordan leaving it to Dizey to determine with whom she will live. I will that my negro Lonon to be supported on this plantation. The plantation on which I live including the Davis tract be valued at a very moderate valuation and that some one of the legatees take it at the valuation. My son in law Alexander Nesbit be executor, 18 Nov 1836. Alex'r Scott (Seal), Wit: Hugh Harris, John M. Harris, Robt Harris. Proved by the oath of Hugh Harris 1 May 1837.

Pages 537-538: Repeat of will of Michael Stedman recorded on pages 478-480.

Pages 538-539: Warrant of appraisement on the estate of John Falls directed to Jno Quinn, Solomon Quinn, Wm Watson, Benj'n Neely and Wm Love 21 April 1837 returnable 21 June. Letters testamentary to James Falls 21 April 1837.

Pages 540-542: Warrant of appraisement on the estate of Aaron Boggs directed to Jas. McElhany, Robert McFadden, Eli Moore, Richard Streight and Wm. Boggs 7 Jan 1837 returnable 7 March. Letters testamentary to Joseph Boggs 7 Jan 1837. Eli McElhany qualified as an executor 16 Jan 1837.

Pages 542-543: Will of Bartlet Meacheam of the district of York... My debts to be paid by my wife who is appointed executrix. To my beloved wife Nancy Meacheam all the property I may die possessed of lands, negroes, horses, hoggs, furniture, 28 Aug 1837. Bart Meacheam (LS), Wit: Wm Withers, Thomas Kimbrel (X), J. H. Rooker.

Pages 543-544: Will of Ann Good of York District... To my brother John Good one half of my cash & notes, also one of my beds & furniture, my clothes trunk, table & little wheel. To my brother James B. Good the other half of my cash & notes, one bed & furniture, one big wheel & one chest. To my niece Patsy Plexco one loom & tacklings. I leave Mary Wallace $2 in cash. To Margaret Plexco $2 in cash. I leave Jean Hemphill $2. I appoint my brother John Good & James Good, exrs., 5 April 1832. Ann Good (LS), Wit: Robert Sheilds, David Hamilton, Wm. Nelson.

Pages 544-546: South Carolina, York District. Will of John Darwin of district aforesaid... To my daughter Pamela one negro woman named Nan. To my daughter Pemala's daughter Elizabeth Maning, Nan's child Melissa. To my grandson Jno, son of Pamela, my negro boy Henry and to my grandson James my negro girl Elvira and further to my grandsons John & James $50 to be applied to their education. To my son Paton B. Darwin 200 acres of land on Broad River. To my daughter Mary Kendrick the tract of land whereon show now resides and at her death to be sold and its value divided equally among her children. To the children of my daughter Rachel the tract of land whereon Rachel with her husband John Powell resides, also my negro girl Rose with her issue except the eldest child. To my granddaughter Jane Powell the oldest child of aforesaid Rose. To my son Robert G. Darwin a horse with $60. To my daughter Matilda the tract of land whereon she with her husband William Barry now lives and a deduction of $420 to be taken out of her divided of my estate. To my two sons in law John Powell & John Moore each five shillings hereby excluding them from any further participation of a divided in my estate. My negroes Daniel & Milly be appraised & to go to the legatee with whom they wish to live & that the mother & their small children not be separated and that the legatees take them at the appraisement by families and my three negro men with the larger children be appraised separately & be taken by the legatees (if they choose) at the appraisement. My unbequeathed land and all my personal estate be sold and the money arising from said sale shall be payable one half in one year & the other half in two years & equal distribution of the amount of the appraisement of the negroes & the sale of the land and other estate be made between the following legatees (viz) Nancy Harrington, Mary Hendrick, William Darwin, Jno B. Darwin, Jane Smarr, Matilda Barry, Pamela Summerford, Payton B. Darwin. [remainder not in will book; completed from checking original will in Case 16, File 666, York County estates]. William Jamison Esqr. and Gordan Moore, Esqr., exrs., 22 Nov 1836. John Darwin (LS), Wit: Williamson Howel, Samuel Howell, Thomas Mitchel. Proved 6 Nov 1837.

End of Book G.

## YORK COUNTY SC WILL BOOK 2 1837-1840

"This Book was bought by John M. Lindsey in Columbia So Ca for Benjn Chambers O. Y. D. on the __ day of January 1838. Price 3.50. Record Book for Wills Caled Book 2."

Pages 1-2: Warrant of appraisement on the estate of Robert Pursley directed to James Hemphill, John Felchet, James Floyd, Robertson McElwee & John Janes 9 Oct 1837 returnable 1 December. Letters testamentary to James Pursley & James Falkner 9 Oct 1837.

Pages 2-4: Warrant of appraisement on the estate of Ann Good directed to Wm Nelson, David Hamilton, Robert Shields, James McCheney & John Brown 30 Oct 1837 returnable 30 December. Letters testamentary to John & James Good 30 Oct 1837.

Page 4: Letters testamentary on the estate of Alexander Scott to Alexander G. Nisbet 1 May 1837.

Pages 5-6: Warrant of appraisement on the estate of Thomas McMakin directed to John Smith, Miles Smith, Wm. Love, John Felchet, Clark Watson 11 Dec 1837 returnable 10 Feb. Letters testamentary to Martha McMakin & J. R. McElwee 11 Dec 1837.

Pages 6-8: Warrant of appraisement on the estate of Samuel Blair directed to David Ayres, Jno Clark, Wm. C. Penick, Benjamin Dowdle & Allen Dowdle 3 Feb 1834 returnable 3 April. Letters testamentary to Jas. H. Alexander, Robert Hays & Wm Jamison, Esq., 3 Feb 1834.

Pages 8-10: Warrant of appraisement on the estate of Elizabeth Sadler directed to Jno G. Black, John Black, Samuel Moore, James Williamson, 4 December 1837 returnable 4 Feb. Letters testamentary to T. B. Collins 4 Dec 1837.

Pages 10-11: South Carolina, York District. Will of William Neely of district aforesaid... To my beloved wife Cyntha Neely the whole of my real and personal estate. It is my will that she shall give unto Wm. H. Neely my nephew for the love & good will I have for him $100. I allow her also at such times as each of the children come of age to give each such property as she may think fit leaving a sufficient portion for support of the family. I appoint Cynthia Neely my wife as executrix and Wm. Sturges assistant and also my son David Neely after becoming of age assistant to his mother, 19 Feb 1838. Wm. Neely (LS), Wit: W. C. Schooly, Samuel Schooly, W. P. Miller, W. Sturges.

Pages 11-16: South Carolina, *Sumter* District. Will of Charles Williams of district aforesaid... To my beloved wife Ann Williams the use of my lands lying west of the Georgetown road with my house, during her widowhood, two feather beds, all of my household and kitchen furniture, a horse and chair of the value of $100 each to be paid for with money arising out of my estate... To my two sons Matthew Williams and Alexander Williams two tracts of land in Williamsburg district viz one tract of 174 acres adj. the lands of Mr. John

Gambol on Turkey Creek, it being part of a tract surveyed for John McCottry; likewise half of a tract of 507 acres surveyed by George White & John McCottry adj. lands of John James Esqr. on Cow head, having sold a tract in Williamsburg District to George Bullons[?] and part of the right of 250 acres being vested in my two sons Matthew & Alexander Williams on condition that they assign that right to the aforesaid George Bullen[?], and I give them $200 each as a compensation. It is my will that a sufficient sum be levied out of my estate for the purpose of educating such of my children who may not have their education, and if there should be a greater sum levied than proves necessary, the balance to be equally divided amongst all of my children. And in case any of the negroes belonging to my estate should become unable to do their work through old age, they should be furnished with victuals & sufficient clothing as long as they live. My lands on the east side of the Georgetown road be rented out during the widowhood of my wife Ann Williams and the money divided amongst my children. At the expiration of the widowhood of my wife Ann the whole of my lands be sold both on the west and east side of the Georgetown Road and the money be equally divided amongst my children. The remaining part of my personal property be equally divided amongst my wife and children viz Matthew Williams, Alexander Williams, Mary Williams, Thomas Williams, Sarah Desant, Charles Williams, Wulgave[?] Williams, John Williams, Louisa Williams, Benjamin Judge Williams, Eliza Ann Williams with any child or children which may be born of my wife in my lifetime or within nine months after my death. If any of my children die before he she or they should arrive to the age of 21 years it is my will that the part of such child or children be equally divided among the surviving part of my children as well the half blood as those of the full blood. I appoint my sons Matthew Williams, Thomas Williams & John Williams, exrs., 28 Dec 1825. Charles Williams, Wit: David Witherspoon, David Witherspoon Junr, James A. Witherspoon.

Warrant of appraisement directed to Wm. Nance, W. Jamison Esqr., Jno Lockhart, Dennis Crosby & Hugh D. Gallaway 23 April 1838 returnable 23 June. Letters testamentary to John Williams 23 April 1838.

Pages 16-19: South Carolina, York District. Will of William Robinson of the district above named... To my wife Isabel I give the whole of the plantation whereon I now live during her natural life & at her death the land shall be sold and the money arising from the sale to be equally divided among all my children. To the deacons of the new Bethel Church $100 for the benefit of said church but in the case of the dissolution of said church, then the same money shall be returned to the hands of my executors. I also give the sum of $75 to be disposed of in the Babtist or Burmah mission. To Melissa my daughter I give one cow and calf. The whole balance of my property to be sold and the money to be equally divided among and between my son James Robisson, Clark Robisson, James Biggers, my son in law William Guinn, Robert Robesson, also my grandsons James Wills, William & Samuel Wills to have a shared divided among them. My wife Isabella Robisson and my son John Robbisson, exrs., 11 ___ 1838. W. Robison (LS), Wit: W. Meek, Geo Wright, John Minter.

Warrant of appraisement directed to Tho Patrick, Wm. Meek, John Burris, Wm. Minter, & Richard Guin 29 March 1838 returnable 29 May. Letters testamentary to James Robinson 29 March 1838.

Pages 19-23: Will of Thomas Boyd Senr of the District of York, 10 November 1834... To my beloved wife Elizabeth Boyd during her natural life the house I now live in & the tract of land whereon it is situate, adj. lands of James Boyd, Samuel Smith, Wm. Boyd, Robert Boyd, & Aquilla Dyson with the exception of a privilege to be hereafter mentioned my daughter Nancy Smith on said land. Also to my wife during her life the following negro slaves viz Virgil, Bacchus, Amanda, Mitchel & Melinda. To my wife Elizabeth Boyd all my household & kitchen furniture, stock, etc., except for certain legacies to be hereafter mentioned to some of my children. To my wife Elizabeth Boyd all my corn, wheat, cotton and crop of any description. To my son John Boyd my wearing apparel. To my daughter Nancy Smith the privilege of living in the house wherein she now resides on my land, to have the use of a spring, fire wood &c., and as much land as she & her children can cultivate, so long as she may live separate from her husband W. Smith and no longer, and to be continued by my son Bennet Franklin Boyd so soon as he becomes possessed of my land after the death of his mother. I have given my son Thomas Jefferson Boyd all that I allow him. I have given my son Robert Boyd all that I allow him. But it is my will and desire that he should at the time my youngest child is 21 years old if my wife is then dear or at her death that he should take my negro boy Virgil at what he may be valued at. To my son James Boyd I have given all that I allow him. To my son Thos Boyd I have given him all that I allow him of my estate. But it is my wish that he should take my negro boy Bacchus when my youngest child is 21 years old. My son Bennet Franklin Boyd at the death of his mother the plantation subject to the incumbrances of my daughter Nancy heretofore named & to my five daughters to be hereafter name, that is the house where I live as a home to them while they are single. To my son Bennet Franklin Boyd after the decease of his mother my negro boy Mitchel, my cupboard and clock. To my five daughters viz Jane, Elizabeth, Mary, Rachel & Louisa, a bed and furniture, bureau, a horse with at least $10, a saddle & bridle, spinning wheel. My thrashing machine on the land I have given to my son William, that it should remain there for the use of all my children. I appoint my wife Elizabeth Boyd and my son John Boyd, exrs. Thomas Boyd (LS), Wit: Wm. Moore, John Guin, John McGill, Wm. Campbell.

Pages 23-24: Will of Hugh Walker of the District of York... to my daughter Sarah and my daughter Martha and my son Andrew five shillings each. To my daughter Margaret the one half of my plantation provided she pays $50 to Mary Ann my granddaughter within 12 months from my decease the land laying along John Remey's[?] side of the plantation, the other half to my granddaughter Mary Ann and her heirs, adj. to Gilfilling including the house and kitchen and barn. She is to take care of Martha and Andrew my daughter and son, and the third of the corn made ont eh place for the year 1838 as rent from John McLain. I leave John Ingram and John McLain exrs., 11 Feb 1838. Hugh Walker (LS), Wit: John Ingram, Elijah Calcot, William Ingram.

Pages 24-25: Will of Mary Steele of York District... After the payment of my just debts, $300 to be paid to my daughter Ann and the balance equally divided between my son Joseph & my daughters Viney & Margaret. I constitute my son Joseph Steele exr., 12 Aug 1835. Wit: John B. Davis James S. Workman, John F. Workman.

Page 25: Letters testamentary on the estate of Wm Neely to Scinthia Neely 3 April 1838.

Pages 26-28: Minor Carroll has applied for letters of administration on the estate of John Carroll deceased with his will annexed, 22 May 1838.

South Carolina, York District. Will of John Carroll of district aforesaid... To my wife Mary I leave three negroes Linda, Mary, and Francis, a note I hold on Andrew McConnell for $178.25 dated 5 April 1826, and a four wheeled carriage commonly called her own, and two horses Tom and Fox, one half of all my household furniture, and I allow her to have the plantation whereon I now live, with farming utensils, one half of the cattle, hoggs, and sheep, and a negro man Elias and a negro woman Juda to work the farm. At her death Elias & Jude to go to my nephew Minor Carroll. To Minor Carroll, my nephew (son of Joseph Carroll), the plantation whereon I now live at the death of my wife Mary, and six other negroes Green, Polina, Thompson, Hicks, Betty & any. Also to Minor half of my household & kitchen furniture with the remaining stock. I also leave my watch & shot gun to Minor Carroll, 29 April 1838. John Carroll (seal), Wit: Wylie L. Harris, And McConnell, Charles McElwain.

Pages 28-31: South Carolina, York District. Will of Joseph Carroll of district aforesaid... To my wife Elizabeth Carroll my negro man Simon & his wife Phillis, with my household and kitchen furniture, the house wherein I now reside & so much of my cleared land as she may be disposed to cultivate and at my wife's decease, I devise the property to my son Minor Carroll. The balance of my estate consisting of lands, negroes, horses & other stock, black smith tools, etc., to my son Minor Carroll. I appoint my wife Elizabeth Carroll and my son Minor Carroll, exrs., 24 Feb 1838. Joseph Carroll (LS), Wit: Minor Sadler, Hugh Warren, Robt W. Wilson.

Warrant of appraisement directed to Andrew McConnell, Thomas Simpson, James Johnston, Philip Sandefer & Minor Sadler, 6 August 1838 returnable 6 October. Letters testamentary to Minor Carroll 6 Aug 1838.

Pages 31-32: Will of Samuel Miller of the district of York, 23 June 1836... All of my debts to be paid out of my plantation lying in North Carolina, Rutherford County. To my beloved wife Jane the plantation I now live on with all my stock, furniture, as long as she remains a widow, but if she should marry then she shall have a bed & furniture & at my wife's death the property to be divided equally among my children & if any of them should go away & leave their mother before they come of age, then they shall have only half a share of that the other shall have. I constitute John McCord, Francis J.

Nickolls, & my wife, exrs. Samuel Miller (LS), Wit: John Davis, Martha Nickolls, John Lowry.

Pages 32-36: South Carolina, York District. Will of Samuel Chambers of the district aforesaid... As the principal part of my estate consists of land & being desirous that my wife & children should always have a comfortable & decent support, my executors shall sell off whenever the necessities of my said wife and children may require such portions of my real estate. To my wife Elizabeth Chambers and my children William Elleson, Samuel C. C., Elizabeth J., John C., Benjamin B., Mary A. Chambers, all of my estate both real and personal in such portions as they will be entitled to under the statute of distribution of South Carolina, manly one third to my said wife and the balance in equal portions to my children. I appoint my wife and my friends Benjamin Chambers and my oldest son Alleson Chambers when he comes of age, and also my son Samuel when he comes of age, exrs., _ April 1838. Samuel Chambers (LS), Wit: Wm. Moore, Jno. A. Brown, Jno. A. Alston. Codicil made 5 April 1838 (same wit.).

Warrant of appraisement directed to Sylvanus Chambers, Stanhope Sadler, S. H. Dinkens, Jno. A. Brown, Saml Brown & Wm. P. Thomasson or John A. Alston, 21 Sept 1838 returnable 20 November. Letters testamentary to Elizabeth Chambers 21 Sept 1838.

Pages 36-37: Warrant of appraisement on the estate of Thomas Boyd directed to John Glenn, David Boyd, Richard Mason, J. L. Wright & John T. Harper 17 May 1838 returnable 17 July. Letters testamentary to Elizabeth Boyd and John D. Boyd 7 May 1838.

Pages 38-39: Warrant of appraisement on the estate of Mary Steel directed to James S. Workman, John F. Workman, Alex'r Steele, Saml Steele & Allen Robinson 18 July 1848 returnable 18 September. Letters testamentary to Joseph Steele 18 July 1838.

Pages 39-42: Will of George Ross of the district of York... To my wife Mary Ross the mansion house in which I now reside with a negro woman Delilah, all my household & kitchen furniture, and my wife may be supported decently off the plantation on which the mansion house is situated and my son Eli A. Ross is to do it inasmuch as I devise the plantation to him. To my son Eli A. Ross the plantation whereon I now reside, about 400 acres, being a part of two tracts adj. J. D. Witherspoon, Daniel James, George Steele, Hellanah McCall & Mrs. Dickey & Thomas B. Hoover. To my son Eli A. Ross three of my choicest negroes to be selected by him at my decease with the exception of the girl Delilah left to my wife. At the decease of my wife remainder to be equally divided among my children Eli A. Ross, John M. Ross & Jane Burris with the condition that James Burris's share is to be held in trust for the support of her and her children. I appoint John M. Ross & Eli A. Ross, exrs., 2 May 1838. Geo Ross (X) (LS), Wit: Arthur Erwin, Francis Miller, J. D. Witherspoon.

Pages 42-44: Warrant of appraisement on the estate of Hugh Walker directed to John Ingram, Robert Gilfillin, Joseph Wylie, Thompson Walker & John Rainey 21 Sept 1838 returnable 21 November. Letters testamentary to John J. McClain 21 Sept 1838.

Pages 44-45: Will of Nathaniel Thomasson of the district of York... To my beloved wife Elizabeth Thomasson all my household furniture, all my stock, all my horses except the stud colt, which my executors are to sell. Tract of land in York District adj. lands of James Thomasson, Barronhill & others be sold to the best advantage and the proceeds to be applied to my just debts and the overplus of said sale if any be divided between all my children. My wife Elizabeth Thomasson live on & hold possession of my home plantation her life time and to keep a negro woman named Fanny her natural life, and at the death of my wife the said negro shall be sold. It is my will that my children now living with me still remain & live with their mother as long as their mother lives. It is my will that my executor compensate my son Lemuel Thomasson for raising & gathering my present crop. I appoint my son Thomas Thomasson exr., 2 Aug 1838. Nathaniel Thomasson (mark) (LS), Wit: Dawson N. Mitchel, Thos M. Neely, James Armstrong (X).

Pages 44-45: South Carolina, York District. Will of John Clerk of the district aforesaid... My wife have her support as usual out of my estate during her widowhood and at my [sic, for her?] death all my estate both real and personal be equally divided between my four children & not others viz William clerk, Mary Miller, James D. Clerk & my daughter Harriet Alexander except that out of my estate I directed that my grandson Pinkney Clerk, son of my son John decd, one horse of the value of $70. I appoint my son James D. Clark and my son in law James T. Alexander, exrs., 15 Jan 1837. John Clerk (LS), Wit: Thomas Wilson (X), John F. Glenn, Robt M. Wilson.

Pages 46-47: Warrant of appraisement on the estate of Nathaniel Thomasson directed to Joel S. Barnett, Jesse Brumfield, Geo Sturges, An'd Giles & Wm. Barron 24 Sept 1838 returnable 24 November. Letters testamentary to Thomas Thomasson 24 Sept 1838.

Pages 48-49: South Carolina, York District. Will of John Barnes of the district aforesaid... To my beloved wife Lucy Barnes all my property both real and personal during her widowhood. Then the plantation whereon I now reside to my son John Barnes provided he allow his sister who are then unmarried a home on the plantation while they remain single. To each of my marriage daughters viz Polly, Sally, Betsey & Lucy, $8 at the death of my wife Lucy Barnes. After the decease of my wife, all property except the land above disposed of consisting of my negro man Edmond, stock, household & kitchen furniture, to be put to publick sale, and the proceeds equally divided between my son John Barnes & my three youngest daughters now living with me. To my three grandsons, the illegitimate children of my daughter Sally, Lucy, & Caroline, William, Samuel & Albertus now living with me, I allow each one $100 when they arrive at the age of 21 years to be paid to them by my son John Barnes, and in case he should fail or refuse to pay, he forfeits his claim to the land. My sorrel horse named Bald I desire my executors to sell and the proceeds to be put at interest for the benefit of my grandson John Glover son of William & Betsey Glover until he arrives at the age of 21 years and then paid to him. I appoint my wife Lucy Barnes & my son John Barnes, exrs., 1 Nov 1838. John Barnes (X) (LS), Wit: Minor Sadler, Harvey Boggs, Alex'r Fewell.

Pages 49-50: Letters testamentary on the estate of Scintha Reeves to Robinson Reeves 15 Dec 1838.

Pages 50-51: Will of Peter Cherry of York District... To my friend Catherine Tate Senr all the money that will be due me as a pensioner, also my bed, bedsted & furniture, with my entire library of books, all my clothing. I appoint my friend Durnay McColm, exr., __ July 1838. Peter Cheery (LS), Wit: Wm. Pressley, Jno Yarborough, R. M. Pressley.

Pages 50-51: Will of Cyntha Reeves of York District... my negro man Eli be sold & from the proceeds of the sale, all my debts be paid and one fourth part of the balance of said sale to be given to each of my three children James Allen, Robinson, and Polly Reeves and the other fourth with $115 now due me by my son James Allen should be equally divided between the children of my daughter Betsey Blalock when they arrives of age or marry. My smith tools to be sold & one third part of the proceeds to my son James Allen & the other two thirds to my son Robinson Reeves. The whole of my furniture, plantation tools, cattle, to be sold and the proceeds of said sale to be equally divided between my son Robinson Reeves & Polly Reeves. I appoint my son Robinson, exr. [no date] Cyntha Reeves, Wit: Jno Springs, Jno Bobbit, Elizabeth Baxter.

Pages 51-56: Citation. James A. Sadler applied for letters of administration on the estate of Daniel Simmons, 16 Jan 1839.

Severally appeared before me Elizabeth Flemming, Matilda Poag & James Isom and made oath that they heard Daniel Simmons on his death bed say he wished there was some person to do some writing for him as respecting his will but as there could be no person had, he called the above named persons to witness his verbal will was to this effect. He owed to William Erwin $8 he wishes that to be paid & the remainder of his estate real and personal he wished James A. Sadler to have it except his bed & loom he wishes Mrs. Elizabeth Flemming to have it. 30 Dec 1838. Elizabeth Flemming (LS), Matilda Poag (X) (LS), James Isom (LS). N. B. The above named Daniel Simmons died the 28 of Decr 1838. Benjn Rowell, J.P. James Isom made oath to the above will 25 Jan 1839 before Benjn Chambers, Q.U.

Warrant of appraisement directed to Thos Robinson, Jos W. McCorkle, Alexr Steele, Wylie Little & Andrew McConnell 21 Jan 1839 returnable 20 March.

Letters of administration with the will annexed to James A. Sadler, 21 Jan 1839.

Pages 56-60: Will of Galloway Senr of York District... To my son James Galloway one horse & two cows & calves, one bed & furniture, one still, and tracts of land, the one I bought from Wm. Alexander & the other I bought from Jones Bailis. To my daughter Margaret Dowdell the half of that tract of land I bought from William Wright south of the tract I now live on and $50. To my son William Galloway the Little Bill the land he did live on to stand for his share of land. To my daughter Mary Dowdle the other half of that tract I bought from William Wright and $50. To my daughter Jane Galloway the tract of land that I now live on & the tract of land adj. the tract I now live on that I bought from John Traves & one horse & saddle, two cows & Calves, one bed & furniture. All the rest of my real and personal estate that remains is to be equally divided to my sons & daughters or their heirs except the now present crop on the farm, it shall remain for the use of my son & daughter James & Jane Galloway. My son James Galloway & John Raney, exrs., 5 Sept 1826. Wm Galloway (LS), Wit: James McCain, Samuel Feemster, Edward Feemster. Codicil: a legacy was given my daughter Jane of my real estate & within the boundary of which land I have since given a writing obligatory to Edward Feemster, giving him liberty to flood a certain spot on the southern side of Alexander's branch, a small stream running into Bells Creek, now I revoke so much of my will as related to the spot of land to be flooded and confirm my daughter Jane in the remainder of the bequest. In my will having given my daughters Margaret and Mary bequests of land, I revoke those clauses & give my son James the whole land not left to Jane on condition that he pay Mary $250 and Margaret $125, dated 23 March 1837. Wm. Galloway (LS), Wit: Isaac Minter, Thos Shearer, James R. Williams.

Warrant of appraisement directed to Isaac Minter, John Rainey, John Hays, Benjn. F. Love & Samuel Feemster 18 Feb 1839 returnable 1 April. Letters testamentary to James T. Galloway 18 Feb 1839.

Pages 60-62: Warrant of appraisement on the estate of Samuel Miller directed to Robt M. Faires, Solomon Guinn, Jno Faires, John Quinn & Dr. Robt Allison or Hugh Allison 14 August 1838 returnable 15 October. Letters testamentary to Jane Miller 14 August 1838.

Pages 62-63: Will of Agness Crawford... having his day by deed disposed of all the estate which I have possessed except two negroes viz Hannah & her child Becky, and it being my anxious desire that they should be emancipated, I do by this my will directed my executors to petition the legislature of this state at its first session after my decease for permission to emancipate said Hannah and her child Becky and their increase. If the Legislature does refuse permission then it is my desire that they be vested in Alexander Crawford, 6 Nov 1834. Agness Crawford (mark), Wit: R. G. Mills, Hugh Drennon, Edward Crawford.

Pages 63-64: Will of Susannah Greer of York District... Whereas no regular division of the property heired by law of the estate of my unckle Robert Greer decd by my beloved sister Mary Greer & myself nor of the property heir by the said Mary Greer and myself by the will of my beloved sister Agness Greer deceased, I do give unto my beloved sister Mary Greer my whole estate. I appoint my friend John Kelley Senr, exr., 13 June 1838. Susanna Greer (LS), Wit: John McElhany, Saml. L. Kelly[?], Thos J. McElhaney.

Pages 64-66: South Carolina, York District. Will of Thomas Guinn of said district... To my wife Elizabeth my two negro boys John & Abram, also on negro girl Rosa & my negro girl Patsey, also my boy Anthony during her natural life, also my girl Jane which last girl she may dispose of as she pleases by will or otherwise. My moveable property of every kind, stock, carriages, tools to my wife during her life and at her death the above property to be disposed of as follows. The moveable property above mentioned to be equally divided among my eight sons viz Richard, John, Littleton, Jesse, William, Jeptha, Thompson, Chesley. Also to my son Richard I give the plantation which now lives [sic], and also confirm to him the property he has before received from me and also $100 in money. To my son John I give the land and other property he has heretofore received from me. To my son Littleton $1000 including what he has already received. To my son Jesse I confirm the land already conveyed to him and $100. To my son William I confirm the tract of land already conveyed to him by me. To Thomas my son I confirm the land I have given to him. To Jeptha my son I confirm the land already conveyed to him. To Chesley my son I confirm the land I have already conveyed to him also my negro boy Abram at his mother's death. To my daughter Mary I give my negro woman Mary & her child Caroline. To my daughter Milley $1200 already paid. To my daughter Sarah my negro girl Emaline & at the death of her mother my negro boy Anthony. If Sarah leaves no heirs, then to the children of my daughter Elizabeth and two negroes Andrew & Amanda also at the death of my wife. To my daughter Elizabeth my negro girl Patsey, said negroes at the death of my daughter Elizabeth to go to the heirs of her body. To my daughter Nancy my negro boy Joe also at the death of my wife my negro girl Rosa. I appoint my wife Elizabeth to be my executrix, 2 Oct 1838. Thomas Guinn (X) (LS), Wit: John Minter, Jesse T. Guinn, Wm. W. Guinn.

Pages 66-68: Will of Andrew Floyd of York District... To my daughter Mary my three negroes Flora, Holly & Curry, my four horses Mide & her colt, my gray horse Bill & a colt of Fancy's, a saddle & bridle, all my household & kitchen furniture not hereinafter dispose of, my farming utensils & Stock of cattle, sheep & hoggs & my loom & tacklings. To my daughter Mary J. for her natural life that part of my plantation on which I reside on the west side of the land & at her death to my son George McWhorter Floyd. To my son George McWhorter Floyd my negro boy Minor & negro girl Margaret. To my son George my negro man called George upon condition that he pay to my son Henry Floyd within six months after my decease the sum of $500. To my son John Floyd my negro boy called Abner. To my two sons James & Robert my tract of land on the waters of Beaver dam, 105 acres to be equally divided between them. To my daughter Dorcus Brown my negro boy named Stephen. To my daughter Rachel Jeans my negro boy Cyrus. To my daughter Margaret B. Jeans my negro girl named Sue & her child called Minerva. To my grandson John Brison Venable a negro boy called Sam, and a brown horse named Mike To my daughter Mary, my clock and my wagon & geers. To my daughter Mary all the remainder of my estate not herein specifically bequeathed & devise & the cash on hand at my death. I appoint my son George executor, 17 April 1838. Andrew Floyd (Seal), Wit: Mary C. Robinson, W. M. Dickson, G. W. Williams.

Pages 68-70: South Carolina, York District. Will of John Black of the district aforesaid... To my wife Eleanor Black all my property not hereinafter name during her natural life with occupation of my dwelling house & outhouses, so much cleared land as may be necessary for her to cultivate for her support & support of her negroes & stock, and after her death all such property to be equally divided between my daughter Margaret Bell and my son John Black. To my daughter Margaret Bell my negro boys Stephen & Sam, my metal clock, falling leaf table & sideboard, a set of china ware & the side board furniture. To my daughter Jane Vickers the tract of land whereon Wm Vickers now resides which was conveyed to me by Matthew Fondren and also a small tract conveyed to me by Zacheriah Bates, also my negro girl Patience and my old riding chair & harness. To my son Leroy Black my negro boy George but the said George is to remain in possession of my wife during her life. To my son John Black my negro Adam and my negro boy Charles, my wagon, black smith tools, cotton gin, cotton screw & thresher with the houses they are in. To my son John at the death of my wife Eleanor the plantation whereon I now reside reserving for the use of my daughter Margaret Bell the occupation of the house during her life or widowhood. To my granddaughter Mary Bell my negro girl Delphy as payment in full for a debt I owe the estate of Joshua D. Bell decd. I appoint my sons David, Leroy and Black [sic], exrs. [not dated]. John Black (LS), Wit: James Williamson Senr, Richard Streight, John N. Williamson.

Page 70: Will of Prudence Harris... To my granddaughter Harriett West all my wearing apparel. To my great granddaughter Prudence West my bed & furniture with all my household furniture. If there should be any more money due me from my son M. T. Hall than will pay all my debts, boarding and funeral expences, I allow it to be divided between my son M. T. Hall, Harriet West & John R. Hall, 8 April 1835. Prudence Harris (LS), Wit: Richard Gillespie, John McElwain, A. Giles.

Pages 70-72: Warrant of appraisement on the estate of Thomas Guinn directed to David Arterberry, John McKnight Esqr., James Robinson, Joseph Hetherington & Robert Robinson 16 Aug 1839 returnable 16 October. Letters testamentary to Elizabeth Guinn and Richard Guinn 15 Aug 1839.

Pages 72-74: Will of Godfrey Beamgard of York District... To my son Adam Beamgard that part of my plantation known by Bennett's Knob adj. John Peters, Mrs. Watson, 130 acres. I desire that my son Isaac have the part of my plantation whereon my son Adam now lives, 100 acres adj. the part allotted to Adam. To my son Samuel & Joseph that part of my plantation whereon the buildings stand, 184 acres. I desire that my son John have the remainder of my plantation between Samuel & Joseph's part & Isaac's part. My executor pay to my son in law Archibald Harvey $10 as his part of estate. My son Samuel have the young coult as his property. My household stuff and all my stock of cattle, etc., for the benefit of my children who now reside with me during the lifetime of my dear wife, then an equal divide be made. My son Samuel & Joseph support & contribute to the necessities of their beloved mother. I appoint my son Adam Beamgard, exr., 9 July 1839. Godfrey Beamgard (LS), Wit: Benjn Neely, Allen G. Lawrance, Myles Smith.

Pages 74-76: Will of Thomas Sherer of the district of York... To my beloved wife Anne Sherer my entire household and kitchen furniture during her life and at her death the same to be sold and the proceeds to be equally divided between my sons and daughters excepting Alaquil Callender. To my said wife my negroes Tom, Eliza, Rachel, Samuel, Simon, Stephen and Rachel and her three children Sarah, Margaret, and John, and at her death I will that Tom be permitted to enjoy the fruit of his own labor for the balance of his laboring days under the guardianship of my executors and should Tom become unable to support himself by his labor, I entrust his support upon my three sons William, Richard, and Thomas Sherer allowing Tom to live with such of them he may prefer. To my son William Sherer the above named boy Samuel at the decease of my wife. To my son Richard Sherer my negro man Simon at the death of my son To my son Thomas Sherer the my negro man Stephen at the death of my wife. To my son William my girl Margaret and my boy John. To my son Richard my negro girl Sarah and to my son Thomas my negro woman Rachel. My wagon & harness my farming utensils & my stock to remain on the plantation for the use of my family. I appoint my three sons William, Richard & Thomas executors, 23 March 1839. Thomas Sherer (mark) (Seal), Wit: Wm. Jamison, James T. Galloway, Benjn. F. Love.

Pages 76-77: Warrant of appraisement on the estate of Susannah Greer to James M. Love, Robt M. Love, Alexr Howie, John McNeel & John McKnight Esqr., 2 Sept 1839 returnable 2 December.

Pages 77-79: Will of Akilles Holt of the district of York... I give to seven of my children (to wit) John Holt, Abraham Holt, Thomas holt, James Holt, Elizabeth Holt, Lucy Holt and Catherine Holt two negro men named George & Dave, the negroes to be sold by my executors on a credit of 12 months and the money arising therefrom to be equally divided. To my son Allen Wyle Holt 70 acres of land on the east side of Buffaloe Creek. To my wife Jane holt two negro men named Jack and Ben, all household & kitchen furniture, tools, etc., during her natural life & to dispose of the same equally to her two daughters (to wit) Eliza Jane and Martha Wylie at such times as she deems proper & she has the privilege to live on the land whereon we now live during her life. The remainder of my real estate being a tract of land in York District on waters of Buffalow Creek, 500 acres to my two sons Allen Wylie Holt & Hercules G. Holt. I appoint Samuel Wylie, exr., 15 Aug 1838. Killis Holt (LS), Wit: Jacob Sterns, James Wylie, Joseph McCosh. Codicil 15 Aug 1838. I revoke the legacy of 70 acres of lane to Allen Wylie Holt and give him $1000. Killis Holt (LS), Wit: Jos McCosh, Jacob Sterns, James Wylie.

Pages 79-81: South Carolina, York District. Will of David Watson... To my beloved wife Margaret my negroes Ame & Dinah, also the place whereon I reside as long as she continues my widow & choose to reside upon it. I also will that 20 acres be added to the place from that formerly owned by Hugh Watson next my father's old place and running to James Watson's line. To my son Samuel $100 in addition to he has already received. To my three married daughters, as follows: to Eliza a negro girl Adaline; to Margaret, Charlotte & to Mary & whatever other things they may have received. To my son William the plantation formerly owned by H. Watson, the aforementioned 70 acres excepted on condition that he pay $400 annually for the support of the family. To my three daughters Elizabeth, Jane & Emily each $200, a horse saddle & bridle, in every respect as their other sisters have received. To my sons David & Franklin my plantation on Crowder's Creek to be equally divided between them and the profits arising before they come of age. To my youngest son Robert the place on which I reside with the addition already mentioned. My negroes Peter, Lot & Minor I allow to remain on my place if it be deemed necessary for the support of my wife & family and after the death of my wife Margaret, they are to be disposed of as follows (viz) to David, Peter; to Franklin, Lot; to Robert, Miner. I nominate my wife Margaret & my son William, exrs., 2 April 1831. David Watson, Wit: Wm Watson, Deborah Watson (mark), Alexander Barnett.

Pages 81-82: South Carolina, York District. Will of Nancy Kimbrell of district above mentioned... My negro wench Rose & her son John to my eldest daughter Jane Armstrong and at her death to be equally divided among said Jean's children. My negro wench Legle[?] and her son Mose remain the loaned property of my youngest daughter Massey H. Hunter and at her death to be equally divided among her children, and if none to be divided between my two sons William & Rush. My daughter Massey is to have two beds & furniture, one folding leaf table, one horse, saddle, one bureau and one set of table spoons silver, tea spoons (silver). To my son William two negro boys Peter & Green & one wench named Fawn, one bureau, two beds & furniture. I direct that my stock with my with my wagon & farming utensils be sold at publick auction and the money arising therefrom to be applied to the discharge of debts. Out of my estate two headstone will be procured and for my first husband Dr. Clawson & the other for myself. I appoint my esteemed neighbor William E. White & my brother George Pettus, exrs., 25 April 1839. Nancy Kimbrell (X) (LS), Wit: Peter K. Ker, James Alderson, Peter Campbell.

Pages 82-84: Warrant of appraisement on the estate of John Black directed to James Williamson Senr, Samuel Moore, Richard Streight, Jno Williamson & Jno S. Bratton 4 Sept 1839 returnable 4 November. Letters testamentary to David Leroy Black 4 September 1839.

Pages 84-86: Warrant of appraisement on the estate of Godfrey Beamgarde directed to Myles Smith, Benjn Neely, Allen G. Lawrance, David Jackson & Henry Carroll 7 October 1839 returnable 7 December. Letters testamentary to Adam Beamgarde 7 October 1839.

YORK COUNTY SC WILL BOOK 2 1837-1840

Pages 86-87: Warrant of appraisement on the estate of Akillis Holt directed to Jacob Stern, James Wylie, James Wood, James Randall & William Moore, 28 Oct 1839 returnable 28 December. Letters testamentary to Jane Holt 28 October 1839.

Page 88: Will of Samuel Bradley of the district of York... Also my estate both real & personal be equally divided among my three children viz Mary P. King, Samuel A. Bradley & Joseph Bradley & as my youngest son Joseph Bradley is not of sound mine, I will that my daughter Mary P. King be the sole agent & guardian for Joseph Bradley, 27 Nov 1839. I appoint Abm Hardin, exr., Sam Bradley (LS), Wit: Jacob Deal, D. A. Fulton, Thos B. Calton.

Pages 88-90: Warrant of appraisement on the estate of David Watson directed to Wm Watson, Hugh Currance, Gaz. Wilson, Josiah Wilson & Wm. Pressley 4 November 1839 returnable 4 January. Letters testamentary to William A. Watson 4 November 1839.

Pages 90-92: Warrant of appraisement on the estate of Thomas Shearer directed to Robt Hays, Robt Wilson, Edwd Feemster, Wm. Jameson Esqr., & James T. Galloway Esqr., 18 November 1839 returnable 18 January. Letters testamentary to Thomas Shearer Jr., 18 November 1839.

Pages 92-93: South Carolina, York District. Will of Wm. M. Bigger... To my beloved wife Mary Bigger my negro girl Ann & boy Allison, and I allow her the possession of my dwelling house & her support off my plantation during her widowhood, also one bed & furniture, my chest of drawers, two milch cows & her choice of my horses & a saddle & bridle .I will that all my property remain on my plantation untill my youngest child arrives to the age of 21 years except such as heretofore bequeathed to my wife for the support maintenance & education of my children & then the personal property to be equally divided between my wife should she remain unmarried & my three children. The two negroes bequeathed to my wife at her death to be equally divided between my children, but the legal title to all property to my two daughters do not vest in them but in my executors. To my son James Lysander Bigger all my real estate not otherwise disposed of. I appoint my wife executors & Dr. David Watson, exr., 15 Dec 1839. Wm. M. Bigger (LS), Wit: Eugene Hill, Arch'd Barron, J. M. Ross.

Pages 94-95: Will of William Chambers of York District being advanced in years & much on the decline of body... To my granddaughter Mary Chambers now the wife of Wm. Compton [Campton?] $80 to be paid in one year after my death. To my granddaughter Scena Chambers my son David's daughter my house clock. My land & all my other property unto my four children viz John Chambers, David Chambers, Elizabeth Neely wife to John Neely & her children after her, and William Maxwell Chambers, equally to be divided between them. Whereas my son Wm Maxwell has been absent in Georgia or elsewhere I have not heard of him for a number of years, if it should so be that he should be dead or could not be found to receive his divided in case, I allow his divide to be equally divided between my other three children above named. I have paid two debts for my son John since he left me, viz one to Wm Gilmore decd & one to John Latta admr, I allow said two debts to be counted up to John in his right to claim. I appoint John McCulloch my executor, 4 Dec 1833. William Chambers (LS), Wit: Robert Denkins[?], John Neely, James P. Neely.

Pages 95-97: Warrant of appraisement on the estate of Samuel Bradley directed to Daniel A. Fulton, Hugh Borders, Edward Bird, T. D. Fallow & Capt. Martin Mullenax 16 December 1839 returnable 16 February. Letters testamentary to Abraham Harden 16 December 1839.

Pages 97-105: Will of Gordon Moore of York District.... My debts & funeral expenses to be paid out of the money now on hand, notes & book accounts, & the following tracts of land (to wit) the land lying in Union District known by the name of Thomas Black's plantation, John Parker plantation, & the Joseph Howell plantation also the tracts of land in York District: one tract of land that I bought from John Darwin Senr, one small tract including the spring that Joseph Logan makes use of that I bought from Amos Davis & if my son John Gordon Moore will make a little from him to the tract of land that Joseph Logan now lives on to my estate, let the same be sold with the foregoing tracts, which I think will promote the sale of the adjoining tracts, then my executors shall be bound to pay unto him the sum of $100 if he agrees to the same in his own right. Also my shares in the Howell plantation, also a part of a tract that I bought from James Plexco on the north side of the Thompson line, to the Howell's Ferry line, adj. Rhoda Smith's line, Mihel Smith's line. If the foregoing are not sufficient to settle my debts, then my executors may sell the following lands: beginning at Doctor Wright's to Payton B. Darwin's, on either tract that I bought from Samuel Barkley. My negroes to be hired out yearly to the carpenter's trade & any other of the negro men if they think it would be more profitable than to work on a farm except my negro man Frank, land at the mouth of the Goyen Moore Creek put in cultivation for the support of my family. My negro Frank and his son Jerry & the negroes that is now on the plantation where my family now lives to remain there to work said plantation under the direction of my son John G. Moore and for his services in carrying on the same, he shall receive $200 annually from my executors, and that my daughters remain where they live now until the youngest arrives to the age of 21 years or marry, then to be divided amongst them. To my son William Thompson Moore all that I have heretofore given him of my estate which will be found charged to him on my books, and one note of hand due from him to me, also one tract of land that I purchased from Jack B. Moore in Union District on Broad River adj. the lands of John Moore & Susan Parker, also one good bedstead but he is not to have possession of the lands until my youngest child shall arrive at the age of 21 years. To my son John Gordon Moore one negro boy equal in value to the boys that William Thompson Moore & Jacob Alexander Moore has already received from me, also one good horse, one good bed & bestead & furniture. To my sons John G. Moore & Jacob A. Moore the following tracts of land: the tract known by the name of the old plantation given to me by my father in York District on the east side of Broad River, also one tract of land bounded by Mitchel's lines & John Darwin decd's lands, and James Currien's[?] grant at or near the Buffaloe stump, Daniel Smith's land, George Darwin grant, also part of two other tracts that I bought from ___ Wilson called the Henderson place & was granted to Joshua Denton on the south fork of the Moore's[?] branch, one good bed, bedstead and furniture. To my daughter Minerva Moore when she arrives at the age of 18 years, one negro girl between the age of eight and twelve, one good bureau, one good bed, bedstead & furniture. To my daughter Temandia when she arrives at the age of 18 years, one negro girl between the age of eight and twelve, one good bureau, one good bed, bedstead & furniture. To my daughter Dianna when she arrives at the age of 18 years, one negro girl between the age of eight and twelve, one good bureau, one good bed, bedstead & furniture, and that she may be sent one year to some good boarding school. To my daughter Colvee[?] when she arrives at the age of 18 years, one negro girl between the age of eight and twelve, one good bureau, one good bed, bedstead & furniture, and that she may be sent one year to some good boarding school. My aged mother remains where she now is and that particular care & attention be paid by my executors to her care & comfort. I do further give to my sons Jno G. Moore & Jacob A. Moore 50 acres of land for which I have Daniel Smith's bond to make me a title between two branches, including my negro quarter. I appoint my three sons William Thompson Moore, John Gordon Moore & Jacob Alexander Moore, exrs., 9 Nov 1839. Gordon Moore (LS), Wit: James Phagan, Charles T. Murphy M. D., James B. Meek, Wm. B. Meek.

State of Mississippi, Winston County. Proved by the oath of James B. Meek & James Phagan before Robert C. Thornton, Judge of the probate for said county, 23 Jan 1840.

Affidavit concerning the will of Gordon Moore 17 Feb 1840 in York District by John S. Moore.

Jos. W. Thompson of Union District attested to the handwriting of Gordon Moore and Charles T. Murphy, witness to the said will, 17 Feb 1840.

Pages 105-106: Warrant of appraisement on the estate of Wm. McBigger deceased directed to Arch'd Barron, Capt. Wm. Barry, Wm May, James Bigger & Wm Carrothers 7 Jan 1840 returnable 7 March. Letters testamentary to Mary E. Bigger 7 Jan 1840.

END OF BOOK 2

## YORK COUNTY SC WILL BOOK 3 1840-1862

**Pages 1-2**: South Carolina, York District. Will of William Hamilton... my landed estate consisting of the tract of land on which I now live & which was willed to me by my father and another tract purchased from Judge Smith adjoining unto, to my beloved son William K. Hamilton, and the said William K. Hamilton do pay out of the value of the aforesaid Land the sum of $400 to the legal representatives of my deceased daughter Eleanor Hemphill when ever legally applied for by the heirs of her body. To my beloved children David Hamilton, Wm. K. Hamilton, Mary Ann Good, Elizabeth Galloway & Janet Starke Davidson, all my personal estate of which I die seized & possessed, share and share alike. I appoint my trusty & Well beloved sons David Hamilton & William K. Hamilton joint executors, 6 Nov 1839. William Hamilton (X) (Seal), Wit: Samuel J. Hovey[?], James H. Alexander, Jas. T. Galloway, Jas. McCluney. Proved by the oath of James McCluney 25 Aug 1840 before Benjamin Chambers. At the same time qualified David Hamilton & William K. Hamilton, executors.

**Pages 2-4**: Will of John Hemphill of State of South Carolina & district of York... my real estate be sold with all my stock etc. out of which I allow my burial expenses & all just debts to be paid. My negro man Amzi & woman Letty, Mills & girl Caroline for the maintainance of my wife Nancy during her natural life or widowhood, my son Samuel G. Hemphill to take charge of them & build her a neat small & comfortable house to live in to herself & see her decently supported. The boy Miles to attend her making fires & doing other like matter at her request. Caroline I allow to be with her to attend & wait upon her at her own discretion & command. If my son Samuel does not or is not willing to take charge of them & her as above named, I allow some of the rest of my sons to do so leaving to her choice which & where to build the house. At the marriage or death of my wife Nancy, I allow my son Samuel G. Hemphill to have Amzi & Letty and my son William H. Hemphill I allow Miles & my son John G. Hemphill I give & bequeath the girl Caroline. At my death I give my boy Ochra to my son James S. Hemphill & my boy Smith to my son John G. Hemphill. To my daughter Martha $100 to be paid out of the price of my real estate & other property, and my son Samuel I allow $200 out of the same for building the house & other necessary buildings for my wife Nancy. My will is that as soon as practicable after my death the respective negroes be appraised & each Legatee named take them at the appraisement at the times above specified. The amount of sales after the different appointments in money are made be so divided among my sons named as to make them equal in the appraisement of the negroes & nett amount of sale except Samuel I allow him $60 more than my other sons as that amt. is due him by settlement. My will is that my sons keep the negroes & not expose them to sale. My wife Nancy keep my gray mare, two of the best beds & furniture, bureau clock & other suitable & necessary furniture to have & to hold the same as the other property. I my son William H. Hemphill's son John my grey filley and my grandson John Sylvanus $150. I appoint my son Samuel G. Hemphill & John J. Plexco as guardians to see that my wife Nancy is well & decently supported & justly done by. My sons James S. Hemphill & John G. Hemphill executors, 15 Aug 1840. John Hemphill (X) (Seal), Wit: Samuel Wright, James G. Good, John G. Brown.

1840 Sept 14th. On 24th of August 1840 James S. Hemphill one of the executors named in the will of John Hemphill Esqr. dec'd petitioner the court of ordinary to have said will proved in solemn form of law, the parties were all cited that was heirs ta law to appear on 3rd September to attend said probate & all appeared by Allen Crosby, but one witness attended & the case was posponed by consent of those parties present until the 7th instant at which time they appeared, all the parties except the widow & A. Crosby. The case was them posponed untill this day 14 September when all the witnesses appeared & the heirs at law except widow & Allen Crosby. I then proceeded to the probate of said will in solemn form by examining the witnesses severally & separately... believing it to be valid. Benjn Chambers, O. Y. D. After the will being established as valid at the same time qualified James G. Hemphill, executor.

We whose names are hereunto subscribed do agree to the following arrangement of the estate real & personal of John Hemphill Esqr decd, provided a paper now filed in the ordinary's office purporting to be the will be established... the said estate after deducting out of the necessary expenses & debts that Samuel G. Hemphill be paid a claim of $150 and the remainder of said estate be then equally divided amongst the four brothers & Mrs. Nancy Hemphill the widow agree her widow in lieu of her life or widowhood estate to take one fifth of the estate aforesaid real & personal. Sept 3rd 1840. Nancy Hemphill (LS), W. H. Hemphill (LS), Jas. S. Hemphill (LS), W. G. Hemphill (LS), Jno G. Hemphill (S).

**Pages 4-6**: Will of Mary Hemphill of District of York... to my son Robert Hemphill the sum of one dollar. To my grand daughter Jane Hemphill daughter of my son Robert one negro boy named George, also to said negro George one bed tick, two blankets, one counterfam[?] and one sheet & one pewter plat. To my son James Hemphill one negro girl called Easther, one white sheet & one pewter bason. To my grandson James A. Hemphill son of James one negro child called Green. My negro woman Amy be valued by three freeholders & that my son James Hemphill take her at the valuation & her value be equally divided between the children of my son Samuel by his first marriage & the children of my son James. To my grandson James V. Hemphill son of Samuel one negro boy named Sigh said negro to remain in possession of my son Samuel untill James becomes 21 years of age. To my son Samuel's three youngest sons one milch cow & calf, one heifer & all my stock of hogs at present 13 head & one stand curtains. To my grandson Alexander H. Hemphill, Samuel's son, one walnut table. To my son Samuel one white sheet also one pewter Bason. To my daughter Jane wife of Wm. Porter the sum of one dollar. To the heirs of my son the sum of $1 each. All loose property found after my death not named in the will be put to sale by my executors to pay expenses that may occur. I appoint Daniel Mishaw & Laban Suggs, exrs., 29 March 1833. Mary Hemphill (X), Wit: David Jackson, Laban Suggs, Jas. L. Jackson. Proved by the oath of David Jackson 28 Sept 1840 before Benjn Chambers, O. Y. D. October 12th 1840 Daniel Meshow one of the exrs. being unwilling to take upon himself the execution of said will do hereby revoke & refuse to qualify.

**Pages 6-7**: South Carolina, York District. Will of Sarah Armstrong of district aforesaid... to my daughter Nancy Malissa me negro woman named Mida & her six children viz Hannah, Amzi, Mansfield, Mariah, Leander & Cresy, with any issue they may have, also all my money on hand & notes in my possession, all my stock, household & kitchen furniture. I appoint Jesse R. Armstrong & Isaac Campbell, exrs., 22 Jan 1840. Sarah Armstrong (LS), Wit: Elizabeth Campbell, Jane Campbell (X), Robt Y. Allison. Proved by the oath of Robt Y. Allison 13 Oct 1850 before Benja. Chambers, O. Y. D.

**Pages 7-9**: Will of Margaret Davison of the District of York... to my son Doct. James H. Davison a certain negro boy named Sam. To my daughter Lucinda Patrick a negro girl named Fanny also another negro girl named Mary. To my grandchildren, the children of Sarah C. Latimore, a negro woman named Sue and her daughter Judy. To my grand child Elias Davison, the son of Franklin F. Davis decd, a negro child named Edmund and a blazed filly called Bet. To my grandchildren, the children of Franklin F. Davison decd, the one half of all my right, title and interest to the plantation or tract of land whereon I now live belonging to the heirs at law of Elias Davison decd. To my grandchildren, the children of Sarah c. Latimore, the other moiety of half of the plantation or tract of land whereon I now live belonging to the heirs at law of Elias Davison decd. My household and kitchen furniture to any children Lucinda Patrick and Sarah C. Latimore to be equally divided between them and their heirs. To my son Elias Davison a balled horse called Ben. To my daughter in law the widow of Franklin . Davidson, one fallen left table. My executors to expose to public vendue my negro boy named Alick and the proceeds of the sale to be applied to the payment of my debts and the balance if any to be equally divided between my son Robert Latimore and my son in law William Scott. The rest of my estate be exposed to public vendue the proceeds of which to be equally divided among my grandchildren namely the children of Lucinda Patrick, Sarah C. Latimore, and Franklin F. Davison. I appoint James Moore Jr. of the District of York, my executor, 27 July 1833. Margaret Davison (X) (Seal), Wit: Jo G. Martin, G. Sandifur, James B. Davison. Proved by the oath of James b. Davison and Jos Martin Esqr, 30 Oct 1805 before Benjn Chambers, ordy. At same time qualified James Moore executor.

**Pages 9-10**: Will of Sarah White of York District... To my well beloved nephew Valdaura Norris Garison, all my monies, notes, bonds, accounts or legacies due to me with two feather beds and all the bedclothes, also one trunk, one pine painted chest with their contents with al my stockings. I also will my wearing apparel to the said V. N. Garison. To my niece Sarah W. Garison my bureau, saddle & Bridle. I appoint my nephew V. N. Garison, my sole executor, 12 Oct 1833. Sarah White (mark), Wit: Myles Smith, John Smith, R. D. Smith. Proved 7 Sept 1840 by the oath of Myles Smith before Benjn Chambers, O. Y. D.

**Pages 10-11**: Will of James Bryan Senr of district of York... To my beloved wife Mary the one third part of the remainder of my estate to be disposed of at her will & pleasure. I allow $2000 to be taken out of the remaining two thirds & distributed amongst my six children by my first wife (to wit) to my son William Bryan $300; to my son Benjamin Bryan $200; to my son Augustus Bryan $150; to my daughter Margaret Matthews $150; to my daughter Nancy Gregory $100; to my son by law Hugh Wallace $6 7 to my daughter Deborah Wallace youngest child $95 to be used by my daughter Delilah if she sees propper to do so. I leave to my four sons by my present wife Mary to wit James, Thomas, Moses & Aaron, the whole of the remainder of my estate, giving Thomas $50 more than James & Moses $50 more than Aaron. 29 Nov 1830. James Bryan (X) (Seal), Wit: S. Melton, Thos H. Smith, Samuel Chambers. Proved by the oath of Saml Melton 2 Dec 1840 before Benjn Chambers, O. Y. D.

**Pages 11-14**: South Carolina, Lancaster District. Will of Isaac Donnom of the state & district aforesaid, planter... I leave to my wife Jane the following negroes for her use, support and maintenance during her widowhood or lifetime, viz, Poll a negro woman, David, Harriot, Eliza, Isaac, Dinah, Sambo, Mars and Richard, also a negro man Ben with their increase. At her marriage or death to be divided in the following manner, viz negroes Ben, Eliza, Isaac and Dinah to my stepson Hall T. McGee. The ballance or remainder to be divided with my other negroes as I shall hereafter direct. To my stepdaughter Martha McGee, a small negro girl Flora, one of negro Tena's children. Should my stepson Hall T. McGee die leaving no living heirs of his body, in that case the said four negroes shall return back to my estate. Should my stepdaughter Martha McGee die without leaving issue I give the said negro girl Flora with her increase to Hall T. McGee & in case both of my stepchildren die leaving no children, them all to return to my estate. I also lend to my wife Jane for her support a piece of land including the improvements to be laid off to her beginning on the Black Jack line between Wm Thomas McDow & myself where the petition fence divides what is usually called the Black Jack field of corn & my cotton field... towards Mrs. Cantzons to where my land stops in that direction, and to my said wife the whole of my household & kitchen furniture with my carriage, one wagon & geers, with tools, four horses, cattle, hogs & sheep. Should the mill be kept up her grinding to be free of to & if Black Smith Dick live to work at his trade her smithing to be done clear of charge. At her death the whole I give to my grandson Isaac Donnam Witherspoon. To my two grandsons Isaac Donnom Witherspoon & Andrew Jackson Witherspoon, the whole of my lands consisting of several tracts with my mills to be equally divided between them with the lands including the improvements that I loaned my wife. My grandson Donnom shall have first choice. In case of both their deaths, I give the whole of my lands to the rest of my grand & great grandchildren. I appoint my grandson Isaac Donnam Witherspoon my sole executor, 2 October 1826. I. Donnom (Seal), Wit: John Sims, Amasa Howard, Eliza J. Jones. Proved in Lancaster District by the oath of Amasa Howard & Eliza J. Jones 4 March 1830 before J. H. Witherspoon, O. Y. D. March 30th 1830. Then qualified Isaac Donnam Witherspoon executor. True copy taken from the original last will & testament of Isaac Donnom (decd), 23 Nov 1840. James H. Witherspoon Junr., Ordinary. Recorded from a certified copy of the will of Isaac Donnom at the request of J. D. Witherspoon January 12th 1841. Benjn Chambers, Ordy of York District.

**Pages 14-15**: South Carolina, York District. Will of Matthew Harper Senior of district aforesaid... My plantation on which I now reside to my two sons John & Robert Harper, John to have the lower part joining lands of Thomas Boyd, to be equally divided between them. To my Margaret Harper, to feather beds & furniture, one horse, saddle & Bridle, one cow & calf, one bureau & chest, & all her wearing apparel. To my daughter Elizabeth, two feather beds & furniture, one horse, saddle & bridle, one cow & calf, one bureau & chest and her wearing apparel. To my daughter Jane, two feather beds & furniture, one horse, saddle & bridle, one cow & calf, one bureau & chest and her wearing apparel. To my son Matthew, one horse, blacksmith tools he now works on. To my son Joseph one horse, saddle & bridle. To my niece Jane Sinclair one cow & calf. To my niece Elizabeth Herdman one cow & calf. To my wife Jane Harper, I allow that her and my unmarried daughters live in the house I now live in & have the land & timber for their support my wife's lifetime and my negroes Torry, Silvey & Curry to work for them. I allow my wife to have one horse and chair & Harness her lifetime, her bed & furniture. At her death the three negroes to be sold & all the unwilled property & proceeds to be equally divided between my five sons James, John, Matthew, Robert & Joseph, and my three daughters Margaret, Jane & Elizabeth. I appoint my son John Harper, exr., 23 Aug 1828. Matthew Harper (LS), Wit: Aaron Wood, David J. Boyd, John Jackson. Proved by the oath of John Jackson, Esqr., before Benjamin Chambers, O.Y.D.

**Pages 15-17**: Will of Jesse White... My executor as soon after my decease as may be proper sell all my personal property and after paying my debts with the proceeds that they turn any balance there may be over to my youngest daughter Elizabeth Elvira White for keeping my two youngest children James Green Willis White & Robert Logan White until they arrive at the age of 21 years. My executors to divide the whole of my real estate equally between my seven children namely Nancey Wilkie, Catherine Wilkie, Lawrence W. White, Thomas M. White, Elizabeth E. White, James Green W. White & Robert L. White. My oldest daughter Nancy Wilkie to take the share on which she & her husband Joseph Wilkie now lives & that they value the same to her as woodland with the present improvements & that they allow my daughter Catherine Wilkie to take the share on which her & her husband Jesse Wilkie now resides & that they value the same to her as woodland with the present improvements. They lay out the share of my son Lawrance W. White with my dwelling house. To my son Thomas M. White the share lying between the shares of Lawrence W. White and Catherine Wilkie & that they lay out to my daughter Elizabeth W. White the lot on which Reese M. Roark lives the present year. I appoint my friend William C. Black the guardian of the persons & estates of my two sons (now minors) James Green Willis White & Robert Logan White untill they arrive at the age of 21 years. I appoint my friends Thomas Breages, Abraham Hardin & Wm. C. Black, exrs., 22 Dec 1840. Jesse White (LS), Wit: Jno Wood, Martin Hardin, Berry Martin. Proved by the oath of John Wood 1 Feb 1841 before Benjn Chambers, O. Y. D. At same time qualified Thos Bridges exrs. Wm. C. Black and A. Hardin declined to qualify 30 Jan 1841.

**Pages 17-20**: Will of Samuel Neely of York District... I will that all my just debts & funeral expences be paid out of the money I have on hand at my deceased. Should not there be money enough on hand, I desire my executors to collect the balance from some of those indebted to me for loaned money. To my daughter Nancy Warran, one dollar. To my daughter Elizabeth McElwee one negro girl named Phebe. To my grandson Samuel, son of Nancy Warren, formerly Nancy Miller, a negro girl named Poll about 8 years of age. To my grandson James, the son of William McElwee, a negro girl named Viney. To my granddaughter Jane, daughter of William McElwee, a negro girl named Elvira. To my son in law John miller, one dollar. To my grand children Drusilla, Jane & Joseph, child of John Miller, one dollar. My executors continue to put out at interest until my wife's decease all the money which I have heretofore loan or may have loaned previous to my death. To my beloved wife Elizabeth all my household & kitchen furniture, my stock of cattle, negroes Tom, Polly & the youngest child of Poll at my decease with half of my ready money after paying debts & funeral expenses. To my wife during her natural life the house wherein I now reside with so much of my land as she may choose to select & work, all my negroes not herebefore bequeathed, all my farming utensils, horses & stock (cattle excepted) and one half of the interest from the money put out at interest. At my wife's decease, I give to my grandson Samuel, son of Benjamin Neely, two of the negroes viz Aron & a yellow girl called Mary or Ma, and the remainder of the property in this item I desire to go to my son Benjamin. To my son Benjamin during the life of my wife, one half of the interest from money loaned. To my wife during her natural life my two houses & lots in Yorkvillle, each lot to contain 3/4 acre. At my wife's deceased, son Benjamin's son Samuel to have the house & lot in Yorkville, the same being the dwelling house which I last built, and my son Benjamin to have my other house & lot in Yorkville. To my son Benjamin all my remaining lots in Yorkville. My wife Elizabeth and my son Benjamin exrs., __ June 1838. Sam Neely (LS), Wit: Benjn Chambers, G. W. Williams, Jas Kuykendall.

February 15th 1841. In the Court of Ordinary. After the heirs at law of Samuel Neely decd being cited to attend to the probate of the will & several heirs at law being present by their attorneys proceeded to qualify the subscribing witnesses to said will & no evidence being introduced by the heirs in contradiction to the testimony of the witnesses, this instrument of writing is the last will of Samuel Neely decd. Benjn Chambers, O. Y. D. At the same time qualified Benjamin Neely, exr.

**Pages 20-21**: Will of Thomas Wilson, 1 December 1837... To my brother William Wilson all that land in York District whereon I now live, believing the same to be 255 acres. To my brother William Wilson a negro man named Allison, also a negro boy named Daniel, a negro boy named Amzi, a negro girl named Nancy, a negro girl named Rachel, all my money and notes after my lawful debts are paid, my household & kitchen furniture, all my horses & cattle & hogs. To my brother John Wilson five shillings sterling. If my brother William's death should happen before this property comes to his hand, then this property is to be sold and the money arising from the sale to go to

William Wilson's children, to James & Thomas Wilson, Sarah Far & Jane Gurdin, & my saddle to Jane. I make Capt. William Nelson & Capt. John Brown, my exrs. Thomas Wilson (LS), Wit: Thomas Whitesides, Lawson Jenkins, Henry Hood. Proved by the oath of Thomas Whitesides and Lawson Jenkins 17 March 1841 before Benjamin Chambers, O.Y.D. At the same time qualified Capt. John Brown executor.

**Pages 21-22**: Will of Susanna Dunlap of York District... I bequeath to my son James P. Dunlap two tracts of land being in the District aforesaid, viz one tract of 200 acres whereon I now live which was conveyed by James Patton to William Dunlap, also one other tract of 160 acres conveyed by said James Patton to said William Dunlap. To my son William B. Dunlap one negro man named Charles, one negro woman named Jemima and her son Isaac, one negro woman Rebecca and one negro woman Susan and two children. To my granddaughter Susannah Dunlap, the one half of the value of a negro girl named Agga and the other half of the value of said Agga to my two grand daughters Lurilla Sussanna Jane and Margaret Catherine Ann. To my daughter Elizabeth Hagins one negro man named Jeff, one negro woman named Patience and three children one negro boy named Sam. To my son James P. Dunlap one negro man named Abram, one negro woman named Cloe, one negro boy named Candy and one negro boy named Charles. To my granddaughter Mary P. Dunlap and my grand daughter Susanna Dunlap to each of them $300 in money provided Robert White gives each of them a negro or should he give his grand daughter Sussanna Fergesson a negro and his granddaughter Mary P. Dunlap none. Then I do bequeath the $6500 to Mary P. Dunlap exclusively at my decease. I do allow that $600 be raised to pay to my two grand daughters Susannah Fergesson & Mary P. Dunlap and that my son William B. Dunlap do pay $250 and my daughter Elisabeth Hagins $250 and my son James P. Dunlap pay $200. I appoint my son William B. Dunlap and my son James P. Dunlap, exrs., 21 Oct 1839. Susanna Dunlap (X) (LS), Wit: Isaac McFadden, William Ware, Jonathon Davis. Proved by the oath of Isaac McFadden 23 March 1841 before Benjn Chambers. At same time qualified James P. Dunlap, executor.

**Pages 22-23**: Will of John S. McClenahan of York District... so much of my personal property be sold immediately after my decease as will pay all my just debts and funeral expenses. The overplus if any to be divided between my two sisters and niece viz Jane McClenahan, Martha Dunlap and Nancy Dunlap. I appoint John Roddey Esqr., executor, 6 March 1841. J. S. McClenahan (LS), Wit: Richard Kirk, William Coonrod, E. T. Crockett. Proved by the oath of William Coonrood 26 March 1841.

**Pages 23-25**: South Carolina, York District. Will of Elizabeth Neely of the district aforesaid... To my daughters Elizabeth McElwee & Nancy Warren, all my household & kitchen furniture, my stock of every description & all the money I may have on hand at my death or which may be owing to me. Should one or both my said daughters die before me, her or their share is to go to her daughters alive at my death. To my daughter Elizabeth McElwee my negro woman Poll & her son Sam on condition that she pay to each of my granddaughters Rachel Miller Letta and Elizabeth Miller $50. To Elizabeth McElwee my Barroach. To my son Benjamin Neely my negro man named Tom on condition he pays to Nancy Warren $100. To my granddaughters Rachel Letta & Elizabeth Miller as above. I bequeath to my negro woman Poll one cow & calf. To Jane Thomasson, Drusilla Simpson and Joseph Miller one dollar each. The rest of my estate to my two daughters Elizabeth McElwee & Nancy Warren, and I appoint them my exrs., 20 March 1841. Elizabeth Neely (X) (LS), Wit: Wm. P. Thomason, Ja Kuykendall, Wm. R. Alexander. Proved by the oath of James Kuykendall, Esqr., 30 July 1841 before Benjn Chambers, O.Y.D. At the date above qualified Wm. M. McElwee in right of his wife Exr and Mrs. Elizabeth McElwee extx and qualified Hugh Warran ex'r in right of his wife Nancy who also qualified.

**Page 25**: South Carolina, York District. Will of William A. Barry... To my beloved wife Elizabeth Barry for her natural life the possession of my dwelling house, lands, negroes, stock & property. Should she marry, she gets a child's part, my property being equally divided between her & my children. To my children I bequeath to them their maintenance and education and other necessaries that my wife should think proper when they marry or come of age. I appoint my wife Eliz'a Barry executrix & Archibald Barron executor, 11 Nov 1850. Wm. A. Barry (LS), Wit: David M. Watson , Joseph Strain, M. E. Barron. Proved 4 Aug 1851 by the oath of Dr. David M. Watson. At same time qualified Mrs. Eliz'a A. S. Barry extx & Arch'd Barron exr.

**Pages 26-28**: Will of John Barron Senior of York District... To my beloved wife Jane Barron the plantation or land I now live on with all the household & kitchen furniture, my library of books, my stock of horses, cattle, sheep, hogs, cotton gin & screw, also my negro fellow Charles & his wife Cass & her daughter Kesiah, her son Sam, her daughter Mary & Elise[?] and her son named Selvanus, also the threshing machine & my old negro woman called Mary. My son Thomas G. Barron together with my wife Jane manage & take care of the plantation & property to the best advantage. To my daughter Jane Barry the negro girl named Jane I have heretofore lent her & at her death to go to the education of her then youngest children Archibald, Andrew & James Barry. My executors pay to my son John Barron out of the proceeds of the property above willed to my wife Jane Barron $100 when called for. to my daughter Elizabeth Parham a receipt which I hold on her husband James Parham of $200. To my grandson William Y. Barron son of my son William Barron decd $100. To my son Archibald Barron my negro fellow named Bailey & my negro boy named Anderson. To my daughter Nancy Wallace a receipt which I hold on her husband James Y. Wallace for $200. To my daughter Violet Baxter a receipt which I hold on her husband Andrew Baxter for $200. To my son Thomas Y. Barron my negro fellow named Starky & my negro boy named Jim. I appoint my sons Archibald & Thomas Y. Barron, exrs., 20 May 1839. John Barron (LS), Wit: A. J. Barron, W. Pressley, John Barry. Codicil made 15 Feb 1840. Wit: Wm. Pressley, A. J. Barron, G. E. Barry. August 4 1851 Proved by the oath of Wm. Pressley Esqr. At same time qualified Thos Y. Barron & Archibald Barron, exrs.

**Pages 28-31**: South Carolina, York District. March the 19th 1841. The following is my last will and testament the division of which my property to be as follows. To Margaret Fewell, to William Barron Junr, to Eliza Pressly, to Jane Thomason, to Archibald G. Barron, to Mary Pressly, to John Barron, to S. L. Barron, to Thomas Barron, to Rebecca Barron (includes one tract of land called the Galland tract with the exception of 15 acres).

Will of William Barron... I wish my wife to have her living off the plantation that I now live on and the following negroes to her use for her lifetime viz John & his wife Sarah, Judy, Mary & Cato with whatever stock, household & kitchen furniture she may wish to keep, the carriage and one wagon. The balance of mt property to be appraised and divided in equal portions among my living children after first paying over to my nephew Thomas Jefferson Thomasson $100 and defraying the expenses of Wm Thomasson my nephew for 12 months from the time he came to my house. Also Eliza Pressly $400 on account of her lane hand. Also Thos Barron $400 on account of his lame hand. There and after that each of my nine children to be made qual according to the previous statement. It is my desire that Asa Fewell, Wm. Pressly, Wm. Barron & A. J. Barron attend to having all my debts paid, money collection & division made, 30 March 1841. Wm. Barron (LS), Wit: A. J. Barron, Alex'r Fewell, Wm Pressly, Wm Barron Jr., John Barron. Proved 20 Aug 1841 by the oath of A. J. Barron, Alexr Fewell, Wm. Barron Jr & John Barron before Benjn Chambers, O. Y. D. At same time qualified A. J. Barron, Alexr Fewell & Wm. Barron Jnr executors.

**Pages 31-32**: Will of John Moore... To my brothers Eli & Zenas my shares in the Charleston & Cincinnati Rail Road Company to be equally divided between them, and they are to pay the installments now or that may become due. Whereas my brother Stanhope for money paid for him as security also by notes & accounts is indebted to me, I do release him from all indebtedness to me. My two negroes Bill and Isbel be sold, the proceeds of which to be divided in the following manner, viz to Zekiel Neely $150, to Leonard Estes $100, to Robert Moore $100, to Thomas Moore, 50, to Stanhope Moore $100, provided the sale of said negroes amounts to $500, but if not the proceeds to be divided in the above proportion. My friend John S. Moore, exrs., 8 Aug 1851. John Moore (LS), Wit: R. S. Hope, Saml Rainey, Samuel Moore. Proved 12 Oct 1851 by the oath of R. S. Hope. October 14th 1851 qualified John S. Moore, executor.

**Page 33**: Will of Joseph Jackson, farmer, of district of York... to Elizabeth my dearly beloved wife full power and authority to settle all my just debts out of my personal estate. To my beloved wife all my estate with all my household goods & moveable effects, all my lands, messages & Tenements, and she is named executor, 28 July 1826. Joseph Jackson (O) (Seal), Wit: John Bennett, Wm. Parks, Jos Parks (X). Proved by the oath of John Bennett 20 Dec 1851 and qualified Elizabeth Jackson executrix.

**Pages 34-35**: Will of William Neely of District of York... enough of my stock of horses or cattle to be sold to settle debts. To my nephew Tillotson S. Neely, son of my sister Elizabeth Neely, my plantation or land whereon I now live that he hold & uses it or sells it for his own advantage; & if he does not sell & should die intestate & have no issued, then my land is to return to the lawful heirs of the Neely family, also to the said Tillotson S. Neely the whole of my personal estate, and I appoint him executor, 27 Oct 1841. William Neely (LS), Wit: Jos. W. McCorkle, Samuel Steele, John Workman. Proved by all three witnesses 14 Feb 1842. At same time qualified Tillotson S. Neely executor.

**Pages 35-36**: Will of Thompson Walker of York District... After all my just debts are paid, to my well beloved wife Jane Walker, all my estate during her life; and at her death to my nephew Hugh Walker. I appoint Samuel G. Brown Esqr. and Nathaniel P. Kennedy, exrs., 6 Feb 1842. Thompson Walker (LS), Wit: Cyrus L. Henry, Robert H. Bigham, Robert Henry. Proved by the oath of Robert H. Bigham 18 Feb 1842. At the same time qualified Saml G. Brown & N. P. Kennedy, exrs.

**Pages 36-37**: Will of David Johnston of District of York... to my beloved wife Mary Johnston four negroes viz Jim, Violet, John & Moriah, the two former during her natural life (Jim & Violet) & at her death they shall be sold & the proceeds be equally divided amongst my children the two latter (John & Moriah) to be her own & subject to her own disposal. My old negro woman Bet shall be kept on the plantation during her natural life. I further give to my wife the use of my plantation, farming utensils, wagon, stock, household & kitchen furniture during her natural life for benefit & support of my children & at her death, my plantation to be equally divided between my three sons James, David & William & in case of the death of either the land to descend to the survivors. The balance of my negroes not otherwise disposed of I give to my children viz Martha Jane, James, David, Sarah, Eliza, Amanda, Emeline, Mary Margaret, & William to be equally divided by lot giving to my wife the use & benefit of these negroes for the support & schooling of my children while they remain with her, each legatee to receive their legacy when they shall arrive at the age of 21 years or marry. The negro girl that I have already given to my eldest daughter Martha Jane to be taken into consideration in her lot. When my children become of age or marry, my wife shall furnish them with a bed, horse & saddle making them equal with my daughter Martha Jane. My wife M. Johnston executrix and my son in law Wm. F. Johnston ex'r, 27 March 1842. David Johnston (X) (LS), Wit: Wm. Glenn, Jno A. Laney, Richard Mason. Proved by the oath of Wm Glenn 6 June 1842. At same time qualified Mrs. Mary Johnston executrix.

**Pages 37-38**: South Carolina, York District. Will of Jesse Hays of the district aforesaid... My stock of horses, cattle, hogs, household & kitchen furniture with my farming utensils, also my land, I allow to my wife Selena A. Hays. I also allow my executor and executrix to sell so much of my horse property as will pay my debts. Samuel W. Faries & my wife to be executor and executrix, 23 April 1831. Jesse Hays (LS), Wit: G. Enloe, Robt B. K. Faries, Jno J. Hays. Proved by the oath of Robert B. W. Faries 11 June 1842. At same time qualified Samuel W. Faries, executor.

**Pages 39-40**: South Carolina, York District. Will of James Crawford Senr of district aforesaid... To my beloved wife Elizabeth, the plantation on which I now live with my stock of horses, cattle, hogs &c., with the household & kitchen furniture, during her natural life & at her death what is left to be divided among my children thus: I allow my son Robert M. Crawford to have one bed & bedsted & the under bed & clothing consisting of one sheet, blankets, pillows & counterpane, also one half of my stone quarry tract of land lying on part of Kings Mountain near the memorable hill called the Battle Ground & the Crowbar between him & his brother William for the use of the quary. Also I allow my daughter Amanda J. Hill at her mother's death the spinning wheel, chards, check, reel shelf & all the furniture thereof, one table, one large oven & lid, one skillet & small pot, one Iron shovel & poker, with all her mother's clothing. Also to my son William N. Crawford at his mother's death the plantation whereon I now live, with all the stock & farming utensils, likewise the half of the quary tract named before. My sons Robert M. Crawford and William N. Crawford, exrs., 4 March 1835. James Crawford (LS), Wit: G. Enloe, John G. Enloe, Asahel Enloe. July 25th 1842, in the court of ordinary. Wm. N. Crawford having petitioned for a citation to the kindred or heirs at law in order to have the said will proved in solemn form Robert M. Crawford was served with a citation, Zenos S. Hill in right of his wife attended in person & Elizabeth Crawford the widow being in a state of derangement was not cited.... after hearing the several subscribing witnesses thereto have declared that the said will bearing date 4 March 1835 as valid. At same time qualified Wm. N. Crawford, executor.

**Pages 40-41**: Will of Eleanor Stanton of District of York... To my son Isom G. Stanton my tract of land, my negro girl named Merievoa & one bed & Furniture. To my daughter Eliza E. McKinzie my negro boy named Fayette, my negro girl named Ann, my horse & Saddle, my chest & clothing, my loom & tacklings, my yarn & wool and one choice bed and furniture, also one large heifer & breeding sow, one hogg in the pen & the present growing crop of corn. The balance of my property to be sold and out of the proceeds thereof my funeral expenses and all my just debts be paid, the overplus to be divided between my two children above named. I appoint my son Isom G. Stanton sole executor, 29 Aug 1842. Eleanor Stanton (X) (LS), Wit: John A. Laney, Jas M. Stewart, Cyntha Timberlake. Proved by the oath of James M. Stewart 5 Sept 1842. At the same time qualified Isom G. stanton executor.

**Pages 41-42**: Will of Mary Unity Mullin of District of York being of sound mind but feeling the infirmities of age... To Sally Costner my daughter the sum of $5. To my daughter Mary Alexander my bed & bedding. My wearing apparel to my daughters Susannah Boins & Mary Alexander. To my granddaughter Eliza daughter of Mary Alexander I give one cow. The balance of my property together with all money due to me by note or otherwise to be divided into three equal shares, one of which I give to my son John Mullin, one to my daughter Mary Alexander and her children and one to my grandson James Boins son of Susannah Boins. I appoint William A. Watson & Susannah Boins executors, 27 Nov 1834. Mary Unity Mullen (X), Wit: David Watson, Elizabeth M. Watson, S. L. Watson. Wm. A. Watson one of the exrs named in the will being unwilling to take on the trouble & duties refuses to qualify 9 July 1842. Proved by the oath of Revd. Saml L. Watson 4 Aug 1842. Qualified Susannah Bowen executrix __ September 1842.

**Pages 42-43**: South Carolina, York District. Will of Henry Rea of district aforesaid... To my wife Mary all my personal estate viz household & kitchen furniture, stock, monies, notes, books of account and all my personal estate except my farming utensils which I bequeath to John Coombes who is now living with me. I appoint A. S. Wallace and Nathaniel P. Kennedy, exrs., 2 Sept 1842. Henry Rea (X) (LS), Wit: Thomas Hogg, Sarah Hogg, William S. Hogg. Proved by the oath of Wm. S. Hogg 5 Oct 1842. At same time qualified A. L.[sic] Wallace executor.

**Page 43**: South Carolina, York District. Will of Mary R. Sadler, widow... my nine negroes now on my plantation be sold after my death by my executor to the highest bidder also horses, cattle, hogs, household furniture & every other property that may belong to me, also one tract of land containing 400 acres or upwards and the proceeds of such sale to be equally divided amongst all my children share & share like. I appoint my son Minor Sadler my executor, 7 Jan 1842. Mary R. Sadler (LS), Wit: Thos Robertson, Rocinda R. Robinson, Nancy J. Robinson. Proved by the oath of Thomas Robinson Esqr 24 Oct 1842.

**Pages 44-45**: South Carolina, York District. Will of Jacob Black, farmer, of York District... To my daughter Jane, wife of Edward Meek of the state of Tennessee, a negro girl now in my possession & belonging to me named Cassy & her son Tom about 24 years old & that the said negroes shall be appraised & the said Jane Meek shall account with my executor for their price. To my daughter Agness Meek, wife of James Meek of York District, a negro woman named Phebe & her son Frank both now in my possession & that the said negroes shall be appraised & the said Agness Meek shall account with my executor for their price. To my daughter Elizabeth Kirkpatrick, wife of Joseph Kirkpatrick deceased, $500 in cash & she is to take this as her share in full against the negroes willed to my other children. To my daughter Eales Love, wife of Eli Love of Chester District, one negro girl Hanah & her son John now in my possession that the said negroes shall be appraised & the said Eales Love shall account with my executor for their price. My sons in law divide my wearing apparel among them & which I desire them to keep or make use of and that my executor divide my books among my children. The balance of my property be appraised & sold and after deducting the $500 above wiled above to Elizabeth Kirkpatrick & deducting from my daughters Jane, Agnes and Eales the price by appraisement of the negroes willed to them, also $40 which I will to my executor for his trouble in attending to the appraisement & division of my negroes, all the balance be so divided as to make equal division among my children named above. I appoint my son in law James Meek sole executor, 21 Aug 1840. Jacob Black (Seal), Wit: James H. Alexander, Robert Black, Robert Sheilds. The will was deemed valid by the testimony of the witnesses 27 Oct 1842. October 31st 1842 qualified James Meek executor.

**Pages 45-46**: Will of James M. Stephenson late of York District, South Carolina, farmer, declared by worth of mouth 12th of September 1842. I will & bequeath to wife Mary the tract of land whereon we live lying on the waters of Turkey Creek containing 75 acres more or less adjoining lands of James Miller, John Miller, John Lockhart, John Gill, Morrison Russel & others and all property in possession at my death to my wife Mary & at her death the land & all property which may not be disposed of during her life time to be given to her brother John Stephenson provided John live with my said wife Polly & takes care of her. Those were the words spoken by the said deceased James M. Stephenson in the presence of us, and we subscribe our names as witnesses 16 Sept 1842. Morrison Russell, James Egger, Hugh Miller, john Lockhart. Proved 9 Nov 1842. At same time James Egger entered into an administration bond with the nuncupative will annexed.

**Pages 46-48**: South Carolina, York District. Will of Robert Cooper of said district... To my brother John Cooper of Kentucky my two negro men Ned & Jack. To my brother James Cooper of George my two negroes Tom and Solomon. To my nephew John Cooper, son of my brother William Cooper of Tennessee, one negro man named Gladman and the whole plantation whereon Stephen Belt now lives including the Cook and Still House places with the stills & vessels. To my sister Elizabeth Davidson of York village my plantation whereon Peter Harris now lives and my negro man named Arnold. I give to my sister Mary Wallace of Virginia my negroes Maria & her children Anderson & Peggy. To my niece Elizabeth Powel daughter of my sister Mary Wallace, my negro girl Patty. To my niece Jane Ferguson of kentucky daughter of my brother John Cooper of Kentucky, one negro girl named Aggy. To my nephew Robert Cooper, son of my brother William Cooper of Tennessee, one negro girl named Falley. To my niece Mary Eliza Alston my negro named Katharine & her child to the said Mary Eliza Alston & her two now living children. The plantation whereon I now live be sold and the proceeds to be divided according to law among the legatees of my wife Mary Cooper decd, viz the children of Nancy Wallace of Alabama & Jane S. Davison of same place. My interest in a family of negroes now in the possession of Jas Kuykendal be valued by Wylie L. Harris and John Chambers and that Jas Kuykendall if he choose to take my interest in said negroes at their valuation and account to my estate for the amount and if not the property to be sold at public auction & my part to be disposed of in the payment of debts. To my namesake Robert Cooper Kuykendal son of my friend Jas Kuykendal $200 to be laid by Jas Kuykendal his natural guardian on his education. All my unwilled property to sold and after payment of debts be equally divided between my brothers James & John Cooper & my brothers son Robt Cooper son of my brother Wm. Cooper of Tennessee. My friend Jas Kuykendal executor. [not dated] Robt Cooper (Seal), Wit: Wylie L. Harris, Peter Harris, Isaac Kuykendal. Proved by the oath of Wylie L. Harris 18 Nov 1842. At same time qualified Jas Kuykendall executor.

**Pages 48-49**: Will of Robert McNeely of York District... To my son James McNeely 100 acres of land on the north east part of the plantation on which I now live. To my daughter Jemima 100 acres on the north side of the same plantation. To my daughter Eliza Ann 100 acres on the west side of same tract. To my wife Margaret the balance of my land which part contains the dwelling house and other improvements. Also to my wife Margaret all my stock of horses, cows, hogs, sheep & other property untill her death at which time I will it to my daughters Mary & Jane. I make N. P. Kennedy executor, 12 Nov 1842. Robert McNeely (LS), Wit: Samuel G. Brown, John Johnson, Sa. Miller. Proved by the oath of Samuel G. Brown 21 Nov 1842. At same time qualified N. P. Kennedy, executor.

**Pages 49-50**: South Carolina, York District. Will of Mary Brian of district aforesaid... To my oldest son Thornton Jones $100 and to my son John Jones $100 & to my daughter Milley Kerr $100 should she be living, if not her proportion to her children. The above money to be paid one year after my decease & to be paid out of a sealed note which I hold on Daniel F. Hall for $850. The ballance of the said note after my debts are paid and my four negroes viz Su[?], Toney, Nancy & Jacob to be equally divided between my four younger sons James Brian, Thos Brian, Moses Brian & Aaron Brian. My negroes to be sold or divided as may suit best the legatees above mentioned. To my daughter in law Susan Brian wife of Jas Brian my wearing apparel, two beds & furniture, two half round tables, one chest & one trunk, five chairs & my saddle & dresser ware. To my son James Brian the horse that he gave to me and my stock of hoggs with the balance of my estate. I appoint my son James Brian sole executor, 8 Oct 1842. Mary Brian (X) (LS), Wit: D. F. Hall, William S. Wood, Joseph R. Howe. Proved by the oaths of Danl F. Hall, William S. Wood and J. R. Howe 13 Dec 1842. At same time qualified Jas Brian, executor.

**Pages 50-51**: South Carolina, York District. Will of William Farris of district aforesaid... to my wife Susanna Farris her maintainance such as is suitable for her health & situation during her natural life. To my son Wm. J. Farris the plantation I purchased from Andrew Baxter which will be included in a state grant with the place I now live on, with all my notes & book accts, also all the stock including horses, cows, hoggs & stock of every description, also including any crop & farming utensils with the wagon & all the aparatus thereunto belonging. To my four daughters Margaret, Jane, Mary & Nancy, all my household kitchen furniture of every description to be equally divided between them. Any other property I leave to my son Wm. J. Farris. My son Wm. J. Farris, my sole executor, 5 Oct 1842. Wm. Farris (LS), Wit: M. T. Hall, Arthur Garison, Wm. N. Kimbrell. Proved by the oath of Major T. Hall [no date indicated]. At same time qualified Wm. J. Farris, executor.

**Pages 51-52**: South Carolina, York District. Will of Henry Tipping... To my beloved wife Margaret Tipping a negro woman named Hester also a negro woman named Ann, two beds & furniture & to live in my mansion house & get her maintainance off this land which she lives & at her death to my son Isaac D. Tipping. The old woman Hester shall be at liberty to choose which of my children she will live with. To my son John C. Tipping a negro woman named Lucy & her children named Jim a boy & three girls Rose, Sarah & Harriott. To my son Henry Tipping a negro girl named Ety also a negro boy named Ned, the offspring of Ety. To my daughter Betsy Flemming & the heirs of her body a negroe girl named Jane, one of Lucy's children. To my nephew John Rainey a negroe woman Charlotte. To my son Isaac D. Tipping a negro man named Sam also a negro girl named Sally also a yellow woman named Caty & four children Harvy, Darky, Calvin, Randolph. It is my wish that Bill, Caty's oldest son should be free at the age of 21. Also the plantation on which I now live with all my stock, household & kitchen furniture, also three negro children Kitty, Charles & Judy, children of Ann. In consideration of what I have bequeathed to my son Isaac D. Tipping, I allow him to pay all my debts & pay my daughter Rosey $100 & my daughter Margaret $20. I constitute James Moore & John C. Tipping, exrs., 4 June 1842. Henry Tipping (LS), Wit: James McElhany, Dudley Jones, John M. Moore.

**Pages 53-54**: Will of Robert Hays of York District... To my wife Salley Hays, all my estate both real & personal during her natural life for the support of herself & family. The property kept together as it is unless in the opinion of my executrix it may be thought adviseable to dispose of it. At the death of my wife, I allow my property both real & personal to be equally divided among my children share and share alike. I appoint my wife Sally Hays the sole executrix and should she live until my son Robert be twenty one years of age, I allow him to be a joint executor with her, 13 Dec 1842. Robert Hays (X) (LS), Wit: John P. Plexco, James Plexco, James Meek. Proved by the oath of James Meek & Col. John T. Plexco 21 Jan 1843. At same time qualified Sarah Hays and Robert Hays exrs.

**Pages 54-55**: South Carolina, York District. Will of Elias Patrick of district aforesaid.. I will & directed as much of the land that will pay my debts to be sold or the whole of it if necessary & if all of it is sold a small plantation to be bought sufficient to make a support for the family. The rest of the property to remain as it is until my son Josiah Clinton comes of age for the support & benefit of the younger children & when he comes of age, the property to be equally divided among the following children & wife. My wife one bed & bureau & her choice of a horse out of the horses that they will be in possession of at the time when the property is divided also & cow & calf & her living off the land during her life or widowhood. To my daughter Mary Elizabeth $25 in money. The rest of my property that is not willed as above to be divided equally between Josiah Clinton, James Reese, George Anderson, Franky Louise & Robert Vaughan, excepting Josiah Clinton to have one horse extra more than the rest. I direct James D. P. Currance to be my executor, 22 Feb 1841. Elias Patrick (LS), Wit: Harbert Lancer[?], James L. Moore, Robert Whitesides. Proved by the oath of J. L. Moore 23 Jan 1843. At same time qualified J. D. P. Currance executor.

**Pages 55-56**: South Carolina, York District. Will of Dorothy Wood, late of district aforesaid, deceased, declared by her by word of mouth 10 September inst. I give to my two nieces the daughters of my sister Mary Lambeth my bed & furniture & my wearing apparel to be equally divided between them, said property to be left in the care of said deceased sister. To my brother Robert J. Wood all my other property to what kind soever, rights& credits, allowing him to pay my just debts, 17 Sept 1842. Wm. H. Johnston, Eliza P. Johnston, Isabella M. Finley.

The above nuncupative will of Dorothy Wood decd the parties residing without the limits of this state was legally notified by publication in the Yorkville Compiler for twelve weeks successively and no one appearing on the day appointed for the probate of said will, in consequence thereof this day I proceed to the probate thereof 13 Feb 1843. Benjn Chambers, O.Y.D. Qualified Robert J. Wood admr with the said nuncupative will annexed.

**Pages 56-58**: Will of William Moore Senr of York District... To my son James O. Moore the plantation whereon he now resides adj. Alexander Barnett & others, also $100 after the decease of my wife Mary Moore. To my son Walter W. Moore the plantation whereon he now resides in Lincoln County, North Carolina, on the waters of Crowders Creek adj. James Craig & others, 175 acres, also $100 to be paid after the decease of my wife Mary Moore. To my son Wm Moore Junr, the plantation whereon I now reside, about 223 acres on waters of Beaver Dam of Crowders Creek adj. lands of Edward Moore Senr & others, but this donation is not to take effect tell the death of his mother Mary Moore. To my daughter Nancy Moore alias Nancy Suggs my two negro girls Milly & Candice, Milly is now in her possession. All the remainder of my estate after paying my funeral expenses & just debts, to my wife Mary Moore during her natural life to be kept on the plantation whereon I now reside for her use & support & at her death to be sold and equally divided among my children: to Walter W. Moore one share, to James O. Moore one share, to Wm. Moore Junr one share. To Nancy Moore alias Nancy Suggs one share. My will is that my wife Mary Moore shall have the plantation whereon I now reside on waters of Beaverdam of Crowders Creek adj. Edward Moore Senr & others during her life then to my son Wm Moore. My son James O. Moore & my son in law Thornton Suggs, executors. 13 Jan 1838. Wm Moore (LS), Wit: Reuben Dulin, Lemuel Eaken, Wm Campbell. Proved by the oath of Reuben Dulin 28 Feb 1843. Codicil witnessed by John Moore, Peter M. Clinton, Wm Campbell. Proved by the oath of John Moore 18 Feb 1843 before Benjn Chambers.

**Pages 58-59**: Will of Elizabeth Cairnes of York District... To my son Robert Cairnes my plantation conveyed to me by John Blair & all my personal property providing he shall provide comfortable boarding & lodging for his sisters Jane, Eliza & Susan while they remain on the place unmarried and the use of a horse to ride when they have occasion and when they marry, they are to have $100 in money or property and $50 to his sister Martha Brown twelve months after my decease and convey to his brother John Cairnes six acres of wood land off said place nighest to where the said John Cairnes lives. I appoint Dr. H. R. Smith, Thomas Patrick & Robert Gilfellon executors, 7 Oct 1841. Elizabeth Cairnes (LS), Wit: John Blair, Wm. P. McFadden, Wm. Wright. Proved 23 Feb 1843 by the oath of John Blair. At same time qualified Dr. H. R. Smith executor.

**Pages 59-60**: Will of William Carrothers of district of York... my beloved wife Dorcas shall have her support on the plantation whereon I now reside during the term of her natural life & she shall have the sole control of all my property of every description whatever until my heir or heirs shall marry or arrive to age or make a demand thereof. My wife shall have an equal share with my other heirs. The firm of Carrothers & May shall be carried on according to the original contract between myself & May for five years from the commencement of the firm. In consideration of three years service of my son Thomas to the said firm, after he arrives of age, he shall have extra $100 yearly for the said service. Dawson N. Mitchell, my son-in-law, and Samuel D. Carrothers, my son, executors. 24 Feb 1843. Wm Carrothers (LS), Wit :James Carrothers, Wm. S. May, James Thorn. Proved by the oath of Wm S. May 6 March 1843. March 6th 1843 qualified Dawson N. Mitchell & Samuel D. Carrothers, executors.

**Pages 60-62**: Will of Mary Greer of district of York... To Mary Hemmingway daughter of William & Henrietta Hemmingway, one bed, bedsted & a sufficient quantity of bedclothing for the same, including one stand of curtains for the said bed & one small walnut chest inlaid in front. To the white woman if any such be living with me at my decease & taking care of me at the time, one half the household & kitchen furniture (exclusive of beds & their furniture & chest above named) & one half of the wearing apparel in my possession at my decease, my loom and all the slays & harness & warping bar belonging to her, but if not such person be living with me then the above property to revert back into my other estate. To my negro woman Nancy & her children, two beds & necessary clothing for the same & all the balance of my household & kitchen furniture & the balance of my wearing apparel. To my negro man Littleton all the carpenter tools in my possession at my decease. To my brother Henry Greer in the state of Alabama but at this time living with me, all the balance of my estate, and Little, Nancy & eight children & all the living children the said woman Nancy may leave at the time of my decease provided the negroes are willing to go to him but if they wish to be sold to other persons then the monies arising from the sale to go to the said Henry Greer, Nancy and her children not to be parted unless they wish it themselves. My executors to sell the negroes at private sale & that the person or persons getting the said negroes do allow each of them the month of October in each and every year during the said negroes lives at a fair hire in case to be paid said negroes for their services during said month for their own use & benefit the above property subject to pay to Malinda Drennon daughter of John Drennon of York District $20 in cash. I appoint my brother Henry Greer and my friend James Ash Senr, exrs., 29 Jan 1842. Mary Greer (LS), Wit: John McElhany, McConnell Curry, Elias N. Pressley. Proved by the oath of McConnell Curry and Elias N. Pressley 8 May 1843. At same time qualified Henry M. Greer exr.

**Pages 62-63**: Will of John McElwee Senr of District of York... All my estate both real & personal to my wife Margaret for & during her natural life & at her death the same to be equally divided between my two daughters Jane Oats & Margaret A. McElwee. To my sons William, George, John R. & James

McElwee & my daughter Gracy all the estate I have heretofore given to them. My wife Margaret executrix & my sons in law William McGill & William Oats, executors, 14 Feb 1843. John McElwee (Seal), Wit: Jas Kuykendall, W. Clawson, G. W. Williams. Proved by the oath of G. W. Williams 17 May 1843. At same time qualified Wm. Oats executor.

**Pages 63-64**: South Carolina, York District. February 27th 1831. Will of James Peters of district aforesaid... I allow as much property sold as will be sufficient to procure suitable head stones for my father John Peters Senr & my mother Martha Peters Senr deceased graves & one suitable for my own grave. To my sister Martha Peter Jnr the whole of the remainder of my estate real & personal, and I appoint her sole executor. James Peters (LS), Wit: Amziah McClain, Benjn Chambers, Samuel Chambers, Wm. Caldwell, G. Caldwell. Proved by the oath of Wm. Caldwell 20 May 1843.

**Pages 64-66**: Will of Elizabeth Davison of District of York... To Wiley L. Harris one negro man called Arnold, the tract of land devised to me by my brother Robert Cooper decd, being the same whereon Peter Harris now resides, my interest being one undivided third share in the brick house and lot in the village of Yorkville owned by the heirs of Robert Davison decd, all my household & kitchen furniture, and all the rest, residue & remainder of my estate, both real and personal, upon the trusts, conditions and limitations, viz to hold the same for the separate use and benefit of my daughter Eliza M. Alston, wife of John A. Alston, not subject to the debts, etc., of her present or any future husband. I appoint James Kuykendal executor, 14 Feb 1843. Elizabeth Davison (Seal), Wit: John H. Williams, F. H. Wood, G. W. Williams. Proved by the oath of G. W. Williams 21 June 1843. At same time qualified James Kuykendall executor.

**Pages 66-67**: Will of James Glenn of York District... To my son John Glenn my negroe woman Miller. To my son James E. Glenn $150 to be considered due six months after my decease. To my sons John & Robert Glenn my wearing apparel to be equally divided between them. All my property not disposed of at my decease to be sold & after paying all my just debts & funeral expenses the remainder to be equally divided between my sons John, Robert & Milton Glenn also Wm Glenn. Those of my children whose names are not herein mentioned have received their full shares heretofore. I appoint my sons John & William Glenn, exrs, 8 Jan 1843. James Glenn (mark) (LS), Wit: John A. Laney, Robert M. Fendley, Walter Quinn. Proved by the oath of Walter Quinn 14 Aug 1843. At same time qualified John and William Glenn, exrs.

**Pages 67-68**: Will of Rezin Tolbert of district of York... To Polly Cook wife of Demsey Cook one negro boy Davy. To my sister in law Rachel Horsley a tract of land on the south side of Rocky Allison Creek which I have lately purchased of the heirs of Wm. Pressley deceased, also a negro woman named Martha Ann & her three children Mary, Jane, & Emaline, and at her decease the right of said property shall be vested in the daughters of said Rachel Horsley viz Rebeckah, Eleanor, Betsy & Nancy, and in case any two or three of them die or marry, the last remaining single one shall become sole heir of the said property. All property not disposed of be divided between Lewis Tolbert's four children viz Thomas Tolbert, Rezin Tolbert, Rachel Fewell & Jane Hall. I appoint my friend Hugh H. Carrothers, exr., 18 June 1843. Rezin Tolbert (LS), Wit: W. H. Neal, Thos B. Price, J. A. Laney. Hugh H. Carrothers qualified 2 Aug 1843. Proved by the oath of Thomas B. Price 28 Aug 1843.

**Pages 68-70**: 8th May 1843. Will of James Dulen of York County... To my youngest daughter Nightwill & her issue 60 acres of land adj. the house wherein I now live including the spring I now use water our of, also another spring next the creek Beaverdam, also a part of the creek. To my fourth daughter Dolly 30 acres of land & a good spring & part of the creek. To my third daughter Sarah 30 acres of land including a spring and part of the creek. To my second daughter Elizabeth 30 acres of land & a good spring including a part of the creek. To my first daughter Salina 30 acres of land including a spring and part of the creek. The mineral spring with ten acres of land around it & part of the creek to the use and benefit of all my children. The balance of my land I bequeath to my two youngest sons John and Daniel to be equally divided between them so as to take in the meadow spring for my son John & the spring nearest Bethel church to be included in my son Daniel's part. If my son Daniel should regain his usual health, it is my further will that he should pay to my several daughters three months work & $10. If any mineral mines should be discovered that may prove profitable that all may have an equal share of the profits excepting Reuben if any mines may be discovered it is my will that he may not have any part in the same. As regards to the estate of my daughter Margaret decd whereon I was executor to the estate of I do desire that my children will not demand anything more of me for the same. It is my desire that my son Reuben should have no part in any of those returns of land unless they all should die without issue. It is my will that my children do pay over to my beloved wife $5 as her share of my estate and that my said wife do not live on any part of the lands bequeathed to my children. My land in North Carolina be sold in order do pay debts or if my son Reuben sees fit to pay the debts against the estate for him to have the land. Also there is a note of hand given by me to E. N. Scott in the hands of my son Reuben for $37. My youngest daughter Nightwill shave have my bed & furniture, also my cupboard, table, stock of cattle & hogs. I also consider that I have done a sufficient part towards my wife in redeeming the two negroes now in her possession and giving them to her as her a legacy. My sons John & Reuben & my daughter Nightwill do remain on the plantation to take care of me during the natural course of my life. My chest of drawers I bequeath to my son John. My son John Dulen, my sole executor. James Dulen (Seal), Wit: W. M. Wilson, Henry C. Duff, Thos M. Wilson. Proved by the oath of Henry C. Duff 25 Aug 1843. Proved by the oath of Thomas M. Wilson 4 Sept 1843.

**Pages 70-71**: South Carolina, York District. November 1841. Will of Rev. Jas. S. Adams... After the payment of all my lawful debts, it is my will that the land on which I live be equally divided between my dear wife Erixene & my youngest son Samuel L. Adams, my wife to hold the part on which the house stands. My married children hold all the property that I have given them & that Elizabeth Davis, Jane Williamson & James H. Adams each receive $100 out of the estate left in the hands of Mrs. Adams. To my son Rufus J. Adams my negro named Frank with 2 horses named Polly & Andy, also a wagon, 2 cows & which plantation tools he may need for farming. My faithful servant Cuffy remain with Mrs. Adams while she lives & if he lives longer than she does that he has his choice of the children to live with. To my dear wife Erixene the balance of my unwilled property except my library which I allow to be divided amongst my children allowing her an equal dividend with them. I will that Mrs. Adams make my son Saml L. Adams equal in negroes, property, stock & farming utensils to his brothers Thomas & Rufus, also my daughter Erixene Susan equal to her sisters that ar married in negroes & other household furniture. My wife Erixene & my son Rufus executors. Jas S. Adams (Seal), Wit: John Jackson Senior, Samuel L. Watson, Augustus F. Anderson. Proved by the oath of Rev. Saml L. Watson 12 Sept 1843. Qualified Rufus J. Adams executor.

**Pages 71-73**: 9th Sept 1843. We the undersigned legatees of the estate of James Sprott decd being over the age of twenty one do authorise our mother Margaret relict of said deceased to act as executrix of the trust imposed upon her in the will of our deceased father. L. Sprott, Jas M. Sprott, Jos F. White, Eliza M. Sprott, Thos D. Sprott, Martha M. Sprott.

South Carolina, York District. Will of James Sprott of said district... To my son Thomas that part of my plantation on which he now lives, where a small tract called the old school path crosses it, to the river including the Island, on condition that he pay $600 to the estate. The balance of my land to b divided between my sons James & Leonidas, James to take the house place containing the improvements. My daughter Elizabeth shall have choice of the negroes when a final division of property is made, that my daughters Elizabeth and Martha shall have the right & sole possession of the north hall room up stairs in my house during life. The remainder of my property at present on the place remain on it during the life time of my wife Margaret. My son James reside on the old place during the life time of his mother. I desire that there shall be no publick sale of my property at any time & ardently hope that all my heirs will amicably agree with one another in the settlement of the estate. The shares of my daughters Elizabeth & Martha if they be living to be equal to those to whom I have willed my land, my sons & my daughter Susan to whom I have before bequeathed the same, 22 July 1843. My son Robert has received his full share. James Sprott (Seal), Wit: John M. Harris, Jas. M. Harris, James McKee. Proved by the oath of Col. James M. Harris 18 Sept 1843. At same time qualified Mrs. Margaret Sprott executrix.

**Pages 73-74**: South Carolina, York District. Will of Daniel Fulton... my just debts be paid out of notes & claims I hold on various persons. The balance o my estate both real & personal to my wife Elizabeth Fulton. D. A. Fulton (LS), Wit: Daniel James, John S. Moon, (Rev.) Ferdinand Jacobs. Proved by the oath of John S. Moon Esq. 9 Oct 1843. October 17th 1843 Qualified Mrs. Elizabeth Fulton executrix.

**Pages 74-75**: Will of Eli Clerk of York District deceased declared by him by word of mouth 11 October 1843. 1st he wishes his debts to be paid. 2nd for his negro girl named Harriet, his beds & furniture, household furniture, two cows & one horse to be kept for the use & benefit of his two children Mary Elizabeth & Nancy Margaret Carlisle & his plantation, his crop & stock of every description to be sold, the money put on interest & when his daughters becomes of age the property & money to be equally divided between them. He also requested that Henry Clerk & Mary A. Rowell should attend to the business of his estate, 14 Oct 1843. James T. Foreman, Allston Clerk, Stourton E. Steele, Mary Ann Rowell. Qualified Henry Clerk and Mary Ann Rowell executors.

**Pages 75-76**: Will of William Henry Anderson of York District... To my nephew John Monroe Anderson the son of John Anderson my brother all my interest in land on waters of Fishing Creek & Also my interest in the land on the waters of Wild Cat on which I now reside, also my slave Toney, also my slave Sam, likewise all my horses, mules & stock of hogs, also my interest in the plantation waggon, also my shot gun, also my part of the crop on each plantation, farming utensils. To my niece Mary Jane Elizabeth Anderson daughter of my brother John Anderson $1000 to be paid to her by her brother John Monroe Anderson out of the property I have willed him, when the said John Monroe Anderson comes to the age of 21. To my niece Mary Jane Elizabeth Anderson, my bed & furniture, my seal skin trunk. To my beloved niece Elizabeth Wherry daughter of William Wherry Senr, $300 to be paid to her by her cousin John Monroe Anderson out of the property I willed him when he arrives to the age of 21. I appoint my brother John Anderson, exr., 18 July 1831. William Henry Anderson (X) (LS), Wit: Jesse Brumfield, A. S. Starr, Jas. P. Henderson. Proved 9 Dec 1843 by the oath of Jesse Brumfield. At same time qualified John Anderson.

**Pages 76-77**: Will of Elizabeth Gwinn of York District... To my daughter Elizabeth McKnight, all the offspring of Past and I also give to Nancy Ruin all the issue of Rin and I give to my son William C. Gwinn my negro girl Jane. I appoint Thomas T. Gwinn executor, 20 June 1842. Elizabeth Gwinn (X) (LS), Wit: John Mcknight, Dixon McKnight, William McKnight. Proved by the oath of Dixon McKnight 4 Jan 1844. At same time qualified Thos T. Gwinn executor.

**Pages 77-78**: South Carolina, York District. Will of John Starr of district aforesaid... To my daughter Cynthia Neely, the following negroes viz Sam, Nancy & child Jane, Scipio & Anson & my bureau & one bed & furniture. To my daughter Lucretia Chambers my negro slaves Alfred, Nelson, Matt & Affy, also my secretary & one bed & furniture. To my son John Starr my negroes Silvy, Sampson, Molly, Charles, Frank & James[?]. To my daughter Jane Latta the following negroes Mariah & child, Joseph, Selena & Tom & one bed and furniture. To my daughter Martha Meek, my negroes Adaline, Flora, Eliza, Ritty & child & one bed & furniture. To my grandson Thomas S. Neely my tract of land known as the Meacham & Erwin land & my girl Dinah & one bed & furniture. The tract of land whereon I now live be equally divided between John Latta Starr & Rufus Starr Meek. To my grand daughter Emery Stewart Starr my negro girl Sarah. The residue of my property be sold & after paying my just debts, it be equally divided amongst my surviving child. My negro man Moses be permitted to chose his master. My son John Starr & John S. Moon, executors, 13 Dec 1843. John Starr (LS), Wit: C. P. Sandifer, R. H. Hope, Wm. Hanna. Proved by the oath of Wm. Hanna 6 Jan 1844. At same time qualified John S. Moon & John Starr Jnr exrs.

**Pages 78-79**: Will of Robert Workman of York District... to my son James Workman the plantation on Taylors Creek now cultivated by him on which Benjamin Hunter is living. To my son Robert Workman the plantation on which I now reside (excepting) 100 acres of said plantation on the north side to my son the said Robert Williams. I give 100 acres of the north side of the plantation on which I am living to my two daughters Martha & Isabella while they remain unmarried, and at their decease or marriage to my son Robert. To my daughter Martha two negroes viz Pol & Henry. To my daughter Isabella two negroes viz Mariah & Tinker. To my two daughters Martha and Isabella, a negro boy named Randall. To my daughters Martha & Isabella each a bureau & one clock. The corner cupboard & brass clock to my son Robert after the death of his mother. The balance of my property to my wife Margaret and after death, Martha & Isabella each have a horse & a pair of geers, the remainder of my negroes & other property to be equally divided among my children, 14 June 1843. Robert Workman (LS), Wit: Thomas Robinson, James S. Workman, Harvey H. Drennon. Proved by the oath of Harvey H. Drennon 26 Jan 1844.

**Pages 80-81**: Will of Elizabeth Jackson of York District... A negro boy called Sam to my son James Jackson. A negro girl called Diana to my daughter Jane Currance. A negro girl called Martha to my son William Jackson. A negro girl called Mary to my son John Jackson. A negro boy called Osburn to be inherited by my son Hamilton Jackson. I desire that my son James get my bureau. I desire that my son William have my walnut table I desire that my son John have my red chest & clock. I desire that Hamilton have my trunk & looking glass. I will one large table waiter to Sam. I allow my bed & Furniture to William, also one to John & two beds and furniture to Hamilton, and I also will for Jane to have four sheets and Eliza Parmela Currance one white stand of curtains with one new bedstead & bedding. My chairs to my sons John & Hamilton. The remainder of my stock to be divided among my three sons Wm. John & Hamilton. I allow my apparel for Jane. My son James Jackson, exr., 17 July 1843. Elizabeth Jackson (LS), Wit: Myles Smith, Jesse K. Armstrong, Samuel L. Watson. Proved by the oath of Myles Smith 5 Feb 1844. At same time qualified James Jackson, executor.

**Pages 81-82**: Will of Benjamin Story of York District... All my stock & other goods such as farming utensils, household & kitchen furniture to be divided among my lawful heirs James Story, Jane Taylor, Joicy Hagins & Benjamin B. Story. To my son Benjamin B. Story, all my land on the head waters of Neelys Creek provided that the other property pays my debts, 19 Jan 1840. Benjamin Story (LS), Wit: Jos H. Abernatha, Wm. S. Hagins, David Roddy. Proved by the oath of Wm. S. Hagins 9 Feb 1844. 1844 Feb 14 qualified Wm. H. Johnston executor.

**Page 82**: Will of Martha Ramsey of York District... To my two daughters Sary and Polly all of my estate after paying debts. My land 200 acres more or less on Wolf Creek where I now live to be equally divided between them. I appoint Morgan Martin Sr., Mannon Martin Sr., Robert Mannin Jr., executors, 20 March 1840. Martha Ramsy (mark) (Seal), Wit: John Martin, Alexandria Martin, Morgan Martin Jr. Proved by the oath of Alexander Martin 4 March 1844.

**Page 83**: January 16, 1842. Will of Jacob Childers of York District, plantation on Neds branch waters of King Creek of Broad River... To my beloved wife Janney Childers all my estate real and personal, only 20 acres of my land on Neds branch where I now live to my daughter Nancy to be run off at that corner above Joseph Mullinax. The childrens names to be after my wife's death Rachel, John, Sary, Lucy, Abraham, Jacob, Nancy, James, Robert, William. Morgan Martin and Robert Mannin, exrs., 16 Jan 1842. Jacob Childers (mark) (LS), Wit: Virgil Owen, Frances Mullinax, Morgan Martin Jr., Thomas Mul-linax (mark). Proved by the oath of Virgil Owen 4 March 1844.

**Pages 84-85**: South Carolina, York District. Will of Margaret Johnston... To my daughter Martha Johnston two negroes Harriet and Polly which in conformity with an arrangement or understanding among the heirs of my late husband John Johnston were to go to my said daughter Martha Johnston at the sum of $700 in part payment of her share of her father's estate which I hereby confirm by vesting the title of said negroes when she becomes of legal age. To my daughter Martha Johnston $300 for the purpose of paying her boarding untill she becomes 21 years old. The residue of my estate be equally divided between my son Samuel Johnston, my daughter Mary Berry and my daughter Martha Johnston. My son Samuel Johnston, exr., 19 Sept 1842. Margaret Johnston (Seal), Wit: Jane Harris, J. M. Ross, Andw McConnell. Proved by the oath of J. M. Ross 11 March 1844. At same time qualified Samuel C. Johnston, executor.

**Page 85**: Will of Alexander Harper of District of York... To my beloved wife Jane Harper, one metal clock, two feather beds and furniture, two chest, one half chest and cooking furniture, and at her death to be equally divided between my two daughters Martha M. C. Harper and Jane Harper. My son John S. Harper, executor, 20 Sept 1843. Alexander Harper Senr (Seal), wit: Jos J. Watson, Robt Patton, Matthew Harper. Proved by the oath of Joseph J. Watson 25 March 1844. At same time qualified John S. Harper, executor.

**Pages 85-87**: South Carolina, York District. Will of Euxine Adams... To my daughter Eliza Davis, my servant girl Peggy and her youngest child now an infant. To my daughter Jane Williams Violet and Ann, children of Mary Ann. To my son Thomas Adams, boy Stephen. To my son James Adams, Henry & Eliza (children of girl Rhena). To my daughter Margaret Crenshaw $100. To my son Rufus J. Adams, my servant girl Mary Ann, Robert her son & her youngest daughter now an infant. To my son Samuel L. R. Adams, the plantation on which I now live subject to the incumbrance hereafter mentioned, also to him my servants Tira, Jack, Rhena & her children Hugh, Martha, Billy & Rhinah, also my girl Amaline to Samuel LeRoy Adams. To my daughter Susan the boy Milton. My daughter Susan have a home in my house & a support & maintenance from my plantation until she marries to finds it convenient to reside elsewhere. My stock of every kind with farming and smith tools to my son Samuel L. R. Adams, also my household and kitchen furniture except the cupboard furniture which I will to be equally divided between my son Samuel L. R. Adams and my daughter Susan Adams. My carriage to my son Samuel Leroy & my daughter Susan Adams. My sons Rufus J. Adams & Samuel Leroy Adams, executors. Euxine Adams (LS), Wit: Saml L. Watson, R. C. Sherrill, H. B. Cunningham. Interlined 8 March 1844 in the presence of Saml. L. Watson, W. H. Neel, and Joseph Adams. Proved by the oath of Saml L. Watson 26 March 1844. March 25th 1844 qualified Rufus J. and Samuel L. Adams, executors.

**Page 87**: Will of John Clark... to Eli Y. Clark my plantation, him being under obligation to support me and my beloved wife so long as we shall live. Wishing my son E. Y. Clark to pay Jas H. Clark for his improvements on said plantation, what Henry Clark and Jas Rattree shall think them to be worth and at our death wishing my son E. Y. Clark to sell all my personal property and divide it equally between the rest of his brothers and sisters, taking an equal share with the rest, 22 March 1844. John Clark (LS), Wit: henry Clark, Jas Rattree, Thomas Rattree. Proved by the oath of all three witnesses [no date] and at same time qualified Eli Y. Clark exr.

**Pages 88-89**: Will of Samuel Farris of South Carolina, York District... To my daughter Margaret A. Watson all the articles I gave her on her marriage and leaving me. I desire that my daughter Editha Gardner have and hold the articles that I gave her on her marriage. I will that Adaline Hays have the articles that I gave her on her marriage. I will that my son R. B. W. Farris have one bed & furniture, one cow and one fourth of the neat proceeds arising from last years cotton crop. I allow Edward T. Farris all that I gave to him since he left me.I allow my son Ausper Harris the mare he now claims also the stock of cattle that he claims also one common bed & furniture. I desire that Eliza C. Harris get one cow & calf, one bed & furniture. I direct Elvey C. D. Farris get and be made equal with my above named daughter. I direct that my son Alex W. Farris get one young horse or mare, one cow & Calf and one bed & furniture, also my shot gun. My still and vessels be sold to meet the demands against me, should they fail & direct my extrs to sell whatever can be the best spare of my personal estate. I desire that all my personal property now already willed be and remain on the premises for the use and support of my dear beloved wife during her widowhood or life, then an equal division to be made of all and everything including the plantation I now reside on, between and among all my children. Should the negro woman prove dissatisfactory, I allow my executor to sell her or trade her for another girl. I appoint my wife extx and my son R. B. W. Farris exrs., 20 Jan 1844. Samuel W. Farris, Wit: Myles Smith, Frances Henry, H. H. Smith. Proved by the oaths of Dr. H. H. Smith and Myles Smith, 6 May 1844. At same time qualified Mrs. Eliz'a C. Farris and R. B. W. executors.

**Pages 89-90**: Will of Robert McLellan Farris of District of York.. After my decease all of my stock of horses, cattle, hogs & sheep and all my household and kitchen furniture except what is hereinafter named be sold & our of the proceeds thereof all my just debts be paid & the overplus to be equally divided among my five children Jonathan, Thomas, William, Rachel & Urias. I give to my son Urias one clay bank mare called Dolly. To my daughter Rachel one Glass knobbed bureau and two beds with their furniture. To my son Johnathan all that part of my plantation which lies south east of Taylors Creek to him upon condition that he shall take my son William who is a cripple under his protection and find him in a comfortable house, clothing & provision during his natural life, and it he should survive my said son Jonathan he shall have his maintenance out of the said land during his lifetime. I give all my land on the north west side of Taylors Creek equally between my two sons Thomas & Urias on condition that they are to jointly pay my daughter Rachel one third value of the said land. I appoint my friend Jesse Spencer my true and lawful executor, 27 Jan 1843. Robt McClellan (LS), Wit: Allen Robertson, Jesse Spencer, D. K. Bates. Jesse Spencer refused to qualify 11 May 1844. Proved by the oath of David K. Bates, Esqr., 13 May 1844.

**Pages 90-91**: South Carolina, York District. Will of Thomas Manning Senior of state & county aforesaid... I will my daughter Catherine, my negro woman Vily to be to here & her heirs. To my son Thomas Manning my negroe boy Sam by him paying to my son Mijamin Manning $150. I also will to my son Mijamin Manning my negro boy Miller. To my grandson Loson my negro girl Febe. My real estate & my negro men Dick & my negro woman Jenny & my stock to be sold and equally divided between my three heirs Thomas Manning, Mijamin Manning & Catherine Scoggins. Robert Manning & John B. Harvin[?], executors, 16 Jan 1840. Thomas Manning (Seal), wit: Thomas McGill, Daniel James, Barton Parker (X). Proved by the oath of Thomas McGill 21 May 844.

**Pages 91-92**: South Carolina, York District. Will of Elizabeth Burris of York District... to my daughter Rachel R. Carrothers my folding table. To my daughter Sarah M. Russell one bed & furniture. To the children of my deceased daughter Mary A. Russell one bed & furniture. To my son John Burris all the rest of my household furniture not mentioned above also my share of all the lands in York District of which my late husband William Burris Senr died seized of I have, being one third. The balance of my property be divided into five equal shares & one share to my daughter Rachel R. Carrothers, one share to my son John Burris, ton share to my daughter Sarah M. Russell, one share to my grandchildren Wm. B. Russell, Robert M. D. Russell, Elizabeth B. Russell, John M. Russell, Isabella R. G. Russell, Eli G. Russell, Charles S. Russell, James J. Russell, Mark C. Russell & Mary Ann Russell, children of my deceased daughter Mary A. Russell, and the remaining share to my grandchildren Nancy C. W. Mitchell & Elizabeth R. R. Mitchell. My son John Burris, exr., 1 March 1844. Elizabeth Burres (X) (LS), Wit J. M.

Ross, R. McConnell, John R. McConnell. Proved by the oath of John M. Ross 21 May 1844. At same time qualified John Burris exr.

**Page 93**: South Carolina, York District. Will of Ruth Moore widow of John Moore, whereas husband in his life had made sundry advancements to his four children & I having some property to dispose & distribute amongst my four children... my children John Moore, Jacob B. Moore, Gordon Moore & Peggy Clerk wife of William Clerk to make them all as near equal was may be practicable charging each one of them with all advancements made to & for them by their father. My son John Moor exr., 27 June 1835. Ruth Moore (LS), Wit: Joseph G. Smith, James McKinney, William A. Nisbit. Proved by the oath of James McKinney 13 June 1844.

**Pages 93-94**: South Carolina, York District. Will of John Boyd... I will that all my property remain as it is untill my youngest son Thomas Jefferson arrives at the full age of 21 for their support and maintainance. My beloved wife Nancy to have the use of every thing belonging to the house & farm as long as she lives for her comfort & happiness. My land be equally divided between my sons David Patton & Thomas Jefferson when the latter arrives at the age of 21. My two sons David Patton & Thomas Jefferson give to each of my daughters $150 (viz) Nancy Clementine, Martha Jane, Sarah Elizabeth, Mary Margaret & Rachel Louisa. My wife Nancy and son David Patton, exrs., 4 June 1844. John D. Boyd (LS), Wit: J. D. P. Currance, David Wallace, James C. Graham. Proved by the oath of all three witnesses 9 July 1844. Same time qualified Mrs Nancy Boyd and David Patton Boyd, exrs.

**Pages 95-96**: Will of John Peters Esqr of York District... To my dear wife Mary one negroe slave named Minter & a boy named Bob; also her support on the plantation I now reside on & I direct for my household & kitchen furniture to be equally divided between her & my daughter Sarah. To my daughter Mary F. Lawrance a negro girl named Harriet. To Mary E. Jackson a negro girl named Pug. To Amelia Lawrance a negro woman now int he possession of A. G. Lawrance & Named Liza. I will to Amanda Lawrance a negro girl named Caroline. To Sarah G. Lawrance a negro girl named Adaline. To D. F. Jackson 286 acres of my plantation the balance being 150 acres I will to John James Jackson & adj. lands of J. C. Watson, Adam Beauregard & Samuel Bearegarde. Immediately after my decease the following negroes viz Joe, Adam, Jess, Cia & Andy, Eliza & Dafney with their descent be appraise & their value be made into two equal divisions; one division to fall to the descent of Sarah Jackson & the other among the children with my daughter Martha Lawrance & Sarah Jackson's descent or when the youngest child of theirs may attain the age of 21. To D. F. Jackson all my livestock and a negro woman named Patty. To D. F. Jackson my fine brass clock. To A. G. Lawrance my claim & interest in the cotton machine also #100 in money. To Martha Lawrance $100 to be paid by D. F. Jackson. I will to my wife Mary the money or notes that may be in my possession at my decease & I allow D. F. Jackson to pay my last expenses. I appoint A. G. Lawrance & D. F. Jackson, exrs., 20 July 1843. John Peters (mark) (LS), Wit: Myles Smith, John Fitchet, James Fitchet. Proved by the oath of Myles Smith

& John Fitchet 13 July 1844. At same time qualified Allen G. Lawrance & D. F. Jackson, exrs.

**Pages 96-97**: Will of William Choat of York District... to my beloved wife Rachel Choat all my personal estate or property consisting of hoggs, horses, cattle, fowls, household & kitchen furniture with my interest I hold in my wagon & blacksmith tools. I further devise she keep with her my son Newton during her natural life. To my daughter Rachel E. Choat a respectable part of rom of my house during her life and at the death of my wife all my personal estate except what I hereafter name to my two sons. To my son Augustine D. Choat jointly with my son James Simeral Choat my interest in my black smith tools wagon at the death of my wife Rachel. Also to the said Augustine D. & James S. Choat the land whereon I now live on both sides of Rocky Allison Creek, down the mouth of Fewells spring branch. My wife Rachel with my two sons Augustin D. Choat & James S. Choat, exrs., 24 Nov 1830. William Choat (LS), Wit: William Anderson, Caleb Gassaway, James Wilkerson. Proved by the oath of James W. Wilkerson 18 July 1844.

**Pages 97-98**: Will of Joseph Wylie of York District... to my son Joseph D. Wylie the plantation whereon I now reside and a bay horse colt 2 years old called Mike. To my wife Margaret my daughters Mary, Lucinda & Elizabeth the remainder or all property other than above named of which I may be possessed at my death. I appoint my son Thomas G. Wylie, exr., 28 July 1843. Joseph Wylie (LS), Wit: S. G. Brown, N. P. Kennedy, R. H. Bigham, Wm. D. Bigham. Proved by the oath of Samuel G. Brown 23 July 1844. At same time qualified Thomas G. Wylie, exr.

**Pages 98-99**: Will of Benjamin Patterson of York District... I will one half of the tract of land on which I live including the houses & improvements to my wife Susan during her life & at her death to be to my son Bobbit, the other half of said tract to go to my son Jackson. One bed & furniture to each of my children Jackson, Bobbit & Susan. The rest of my property to be sold at publick sale & the money rising from the sale to be divided amongst my wife and children: to my wife Susan, one third, to my sons Smith, Jackson & Bobbit & my daughters Isabella Hunter & Susan share & share alike. The son of Emily Burton being a son of my deceased daughter Margaret do not come in for any portion of my estate. I appoint my son Jackson Patterson sole executor, 16 April 1844. Benjamin Patterson (X) (LS), Wit: Joseph F. White, Jno T. Withers, Augustus McKinney. Proved by the oath of John T. Withers 6 Aug 1844.

**Pages 99-100**: South Carolina, York District. Will of Gilley Moss of district aforesaid... to my youngest son John all the land I am in possession of by his maintaining my wife Polly & my daughter Patty & my grand daughter Eliz'a so long as they see proper to live with him. To my son Howell one dollar. To my son James one dollar. To my son Lewis one dollar. To my son Ephraim one dollar. To my daughter Fanny one dollar. To my son Wylie on dollar. The rest of my property to my beloved wife Polly during her life and at her death to be sold & divided equally with my sons Jeremiah & John & my daughters

Sarah, Molly, Giley & Patsey. My sons Jeremiah & John executors, 2 Feb 1841. Gilley Moss (mark) (Seal), Wit: A. Hardin, J. B. Fulton, T. D. Fulton. Proved by the oath of T. D. Bulton 5 Aug 1844. At same time qualified Jeremiah & John Moss, exrs.

**Pages 100-101**: Will of Frederick Hambright of district of York... To my daughter Charlotte Carpenter one carriage or sulkey to make her equal with the other legatees of my estate. To my daughter Sarah Dillingham a clay bank colt to make her equal with the other legatees. I will that my executor as soon as practicable after my death advertise & sell all the personal property except two beds & furniture that I have heretofore give to my daughters Sarah Dillingham and Charlotte Carpenter but they are left with me during my life. All the rest of my estate to be divided between the following persons or legatees viz James Hambright, Sarah Dillingham, Michael A. Hambright, Jefferson Hambright, Madison Hambright & Charlotte Carpenter & Liddia Hambright, John Hambright's daughter in the room of John Hambright. I appoint James Hambright the sole exr., 6 May 1844. Frederick Hambright (LS), Wit: Aaron Whistenant, Robert M. Crawford, A. Hardin. Proved by the oath of A. Hardin 5 Aug 1844. At same time qualified James Hambright, exr.

**Pages 101-103**: South Carolina, York District. Will of Samuel Wright of district aforesaid... My old negroe woman Jenney & also my negro girl Mariah under the advice & direction of my son William live with such of my children as Jenney may desire, Jenny to take with her & keep to her own use all the bedding, cooking utensils & other articles that she may claim & own at my death and Mariah is to stay with her & attend to her. After Jenney's death Mariah is to belong to the person with whom she & Jenny may have lived. The remainder of my estate be equally divided amongst my children William Wright, James L. Right, Nancy McElwee, Eliz'a McGowan, Catherine McGowan & the children of my deceased daughter Mary Robinson. My negro girl Ann be taken by my son James L. Wright at appraisement. My son William Wright, exr., 4 June 1844. Saml Wright (Seal), Wit: James Jefferies, G. R. Ratchford, G. W. Williams. Proved by the oath of G. R. Ratchford 9 Sept 1844. At same time qualified Col. Wm. Wright, exr.

**Pages 104-105**: Will of Francis Miller... All my just debts be paid and tomb stones be placed over the graves of my mother & two sisters if I should not have it down before my death and also a tomb stone to myself and my wife should she died before me. To my beloved wife my negroes Led & Henry, two beds & such other household articles as came by her at our marriage. To my wife all the rest and residue of my estate consisting of land and negroes, stock, etc., during her natural life not to be removed out of this district on pain of forfeiture. If my wife should die before me, my two negroes Led and Henry, the two beds aforesaid &c., to my wife's niece Jane Erwin daughter of Arthur Erwin. The remainder to be divided into three equal parts, one part to my nephew John M. Ross, one part to my nephew Eli A. Ross, and one part of John M. Ross. My nephew John M. Ross, exr., 30 Dec 1841. Francis Miller (LS), Wit: G. W. Williams, W. J. Clawson, John A. Alston. Proved by the oath of W. J. Clawson 26 Oct 1844 before Ja Kuykendal, O. Y. D. John M. Ross qualified as executor 26 Oct 1844.

**Pages 105-106**: Will of Jane Crawford living on Clarks Fork, York District.... To my sister Ann Crawford all my interest which is the equal half in the following property viz one negro man named Isaac and his wife Linda, one girl named Nancy, one girl named Pasty, one girl named Margaret and one girl named Mariah,also my interest in equal half of two horses and the same of all the stock of cattle, sheep and hogs, and half of four feather beds and furniture, household and kitchen furniture and farming utensils. To my sister Ann Crawford, all the cash, notes of hand and book accounts that may be in my possession at my decease. To my sisters Mary Henry, Martha Neil, Margaret McElwee, Elizabeth Crawford, and my brother James Crawford, five shillings sterling. My brother James Crawford and my sister Ann Crawford, exrs., 15 Sept 1842. Jane Crawford (X) (LS), Wit: W. M. Dickson, John McCoy, Wm. Crawford. Proved by the oath of William Crawford 8 Nov 1844. James Crawford qualified as executor 8 Nov 1844.

**Pages 106-107**: South Carolina, York District. Will of William Given of state and district aforesaid... To the four minor children of Samuel E. Given decd in equal shares the following negroes Jim and his wife Caroline and their four children Thomas, Harriet, Milly, and Jane. The said negroes to be hired out by my executor until the youngest legatee comes of age. To William Poag, son of Joseph Poag, my gold watch. To my niece Mary Harriet Poag $100. The balance of my property real and personal be sold to the highest bidder and after paying my just debts, and furnishing a decent slab letter with gold leaf to my grave, be equally divided between my four sisters Polly Ash, Esther Poag, Isabella Walker, and Margaret Sadler. Zenus A. Walker, my executor, 23 Nov 1844. William Given (LS), Wit: J. L. Howe, J. M. Moore, John Burris. Proved by the oath of John Burris 3 Dec 1844. Qualified Zenus A. Walker executor 3 Dec 1844.

**Pages 107-108**: South Carolina, York District. Will of Catharine J. Alexander... I leave in the care of my son Stephen H. J. Alexander a negro woman named Eunice about 17 years of age together with her increase if she should have any for the use and benefit of himself and his family until the youngest child that said Stephen H. J. Alexander has comes to the age of 21 years, the said negro woman Eunice to be set free. To my son Stephen H. J. Alexander my carryall, provided my son Alfred R. Alexander does not call upon my son Stephen H. J. Alexander for said Carryall in three years after my death. To my son Alfred R. Alexander one dollar. To my son Eli O. Alexander one dollar. To my daughter Emeline Lowe (wife of Mr. Lowe) one dollar. To James Alexander who was husband formerly of my daughter Elizabeth C. Alexander one dollar. To my granddaughter Catharine J. Alexander, daughter of Stephen H. J. Alexander my bed with all the bed clothes. My son Stephen J. H. Alexander exr., 11 May 1840. Catherine J. Alexander (Seal), Wit: Wylie L. Harris, W. J. Kuykendal, G. W. Harris. Proved by the oath of Wylie L. Harris 10 Nov 1844. Qualified S. H. J. Alexander as executor Decr 10th 1844.

**Page 108**: Will of Mary Wallis of the District of York... to my son Robert Bratton $100 to be paid to him one year after my decease and to my granddaughter Betsey E. Bratton, one negro girl named Diana and the first child that my negro woman Caroline has and for my son Isaac M. Wallis if she marries to fix her off in common furniture for housekeeping and for her to get one side saddle, and I allow her to have her living with my son Isaac whilst living single. To my grandson James C. Bratton one bed and furniture and to my son Isaac M. Wallis the balance of my negroes & stock. I appoint James B. Good and my son Isaac M. Wallis, exrs., 12 Sept 1842. Mary Wallace (X) (LS), Wit: James A. Murphy, Zenus A. Walker, Henry Tipping. Qualified Isaac M. Wallace as executor March 1844.

**Pages 109-110**: South Carolina, York District. Will of William Nance of district aforesaid... To my daughter Rebecca Nance, a negro girl called Nelly and a negro boy named Little John. To my daughter Lucy Youngblood a negro girl called Maria & a negro girl called Caroline. To my son Thomas Nance three negroes Peter, Matilda, and Reuben. To my son Alexander Nance $1000 to be raised in the manner hereinafter provided, $100 one year after my decease, $100 annually thereafter until the whole $1000 are paid. To my wife during her life ore widowhood a negro girl called Nancy, the one called Louisa, one called Adaline & a negro boy called Big John, two horses called Dove & Charley, two cows & calves, two beds, bedstead & necessary bed furniture, my household and kitchen furniture. At the death of my wife the negro girl called Adaline to Thomas Nance, the girl Louise to my daughter Rebecca and to my daughter Lucy Youngblood, Big John & to my grandson William Crosby the negro girl Nancy. To my grandson William Crosby two negro boys named Bed & Beverly on his arriving to the age of 21 years, the said negroes are to remain in the possession of my daughter Rebecca until the period aforesaid. Should she die before the said William comes to 21 years of age then Samuel Youngblood is to have the negroes upon the same terms. I appoint Samuel C. Youngblood, exr., 11 Jan 1841. William Nance (Seal), Wit: W. J. Clawson, Ja Kuykendal, G. W. Williams. Qualified Samuel C. Youngblood as executor Jany 3 1845.

**Pages 110-111**: South Carolina, York District. Will of Archibald Hammel of York district... To my wife Rachel Hammel after the payment of all just debts, all my property both real and personal for her support and the raising, maintaining & schooling of my children, until my youngest child comes of age, consisting of the plantation whereon I now reside, my negro boy named John, two horses, a pony and bald horse, all my stock of cattle & hogs, etc. When my youngest child comes of age, all my property to be sold and an equal distribution be made between all my children. I have furnished the daughter that has left us and to the boys a horse & stock. To my son John the colt he now claims. My wife and my friend James McElwee, exrs., 13 Dec 1844. Archibald Hammel (LS), Wit: J. D. Currence, James McElwee, A. J. Barron. James McElwee relinquished his appointment as executor 9 Jan 1845. Proved by the oath of James McElwee 9 Jan 1845. Qualified Mrs. Rachel Hammel as extx 9 Jan 1845.

**Pages 111-112**: York District. Will of George Pettus of district aforesaid... All the property I got by my beloved wife Jane viz all the land whereon she lived when I married her and negro woman Caroline and her four children Harriet, Sam, Mary and Emeline, one folding leaf table, six sitting chairs, one looking glass, etc. What property may be after my debts are paid shall be kept together and hired out for the benefit of my five children Stephen D. Pettus, Hannah Jane, Eliza Ann, Benjamin Russ, Mary Elizabeth, until my oldest son Stephen D. Pettus shall arrive at the age of 21, then the whole to be divided between them that are living. Joseph Glover my step son shall have $30 for services rendered heretofore. Dated ___ 1844. George Pettus Jun (Seal), Wit: Edward Smith, J. Smith, Thomas N. Pettus. Proved by the oath of Edward Smith 10 Jan 1845.

**Pages 112-113**: Will of William Smith... To my two sisters Caroline and Sarah Ann all my interest in my brother James' land in the Mississippi. To my nephews John S. B. Erwin, Wm. Edwin Erwin, my horse and $200 in cash. To my cousin Amanda S. Henry one negro boy named Amos and one negro from 15 or 18 years old now in possession of John M. Smith in the Mississippi. To my sister Mary one negro girl named Selena and all that I am nw possessed of notes, money and negroes. I appoint George Steel and Edward G. Byers, my exrs., 27 Aug 1844. William M. Smith (LS), Wit: J. N. McElwee, Mijamin Smith, John Brown. Proved by the oath of J. N. McElwee and John Brown 27 Jan 1845. Qualified Edwards G. Byers executor 27 Jan 1845. George Steele renounced his appointment as executor 27 Jan 1845.

**Pages 113-114**: Will of James Franklin Watson... To my brother Samuel L., also sister E. A. G. Barry, also sister M. E. Barron, also sister M. A. Bigger, also sister E. M. Currence, also sister J. S. Barnett, each one of those the sum of $30. To my niece M. A. Watson $15, also my nephew Wm. D. Watson $15, payment to guardian. To my brother David $60. To my sister E. K. Watson $160 payable to her by Robert through the gift of a negro boy named Lot. I also allow my horse, saddle and bridle to be sold and also a fine suit of clothing, Medical Library & Medicines. To my brother Robert my negro boy named Lot. W. M. Watson and R. A. Watson, exrs., 6 Jan 1845. J. F. Watson (LS), Wit: Albert W. Watson, John L. Watson, John Harrison. Proved by the oath of Albert W. Watson 29 Jan 1845. Qualified Dr. D. M. Watson & Robt A. Watson executors 29 Jan 1845.

**Pages 114-117**: Will of William Wylie of York District, planter... To my son William Wylie the occupancy of all my land on the east side of Neely's Creek which originally was my father Wm Wylie's except a small crap of about one acre now closed by my fence conveyed to me from Henry F. White, all of which lies on the said east side of the north fork of said Neelys Creek. To my son William the following negroes and other personal property Patsy, Rachel, Betsey & Leroy, Bob, but the negroes not to be removed from this state or be disposed of by him or any other person, my stock of hogs, and a mortgage which I hold of $300 on certain property of my said son William and duly recorded when the same is foreclosed I will that the whole product arising from the same tbe given to my daughter in law Caroline, wife of my said son

William. To my daughter Elizabeth White, my negro woman Mariah and her four children Ben, Martha, Taylor & Sam, and my negro woman Rhody and negro girl Becca and my negro girl Gean. To my son Thomas G. Wylie all the rest of my land where I now live both in York and Chester District (except what I have already willed, also my negro woman Harriet and her two children Carter & Green, also my negro man Julius or Bug and George my negro boy about 15 years old, also my negro woman Siley and Charlotte also my old negro woman Siby. If Thomas G. Wylie should die having no heirs, then to my son William and daughter Elizabeth aforesaid. To my said son Thomas G. Wylie two of my horses and four head of sheep, to pay within two years after my decease to James & Jean Kenmore $30. I appoint my son Thomas G. Wylie and Henry F. White (my son in law), exrs., 3 Jan 1845. William Wylie (Seal), Wit: John Roddy, James Kenmore, John Kenmore. Codicil mentioning the scrap of land which was conditionally by me sold to Augustus Parish, and executors to make a title to it, 13 Jan 1845. Wit: John Roddy, Isaac McFadden, John Kenmore. Proved by the oath of John Roddy 3 Feb 1845. Qualified Henry F. White as executor 3 Feb 1845.

**Page 117**: South Carolina, York District. Personally appeared Mrs. Sarah Hogge, Hugh McGinness & Thos H. Lominack & made oath that in his last illness about eight hours before he died Thomas Bradshaw called the witnesses & others to bear witness that the following was his last will & testament. First, he desired all his just debts to be settled, that he wishes the family all stay together, the property all to be his wife's during her lifetime & at her death to be equally divided amongst his children. He states that he had intended to have had his will written & executed as is usual but that when he was speaking he had not an oppertunity to do so... 19th of this instant. Sarah Hogge (mark), Hugh McGinness (X), Thomas H. Lominack (Seal), 22 March 1845.

**Pages 117-118**: South Carolina, York District. Will of Elizabeth Patrick of district aforesaid... To my beloved son David Josiah Jesse, two negro boys Sam & Tom & my clock & bureau, also bed & furniture & Also waggon & harness & car bello & his choice of two horses & cow. To my beloved daughter Mary Caroline, two negro girls Violet & Viney, my cupboard & ware & her bed & furniture, and a horse called bully. I will that a negro boy called Minor to be equally divided between my son and daughter. To my beloved daughter Elizabeth Olivia McCarter my saddle. The remaining property to be divided between my children equally as follows, John Allison, Elizabeth Olivia, Eleanor Paulina, Rebecca Irrebella, Mary Caroline & David Josiah Jesse. Thomas J. Clinton, exr., 10 March 1845. Elizabeth Patrick (X) (LS), Wit: J. D. P. Currence, Daniel Currence, Wm. A. Currence.

April 15th 1845. In the matter of proving the will of Eliz. Patrick decd, the parties or heirs at law being cited appeared. James D.P. Currence was present and believes and she was of sound mine. Daniel Currence was present and believes that she was of sound mind. Wm. A. Currence states that his evidence is the same.

**Pages 119-120**: Will of William Summerford of York District... To my wife Piety Summerford my negro girl Mariah in lieu of her dower, and at her death to be sold & the proceeds be equally divided among all of my children and also two work horses for the use of the family, three milk cows, three young cattle, stock of hogs. The money that may be coming to me on my pention to the schooling of my two younger sons Loami & samuel & my daughter Elvirah and as I have gave to my son Isaac Summerford $100 my will is that that much viz $100 be taken off his share of my estate. I have given my son William Summerford $100 my will is that that much viz $100 be taken off his share of my estate. To my son Rueben Wilson, I hold a note on him for about $250 which said note I want take out of his share of my estate, all except $75 that I give unto him. The balance of my property to be sold & equally divided among all of my children as my daughter Elizabeth Jane, Isaac, Edward, Crossey, John, Polly, Malinda, Abraham, Elial, Elvirah, Loami, Samuel, William and Nancy. My friend Peyton B. Darwin, exr., 26 Feb 1844. William Summerford (LS), Wit: J. W. Thomson, T. J. Wilkerson, Wmson Howell. Qualified Peyton B. Darwin exr. April 15th 1845. Proved by the oath of Wmson Howell 15 April 1845.

**Pages 120-122**: South Carolina, York District. Will of John H. Barry of district aforesaid... To my son James H. Barry, the plantation whereon he now resides & two negroes Alexander & Charles. To my daughter Margaret Barry, two negroes Mary & Harriet, one horse, saddle & bridle, bureau, 2 beds, & other articles similar to those received by her married sisters, also $200 in cash. To my granddaughter Martha Ann Barnet, one girl called Amy, horse, saddle & bridle, one bureau, feather bed. To my grandson John B. Barnet, my silver watch. To the Rev. P. E. Bishop, Pastor of the Presbyterian Church at Ebenezer, $100 in trust for the support of foreign missions. To my beloved wife Violet the plantation whereon I reside & all the rest of my property, and at her death or marriage to be divided amongst my children Margaret Barry, Jane Partlow & my grandchildren John R. Barnet, Violet A. Barnet, Jane E. Barnet, Margaret Barnet & Martha Ann Barnet. My son James H. Barry & my wife Violet, exrs., 27 Nov 1845. John H. Barry (LS), Wit: Jesse Niven, F. H. Wood, G. W. Williams. Proved by the oath of G. W. Williams 5 May 1845. Qualified Jas H. Barry as executor 5 May 1845.

**Pages 122-123**: Will of John Anderson of York District... To my beloved son J. M. Anderson all my land, my entire interest in the plantation on which I now live, my entire interest on the plantation on the waters of Fishing Creek, now owned jointly by myself and my son J. M. Anderson, also the two parcels of land which I recently entered as vacant land. To my said son J. M. Anderson, my two negroes named Dave & Black Bill, my stock of mules, wagon, and farming tools. To my beloved daughter Mary J. E. Anderson, my four negroes Letty, Yellow Bill, Milton & Ross, my sorrel mare & colt, and her support on my plantation during her single life. My son J. M. Anderson to maintain & support my poor & unfortunate daughter Margaret Sarah Anderson. My son J. M. Anderson, exr., 15 April 1845. John Anderson (LS), Wit: John Johnson. S. M. Roach, J. W. Rawlinson. Proved by the oath of John Johnson 5 May 1845.

**Pages 124-125**: South Carolina, York District. Will of Rebecca Evans of district aforesaid... My two plantations known as the Smith Tract & the Ellis Tract descend to my son James Chancey Evans, and my negro man Caeser & negro boy Booker, negro girl Silvey & negro woman Amy or sometimes called Sue. To my son said Jas. C. Evans my sorrel horse called Charley & my bald horse called Ball,etc. To my son Thomas Howell Evans, all my right, title & interest in this plantation where on I now live, also a court judgment which I hold against two of my absent sons Halcut Clark Evans & Allen Jones Evans. To my said son Thos H. Adams [sic], negro woman Dorcas & her children Abram, Lucy, Hannah & Julia & my negro Levi & man Tom, boy Jenkins. My cotton gin & screw shall belong to my son Thos H., only that my son Jas. C. shall have the use of them for picking & packing his own cotton annually. My negro woman Amy descend to my niece Rebecca Hetherington, and my side saddle & wearing apparel & one bed. My negro boy Anthony descend to my son Thos H. Evans. Wm. B. Dunlap, my sole executor, 4 Sept 1842. R. Evens (LS), Wit: John Roddey, Elias B. McClellan, James L. Murphey. Proved by the oath of John Roddey 2 June 1845. Qualified Wm. B. Dunlap as ex'r June 2d 1845.

**Pages 125-126**: Will of Ann Swann of York District... To Moses Barnet Swan, my tract of land whereon I now live, it being inherited by me under the will of my father John Swann, part of the land whereon he died, on the NE side of Beckeys branch near the meeting house, near the brickyard, by estimation 156 acres. To Moses Barnet Swann all my household & kitchen furniture, and appoint him executor, 28 July 1838. Ann Swann (LS), Wit: Jo. G. Martin, James A. Murphy, James Bratton. Proved by the oath of James Bratton 7 July 1845.

**Pages 126-129**: South Carolina, York District. Will of Randolph Weathers of district aforesaid... To my wife Sarah M. Weathers, the plantation whereon I now reside, 535 acres and granted to me 15 Dec 1841, also four negroes, her choice of my whole stock of negroes, all my household & kitchen furniture, carriage and harness. To my three youngest sons (namely) B. F. Weathers, Wm. R. Weathers & Isaac Newton Weathers, $300 over and above the distribution hereafter to be mentioned, to be laid out or disposed of for the completion of their education. All the rest of my estate both real & personal to be divided between all my children or their representatives according to the Statute of distribution of the State of South Carolina. I appoint my sons Thos J. Weathers and John B. Weathers, and Jesse Brumfield executors, 7 July 1842. Randolph Weathers (Seal), Wit: Minor Sadler, Wm. T. Hart, Wm. N. Simril. Codicil provides that his son John B. Weathers shall be allowed to retain his such of that portion of my tract of land lying on Sugar Creek & on both sides of the public road leaving to Charlotte, North Carolina, which I have already permitted him to use & cultivate. I direct my executor to pay to my daughter Amanda $50 not to be accounted for by her and a negro girl called Fan, dated 23 Dec 1843. R. Weathers (Seal), Wit: P.E. Bishop, Jas Boatright, W. J. Faris. Will proved by the oath of Wm. N. Simril 15 Aug 1845. Codicil proved by the oath of Wm. J. Faris 15 Aug 1845. Qualified T. J. Weathers, J. B. Weathers, and Jesse Brumfield as executors 15 Aug 1845.

**Pages 129-130**: South Carolina, York District. Will of Sarah McCarter Senr, 12 May 1841... To my eldest daughter Eliz. Love one dollar. To my daughter Jane one pewter dish, one chair. To my daughter Sarah one pewter dish & chair & table between them. To my daughter Nancy Husky one dollar. To my son Andrew & daughter Margery my part of the land to be equally divided between them. To my son Andrew one pot & blanket. To my daughter Margery one bed & furniture, one chest, 2 chairs, one pewter dish, 1 reel. To my granddaughter Sarah McCarter my wheel. After my death my wearing apparel be equally divided between my three daughters Jane, Sarah & Margery. Sarah McCarter (X) (LS), Wit: Robt Caldwell, Jas Caldwell, Sarah T. Caldwell. Proved by the oath of James Caldwell 12 Sept 1845.

**Pages 130-131**: Will of Morrita Black of York District... To my niece Mary Angelina Black $100; to my niece Margaret L. Black $100; to my sister Jane Neely all my household furniture and wearing apparel and $300; If there should still be a balance left, to the Bible Society for York District. My nephew David L. Black, exr., 27 Sept 1842. M. B. (Seal), Wit: James Williamson, Francis M. Steele, Leroy Williamson. Proved by the oath of Gregg Williamson 1 March 1845. Qualified David L. Black exr 3 March 1845.

**Page 131**: Will of Saml D. Smith of York District... To my beloved wife Jane my negro man John and my negro woman Eliza & her two children Mary & Harriet, , two of my horses, one half of my cattle, hogs & sheep, etc, and to pay all of my debts and & pay to my daughter Elizabeth Nolen & my son Zadok D. Smith each of them $100. To my son Zadok D. Smith my negro man Newton & my negro woman Charity & negro girl Ann, all my employments of husbandry, and the balance of my stock after my wife makes her selection. To my daughter Elizabeth Nolen $100 to be paid to her by my wife. My son Zadok D. Smith exr., 7 April 1842. Saml D. Smith (LS), Wit: Wm. Glenn, E. D. Thompson, W. J. Good. Proved by the oath of Ephraim D. Thompson 6 Oct 1845. Qualified Zadok D. Smith executor 6 Oct 1845.

**Pages 132-134**: South Carolina, York District. Will of David Hutchison of district aforesaid... My body may be buried in the simplest manner in a plain pine coffin not stained or lined & no headstone or monument put at my grave by any of my relations. In the end of the year after my decease, all my debts be paid and the Rev. McGilvrey who married my daughter Elizabeth (I think him an honest man), $100. To the Rev. A. Whyte (who has from our first acquaintance been a good neighbor), $20 worth of books of his own choice out of my library as a remembrance. To the Rev. P. E. Bishop, my Encyclopaedia Britania in ten volumes I purchased it at second hand at $75. To my two daughters Mary & Adeline, each a bed & bedstead equally furnished as the bed that was given to Ann & Rebecca. To the Rev. Mr. Gilland my son in law who was married to my daughter Rebeca, the books he received from me amounting to about $80 or $90. I hold a note & receipt on the Rev. Mr. Gilland which will amount to $4000 or upwards, I bequeath to Jenny Gilland the surviving child of my Rebecca as her full share when she arrives at the age of 21. The receipts I hold on Hiram & Mary Ann & Adeline, I allow to be taken in to the appraisement bill and divided into five shares or as many shares as I have children then living, at this time they are Hiram, Mary, Ann, Adeline & Eugene, to have it in equal portions. Hiram & George White are more experienced in business & can manage the balance. dated __ Aug 1845. David Hutchison (LS), Wit: A. Whyte, John Hart, H. H. Hart. Proved by the oath of Rev. A. Whyte 16 Oct 1845. Qualified George P. White one of the executors 16 Oct 1845.

**Pages 134-135**: Will of Hezekiah Thorn.. to my beloved wife my negro man named Burrell and after her death to be sold & equally divided amongst my children. I allow my property after my death to be sold & divided as described above with the exception of what would be coming to Samuel Barron & his heirs, known that Archibald Barron his brother holds a note on him which note is in my hands & after satisfying said note out of said share. What property I give to my children during my life I don't allow it call'd back for a divide. 20 March 1845. Hezekiah Thorn (h) (LS), Wit: M. T. Hall, John R. Hall, M. t. Hall Sr. Proved by the oath of M. T. Hall esqr., 28 Nov 1845.

**Pages 135-136**: Will of Edmund Weathers of York district... To my son John G. Withers the tract of land he now lives upon & for which he has a plat now in his possession. To my son Benj. J. Weathers the tract of land whereon I now live with one horse & saddle, two feather beds & furniture, one cow & calf, one sow & pigs, $50 in money with such other household furniture as my other children that have left me have recd. To my daughter Pheby Jane Wethers one good horse, bridle & Saddle, one cow & calf, the choice of my stock, and such household furniture as her oldest sisters have received. The balance of my property to be sold and the proceeds equally divided among my six female children Malinda Elms[?], Ellen Crocket, Eliz. Miller, Patsy Cheek Glover, Pheby Jane Weathers & my two grand children sons of my daughter Hicksey Cook, to receive one share between them. Silas C. Cook & Thos J. Cook & such property as may be received by said daughter from the proceeds. My son Benj. P. Weathers have my entire stock in the tan yard .I appoint my two sons John G. Weathers & Benj. P. Weathers, exrs., 20 April 1845. E. Weathers (LS), Wit: John Bell, E. Elms, J. Smith. Proved by the oath of John Bell 27 Oct 1845. Qualified Jno G. Weathers & Benj. P. Weathers, exrs., 27 Oct 1845.

**Pages 136-137**: South Carolina, York District. Will of John Fewell, planter, of district aforesaid... Having heretofore given to each of my children who have married a certain amount of property which I intended to be equal & which I hereby confirm to them, I now bequeath to my daughter Amanda the following property which is intended to be equal to the amount receive by her brothers & sisters (Viz) one negro called Matilda & one called Theresa, one horse, saddle & bird, 2 cows, one bed & furniture, one table and bureau. After my decease an equal distribution of all my other property take place & that my sons Alexander, Robert, Stanly & my daughters Betsy Nichols, Rachel Millinder, Amanda Fewell, Lavinia[?] Barron, Arabella May & Matilda Steedman & my daughter in law Fanny Fewell (widow of my son John) share alike. The share falling to my son Robert & my daughters Betsy & Rachel at their decease descend to their children. I confirm to the use of my son Robert the lands on which he now lives. My son Alexr Fewell, exr., 20 Jan 1844. John Fewell (LS), Wit: A. Whyte, A. S. Fewell, T. C. Barron, Jno Sturgis. Proved by the oath of A. F. Fewell, 17 Nov 1845. Qualified Alexr Fewell executor 17 Nov 1845.

**Pages 137-138**: South Carolina, York District. Will of Richard Gwin of district above mentioned... To my wife Mary Gwin, the plantation & tract of land whereon In now live, all my stock of every king, with tools, etc, and my negro woman named Milly, negro boy named Peter which she will receive at the death of her step-mother. I also allow my wife to dispose of all or any of the above named property for her support or the support of the family. I appoint my wife executrix, 27 Nov 1839. Richard Gwin (LS), Wit: Thos T. Gwinn, Elizabeth Gwinn, D. Attleberry. Proved by the oath of Thomas T. Gwinn 17 Nov 1845. Qualified Mary Gwinn as executrix 17 Nov 1845.

**Page 138**: South Carolina, York District. Will of John Neely of district aforesaid... To my wife Mary the following property: all that part of my land lying south & west of the branch, being the side the dwelling house is on, all my household & kitchen furniture, tools, etc. Also to my wife the negro woman Sally. The balance of my estate to my two sons Alexr & Hyde. The use of my land and negroes I lend to my wife as long as she is a widow or Alexander becomes of age, the land to be worked in corn only one year out of that if the boy Chess he becomes unmanapable[?] to be sold & the money put to int. for the benefit of my two sons. [not dated]. John Neely, Wit: Thomas McClelland, Wm. McClelland, Allen Robertson. Proved by the oath of Allen Roberts 24 Nov 1845.

**Page 139**: South Carolina, York District. Will of James Campbell of district aforesaid... To my son Thomas Campbell the plantation whereon he now lives. To my son Robert my plantation whereon I reside also my negro boy Aaron. To my sons Elias & James and to my daughter Mary Sutton each $20 and to my granddaughter Elizabeth Campbell $50. To my daughter Jane my negro boy Stephen & that she have her maintenance off the plantation willed to my son Robert. The balance of my property to be equally divided between my son Robert & my daughter Jane. My sons Thomas & Robert, exrs., 20 May 1841. James Campbell (LS), Wit John S. Moore, H. F. Adickes, S. R. Moore. Proved by the oath of John S. Moore 24 March 1846. Qualified Robert Campbell exr. 28 March 1846.

**Pages 139-140**: Will of Grizzell McCall of Yorkville... To my son Hellinah McCall, my negro woman named Cindah. To son Alfred McCall, my negro boy child son of Cindah named John. To my granddaughter Lucinda McCall, the bed and furniture known as that once belonging to her aunt Lucinda for whom she was named. To my son Alfred the bed & furniture he now uses. Remainder divided among my three sons Alfred, Hellinah and John. My sons Hellinah and John McCall, exrs., ___ Feb 1839. Grizzell McCall (LS), Wit: J. M. Ross, Caroline Boggs. A. S. Hutchison. Proved by the oath of Miss

Caroline Boggs 30 March 1846. Qualified Hellienah McCall, exr., 30 March 1846.

**Pages 140-141**: Will of John Bennett of York District... all my lands and property whether moveable or immovable may be sold and divided among my seven legatees, viz Jos. P. Bennett, Rebecca Kimbrell, Lucretia Meritt, Margaret Glover, Mary Fields, Alsey F. Bennett and Tirza M. Bennett, 12 March 1846. John Bennett (LS), Wit: Nath. Harris, John S. Alderson, M. Shurley. Proved by the oath of Nathl Harris 9 April 1846.

**Pages 141-142**: South Carolina, York District. Will of Joseph McCorkle of district aforesaid... The whole of my estate both real and personal to my wife Jane B. McCorkle, that is to say the plantation on which I now reside, also all my negroes say 16 in number viz David, Jacob, Albert, Monroe, Rachel, Billy, Harriet, Fanny, Mariah, Juliet, Hamilton, Frank, Violet, Mary, Abraham & Sylvanus, also my stock, furniture, carriage, harness and silver watch. I appoint my wife Jane B. McCorkle, extx, 18 Jan 1846. Joseph W. McCorkle (LS), Wit: T. Neely, Wm. P. Thomasson, J. D. Witherspoon. Proved by the oath of Tillotson Neely and J. D. Witherspoon 21 April 1846. Qualified Jane B. McCorkle as extx 21 April 1846.

**Pages 142-143**: Will of James Quinn of York District... to my beloved wife Margaret Quinn, my dwelling house and kitchen, with three acres of land attached thereto including the garden, orchard & spring. Also to my wife during her life time a negro girl Patsey & child Isabella, household & kitchen furniture, one milch cow, loom & tacklings. To my son James Quinn, a negro man Toney but my son James is to pay half the value of Toney to John Quinn. To my son Walter Quinn the plantation on which I now reside with the exception of that part left to my wife, and at the death of my wife my son Walter to have that part of the plantation left to her. I give to my son Walter a negro girl called Rachel. At the death of my wife I give to my son Solomon Quinn the negro girl Patsey & child Isabella. I also give to my son Solomon my black smith tools, waggon & harness. At the death of my wife I give all the household and kitchen furniture to be equally divided amongst the females of my son Solomon & Walter. The loom and tacklings at the death of my wife to Margaret Crawford. The rest of my estate to be sold and the remainder after payment of debts to be equally divided amongst my sons Solomon & Walter. I appoint my son Solomon Quinn exrs., 6 Oct 1840. James Quinn (LS), Wit: J. Bolton Smith, Ed H. Gunning, A. S. Hutchison. Proved by the oath of J. Bolton Smith 29 June 1846. Qualified Solomon Quinn as executor 27 June 1846.

**Pages 143-144**: South Carolina, York District. Will of Foster H. Wood... All my estate of whatever nature to my wife Katharine in full and absolute fee simple, 6 April 1846. F. H. Wood (LS), Wit: W. C. Beatty, Wm. H. McCorkle, G. W. Williams. Proved by the oath of George W. Williams 28 June 1846.

**Pages 144-145**: Will of James P. Henderson of York District... to my beloved wife Elizabeth Bowie Henderson the one half of all my lands, the half of the plantation on which I now reside provided she does not marry again; to my daughter Mary Ann Henderson the remaining half of my plantation, and the half mentioned in the first item at the death of my wife or upon her second marriage. To my wife my negro boy named Simon. To my daughter Mary Ann my negro boy Absalom. to my daughter Mary Ann all my books with the condition that her mother have the use of them. AS I am somewhat indebted, my executors to sell my distillery and all the balance of my property not heretofore mentioned for the payment of my just debts. In case my daughter should die without issue before the death of her mother, then property shall belong to my nephew James Franklin Henderson of Alabama. My friends James Brian Sr. of York District and J. Monroe Anderson, exrs., 20 April 1845. Ja P. Henderson (LS), Wit: Jesse Brumfield, James S. Jones, John Johnson. Proved by the oath of James S. Jones 21 July 1846. Qualified J. M. Anderson & James Brian, exrs., 18 Sept 1846.

**Page 146**: Will of George Smith of York District... to my beloved wife Cary Smith the lands I now live on known by the name of the Saw Mill Place on the waters of Turkey Creek, also a small tract of land lying west of Galbraiths place adj. McLure, Read, Miller & Galbraith,; also two tracts of land on Gallatin County, Illinois, one of 80 acres and the other 183.96 acres described by their grants. Also my silver watch, chain and guard. To my stepson Elias Davison my rifle gun and shot bag and pistols & trunk & all my books and manuscripts. To my wife Cary Smith all my cattle, household furniture, etc, and my negro man Stanhope. My wife Cary Smith, extx, 22 June 1846. George Smith (LS), Wit: Enoch Doster, James Laughridge, Samuel Laughridge. Proved by the oath of Samuel Laughridge 9 July 1846. Qualified Cary Smith 9 July 1846.

**Pages 147-148**: South Carolina, York District. Will of Sarah M. Withers of district aforesaid... I wish my four youngest children viz Amanda C., Benjamin F., Wm. Randolph and Isaac N. Withers to have my dwelling house with the plantation including the tracts of land known as the Chriswell & Gallant tracts, farming tools, etc., as joining property until the marriage of Amanda or until Isaac shall have come of age. Then it to be sold and the money divided unless on the marriage of Amanda if she prefers she may keep the dwelling house with one fourth of the land. Exception 1st all the carpeting pertaining to the house, the brass fender, one pair of trass[?] and irons, one folding leaf table, two beds with the bedding, with a horse, bridle and saddle to be the property of Amanda. Also, to her one dozen can bottomed chairs, one arm chair, one half dozen silver table spoons, one half dozen silver tea spoons. Except 2d. To each of my sons Benjamin F., Wm. Randolph & Isaac, one bed with the bedding. To Amanda a negro woman called Runy with her child named Adelaide. To my granddaughter Sarah R. Adickes, a small negro girl called Caroline and my tea table with its cover. I wish my son John B. Withers to hold the buildings he has erected and in which he now resides with one care of land if he wish to do so, but if he prefer it, Franklin Randolph & Isaac to purchase his buildings. I wish Amanda, Franklin, Randolph & isaac to pay for the negroes which I bought at the sale of my deceased husband Randolph Withers. The portion of my estate to which my daughter Rosinda

Sims is entitled to be sold should she wish it, she is at liberty to purchase one negro but the remaining portion of her legacy placed out at interest. Jesse Brumfield, Exrs., Capt. Wm. Faris & Hennery F. Adickes exrs., 24 Aug 1846. Sarah M. Withers (X). Wit: Alex Fewell, W. N. Simril, P. E. Bishop. Proved by the oath of Rev. P. E. Bishop 19 Oct 11846. Qualified H. F. Adickes executor 19 Oct 1846.

**Pages 148-149**: Will of Ann Crawford living on Clarks fork, York District, So Carolina.... To my sister Mary Henry one bed and furniture. To my sister Martha Niell, one bed and furniture. To my sister Margaret McElwee, one cow and calf. To my brother James Crawford one bed and furniture and to my sister Elizabeth Crawford one walnut bureau. To each of my sisters above named an equal share in my body clothes. To my nephew James Crawford, son of my brother Jas Crawford, all of my property that may be here at my death, whether negroes, horses, cattle, etc. I appoint my brother James Crawford and his son James Crawford, exrs., 16 Nov 1844. Ann Crawford (O), Wit: A. H. Neill, Robt Quinn, Wm. Crawford. Proved by the oath of Wm Crawford 15 Dec 1856. Qualified Jas Crawford and James Crawford Junr, exrs., 15 Dec 1846.

**Pages 149-151**: South Carolina, Chester District. Will of John Minter of said district. I wish my moveable property to be sold except for my patent clock, one bed and covering) and the money to be dispose of as follows. Wm. Sherer & wife Martha to get one fourth part and also the above except bed and covering; Jesse Gwinn & wife Mary A. Gwinn to get one fourth part and one half of the said bequest to the sole and separate use of the said Mary if the said Jesse continues in his present deranged state of mine; to Elizabeth Minter widow of Jesse J. Minter an eighth part & and one eighth part to her four children Rebekah, Junius, John & Jackson. Also to the said Elizabeth Minter the plantation whereon she now lives including her house and farm adj. Wm. Winter, McAlilly, 80 acres. To William Minter I give a corner of land on the east side of the creek and north of the Chester line, one or two acres and I now confirm to him the said Wm Minter the land I have heretofore conveyed to him. John L. Minter has a conveyance for his share which I now confirm to his use. To Isaac Minter I give the plantation whereon I now live, 80 acres including all my land not conveyed by deed nor by this will, also my patent clock. The remaining fourth part of my moveable property to be equally divided among Wm Shearer, Isaac Minter, Wm. Minter, John T. Minter, Elizabeth Minter & Mary A. Gwinn. I appoint Wm Minter & John T. Minter, exrs., 2 March 1839. John Minter (LS), Wit: Robert Hays, Mary C. Hays, Ethalinda Minter. Proved in York District by the oath of Ethalinda Minter 13 Jan 1847. Qualified Wm Minter as executor 18 Jan 1847.

**Page 151**: South Carolina, York District. Will of Elizabeth Shirley of said district... I desire that the following legacies be paid out of my property to Meredith Sherley my oldest son, $10; to Philaman Sherley my second son $10; to Ruth Wright my oldest daughter $10; to Elizabeth Sherley my second daughter $10; to Nancy Quick my third daughter $10; To James Sherley I give $10; all the remainder of my property after the above legacies and my debts are paid to my youngest son Eli Clawson Sherley and he will be executor, 20 Oct 1841. Elizabeth Sherley (X), Wit: S. D. Barron of Chesterville, A. F. Fewell, B. D. Sturgis. Proved by the oath of Benjamin D. Sturgis 3 Nov 1846. Qualified Eli C. Sherley as executor 3 Nov 1846.

**Pages 151-154**: South Carolina, York District. Will of Nancy McCaw of said district... To my executors hereinafter named my brick house & lot in the village of Yorkville, my tract of land near the said Village containing 381 acres according to a plat made by Wm. Campill, deputy Surveyor, 26 April 1839, my negroes Molly & her two children, Ellen, Ben, Joe & his three children, to hold for the use of my son Robert McCaw. My executors to sell the remainder of my real and personal estate and that belonging to me under the will of my son John McCaw decd except my negro Peter, Betty & Lucy who are to be disposed of as hereinafter directed, the sales when collected to be vested in some sound & safe bank stock or to be leaned out to individuals, the payment well secured and the interest to be paid annually. The interest to be applied to the support of my son Robert. Upon the death of my son Robt McCall, the property to such children of said Robert McCaw as may then be alive. Should my son Robt at his death leave no child or grandchild, then I will my brick house & lots in the village of Yorkville, also my Miller tract to Agness Bratton daughter of John S. Bratton decd. If she should leave no children at her death, then to the sisters of said Agness Bratton who may be alive at her death. To Agness Bratton my gold watch, furniture, etc. To John S. Bratton & Mary Bratton children of my brother Wm each $200. To my nephew Francis Erwin $200. My slaves Peter, betty & Lucy be permitted to live with whom they please without any person exacting any service or labor from them and that they be maintained in comfort & ease. Wm. Hacket, G. W. Williams & William Wright, exrs., 23 Octr 1845. Nancy McCaw (Seal), Wit: John S. Moore, John H. Adams, J. M. Ross. Feby 2d 1857. For the purpose of enabling R. G. McCaw to administer on the estate of Nancy McCaw decd with the will annexed we renounce & relinquish our executorship: G. W. Williams, W. Wright, Wm. Hacket. Proved by the oath of John H. Adams 2 Feb 1847.

**Pages 154-155**: Will of John Jackson... To my son Wm. B. Jackson 130 acres of land where he now resides, the plantation to be so divided as to include the dwelling house & what is called the black jack field. To my son James B. Jackson, my daughters Mary M. Hunter & Violet A. Anderson, the sum of $100 each. To my son James B. Jackson 12 acres of land adj. him including the field known as the fork field to be limited on the northern boundary by the creek. To my son Saml W. Jackson a tract of land formerly bought of Thos Greer Esqr 105 acres adj. lands of Abram Stowe & Leroy Adams & my lower plantation. Also the remainder of my lower plantation not already bequeathed to my sons William & James. To my son James B. Jackson the plantation on which I now reside reserving so much of it as maybe necessary for a tan yard where my son Samuel has commenced one. To my son Samuel W. Jackson my servants Billy & Enos, also my young gray mare. To my son John B. Jackson my servants Isaac, Rachael & Milton. My servant Rhoda I give to my sons Samuel & John. My servant Lucy be sold, also all my stock, tools, etc., for the purpose of paying the above legacies. My friend Hugh M. Jackson & my son

James B. Jackson, exrs., 22 March 1847. John Jackson (LS), Wit: Saml L. Watson, James McCully, Elias M. Jackson. Proved by the oath of Saml L. Watson 6 April 1847. Hugh M. Jackson relinquished his appointment 6 April 1847. Qualified James B. Jackson as executor 6 April 1847.

**Page 156**: South Carolina, York District. Will of J. R. McElwee of district aforesaid... all my real estate in the village of York consisting of the tavern lot on which I live, the lot on the opposite side of the street known as the Suggs lot, and the lot opposite the lot in which Mr. Lewis now lives, known as the grove lot, be sold and the proceeds applied to the payment of my debts. To my beloved wife Rebecca McElwee the one third part of the whole of my estate both real and personal and after the payment of my debts to my son Wm. Meek McElwee. The remaining two thirds of my estate be equally divided between my three children Jane E. McElwee, John N. McElwee, and Rachel D. McElwee. I will that a reasonable sum be set apart to complete the education of my son Wm. M. McElwee for the ministry. Jonathan N. McElwee my brother in law, executor, 24 May 1847. J. R. McElwee (LS), Wit: W. J. Clawson, James McElwee, Nancy Ross. Proved by the oath of W J. Clawson 2 June 1847. Qualified Jon'a N. McElwee, executor 2 June 1847.

**Page 157**: Will of John Albright... To my dear wife Elizabeth all my estate both real and personal as long as she may remain my widow. After her death, all my property be sold and the proceeds thereof be equally divided among my children. I appoint John McCoy executor, 29 April 1847. John Albright (LS), Wit: James Jefferys, S. Melton, J. S. Lewis. Proved by the oath of James Jefferys 2 June 1847. John McCoy relinquished appointment as executor 2 June 1847.

**Pages 158-160**: South Carolina, York District. Will of John Miller... All my negroes and all my other personal property be kept together on my farm after my death & continue to work the same until my youngest child arrives to the age of fourteen years. To my sons John, James G. Dickson, Thomas & Calvin, all my lands. My son Charles Gerome receive a good classical education & that he study some of one of the learned professions and on the completion of his education, my executors to pay him $200. To my wife all my household furniture to be divided amongst her & her children as she sees fit & the remainder of my property to be divided equally amongst my wife & all my children. In my wife's share a negro woman called Julia to be included and that of my son Calvin to include a negro girl called Caroline. My negro blacksmith called Jim Williams & my carpenter called Jack Williams are to remain on my plantation with my wife until the division of my estate. I appoint my wife Mildred executrix & my sons Joseph & John and my friend G. W. Williams, exrs, 23 Jan 1840. John Miller (LS), Wit: Jas Kuykendal, W. C. Beatty, W. H. Wood. Proved by the oath of James Kuykendal 7 June 1847. Qualified Joseph Miller & G. W. Williams as exors 7 June 1847.

**Pages 160-161**: South Carolina, York District. Will of John Wilson of district aforesaid... to my daughter Mary McSwain $5. To my wife the plantation whereon I now live during her natural life and all the remainder of my property remain on the plantation under the management of my son Wm. J.Wilson during the life time of my wife for the support and maintenance of my wifes son William J. and daughter Sarah. Should my daughter Sarah not marry before the death of her mother, I devise 50 acres of land including the buildings I now occupy and the land around them to my daughter Sarah but on her death or marriage that land to go to my son William J. Wilson on condition that he pay to my daughter Sarah if she marry $50. To my son Wm J Wilson in trust for the use of my daughter Sarah Wilson my negro woman Silvey & one half the increase which she may have at the death of my wife. To my daughter Sarah Wilson a horse worth $60, a saddle and bridle, a fine jack bed stead, four beds and furniture, wheel & cards, loom & Tackling, etc. To my son William J. Wilson after the death of his mother the plantation on which I reside 350 acres except such part as devised to my daughter Sarah, also my negro boy Allison. I appoint my son Wm. J. Wilson exr., 30 April 1847. John Wilson (Seal), Wit: R. S. Moore, B. F. Withers, W. A. Moore. Proved in solemn form by all three witnesses 26 June 1847. Qualified Wm. J. Wilson exr.

**Pages 162-163**: Will of Margaret A. Jackson of South Carolina, York District... to my son William a negro boy named Sam. To my daughter Elvira a negro girl named Martha. To my daughter Mary Moore a negro girl named Eliza. To my son Alexander a negro girl named Amanda. I direct that my executor sell a negro woman named Mary for the purpose of paying my debts. My son James to have $150. As I hold a claim and interest to the one third of all the lands owned by my deceased husband, I direct that 100 acres be laid off to my son William including the improvements I now reside on, the balance if any fall equal between my other two sons James & Alexander and that Elvira have her living during her single life on the part of land allotted to William. I allow Elvira the white curtains over the bed in the room. My friend Miles Smith exr., 25 May 1847. Margaret Jackson (LS), Wit: John Thomas, John Smith Elias M. Jackson. Proved by the oath of Elias M. Jackson 12   July  1847. Qualified Miles Smith as executor 12 July 1847.

**Pages 163-164**: Will of John McNeel of South Carolina, York District... To my wife Esther McNeel my negros Will & Sylvia, the plantation whereon I now reside with the crop at present on it, all my farming utensils, the machinery belonging to my Gin House, etc., and at her decease the property remaining be sold & equally divided among my several children or their bodily heirs. Also to my wife Esther McNeel $800 in money & notes for her special use. I appoint my sid wife executrix, and my nephew Wm R. McNeel, exr., 28 June 1847. John McNeel (LS), Wit: Wm. J. L. Boyd, John Misskelly, Andrew Brown. Proved by the oath of Wm. J. L. Boyd 30 Aug 1847. Qualified Esther McNeel & Wm. R. McNeel, exrs., 30 Aug 1847.

**Pages 164-165**: South Carolina, York District. Will of James Moore of district of York... to my niece Sarah Adickes the land whereon she now lives including all that lies on the north east side of Fishing Creek and also a negro man called Aleck. To my nephew Wm Moore a negro boy called Henry. To my grand niece Dorcas Antoinette Adickes a negro girl called Little Rose. To my niece Maria Ervin wife of Thos Ervin a negro girl called Lovey. The remainder of the land on south side of Fishing Creek with all my negroes not named above, stock, etc., to be sold and the money arising from the sale to be equally divided amongst my lawful heirs. I appoint Wm. Moore sole executor, 17 July 1845. James Moore (LS), Wit: E. A. Crenshaw, S. E. Moore, W. B. Byers. Proved by the oath of Wm. B. Byers 30 Aug 1847. Qualified Dr. Wm. Moore as executor 30 Aug 1847.

**Pages 165-166**: South Carolina, York District. Will of Winefred Smith of district aforesaid... My negro man Sampson be sold & proceeds to be equally divided among my eight children viz Edmund Kendrick, Sally Cunningham, Elizabeth Darnall, Lucy Russell, William Smith, John R. Smith and Mary Glover and Samuel Smith. I will to my daughter Mary Glover the lot of land on which I now live, about 17 acres. To my granddaughter Mary Jane Smith my bed and stead and furniture. Wm Boyes to execute this will, 7 July 1847. Winefred Smith (Seal), Wit: Jos Smith, H. Smith, Samuel Smith. Proved by the oath of Joseph Smith 3 Sept 1847. Qualified William Boyes as executor 3 Sept 1847.

**Pages 166-167**: South Carolina, York District. Will of Ann Anderson... to my daughter Elizabeth Wren my negro girl Sarah & her child Loe. To my grandchildren Henrys namely Isaac N. Henry, James J. Henry, John A. Henry and their sisters daughter Margaret A. Abernetha my negro man Isom to be sold and equally divided between the four named in this clause. To my two grandsons Francis T. Wren & Jeremiah L. Wren $25 in cash. To my grandchildren Andersons namely Robt F. Anderson, Sarah S. Anderson, Amelia D. Anderson, Mary Anderson, Ann E. Anderson & Isaac Anderson, $350 & the money that my bed and clothing thereon will bring at sale to be equally divided between the above named six Andersons. To my daughter Mary C. Nelson $150. I allow my two little negroes Ben and Sam to be sold to make up the above named amounts of money if required, if not I allow the proceeds of their sale to go to my sons John Anderson & William Anderson, 29 Nov 1846. I appoint David Roddy my executor. Ann Anderson (X) (LS), Wit: Wm Abernethey, Milton Abernethey, Sarah C. Wylie. Proved by the oath of Milton Abernethey 4 Oct 1847. Qualified David Roddy as executor 3 Oct 1847.

**Pages 167-169**: South Carolina, York District. Will of William Currence of district aforesaid... To my wife Hannah Currence during her widowhood my plantation whereon I live and all my personal estate. To my son Daniel A. Currence the plantation whereon I reside, new waggon & Harness, my negro boys Ned, Big Peter, negro woman Affy and negro girl Peggy. To my son Robert F. Currence my negro man Henry and negro girl Violet, the black smith tools and coal which may be on hands at his mother's death. To my son William A. Currence my negro man Tom and negro boy Sam at his mother's death. To my son James D. P. Currence my negro boy little Peter now in his possession and my negro girl Sally at his mother's death. To my son Milton H. Currence my negro boy Amos now in his possession and my negro woman Winny at his mother's death. To my sons James D. P. Currence and Wm. A.

Currence in trust for the use of my daughter Eliza A. Barnet my negro woman Ela at their mother's death. To my daughter Eliza A. Barnet my negro woman Rhena which she has in possession. To Martha Currence widow of my decd son J. N. Currence my negro boy Ben now in her possession. To my granddaughter Margaret H. Currence my negro child Allison at her grandmother's death. My sons Wm. A. Currence and James D. P. Currence, exrs., 8 Jan 1846. William Currence (LS), Wit: Daniel Currence, Elias McCarter. Proved by the oath of Daniel Currence 4 Oct 1847. Qualified William A. Currence and James D. P. Currence, exrs., 4 Oct 1847.

**Pages 169-171**: Will of John M. Lindsay of York District.... To my beloved wife Catharine Lindsey, the one third of the balance of my personal estate and to occupy my mansion house during her natural life. To my son Robert M. Lindsey my negro boy Grandison as compensation for $280 which he received for his services as deputy Sheriff and loaned to me. The remainder of my personal estate not above willed to be equally divided amongst my five children viz Robert M., James G., John F., Philip W. & Henrietta E. Lindsey. All my real estate to be equally divided and that my son Robert M. is to have his share so laid off as to include my mansion house in his portion. My son Robert M. Lindsey guardian of my daughter Henrietta E. Lindsey until she arrives to the age of 21 years or marries. Should the stock I have subscribed to the Charlotte & South Carolina Rail Road be required to be paid, I direct the payment to be made before a division is made of my estate. I appoint my sons Robert M. Lindsey and James G. Lindsey, exrs., 8 Nov 1847. John M. Lindsey (LS), Wit: Robert Lindsey, Robert Miller, Moses Linsey. Proved by the oath of Robert Lindsey 8 Dec 1847. Qualified Robert M. Lindsey and James G. Linsey, exrs., 8 Dec 1847.

**Pages 171-172**: South Carolina, York District. Will of Mary Rea... to Cynthia Palmer widow of Joshua Palmer $50 and also to Emeline E. Hays one feather bed and furniture, one walnut chest, wheel and reel, also Mary M. Bigger the balance of my estate, and it is understood that my funeral expenses include stones for my grave which I desire to be purchased by A. S. Wallace and N. P. Kennedy, exrs., 6 Sept 1845. Mary Rea (X), Wit: John Coombs, Catherine Coombs, Mary Gunter. Proved by the oaths of Wm. Currier & Elijah Carroll who swore that the witnesses have removed to live beyond the limits of this state and testified to the handwriting of John Coombs, 27 Dec 1847. Qualified A. S. Wallace as executor 28 Dec 1847.

**Pages 172-173**: South Carolina, York District. Will of James R. Gallaspie of district aforesaid... To my wife Mary M. Gallaspie during her life one tract of land that I now live on containing 5 acres, and one other tract known as the Hogg tract estimated at 270 acres, a negro boy called Addison & one called John, household furniture, etc. After my death my executor sell all the rest & remainder of my estate both personal and real and to be equally divided between my wife and the heirs of my body. I appoint Samuel C. Youngblood, executor, 24 Jan 1848. James R. Gillespie (LS), Wit: Robert Rainey, Robert Latham, Jeptha Neal. Proved by the oath of Jeptha Neal 20 March 1848. Qualified Saml C. Youngblood as executor 20 March 1838.

**Pages 173-174**: South Carolina, York District. Will of Ezekial Gillam... To my son Ezekiel Gillam all my estate of all kinds whatsoever both real and personal. I appoint my friend Jane Black to take charge of my son and his estate as his guardian. John McSwain, Croker Howell, exrs, __ Jan 1847. Ezekiel Gillham (Seal), Wit: John G. Brown, William Jamieson, William M. Smith. Proved by the oath of William M. Smith 14 Feb 1848. Qualified John McSwain as executor 22 Feb 1848. Qualified Jane Black as guardian 10 Oct 1848.

**Pages 174-175**: South Carolina, York District. Will of William H. Patrick of district aforesaid... To my beloved wife Catharine Patrick all my property both real and personal except so much as may be necessary to pay my lawful debts, 24 Feb 1848. William Patrick (LS), Wit: Elias M. Jackson, John T. C. Patrick J. B. Hunter. Proved by the oath of Dr. John B. Hunter 6 March 1848.

**Pages 175-176**: South Carolina, York District. Will of Jefferson Hambright of district aforesaid... To my wife Sarah one negro boy called Jesse, also my household furniture excepting two beds & furniture, all my stock, and the use of my land for the support of my children as long as she remains my widow. TO my daughter Vina Catherine one negro girl called Cinda also one bed & furniture. To my daughter Mary Amanda one negro girl named Eva & one bed and furniture. To my son James Madison one negro girl called Jenny. To my son Philip Boyd one negro girl named Eliza. At my wife's death of if she should marry again, my land or both plantations to be sold and equally divided between all my children. I appoint Madison Hambright and Joseph Mannin exrs., 5 March 1848. Jefferson Hambright (LS), Wit: Robt S. Allison, Aaron W. Whisonant, James H. Etters. Proved by the oath of Aaron W. Whisonent 3 April 1848. Qualified Madison Hambright as executor April 3d 1848. Qualified Joseph Manning.

**Pages 176-178**: North Carolina, Cleveland County. Will of Abner McAfee... After paying all my just debts, I give Tilman McAfee, Randal & the lot of land on Hickory Creek joining the widow McEntires land at my death. I also give Pinckney McAfee, Joseph & the lot of land on little Broad River adj. lands of Saml McBrayer at my death. I also give Lawson A. McAfee, Howard & two tracts of land one on Hickory Creek adj. lands of William Putman & the other on the Rut[?] Road joining lands with the heirs of Wm. Graham decd at my death. I also give Green T. McAfee half of two tracts of land one on Washitaw River the other on the Suder waters of said River, also Leggat, Dulcina & Lucretia that I have formerly given heretofore. I also have given the half of two tracts of land to C. E. McAfee on Washetaw River the other on the Suder waters of Sd River. I also have given Polly Trimmier, Sam & Hannah, one bay mare, two feather beds & furniture. I also gave Eliza Morgan five shillings at my death. I also have been given out of my fathers estate that was coming to me from my father, Philes, one mare, one bed & furniture to Nancy Starns. I also have Sendavella gave Bett & her increase. I also have Amelia McAfee one horse, bridle & saddle & feather bed & cow, calf, also Cass, Bill, Mariah, Mary, Rachel, Hicks, & Ben. I also give Emily Jane McAfee one horse, bridle & Saddle, cow & Calf, feather bed & furniture at $75, also Tom, Hannah, Cinda, Susannah, Sylvia, Jordan Lucy & Ned. I also give Manda Elvira McAfee one horse, saddle & bridle at $75, one cow & Calf, feather bed & furniture, Nero, Phebe, Henry Griffin, Peter, Hester, Cinda. To George Wellington McAfee half of the different tracts of land where I now live between him & Leroy McAfee, also Rueben, Siller, Osamy, Jesse, Ellison, Anderson, Pat at my death or his marriage. I also give to Leroy McAfee one horse, bridle, saddle, also half of the different tracts of land that I now live on, the other half before willed to George Wellington McAfee, also Gabe, Margaret, Nelse, Rice, Harriet, Lewis, Clarissa. I also give Amzi McAfee one horse, bridle, saddle, also half of different tracts of land on Bullocks Creek in York District, South Carolina, the other half to his mother Eliza McAfee during her widowhood then to Amzi McAfee, also Martin, John, Mal, Vice, Riley, Adaline, Dulcina. I also give to my wife Eliza McAfee, Mill, Mira, Jacob, Barbe, Berry, Delph, Lissa, Sal, Adam and at her death to be equally divided amongst her daughters namely Amelia McAfee, Emily Jane McAfee, Manda Elvira McAfee. I authorize my wife Eliza McAfee, exrs., 17 Jan 1844. Abner McAfee (Seal), Wit: Charles Blanton, William Wray, John R. Logan. Copy certified by Richard Champion, Clerk of the Court of Pleas and Quarter Sessions for Cleveland County, NC. J. R.Logan, Chairman of the County Court, certified that Richard Champion is Clerk. Qualified Eliza McAfee executrix 10 Feb 1848.

**Pages 179-180**: Will of Martha Ramsay of York District... To my son Thomas Misskelly 40 acres of land of the plantation whereon I reside to embrace my dwelling house and other out buildings, also bed and furniture, etc. To my grandson DeKalb Misskelly (son of James Misskelly) and Samuel Misskelly (son of Newton Misskelly) the residue of my lands being part of a plantation above mentioned. To my grand daughter Martha Carson my negro girl Hannah and my wearing apparel. My negro woman Lena to my daughter in law Elizabeth Misskelly (wife of my son James Misskelly). My negro girl Jane to my granddaughter Sarah Jane Misskelly. My nero boy Jim (Lena's son) to my granddaughter Elizabeth Catharine Misskelly. To my grandson Lucian Misskelly one bed & furniture. To my daughter in law Elizabeth Misskelly and the heirs of her body all the rest of my property. I appoint Lucien P. Sadler my sole executor, 15 Jan 1848. Martha Ramsay (LS), Wit: Green Gordon, N. Marion Sandefur, J.M. Martin. Proved by the oath of N. Marion Sandefur 10 June 1848. Qualified Lucien P. Sadler as executor 10 June 1848.

**Pages 180-181**: South Carolina, York District. Will of John Brown of district aforesaid. To my beloved wife Mary Elizabeth all the property & effect which I received with her at our marriage. My mother and sister Terza should live together on the farm as long as my mother lives & my sister remains unmarried. My brother in law Thomas Whitesides should live on the farm & take care of my mother & sister and I bequeath to him the said land at my mother's death or sister Terza's removal. I appoint Thos Whitesides executor, 18 March 1848. John Brown (LS), Wit: V. Y. Cowen, James Faulkner, Robt Y. Allison. Proved by the oath of James Faulkner 5 April 1848. Qualified Thomas Whitesides as executor 5 April 1848.

**Pages 181-183**: South Carolina, York District. Will of William R. Erwin late of York District now of Chester District... to my son Francis Erwin my house and lot in Yorkville, my negro boy Green, and my negro woman Malinda and her child Fanny. To my daughter Martha E. Smith my negro woman Nancy & girls Sophy, Amanda, Louisa & Caroline & boy Hampton. I allow my negro woman Margaret to live with either my son Francis or daughter Martha she may choose and desire them to treat her kindly. To John and Edwin Erwin children of my deceased son Wm. Erwin to be equally divided between them the money arising from the sale of my plantation called the Wallace tract about 216 acres, my executor to sell and money to remain in his hands without interest until Edwin arrives to the age of 21 years. The remainder of my estate to be sold to pay debts and any residue to my son Francis. I appoint my son Francis Erwin executor, 4 May 1847. Wm. R. Erwin (Seal), Wit: W. J. Clawson, S. Mellon, J. M. Ross. Proved by the oath of Wm. J. Clawson 14 June 1848. Qualified Francis Erwin as executor 14 June 1848.

**Pages 183-184**: Will of James Floyd Senr of York District... To my son James N. Floyd the plantation whereon I now reside with personal property my thresher & fan, walnut chest, etc. To my daughter Elizabeth two beds & bedding, one bureau, etc. To my daughter Sarah Ann two bureaus, two beds & bedding, etc. My beloved wife Sarah have her living on the above named plantation, the remainder of my household furniture, and at her death fall equally between my three children Elizabeth, Sarah Ann, and J. N. Floyd. My son J. N. Floyd to give my grandson James A. Bell good English schooling. Should my grandson Izard Floyd return & wish to remain, I allow him the use of the Tan yard, the crop and provisions on hand at the time of my decease. As respects my other children viz Nathan Floyd, Rebecca Houser, & the children of my son Andrew Floyd and daughter Nancy C. Bell, I advanced them in property on their having a share equal to that allow my children now living with me. I appoint my son J. N. Floyd executor 31 Jan 1848. James Floyd (LS), Wit: John Janes, G. R. Boleyn, Myles Smith. Proved by the oath of Myles Smith 24 July 1848. Qualified James N. Floyd as executor 24 July 1848.

**Pages 185-192**: Will of John Blair of Yorkville... My body to be interred at the foot of my former wife's grave in Sharon Graveyard with a monument erected over my grave similar to the one erected over the body of the late Robert McCaw of Yorkville, with the addition of an iron inclosure, & if my wife should survive me & she should desire it, her body at her decease should be buried with mine in the same grave. To my wife Nancy Blair in trust my forty shares of stock in the Bank of the State of North Carolina, my fifty shares of stock in the Merchants Bank Chirah, 200 acres of my stock in the Commercial Bank Columbia, and my [note?] against Alexander Huggins. At my wife's deceased to the payment of debts & her bond then due to the exors of her brother Jas Irwin's estate. I also give to my said wife during her natural life the house & two lots whereon we now live, the four acres of land adj. which I purchased of Thos Hoover, 14 3/4 acres purchased from John McCoy; the lots purchased from Shff Brian & formerly Doctor Jennings property; my plantation of 367½ acres, purchased of Benjn Neel & wife and all the negroes, live stock, etc. Let the negroes individually have their choice amongst the said legatees of those whom they may prefer to live with but to let not more than two negroes be given to any one of the said legatees. To Saml B. Alexander son of my late niece Isabella Alexander, 30 shares of my stock in the Broad River Bridge Co. and 11 shares of my stock with the South Carolina Rail Road & its bank; also the negroes Golden, George, Jude, Alick, and Henry and the personal property which I purchased from Thos E. Suggs assignees of Jas H. Alexander. Also to the said Saml B. Alexander & his children my two lots in Pinckneyville at 26½ acres; and my plantation on Pacolet River 238½ acres purchased also from said T. E. Suggs & Jas. H. Alexander, and I appoint the said Jas H. Alexander as guardian for his son the said Saml B. Alexander until he comes of age to receive the dividends arising upon said stocks. If said Saml B. Alexander should die without heirs, then to be divided between his uncle Saml Blair and his cousin Eliza Jane Smith. To Eliza Jane Smith daughter of my late niece Mary Smith 40 shares of my stock in Broad River Co. & my negroes Perry & his wife Dilsey & her two children & I appoint my second cousin Robt Gilfillen to be her guardian. If she should die without heirs then her property be equally divided between her uncle Saml Blair & her cousin Saml B. Alexander. To my nephew Saml Blair 120 acres of my stock on the Commercial Bank Columbia, the negro girl Catharine and her offspring, my tract of land at Blairsville conveyed in four parts by More, McKenney, Jas & Jos Jamieson to the heirs of John Dickey, 287 acres, also my tract of about 450 acres conveyed to me by James S. Guignard assignee of Wm. Ed. Hayne but should my said nephew die without issue, then my exors will sell 40 shares of the bank stock and commit the proceeds to the care of suitable trustees for the purpose of building a brick schoolhouse upon any one acres of land of the Blair tract and the remaining 80 shares to the minister & elders of Sharon Congregation. To my nephew John B. Lowry, 60 shares of my stock in the Camden Bank, one half of the dividends arising upon which he will pay to his father & mother during their life, but if he should die without issue, then to become the property of my nephew Saml Blair & third cousin John Latta. To my second cousins John Carnes, Martha Moore, Robert Carnes, Eliza Carnes & Susan Carnes to each of whom 30 shares of my stock in the Bank of Hamburg and to Robert Carnes & his sisters Eliza & Susan until some one of them marries, the negro fellow Edward now in their possession. Also the negro fellow Simpson to the said Martha Moore and her children also the negro girl Isabella. To second cousins Eliza Patrick, John Patrick, Joseph Patrick, Alexander Patrick & Samuel Patrick, 30 shares of my stock in the Bank of Hamburg, conjointly but equally the negro woman Mariah & her child now in their possession and that part of a tract on waters of Turkey conveyed to me by Wm Jamieson & laid down in a mal of said land by Wm. Campbell marked No. 3, 190 4/5 acres. To the three children conjointly of my late second cousin Rebecca Mitchell namely Mary Francis, Thomas & Henry, 30 shares of my stock in the Broad River Company, and the tract conveyed to me by John Carnes, 200 acres for which I made a deed of trust to their father Jos Mitchell whom I hereby appoint to be their guardian. To my second cousin Robert Gilfillen in trust for his wife and children 20 shares of my stock in the So Car Rail Road and its Bank. To my second cousin Wm Latta, 80 shares of my stock in the Commercial Bank of Columbia.

To my half cousin James Blair sen during his natural life and in trust for his children 30 shares of my stock in the Camden Bank & 15 of my shares in the So Car Rail Road & its Bank, also two sections of the tract of land conveyed to me by Wm. Jamieson, Nos. 2 and 3, 370 7/10 acres. To the following relatives, I give & bequeath the several sums annexed to their names, viz To Garrison Blair $200; to Betsey Blair (widow of Jas Blair) & children $300; To the orphan children of the widow D. Hall decd $300; To Joseph Reid's wife & children $130; To Saml H. Smith $100; to Polly Gribble $300; To the late Wm Blair's widow & children $200; To Rachel Dickson $200; To Rebecca Prescot's son $200; To David Blair's widow & her two youngest sons $300; To Elijah Patrick, Marion Alabama, $500; To Jane Cairnes now Cunningham, Ashville NC, $500; To the five children conjointly of Jas Stephenson deceased $2150; To John Semple (for his wife & children by her) $166 2/3; To Wm Rankers[?] and his sister Mrs. Young conjointly, $666 2/3; To Wm Miller for his wife and children $266 2/3; To the three children of my half uncle David Blair decd, $266 2/3. The six legacies first mentioned my friend W.. W. Elms can convenient pay off for it may be remitted to John W. Blair, Petesburg as my agent to pay the same. E. Patrick may be remitted to her brother Jno Patrick Marion the legacy to Jane Cunningham may be remitted to her husband. the last seven legacies may be remitted to Alex Gwyn, Londonderry, as my agent. But as I intend to pay the legacies in this clause myself if spared in two years,my exors will therefore only have to pay such legacies as they find to be unpaid. To the treasurer of the Erskine Seminary of the A. R. Church locate at Due West Corner, Abbeville District, 30 shares of my stock in the South Carolina Rail Road & its Bank. To the Treasurer of the Theological Seminary in Columbia 200 shares of my stock in the Farmers & Planters Bank, Baltimore. To the Treasurer of the Southern Board of Foreign Missions 80 shares of my stock in the Farmers & Planters Bank, Baltimore. To the Treasurer of the American Tract Society, New York, 80 shares of my stock in the Farmers & Planters Bank, Baltimore. To the Treasurer of the Hibernian Society of the City of Charleston 60 shares of my stock in the Farmers & Planters Bank Baltimore. To the legislature of South Carolina in trust 30 shares of my stock in the South Carolina Rail Road & Its Bank, to the support of a free school in Yorkville. My brother in law Wm. Wright and my friends Dr. John B. Hunter and John M. Ross, exrs., 5 Aug 1846. John Blair (LS), Wit: John S. Moore, John H. Adams, S. R. Moore. Codicil made 9 Aug 1848, witnessed by W. H. McCorkle, T. S. Jefferys, J. A. McLean. Proved by the oath of John H. Adams and Joseph A. McLean, 12 Nov 1848.

**Pages 192-193**: Will of Tabitha Donaldson... To my daughter Nancy Wilkenson all my tract of land that son James settled and containing 9 acres, one cow and calf, two feather beds, one loom & one dye pot. To my son Charles E. Wilkenson the piece of land that I bought from William Carson containing 9 acres. To my son Thomas J. Wilkenson one feather bed & bedding. My daughter Elizabeth Burns [Burris?] is to be charged with all that she bought at her father's estate. I appoint Peyton B. Darwin, exr., 8 Dec 1848. Tabitha Donaldson (X). Wit: B. S. Carson, Williamson Byers, Frank S. Carson. Proved by the oath of Williamson Byers 31 Jan 1849. Qualified Peyton B. Darwin as executor 31 Jan 1849.

**Pages 193-196**: South Carolina, York District. Will of James Thomasson Senr of district aforesaid, being aged and feeble in health... to my son James C. Thomasson a negro man named Henry, a negro woman Letta, the tract of land on which he now resides called the Beatty tract, some stock & household furniture. Whereas I have given to my son Wm. P. Thomasson as negro man named Rener, a woman Harriet, also stock & household furniture of equal of that given to my other sons, it is my wish that his title to the same be confirmed and I will to him the tract I gave to my son William I afterwards purchased of him. The property which I have given to my son Hiram C. Thomasson the negro man named Isom, girl Vena, stock household furniture equal with other sons, also the tract of land on which he now lives, 215 acres according to survey and plat made by Wm. Campbell deputy surveyor, 4 Sept 1845, I will & devise to him. The property which I have given to my son P. A. Thomasson a boy named Henry, girl Louisa and a tract on which he now lives 150 acres, and household furniture equal with my other sons. I have given to my son Doctor D. H. Thomasson the sum of $836 to complete his education, the same shall stand to him in lieu of the tract of land which I have given to each of my other children, the boy Daniel and the girl Sue I will & devise to him. I will to my son G. L. Thomasson a negro boy named Albert, girl Margaret, tract on which I now live, known as the McWhorter tract, being the balance of the Porter tract after taking off that part which I have given to my son Hiram C. Thomasson and the Henderson tract, about 111 acres and furniture to be selected by him, a horse & saddle which he now claims. To my son Hiram C. Thomasson a negro girl named Harriet in trust for the benefit of my son Doctor Alfred Thomasson. To my son James C. Thomasson a negro boy Allison, the tract known as the Allison tract, about 117 acres, also the tract known as part of the Wright tract, 103 acres, per plat made by William Campbell 5 Sept 1845 in trust for the benefit of my son Simon B. Thomasson. All the property not herein before devised be sold by my executors and the proceeds divided between my eight children herein mentioned. I appoint James C. Thomasson & Wm. P. Thomasson my sons, exrs., 1 Sept 1847. James Thomasson (LS), Wit: W. J. Clawson, Wm. L. Brown, Hance Neely. Proved by the oath of W. J. Clawson 15 Jan 1849. Qualified James C. Thomasson executor 15 Jan 1849.

**Page 196**: South Carolina, York District. Dorcas M. Stephenson of district aforesaid for love and affection towards my brother James G. Stephenson give him all my personal goods & effects, one sorrel horse & side saddle, two cows, five feather beds & furniture, etc., 16 Feb 1849. Dorcas M. Stephenson (LS), Wit: J. M. Hope, E. G. Byers, Saml Black Proved by the oath of J. M. Hope 12 April 1849.

**Pages 196-197**: South Carolina, York District. Will of Jane McClenahan of district aforesaid... to my sister Martha Dunlap my negro woman Ruthy, one bed & furniture, one half of my other household furniture, one half of my stock of cattle, etc, and at her death to go to my niece Nancy Rogers & her children. To my nephew James E. Rogers all my interest in the tract of land whereon we now live (i. e.) one third of said tract, and also my negro woman Cynthia and my two mares Patsy & Doll, one half of my cattle. To my niece

Nancy Rogers my negro girl Juliet, two beds & furniture, one half of my other household furniture. To my grand niece Mary Jane Rogers my negro boy Jesse, Ruthy's child. The balance of my estate to be sold and the money arising from the same to be divided between my sister Martha Dunlap & James E. Rogers. I appoint Martha Dunlap and James E. Rogers, exrs., 25 Jan 1849. Jane McClenahan (X) (LS), Wit: Isaac McFadden, A. H. McFadden, E. F. Crockett. Proved by the oath of Isaac McFadden 10 April 1849. Qualified James E. Rogers executor 10 April 1849.

**Pages 198-200**: South Carolina, York District. Will of Edward Smith of district aforesaid... To my beloved wife Fanny Smith, my two horse carriage & harness, my riding mare called Fly, one or two feather beds & furniture, one set of silver table spoons, one set of silver tea spoons, one bureau, one set of china ware, and also a child's part of my estate or a sum not exceeding one third of said distributive share. My son Robert being afflicted & like to remain so through life, one of the children take him and his legacy & give bond & security. To my son William Smith the plantation on which he now lives, 200 acres, valued at $1200. To my daughter Elizabeth J. Boyd the property charged to her in my family book as already received, and also my home plantation. To my daughter Margaret H. Bowden an equal share of my estate with the rest of my children, she has received a note made to me by her husband Wm. R. Bowden. To my son John R. Smith the property heretofore advanced to him with the plantation on which he now lives, also the River hills known as the Peter place whereon Zack Caps now lives, 120 acres. To my daughter Emeline Greer, all that has been advanced to her, and if she dies having no other child my will is that the one third of her legacy to the use of her son Samuel D. Bowden. To my granddaughter Sarah D. Fuller $500 to be put out at interest until she arrives of age, and I appoint my son Wm. Smith to act as her guardian. To my grandson Edward Smith my young cold now sucking Fly, one saddle & bridle. The balance of my property to be equally divided between my wife Fanny Smith, Wm. Smith, John R. Smith, Robert W. Smith, Elizabeth J. Boyd, Margaret R. Bowden and Emeline Greer. I appoint my son Wm Smith and son in law James Boyd executors, 1 Sept 1848. Edward Smith (Seal), Wit: Robert S. Warren, Robt A. Ross, Isaac S. Guyer. Proved by the oath of Robt A. Ross 9 Feb 1849. Qualified Wm. Smith and James Boyd executors 9 Feb 1849.

**Pages 200-201**: Will of William Amberson of District of York, 21 June 1848... After my decease and debts paid, to nephew James S. Jones my land, my two negro boys Ned & Edmond, my stock, farming utensils, household & kitchen furniture, enjoining it on him to take special care of my two sisters Agnes Jones & Margaret Whitesides. I appoint my nephew James Jones, exrs. Wit: R. H. Hope, A. T. Black, Jas. B. Steele. Proved by the oath of A. T. Black 1 June 1849. Qualified James S. Jones as executor 1 June 1849.

**Pages 201-202**: Will of John Brown of York District... To my daughter Margaret Steele and her children that may be living at her death the interest of $200 which my executor will loan out and pay over to my said daughter annually and not to be subject to the contracts of her husband James Steele and at the death of my said daughter the said $200 to be equally divided amongst all her children that may then be living. To my granddaughter Minerva Adams $50. To my grandson Watson Adams $50. To my grandson John G. Adams $50. To my grand daughter Amanda Adams $50. To my son Robert Brown the balance of my personal estate and the plantation whereon I now live but should my said son note survive my wife Elizabeth, then said property to his child or children that may then be living. I appoint my son Robert Brown executor, 19 Jan 1843. John Brown (LS), Wit: Julia B. Rainey, S. W. McNeel, Saml Rainey. Proved by the oath of S. W. McNeel 30 June 1849. Qualified Robert Brown as executor 18 June 1849.

**Pages 202-203**: Will of Robert Mitchell of District of York... To my beloved wife Catharine the plantation whereon my mansion house is situated and for the purpose of supporting her and the children until the youngest child arrives of age or marries. My interest in my horse Streak which is the one half, the other half being vested in Resen Talbert, after the season is out, be put to sale by my executor. I appoint my brother Dawson[?] N. Mitchell, exr., 23 May 1849. Robert R. Mitchell (LS), Wit: M. O. Mitchell, George Pettus, James Thorn. Proved by the oath of George Pettus 7 July 1849.

**Pages 203-205**: South Carolina, York District. Will of Sarah McCarter (widow) of district aforesaid... To my grandchildren, children of my son Minor McCarter, viz. David Byers McCarter, Simpson Hervey McCarter, and Eli Erwin McCarter, the plantation or tract of land whereon I now live, also one negro boy named Dick Perkins, one negro boy child named Andrew Jackson, one negro woman named Temay and her child Emalene, one negro woman named Amy and her two children Flora & Hannah Mahela, also three head of horses. To my granddaughter Margaret Hermon, one feather bed and furniture. To my daughter Elizabeth McCarter, $2 in cash. To my daughter Sarah Dickson (wife of Thomas Dickson) $2 in cash. To my son in law John Herman, $2 in cash. To my son Thomas McCarter, $2 in cash. To my son Minor McCarter $2 in cash. I appoint my son in law Clesby Cobb & my son Minor McCarter, exrs., 6 Dec 1836. Sarah McCarter (X) (Seal), Wit: W. M. Dickson, Betsey C. Floyd, James Floyd. Proved by the oath of Betsey Caroline Floyd 4 July 1849.

**Pages 205-206**: South Carolina, York District. Will of Elizabeth Moore of district aforesaid... To my sister Nancy Craig all my lands except 30 acres at the lower end of the plantation and at her death the land be given to Alexander Fuller. The above named 30 acres to my brother John Moore during his life & at his death to my brother Henry Moore (should he survive the said John). I give my horse and one bed and furniture to Alexander Fuller and the other bed to my brother Henry Moore. The balance of my stock and effect to said Nancy Craig. I appoint Clark Moore, exr., 5 May 1849. Elizabeth Moore (X) (LS), Wit: A. S. Wallace, Casinda Moore, Cyrus Moore. Proved by the oath of A. S. Wallace 4 July 1849. Qualified Clark Moore as executor 4 July 1849.

**Pages 206-207**: South Carolina, York District. Will of Thomas Robertson of district aforesaid... To my son Wm. L. Robertson the tract of land whereon I now live, 290 acres by a late survey made by J. H. Crawford, 70 acres of which is taken off another tract joining which was granted to me at the same time, 11 Dec 1841. This bequest is made with the perfect understanding that his mother is to have the use of the plantation during her natural life. To my daughter Rosinda R. Robertson a part of my tract of land adj. the above bequest, 200 acres between the creeks of Tools Fork and Fishing Creek, but is said Rosinda should die without issue, then the above property is to revert to my estate and be equally divided among my surviving legatees. To my wife Rebecca Robertson during her life or widowhood the tract of 290 acres bequeathed to my son Wm. L. Robertson. I appoint my son Allen Robertson, exr., 4 Aug 1847. Thomas Robertson (LS), Wit: James W. Long, Martha E. Robertson, S. Sadler. Proved by the oath of Stanhope Sadler 5 Aug 1849.

**Page 207**: South Carolina, York District. Personally appeared Dr. John Hall, Philip Williams & Thomas J. McElhenny and made oath that on the 15th of this instant John McLure called upon the deponents to bear witness that he was about to make his last will and testament and that he "willed and devised to his brother WM. Mclure the plantation on which said William McLure then resided except that he allowed his brother Robert McLure to have as much of the land to cultivate for the next year. And that he willed al the remainder of his property to his brother Robert McLure for and during his life" ... he died the next day after. John Hall, Philip Williams, T. J. McElhenny, 20 April 1848.

**Page 208**: Will of Henry M. Greer of York District... To Mary Margaret Jane Greer and Edward Henry Greer the land I now live on to be disposed of until they come of age as my executors Alex Erwin and Milton Wallace may think most to their profit... $300 to be applied for schooling, clothing & boarding the above two minors. To John Cockerham's oldest son Henry Rufus $100. To Wm. Greer's son Henry $100, the donations of the last two is for their names and the remainder after my debts is paid to be equally divided into four shares one fourth part to Edward Henry Greer, one fourth part to Mary Margaret Jane Greer, one fourth to son Wm. Greer and the last fourth to be equally divided between my daughters children to Cockerham. The kitchen furniture and carpenter tools were left to them negroes by Mary Greer 7 May 1843. I was her executor and is on record... dated 7 July 1849. Henry M. Greer (LS), Wit: McConnell Curry, John Mc. Curry, Wm. Curry. Proved by the oath of John M. Curry and William Curry 21 Sept 1848. Qualified F. Alexander Erwin & S. Milton Wallace exors 21 Sept 1849.

**Pages 209-210**: Will of James Moore of Indian Land, York District... To my beloved wife my carriage & two horses each worth $75, the plantation on which I now reside & the following negroes Old London, George, Young London, Penny, Pleasant, Milly & Phillis, and desire that she shall give a classical education to my two youngest sons Alberta A. Moore & Eli P. Moore, and at the death or marriage of my said wife, all the property bequeathed to her to be sold & the proceeds be equally divided between my six youngest sons. To my son Richard S. Moore my negro girl Caroline & a horse with $75. To my son James Moore my negro man named John & girl Adaline, a bed & furniture, & a horse worth $75. To my son William A. Moore my negro man named Jack & girl Amanda, a bed & furniture, & a horse worth $75. To my son Maurice A. Moore my negro man named Simon & girl Ann, a bed & furniture, & a horse worth $75. To my son Alberta A. Moore my negro boy named Ned & girl Amy, a bed & furniture, & a horse worth $75. To my son Eli P. Moore, my negro boy named Sampson & girl Eliza, a bed & furniture, & a horse worth $75. All the remainder of my estate both real & personal be sold and the proceeds divided into ten equal shares, one of which to each of my six youngest sons & my daughters Dorcas E. Murphy & Jane A. Campbell. one of the remaining shares to the children living at my death of my son Alexander L. Moore & the remaining share to my son Wm. A. Moore in trust for my daughter Cynthia L. Bynum. I appoint Richard S. Moore and James L. Moore, exrs., 15 Sept 1849. James Moore (X) (LS), Wit: J. M. Ross, R. C. McCaula, David B. Miller. Proved by the oath of R. C. McCaula 6 Nov 1849. Qualified Richard S. Moore & James L. Moore as exors.

**Pages 210-211**: 26 Oct 1847, Will of Jane Boyd of the District of York... To my daughter Mary one negro girl named Violet. To my daughter Margaret one negro boy named Sam. To my daughter Margaret my young sorrel horse. My negro boy John with all my other property to be sold & all my just debts to be paid and remainder divided between my daughters Jincy & Permelia & my grandson Andrew N. Smith. I appoint my friends John Glenn & Rufus J. Boyd, exrs. Jane Boyd (X), Wit: Wm. H. Johnston, T. M. Boyd, John A. Laney. Proved by the oath of T. M. Boyd 28 Nov 1849. Qualified John Glenn & Rufus J. Boyd as executors 28 Nov 1849.

**Pages 211-212**: Will of James Plexico of the District of York... To my two sons John T. Plexico & James G. Plexico all my lands or real estate, the crop now on hand of last year, and the crop now growing at present, all debts due the estate and bind them to settle or pay all just debts against the estate. To my son John T. Plexico my negro man named Billy, a small girl named Adaline, one bed & furniture and a cow & calf. To my son James G. Plexico my negro woman named Viney, a small girl named Margaret, one bed & furniture and a cow & calf. To my executors $400 in trust for Pamela Garrison and her children. To my daughter Jane Plexico my negro girl named Clarissa, two beds and furniture, feathers for another bed which she has now on hand, one bureau, two cows & calves, and a horse & saddle & while she remains single her living off the land for a home. To my son Henry G. Plexico a negro girl named Liza and $100 to be paid if he comes back to live in this country, if not I allow him $450 out of my estate. To my sons James & James, all the balance of my personal estate. My sons John T. Plexico & James G. Plexico, executors, 27 Dec 1848. James Plexico (Seal), Wit: Jas S. Hemphill, John P. Hood, John S. Plexico. Proved by the oath of John P. Hood 16 Jan 1850. Qualified James G. Plexico as exor 16 Jan 1850.

**Pages 212-213**: Will of William Wherry of York District... To my wife Elizabeth Wherry the whole of my estate real and personal and after her death to my daughter Elizabeth Wherry the plantation on which I now reside. The balance of my estate to be equally divided amongst my children. I appoint my son Andrew Wherry, exr., 23 Feb 1850. Wm. Wherry (LS), Wit: Harvey H. Drennan, Archibald Steele, Mathew H. Williams. Proved by the oath of Harvey H. Duncan 12 March 1850. Qualified Andrew Wherry as executor 12 March 1850.

**Pages 213-214**: South Carolina, York District. Will of Elijah Carroll of district aforesaid... I desire that my executors herein after named take the management of my whole estate real and personal & without sale pay all my just debts & keep my property now life with the increase of the same all together for the support and education of my children until the youngest child issue of my said marriage shall be 21 years of age at which time I desire that all of my personal estate be equally divided among all my children except Sarah Rainey who has got her share. My beloved wife Cynthia Carroll to have an equal share should she be living at the time of distribution. My wife Cynthia with my other executor have the entire control of all my real and personal estate. After her death all my real estate to my youngest son Rufus Monroe Carroll. I appoint Cynthia Carroll my wife and my son Silas E. Carroll, exrs., 29 July 1850. Elijah Carroll (LS), Wit: John Rainey, John Ingram, A. S. Wallace. Proved by the oath of John Rainey 9 Sept 1850. Qualified Cynthia Carroll as executrix 9 Sept 1850.

**Pages 214-215**: South Carolina, York District. Will of Robert Wilson of district aforesaid... to my wife Sarah Wilson the whole of my personal estate including also my land property. At the death of my said wife Sarah my land fall to John Gilmore Junr and he is to take care and support my three old negroes George and his wife Sarah & Rena, & whereas my negro man Wilson was originally the property of my said wife, it appears to me equitable and right that she should have the entire right to said negro man Wilson. I fell a desire to place my negroes Aly, Eleanor, Mary Jane and Charleston in as comfortable & agreeable situation as possible, I will that each choose their own master or mistress. At the death of my wife Sarah the balance of my property, one half fall to her heirs and one half to my heirs at law. I appoint Jas S. Hemphill, exr., 12 May 1848. Robert Wilson (X), Wit: Richard Sherer, John M. Sherer, Robert W. Sherer. Proved by the oath of Richard Sherer 14 Oct 1850.

**Pages 215-218**: South Carolina, York District. Will of William Hacket of district aforesaid... to Robert G. McCaw of said District my plantation on Turkey Creek known as the Latimer tract of land, about 240 acres, my house & lot in Yorkville known as Lot. No. 19 whereon I now reside & my tract of land near the village of Yorkville known as the Chambers tract about 80 acres (reserving one acre of the Chambers tract adjoining the Graveyard of the Independent Presbyterian Church) in trust for the said Robert C. McCaw to hold the said tracts for the use and benefit of my brother Hugh Hacket, if alive at my death, now residing in the North of Ireland, Drumahagles, near

Balleymaney, County of Antrim, the legal title to remain & be vested int he said Robert G. McCaw until such time as the said Hugh Hacket now an alien shall become duly qualified according to Acts of Congress of the United States of America to take & hold said real estate. To my said brother Hugh Hacket if alive at my death, my negroes viz Isaac, Sealy & son Ben, Till & her daughter Laura, Hiram, Delhi & her children Orseola, Charles, Wyona, New and Harriet, Margaret & the increase of said female slaves. To my said brother Hugh Hacket my negroes Alsey, Mary & her daughter Louisa & Dick, that as soon as may be practicable after my decease he do erect a comfortable house for them to live in upon the Chambers tract. Should my brother Hugh Hacket not be alive at my decease, then the real estate to my nephew William Hacket, eldest son of said Hugh Hacket). If both of them be dead, then to my nephew James Hacket, son of said Hugh Hacket. To my nephew James Hacket my negroes Adam & Patience. To my sister Jincy Mallet $2000. To my niece Elizabeth now Mrs. Ratchford, $500. To my niece Martha Mallet $1000. To the daughters of my brother Hugh Hacket $500 each. I appoint Robert G. McCaw, J. Bolton Smith & James R. Bratton, exrs., 16 Oct 1847. Wm Hacket (Seal), Wit: James Brian, R. S. Moore, Jas Kuykendal. Proved by the oath of R. S. Moore 22 Oct 1850. Qualified J. Bolton Smith as executor 24 Oct 1850.

**Pages 218-219**: South Carolina, York District. Will of James Faris of district aforesaid... All my estate real and personal to my daughter Eliza Youngblood, wife of Henry Youngblood, not subject to the debts, etc., of her husband. Whereas my wife Mary is now alive & may live longer than myself, she be supported and maintained out of the estate given to my daughter. I appoint Elijah A. Faris, exr., 18 Feb 1844. James Faris (Seal), Wit: Simpson B. Wallace, Thomas Faris, Catharine S. Faris. Proved by the oath of Catharine S. Faris 4 Nov 1850. Qualified Elijah A. Faris as executor 4 Nov 1850.

**Pages 219-220**: South Carolina, York District. Will of John Dennis of district aforesaid... To my beloved wife Mary, my negro man Philip and my negro woman Nancy during her lifetime, and at her death to belong to my son John Dennis. To my son John Dennis all my negroes of every description to wit Philip and Nancy as stated above, Old Sarah, young Sarah, Isaac, Harding[?], Hannah, Caroline, Charles, Esther, Ned, David, Joe, Lucy, Peter, Kiziah, Jude, Tom, William, Mander, Peggy and Phillis. To my son John Dennis all my land, all stock, all my blacksmith tools. My wife Mary and son John executors [not dated]. John Dennis (LS), Wit: Wm. Hacket, E. H. Gunning, James Kuykendal.

**Pages 220-222**: Will of Benjamin Dunlap of District of York... My negroes Smith, Harriet and her two children John and Mary to my three grandchildren Joseph Dunlap, Thomas Dunlap, and William Berry Dunlap, as they severally come to age. If all of my said grandchildren shall die leaving no issue, then to the heirs of Wm. B. Dunlap, Elizabeth Hagans, and James P. Dunlap equally. My executor to sell all my real estate consisting of a plantation on the Six Mile Creek, and to collect all my dues by notes, book accts, &c., and to expose to sale all of my goods not herein before mentioned and out of the proceeds thereof after paying all debts to buy and put up suitable tombstones for myself and wife and all my deceased sons and daughters interred in the Stone Graveyard. William B. Dunlap, exr., 2 Jan 1850. Benjamin Dunlap (LS), Wit: John Roddey, Wm. D. Rogers, John Polk. Proved by the oath of John Roddey 11 Nov 1850. Qualified Wm. B. Dunlap as executor 1 Nov 1850.

**Page 222**: South Carolina, York District. Will of John James of district aforesaid... In as much as I have in my life paid off to my four children Polly the wife of Joseph Stoup, to Thomas James, to Hannah the wife of W. L. Boyd, and Elizabeth wife of Aaron Peler, each $250, that my executors shall pay to my daughter Anna the wife of James Sandland $132 and also pay to my daughter the wife of William Harvey $38.08 and to pay to my daughter Susan the wife of Daniel Peeler $31 and pay to my daughter Catharine the wife of Wm. Smith Bird $82.75 which sums with what I have advanced them will make them each $250. Inasmuch as I have given off to my sons John James and Daniel James by deed all my plantation, they shall not receive any part of my estate. All my household and kitchen furniture with other personal property (but now including a note I hold on my son Daniel for $286.55) to my wife Elizabeth during her natural life and at her death to be equally divided between my seven daughters. I appoint my friends Thomas McGill and John Whisonant, executors, 29 Dec 1847. John James (X), H. C. Black, James McGill[?], A. J. McGill.

**Pages 223-225**: Will of John Niven Senior, planter, of District of York... To my beloved wife Pricilla Niven the plantation I now live on including all the improvements and spring of water and at her death of marriage, my executors do sell said plantation and divided the money arising from such sale equally amongst my grandchildren they taking the share which would have been due their parents if alive. Also I will that my grandchildren whose parents may be alive at the time of my death likewise the share which would be due their parents. To my wife Priscilla three of my negroes Tabitha, Jim, and Ransom, and at her death or marriage to be sold and the money divided as above. I give to my said wife Priscilla my negro girl Harriet and her child Lewis, also cattle, kitchen furniture, etc. I will my plantation on which my son Daniel Niven now lives to my two grandchildren William Harvey Niven and James Niven, sons of Daniel, but they are not to exercise any acts of ownership during the lifetime of said Daniel. My river plantation to be sold and the proceeds divided as before directed. To my grandson Joseph Green Niven my negro girl Kizzy and it is my wish that he remain on the plantation with my widow until he arrives at 21 years of age. My negro girl Harriet be allowed to keep a bed clothing as her own property, she having made and acquired the same herself. I loan to my daughter in law Patience Niven one negro girl named Ann which she has in possession at this time and at her death to go to the use of her children by James Nivens. I also loan to my daughter Elizabeth Bennett one negro girl named Mary which she now has in possession. I will the amount of a note due Jesse niven deceased of the state of Alabama to me for which I hold a receipt of Joseph S. Bennett in the event of said Bennett making no return to me for the amount of said note, the said amount to be deducted from the share of my estate falling due to the said Bennet's children born of my said daughter Elizabeth. I appoint my friend Joseph F. White sole executor, 25 Feb 1850. John Niven Sen (X) (Seal), Wit: John L. Lanier, Wm. N. Faris, Jas. M. Smith. Codicil dated 25 Feb 1850. My intentions are that my will was to give property to my grandchildren who might be in existence at the time of my death and not to such as might be born after my death. John Niven (X), Wit: C. R. Perry, S. D. Carothers, Wm. N. Faris.

**Pages 225-226**: Will of James McKee of District of York... After my just debts are paid, the remainder of my estate, both real and personal, shall be divided as follows, viz. one sixth part to be equally divided between my son Samuel's daughters Mary C. and Louisa C., and two sixths to my grandson Robert H. Fulwood; the remaining three sixths to be equally divided between my son James M. and my daughter Margaret Jane the wife of Thos. D. Spratt, but if my grandson Robert H. Fulwood above named should die without leaving heirs, the portion left to him shall revert equally to my son Jas M. and my daughter Margaret Jane. It is my will that my daughter Margaret Jane shall receive as a part of her portion a small strip of land lying on the back Branch, beginning at White's path near the mouth the Schoolhouse branch including all of the woodland between the old field and the center of the branch bottom down to Wm. E. White's line. I appoint Franklin H. Harris of this District my executor, and also the guardian of my grandson Robert H. Fulwood, 3 Jan 1851. James McKee (LS), Wit: Robert P. Harris, John A. Hunt, John Farrar. Proved by the oath of Robert P. Harris 20 Jan 1851. Qualified F. H. Harris as executor 20 Jan 1851.

**Pages 226-227**: Will of Alexander Crawford impressed with the belief that I have not long to live... To my wife Sarah the negroes Jim, Becky, Kate and Betsey; also my waggon and harness, carriage and harness, the two mules and the mare; also her bed and the kitchen furniture, and my lands during her lifetime and at her death to my daughters Margaret Jane and Susan Isabella jointly, should they be living, and in case they should not, then it to be sold and the proceeds be equally divided amongst my three sons James Harvey, Alexander Lafayette, and Edward Newton. To my son James Harvey, Becky's youngest child; to my son Alexander Lafayette the negro boy Jack; to my son Edward Newton the negro boys Silas and Ben, and the mar Penick. To my daughter Margaret Jane the negro girls Anna and Narcissa, also the piano and the mare Age and one bed. To my daughter Susan Isabella the negro girls Sileah and Betty, also the younger mare colt and one bed. All property not herein mentioned or specified to be sold. If there be any overplus that it be applied to the education of my daughter Susan Isabella [not dated]. Alexander Crawford. Wit: J. S. Chambers, Jas T. Goudelock, Job L. Neely.

**Pages 227-228**: South Carolina, York District. Will of William Smith of district aforesaid... To my wife during her life a negro girl called Esther, one cow and calf, two beds, bedstead and necessary bed furniture, one third part of my household and kitchen furniture, and the plantation that I now reside on, and at the death of my wife to be equally divided between my nine children viz Katherine, John, J. William, James, Jesse, Eli, Jane, Sarah, Elizabeth. I bequeath to my daughter Avolina $5 which shall be her full share of my estate, dated 9 Feb 1851. William Smith (LS), Wit: S. C. Youngblood, J. Ross,

James M. Griffin.

**Page 228**: South Carolina, York District. Will of A. S. Fulton of district aforesaid... to my son James W. Fulton my little gray horse and one horse waggon and harness with 30 bushels of corn I have at James Brian. The ballance of my property to be sold and equally divided with my six children Horatio S. Fulton, James W. Fulton, T. D. Fulton, E. P. Featherston, A. C. James, and the heirs of D. A. Fulton. I also will that my executor pay to the heirs of my daughter Rachel O. Wheeler one dollar. My son Horatio to have my black boy Joseph to constitute his part of my estate. I appoint T. D. Fulton executor, 18 Feb 1851. A. S. Fulton (X) (LS), Wit: B. T. Wheeler, R. S. Barry, Miles Johnson.

**Pages 228-229**: Will of Margaret Hemphill... To my son James Hemphill all my claim, title, and interest to and in the land I now reside on, and a negro boy named Ellis, my household and kitchen furniture, also the crop hands, my waggon and appendages, my thrasher and gearing, all my live stock, loom and tacklins. I direct my son Jas Hemphill to pay over to my three daughters viz Narcissa Brian, Elizabeth Pursley and Mary Howe, $5 each. I direct that he pay all my just debts and I appoint him executor, 18 Feb 1851. Margaret Hemphill (LS), Wit: Samuel Hemphill, W. J. Good, Myles Smith.

**Pages 229-230**: South Carolina, York District. Will of William Bridges of district aforesaid... I will that all my real estate consisting of the plantation whereon I now reside, about 176 acres to my daughter Lucy Bridges and Cecilia Bridges with the condition that they allow their sister Nancy Husking, the wife of John Husking, the enclosed part of 30 acres I purchased from William Jeffries. All my personal property to my daughters Lucy and Celia Bridges, and that they maintain and support their mother Polly Bridges during her life. I appoint my friends John Morris[?] and William C. Black executors, 10 Aug 1850. William Bridges (LS), Wit: John L. Bridges, James J. Eskridge, Benjamin Talbert.

**Page 230**: Will of Holloway W. Daniel of York District.... To William Benjamin Dunlap $100. The balance of my property to be equally divided one half to my brothers John and William and sister's children, the other half to my wife. I appoint my brother Joseph J. Daniel, exr., 11 Jan 1851. Holloway W. Daniel (LS), Wit: Jas A. Clark, Harvey H. Drennan, Thos W. Sturgis.

**Pages 231-232**: Will of Henry G. Harris Sen, planter, of York District... To my beloved wife Patience Harris all my lands during her natural life and at her death my son H. G. Harris take the Austin Saville place and my son Isham W. Harris take the home place. To my daughter Mary Wilson a lifetime on my Green pond place, it being part of my home place. I will my negro boy Smith to my daughter Elizabeth Wilson now in the State of Georgia or the sum of $400 if she prefer it. I will to my wife the rest of my negroes great and small her lifetime. My sons H. G. Harris and Isham W. Harris jointly to use and occupy my cotton gin and screw. My son Isham go one year to school and it to be paid out of my property left to the use of my wife, and my youngest daughter Eliza Anne shall go two years to school. My son H. G. Harris sole executor, 11 April 1851. H. G. Harris (LS), Wit: Joseph F. White, H. M. Saville, J. B. Saville. Codicil: to my youngest daughter Eliza Anne one negro girl named Martha and a bed and furniture, and to my two sons H. G. Harris and Isham Harris each a bed and furniture, 15 April 1851. [same signature and witnesses].

**Pages 232-233**: South Carolina, York District. Will of Alexander Barnett... To my wife Rachel Barnett the use of my plantation as long as she lives for her benefit and support and my negro woman Philis and girl Amanda, a choice of my horses, a choice cow, buggy, good bed and bedstead, and a lifetime interest in the boy Cubit and woman Nell. To my son James A. my boy Kit and the third choice of horses. To my daughter Margaret C. Wallace my boy Ben and $50 to be paid to her from my daughter Martha Currence, it being part of a girl Louisa[?]. To my son Wm. A. Barnett my boy Sylvanus and the blacksmith tools and my waggon and harness, but it remain on the plantation as long as my wife Rachel lives. To my daughter Martha P. Currence her boy Isaac and a girl Laura and she is to pay $50 to Margaret Wallace. To my daughter Catherine a negro woman Ann and child Violet, second choice of my horses, cow and calf, etc. To my grandchildren Ann Bigger, Alexander and Andrew Bigger, $5 each. I bequeath a year's provisions to be made for my wife and daughter Catherine and the money and notes I have on hand to be divided between Rachel and Catherine, Rachel two thirds and Catherine one third. My property not above named to be equally divided between my wife and six children James, Margaret, Wm., Martha, Eliza Alexander, and Catherine. sons Wm. A. and Hamilton A. Barnett, exrs., 24 Dec 1849. Alexander Barnett (LS), Wit: Jas O. Moore, James A. Wallace, D. M. Watson.

**Pages 234-235**: South Carolina, York District. Will of John McKoy of Yorkville in the district aforesaid... Immediately after my decease my executors do employ some suitable person to work out the hides I may have in tan and to make and finish the same into leather. My executor shall sell all my personal estate to the highest bidder except my finished leather. My executor do sell my finished leather at private sale. To my dear children viz William, Mary, John, Ira, Julia, Elizabeth, and George Andrew, my rail road stock in the Kings Mountain Railroad Company consisting of six shares to be equally divided amongst them. My executor shall sell my house and lot wherein I now reside in Yorkville, my Tanyard tract or piece of land in the vicinity of Yorkville and my tract adj. my tanyard tract, and all my other lands in York District. After the payment of all my just debts, to my wife Sarah, one third part of the remainder of my estate and the remaining two thirds to my dear children viz William, Mary, John, Ira, Julia, Elizabeth, and George Andrew, the share of any coming to the child or children dying before he she or they become of age, shall be equally divided amongst my surviving ones. My executors to send my said children to school to learn the rudiments of a plain education such as reading, writing, and arithmetic at least as far as the rule of three. I appoint my friend James Jeffries executor, 6 Feb 1851. John McKoy (LS), Wit: S. Melton, J. J. Evans, G. W. Lowe.

**Pages 236-237**: South Carolina, York District. Will of Samuel Given of district aforesaid... to my son in law Samuel Ash all my tact of land whereon I now reside with al the improvements and interested with the machine attached, by his paying $2 per acre for said land to the ballance of the legatees. To the three minor children of Samuel C. Given deceased a negro man Jacob and his wife Susan and her increase, hereafter if any), and their five children Hannah, Elvira, Narcissa, Jane and Berry, to be equally divided when Samuel W. Givens arrives to the age of 21 years. To the two youngest children of Louisa Poag deceased each $100 at the death of my wife. To my loving wife Mary Given all my household and kitchen furniture. I also will that Jacob, Susan and their five children remain with her during her life and Nero and his wife Selena and their young child also to e with her. My negro woman Malinda and my girl Susan to my wife Mary Given to be disposed of by her according to her pleasure. To my grandson Samuel J. Walker a negro boy Smith son of Malinda, this being all I allow him out of my estate. To Solomon W. Given my grandson a negro Henry. All the property not disposed of in this will shall be sold at my death and the proceeds to be equally divided into four shares counting $450 already received by Margaret as part of her share, the said four to be received one by Polly Ash, one by Esther Poag, one to be equally divided between the three minor children of Louisa Poag deceased, and the remaining share viz Margaret it is my will that Francis A. Erwin shall with Margaret's share purchase a negro boy at the same for the use of Margaret. I appoint Saml Ash my executor, 22 March 1848. Samuel Given (LS), Wit: James Ash, R. McConnell, Francis A. Erwin.

**Pages 238-239**: South Carolina, York District. Will of James B. Good of York District... To my daughter Margaret J. Good my negro girl Violet and my boy Jiles, the girl to be hers at my decease but the boy to remain on the plantation until my son Milton arrives at the age of 21 years, also one horse with $65, one side saddle, on bed and furniture and one bedstead. To my son James W. Good my boys Patrick and Foster they to remain on my plantation until my son Milton arrives at the age of 21 years, also the choice of the horses that may be on my plantation when he arrives of age and also the cotton that is growing on his patch this year. To my son George M. Good my boy Dan and girl Feeby, they to remain on the plantation until he comes of age, also one horse and saddle such as the others got. To my daughter Elizabeth M. Good my boy Sam and my girl Sarah, one horse worth $65, etc. To my son John H. Good the tract of land on which he now lives called the Nelson tract, also the use of the spring that he now uses water from so long as he may remain there. All the ballance of my real estate to be divided equally between my two sons James W. Good and George M. Wood. I allow my daughter Mary Ann Sherer the first child that my girl Feeby has to be deliver at the age of two years if living. My grandson Robert Brown to be boarded in my family free so long as he may stay. I appoint my son William J. Good, exr., and guardian for the minor legatees, 21 June 1850. James G. Boos (LS), Wit: J. P. Good, B. E. Feemster, J. G. Plexico.

**Page 239**: 18 June 1851. South Carolina, York District. Will of William B. Jackson of district aforesaid... To my wife Mary all my property real and personal including money notes and accounts. It is also my will that when any of my children marry or come of that my wife give them so much as their necessities require and the interest of my family will allow. I appoint my brother James B. Jackson, exr. W. B. Jackson (LS), Wit: Peter McCullum, D. A. McCullum, S. L. Watson. Qualified James B. Jackson as executor July 14th 1851.

**Page 240**: Will of Jedediah Coulter of York District... Whereas 60 acres of the homestead tract of land and my negro man named Nemo[?] (in part) and my negro woman Adaline and her children were inherited by my deceased wife Rachel, I direct the same to be valued by three disinterested men selected by my executors and the same descend to my son Alexander A. Coulter. I bequeath to my wife Julia out of my estate an amount equal to the value of the aforesaid land and negroes. Should there be an excess belonging to my estate the same is to be equally divided between my wife Julia L. Coulter and my son A. A. Coulter. I appoint my friend Saml Rainey, Esquire, my son A. A. Coulter, and my wife Julia executors, 11 Aug 1850. Jedidiah Coulter (LS), Wit: Jno Coulter, Ezekiel Wilson, Elkanah P. Coulter.

**Pages 240-242**: South Carolina, York District. Will of Peter Morgan of district aforesaid being infirm in body and of a good old age.... My executors shall sell all my property at public auction, and divide the amount between my children Mary the wife of Thos Camp, John Morgan, Anthony Morgan, Delilah the wife of Saml Lister, Elias Morgan, Spencer Morgan, Louis the wife of Wm. Griffin, Saml Morgan and Adaline the wife of Noah Duffin. In paying out the legatees my executors shall pay the share of John Morgan to his wife Louisa A. Morgan in trust for the children. My granddaughter Vina the wife of Hiram Mayner shall not receive any part of my estate. The share of my daughter Louisa the wife of Wm. Griffin shall go to her during her natural life and at her death to her children. I appoint my sons John Morgan and Elias Morgan executors 5 June 1849. Peter Morgan (X) (LS), Wit: W. C. Black, L. Nance, T. M. White.

**Pages 242-244**: South Carolina, York District. Will of James Simral... To my beloved wife Jane Simril my negro woman named Hannah and her child Harriet. I will and bequeath the sum of $300 to my [daughter?] Jane Rosinda Simril to be paid to her within two years after the death of my said wife. To my daughter Mary Emeline Simril the sum of $300 to be paid out of the proceeds of the sale of the negroes and the balance of such sale shall be equally divided between my children Andrew B. Simril, William D. Simril, Jane Rosinda Simril and Mary Emeline Simril. My wife should reside on the plantation on which I now live during her natural life and to be maintained and comfortably supported off the proceeds. I bequeath the tract of land whereon I now reside to my sons Andrew B. Simril and William D. Simril jointly. To my son Andrew B. Simril my negro boy named White. To my son William D. Simril my negro boy named Henry and my sorrel filley called Hag. To my daughter Nancy E. Hogue the sum of $200. I bequeath $200 to my grandson Robert Eton Simril eldest son of Miles G. Simril. My executors at my death should sell my tract of land on Catawba River in York District adj.

lands of James M. Harris, John Hart and Jesse Brumfield Esquire, and after the payment of legacies the balance to be equally divided between my children Andrew B. Simril, Wm. D. Simril, Jane Rosinda Simril and Mary Emeline Simril. As to my other children Salina Kendrick, Franklin H. Simril, Miles G. Simril, and Violet D. Simril, I have already done a good part by them and therefore give to them each $1. I appoint my son Andrew B. Simril my sole executor, 15 Sept 1850. James Simril (LS), Wit: James Carrothers, Austin Garrison, John A. Alston. Codicil bequeaths to two grandsons James Franklin Simril and James Benjamin Houge each $150, 2 May 1851. James Simril (LS), Wit: James Carrothers, Austin Garrison, John A. Alston.

**Pages 244-245**: Will of William Hetherington of York District.... To my son Joseph Hetherington all my land & that his brother James Hetherington has a support on the said plantation while he lives. Also to my son Joseph my negro boys Jack & George but George to remain with James Hetherington during his life to assist him in making a support for his family. Also to my son Jos. Hetherington my negro girl Ann. To my daughter Mary McClelland my negro girl Lot with her youngest child Bill. I also bequeath my negro boy Lindsay to my grandson James Hetherington. I also bequeath to my son Joseph Hetherington my two negro boys Daniel & John. To my two daughters Elizabeth Robison & Mary all my household & kitchen furniture to be equally divided between them. I also bequeath to my children all my stock of horses, cows & hogs. I appoint Joseph Hetherington & John McKnight executors, 17 Nov 1844. William Hetherington (X) (LS), Wit: John Hall, William Robison, R. C. McAlla. The will having been established by the court of common pleas, qualified Jos Hetherington as executor 20 Nov 1851.

**Pages 245-246**: Will of Susannah Horsely of the District of York.... To my nephew Richard R. Horseley my tract of land whereon I now reside. To my said nephew R. R. Horseley for the use and benefit of his three children viz Abram Roberts, Nancy Amanda Jane & Susannah Matilda to be equally divided between them all the remainder of my property, dated 30 Dec 1850. R. R. Horsely, executor. Susannah Horsely (X) (LS), Wit: Jas. M. Stewart, J. J. Stewart, John A. Laney. Proved by the oath of James M. Stewart 30 Dec 1851.

**Pages 246-247**: South Carolina, York District. Will of John Workman of said district... To my sister Elizabeth Steele my negro woman called Tina. To John Newton Steele son of N. A. & Elizabeth Steele my silver watch. I desire that N. A. Steele take my land at $8 per acre should he be unwilling to take the land at that price I will that it be sold to the highest bidder. All the balance of property be sold and together with the proceeds of my land be equally divided between my sisters Elizabeth Steele, Martha Steele, Sarah Roach's children & the guardian hereafter appointed for my brother Robert P. Workman. I appoint Newton A. Steele executor. John Workman. Wit: W. P. Thomasson, Saml Steele, R. H. Hope, D. S. Patton. Proved by the oath of Saml Steele and Dr. R. H. Hope 15 Dec 1851.

**Page 247**: Will of Wm. T. Hart of District of York... to my beloved wife Mary all my property real & personal and I appoint her executrix, 25 Nov 1851. Wm. T. Hart (LS), Wit: Thos C. Neal, Wm. Wilson, J. M. Anderson. Proved by the oath of Rev. J. M. Anderson 10 Jan 1852.

**Pages 248-249**: South Carolina, York District. Will of John H. Orr of said district... to my grandchildren Augustus & the other two children of my son James Harvey Orr four negroes viz Elim, Cinda, Leander & Frank. To my granddaughter Mary Adaline Parks $50 in cash. To my daughter Hannah Emily Starr the negroes I have already given her & $50 in cash. To my daughter Eliza A. Steele the following named [negroes] Osborne, Susan, Fanny, Tom and Charity & her choice of two of my best horses. To my son Moses Manlius Orr the following named negroes Jim, old Ben, Young Ben, Old Jane & Young Jane, Aleck, Van Buren, Malinda, Kitten & Kiah. To my said son M. M. Orr all my lands in York District, all my horses, cattle, hogs farming tools, etc. I appoint my said son Moses Manlius Orr executor, 24 March 1832 [sic]. John H. Orr (X), Wit: W. P. Thomasson, R. H. Hope, R. Sadler, W. G. Erwin, Wm. L. Robertson. Proved by the oath of R. Sadler, Wm. G. Erwin, Wm. L. Robertson & R. H. Hope 30 March 1852.

**Pages 249-250**: South Carolina, York District. Will of Ann Yarborough of said district... I desire that my daughter Minerva shall after my death by my sole heir of my estate consisting of the plantation whereon I now live or all my interest in it and also all my cattle, hogs & horses, all furniture, etc. I appoint my son in law Edmund Nickols, executor, 23 July 1839. Ann Yarborough (X), Wit: Ezekiel Fewell, Gilbert Shaw, James N. Fewell. Proved by the oath of Ezekiel Fewell 10 Aug 1852. Qualified Edmund Nickols as executor 10 Aug 1852.

**Pages 250-251**: South Carolina, York District. Will of John Black of York District... To my wife Jane Blake during her lifetime all the balance of my estate real and personal after the payment of my debts with the following exceptions to wit my gin house and gin & running gears and ten acres of land attached thereto and negroes Sciss & Jacob. At the death of my wife all the estate left to her to my daughter Susannah Lominack. My wife and myself are in the possession of the following slaves Rebecca, Rachel and Henry which said negroes when left to my wife in and under the will of her father Thomas K--- the negroes I do not claim as my property and I regard them as limited to my wife. I appoint Thomas K. Mickle executor, 31 May 1848. John Blake (LS), Wit: J. S. Moore, T. A. Moore, S. R. Moore. Proved by the oath of T. A. Moore 14 Sept 1852. Qualified Thomas K. Mickle as executor 14 Sept 1852.

**Pages 251-253**: South Carolina, York District. June 8th 1852. Will of Samuel McCully... To my beloved wife Jane my negro man Charles, my mare Gin with Saddle & Bridle, with all household & kitchen furniture which she brought with her, also my clock and one half of the loom & all that pertains to it, also two cows & calves, with one half of my buggy, and she to have her support from the plantation on which i now reside. To my daughter Frances Patterson a negro boy named George. To my daughter Ervine a negro girl named Mary, a bureau, mare, cow & calf, half of the loom and half of my buggy and to have a support from the plantation as long as she may reside on the same. To my daughter Rebecca Adams a negro boy named Cubit. To my son James a negro boy Henry also my old waggon, and one half of my blacksmith tools. To my daughter Margaret Craig my negro woman Grace and one girl named Amanda. To my sons Samuel and John my negro man Harry, Joseph and Milly together with any children she may have, the plantation on which I now reside subject to the incumbrance above specified. To my sons Samuel & John my waggon and all my farming tools with one half the Blacksmith tools. To my son Samuel a colt and to John my horse called Buck. It is also my will that Hary remain on my place and that he be properly cared for should he lived to be unable to labor. I appoint my son James R. McCully executor and my wife Jane the guardian of my sons Samuel and John. Samuel McCully (LS), Wit: John Riddle, Mary M. Hunter, Samuel L. Watson. Proved by the oath of Rev. S. L. Watson 11 Oct 1852. Qualified James L. McCully as executor 11 Oct 1852.

**Pages 253-254**: Will of William Parks of District of York, planter... to my son in law John Alderson and his wife Mary one half of my tract of land including the improvements and spring of water, where said John now lives on the west side of Steele Creek, and the other half of my said tract to my [son] Joseph Parks including the improvements and spring of water where I now live on the east side of said Creek. To my son Henry Parks $20. To my grandson William Clawson $10 on his arriving to 21 years of age. I appoint my son Joseph Parks and John Alderson executors, 26 Dec 1851. Wit: R. Stewart, A. J. Giles, S. H. Giles, Joseph F. White. Proved by the oath of Robert Stewart 3 Nov 1852. Qualified Joseph Parks as executor 3 Nov 1852.

**Pages 254-255**: South Carolina, York District. Will of Sarah C. Smith. I want all of my just debts paid, my body decently buried, and the remainder of my property to be equally divided between my son Daniel W. Smith and my daughter Sarah C. Smith and my son John T. Smith, and in case that John T. Smith who is now a minor should die before he is of age, then his part to be equally divided between Daniel W. Smith and Sarah E. Smith, 12 Jan 1853. Sarah C. Smith (X) (LS), Wit: John Cheek Smith, Geo W. Kimbell, SC. L. Clawson. Proved by the oath of George W. Kimbell 26 Jan 1853.

**Page 255**: Will of Button Boleyn of District of York... To my grandson John A. Boleyn $2.50 in cash. To my sons and daughters G. R. Boleyn, Jane Boleyn, Elizabeth Boleyn, Joseph Boleyn & John Boleyn, all my ready money, also all my lands, mall my stock consisting of one gray hose, one mule and one colt, also all my cattle, hogs and sheep, also my waggon harness &c., household and kitchen furniture, all aforesaid property shall be divided equally between my sons and daughters except the colt which I allow my daughters Jane & Elizabeth to have. I appoint my friends Wm. McGill, G. R. Boleyn & John Boleyn executors, 25 March 1853. Button Boleyn (X), Wit: W. M. Packard, C. L. H. McCarter, James L. McCarter. Proved by the oath of

Christopher L. McCarter 22 April 1853. Qualified George R. Boleyn and John Boleyn as executors 12 Sept 1853.

**Pages 255-256**: Will of Joseph Black of York District... to my wife Elizabeth Black the whole of my personal and real estate during her natural life and after her deceased I desire that the land be divided commencing at a hickory on McSwain's line and running to the branch the passes nearest my house leaving my son Andrew Black the spring that he now uses water out of, and leave my son Robert Black's house to the left of said line, to Jamieson's line. After the death of my wife, all the balance of my estate be divided between the remainder of my children to wit Pamela Black, Rebecca Smith, Hester Black, Jane Bankhead, Woods Black, Anna Foster. I appoint my wife Elizabeth Black executrix, 11 Feb 1852. Joseph Black (X) (Seal), Wit: Wm. M. Smith, Moses Leathum, Robert Jamieson. The reason that Mr. J. Black made his mark is because that he is palsyed in his hand and cannot write. Wm. M. Smith. Proved by the oath of Robert Jamieson 28 Apr 1853. Qualified Elizabeth Black as executrix 28 April 1853.

**Pages 257-258**: South Carolina, York District. Will of James Bigger of District aforesaid... to my sister Elizabeth Patterson all my lands, my household furniture, and my negro boy named Anthony, and at her death my executor to sell said boy and furniture and divide the proceeds equally between Alexander B. Biggers, Ann E. Biggers, Moses A. Biggers, and Martha C. Maclean. Also the land to be divided amongst them if it can be conveniently done and they agree to the division made, otherwise my executor is to sell the land and divide the proceeds amongst my nephews and nieces above named. To my sister Elizabeth Patterson my gray mare, one third of my stock of cattle, hogs & sheet, and my interest in the Barouche and harness now owned by her and myself. To my niece Anne E. Bigger, my gray Archy horse and my patent lever watch. I appoint my friend G. W. Williams executor, 20 Aug 1850. James Bigger (LS), Wit: E. T. Brandon, S. L. Campbell, Elias McCarter. Proved by the oath of Elias McCarter 29 April 1853. Qualified G. W. Williams as executor 11 May 1853.

**Pages 258-259**: South Carolina, York District. Oct 12th 1852. Will of James McCully of District aforesaid... To my beloved wife Jane my negro woman Dinah, also my bay horse Mike. To my son James C. McCully that part of my plantation on which I now reside lying south east of a line between my residence and Mr. Dulen's house, to a spring in my field known as Reeves spring, Crowders Creek, 100 acres, my horse Boney, one road waggon and one half the farming tools. It is my will that my wife Jane have her support from the plantation and that my daughter be allowed to reside on the same as their home as long as they wish. To each of my children Rebecca, Mary & Jane, one bed and bedding. My cattle to be equally divided between my wife Jane and my children James, Rebecca, Mary and Jane, giving to each an equal portion. To my son James one lot of blacksmith tools. I appoint my son James C. McCully executor. James McCully (LS), Wit: Saml L. Watson, Coffey C. Smith, Martha S. Smith. Proved by the oath of the Rev. Saml L. Watson 20 July 1853. Qualified James McCully as executor 1 Aug 1853.

**Pages 259-260**: South Carolina, York District. Will of Mansfield Gordon... To my son Calvin Gordon the following negroes viz Charles, Jean and her child named Randolph. To my son Green Gordon the following negroes viz Aleck, Wilson & Bob and my bay horse John and 40 bales of cotton now in my possession. To my son David A. Gordon the following negroes viz Phillis, Frank & Sandy. To my son William M. Gordon the following negroes viz Sam, Henry, Eli & Jack. To my daughter Elizabeth A. Gordon the following negroes viz Ben, Margaret, Norris, Tom, Rose, Hannah, Melissa, Dinah, Peter, Violet, Newton & Chloe, and a bay mare named Bat. To my four sons Calvin Gordon, Green Gordon, David A. Gordon & Wm. M. Gordon, all my real estate except as herein after devised. To my two sons Calvin Gordon & Wm. M. Gordon a small tract of land lying near Yorkville purchased by me from John Russel. The remainder of my personal estate not herein bequeathed after the payment of my debts be equally divided amongst all my children. I appoint my son Covin Gordon and Green Gordon, exrs., 17 March 1853. Mansfield Gordon (LS), Wit: G. W. Campbell, Caroline Lowry, J. M. Ross. Proved by the oath of Dr. George W. Campbell 18 Sept 1853. Qualified Green Gordon as executor 19 Sept 1853.

**Pages 260-262**: Will of David S. Patton of York District... I direct that the negro property I obtained by my wife be and remain her absolute property with the three following named negroes excepted, first a negro boy called Isaac having bought him I intend he shall go to my children, the other two exceptions viz Penelope and youngest child at the time of the division of my estate being made and George I also will to my wife's son John Faris, and that John Faris should receive from my estate one horse, saddle and bridle. I also will my negro man Lum to my wife in lieu of the two negroes Charlotte and Harriet. I also will that my wife shall receive one third of my household furniture, the other two thirds to be divided between my son Robert and granddaughter Mary Elizabeth Watson who I wish to live with my wife and negro Blacksmith Peter to work for her support, schooling, etc., as long as she remains with my wife. It is also my will that my wife should have the upper part of my plantation (containing the house where I now reside). At the death or marriage of my wife, my plantation on which I now reside should be divided equally between my son Robert and granddaughter M. E. Watson and that $200 should to each of my son Robert's children to be taken from my granddaughter M. E. Watson's interest in my estate. It is also my will and my son Robert Patton have the use of the lower part of my plantation on the river free of rent. I bequeath to Hetty Strain $50, also the same amount I give to Laura Giles, also to David P. Steele. Plent to be sold and sent out of the state. I ordain my son Robert Patton and Joseph Watson, executors, 2 Feb 1853. D. S. Patton (Seal), Wit: R. A. Springs, C. L. Clawson, D. G. Bennet (X). Proved by the oath of D. G. Bennet 21 Sept 1853. Qualified Robert Patton and Joseph Watson as executors 21 Sept 1853.

**Pages 262-265**: Inventory and valuation of the property and effects of John Springs, 4th July 1853. negroes Wheeler aged 53, Jake aged 21, Dana aged 20, Alfred aged 18, William aged 16, Tom aged 12, John aged 10, Rufus aged 8, Charles aged 5, Joe 1 year old. Nancy aged 39, Jincey aged 13, Margaret aged

3. Shares of stock in a number of companies and banks. Negroes, Lands, Cash & Effects given off to my children: Richard A. Springs, Leroy Springs, Mary L. Davidson, Andrew B. Springs, Sophia C. Myers. A List of property belonging to my wife which I intend her or heirs to have at my death: includes negro man John 30 years of age.

Will of John Springs... I leave to my beloved wife all the property and effects named above. To Unity Church the church of my childhood ten shares in the Charlotte & S. Caroline R. Road. To my wife during her life my portrait and at her death to Sophia C. Myers. To my granddaughter Margaret Springs my mahogany wardrobe, my voltair chair and four office chairs. To Julia Amanda Springs my mahogany bureau, slab and glass and my large tea table. To Mary L. Davidson my French mahogany bedstead, and to JohnS. Davidson my negro girl Jincey. To John S. Myers my small negro girl Margaret. To Eli B. Springs Nancy's youngest boy Joe. To Julia Amanda Springs, Nancy's boy Charles. To my son Richard A. Springs the whole of my lands on the west side of the Catawba River by a plat of survey made by William Campbell, containing 1649 acres more or less with all the negroes I have heretofore given him and also my negro man Wheeler and boy William. To my son Leroy Springs the buck corner house in Charlotte, the lots and appurtenances and my negro boys Tom and John. To my daughter Mary L. Davidson my buck house Dixon plantation in Lincoln County, 889 acres and all the negroes I gave off to her after her marriage and also my negro boy Alfred. To my son Andrew B. Springs the whole of my lands in York District on the east side of the Catawba River, 1658 acres and the whole of the negroes I have given him and my negro woman Nancy and boy David. To my daughter Sophia C. Myers the whole of the land I own on Sugar Creek, Lancaster District, 1226 acres with all the negroes I gave off to her at her marriage and my negro man Rufus and boy Jake. And as it seems to be and has long been the custom of this Country to give the lands to the sons, it is my will in the division of my estate that my sons have each $5000 more than my daughters. To Margaret Springs (alias Bullinger) $800 and to Adaline Springs (alias Flowers) $500 (reputed daughters of Adam A. Springs), and leave it int he hands of Leroy Springs as trustee. Deeming my unfortunate brother Richard C. Springs incompetent from his natural defect of transacting his business, and having at the particular request of his father acted as his agent for nearly 20 years, it is my will and my son A. B. Springs will in like manner act as his agent or trustee. I appoint Andrew B. Springs and Wm. R. Myers, exrs., 19 July 1853. John Springs (Seal), Wit: Hugh M. White, H. H. Colthorp, T. B. Withers. Proved by the oath of Hugh M. White 23 Nov 1853.

**Pages 265-266**: Will of John Ratchford of York District... After the payment of my debts and funeral expenses every item of my estate of which I may die seized both real and personal to my wife Sarah Catharine Ratchford. I appoint my friend and kinsman A. S. Wallace and my [wife] Sarah Catharine Ratchford, exrs., 17 May 1853. John Ratchford (Seal), Wit: J. H. Walker, James M. Pardue. G. H. Letson. Proved by the oath of J. H. Walker 29 Oct 1853.

**Pages 266-267**: South Carolina, York District. Will of Hannah Ellwell... to my dear niece Charlotte J. Reynolds all my property of whatever description real or personal. I appoint Charlotte J. Reynolds executrix, 4 Aug 1853. Hannah Elwell (Seal), Wit: R. S. Moore, W. C. Bennett, J. H. Harris. Proved by the oath of R. S. Moore 27 Dec 1853.

**Pages 267-268**: South Carolina, York District. Will of Henry Carroll of district aforesaid... to my wife Eve all that parcel of land whereon I now reside lying northwest of the Campbell branch also a negro girl named Eliza, one grey mare with all my cattle and sheep, also half of my hogs, at the deceased of my said wife, the parcel of land and the negro girl fall into the possession of my son Zimri. To my daughter Isabella a negro boy Hugh, also the Cherry Cupboard but must pay to my executor $55 to pay my debts. To my son Zimri in trust for my daughter Martha one negro girl named Rachel to be held by him in trust. To my son Zimri the balance of my said plantation with the use of the Campbell house if he wishes. I allow him the note on Briggs, one horse named Mike, also the smith tools, the wagon, etc. I appoint my son Zimri executor 16 Nov 1853. Henry Carrol (Seal), Wit: Wm. B. Pursly, A. P. C. Campbell, Myles Smith. Proved by the oath of Myles Smith and Wm. B. Pursley 20 Dec 1853.

**Pages 268-269**: South Carolina, York District. Will of John Caveny of York District... to my three daughters Mary J. Caveny, Isabella N. Caveny and Nancy S. Caveny, all my real estate consisting of about 120 acres bounded by lands of R. C. Caveny, William Crawford, Joseph Mullinax. My beloved wife Mary Caveny shall have the right and privilege of living on my land and getting her support from the same in common with my three above named daughters. My friends James Caldwell, and John N. Whisonant, executors, 17 Sept 1853. J. Caveny (Seal), Wit: W. C. Black, Thomas H. Mullinax, Wm Crawford, R. C. Caveny. Proved by the oath of Thomas H. Mullinax 1 Dec 1853.

**Pages 269-270**: Will of Joseph Jamieson of District of York... to my son William Jamieson the tract of land he now lives upon which I purchased [from] Joseph Scott, 100 acres, and to my son Joseph Jamieson that part and portion of the plantation or tract I now reside upon on the north side of Bells' Creek including the side where he now resides, also including all his improvement, also including a small piece of wood land on the south side of said Bell's Creek which I in the presence of Joseph Black and others marked out with the express design that he might have the benefit thereof both as to land and timber. To my son Allen Rowe Jamieson the remainder of said tract of land upon which I now reside after the bequest to my son Joseph and my negro boy Humphrey hoping that the said Humphrey will be kindly and tenderly raised and humanely treated according to his station. My negro woman Dorcas be sold and the amount of the sale be equally divided between my said son Allen Rowe Jamieson and my daughter Barbara Chambers, and to my three sons James, John & Milton Jamieson (all absent), the sum of $20 each to be paid at any time after my decease if applied for. to my little granddaughter Eliza Ann Jamieson daughter of Allen R. Jamieson and Nancy

Jamieson my negro bon Amzi. I appoint my son Allen Jamieson and James B. Good exrs., 21 May 1842. J. (Seal), Wit: John G. Brown, John H. Good, William J. Good. Proved by the oath of William J. Good 18 Oct 1853.

**Pages 271-272**: South Carolina, York District. Will of John T. Plexico of district aforesaid... my body to be decently buried and a tombstone erected to my memory. My executor hereafter named shall take charge and control of all property hereafter bequeathed by me to my brother Henry G. Plexico in trust for him during his natural life and at his death to be equally divided among his surviving heirs. To my brother Henry G. Plexico the following lands: viz the plantation known as the Palmer tract also the Penic tract provided brother James relinquishes his claim to said Penic tract, or should James refuse to relinquish his claim, to my brother Henry all my title and interest to the plantation on which we now live, also the negro man Bill the horse Logan, the mule Dave, one sideboard, one bed and furniture (square posts), one folding leaf table, also my interest in the cotton gin and appurtenances with two cares of land around the gin house, also two judgments I hold against on assigned by Crosby to me the other by Steel. To my brother James my right and interest in a negro woman named Mariah provided James G. Plexico relinquished his claim to the negro girl Martha in favor of James E. Plexico (son of James G. Plexico), also all the notes and accounts I hold against my father's estate provided he James does not produce any accounts against my estate for services rendered. I also give to James G. Plexico all my right, title and interest in the plantation whereon we now live excepting two acres around the gin house previously disposed. To sister Jane Latham a negro girl named Eliza. To John T. P. Latham (son of Jane Latham) a negro girl named Adaline. Should John T. P. Latham die before he is 21 years of age, leaving neither brothers or sisters of full blood, then said girl Adaline to revert to John Ager Plexico. To James son of Henry Plexico my watch. To Joseph Plexico my rifle Gun. To J. Edward Plexico a negro girl named Martha provided Brother James do relinquish his claim to said negro, also one bed and furniture (round posts), one bureau & mettle clock. My executors to procure headstones for my father's, mother's, and sisters' Martha & Emeline's graves. I constitute James S. Hemphill, executor, 15 Oct 1852. J. T. Plexico (seal), Wit J. G. Kell, James C. Hicklin, H. N. Hambrick. Proved by the oath of J. G. Kell 7 Nov 1853.

**Pages 272-273**: Will of Elizabeth Burns... all estate after the payment of debts to my four daughters Mary Young, Elvira Burns, Elizabeth Burns, & Jane Burns. I appoint David S. Patton, exr., 10 April 1849. Elizabeth Burns (X) (Seal), Wit: Thomas Thomasson, T. G. Wylie, J. M. Ross. Proved by the oath of Thomas G. Wylie 11 Oct 1853.

**Pages 273-274**: South Carolina, York District. Will of Edward H. Gunning of Yorkville... to Joseph H. Gunning my son now at Wylie L. Harris's &under my care and control, all the remainder of my estate of every description, but if he should die before he arrives of age, then to my sisters to be equally divided between them. I appoint George Steele executor, 28 Jan 1852. E. H. Gunning

(Seal), Wit: R. S. Moore, James Mason, J. M. Ross. Proved by the oath of R. S. Moore 7 Feb 1854.

**Pages 274-275**: South Carolina, York District. Will of William Watson a citizen of the state & district aforesaid... to my beloved wife Margaret T. Watson formerly Parks, for her own use and benefit during her natural life the plantation whereon I now live, 312 acres, my negro man Isaac & his wife Lucy and their son Jesse (Jess), all my horses cattle, stock, household and kitchen furniture, etc. To my son Samuel Davis Watson my negro man Charles. To my son Hugh Parks Watson my negro girl Lucinda and her boy child named Andrew. To my daughter Mary Hopkins Wilson formerly Watson my negro man Ben. To my daughter Elizabeth Ann Hall formerly Watson my negro boy George. To my son William Marion Watson my negro man Joseph (Joe). To my son John Lykin Watson my negro man Thomas (Tom). To my son Andrew McWhorter Watson my negro boy Jim. To my daughter Margaret Jane Watson my negro girl Ellen. To my sons William Marion and John Lykins my said plantation to each an undivided one half after the death of my wife Margaret T. Watson upon the payment by each of #100 into the joint estate to be divided. After the death of my wife my negro man Isaac & his wife Lucy and their son Jesse as well as $200 to be paid into the joint estate as aforesaid by William M. & John L. Watson. To my sons Samuel D., Hugh P., and Andrew Mc. Watson and my daughters Mary H. Wilson, Elizabeth A. Hall and Margaret Jane Watson to be equally divided between them by sale or otherwise. I appoint my sons William M. Watson and John L. Watson, executors, 25 Dec 1852. Wm Watson (Seal), Wit: John C. Wilson, John R. Wallace, John M. Bowen. Proved by the oath of John C. Wilson 24 March 1854.

**Pages 275-276**: South Carolina, York District. Will of Jacob Starns of district aforesaid... to my wife Nancy all my effects both real and personal during her life and at her death to my daughter Mary C. Wylie one negro boy Austin. To my daughter Susan M. Kendrick one negro girl Julia. To my son J. G. two negroes: Ned and Lucy. The balance of my negroes will to the rest of my daughters viz the heirs of Eliza Wilie and E. C. Martin, Minerva Walker, Pamelia McAfee. My plantation to be equally divided with my three sons Montgomery, John and Green. The ballance of my personal property to be equally divided with all my children. I appoint my wife Nancy and T. D. Fulton, exrs., 19 Feb 1853. Jacob Starnes (Seal), Wit: A. C. Webber, J. G. Wood, H. Martin. Proved by the oath of Henderson Martin 10 April 1854.

**Pages 276-277**: South Carolina, York District. Will of Simpson Glass of district aforesaid... I direct that my mother Sarah Glass have her support on the plantation whereon I now reside, also the use of my slave Caroline during her life, also $10 in money. To my brother Alexander Glass the plantation whereon I now reside, also the negro girl Caroline at my mother's death, also one horse (bob) also the Bsmith Tools. I direct that my waggon, the sorrel mare, and mule be sold and the proceeds be equally divided between my three sisters viz Isabella Robinson, Martha Neil & Margaret Wallace. My brother A. Glass have what money I have on hand and I enjoin on him to pay all my debts. I appoint A. Glass, my exr., 10 March 1854. Simpson Glass (Seal), Wit:

John Smith, Zimri Carroll, Myles Smith. Proved by the oath of Myles Smith 10 April 1854.

**Pages 277-278**: Will of Hugh Currence of York District... to my beloved wife Susannah Currence, my negroes Ephraim, Lot, Winney, Charity, Patience and her children Amaline, George, Cynthia & Martha with their future increase, also my waggon & four horses. I also will to my said wife during her natural life all my lands except the Harper tract and except a sufficient of the cleared land for the hands of my daughter Elizabeth Watson to cultivate for the term of two years after my death, then the whole plantation to be my wife's until her death. Also to my said wife my negro girl Emily and at her death to my grandchildren Margaret A. Watson & Wm. D. Watson. To my daughter Margaret Harper the plantation on which she now resides on condition she pays to my estate $180. To my wife the one half of the cash I may have on hand at my death. All the remainder of my personal estate except my negroes be sold and proceeds divided among all my children. All the remainder of my negroes not herein bequeath be equally divided among all my children and for this purpose they are to be appraised and put into lots by my friends Wm. Watson, Duncan McCallum, Andrew Tate & James Wallace. I appoint John D. Currence and George T. Wallace, exrs., 12 Nov 1851. Hugh Currence (Seal), Wit: Martin L. Tate, David M. Campbell, John M. Ross. Proved by the oath of Martin L. Tate 10 April 1854.

**Pages 278-279**: South Carolina, York District. Will of James Carothers... to my daughter Nancy Adaline Erwin $500. To my daughter Martha N. Harris $500. To my sons John Newton & Thomas Milton [Carothers] each a good horse, saddle and bridle, and all my household and kitchen furniture to be equally divided between them. The tract of land whereon I now reside including the Thompson tract in the Wm. Carothers tract to the mill be divided having due regard to quality and quantity so as to make them equal and being so divided I give the home tract to my son Thomas Milton, & the Wm. Carothers tract to my son John Newton, and the Thompson tract to my son James Franklin. I have through proper to give off the small legacies to the legatees above named in order to make them in the first place as nearly equal as possible to my son Samuel D. to whom I have advanced $1000 and to my son William Neely to whom I also have given $1000 and to my daughter Margaret Neely to whom I have given a negro girl and land to the value of $600, and to my daughter Nancy Adaline Erwin to whom I advanced a negro girl and to Martha N. Harris to whom I advanced a negro girl. All the negroes which I may be possessed of at my death should be equally divided between my sons Samuel D., John N., James F., William N., Thomas M., my daughters Nancy Adaline Erwin, Martha N. Harris and the children of my deceased daughter Margaret H. Neely. I appoint my three sons James F., John N. & Thomas M. Carothers, executors, 17 May 1853. James Carothers (Seal), Wit: John A. Alston, Austin Garrison, John Garrison. Proved by the oath of John Garrison 5 April 1854. Qualified James F. Carothers & Thomas M. carothers as executors 5 April 1854.

**Pages 280-282**: South Carolina, York District. Will of John B. Darwin of district aforesaid... I will that all of my gold mines in Union District be kept leased out and the profit be put in as general funds to be divided among all of my children, also all of my gold mines in York District in the same situation. The iron stock I want kept as general funds till it can be sold at par. AS to my wife Gilly Darwin if she should change her situation in life that is get married, my will is that all of my property be appraised (that is I have not willed away) and she take a child's part in lieu of her dower. As to my son James C. Laree[?] I have his receipt for $1385.73 which amount I want take out of his share of my estate. As to my son in law David A. Chamblain, I have his receipt for $1705.06 which amount I want take out of his share of my estate. As to my son in law Abraham Guiton, I have his receipt for $1319.60 which amount I want take out of his share of my estate. I also give to my daughter Nancy M. Guiton my negro girl Patience about seven or eight years old to be appraised at the time she receives her and that amount be taken out of her share of my estate. As to my son John W. Darwin, I have his receipt for $1964.33 which amount I want take out of his share of my estate. I have also given him a tract of land that I bought from Wm. Fearnell lying in Union District on the Pinckney road, 275 acres on waters of Mitchells Creek adj. Wm. S. Howell, Wm. Ison[?], Col. Clowney, H. F. Means. I want my land in Union District (the gold mines excepted) to be equally divided between my two sons Elnathan D. & Robert T. Darwin, my son Elnathan to have the upper end of said tract. I also give to my son Elnathan D. my negro boy named Henry[?] about 16 or 17 years old. I also give to said Robert my negro boy Amzi about 15 years old. As to my daughter Sarah R. Smith, wife of James A. Smith, I have her receipt for $1285 which amount I want take out of her share of my estate. To my four sons Martin V. and Presley P. and Elssly S. and James M. Darwin all my tract of land that is the home tract and also the Childers tract on Wolfs Creek. My son James M. to have the lot about the dwelling. Also to my son Martin V. my negro boy George about 13 years old. I also give to my son Presley P. my negro boy Lewis about nine years old. I also give to my son Elsey S. my negro boy named Calhoun about 5 years old. I appoint David A. Chamblain, Peyton B. Darwin & Elnathan D. Darwin, executors, 23 Oct 18--. J. B. Darwin (Seal), Wit: William Mitchell, Nancy M. Wilkinson, George M. Hamrick.

The executors named in said will having filed their petitions to be permitted to swear and examine witnesses for the published and confirming thereof and all persons entitled to distribution if decd had died intestate, 20 May 1854. [Will was confirmed.]

**Page 283**: Will of Isaac McFadden... to my beloved wife Nancy one negro boy Shadrach, one negro girl Sarah & one horse, any one that she may choose, my barouche & harness, two beds & bedsteads, her bureau, and $500 in cash. To my son William P. McFadden one negro man Albert, man Lewis, woman Emily & child Jane. To my daughter Elizabeth S. Dunlap one negro man Daniel, woman Charlotte, one boy Washington, one boy Edmond, one girl Condy, one girl Isabella, one girl Rine. To my daughter Amelia G. hope one negro man Henry, one woman Nancy, one boy Ned, one boy John, one woman Alsey. I appoint my son Wm. P. Mcfadden, exr., 19 Sept 1853. Isaac McFadden (LS), Wit: William Wylie, O. G. Stewart, Wm. Wilkinson. Proved by the oath of O. G. Stewart 30 June 1854. Qualified Wm. P. McFadden as executor 30 June 1854.

**Pages 283-284**: Will of Rufus J. Withers... all my estate to my brother Walter C. Withers, consisting of my tract of land on York District about 7 miles east of east of Yorkville on the waters of Little Allison Creek contracted for by myself and said brother Walter from Alexander McIlwain, and to which said Walter is entitle to one half, also notes and accounts on various persons in both North & South Carolina, also any tools. I appoint my said brother Walter C. Withers, exr., 12 June 1854. Rufus J. Withers (Seal), Wit: Wm. Johnston, John C. Hardister, William B. Lay. Proved by the oath of Wm. B. Lay 8 July 1854. Qualified Walter C. Withers executor 8 July 1854.

**Pages 284-285**: South Carolina, York District. Will of Mary Laughridge of district aforesaid... to my living children James, Samuel, Mary McWhorter & Margaret L. Laughridge, all my real and personal estate to be equally divided amongst them with the exception of the share now left to my beloved daughter Mary McWhorter who is now very low, which share in case of her death I give to her two children Margaret Ellen McWhorter and Mary Laughridge McWhorter. I appoint my beloved son Samuel Laughridge executor, 23 June 1854. Mary Laughridge (X), Wit: A. S. Wallace, R. E. Gettys, R. J. Davison. Proved by the oath of R. E. Gettys 7 July 1854. Qualified Samuel Laughridge executor 7 July 1854.

**Pages 285-286**: South Carolina, York District. Will of Mary Givens of said district being advanced in years.... to my granddaughter Louisa J. Poag my negro girl Susan with her issue if any that she may have living at my death, said negro girl to remain in the possession of my son in law Samuel Ash until said Louisa J. Poag marries or becomes of age. If said Louisa J.Poag dies & leaves no issue, then the Susan and her issue be appraised and one half the appraised value belong to my granddaughters Mary H. & Jane E. Poag and the other half divided amongst my three granddaughters Mary M., Louisa Ann & Eleanor S. Ash. The remainder of my estate be divided amongst Mary Ash, Esther Poag, Margaret Sadler, Samuel Walker, Mary H. Poag & Jane Elizabeth Poag. I appoint my son in law Samuel Ash, executor, 27 Jan 1852. Mary Givens (X) (Seal), Wit: R. M. McConnell, Robert Ash, G. W. Williams. Proved by the oath of Ruben McConnell 17 Aug 1854.

**Pages 287-289**: South Carolina, York District. Will of John Chambers of district aforesaid... To my beloved wife Margaret all my real estate with all my personal property during her natural life. As soon as practicable after the death of my wife Margaret bring to public sale all my estate and personal property including negroes, horses, etc., bank stock Rail Road stock, and the proceeds arising therefrom to be equally divided between my children viz Alexander H., John, Elizabeth Ann Spain, James S., Mary S. McElmoyl, Serena L. Davis, Ptolemy P., Margaret J. Patterson, Mijamin W., Elvira J. Kuykendal & Benjamin W. Chambers, except that of the share of Mary S.

McElmoyl, one fourth to my granddaughter Margaret, wife of John A. Davidson, also $50 to be deducted being advanced to Daniel McElmoyl husband of said Mary S. McElmoyl by giving him ten acres of land at $5 per acre, also out of the share to my daughter Elvina J. Kuykendal the sum of $275 to be deducted the same having been advanced to her and S. J. Kuykendal by gift of the girl Emeline. I appoint my son Mijamin & son in law Samuel J. Kuykendal, exrs., 29 April 1851. John Chambers (LS), Wit: John Steedman, James A. Scott, Y. J. Bell. Codicil specifies that the executors note to separate by sale the boy Youngue from his wife Peggy but they be sold together. Also my girl Margaret and all her living children under six years old be sold to the same purchaser, 23 May 1851. (Same wit.) 2nd Codicil... since Margaret wife of John A. Davidson has died, the said one fourth part back to said Mary McElmoyl, 6 Feb 1854. Wit: James A. Scott, John Steedman, John McClennan. Will and both codicils proved by the oath of John Steedman 9 Sept 1854.

**Pages 289-300** [error in pagination; skips from pages 289 to 300]: South Carolina, York District. Will of J. A. Campbell of said district... To my son S. L. Campbell a tract of land lately surveyed and laid off being the southwestern part of my old tract adj. lands of Elias & G. A. McCarter. To my son Wm. E. A. Campbell a tract of land known as the Laurence tract with an addition from my corner on Campiun branch, south of my black smith shop. To my son A. P. C. Campbell a tract of land say south eastern part, near the main road with the York to Currence Road to J. K. Armstrong's line, Emelina Barnett's land, Hunter's. The remainder of my land I allow for D. M. Campbell. In case any of my sons should die leaving no lawful descendants, the portion of land by me assigned them to be equally divided among my surviving sons. To my daughter Mary J. Jackson a negro girl named Creesa. To my daughter C. L. Wallace a negro girl named Harriet. To my daughter C. A. Campbell a negro girl named Amy. To S. L. Campbell a negro named Nolen. To my wife Elizabeth a negro woman named Hannah but all the descendants of Hannah from this time be equally between my wife Elizabeth & son William. I allow Mark for my son William. I allow Miles for A. P. C. Campbell. I allow the household & kitchen furniture with the Loom for my wife Elizabeth, and the barouche. The waggons & farming utensils for William and my wife and the smith tools for Samuel. Dated 19 Jan 1854. J. A. Campbell (Seal), Wit: Jefferson Black, J. Blair Hunter, Myles Smith. Codicil. Whereas a negro child has of late been added to my slave family, the child Adaline fall to and be the property of my wife Elizabeth, 2 June 1854. J. A. Campbell (Seal), Wit :Mary Jane Barnett, J. Leander Adams, Myles Smith. Will and codicil proved by the oath of Myles Smith 8 Aug 1854.

**Page 301**: South Carolina, York District. Will of James McCants of district aforesaid... After paying debts, the remainder of my property to my wife Tirzah for her natural life or widowhood and at her death the whole of the property real and personal be sold and the money arising therefrom be divided between my three children Henry Matthew, Jesse Franklin & Margaret Jane. If any of my children should die before they attain the age of 21 years, their portion go to the survivors. I appoint Thomas W. Sturgis, executor, 31 July

1854. James McCants (Seal), Wit: Henry H. Drennan, George M. McCants, Henry C. Hudson. Proved by the oath of Henry C. Hudson 21 Aug 1854. Qualified Thomas W. Sturgis as executor 21 Aug 1854.

**Pages 301-303**: South Carolina, York District. Will of James C. Thomasson of district aforesaid... After my debts are paid, the balance of my estate be kept together for the joint support of my wife and maintenance and education of my children, until the youngest child shall arrived to the age of fifteen years, or until the decease of my wife. If my executors should deem it more advantageous, then sell the lands which for the benefit of my family. As my children severally arrive to the age of twenty one years or marry, my executors give to them such portions of my estate as can be best spared. At the death of my wife my estate be partitioned among my children. I appoint my wife my executrix and Hiram C. Thomasson & Joseph Miller my brother and brother in law executors, 9 Aug 1854. James C. Thomasson. Wit: Jerome C. Miller, D. H. Thomasson, W. J. Clawson. Proved by the oath of Dr. D. H. Thomasson 22 Aug 1854. Qualified Jane S. Thomasson & Joseph Miller as executors 22 Aug 1854.

**Pages 303-304**: Will of James Stewart of District of York, planter... My wife Nancy do live and remain on my plantation and that all my property both personal and real remain subject to her management and control during her natural life and assisted by my two sons John Stewart and William Stewart. On the event of any of my negroes becoming uncontrollable by my said wife Nancy, she is empowered to make sale of such stubborn and uncontrollable slaves or slave. At the death of my wife my two sons John and William shall take charge of my property and they do raise and educate all of my young and uneducated children in the same manner and style as I would have done myself. As my young children may arrive at the age of 21 years or marriage, they shall have an equal portion of my estate. My son Josiah Stewart who is now at Davidson College continued and go through his College course and that my son John do sell that my said son be furnished with money until he shall get through at College. To my son William Stewart absolutely my Perry plantation and my two negroes Rose and Taylor and every species of property that he has on said plantation exception the one half of the stock of hogs which are to be returned to the plantation on which I now live. To my son John Stewart 100 acres of land to be taken off the lower end of my Spears plantation and he is to pay one half of the value of said land to his brother > J. Stewart. My son John do take my fourth part of the saw and grist mills at Kings bottom, Lancaster District, and sell to educate the younger children. I will that J. J. Watson keep and retain the 13 or 16 acres of land which I had formerly gave him on the west side of the Blackberry branch. I will that my son William has received from me all that I new feel able to give him. My son John to take my Island land lying in the Catawba river. I will that there be no public sale of my estate at any time. Dated 15 June 1854. James Stewart (LS), Wit: J. J. White, Smith Patterson, J. F. White. Codicil stating that my scholarship in Davidson College to remain undrawn and to be used for the benefit of my grandsons, also my stock in Charlotte Rail Road, 16 June 1854. James Stewart (LS), Wit: J. F. White, J. M. Morrow, Wm. C. Doby. Proved by the oath of John J. White 7 Sept 1854. Qualified Nancy Stewart as executrix 7 Sept 1854.

**Pages 304-305**: Will of David M. Watson... My interest in the store belonging to the firm of D. M. Watson & Co. shall be sold during the ensuing winter & the proceeds of the sale with my interest in the notes & accounts of the same firm, and all notes and accounts otherwise due shall be collected as early as practicable and the same after payment of debts shall be loaned out by my executors. My farm with all its stock &c shall be continued and the proceeds be used in the support of my family to the education of my children. My dear wife and children shall each have an equal share of my entire estate and whenever as my children shall come to the age of 21 years or my daughters shall marry, my executors shall pay to each a sum not exceeding $1000. Miss Emily Watson my dear sister & my niece M. E. Bigger shall live in my house free of board for their kind attentions to my children so long as they remain unmarried. I appoint my brother in law J. D. Currence & my wife executors, 27 July 1854. David M. Watson (LS), Wit: A. L. Choat, Richard Gillespie, John L. Watson. Proved by the oath of A. L. Choat 8 Sept 1854. Qualified John D. Currence & Mary J. C. Watson as exors. 8 Sept 1854.

**Pages 305-306**: Will of Philemon Shurley of District of York, farmer... The tracts I gave to my sons Absalom Shurley and Eli Washington Shurley be valued at $60 each, which amount is to be deducted from their portion in the further division of the remainder of my estate. The remains of my estate after debts are paid be divided into eight equal shares, that one portion fall to my wife Lucretia Shurley, one to my daughter Melinda Lock wife of Len Lock, one portion to my daughter Lucinda Bennett, one portion to my daughter Lucretia Shurley, ton portion to my daughter Emmeline Ferguson, one portion to my son Absalom Shurley $60 to be deducted, one portion to my son Eli Washington Shurley $60 to be deducted, the remaining portion to be divided between my two grandchildren viz William C. Schooley son of my daughter Elvira Schooley deceased and George W. Sturges son of my daughter Barbara Sturges deceased. I appoint Franklin D. Scholey and my son Eli Washington Shurley, exrs., 5 July 1854. Philemon Shurley (Seal), Wit: John D. Brown, William B. Sims, J. A. Hill. Proved by the oath of J. A. Hill 26 Sept 1854. Qualified Eli W. Shurley as executor 26 Sept 1854.

**Pages 306-307**: South Carolina, York District. Will of John G. Kell of district aforesaid... To my beloved wife Elizabeth S. all my property real and personal to be subject to her management until my youngest child is of age, or during her widowhood, to support the family and education the younger children. When youngest child is of age, half of my personal estate be sold & divided equally amongst my children if my wife is at that time a widow, I give to her all the residue of my property to be hers during her natural life and at her death to be equally divided between my children. I hereby authorize my executor to make a deed of transfer of the following tract of land to Jas. S. Hemphill... on the Quinns road. I appoint Jas. S. Hemphill executor 2 Dec 1854. J. G. Kell (LS), Wit: S. Wright, John S. Crosby, Robert Nelson. Proved by the oath of John S. Crosby 23 Dec 1854. Qualified James S. Hemphill executor 28 Dec 1854.

**Pages 307-309**: South Carolina, York District. Will of Robert Manning of York District, planter on Broad River & Kings Creek.... to my beloved wife Mary Ann Manning all this tract of land where I now live with the household and kitchen furniture and farming utensils and seven negroes: Charles, Dick, Sarah, Jackoles, Pickens, Margaret, Ann, to hold during her natural life then to go to my six sons: Joseph B. Manning, Thomas W. Manning, Robert L. Manning, John M. Manning, William C. Manning & Commodore P. Manning. I give to my daughter Sarah C. Hill one negro girl named Vina. To my daughter Jane C. Kennedy one negro girl named Eliza. To my daughter Levina R. Carpenter one negro girl named Susy. To my daughter Mary M. Manning one negro [not named]. I leave five negroes to be sold at my death by my executor with all notes, money and debts to pay my just debts. The negroes to be sold are Lewis, Suckey, Giles, Pickens, Jim. To my wife Mary all my stock of every kind during her life then to be equally divided between my six sons and my interest in a tract of land of Thomas Manning decd on Bogan's branch to be equally divided between my six sons. I give to Alexander Hill my son in law $1. I give to Madison Hambright my son in law $1, also John Kennedy $1, also to Isaac Carpenter $1. I appoint Joseph B. Manning sole executor, 15 __ 1854. Robert Manning (LS), Wit: R. W. Hughs, Eli McDaniel, Morgan Martin. Proved by the oath of R. W. Hughs and Eli McDaniel 30 Nov 1854. Qualified Jos. B. Manning as executor 30 Nov 1854.

**Pages 309-310**: South Carolina, York District. Will of Wm White being on a bed of sickness... my land be sold & the proceeds thereof go to pay all my lawful and just debts likewise my stock, cattle & hogs. My two daughters F. L. and A. V. White do have two beds apiece, my son J. H. White one bed & cupboard, my [son?] J. D. White one large falling leaf table, my daughter F. L. White one bureau, A. V. White my slab. My two daughters F. L. & A. V. White do have my negro girl Polly. My son J. H. White do take care of the old man Antony. I leave my son J. H. White to executor this will, 23 Jan 1855. Wm. White (LS), Wit: J. J. White, J. F. Harris, Jas. H. White. Proved by the oath of John J. White 2 Feb 1855. Qualified James H. White as executor 1 Feb 1855.

**Pages 310-311**: South Carolina, York District. Will of Eleanor Webb of York District... To my sister Nancy Stuart my plantation where I live with all the things belonging to it, and all my negroes except Daniel. I will him to be sold. I will to my sister Nancy Stuart's children $300. I will to Sarah Watson's children $300. I will T. W. daughter Elizabeth Cooper $300. I will sister Sarah Dier $30. I will Margaret Patton one cow & calf if there should be any money left from the sale of the boy Dan. If there be any money left I will it to be divided between N. S. children. Eleanor Webb (LS), Wit: J. D. White, J. P. Stuart, Jos. J. Watson. Proved by the oath of Joseph J. Watson 15 March 1855. Qualified Nancy Stewart as executrix.

**Pages 311-312**: Will of Mary Miller... my brother Robert & sister Ibby shall have and hold my negro boy George for their use and at the death of the survivor, to my nephew James Miler son of the widow Betsy. I will my other property to belong to my brother Robert and sister Ibby, and at the death of the survivor to be equally divided between the daughters of the widow Betsy Miller except a feather bed which I give George. I will that James Miller erect a tombstone over my grace. Some time since I gave a cow & calf to Nancy who has been a faithful servant, I do not wish any one to take said cow & calf from Nancy. I appoint Joseph Black & Wm. J. Bowen executors [not dated]. Mary Miller. Wit: J. Monro Anderson, Alexr Fewell, R. F. Anderson. Proved by the oath of J. M. Anderson 21 Feb 1855. Qualified Joseph Black as executor 21 Feb 1855.

**Pages 312-313**: South Carolina, York District. Will of Edward Feemster... The whole of my property both real and personal be sold and that the proceeds be divided as follows viz, one third to my wife Anna, and the balance equally amongst my six children Bond E.Feemster, Nancy R. Hood, Margaret L. Goode, Emeline N. Plexico, Mary Ann Goode & Catherine Feemster. I appoint my son B. E. Feemster executor, 31 Oct 1854. Edward Feemster (LS), Wit: Joseph Feemster, E. G. Feemster, Saml W. Boyd. Proved by the oath of E. G. Feemster 27 Nov 1854. Qualified Dr. B. E. Feemster executor 29 Nov 1854.

**Pages 313-314**: South Carolina, York District. Will of Mary Emeline Simril... To my sister Jane Rosinda Simril all my interest mentioned in my father's will and also my bed, bedstead and clothing and bureau. I appoint my brother F. H. Simril my sole executor, 5 Feb 1854. Mary E. Simril (LS), Wit: Mark Garrison, P. A. Garrison, J. T. Mathews. Proved by the oath of J. T. Mathews 11 Oct 1854.

**Pages 314-315**: Will of Mary Brumfield of the District of York... to my son in law Thomas Whitesides one half of my plantation whereon I now reside including the improvements, and at his death to be equally divided between his sons James, John & Austin Whitesides. To my son George Brumfield all my negroes viz Peggy, Stephen, Amy, Leander & Bonnaparte, on condition that he pay to my executor $1200. My executor shall sell the balance of my land after setting off Thomas Whitesides's portion. My executor to pay to my daughter Violet Neely $600, and to each of my daughters Harriet Daniel & Elizabeth Tharp $350, and the balance of my estate equally between my daughters Elizabeth, Harriet, Violet& Mary. I appoint J. M. Anderson executor, 6 Oct 1854. Mary Brumfield (X) (LS), Wit: W.J. Rice, R. P. White J. Brem. Proved by the oath of David J. Rice 14 Dec 1854. Qualified J.M. Anderson as executor 14 Dec 1854.

**Pages 315-316**: Will of Henry Smith... to my daughter Amanda daughter of Elizabeth Lowry living in Mississippi $100 when she marries or becomes of age. My executors sell all of my property both real and personal and that my wife Jane Smith be allowed to have her choice the one third of a child's part of all the balance. I appoint my brother James Smith, John Smith & Ryton B.

Darwin my executors, 14 Sept 1854. Henry Smith (LS), Wit: Emsley Osborn (X), Cynthia P. Corry, Eleanor M. Lowry. Proved by the oath of Emsley Osborn 11 Oct 1854.

**Pages 316-317**: Will of George Allen of District of York, 1st November 1854... to my beloved wife Rebecca Allen all my lands, stock, farming utensils, household & kitchen furniture, not touching anything belonging to my two daughters Mary and Rebecca Allen. At the death of my beloved wife and after her debts are paid, to my daughter Jane Henry $10 and to my daughters Mary & Rebecca Allen my land & all the residue of my effects. I appoint Rebecca Allen executrix. George Allen (X) (LS), Wit: J. S. Jones, John Campbell, Joseph Black. Proved by the oath of James S. Jones 13 Jan 1855. Qualified Rebecca Allen executrix 13 Jan 1855.

**Pages 317-320**: Will of William McElwee of York District... to my son John McElwee now of the State of Mississippi all the written obligations I hold on him. To my daughter Rebecca McElwee my bay mare. To my son Jonathan N. McElwee my hat, saddle, overcoat. To my daughter Naomi Kennedy $300 in cash. To my granddaughter Martha Caldwell (daughter of Gabraith Caldwell) $100 in cash. To my granddaughters Rosanna Lesley, Emmeline McGill & Isabel Adams (wife of John Adams) $500 in cash, each one to receive $167.66 2/3. My executors shall pay to my son James McElwee $100 to be by him paid over in five equal installments to the officiating minister of Bethany Church as my stipend. To my daughter Agnes McElwee the tract of land on both sides Clarks Fork known as the Galloway tract (the other part of the tract I have conveyed to my daughter Rachel McGill wife of John McGill). I bequeath to my daughter Agnes McElwee the following negroes to wit Nelly, Ann, Charlotte and her six children Caroline, Sarah, Ann, Sam, Tom, and Alfred and Ross, Jim and Miles. Also to my daughter Agnes McElwee my sorrel horse, one bay horse, and two dark bay horse colts, also half of my cows, sheep & hogs, one half of all the grain and provender, also one clock, one cupboard, and the contents of the said cupboard as usually furnished, one half dozen of table & one half dozen of tea spoons, also one half dozen sitting chairs, one bureau, one pair of fire dogs, shovel and tongs, two looking glasses, one large spinning wheel, three beds, bedsteads and all their furniture, one falling leaf table, one large chest, one set of knives and forks, and one half of all my books. If she should die not leaving any children, then this property to any brothers and sisters and the children of any deceased brother or sister residing in this state at the time of her death. To my son James McElwee, the plantation whereon I now reside, 700 acres known as the home tract, also the tract known as the Jonathan Newman tract adj. my house tract, 367 acres, and adj. lands of William Crawford, James Biggers. To my son James McElwee, the following negroes Jack, Grace, and Joe, also one mule, two road wagons, one set of blacksmith tools, one still & vessels, one rifle gun, one shot gun, the one half of my cows, sheep, hogs, desk and bookcase, half of my books, one cloak, one other desk or tall boy, my sitting chairs, half of my grain and provender. To my sons Jonathan N. McElwee & James McElwee my five shares in the Kings Mountain Rail Road Company. To my daughter Rachel McGill, wife of John McGee, my one share of stock in the

King Mountain Iron Company and $50 in cash. Remained to be divided between my legal heirs with the exception of John McElwee, Jonathan N. McElwee, William Meek McElwee, James McElwee and Rachel McGill, who shall not receive any part thereof. I appoint my sons Jonathan N. McElwee and James McElwee executors, 15 June 1853. William McElwee (LS), Wit Wm. Black, John V. Whisonant, J. L. Crawford. Proved by the oath of John Whisonant 23 Nov 1854. Qualified Jona. N. McElwee and James MCElwee as exors 23 Nov 1854.

**Pages 320-322**: Will of Richard Gillespie... To my beloved wife Elizabeth E. Gillespie all my estate after payment of debts to remain with her for the special use to raise, support & educate my children, and after any one of my children comes of age and wish to leave their mother, then my executors shall call some three of their good and discreet neighbors to their assistance to appraise any property their Mother may thing proper to give them and their shall be a record of the same kept until the youngest child comes of age or marries and then what remains to be equally divided according to what had been given off. I appoint my wife Elizabeth and her brother John R. Hall and Peter Garrison, exrs., 17 Nov 1854. Richard Gillespie (LS), Wit: William J. Faris, Jas. C. Hicklin, Ezekiel Fewell. Proved by the oath of W. J. Faris. Qualified Elizabeth E. Gillespie, John R. Hall, and Peter Garrison as executors 8 Dec 1854.

**Pages 322-323**: Will of John Scott.. My daughter Mary Scott pay my funeral expenses and just debts out of such property as I may will her. To my son William Scott one dollar in cash. To my son John Scott two thirds of my plantation to be laid out on north side of my plantation so as to give him the house where he lives and all the out buildings. To my daughter Mary Scott the balance or one third of my plantation to be laid out so as to give her the house where I live and all the out buildings and also my stock of cows, hogs and other loose property. To my granddaughter Sarah Jane now living with me a living out of that part of the plantation which I have willed to my daughter Mary Scott, 3 Aug 1854. Wit: L. H. Massey, Thomas Wylie, W. McFadden. The testator appointed his son John Scott the executor of this will. Proved by the oath of Wm. P. McFadden 6 Dec 1854. Qualified John Scott Jr. as executor 8 March 1855.

**Pages 323-325**: South Carolina, York District. Will of Hugh Harris of district above mentioned... to my wife Mary Harris all the property of every description that she brought with her at her marriage, viz negroes, horses, cattle, household and kitchen furniture, also to have full & free possession of my house except some of the rooms for my children, a comfortable support from my plantation during her life, my carriage & harness and all stock and stools, and it is my further wish that my negro man Solomon should be left on the plantation to manage the farm for my wife. To my eldest son John L. Harris a part of the plantation on which I now reside at the death of my wife, one horse, saddle & bride and my sett of mahogany dining tables. To my son Hugh C. Harris one half the value of the plantation on which he now resides containing 267 acres but as he had paid me the different in the half value he does not owe me now anything for the whole plantation and it is therefore all given to him. I give to my grandson Samuel Harris Orr, son of my deceased daughter Martha M. Orr, $500. To my son Robert Harris a horse, saddle & bridle, my negro boy Sam, one bed & furniture, and the tract of land on the east side of the Nation Ford Road on which William Gibbons & Washington Boatwright now resides together with a cow & calf. To my daughter Eleanor Jane, one hose, saddle and bridle, one bed & furniture, one negro girl of her own choice, one bureau and all the balance of the plantation or tract of land lying west of the Nation Ford Road, on which free Suck and Chandler now live, together with a cow & calf. To my daughter Eliza Isabella one horse & saddle & bride, one bed & furniture one bureau of equal value as the one Ellen may get, one negro girl of her own choice, one cow & Calf, & the balance of the plantation on which I now reside. I wish that my mills and the plantation on which they are located my lands in Indiana and sufficiency of the unwilled property be sold to pay all debts against my estate. The property given to my children should be appraised so that each child should receive as near as equal except my grandson Samuel H. Orr whose legacy is specific except as to the residue and remainder. It is my wish that each of my give mentioned children should realize the sum of $1500 each, that in the case I give the sum of $300 to my son Hugh C. Harris, William Boyce & James Boyd in trust for the sole use of Lower Steel Creek Church the interest arising from said sum to go to the support of the preaching of the Gospel at said church. I give my library to my several legatees to be equally divided between them, Saml H. Orr if he arrives at the age of 18 year to receive a full share with the others. I give my executors full power to sell all of my property at private sale especially the negroes avoiding the separation of man and wife as much as possible. I appoint my three sons John L., Hugh C. & Robert H. Harris, exrs., 9 Jan 1855. Hugh Harris (LS), Wit W. H. Neal, Jas. Boyd, Thos. P. Greer. Proved by the oath of James Boyd 18 Jan 1855. Qualified Hugh C. Harris & Robt Harris as executors 18 Jan 1855.

**Pages 325-326**: Will of John Brumfield... to my neice Mary C. Whitesides $450. To my neice Margaret E. Whitesides $450. To my nephew John B. Whitesides $100. To my nephew Austin S. Whitesides $100. To my brother in law Thomas Whitesides my bay horse Charley. To my neice Frances Neely $250. To my brother George M. Brumfield $250. To my sister Violet Neely my black mooley cow and calf and whatever may be left of my estate. I appoint Thomas Whitesides my executor, 29 Aug 1854. John Brumfield (LS), Wit: W. P. McFadden, F. J. Rice, J. C. Whiteside. Proved by the oath of D. S. Rice 11 Oct 1854. Qualified Thomas Whitesides as executor 11 Oct 1854.

**Pages 326-328**: So Carolina, York District. Will of James Wood, planter, of district aforesaid... I lend unto my beloved wife Polly Wood all my estate during her life or widowhood. If my said wife should marry, I give unto her four choice negroes and the third of my plantation where I now live & at her death to be equally divided among my children. I give her one good horse, saddle & bridle with $120, three cows & calves, also my hogs & sheep, after my children have received their share or shares. I give to my oldest daughter Nancy Minerva Mooney $1532 which she has heretofore received. I give to the heirs of Jacob Pinckney Wood my eldest son $780 which he has heretofore received. I give to my second son John S. L. Wood $1140 which he has heretofore received. I give to my daughter Elizabeth Frances Elvaline Ross $1037.84 which she has heretofore received. I give to my son Joseph George Wellington Wood a tract of land on the waters of Thickity in Spartanburg District which I value to be worth $1246.25, a suit of clothes worth $40, one bed & furniture which I value at $75, one cow & calf at $12.50, which I authorize my executors to give him when he comes of age or marries. I also authorize my executors to give to my daughter Mary Rippy Wood one likely negro girl worth $600, one horse, saddle & Bridle at $95, two cows & calves at $25, one bureau at $25, two beds & furniture at $50, one walnut table at $4, a wedding & infair suit, and also $240 cash whenever she become of age or marries. I authorize my executor to give to my daughter Nancy F. Susannah Dill Wood one likely negro girl by the name of Rose and one horse, saddle & bridle at $95, two cows & calves at $25, one bureau at $20, two beds & furniture at $50, one walnut table at $3, a wedding and infair suit, and also $240 cash whenever she becomes of age or marries. To the heirs of Jacob Pinckney Wood deceased Jacob Ferdinand & James Pinckney Wood $3450 each on arriving at 21 years of age. I appoint my wife Polly Wood executrix and James Madison Wood and my son Joseph George Wellington Wood my executor when he comes of age, dated 13 Jan 1852. James Wood (LS), Wit: Jesse Blanton, Peter Seapaugh, Bird Martin. Proved by the oath of Peter Seapaugh & Bird Martin 13 Oct 1854. Qualified Mary Wood & James M. Wood as executors 13 Oct 1854.

**Pages 328-330**: South Carolina, York District. Will of Elizabeth Patterson of the district aforesaid... I give to nieces Jane E. & Margaret E. & my nephew James L., children of my deceased brother William M. Bigger, the sum of $300 to be equally divided amongst them. To my nephew & nieces James, John, Martha & Amelia Neagle, children of my deceased sister Mary Ann Neagle, $300 to be equally divided amongst them. I bequeath one feather bed to my niece Mary E. Bigger. My plantation on Allison Creek be sold and the proceeds be equally divided between Alexander B. Bigger, Moses A. Bigger, Ann E. Bigger & Martha E. McLean. To my neice Ann E. Bigger my negro boy Lark, and my interest in the buggy & harness now owned by her & myself jointly. To my niece Martha E. McLean, my negro woman Minny. To my nephews & nieces Alexander B. Bigger, Moses A. Bigger, Ann E. Bigger & Martha E. McLean, all my negroes not herein before dispose of. My barouche & harness to be sold and the proceeds to be equally divided between Alexander B. Bigger, Moses A. Bigger, Anne E. Bigger & Martha E. McLean. I appoint G. W. Williams executor, 6 June 1853. Elizabeth Patterson (LS), Wit: M. C. Partlow, D. P. Partlow, G. W. Mason. Proved by the oath of R. C. Partlow 11 Oct 1854. Qualified G. W. Williams as exor 21 Oct 1854.

**Pages 330-333**: South Carolina, York District. Will of Robert Smith of the district aforesaid... to my daughter Mary Smith 100 acres of my plantation which I bought of Daniel Nichols the same to be run off to her from the lower end of said tract next to the mill. To my daughter Caroline Kennedy a small parcel of land adj. a tract I have heretofore given her and on the side next to

D. R. S. Allison and Vincent Cowan. To my daughter Sarah Ann Goode a negro boy called Charles, son of Lucinda, and $400 in case. To N. P. Kennedy $100 to be help by him for and applied from time to time to the use of my daughter Pamela Chambers. To my daughter Isabella Steele my four shares in the Capitol stock of the Kings Mountain Rail Road Company. My negro Lucinda and her children Adolphus, Oscar and the one now she has at her breast be sold and the proceeds of sale be divided between Eliza Meek and John Smith. To my wife the household furniture &c she brought to my house on her marriage with me. To John Mason and James Mason each the sum of $100. To my daughter Margaret Elizabeth the tract of land I purchased from the commissioner in equity for York District called the Barker tract and also the tract of land I bought of William Givens, about 160 acres-- my wife and all her children by me are to have the use of said tract until my said daughter Margaret Elizabeth becomes of age or marries when she is to take exclusive possession of the same. To my son Robert Bailey my plantation composed of the tracts I purchased of G. F. Ferguson and Vincent Cowan and the balance I own which I bought of John Wood. To my two youngest sons Mijamin Randolph and Benjamin Felix all the balance of my lands consisting of the plantation I reside on on Bullocks Creek and the lands attached thereto. If said Mijamin R. or Benjamin F. should die before arriving at the age of 21 years, or die unmarried, then the share of said deceased son to be equally divided among the surviving full bothers & sisters of said deceased son. My negroes and other property not bequeathed remain together for the support of my wife and her five children by me. To my daughter Carolina $300. I appoint N. P. Kennedy my executor, 26 Jan 1853. Robert Smith (LS), Wit: J. A. McLean, John H. Adams, W. C. Beatty. Proved by the oath of John H. Adams 17 Nov 1854.

**Pages 333-334**: Will of Michael Whisonant of District of York... to my daughter Elizabeth Bell $2 having received her distributive share of my estate heretofore. I will to my son David W. Whisonant $50 to make up his full distributive share of my estate. To my daughter Martha F. Morrow $2 as she has received her distributive share of my estate heretofore. Whereas I had given to my daughter Lucy B. Harden a deed of gift for 200 ares reserving my right thereof during my natural life time and since then have bought back the 200 acres of land that I gave to my daughter Martha F. Whisonant now Martha F. Morrow, I will that my said daughter Lucy B. Harden have the whole tract of 404 acres after the death of myself and my beloved wife Margaret Whisonant. To my beloved wife Margaret Whisonant the tract whereon I now live during her life and then to descend to my son in law David D. Hardin and Lucy B. Hardin his wife, and to my wife Margaret Whisonant all my household & kitchen furniture, stock of horses, cattle, hogs and sheep and a road waggon with harness to be her own property and subject to her own disposal and discretion. I appoint Davy D. Hardin and Abraham Hardin, executors, 29 Jan 1853. Michael Whisonant (X) (LS), Wit: Phillip Etters, Samuel Etters, D. S. Wilson (X). Proved by the oath of Samuel Etters 20 Nov 1854. Qualified David D. Hardin as executor 20 Nov 1854.

**Pages 334-335**: Will of Vincent Davis of York District... To each of my daughters viz Elizabeth Davis, Mary Davis, Sarah Davis & Catherine Davis one horse and one cow and calf to be delivered to them when they marry. I have already given my other daughters their share. All the rest & residue of my estate both real and personal to be equally divided between my two sons Joseph G. Davis and Benjamin Davis but I will that my wife shall remain on my plantation and be supported by my sons out of the profits thereof during her natural life or widowhood. I appoint my son Joseph G. Davis executor 15 Nov 1852. Vincent David (LS), Wit: John G. Enloe, A. Stillwell, J. W. Ross. Proved by the oath of John G. Enloe 18 Oct 1854. Qualified Jos. G. Davis as executor 18 Oct 1854.

**Pages 335-336**: Will of William D. Lesslie of York District... To my daughter Mary Elizabeth a negro girl Harriet. To my daughter Eleanor Jane a negro girl Margaret. To my daughter Isabella Henry a negro girl Angeline. To my daughter Rachel Emmeline a negro girl Manda. To my son Thomas Henry a negro boy Anderson. After payment of debts, all the resident of my negro property not above named belong to my dear wife Rosanna Jane, viz Frank, Susan his wife, Nancy, Isaac, Wesley, Sam. As I yet hold the rights of the tract of land known as the Caldwell place, I bequeath the my wife Rosanna Jane give rights so early as the terms of sale are complied with and that my wife have the control of the money. Dated 25 Oct 1854. William D. Lesslie (LS), Wit: James McElwee, Thomas C. Henry, E. E. Boyce. Codicil named Newman McElwee as executor. Proved 28 Nov 1854.

**Pages 337**: Will of Charles McIlwain of the District of York... to my beloved wife 150 acres of land to be run off of the west end of the tract of land whereon I now reside including the dwelling house and other buildings including the spring with provisions to support the white family now residing with me for one year, and after her death to be equally divided between my son Charles and daughter Margaret. The balance of my estate to my son Charles and my brother David. I appoint my said son Charles and my friend Calvin P. Sandifer to be executors, 18 Oct 1854. Charles McIlwain (LS), Wit: Jas Johnston, Albert P. Johnson, C. P. Sandifer. Proved by the oath of Albert P. Johnson 29 Nov 1854.

**Pages 338-339**: Will of Thomas L. Good of York District... I desire my wife Mary A. Good to have all the balance of my estate after payment of debts. If she should marry I allow her to have a bed and bureau but all the balance of my property to go to my lawful heirs equally. At her death all my personal property to be sold except my negroes and I allow my executor to heir them out privately to such people as will not abuse them and I allow my executor to rent the land that my father allows me to such men as will not abuse it or destroy the timber until my children may arrive at the age of 21 years. I desire that my son John E. Good to take all of my affairs if he should live to the age of 21 years and manage the affairs during his mother's life, provided she is still a widow. I appoint David J. Goode my executor until my son John E. Good arrives at the age of 21, 11 Feb 1854. Thomas L. Good (LS), Wit: John G.

Davidson, J. M. Roberts, J. P. Hood. Proved by the oath of John G. Davison 10 Jan 1855. Qualified David J. Good as executor 10 Jan 1855.

**Pages 339-340**: Will of William E. Anderson of York District... I will that my wife and children be kept on the land as a home and that my children be schooled out of the said effects (if any remain). My beloved wife Mary Ann Anderson and my daughter Mary Rebecca and Sarah Elizabeth and William Jasper Anderson have the balance of the whole of my estate to be equally divided between them in four equal shares. I appoint my friend Robert C. Partlow to execute this my will and I have called on Dr. John A. Barnett and David H. Anderson with James C. Hicklen to witness the due execution of this will. Wm. E. Anderson (LS). Proved by the oath of David H. Anderson 12 Jan 1855.

**Pages 340-341**: South Carolina, York District. Will of Mary C. Barnwell of district aforesaid... To my sister Cynthia E. Barnwell all my interest or part in the household and kitchen furniture and also my interest in the stock of very kind that I have in our plantation. To my sister Cynthia E. Barnwell my interest if any in my brother John's estate. To my sister Cynthia E. Barnwell my negroes (viz) Mary and her three children Nelson, Margaret and Bob. After her death to my brother James A. Barnwell. To my sisters Hannah Morrison and Elizabeth C. McCarter $1 in money to each in money, 17 Sept 1846. Mary C. Barnwell (X) (LS), Wit: J. D. P. Currence, J. H. Hemphill, Wm. B. Jackson. Proved by the oaths of all three witnesses 24 Jan 1855. Qualified James A. Barnwell as executor 24 Feb 1855.

**Pages 341-342**: Will of Thomas Martin of York District... to my beloved wife Elizabeth one third part of the land that I may be in possession of at my decease, to include the Mansion House. The balance of my land be divided into lots by my executors so as to make suitable settlements, and those lots be exposed to the highest bidder amongst the legatees and the moneys therefrom to be so paid over as to make my children all equal. A part of them having received the following sums (viz) Priscilla Moreland $100, Laben Logan $75, Gabriel Martin $57.50, T. M. Martin $57.50, Bird Martin $57.50, Benjamin Martin $57.50, Rhoda Collins $80, Nancy Collins $70, Josey Martin $57.50, William Martin $57.50, Andrew Martin $42.50, Elizabeth Goforth $56, Henderson Martin $57.50, my two daughters Mary and Lakey and my two sons Absalom and Perry who have received nothing. Hicks Martin has received $57.50. I appoint Henderson Martin and S. D. Fulton executors, 17 April 1846. Thomas Martin (X) (LS), Wit: James Wood, John Wood, Abraham Hardin. Proved by the oath of Abraham Martin 6 Aug 1855. Qualified Henderson Martin as executor 6 Aug 1853.

**Pages 342-344**: South Carolina, York District. Will of Robert Burris of York District... my wife shall have her support off my plantation during her life. I further will to my wife all my negroes and as much of my stock as shall be necessary for her comfortable support. I further direct that no lands be cleared nor any more timber be cut than may be necessary to keep up the plantation until it comes into the possession of my grandsons as hereinafter devised. My plantation after the death of my wife to my grandsons Robert Walker Burris & Reuben McConnell Burris, but if either of them should die before arriving of age, his part shall descend to the other, but my said grandsons are required to pay to my granddaughter Mary Burris their sister $300 viz each of them to pay her $150. I also will that Mary Burris the mother of the above named children remain on the plantation & have her support off it during her widowhood. At the death of my wife my negroes be divided amongst my legal heirs by lot or by ballot, but the above division to be so made that my negro Alfred if alive fall in share of my grandchildren aforesaid the children of my deceased son R. Mc. Burris. The share of my negroes which may be allotted to my daughter Esther Serefina McConnell is bequeathed to her during her life & at her death to any children she may then have living. The share allotted to my son Robert N. Burris shall not go to him but to any children which he may have living at the time of the division. I appoint David Z. Burris and John McConnell Jr., exrs., 4 May 1853. Robert Burris (LS), Wit: John Burris, Robert Ash, A. S. Wallace. Proved by the oath of John Burris 12 Sept 1855. Qualified Davis Z. Burris & John McConnell Jr. as executors 12 Sept 1855.

**Pages 344-345**: Will of Janet White... of the property which a kind providence has given me, I would make the following distribution, viz to my brother in law John White $15. To Mary White my sister in law $5. To Mary Caroline White $13. To James White, Isaac White's son, $4. These legacies to be paid after the decease of my sister Elizabeth Scott. The remainder of all my real estate and personal property to my sister Elizabeth Scott and after her death to my brother Ebenezer Scott. I appoint my friends Messrs James R. McCully and Josiah C. Patrick, exrs., 8 Sept 1855. Janet White (LS), Wit: S. W. Jackson, R. E. McCully, J. C. Patrick. Proved by the oath of S. W. Jackson 29 Nov 1855. Qualified J. C. Patrick as exor 29 Nov 1855.

**Page 345**: Will of David C. Crawford being in a low state of health... to my son Edward A. Crawford the three following negroes viz my boy Burwell and Eliza and her daughter Molly Esther. My executors sell for the purpose of paying my debts negroes Harvey and Rebecca & her son Jimmy. The remainder of my estate both real and personal to my wife Mary S. Crawford, and in the event of my marriage to be equally divided between her and her children each share and share alike. I appoint my friends Robert Hope and Robert S. Hope, exrs., 8 Jan 1856. David C. Crawford (LS), Wit: William Hannah, Silvanus Williamson, C. P. Sandifur. Proved by the oath of Dr. C. P. Sandifer 24 Jan 1856. Qualified Robert H. Hope and Robert S. Hope, exrs., 24 Jan 1856.

**Pages 345-346**: South Carolina, York District. Will of Robert Leathem of said district... my estate to be divided between my beloved wife Elizabeth L. Leathem and my four sons, J. W. Leathem, Andrew A. Leathem, Robert T. Leathem, and James G. Leathem, with the exception of my negro woman Netty which I allow to belong to my said wife and allow $5 to be paid to my grandson Asbury H. Anderson. Dated 14 Jan 1856. Robert Leathem (LS),

Wit: G. D. Hood, J. G. Plexico, J. P. Hood. Proved by the oath of John P. Hood 9 Feb 1856. Qualified John W. Leathem as executor 9 Feb 1856.

**Pages 346-347**: Will of George Ratchford of York District... To my beloved wife my mansion house & her support off the plantation on which I reside during her natural life, and all my household and kitchen furniture to be disposed of by her as she chooses. To my son James A. Ratchford the plantation on which I reside subject to the support and maintenance of his mother and the support of my daughter Eliza J. Ratchford while she remains unmarried also subject to the payment of $100 to my son R. W. Ratchford. To my son Robert W. Ratchford my plantation on the waters of Turkey Creek called the Ditty place. To my grandchildren James W. Ratchford and Margaret J. Ratchford each $100. The remainder of my personal estate be equally divided between my children George R. Ratchford, Robert W. Ratchford, John Ratchford, James A. Ratchford, Nancy L. Wallace and Eliza Ratchford. I appoint my son Robert W. Ratchford and son in law Alexander Wallace executors, 29 Jan 1850. George Ratchford (LS), Wit: Thomas J. Bell, Stanhope Sadler, B. J. Kuykendall. Proved by the oath of Thomas J. Bell 7 March 1856. Qualified Robert W. Ratchford & Alex S. Wallace as executors 7 March 1856.

**Pages 347-348**: South Carolina, York District. September 29th 1855. Will of Robert Campbell of district above mentioned... To my two sisters Ann & Rachel Campbell or either of them that may survive me, all of my property both personal & real. Robert Campbell (X) (LS), Wit: J. Leander Adams, John Moore, D. A. McCallum. Proved by the oath of D. A. McCallum 7 April 1856.

**Pages 348-350**: Will of William Crawford Sr. of York District... To my beloved wife Elizabeth during her natural life all my real estate and at her death to become the property of my son Robert, should my said wife not cultivate all the above land so devised to her, it is my request that she suffer my son Robert to enjoy the use thereof, but this is at her discretion. To my said wife all my negroes and at her decease said negroes are to be equally divided among my sons James, John, Robert & William. I also give my said wife one share of stock in the Kings Mountain Rail Road Company. To my son James one share of stock in the Kings Mountain Rail Road Company. To my son Robert one share of stock in the Kings Mountain Rail Road Company. To my daughter Jane the one share of stock in the Kings Mountain Rail Road Company given to my wife during her life, and while she remains unmarried she shall reside on the tract herein devised to her mother. To my sons John, James, Robert, and daughter Jane one share of Kings Mountain Rail Rock stock to be equally divided among them in interest. As several of my children are not named in my will, I would have it understood that I have heretofore given and provided for each and every one. I appoint my sons William & James exrs., 31 July 1855. William Crawford (X) (LS), Wit: W. H. McCorkle, W. C. Beaty, G. W. Williams. Codicil including daughter Jane in the division of the negroes, 20 Aug 1855. William Crawford (X) (LS), Wit: G. R. Ratchford, W. C. Beaty, W. H. McCorkle. Proved by the oath of W. H.

McCorkle 4 Aug 1856. Qualified William & James Crawford as executors 4 Aug 1856.

**Pages 350-351**: Will of Sarah Starr widow & now residing in Yorkville... I order at my decease that plain tombstones be placed at the head of the grave of myself as also the graves of my father & mother. To my niece Sarah Shillinglaw a negro boy named Esau. To my niece Sarah Watson a negro boy named Jacob. The balance of my estate including lands, negroes, bonds, notes, etc., to my nephew J. Monroe Anderson. I appoint J. Monroe Anderson my executor, 29 Jan 1855. Sarah Starr (X) (LS), Wit: Eli Meek, S. R. Moore, J. D. Witherspoon. Proved by the oath of S. R. Moore 29 Sept 1855.

**Pages 351-352**: Will of James M. Harris... I will that all my estate real and personal to be sold after my death and the proceeds thereof with all moneys, etc., to be equally divided between all my children, the children of my deceased daughter Margaret E. Carrothers taking among them the share their mother would have taken if alive, but the share of my daughter Rebecca A. Perry is to remain in the hands of the administrator with my will annexed for I do not intend to appoint an executor, until the Ordinary of York District shall appoint a trustee to receive it. Dated 13 Dec 1856. J. M. Harris, Wit: T. D. Spratt, J. M. Stewart, B. F. Powell. Proved by the oath of J. M. Stewart 9 March 1857. Qualified F. H. Harris as admr. with the will annexed, 9 March 1857.

**Pages 352-354**: South Carolina, York District. Will of Major T. Hall... It is my will that if my lands in Florida are not sold prior to my death my executors should sell the same & I authorise them to execute good titles and the proceeds of the same to be divided as hereafter directed. I will $5000 of my estate to John R. Hall & Peter Garrison to dispose as they may think proper. I will to James Temple Hall & Robert McCaw Hall sons of my deceased son A. N. Hall each $1000 & if that does not make them equal with my other four legatees, that they should be made equal. I will to Major Thomson Hall the son of John Hall deceased of Arkansas $100, to Major Temple Hall son of Eliza Hall of Tennessee also 41000, to Mary Garrison daughter of my brother William Hall decd to be pd to them as soon as convenient after my death. My executors should sell in any manner they may think proper my negro man named Johnson, my horse, saddle, bridle, & waggon & any other articles. Money to be divided between my four children J. R. Hall, E. E. Gillespie, C. L. Garrison & R. F. Hall in such a manner that each one of them shall receive no more of my estate upon a final division than the children of A. N. Hall. AS to my son Saml B. Hall, I will him one dollar. I appoint my son John R. Hall & my son in law Petter Garrison, exrs., 23 June 1854. M. T. Hall (LS), Wit: Jas. C. Hicklin, Jno. W. Choat, Wm. Bobbett. Proved by the oath of Jas. C. Hicklin 1 July 1857.

**Page 354**: Will of Martha Byers... After payment of debts, the remainder of my property be equally divided amongst my brother William Adams children. I appoint John S. Moore to execute my last will [not dated]. Martha Byers (mark), Wit: Mary T. Curry, Martha Boggs, Joseph Black. Proved by the oath of Joseph Black 19 March 1857. Qualified JohnS. Moore as exor 19 March 1857.

**Page 355**: South Carolina, York District. Will of Elizabeth Bates of district aforesaid... I give the plantation I now reside on to my nephew Thaddeus Kennedy Bates, and my brother Thomas A. Bates is to have his maintainance or support as long as he shall live of the above named plantation. To my said nephew Thaddeus Kennedy Bates all my stock of horses, cattle, and hogs, loom, household and kitchen furniture. I appoint my brother David K. Bates, executor, 19 April 1848. Elizabeth Bates (X) (LS), Wit: Harvey H. Drennan, Archibald Steele, John M. Steele. Proved by the oath of Archibald Steele 11 March 1857. Qualified D. K. Bates as executor 11 March 1811.

**Page 356**: Will of William T. Stewart, planter, of district of York... to the officers of Unity Church $50, the interest of which sum to be used by said officers towards employing a minister in preaching at church. All the remainder of my property be sold at public sale and the proceeds to be equally divided between my brother J. S. Stewart and sisters Nancy M. Poag, E. K. Stewart, & E. L. Stewart, M. M. Stewart, J. A. Stewart and A. L. Watson and R. J. Watson, the minor children of a deceased sister, these children to take their mother's share. My executors to call in some three or four men of judgment to say what the hire of the boy Dan shall be worth for the time that he has been working on my plantation and at the close of this crop season let the said Dan go back to the estate Eleanor Wells to which he original [sic] belonged. I appoint my brother James H. Stewart, sole executor, 6 April 1857. Wm. T. Stewart (LS), Wit: Joseph F. White, Eli Stewart, E. L. D. Johnston. Proved by the oath of L. D. Johnston 21 April 1857. Qualified J. H. Stewart as executor 21 April 1857.

**Page 357**: South Carolina, York District. March 6th 1848. Will of Rhoda Smith... to my two sons Charles Smith and Robert Smith all my lands which I now hold in my possession to wit one tract on the east side of Broad River in york District adj. lands of Luke Smith, W. G. Smith, H. H. Thompson; one tract of 100 acres adj. lands of Edward Leach & Jenny Moss and Josiah Smith; one tract of 22 acres adj. lands of Dr. Samuel Wright to be divided between them equally. My other effects to wit, all the negroes, horses, stock and household furniture to be equally divided among my daughters and grand daughter Eliza Jane, daughter of my son Henry decd, one fourth to Martha Archer, four to my daughter Margaret Forbes, fourth to Mary Nelson, one fourth to my granddaughter Eliza Jane Smith. I will all the above to my beloved wife if she out lives me her natural life time for her support. I appoint Charles W. Smith and Robert J. Smith, exrs., 6 March 1848. Rhoda Smith (LS), Wit: Wmson Howell, John P. Smith, Wm. G. Lackey. Proved by the oath of Williamson Howell 10 March 1857. Qualified Robert J. Smith as executor 10 March 1857.

**Page 358**: Will of John Hays of York District... To my daughter Ann Hays the plantation known as the Creek tract whereon Alison Hays now lives and after her death the said premises to be my grandson's Alison Hays. I give my plantation whereon I now live to three of my children viz Amelia Hays, Mary Hays & Susan Hays to live upon jointly. I appoint H. Mitchell, Wm. Nelson my sole executors, 26 Feb 1857. John Hays (LS), Wit: C. C. Daniel, Wm. White, J. H. Meek. Proved by the oath of John H. Meek 23 July 1857. Qualified C. Mitchell & Wm. Nelson executors 23 July 1857.

**Pages 358-359**: South Carolina, York District. Will of Robert Adams Sen of said district... to the children of my son Wm. Adams $100. To my son J. B. Adams one negro boy named Edwin. To my son James Adams one negro boy named Stephen. To my son Joseph Adams one negro boy named Henry. To my son D. A. Adams one negro boy named George with $100 also the cotton gin & screw, also the smith tools. To my daughter Mary M. Carigan one negro girl named Dorcas also one bed & bed clothes. To my daughter S. M. Clinton on negro girl named Mary and the bed she has in possession. To my daughter M. E. Adams one negro woman named Eve & her son William also her child Mary Ann, also Susan and one bureau. To my daughter Eliza Adams one negro girl named Violet and her child Adam, also one negro boy named Isaac and one bureau. To my daughter E. J. Jackson one negro one negro girl named Betty also one boy named Sam. To my daughter Isabella R. Wood a parcel of land on the northern part of my tract on the Lincoln Road north west of the Smith ford road, adj. Wilson line, James Adams' corner, to the York road, also one negro girl named Amy also one bureau, a cow & calf. The balance of money or all specialties to be equally divided between my two daughters Margaret & Eliza. All my property not otherwise of above including the remainder of land with all my live stock, etc., to be equally divided between my daughters Margaret & Eliza. I appoint my two sons James & D. A. Adams, 26 Aug 1856. Robert Adams (LS), Wit: Elias M. Jackson, Mary M. Jackson, Myles Smith. Proved by the oath of Myles Smith 28 May 1857. Qualified David A. Adams as executor 28 May 1857.

**Pages 360-362**: South Carolina, York District. Will of James S. Hemphill... to my beloved wife Martha G. Hemphill my family carriage, my riding horse & two mules viz Nell & Dine, all my household & kitchen furniture, all the negroes she brought with her with the two negroes viz Henry & George which I bought at her father's John Rosborough's sale subject however to the debts. To my wife all necessary provisions for one year after my decease, as well as farming utensils, etc., for the support of my said wife and son James S. Hemphill. Also to my wife my home plantation during her life ore widowhood and at her death or marriage to go to my son James S. D. Hemphill. I further desire that my executors to carry out the contract with Mrs. Nelly Rosborough in regard to a tract of land purchased by me at the sale of the late John Rosborough deceased & receiving the title. Also my Hanbreak or Blair plantation he may sell. The negroes Dan, Nan, Antony, Giles, Ric & Amy to remain unsold on my plantation for the benefit of my son & wife as long as said negroes behave. The said Nan to be supported out of my estate in case she becomes helpless or a charge from age and i place at the disposal of my executor my stock in Davidson College, Mecklenburg County, N. Carolina to be used as he may think proper excepting so much as may necessary for my son's education in said college. I appoint my beloved brother Samuel G.

Hemphill executor and guardian of my son James S. D. Hemphill, 8 Jan 1857. James Hemphill (X). Wit: S. L. Love, G. C. Mitchell, R. H. Leathem. Proved by the oath of S. L. Love 27 Jan 1857. Qualified J. G. Hemphill as executor 27 Jan 1857.

**Pages 362-363**: South Carolina, York District. Will of Solomon Kimbel, planter of District of York... I give to my son Sargent Jasper Kimbel the plantation on which I reside after the death of my wife Dicey who shall have the use of said plantation during her life. I will all my negroes great & small to my said wife Dicey her life time & then to my children by appraisement & in said appraisement I allow to each of my daughters $200 each more than my two sons. If any personal property of my estate remaining at the death of my wife, I allow the portion due to such deceased child to be distributed to the children of the deceased parent. I will that the share of negroes allotted to my daughter Nancy Saville be retained by my executors who are impowered to hire said negroes & give from time to rime said hire to her & her children. I will tract of land lying on Big ___ Creek to my son Harris Kimbell at the death of my wife Dicey. All the remainder of my personal property to my children share & share alike. I appoint my son Sargent Jasper Kimbell & D. Gibbons, exrs., 21 April 1855. Solomon Kimbel (X) (LS), Wit: W. E. White, T. B. Withers, Jno. M. White. Proved by the oath of John M. White 10 Aug 1857. Qualified Sergent J. Kimbel & Jon. G. Gibbin executors 10 Aug 1857.

**Pages 363-364**: South Carolina, York District. Will of Nancy Stewart of District of York... To my daughter Alice E. Stewart my negro girl Ann, my daughter Mary M. Stewart negro girl Crecy. The balance of property given to me by my sister Eleanor Webb namely a negro woman Nancy's child Shed, Martha & Abraham & plantation one bay horse which I design shall be divided equal among my six remaining legates namely J. J. Watson, two children Araminta & Robert James, Nancy M. Pog, W. T. Stewart, E. R. Stewart, I. J. Stewart, & E. L. Stewart. I desire that my daughter Mary M. Stewart be made $200 more than the six older legatees. Likewise Alice E. Stewart be made $300 better. The other legatees made up the sum of $50 for my sister Sarah Dyer & also a small bureau. My daughters E. R., E. L., M. M. A. C. Stewart to have each one of them a bed. I appoint W. T. Stewart executor, 23 Dec 1856. Nancy Stewart (X) (LS), Wit: J. J. White, Smith Patterson, J. J. Watson. Proved by the oath of J. J. Watson 13 Feb 1857. Qualified W. T. Stewart as executor 13 Feb 1857.

**Pages 364-366**: South Carolina, York District. Will of Gazaway Wilson of District of York... The balance of the proceeds of sale after payment of debts to be equally divided between my eight children viz Eliza P., Margret, Jemima McCarter, Sarah D. Watson, Josiah, John, Robert, & William Wilson. I give to my wife Sarah Wilson my negro boy Sam & girl Priscilla during the natural course of her life and at her decease to be sold & equally divided between my eight children. My furniture, bureau, cupboard, falling leaf table, clock, six chairs, two wheals & cards. My land containing ___ acres adj. lands of Josiah Wilson, Luther ___ Robert W. Wilson, be for the use of my wife Sarah and daughters Eliza & Margret if they remain single. My home tract that I now live on be kept for a home for my wife Sarah and daughters Eliza & Margaret. My son John C. Wilson, exr., 13 Nov 1856. Gazaway Wilson (LS), Wit: R. C. McCarter, W. J. Jackson, R. M. Wilson. Proved by the oath of Robert C. McCarter 6 Feb 1857. Qualified John C. Wilson as executor 6 Feb 1857.

**Page 366**: South Carolina, York District. Will of Rebecca Robertson of District of York being old & infirm... to my three sons who have gone to the west viz James & Tom & S. Robertson each $300. Any remainder to be divided amongst all of my children as well those above named who are in the West as those who reside in this country. I appoint my son Allan Robertson executor 25, July 1851. Rebecka Robertson (LS), Wit: S. Sadler, G. S. Sadler, M. A. Sadler. Proved by the oath of S. Sadler 16 Feb 1853. Qualified Allen Robertson as executor 16 Feb 1857.

**Pages 366-367**: South Carolina, York District. Will of William Patrick of said district... To each of my grandchildren, the children of my daughter Jane Tate deceased, the sum of $100. To my youngest grandchild D. Yates I also give one feather bed & furniture. To my grand nephew William D. Patrick son of Clinton Patrick my rifle gun. the remainder of my property to my daughter Mary H. Patrick. I appoint my friend Josiah C. Patrick & my daughter Mary H. Patrick executors, 18 Dec 1854. William Patrick (LS), Wit: J. D. Watson, J. A. Barnett, J. B. Jackson. Proved by the oath of James B. Jackson 16 Dec 1856. QQalified Josiah C. Patrick executor 16 Dec 1856.

**Pages 367-368**: South Carolina, York District. Will of James Wallace of District of York... To James McCarter all my land lying on the east side of the creek and $100. To Eliza Gamelin the one third of all the balance that I possess. I also give Rebecca Rhea of Pike County, Missoura, one third of estate. To Margret Wallace of this District one third of all my estate. I appoint James Caldwell my executor, 14 Nov 1856. James Wilson (LS), Wit: R. Neeland, A. Neeland, J. W. Whitesides. Proved by the oath of R. Neeland 19 Dec 1856. Qualified James Caldwell as executor 19 Dec 1857 [sic].

**Pages 368-369**: South Carolina, York District. Will of Christina Howser... I will to my daughter Mary Hoover $200 in cash. I will to the three youngest children of my son John Houser namely Polly, Nancy, and Doctor, $33.33 each provided they claim the said legacy within three years after my death. If they do not their share to go to my daughter S. Whisonant. I will to my son in law John N. Whisonant my negro man Wilson and at his death to my grandson T. P. Whisonant, having sometime since conveyed this negro by deed of gift to my son in law John Whisonant & which deed having been burnt up in the house of said J. M. Whisonant. To my three daughters Mary Hoover, Lidia Dixon, S. Whisonant, all my wearing cloaths, bed & furniture. I appoint my friend William C. Black & J. N. Whisonant as executors, 23 Sept 1858. Christina Houser (LS), Wit: Thomas McGill, James H. McGill, Daniel James. Proved by the oath of James McGill 12 Nov 1856. Qualified Wm. B. Black as executor 2 March 1857.

**Pages 369-370**: South Carolina, York District. Will of Cynthia E. Barnwell of district aforesaid... I will all my part & interest of the household & Kitchen furniture to my sister Mary C. Barnwell, also my part and interest in the plantation and stock of very kind. I will my part & interest in my brother John's estate if any to said Mary. After the death of my sister Mary C. Barnwell, to my brother James A. Barnwell excepting one bed and furniture to a negro girl called Margaret. To my sisters Hannah Morrison & E. McCarter $1 each in money. I will that my brother James A. Barnwell do execute this will, 17 Sept 1846. Cynthia Barnwell (X) (LS), Wit: D. H. Tomason, G. H. Hempill, Wm. B. Jackson. Proved by the oath of J. H. Hemphill & W. B. Jackson 21 Feb 1857. Qualified James A. Barnwell executor 21 Feb 1857.

**Page 370**: South Carolina, York District. Will of Jacob Pugh... To my brother John Pugh & his heirs the plantation on which i now reside, also my negro girl Dorcas & boy George, my two cows & calves, with stock of hogs, corn & fodder. To my sister Rebecca Pugh my interest in my mother's plantation & my [negro?] Jack. I also will my interest in a tract of land in North Carolina on the waters of cany fork Drowsy Creek be equally divided between my brother John Pugh & Rebecca Pugh. I appoint my brother John Pugh executor, 11 Nov 1856. Jacob Pugh (X) (LS), Wit: John McKnight, J. M. Brian, T. Pugh. Proved by the oath of Tomas Pugh 21 Dec 1856. Qualified John pugh as executor 5 Jan 1857.

**Page 371**: South Carolina, York District. Will of Joseph Robison... all my estate to my wife during her natural life, and at her death to be equally divided among my children but the legal title of my daughter Elizabeth Jenkins is to vest in my executors who are direct to pay over to her annually the interest on her share. I appoint my sons Andrew E. Robison & William Robison, executors, 7 April 1856. Joseph Robison, Wit: J. N. McElwee, W. S. Plaxico, J. Crawford. Qualified Andr E. Robison & William Robison as executors 15 Dec 1856.

**Pages 371-372**: South Carolina, York District. Will of James T. Bennett of the District of York... To my well beloved wife Elizabeth all of my property both real and personal consisting of the plantation on which I now live, also negro woman named Mint & girl Milly & one boy Calvin, one girl Lucinda, and one boy Washington.I appoint my said wife Elizabeth and my son Thomas C. Bennett executors, 29 July 1857. James S. Bennett, Wit: D. K. Bates, R. Strait, R. W. Coleman. Proved by the oath of Richard Strait 31 Aug 1857. Qualified Elizabeth Bennett & Thos C. Bennett as exors, 31 Aug 1857.

**Pages 372-373**: South Carolina, York District. Will of Margaret Whitesides of District of York, 10th Jany 1855. I will to my three nieces namely Margaret Johnson, Sarah Thorn & Jane Fewell my bed & bedsteads & furniture, body clothes, saddle, wash pot, wheel, two trunks, one small table. But if they can't make division to suit themselves, they can sell the said article and divide the proceeds. I also will to my nephew Mathew Nichols $10 in cash. The balance of my cash & my notes to my nephew James S. Jones. I appoint my nephew

James S. Jones executor. Margaret Whiteside (X), Wit: A. T. Black, Rebecca Allen, Rebecca E. Minges. Proved by the oath of A. T. Black 31 Aug 1857. Qualified James S. Jones as executor 31 Aug 1857.

**Pages 373-382**: South Carolina, York District. Will of William Wright of Yorkville...

Item 1. To my wife Mary Wright during the term of her natural life my houses and lots in Yorkville and all my lands near to and adjacent to said village except as hereinafter direction, all my negroes, household & kitchen furniture, my carriages, waggons, buggy, hoses, mules, cows & hogs, all my farming tools.

Item 2. To my said wife the dividends arising from 250 acres of Capital Stock in the Bank of the State of North Carolina.

Item 3. As my object & is to provide a comfortable home and liberal income for my said wife, I direct that the houses, lots and lands be kept in repair by my executors.

Item 4. If the dividends from the stock are not sufficient for her comfortable support, my executors to pay over to her such sums of money as they may think proper.

Item 5. At the death of my wife, my executors sell the said 250 acres of stock and first pay to the executors of James Irwin a bond they hold on me & my wife for about the sum of $19,0000.

Item 6. To Margaret Stockton for the use of herself and children $2000. To Mary H. Moore for the use of herself and children $2000. To Joel A. Huggins for the use of himself & his children $2000. To John Huggins for the use of himself & his children $2000.

Item 7. To my niece Margaret E. Wright now residing with me, at the death of my wife, all the property real & personal given to my said wife.

Item 8. To my said niece Margaret E. Wright 200 shares of Capital Stock of the Bank of Hamburg and 300 shares in the Capitol Stock of the Commercial Bank of Columbia, South Carolina.

Item 9. I give to my brother J. L. Wright my wearing apparel.

Item 10. I give to my nephew James Spratt Wright my interest being one undivided half part in the ferry on Catawba River called Wrights Ferry and the landings, privileges, and rights attached thereto.

Item 11. I give my watch and chain to my nephew Wm. Irwin McGowan.

Item 12. I give to my niece Mary Jane McNeil my barouche and the harness belonging to it.

Item 13. To Robert McGowan and John L. McGowan each ten shares in the capitol stock of the Graniteville Manufacturing Company, to William Irwin McGowan, James Spratt McGowan & Mary Roberts McGowan, each 80 shares in the capitol stock of the Bank of Hamburg and to William Irwin McGowan 20 shares in the capital stock of the Bank of Chester, none of said shares of stock to be transferred until after the death of my wife.

Item 14. To my niece Mary Jane McNeel for the use of herself and children 50 shares in the capital stock of the Bank of Hamburg and 100 shares in the capital stock of the Peoples Bank of Charleston, none of said shares of stock to be transferred until after the death of my wife.

Item 15. To my niece Eliza Adams for the use of herself and children 160 shares in the capital stock in the Bank of Chester and four shares of stock in the South Carolina Rail Road and the South Western Rail Road Bank. I also give to my niece Nancy H. Gill for the use of herself and children 160 shares in the capital stock in the Bank of Chester and ten shares of capital stock of the Bank of Camden.

Item 16. To my grandnieces Mary & Martha Harris, children of J. L. Harris, 160 shares of stock in the Bank of Chester and eight shares of stock in the South Carolina Rail Road and the South Western Rail Road Bank.

Item 17. To my grand nephew Robert R. McCorkle, son of W. H. McCorkle, 160 shares of stock in the Bank of Chester and eight shares of stock in the South Carolina Rail Road and the South Western Rail Road Bank.

Item 18. To my nieces Margaret W. McElwee, Mary E. McElwee & Catharine McElwee each 50 shares in the Capital stock of the Bank of Hamburg and 100 shares in the capital stock of the Peoples Bank of Charleston. To my nephews William W. & Samuel A. McElwee, each 50 shares in the capital stock of the Peoples Bank of Charleston. To my nephew James L. McElwee 50 shares in the Capital stock of the Bank of Hamburg.

Item 19. To my three nephews William W., Samuel A. & James L. McElwee my tract of land in York District which I purchased of Elizabeth Patterson to be equally divided among them.

Item 20. To my three nephews William W., Samuel A. & James L. McElwee each the sum of $1000 to be vested in negroes for the purpose of working their shares of the land herein given to them.

Item 21. To Eliza Jane Miller for the use of herself and children 40 shares in the capital stock of the Bank of Newberry and 10 shares of stock in the Bank of Hamburg, also a negro girl called Edy and her children. And whereas under a certain trust deed heretofore made by me to J. L. Wright, the said Eliza Jane Miller and her brother and sister William W., Samuel A., James L. & Catherine E. McElwee own said negroes, I declare all the legacies given in this my will to said Eliza Jane Miller and her brothers & sister release to her their interest in said negroes.

Item 22. I give to the Synod of the Associate Reformed Presbyterian Church South 30 shares stock in the South Carolina Rial Road and South Western Rail Road Bank, the divided therefrom for the benefit of the churches or college under its car. Also to said Synod 50 shares of stock in the commercial Bank of Columbia, the dividends to be applied to the support of Foreign and Domestic Missions.

Item 23. To my executors 20 shares in the capital stock of the Bank of Camden in trust to receive the dividends and apply $50 of the same annually to the support of the minister in charge of the Associate Reformed Presbyterian Church at Yorkville.

Item 24. To the Yorkville Female Collegiate Institute a bond and mortgage executed to me by said corporation for the sum of $500 on condition they will release my estate from the payment of $200 due by me on a subscription list in favor of said Institute.

Item 25. As soon after my death as my executors think proper they place $2500 in the hands of J. L. Harris and that said J. L. Harris invest the same in a check in some Northern Bank payable to the order of Henry Harris, Maury County, Tennessee, and out of the proceeds pay tot he family of my deceased uncle James Wright viz $600 to William J. Wright, $600 to Robert

Newton Wright, $300 to the widow of Joseph Wright decd, $300 to Mary Freeland, $300 to John F. Wright, $200 to Samuel Wright, and $200 to Andrew J. Wright.

Item 26. To George W. Williams a small parcel of land in Yorkville adjoining his lands being that portion of my field cut off from the balance thereof, by the opening of anew street in Yorkville.

Item 27. I direct my executors to sell my two shares of stock in the Kings Mountain Rail Road Company.

Item 28. I give to John F. Irwin a note I hold on him for the sum of $2000.

Item 29. I give to the Rev. Aaron F. Quay the sum of $500.

Item 30. I give to David Wright Hunter $300 to be applied to the purposes of his education.

Item 31. Should my executors think it advisable and proper, they are to be at liberty to sell any of my stocks in Banks and Companies mentioned in this will and invest the proceeds in other stocks to be held ont he same terms.

Item 32. My executors will receive the dividends on all stocks I may die possessed of and not disposed of in this will and either reinvest the same in other stocks, apply said dividends to the use of my wife or the payment of cash legacies as they may think property.

Item 33. No dividends are to be paid over by my executors except to my wife and except also to my niece Margaret E. Wright for the purposes mentioned in item 8th until all my debts, funeral expenses and charges and the cash legacies mentioned are paid.

Item 34. I give to each of my executors in lieu of commissioners out of my estate, 20 shares in the capital stock of the Bank of Camden.

Item 35. My executors may need advice from time to time and also aid int he transfer of stocks and other property, and I request them to apply for such advice and assistance to my friend G. W. Williams, and for his said services, I give to said G. W. Williams eleven shares in the capital stock of the Bank of Camden.

Item 36. In transferring the stocks bequeathed in the 13th, 14th, 15th, 16th, 17th, 18th and 21st clauses of this my will, the person to whom the bequest is made, is to have the use of the stock bequeathed for & during his or her lifetime, and after his or her death, the said shares to be divided equally amongst the issue of such legatees.

Item 37. None of the stocks bequeathed is to be transferred until the death of my wife except those mentioned in the 34th and 35th clauses of my will.

Item 38. Whereas in item 7th of this my will I have directed if my niece Margaret E. Wright should die leaving alone no issue, the property should be distributed equally amongst my nephews and nieces then living per capita, now I declare that if any of my nephews and nieces should have died before that time, leaving issue then alive, the issue of such deceased nephew or niece shall take among them the share. I hereby declare that my nephew James Spratt Wright is not to be entitled to any part of share of said property. I hereby revoked that part of my will that 300 shares of stock in the Commercial Bank go to my niece Margaret E. Wright, but in place 200 shares of stock in said Commercial Bank.

Item 39. I revoke the bequest of 160 shares of stock in the Bank of Chester to Robert R. McCorkle, and give him in lieu 160 shares of stock in the Bank of Newberry.

Item 40. I hereby revoke so much of the 18th clause of my will as directs the dividends received on stock bequeath to James L. McElwee, Margaret W. McElwee, Mary E. McElwee & Catharine McElwee, to be paid to them before the death of my wife, and direct said dividends so received to be reinvested in stocks or negroes.

Item 41. I give to my niece Eliza Jane Miller $500 to be vested by my executors in a negro girl to be held by said Elizabeth Jane Miller. In said clause in naming the brothers and sisters of said Eliza Jane Miller, I have erroneously called Catherine McElwee, Catherine E. McClure and omitted the name of Mary E. McElwee.

Item 42. I will that at the death of my wife all the rest, residue and remainder of my property and estate be divided amongst my nephews and nieces.

Item 43. I appoint John Irwin of Charlotte, J. J. Blackwood of Hamburg, and John L. Harris of Chester, exrs., 13 June 1857. Wm. Wright (Seal), Wit: John H. Adams, James Jefferys, J. A. McLean, W. H. McCorkle. Proved by the oath of John H. Adams 3 Oct 1857. Qualified John L. Harris as executor 3 Oct 1857.

**Pages 382-384**: Will of William Brown of the District of York... To my beloved wife Tabitha D. Brown, tract on which I now reside being the tract purchased of Samuel Curry, bounded by lands of John Brown, William L. Brown, James Thomasson Sen. & Jefferson Black, and at the decease of my said wife, to my son Wm. L. Brown. Also to my said wife Tabitha D. Brown, my negro man named Stephen, my negro woman named Betty. To my son John brown my negro man named Ben. To my two sons John Brown & William L. Brown my plantation in York District on the waters of Bullock's Creek, purchased from Robert Brown dec'd. To my daughters Margaret E. Floyd, Eliza D. Duff James Glenn & Mary D. Brown each $10, having already given them that portion of my estate which I allow them. To my daughter Harriet my negro girl Minny, and in case my said daughter should die without issue, then said negro girl to go to my daughter Usry D. Brown. To my daughter Harriet A. Brown $10. I appoint my wife Tabitha D. Brown executrix & my two sons John & William L. Brown, executors, 12 Sept 1845. William Brown (LS), Wit: J. A. Brown, Hance Neely, P. A. Thomasson. Proved by the oath of John A. Brown 5 July 1858. Qualified John Brown as executor 19 July 1858.

**Pages 384-385**: South Carolina, York District. Will of Frances Barron of York District... To my daughter Margaret Fewell wife of A. Fewell, to my son Wm. Barron & to my daughter Elizabeth Pressley wife of Wm. Pressley, to my son A. J. Barron, to my son in law R. M. Pressley, to my son Thomas Barron & to my son John Barron, whatever amount may be due to me for annuity interest at the time of my death; each to receive the individual claims I hold against hem, but no part of each others indebtedness. Whatever is remaining due me from the estate of James G. Corry for annuity interest be collected from his estate, and that $300 of the same be applied by A. J. Barron for schooling & fitting up my grandson Wm. Corry, son of my daughter Rebecca

Corry for business. To my grandsons Wm. B. & F. J. Thomasson sons of my daughter Jane Thomasson having received by settlement with the executors of my husband Wm. Barron their full share of my estate. Should any funds be recovered from these claims which include lands, town lots, notes & a negro boy, my will is that an equal distribution of it be made between A. Fewell, Eliza Pressley wife of Wm. Pressly, Wm. Barron, A. J. Barron, R. M. Pressley, John Barron, Thomas Barron & my grandson Wm. Corry. I appoint Alexander Fewell and A. J. Barron, exrs., 22 Feb 1856. Frances Barron (X), Wit: W. J. Bowen, John G. Enloe, J. J. Snider.

**Pages 385-386**: 15th January 1838. Will of Mary H. Swann of the District of York... To my two sons Joseph Addison & Edward Eaton both their living off a tract of land willed to me by my father John Swann, 100 acres near Charleston road south of Swann's bridge on Becky's branch in Kuykendall's old line, adj. Strait. At my death I do allow my two sons above named an equal share of the above land divided by lot. I appoint my trust brother John B. Swann executor. Mary H. Swann (X), Wit: Moses B. Swann, James Bratton, William Bratton. Proved by the oath of Moses B. Swann 5 April 1858. Qualified John B. Swann as executor 6 Sept 1858.

**Pages 386-387**: South Carolina, York District. Will of Elizabeth Reeves of district aforesaid... I will unto Free Andy Cathcart my negro woman Franky to him, the said Free Andy paying $100 to my executors. To Sarah Ward my three negroes Martha & two children Monroe & Mary. To Nancy Reeves my three negroes Thom, Eliza & Synthia. All my real estate consisting of the place where I now live, with all my personal property not above mentioned, to be equally divided between my two step daughters Sally Ward & Nancy Reeves. Said Sally Ward and Nancy Reeves shall maintain and keep their father John Reeves my beloved husband on the lands willed to them during his lifetime. The negro woman Franky willed to Free Any is to him for his use, but I appoint Mr. Archibald Barron his guardian. I appoint my friends Peter Garrison & Wm. B. Allison, executors, dated 28 Nov 1857. Elizabeth Reeves (LS), Wit: Joseph Miller, Wm. B. Allison, Duncan McCallum. W. B. Allison refused to qualify as executor 5 Jan 1858. Proved by the oath of Duncan McCallum 8 March 1858. Qualified Peter Garrison as executor 8 March 1858.

**Pages 387-387** [there are two pages numbered 387]: South Carolina, York District. Will of John H. Good... To my wife Margaret L .Good all the balance of my estate both real & personal after payment of debts, to dispose of as she may think best for her & or children (by the consent of my executor). I appoint Dr. B. E. Feemster my executor, 10 Feb 1858. John H. Good (LS), Wit: James W. Good, J. P. Hood, W. N. Nelson. Proved by the oath of John P. Hood 1 March 1858. Qualified Dr. B. E. Feemster as executor 1 March 1858.

**Pages 387-388**: South Carolina, York District. Will of Rachel Barnett... To my daughter Margaret E. Wallace my set of drawer & 10. To Jas. A. Barnett one cow & Calf & two ewes & lambs. To my son Wm.A. Barnett my mare Dicy also one cow & calf. To my daughter Martha P. Currence my buggy an $50.

To my daughter R. Eliza McKenzie my bed and furniture and $50. To my son Alex H. Barnett $100 also a sow & pigs. To my grandson Moses A. Bigger my sorrel, and to my grandson Alex B. Bigger & my granddaughter Ann Bigger & Martha E. McLean $10. To my daughter Mary C. Barnett my negro Mary C. Barnett my negro girl Amanda with the balance of my property except my negro woman Phillis which I will to my daughter R. Eliza McKenzie. My son Wm. A. Barnett executor, 3 May 1850. Rachel Barnett (X), Wit: John A. Laney, Rubin Dulin, George A. Patrick. Proved by the oath of Reuben Dulin 11 Dec 1857. Qualified Wm. A Barnett as executor 11 Dec 1857.

**Pages 388-389**: Will of Robert Miller... I give the plantation & tract of land whereon I reside to my two nephews David Miller & James Miller equally to be divided between them. I give my negro woman Nancy to my niece Isabella Miller. I give my negro man Peter to my nephew James Miller. I will that all my household & kitchen furniture be divided between the aforesaid James, David & Isabella Miller. The remainder of my estate to be sold by my executor and the proceeds to be equally divided between the aforesaid James, David & Isabella Miller. I appoint Joseph Black executor, 14 Dec 1853. Robert Miller (LS), Wit: David McDowell, Mary A. Black, A. D. Black. Proved by the oath of David McDowell 13 Feb 1858. Qualified Joseph Black as executor 5 March 1858.

**Pages 389-390**: South Carolina, York District. Will of Nancy M. Poag of district aforesaid... to my daughters Selena Poag, Nancy Adeline Poag & Dorcas M. Poag, the tract of land on which I nor reside, 160 acres, to be divided between them equally. In case of the death of one or more of my said daughters without leaving heirs, then the share of such deceased shall go to the survivors. Also to my said daughters all household & kitchen furniture. To Mary Elizabeth Poag the daughter of Dorcas M. Poag, one bed & furniture. I appoint James Poag executor. [not dated] Nancy M. Poag (S), Wit: G. Gordon, J. S. Tipping, James Long (X). Proved by the oath of Green Gordon 26 Feb 1858. Qualified James Poag as executor 26 Feb 1858.

**Pages 390-391**: South Carolina, York District. Will of Robert Caldwell of district aforesaid... To my niece Margaret Ann Caldwell $200. To my nephew Robert A. Caldwell $600. To my nephew Hugh G. Caldwell $300. To my nephew William Caldwell $200. To my niece Martha K. Meek $200. To my sister Sarah Smith $200. To my brother Gilbreath Caldwell $200. To my nephew Robert C. Smith of Arkansas $300. To James Caldwell my brother my negro woman Mary & her child. To Margaret Whisonant's Mary & Sarah $50 each. To Bersheba Church all my stock in the Kings Mountain Rail Road. My wearing apparel to be equally divided between my nephews & I appoint Robert A. Caldwell, my sole executor, 27 March 1858. Robert Caldwell (LS), Wit: A. M. Henry, James L. Harris, William Love. Proved by the oath of A. M. Henry 19 April 1858. Qualified Robert A. Caldwell as executor 19 April 1858.

# YORK COUNTY SC WILL BOOK 3 1840-1862

**Pages 391-393**: South Carolina, York District. Will of Isaac Donnom Witherspoon, a planter and attorney at law, of Yorkville... To my wife Nancy during her lifetime or widowhood, the following real & personal estate: my house & lot with the household & kitchen furniture including the lot on which my law stands int he village of York, with a tract of land near Yorkville where I have a small farm on the right of the public road from York to Pinckney, as likewise the following negroes Sophy (my cook), Adianda, George & Betty with Betty's present & future increase. Also my carriage & carriage horses. The balance of my estate both real and personal including negro, stock, money, debts due me, law books, rail road stock) to be divided between my wife Nancy and such of my children as may be alive at my decease, my daughter Nancy not to be included in this division having heretofore made her equal by advancements. I appoint my wife Nancy so long as she remains a widow as executrix, & my son Donnom & my brother George Mc. Witherspoon, executors, 21 Feb 1853. J. D. Witherspoon (LS), Wit: William B. Wilson, John G. Enloe, J. M. Ross. Proved by the oath of John G. Enloe 10 Sept 1858. Qualified Nancy Witherspoon & J. D. Witherspoon Jun as executors.

**Pages 393-394**: South Carolina, York District. Will of Samuel Wright of said district... I give my wife of my estate $2000 which she may take in money or in such property as she may choose, at the appraised valued, the same to be accepted by her in lieu of dower. The residue of my estate, I give to my children. The estate of my children be held together for their maintenance and education. As each child shall attain the age of 21, such child shall then have allotted to him or her the share to which he or she may be entitled. I appoint my wife as executrix, 9 Aug 1855. S. Wright, Wit: Saml W. Melton, Amanda Galbraith, J. M. Smith. Proved by the oath of Samuel W. Melton 13 Oct 1858.

**Pages 394-395**: Will of Thomas Faris of York District... I will that there be no useless expences attend my burial, nor no tomb stone be placed at my grave nor no funeral preached on the occasion. To my daughter Mary B. Garrison no more than what I have given her with the exception of the equal part of my library to be divided amongst all my children except my family table which I devise to my two daughters Catharine S. Faris and Harriet E. Faris (jointly). To my daughter Sarah G. Faris $5. To my daughter Eliza S. Wallace a note of upwards of $60 I hold against James A. Wallace her husband subject to some credit I owe him for some work done for me. To my son Elijah A. Faris, the land I have designated under a bonded title or deed of gift dated 20 Dec 1848, also water privileges are open way to my spring. To Mariann J. Youngblood the one[?] of all the money or cash on hand after the settling of all my debts and dues. To my two daughters Catharine S. Faris and Harriet E. Faris jointly the balance of two thirds of all cash on hand as balance equal with my daughter Marianne J. Youngblood, also my Bible in which is my family record, also all estate real and personal not designated to my son Elijah A. Faris. I also desire that there be no sale of any property to debts, as I suppose there will be enough money on hand and a surplus to settle my debts & dues. I appoint my son Elijah A. Faris executor, and that I at my own requested have called in Joseph Starnes, Robert T. Starnes and William

Anderson in the presence of each other to see me sign and seal the same, 23 Nov 1858. Thomas Faris (X) (LS). Proved by the oath of Joseph Starnes 3 Jan 1859. Qualified Elijah A. Faris as executor 3 Jan 1859.

**Page 396**: South Carolina, York District. Will of Ann Campbell of district above written... To my niece Elizabeth Campbell the residue of my estate after payment of debts, consisting of money, notes, household & kitchen furniture, and anything real or personal, 4 May 1859. Ann Campbell (LS), Wit: J. L. Adams, M. C. Armstrong, J. T. Armstrong. Proved by the oath of J. L. Adams 30 May 1859.

**Pages 396-397**: South Carolina, York District. Will of Samuel R. Dickey of district aforesaid... To my sister Ann Dickey all my interest in the land and negroes in this state owned jointly by us and all my intestate in the State Of Texas owned jointly by us. Also to my said sister all the estate both real and personal which I have, 1 March 1859. Samuel R. Dickey (Seal), Wit: Wm. B. Wilson, Simpson Rawls, William Rawls. Proved by the oath of Wm. B. Wilson 8 July 1859.

**Pages 397-398**: Will of Catharine Moore... My negroes Leander, Leonard, and Cinda to be sold at my death and out of the sales my debts & funeral expenses to be paid. To my son Peter Marion $500, to my grandson Francis E. Moore $400. To my grandson Wm. L. Sandefur $200. To my grandson Nathaniel M. Sandefur $200, and the remainder of said sales if any to be equally divided among the children of my late daughter Eliz. A. Moore decd. To Calvin P. Sandefur & Wm. L. Sandefur my negro woman Renah & her son Rufus in trust for the use of my granddaughter Jane Catharine Sadler. To my granddaughter Emma K. Hemphill my negro girl Emmy and boy John. To my grand daughter Jane A. Williams my negro girls Savilla & Rena. To my granddaughter Eliza C. Lindsey my negroes Margaret and Jacob. To my grandson Joseph P. Moore my negro child Louisa daughter of Emmy. I appoint my grandson Jos P. Moore & James M. Williams, executors, 1 Sept 1858. Catharine Moore (X) (LS), Wit: J. C. Tippeng, David M. Pressley, J. M. Ross. Proved by the oath of J. C. Tippeng 26 Aug 1859. Qualified Joseph P. Moore and James M. Williams as executors.

**Pages 398-399**: Will of Daniel Mesheau... To my wife Nancy Mesheau the following negroes viz Amy, Bob, Ed, Harriet & Margaret, and during her life my plantation and stock of all kind, farming utensils, household furniture & crop growing. To my daughter Mary Ann Bolen the following negroes viz Milly & Dick, and the plantation & other property willed to my wife during her life, but my daughter is bound to support and take care of my son Allison P; .Mesheau for and during his life. To my granddaughter Nancy Jane Bolen my negro girl Patsey. To my said wife, all the residue of my estate, 6 May 1857. Daniel Mesheau (LS), Wit: James Felchett, Jonathan Felchett, W. R. McCorkle. Proved by the oath of Jonathan Felchett 26 Aug 1859.

**Pages 399-401**: South Carolina, York District. Will of William H. Johnston... to my beloved wife Susan E. Johnston all my household and kitchen furniture, my cow & calf and amply supply of provisions for my family for one year. Also the one third part of the balance of my estate real and personal. To my children George Augustin, Margaret Dorcas & Anna Cora the remaining two thirds of my estate real and personal to be divided equally among them. It is my will that my library be kept for the benefit of my family, my executors however have the right to divide the same amongst my children when she may deem it necessary or property. I will that my beloved wife Susan E. Johnston whom I have hereinafter the guardian of my children shall educate them as liberally as their circumstances will warrant her doing. My said executrix shall have the liberty of disposing of certain classical & theological books which in her opinion would not be of any considerable benefit to my family. I appoint my wife Susan guardian of my children and executrix of my will, 17 Jun 1859. Wm. H. Johnston (LS), Wit: J. M. H. Adams, M. E. Crenshaw, J. J. Smith. Proved by the oath of J. M. H. Adams 8 Aug 1859. Qualified Susan E. Johnston as executrix 8 Aug 1859.

**Page 401**: Will of Margaret Graham of York District... to my granddaughter Margaret Graham my bed and furniture. To my son Arch'd Graham my house & lands on which I now live and all the balance of my property including the legacy left me by my brother in North Carolina. I appoint my son Archibald Graham executor, 1 May 1854. Margaret Graham (X) (Seal), Wit: John Cheek Smith, Wm. Felts Sen, Silas Felts. Proved by the oath of John Cheek Smith and Silas Felts 21 Sept 1859. Qualified Archibald Graham as executor 21 Sept 1859.

*N.B.* Pages 402-405 are missing on the South Carolina Archives microfilm and on the older LDS microfilm. Therefore, I assume that the pages are missing from the original book. By checking the index in the front of the volume, I was able to ascertain which wills were recorded on those pages. I have made abstracts from the original loose wills on South Carolina Archives microfilm. The proper references to the original records are included with these abstracts.

**York County Estates, Case 42, File 1786**. South Carolina, York District. Will of John S. Moore... to my sons Theodore A., Samuel R. and William A. Moore in trust for the use and benefit of my granddaughters Amanda J. Springs, Lana B. Springs and Buennet Springs, each $10,000 when they arrive to the age of 18 years old and should either of them die then to her issue but if either die leaving no issue alive, then to her surviving sisters my granddaughter Margaret Lyon being one of them. The remainder of my property both real and personal to my sons Theodore A., Samuel R. and William A. Moore to be equally divided amongst them, and I appoint my said sons my executors, 7 Jan 1858. John S. Moore (S), Wit: Eli Meek, E. M. Kirkpatrick, W. B. Byers. Proved by the oath of W. B. Byers 4 Jan 1860. Qualified Saml R. Moore, exr., 4 Jan 1860.

**York County Estates, Case 41, File 1738**. North Carolina, Gaston County. Whereas, by an agreement heretofore made and entered into between my husband William W. Garvin and myself and one Alexander S. Wallace, it was provided that certain property and estate should be conveyed to and held by the said Alexander S. Wallace for my use and benefit during my life, and that I should have the right to dispose of said estate by my will, as though I were a feme sole. I direct that my executors to sell and convey all my real estate in South Carolina and to sell and convey all my real estate in North Carolina, but as I own a tract of land in Gaston County, containing about 271 acres in which my mother has a claim of dower, I leave it discretionary with my executors either to sell said real estate which she lives with the encumbrance of dower, or to postpone the sale until after her death. To Leroy Adams during the lifetime of my mother Elizabeth J. Stowe, one negro girl named Jeneva and her child Roxana in trust for the said Elizabeth J. Stowe. To my late husband's nephew Robert M. Wallace, one negro boy Zimri. To my nephew Gaban Stowe, son of my sister Margaret Stowe, my gold watch. To the Rev. Robert Y. Russell one of the ministers of the Independent Presbyterian Church $500. $100 in trust for the use of my two nieces Susan Elizabeth Stow and her infant sister not yet name, children of my sister Margaret Stowe. I appoint George W. Williams and Samuel W. Melton, Esquires, to be executors, 11 July 1859. Sarah C. Garvin (LS), Wit: J. Blair Hunter, J. F. Wilson, Robt Wilson. Proved in York District by the oath of J. B. Hunter 5 Nov 1859. Qualified G. W. Williams as executor 7 Nov 1859.

**York County Estates, Case 41, File 1737**. South Carolina, York District. Nov. 15th 1859 Will of Miss Jane Farris... my sister Margaret to have $200, sister Nancy $125, sister Mary H. Hare $100, my niece Susan Jane Hare $100 to be disposed of as Wm. J. Farris thinks property untill she is of a proper age. My aunt Jane Sloan $50. The balance of my estate to my brother W. J. Farris also the balance due me from my brother deceased to be included in this will and given to my brother W. J. Farris, also my sun flower quilt and one of my last woves. I leave my bed and the balance of my bed clothes to my sister Margaret. I wish no sale or appraisement of my property, and I appoint my brother W. J. Farris executor, 25 Nov 1859. Jane Farris (X) (LS), Wit: J. W. Robison, John H. Bailey, W. B. Fewell. Proved by the oath of Wm. B. Fewell 2 Jan 1860.

**Page 406**: Qualified Wm. G. Faris as executor 16 January 1860.

**Pages 406-408**: Will of Wm Moore Sen of York District... I will my negro woman Mariah & her four children Cynthia, Tena, Lucinda, & Nancy to my children John Moore, Orson Moore, Wm Moore Jr., Welborn Bridge wife of Wm Bridges, Isaac W. Moore, Jonathan Moore & my grandchildren the children of Francis J. Moore decd. The negro woman Fanny & her children shall go to the daughters of my wife Ruth B. Moore by her first husband Abraham G. Smith in according with the settlement made of said negro woman Fanny on my wife and her daughters by her grandmother Ruth B. Moore decd. To my stepson James M. Smith the son of Abraham G. Smith decd the plantation on which I now reside containing 223 acres on Gion Moores Creek & waters of Broad River adj. Sally Smith, John G. Smith, James Scoggins & others, said James M. Smith not to receive said land until the death of my wife. My negro woman Ellen shall go to my wife Ruth during her life and at her death said negro woman Ellen shall be appraised and my stepson John M. Smith shall pay the appraised price to my executions who shall pay the one half of the same to my children by my first wife and children of my son Francis J. Moore decd. At my death my executors shall apportion off to my wife Ruth B. Moore as much as they may think sufficient to do my wife for one year of corn, fodder, meat & cows, horses, sheep & hogs, and furniture, for my wife to carry on her business on the farm, and any surplus shall be divided equally between my own children and my three step sons A. T. Smith, John M. Smith & Jos. W. Smith. Whereas I am the guardian of my step son Jas M. Smith now a minor, if I die before I have made a final settlement with my said ward, my executors shall settle. I appoint my son Wm. Moor Junr, my step son John M. Smith and my friend John J. Wylie executors, 27 Aug 1848. William Moore (LS), Wit: Wm. C. Black, John Moore, John L. Briges. Proved by the oath of John Moore 24 Oct 1859. Qualified Wm. Moore Jun, John M. Smith & John J. Wylie as executors, 24 Oct 1859.

**Pages 408-409**: Will of William Camp of York District...To my beloved wife Mary Camp all my estate both real & personal of every description and at her death to be equally divided among my six children Harris B. Harden, Lawrence S. Camp, Joseph P. Camp, Mary Caroline Starnes, Amanda F. Palmer & Adalissa Camp. I empower my wife & executors if they should think necessary to partition off a portion of my estate equally among my children or to set off any portion that may be necessary to pay debts. I appoint Laurence S. Camp, Noah Hardin & John Starnes Junr exrs., 28 May 1858. William Camp Sen. (LS), Wit: John Moore, John Young, Wm. C. Black. Proved by the oath of John Moore 12 Oct 1859. Qualified L. S. Camp, Noah Harden & Jno Starnes, exrs., 6 Feb 1860.

**Pages 409-410**: South Carolina, York District. Will of Jane Campbell of said district... To my niece Jane Jenkins $100 if living if not then to her daughters equally. To my niece Jane McCully my trunk & all that is in with all my apparel. To Mary, Rebecca & Jane McCully $25 each. I allow Emelia Barnett $30. I allow Jane C. Craig my bureau also $25 to be paid to her father and to be kept for her use. I allow Martha E. Campbell, Elizabeth J. Jackson, & Eliza A. Campbell $25 each to be paid to their fathers for their use. I allow E. A. Campbell my wheel and card, one small table. I allow Saml Campbell to have his note I hold on him also my arm chair and large Bible. I appoint my friend Eliz. Campbell $30. I allow Wm. Campbell my R. R. Stock also one bed & clothes that belong to it. I allow Ann Barnett the bed I slept on with the clothes. The remainder of my money to be dispose of equally between my friend Eliz. Campbell and her children. I wish my friends A. P. C. Campbell and Myles Smith to execute this will, 6 April 1854. Jane Campbell (X) (LS), Wit: Robt P. Smith, John Smith. Myles Smith. Proved by the oath of Myles Smith 15 March 1860. Qualified Dr. Andr P. C. Campbell as executor 15 March 1860.

**Pages 410-411**: Will of Deborah Watson of District of York... To my daughter Jane I bequeath Myles & the plantation I now live on, to my daughter Jane

& her son Albert equally and likewise one bed, household & kitchen furniture, my old negro Kate in consideration of which they must pay to my [daughter?] Elizabeth's children the sum of one dollar. To my son James Children $10 to be divided equally among them and to my daughter Margaret $5,one bed & furniture. I give my cloth to my grandson Saml. W. Jackson. My wearing apparel I leave to be divided betwixt my two daughters. I allow my daughter Jane to pay her Drucilla $10. I nominate Wm. Watson & my grandson Alberta as executors, 8 Dec 1846. Deborah Watson (X) (LS), Wit: David M. Watson, Wm. Watson, Rich'd Gillespie. Proved by the oath of John L. Watson & John R. Hall who testified that David M. Watson, Wm. Watson & Richd Gillespie who were witnesses are all dead and the said John L. Watson made oath to the handwriting of David M. Watson & Wm. Watson and John R. Hall made oath to the handwriting of Richard Gillespie, 13 March 1860. Qualified Albert Watson as executor 13 March 1860.

**Pages 411-412**: South Carolina, York District. Nov. 21st 1859. Will of James Boyd of district aforesaid... To my daughter Margt E. Boyd that portion of property that I have given her. That portion of property I have given to my daughter Fanny R. Garrison to her. To my daughter Mary J. Simril provided she leaves her mother $1000. I invest my wife Eliz J. Boyd with full power to dispose of my property during her lifetime. I appoint Rufus Boyd sole executor and provided he be not living, I appoint my son John Boyd to act in his place, 21 Nov 1859. James Boyd (LS), Wit: John L. Erwin, John R. Smith, R. G. Kendrick. Proved by the oath of John R. Smith 13 March 1860. Qualified R. F. Boyd as executor 13 March 1860.

**Pages 412-413**: York District, So Car. Will of Jerusha Leech... To my beloved sister Martha all my undivided half of property which now own in common. At her death or sooner if she chooses to do so, I will that my share or interest in Coly & her two children be equally divided between my two beloved nieces Martha & Jerusha Moss. The remainder of my share of interest in all property to be disposed of by my sister Martha. I appoint my sister Martha executrix, 27 April 1855. Jerusha Leech (X) (LS), Wit: Samuel Wright, Martha Archer, John M. Goza. Proved by the oath of Martha Archer 27 July 1860. Qualified Martha Leech as executrix 28 July 1860.

**Pages 413-414**: South Carolina, York District. Will of Sarah C. Smith of district aforesaid... To my daughter Margaret Whisonant all my real estate, my negro girl Jane also one half of my personal property exclusive of my notes, accounts & cash on hand. To my daughter Martha M. Whisonant $500 in cash and the one half of my personal property exclusive of my notes. To my other three children viz Jno Smith, Robt C. Smith & Nancy Whisonant the remainder of my money, notes and accounts after paying debts and the legacy of $500. I appoint Henderson Whisonant executor, 9 March 1859. Sarah Smith (X) (Seal), Wit: James Caldwell, William Love, Robert A. Caldwell. Proved by the oath of James Caldwell 27 July 1860. Qualified Henderson Whisonant as executor 27 July 1860.

**Pages 414-415**: Will of John Smith of York District, feeling the infirmities of age... To my son Myles Smith I give him my servants Hannah, Leander, Phebe, $200 in cash (my stock (1 share) in the K. M. Rail Road & my cupboard. To my grandson Robt P .Smith my servants Billy, Carey, Ann, Rufus, Jackson, Jane, Warren & $600. To my grandson John J. Smith my servants Waties, Sam, Amanda, Foster & Mary & her child Eliza, Ellen & Morris, also my side board, two half round tables, small mahogany table, my chest, a large pitcher, silver spectacles, shaving glass & razor, large looking glass, clock, iron pot rack & $600. To my grandson Wm. B. Smith my plantation known as the Faulkner tract, Ephraim my servant & also Adaline, Wesley, Cuffy & Andrew, my square walnut table, $600, the property to remain in charge of my son Myles Smith till said Wm. B. Smith comes of age. I nominate my grandsons Robert & John Smith, executors, 2 May 1860. John Smith (LS), Wit: A. Glass, J. E. Pursley, S. L. Watson. Codicil: the balance of my land known as the Burns, Polly Floyd, Ramseys & Howe tract, be divided between my grandsons Robert & John adj. Rays corner, 2 May 1860. Proved by the oath of W. L. Watson & Alex Glass 16 July 1860. Qualified Robert P. Smith as executor 16 July 1860.

**Pages 415-416**: South Carolina, York District. Will of Esther Bigger of said district... To my son Andrew Bigger the plantation whereon I now reside with my bed & bedding, also my share of the kitchen furniture. It is my desire that my daughter Margaret have her living on said plantation during her single life and $10. To Mary Quinton $10. My wearing apparel to be equally divided between my three daughters Margaret, Mary & Maria. As respects my two sons James A. & Robt P. Bigger from the ungrateful treatment they executed towards me, I feel under no obligation to will them any portion of my estate. I appoint my son Andrew Bigger my executor, 2 Jan 1852. Esther Bigger (LS), Wit: John Hall, John Smith, Myles Smith. Proved by the oath of Myles Smith 16 July 1860. Qualified Andrew J. Bigger as executor 16 July 1860.

**Pages 416-417**: Will of Jesse K. Armstrong... My wife Jane W. Armstrong to remain on my plantation & receive a comfortable support from the same. My servants Watson, Mingo, Gilbert, Matilda, Adaline & Mary remain on my place during the life of my wife to aid in the support of my family. All my personal property not otherwise disposed of to be equally divided between my wife Jane & my children, as my children severally marry. The plantation on which I now reside to my son Lawson Kingsbury encumbered as above. At the death of my wife Jane, my servants Watson, Mingo, Gilbert, Matilda, Adaline & Mary to him. My lower plantation (formerly my brother Robert's) to remain for the support of my family until my youngest child comes of age then to be sold & the proceeds divided between my wife and children. My mill on Allison Creek to be returned for the use of my family. I nomination my daughter Isabella guardian of my daughter Sarah Jane. I nomination my wife Jane & my daughter Mary Clinton the executrixes, 23 March 1860. J. K. Armstrong (LS), Wit: E. G. Campbell, W. E. Campbell, S. L. Watson. Proved by the oath of Rev. Saml L. Watson 14 May 1860.

**Pages 417-418**: South Carolina, York District. March 13th 1859. Will of Joseph Adams... To my son John H. Adams in addition to what I have already given him, my boy George. To my daughter Amanda Caroline Adams, my servants John, Sye & Harriet & her children, also my waggon & two horses or mules with harness, household & kitchen furniture. To my grandson Richard A. Sherrel (son of my daughter Emily decd), should he live to the age of 21 years, $400. My servants William & Jane children of girl Lydia to my children Wm, John, James, Leander, Amanda Caroline, to be equally divided among them. The balance of my property to be equally divided among my children Jane M. McLean, Wm. E., John H., James L. M. & Amanda C. Adams. The corner of my place where Jas Davis & Robt E. Adams also corners, and with myself & A. Stowe also corners. Should my son Wm. E. Adams wish to possess as much of the plantation on which I reside, he be allowed to have it at a fair price. Should my son J. Leander Adams desire my plantation adj. him, he be allowed to retain it by paying a fair price. I appoint my sons Wm. E. Adams & John H. Adams, exrs. Joseph Adams (LS), Wit: S. L. Watson, S. N. Watson, D. A. A. Watson. Codicil mentions grandson Jos. A. McLean, 18 April 1859. Jos Adams, Wit: S. L. Watson, D. A. Adams, Robt E. Adams. Proved by the oath of S. L. Watson 14 May 1860.

**Pages 418-419**: Will of John Kennedy... To my beloved wife Naomi Kennedy the plantation on which I now live and after her death the said plantation to be sold and the proceeds to be equally divided between my three children James R., Wm. M. & Rachel N. and to my wife the following negroes Henry & wife Sarah, Hannah, George Russell, Solomon & Alfred and at her death to be equally divided between my three children James R., Wm. M. & Rachel N. To my son James R. a negro girl Caroline & her four children. To my son Wm. M. my negro girl Margaret & her four youngest child. To my daughter Rachel N. negroes Harriet, Jane, Emily Ann, Amanda Eliza & Sam. To my three grandchildren, children of my daughter Nancy E. Ross, the following negroes Naomi, her eldest child my negro girl Cinda; to Jane her second daughter my boy Andy, and to Samuel her youngest son I give boy Amzi. I appoint my sons James R. & Wm. M. executors, 2 April 1860. John Kennedy (LS), Wit: J. M. Meek, J. S. Plexico, G. Caldwell. Proved by the oath of J. M. Meek 11 May 1860. Qualified James R. & Wm. M. Kennedy as executors 11 May 1860.

**Pages 419-420**: South Carolina, York District. Will of A. G. Lawrence... To my daughter Amelia Hunter, Phebe Ann with her increase for her sole & separate use during her life not subject to the debts of her husband & at her death said negroes to be vested in the child or children that said daughter may have. To my daughter Amanda McNinch[?], Adaline Jane on the same principles as Amelia. To my daughter Francis, Harriet & Clementine on the same principles as above, also to receive household furniture & stock equal to Amanda. To my daughter Margt, Louise, Mellon & Susan on the same principles as above, also house hold furniture & live stock equal with the others. To my daughter Emma Green, Candace & Calvin on the same principles as above, also house hold furniture & live stock equal with the others. To my son John William, Anthony & Viny & Tom with a bay colt he now claims, also the plantation with all the farming implements and appendages with his choice of four mules at his mother's demise. To my wife Martha her living on my plantation with the care & direction of all & eery thing not disposed of to manage ever matter the same as I have or would do. At her death all not disposed of to be equally divided among my daughters ont he same terms as I have directed above the two little girls to be schooling something equal to the other girls, my debts & the Jackson estate to be paid out of the monies or notes on hand. I request my friend J. B. Hunter to assist my wife in the execution of this my will, June 14, 1860. A. G. Lawrence (LS), Wit: John P. Hogue, A. Glass, Myles Smith. Proved by the oath of Myles Smith 30 July 1860. Qualified Martha Lawrence & Jas. B. Hunter as executors 30 July 1860.

**Pages 420-422**: South Carolina, York District. Will of Sarah McFaddin... to my son Samuel McFadden $200 in money & a negro boy called Lawson Henderson. To Jefferson V. McFadden $500 in money in trust however for the alone & separate use & benefit of daughter Caroline wife of Wm. Wylie. To Robert McFadden $100 in money & a negro girl called Mary Jane for the alone & separate use & benefit of my daughter Susan wife of Wm. Beatty. To my son Jefferson V. McFadden a negro woman named Julia & her child Margaret Willoughby my waggon, half of my farming tools & one half of my cows, hogs & sheep. To my son Thomas McFadden $500 in money. To my son Henry McFadden $500 in money. To John McFadden $100 in money in trust for the use and benefit of my son James McFadden & his family. To my five daughters Caroline Wylie, Susan Beatty, Mary McKnight, Emily McConnell & Eliza Rowell my household & kitchen furniture to be equally divided between them. I have give n no part of said furniture to my daughter Jane Rowell simply for the reason that she resides at a great distance from me & not from any want of love & affection towards her. After payment of any debts and expenses of my funeral & the cash legacies above stated, the balance of my estate to be equally divided amongst nine of my children viz John McFadden, Thos McFadden, Robt McFadden, Wm. McFadden, Henry McFadden, Mary McKnight, Emily McConnell, Eliza Rowell & Jane Rowell. I appoint my three sons Henry, Robert, Jefferson V. McFadden, executors, May 12th 1859. Sarah McFadden (X) (LS), Wit: G. W. Williams, James Jefferys, Saml W. Melton. Proved by the oath of James Jefferys 10 Feb 1860. Qualified Henry, Robert, & Jefferson V. McFadden as executors 20 Feb 1860.

**Pages 422-426**: South Carolina, York District. Will of John Roddy... To my beloved wife Mary G. Roddy my negro man Nelson, my negro woman Ibby and their issue, also four head of horses or mules as she may choose, four milch cows and calves, my entire stock of hogs & sheep, one waggon and gearing, also my old buggy & harness & one new buggy to be made by Wm. P. McFadden & harness, also blacksmiths tools, one thrasher & fan, all my plows & plow irons, etc. To my beloved wife Mary G. Roddy my negro girl Mary during her life or widowhood, then to be divided between my three sons David C. Roddy, Thos. E. Roddy & Wm. L. Roddy. Also to my wife Mary the plantation whereon I now live known as the McFadden, Horne & Story tracts about 700 acres for her own use & the boarding of my four daughters & little son Jos. W. Roddy, this being her full consideration of all dower claims, and should she marry or at her death, then said lands be sold and the proceeds equally divided between my four sons David C., Thos E. Wm. L. & Jos. W. Roddy. To my daughter Nancy Jane Roddy my negro girl Sarah & negro boy Lee & their issue. To my daughter Sarah L. Roddy my negro woman Septima[?] and negro girl Cinda. To my daughter Mary J. Roddy my negro boy Bill, negro girl Laura & boy Mars. To my daughter Martha A. Roddy my negro man Lewis, negro girl Harriet & their issue. To my son Joseph W. Roddy my negro woman Tilla & negro boy Ben & their issue. To my son David c. Roddy over & above his former advancement my negro boy Hiram. To my son Thos E. Roddy over & above his former advancement my negro boy Monro. To my son Wm. L. Roddy over & above his former advancement my negro boy Eli. I also will that my two negro girls Caroline & Louisa be appraised & either of my three oldest sons be allowed to take them by paying up the appraisement. My negro boy Allen be sold and all my unwilled personal property also that my lower plantation about 227 acres & two acres being my part of the mill seat making 229 acres. our of the money there be erected a monument over my grave to cost about four of five hundred dollars to be of fine Italian marble with suitable inscription. For the purpose of assisting[?] an additional building to Neelys Creek Church it having been my lifetime place of worship the sum of $150. Also $100 to each of my oldest sons David C. Roddy, Thos E. Roddy & Wm. L. Roddy, the remainder of all my money to be divided between my wife & all my children. I appoint my wife Mary G. Roddy, David C. Roddy, Thos E. Roddy & Wm. L. Roddy, exrs., 31 May 1860. John Roddy (Seal), Wit: Saml Wylie, David T. Lesley, David Roddy. Codicil leaving daughter Nancy G. Roddy $400, my daughter Sarah L.Roddy $100, my daughter Margaret J. Roddy $300, my daughter Marthan A. $300, to my son Joseph W. Roddy $300, and to my wife Mary G. Roddy $250, dated 23 June 1860. John Roddy (LS), Wit: Saml Wylie, David T. Lesley, David Roddy. Proved by the oath of David Roddy 16 July 1860. Qualified David C. Roddy ,Thos E. Roddy & Wm. L. Roddy as executors 16 July 1860.

Page 427 is blank.

**Pages 428-431**: Will of Nancy Blair of Yorkville... That I may be decently buried according to the arrangement made by the executors of late husband. of the estate or property left to me for life by my late husband John Blair, by his will, with the request and advice that I devise the same to such of the legatees of his said will in York District as I might select, I hereby exercise that power and give to Susan Elizabeth Moore daughter of Clark Moore and his late wife Martha, $500; to William, son of the same Clark and Martha Moore, $500, John Cairnes to be guardian of said children. I bequeath to James P. Blair ten shares of South Carolina Railroad stock and $500 in money and to his son Irwin, $750. To William Latta Senior $500 and to Nancy, daughter of John Latta, $500, said William Latta to be guardian for his said granddaughter Nancy. To Mary Frances, Thomas, Henry and Nancy Irwin, two sons and two daughters of Joseph Mitchell, 30 shares of Bank of Hamburgh stock and $1500 in money. and to said Mary Frances and Nancy Irwin in addition to the above, each $500. To Robert Gilfillan $500 and to his daughter Martha Love, $500. To John B. Lowry, 80 shares of Farmer's & Planter's Bank stock of Baltimore, Maryland. To Samuel Blair, near Blairsville, the remainder of said estate. Of my individual and absolute estate, I give to William H. McCorkle of Yorkville, my common wearing apparel, my common bed-clothing, my farming tools of all kinds excepting the wagon, my hogs, provisions and groceries on hand. The sum of $2000 to be reserved and placed in the hands of William Wright and William H. McCorkle who are earnestly requested to place said sum at interest and spend the interest in providing clothing, sugar, coffee and such other necessaries for the comfort of the negroes Isaac, Jacob, Adeline, and such other of my negroes that may abe alive at my death. Remainder to be equally divided between Mary Margaret and John Blair, children of Margaret B. Stockton and Martha and Ann Blair, daughters of Mary H. Moore. To Mary H. Moore and Margaret B. Stockton to be equally divided between them all my fine wearing apparel and all my fain bed-clothing. To Nancy Irwin daughter of the late Dr. J. B. Hunter, $500 and I constitute her mother to be her guardian. To Ann M. Beatty, wife of W. C. Beatty, for her sole and separate use,$200. To Caroline G. Boggs, $100. Of my individual estate, one third thereof to Margaret B. Stockton and her children, one third to Mary H. Moore and her children, one third to Joel Huggins and John F. Irwin to be equally divided between them. I appoint William Wright and W. C. Beatty, exrs., __ Jan 1855. Nancy Blair (Seal), Wit: J. H. Adams, J. A. McLean, E. F. Meek. Codicil leaving to William H. McCorckle $4400, and appoint him to served with W. C. Beatty as executor in place of Col. Wm. Wright now deceased, 5 March 1858. Nancy Blair (LS), Wit: Joseph Herndon, J. A. McLean, J. J. Smith. Another codicil giving to W. H. McCorkle $1100, 13 July 1858. Wit: John H. Adams, John J. Smith, G. W. Williams. Proved by the oath of J. A. McLean 2 Nov 1860. Codicil proved by J. J. Smith 2 Nov 1860. Qualified William C. Beatty and William H. McCorkle, exrs., 2 Nov 1860.

**Pages 432-433**: South Carolina, York District. Will of James A. Burnett of the district aforesaid... I will that my negro girl named Candes be sold in order to settle my debts and the balance of the money to be equally divided between my daughters Mary, Hannah, and Adeline, after my son James Josiah receives $25. My negro girl Sarah to my wife Eliza and my four horse wagon & bay horse. My small wagon to my daughter Mary. My buggy to my daughter Margaret. My bald horse to my son Robert. To my son John the gray colt and silver watch and saddle. My stock of cattle, hogs, household and kitchen furniture & farming utensils left to my wife Eliza, for the use of the family, for her to dispose of as she sees proper. To my wife Margaret & John the land whereon the house is situated, commencing on Biggers' line, and Wm. A. Burnett's line. That balance of the land be equally divided between my sons Alexander & Robert. I desire that William A. Burnett & J. D. P. Currence execute this my will, 6 Oct 1860. Jas. A. Burnett (LS), Wit: R. L. Simmons, H. A. Wallace, S. L. Campbell. Proved by the oath of R. L. Simmons 12 Nov 1860. Qualified William & Burnett & J. D. P. Currence executors 12 Nov 1860.

**Pages 433-434**: York District, S. C. Will of John B. Swann of the district above named... To my son John M. Swann the south division of my land on Neil Branch, Beckey's branch [metes and bounds included]. To my son H. L. Swan the north division of my land new Old Brick yard and Still-house adj. Strait, the Meeting-house lot, B. J. Mendenhall [metes and bounds included]. To my son John M. Swann my negro boy Simmon for his only use. To my son H. L. Swann my negro girl for his only use. To my grand daughter Jane A. Swann the first girl child my negro girl Ann may have. To J. M. Swann my truffle horses and H. L. Swann my rounoak horse. I give to my sons my black smith, carpenter tools, and waggon provided J.M. Swann comes home in his right mind. I allow my negro woman Mariah to be sold and her price equally divided between my two sons. I appoint J. M. Wallace agent for my son John M. Swann, as long as he is not in his right mind here at home or in the Asylum. I appoint H. L. Swann executor of my will, 16 Feb 1848. John B. Swann (LS), Wit: J. M. Wallace, Wm. Smith, Eaton Swann. Proved by the oath of J. M. Wallace 10 Dec 1860. Qualified H. L. Swann executor 10 Dec 1860.

Note: John M. Swan was admitted to the Asylum on August 5, 1857, and cured and sent home on May 25, 1859. See the *South Carolina Magazine of Ancestral Research*, Volume XXIX, #3, (Spring, 2001), page 97.

**Pages 434-435**: Will of Mary Patrick of York District... My will is that my negro boy Calvin, about 23 years of age, be sold to pay my debts & if not enough money arising from the sale of my negro boy Calvin, my negro woman Suff to be sold. I give unto John D. ___ my negro boy Walker, 38 years of age, also my negro girl Betty, 26 years old, and if enough money from the sale of Calvin, he is to have negro woman Suff, all for the use of Thomas Patrick. To my niece Margaret Bigger one feather bed and furniture. I give to my brother Robert Patrick, one feather bed & furniture. I give all the balance of my beds, clothing, furniture, to John C. McLean for the use of Thomas Patrick. I give the plantation I now live on lying on the waters of Mill Creek, 150 acres adj. John McGill & others to John D. McLean for the use of Thomas Patrick. To my niece Margaret Bigger & my three sisters Margaret Duff, Esther Bigger & Martha Cawley, all of wearing clothes. I appoint my friend John D. Mclean my sole executor, 5 July 1849. Mary Patrick (X) (Seal), Wit: David C. Duff, Robt. M. Wilson, Thomas L. Brandon. Proved by the oath of Robert M. Wilson 11 Feb 1861. Qualified John M. Wilson executor 11 Feb 1861.

**Pages 435-436**: South Carolina, York District. Will of Andrew McCarter of York District... To my wife Mary one saddle and one little wheel and spotted heifer and one third part of all my household and kitchen furniture and one spotted cow. To my son Samuel W. McCarter one rifle gun, one half of my hogs and sheep and one half of my farming utensils, and one bed & furniture to my two sons Samuel and Andrew J. McCarter. To my son Andrew J. McCarter one short gun, one half of my farming utensils and one bed and furniture to my two sons Andrew J. McCarter and Samuel W. McCarter. To my daughter Sarah L. McCarter one black heifer and one third part of all my household and kitchen furniture and one brindle heifer. To my daughter Isabella J. McCarter one large wheel and one white heifer, and one third part of all my household and kitchen furniture. To my grand son Oliver J. McCarter $10 to be paid by my executor when he arrives at the age of 21 years. To my grand daughter Nixency V. C. McCarter $10 to be paid by my executor when she arrives at the age of 21 years. I nominate my brother in law Andrew M. McCarter, exr., 1 Sept 1859. Andrew McCarter (Seal), Wit: Joel McCarter, Margaret McCarter Samuel McCarter. Proved by the oath of Samuel W. McCarter 25 Feb 1861. Qualified Andrew McCarter executor 25 Feb 1861.

**Page 437**: Will of Sarah Rooker of the District of York... To my daughter Mary A. M. J. Finley, wife of Wm. G. Finley, my tract of land whereon I now live and at her death the same be sold and the proceeds be equally divided amongst the heirs of her body. I allow W. G. Finley (my son in law) the use of the above property during the life of his wife. I appoint Zada D. Smith executor 7 Oct 1860. Sarah Rooker (X) (LS), Wit: John T. Harper, Thos E. Harper, Robert Latta. Proved by the oath of John T. Harper 13 March 1861. Qualified Zadoc D. Smith executor 13 March 1861.

**Pages 438-439**: Will of Mary A. Rowell... To my niece Mary E. Clark the plantation on which I now reside, also all of my household & kitchen furniture, also all of my farming utensils, with all my stock. To my said niece Mary E. Clark my two slaves named Isaac & Henry. Should my niece die without any bodily heir, all of the above mentioned property shall revert back to my brother Benjamin D. Rowell. My sister Nancy W. Rowell shall remain on the plantation during the term of her life. I give to my brother Benjamin D. Rowell one slave named Joe & $1000. I give to my niece Mary E. Clark my two slaves Patty & Jane. My five slaves Sarah, Ephraim, Louisa, Molly & Perry shall be sold and out of the proceeds thereof I give to my sister Mary J. Poag, my sister Margaret E. Sloan, my niece Mary A. Foreman, & my niece Mary E. Rowell $400 each and the balance be equally divided between my two nieces Mary E. Clark & Sarah C. Logan. I appoint my brother Benjamin D. Rowell my executor, 25 April 1861. Mary A. Rowell (LS), Wit: D. K.Bates, Silvanus Williamson, J. N. Bratton. Proved by the oath of J. N. Bratton 7 May 1861. Qualified Benjamin D. Rowell executor 7 May 1861.

**Pages 439-440**: South Carolina, York District. Will of John McGill... I will that so much of my land upon which I now reside shall be sold and the money applied to the payment of my just debts. The balance of said tract I leave to my daughters Jane A., Clarissa H., and Amanda C. McGill, and to my granddaughter Avelina McGill. To my daughter Eliza M. Campbell $800 in cash. To my daughter Martha M. Stanton my negro man Minor with the provision that she pay into my estate the sum of $500. To my daughter Sarah A. Brandon the negro woman Sylvy. To my daughter Margaret A. Oats the negro girl Laura. To my daughter Zeverah[?] Johnston, the negro girl Emeline (which she now has in possession). To my daughter Clarissa H. McGill, the negro girl Martha. To my daughter Jane. A. McGill the negro girl Eliza. To Amanda C. McGill, the negro girl Violet. To my granddaughter Avelina M.

McGill the nero girl Ann. To Wm. McGill's widow and her son by the said Wm. McGill, one dollar cash. The negro woman Amy with the rest of my estate to my daughters Jane A., Clarissa H., and Amanda C. Mcgill. I appoint my friend David J. Glenn, sole executor, __ Dec 1860. John McGill (Seal), Wit: J. B. Hunter, R. L. Simmons, Thomas H. Turner. Proved by the oath of J. Blair Hunter 10 May 1861. Qualified David J. Glenn executor 15 May 1861.

**Pages 441-442**: South Carolina, York District. Will of Mary J. Floyd of district aforesaid... I allow my servant man Cury to choose his own master, who will pay to my executors $590 & $10 to Cury. I allow George to Izzeral E. Floyd & he to give up all demands against me to my exors & Give $10 to the boy George. I allow Flora, Holly & her youngest child, also Siah & Lizzie to J. Brison Venable. I allow Jeff a darkey to my sister Darcus Brown. I bequeath Bill to Elizabeth C. Floyd, Minerva to Mary Brown, and Bob to Margaret Floyd. I allow my old horse & black horse to J. B. Venable. I give my __ to Darcus Brown, my mule to Margaret Floyd, my cat[?] to J. A. Bell, and the 2 yr old Filley to be sold. I allow J. B. Venable to have 4 head of cows, his choice & Mary A. Floyd one the next choice, and the balance to be sold. I allow my sheep to be equally divided between Darcus Brown, Margaret Floyd & J. B. Venable. I allow $300 to be equally divided between Peggy Floyd & her children, ie. my Bro. John widow and children. I allow my buggy & harness to Eliz. B. Floyd & she to give up all demands against me. I give my land and all other property to J. B. Venable, I allow him to pay all my debts & last expenses. I appoint Alex. Glass & J. B. Venable to execute this my late will, 19 May 1861. Mary J. Floyd (X) (Seal), Wit: Robert Pursley, David McCulloh, A. P. Campbell. Proved by the oath of Dr. A. P. C. Campbell 16 July 1861. Qualified Alex Glass & J. B. Venable executors same day.

**Pages 442-443**: Will of James Crawford... I will four negroes to my wife namely Hannah, Maria, Anthony, Nercissa, and I will that my wife Mary Crawford and her two daughters namely Mary McGill, Martha A. Margaret Crawford do have their right to the dowery of my land during their natural lives or one third of my real estate, also all of my household and kitchen furniture claimed by my two daughters namely Mary & Martha which is two beds a piece and one bureau a piece. If the daughters marry, they are to have no right to my real estate. To my daughter Mary McGill a negro boy called Walker and a horse or $100 cash to be paid by my son John Crawford. I will to my daughter Martha A. Crawford a boy Ben and a horse or $100 cash to be paid by my son John Crawford. I will all of my lands to my son John Crawford and the improvements thereon bounded by Davises land, John McCarter & Wm Oats, 500 acres, a tract on the Burk road bounded by Wm. N. Crawford and Jane Crawford, 222 acres, also my smith tools and carpenters plains, and a negro boy named Henry. I will that all money and notes and accounts be equally divided between my wife Mary Crawford and my daughters Mary & Martha & my son John Crawford. I appoint my son John Crawford as executor, 7 July 1858. James Crawford (LS), Wit: Wm. Oates, Wm. B. Davison, James McElwee. Proved by the oath of Wm. Oats 12 Sept 1861.

**Pages 444-445**: Will of J. N. Stewart Jun of York District... I bequeath to my beloved wife the land, appurtenances thereon, known as the McFarlin tract on Bell's branch in York District, my blind mare, waggon & harness, one lot of hogs 7 head of sheep, my wheat crop this year, my clock, bureau, and looking glass, also my violin and body clothing. To my step-daughter Louisa Stewart for her benefit, all the residue of remainder of my real and personal estate to my wife now at my decease. I appoint S. H. Anthony and A. J. McGill, exrs., 12 July 1861. J. N. Stewart (X) (Seal), Wit: M. L. Sanders, M. V. Wilson, John N. Whisonant. Proved by the oath of M. V. Wilson 23 Sept 1861.

**Page 445** [appears to be fragment of will here]: South Carolina, York District. Will of William Moore of district aforesaid... to my daughter Jane C. Rawlinson, negroes that I have already given her: Margaret and her child Fed & Adaline, and also Jo, Dallas, Peggy, Julie & Lucy. To my son William S. Moore, the plantation he now lives on and 200 acres of land taken off the Rowel plantation on the side next to William Erwin & McFadden's land, that I have had surveyed & laid off for him, and also the negroes I have already given him Neel, Rachel, Sam, Mary Susan, Alfred, Jane & I also will him Little Jim and Mary & Henry. To my son H. Baxter Moore the one half of the plantation that lies on the Catawba River on both sides of the river, to be equally divided & Frederic E. Moore and I also will to him the following name negroes Bob, Toney, Jake, Dan, Ann & her oldest child, younger Nancy & her child. [see pages 451-452 on the following page].

[Page 446 is blank.]

**Page 447**: South Carolina, York District. Will of Hannah Currence of the District aforesaid... To my son D. A. Currence his choice of two beds with the common covers of summer & winter, also the bureau and folding leaf table, also the painted cupboard and choice of the contents, also the clock. To my daughter Eliza Barnett my buggy & harness, also one bed and covers, being the third choice. I will to R. F. Currence, M. H. Currence & J. D. Currence, one bed and covers to each, and to have choice as their names are written. I will $5 in cash to each of my grandchildren who were called for me to be paid within or their parents to be disposed of as they fit for their benefit. The remainder of my effects be equally divided among my children but the share of my son Nelson (if alive) to be equally divided between his three daughters. I appoint my son J. D. Currence to execute this will, __ April 1858. Hannah Currence (LS), Wit: Daniel Currence, James Turner, Myles Smith. Proved by the oath of James Turner 29 Nov 1861.

**Pages 448-450**: South Carolina, York District. Will of Charles Hopper... I will all of my estate both real and personal consisting of the tract of land whereon I now reside containing 160 acres and all my stock, etc., to my wife Barbara Hooper during her life and at her death to be disposed of as herein after direction. To my son Anthony Hopper all that tract of land willed to my wife during her life, 160 acres adj. lands of O. Sarratt, Jno. G. Webber, Geo. W. Quinn, estate of James Wiley decd, and on Broad River. The said Anthony shall not account to my estate for said tract as an advancement but shall take said land over and above his original share of the rest of my estate and shall have the right to live on the tract with his mother. I will and bequeath that of my several children to whom I have made advancement shall not be made to account for said advancement, but each of the following named children shall on final settlement with my executor pay back the following sums as a part of my estate namely my son Jefferson S. Hopper shall pay $74; my son Humphrey Hopper shall pay $119; my son Charles G. Hopper shall pay $350; and my son John S. Hopper shall pay $266; my daughter Eliza wife of Brison Moore shall pay $1; my daughter Eulisses wife of Henry K. Kester shall pay $12; my daughter Mary wife of Edward Rippy Junior shall pay $12; the children of my daughter Selina Rippy decd shall pay $22; the children of my daughter Nancy Moore decd shall pay $2; my son Anthony hoper shall pay $200. To my daughter Eulisses wife of Henry K. Kester my negro boy Stanford during the life of my wife Barbara free from hire or charge but at the death of my wife Barbara, my daughter shall return my said negro boy Stanford to my executors. To my daughter Mary wife of Edward Rippy Jr. my negro boy Bruce during the life of my wife Barbara free from hire or charge but at the death of my wife Barbara, my daughter shall return my said negro boy Stanford to my executors. To my daughter Eliza wife of Brison Moore my negro boy Dave during the life of my wife Barbara free from hire or charge but at the death of my wife Barbara, my daughter shall return my said negro boy Stanford to my executors. I appoint my son Humphrey P. Hopper and my friend William C. Black, exrs., 3 May 1859. Charles Hopper (X), Wit: Joseph McCosh, John Moore Jr., John L. Bridges. Proved by the oath of Joseph McCosh 25 Nov 1861.

**Pages 451-452**: South Carolina, York District. Will of William Moore of district aforesaid... to my daughter Jane C. Rawlinson, negroes that I have already given her: Margaret and her child Fed & Adaline, and also Jo, Dallas, Peggy, Julie & Lucy. To my son William S. Moore, the plantation he now lives on and 200 acres of land taken off the Rowel plantation on the side next to William Erwin & McFadden's land, that I have had surveyed & laid off for him, and also the negroes I have already given him Neel, Rachel, Sam, Mary Susan, Alfred, Jane & I also will him Little Jim and Mary & Henry. To my son H. Baxter Moore the one half of the plantation that lies on the Catawba River on both sides of the river, to be equally divided & Frederic E. Moore and I also will to him the following name negroes Young Charles, Rachel, Titus, Isabella, Dawson, Penny, Jim, that I purchased of Franklin Rawlinson & Mima. To my son Frederick E. Moore the remaining half of the above plantation named to H. Baxter Moore and also the following negroes Bob, Toney, Jake, Dan, Ann & her oldest child, younger Nancy & her oldest child Patience & her two eldest children Suffy & Emeline Ann. I also will $800 to cash. To my daughter Dorcus E. Moore the following named negroes Young Simon, Rena & her daughter, Adaline, Tim, Philis & her child, Chloe & her child, Ninah, Nelson, John & Hariet, and also $800 in cash. The legal title to said negroes shall rest in my son Frederick E. Moore to hold the same in trust for her. The lot I reside on & the land I possess near Yorkville be sold & the proceeds be equally divided between my daughters Jane C. Rawlinson & Dorcus E. Moore. I appoint my son Frederick E. Moore, exr., 16 Aug 1860.

Wm. Moore (LS), Wit: J. N. Withers, W. B. Byers, H. F. Adicks. Proved by the oath of H. F. Adicks __ Dec 1861.

**Page 453**: South Carolina, York District. Will of Martha Black of district aforesaid... To John Miskelly, a boy now living with me, $50 to be paid when he comes of age. To my brother John Black of State of Texas, one half of my whole estate, both real and personal. The other half of my estate to be equally divided between my brothers Samuel Black, William Black, and my sister Mary Freeman. I appoint my nephew Robert A. Black my executor, 6 April 1860. Martha Black (X) (LS), Wit: J. M. Hope, Joseph Howell, J. F. Burns. Proved by the oath of J. M. Hope 10 March 1862.

**Page 454**: South Carolina, Johns Island. Will of James Turner... after payment of debts, the remainder of my personal estate, consisting of one gun, notes, corn and cattle in York District, to my mother Barbery Turner, during her natural life and at her decease to be given to my brother Gordon Turner. I appoint (Baby) John Smith executor, 23 Feb 1862. James Turner (X) (Seal), Wit: John A. Witherspoon, Wm. H. Smith, J. B. Whitesides. Proved in Charleston District by the oath of John A. Witherspoon 3 March 1862 before Walter B. Metts, Magst Ex. off.

**Pages 455-456**: South Carolina, York District. Will of Johnson Goforth of district aforesaid... My wife Hannah and my family that is yet to be raised to have the use and benefits of my home plantation of 674 acres, except the bureaus and beds and furniture designed [sic] for my daughters Sarah and Eliza. I also will that one road wagon and one two horse wagon with all the harness belonging to them and the wood work of one other, and one sett of blacksmith tools be also left with my wife Hannah, and all the negroes that I am seized of be left with my said wife, if she can control, but if she cannot, then the executors are to sell them. I will to my daughter Sarah Moore one horse, bridle, and saddle, one bureau, one bed and furniture, and $150 in cash. The executors will proceed to sell my other lands and mills not heretofore mentioned, in lots: the Buffaloe Mills with a proper portion of land, also the mill in the Martin settlement, and balance in lot or lots as may seem best, and that they proceed to sell a cotton gin and threshing machine. And as I have left the house plantation and negroes and horses with my wife and children as before mentioned, I now add or until my youngest child shall arrive to the age of 21. My several children then to receive equal shares, viz Sarah Moore, Eliza, William, Reuben, Andrew, Preston, and one not yet born. I appoint John Moore and Henderson Martin, exrs., 13 March 1862. Johnson Goforth (LS), Wit: J. Gist Davis, J. S. Dawson, A. Hardin. Proved by the oath of J. S. Dawson 4 April 1862.

**Pages 457-458**: South Carolina, York District. Will of William D. Watson... To give to my mother Elizabeth R. Steele for life and at her death to my two half-sisters Susan & Eliza Steele, my negro woman Sarah & the child she now has. I give my horse to my grandmother Susan Currence, and at her death to my sister Margaret Roach. I give my interest in negro woman Emily & child to my mother E. R. Steele and at her death to my two half sisters Susan &

Eliza Steele. I bequeath the whole balance of my estate to my sister Margaret A. Roach. I appoint George F. Wallace, exr., 12 April 1861. William D. Watson (LS), Wit: G. R. Ratchford, W. H. McCorkle, G. W. Williams. Proved by the oath of G. W. Williams, 18 Aug 1862. 18 Aug 1862 qualified G. F. Wallace as executor.

**Pages 458-462:** Will of Susan Currence... To my granddaughter Susan Elizabeth McDowell Wallace, daughter of G. Franklin & Adeline Wallace, my negro woman Emeline & one bed & furniture. To my granddaughter Clementine Virginia Wallace, daughter of G. F. & Addeline Wallace, an infant negro child named Roseline (child of Emeline). To my grandson Wm. Rufus Wallace, son of G. F. & Addeline Wallace, my negro girl Martha, and to my grandson Joseph Wallace, one horse, he to have the liberty of his own choice out of my stock of horses. To my granddaughter Margaret Adams Watson, my negro girl Cynthia & also the stand of drawers made by Simon Flodin. I also will to my grandson William David Watson my negro boy Andy, and the colt he now claims, bed, and my secretary. To my daughter Mary Allison, wife of W. B. Allison, my old negro woman Minny, and my negro woman patience, and to the children of my daughter Mary & W. B. Allison: to Susan Jane Currence Allison, my negro girl Simon; to Hugh Parks Allison my negro boy George; and Robert Rufus Allison, my boy Jeff. To my two granddaughters Catharine Suggs & Susan Steele, each $100 out of the proceeds of the sale of my property, when they shall have arrived at the age of 21. To my daughter Margaret Harper my old negro woman Charity with $50. To W. B. Allison & G. F. Wallace, my two sons in law, my negro man Lott in trust for the use of my daughter Margaret Harper. At the death of my daughter Margaret, they to transfer their title to my grandson Hugh Harper. To my grandson Hugh Harper a $50 note on his mother Margaret Harper which I now hold. The balance of my property be sold at public sale, and after paying my expenses and debts and the special legacies, be equally divided among my six children viz Addeline Wallace, Margaret Harper, John D. Currence, Elizabeth Steele, Mary Allison & Eliza Suggs. I appoint Wm. B. Allison and G. Franklin Wallace, exrs., 20 April 1859. Susan Currence (X), Wit: S. E. Moore, Alfred Stilwell, J. G. Enloe. Proved by the oath of Alfred Stilwell 18 Aug 1862.

August 18th 1862. Qualified George F. Wallace as executor of the above will and the codicil thereto dated 12 April 1861.

Codicil. To my granddaughter Susan E. Wallace, a negro girl Eliza, child of Emeline, and all issue of Emeline. To William Rufus Wallace my grandson all the issue of my negro woman Martha. To my granddaughter Margaret A. Roach named in my said will Margaret Adams Watson, all the issue of my negro girl Cynthia. I revoke so much of the fifth clause of my will as gives my negro boy Jeff to Robert Rufus Allison, and instead of said negro I give him the youngest child of my negro woman patience, a boy not yet named. All the issue of Sinah to go with the mother & belong to Susan Jane Currence Allison. I revoke the legacy of $50 to my daughter Margaret Harper and to my grandson Hugh Harper the $50 note, and I hereby give said note & all interest due to my said daughter Margaret Harper. I give my old negro man Ephraim to my son in law G. F. Wallace and his wife Adeline and I recommend him to their care. Dated 17 Sept 1861. Susan Currence (X), Wit: W. P. McFadden, D. F. Jackson, G. W. Williams. Proved by the oath of G. W. Williams 18 Aug 1862.

**Pages 462-463**: South Carolina, York District. Will of McCastland Wallace of district aforesaid... Having given my children & grandchildren except my son Alexander S. Wallace all that I wish or intent to give them, I give to my son Alexander S. Wallace all my estate both real and personal. I appoint my said son Alexander S. Wallace, exr., 28 Dec 1847. Mc'nd Wallace (LS), Wit: Jas Brian, J. Bolton Smith, S. W. Melton. Proved by the oath of J. Bolton Smith 21 Aug 1862. Qualified A. S. Wallace as executor 28 Aug 1862.

**Pages 463-464**: Will of John J. Gilmore of the District of York... To my brother Charles M. Gilmore of Chester District my negro woman Amanda and her four children, also Isabella, Leca, & Shelton. To my brother William C. Gilmore of said Chester District the following negroes viz Dorcas, Charles &U Mary. I will to my aunt Sally Wilson of York my negro man named Ellison during her life and at her deceased to my said brothers Charles M. Gilmore & William C. Gilmore. I will to the said Charles M. & William C. Gilmore the residue of my estate. I appoint my said brothers Charles M. & William C. Gilmore, exrs., 30 Dec 1861. J. J. Gilmore (Seal), Wit: S. J. Kuykendal, A. M. Jackson, J. Bolton Smith. Proved by the oath of J. Bolton Smith 25 Apr 1862. Qualified Charles M. Gilmore and William C. Gilmore executors 29 Aug 1862.

**Page 465**: Will of Joseph B. Manning of Union District... My executor to expose to sale all my estate both real and personal. I do bequeath to my beloved mother Mary A. Manning one half of the clear residue of my estate & the remaining half to be equally divided among my five brothers Thomas W. Manning, Robert L. Manning, John M. Manning, William C. Manning, Commodore P. Manning. I appoint my brother Thomas W. Manning, A. F. Smith and John Smith, exrs., 7 Nov 1861. J. B. Manning (Seal), Wit: J. Herndon, W. B. Byers, J. Bolton Smith. Proved by the oath of J. Bolton Smith 1 Sept 1862. The original will filed at Union.

**Page 466**: South Carolina, York District. Will of J. B. Venable of said district... I will to Betsy Floyd a negro woman named Holy and her two youngest children. I will to Alex Glass a negro woman named Flora also Cyrus, John, Annie and Lizzy and George, and I allow him to pay all I owe including my last expences. I will to Jane E. Jackson my black mare. I will to Katharine Jackson my gray mare. I allow Holly one bed & appurtenances. The remainder of my property including my lands to my friend Alex Glass. I appoint Alex Glass executor, 12 July 1862. J. B. Venable (X) (LS), Wit: Robert Pursley, Ezekiel Fewell, Myles Smith. Proved by the oath of Myles Smith 18 July 1862.

**Pages 467-468**: South Carolina, York District. Will of Robert L. Manning of York District... I will that all of my estate real and personal and claims and interest of all kinds shall be sold by my executors and my notes and accounts to be collected. After my just debts are settled, my beloved mother Mary A. Manning is to have one half of the remaining balance. The other half to be divided among my five brothers Jos. B. Manning, Thomas W. Manning, John Manning, William C. Manning, and Perry C. Manning. I appoint Jo. B. Manning and Thomas W. Manning, exrs., 27 July 1861. R. L. Manning (LS), Wit: W. R. Hughs, Moses Martin, Morgan Martin. Proved by the oath of Moses Martin 12 Sept 1862. Qualified Thomas W. Manning, executor, 12 Sept 1862.

**Page 468**: South Carolina, York District. Will of Wm. R. Glenn of district aforesaid... My will is that my beloved mother Eliza Glenn do have all my estate (except my mule & interest in my thrashing machine) consisting of one negro boy Sam, one negro girl Mary, with other property. My will is that my brother David J. Glen do have my brown mule and my interest in a thrashing machine. My will is that my cousin John F. Glenn, Junr, be my executor, 11 April 1861. Wm. R. Glenn (Seal), Wit; W. G. Melton, Albert Bradley, Sarah O. Glenn. Proved by the oath of George W. Melton 24 Sept 1862.

**Pages 469-471**: South Carolina, York District. Will of David Byers of York District... To my son Alemith Byers $500. To my son James Byers $500. To my daughter Elizabeth N. Penick $500. To the three children of my deceased son John, jointly $500. The legacies in the foregoing clauses are to be paid by my executors either in cash or negroes of same value. To my beloved wife Mary my negroes Sarah & her children, Amanda & Margaret, my buggy, a bureau, two of my best beds & furniture. My wife Mary to live in my dwelling house and be comfortably maintained, supporting and taken care of by my sons Edward & Theodore. To the widow and children of my deceased son John any debt or demand I may have against his estate for money advanced to him. To my wife Mary my negro boy named John. The balance of my estate both real and personal to my two sons Edward G. & David Theodore. I appoint my sons Edward G. & David J. Byers & my friend R. T. Allison, exrs., 5 Feb 1850. David Byers (Seal), Wit: E. H. Gunning, S. G. Brown, G. W. Williams. Codicil: Since my will dated 5 Feb 1850, I have paid to my daughter Elizabeth N. Penick $600, and I do revoke the 3rd item of this will and give to my wife Mary, Charles a child of Sarah. I have disposed of my real estate by deed to my sons E. G. & D. T. Byers, I do hereby revoke that portion of the 11th item, 30 April 1852. David Byers (Seal), Wit: John Kennedy, Samuel Black, Mary M. Brown, S. G. Brown. Codicil: Since the will and codicil, I have disposed of by deed of gift the property willed to my wife Mary to my son E. G. Byers, I revoke the 6th item of said will made 5 Feb 1850. Dated 14 March 1857. David Byers (LS), Wit: John Kennedy, Samuel Black, Robert S. Chambers, S. G. Brown. Proved by the oath of S. G. Brown 24 Sept 1862.

**Pages 472-473**: South Carolina, York District. Will of Elias M. Jackson of said district... To my wife Mary a negro boy named Frank one bed, sipping wheel & cards, one cow & calf, one bay mare named Pat, 100 acres of land with the improvements, then to go to my son Samuel, also the pot ware, cupboard & ware, also a sufficiency of provisions on hand of corn, wheat &c. that will support her and the family for 12 months. To the children of my son Robert 100 acres of land. To my son John 100 acres of land. To my daughter Mary one negro named Adam, also one horse, one bed & wheel, and her saddle & one cow. To my daughter Erixana one negro named Cato, one horse & Saddle, one bed & wheel, also one cow. To my daughter Susan one negro named Stephen, one bed, also one cow, also one of the colts. To my daughter Jane one negro girl named Ann. To my son Samuel 100 acres of land, one horse named Charley, also all the farm tools, wagon & smiths tools, one cow and sheep. I allow 100 acres of land for my three daughters jointly Mary,, Erixana & Susan. I allowed David 25 acres, also John & samuel and Robert children the same manner as above. My Union land I allow it to be sold and the proceeds divided among all my children. I allow one negro named Mary Ann for my wife Mary and at her deceased go to Samuel. I desire my son David to execute this will, 24 Sept 1861. Elias M. Jackson (LS), Wit: H. M. Jackson, W. T. Jackson, Myles Smith. Proved by the oath of Myles Smith 2 June [Jan?] 1861.

**Pages 473-474**: Will of Mary Wright of Yorkville... I give one fifth part of my estate remaining after the payment of debts to my nephew John Irwin Huggins residing at Athens in the state of Georgia. I give one fifth part of my estate to my niece Margaret Brevard Stockton, wife of Joseph W. Stockton & now residing at Statesville in the state of North Carolina. I give one fifth part of my said estate to my niece Mary Hall Moore now residing at Statesville, North Carolina. I give one fifth part of my said estate to my nephew Joel Huggins now residing in the State of Texas. I give one fifth part of my estate to my nephew John F. Irwin son of my deceased brother William. I appoint John H. Adams executor, __ Dec 1861. Mary Wright (Seal), Wit: M. E. Witherspoon, J. H. Witherspoon, G. W. Williams. Proved by the oath of G. W. Williams 6 Oct 1862. Admitted to probate in common form and at same time qualified John H. Adams as executor, October 6th 1862.

END OF BOOK 3

# YORK COUNTY SC WILLS (UNRECORDED)

**York County Estates: Case 1, File 7** [SC Archives microfilm C1997]:
Will of Hannah Oldrage living in Lincoln County, North Carolina, 6 November 1826... I allow all my clothing to my granddaughter Hannah Bennett except two homespun frocks that I leave to my two granddaughters John Bennet's two oldest daughters. I will to my granddaughter Hannah Bennet the wheel and cards, etc., my feather bed. I will that my son William Bennett shall have my share of the land that Samuel Neely now lives on. Hannah Oldrage (mark), Wit: James Mtgomery [Montgomery], Eb. Davis. Proved 26 Jan 1831.

**York County Estates: Case 11, File 490** [SC Archives microfilm C2009]: South Carolina, York District. Personally appeared Dr. John Hall, Philip Williams & Thomas J. McElhenny and made oath that on the 15th of this instant John McClure called upon the deponents to bear witness that he was about to make his last will & testament and spoke as follows that he "will & devised to his brother William McClure the plantation on which said William McLure then resided except that he allowed his brother Robert McLure to have as much of the land to cultivate as he wishes for the next year. And that he willed all the remainder of his property to his brother Robert Mclure for and during his life." Sworn 20 April 1838 John Hall, Philip Williams, T. J. McElhenny, before J. M. Ross, O. Y. D.

**York County Estates: Case 18, File 770** [SC Archives microfilm C2018]: Will of James Graham... I devise all that tract of land on the Catawba River known as the Lefer tract to my brother William A. Graham, supposed to contain upwards of 1000 acres in York District, South Carolina, also in Gaston County, North Carolina. To my brother William A. Graham all the slaves that I own and now in possession of that Lefer land including Turner and his family, also Ben, Jim, Jack, Harvey, Mary, and her children, also Carter. All the stock on that plantation to my brother William A. graham, including all the corn, cotton, wheat, oats and rye that have grown there during the year 1848, all my household furniture at the Lefer place. To my brother William A. Graham all my land in Lincoln County, including the Earhardt place, the Bradshaw tract, the Moody place and the land which I purchased of J. R. Witherspoon and my sister Sophia amounting in different surveys to about 1600 acres, on William's, Anderson's, and Snyder's Creek. To my brother William A. Graham all my negroes that I own on my Earhardt place with all the stock, etc. I won upwards of 3000 acres of land in the state of Tennessee lying in Tipton and Haywood counties and which I hereby devise to my three sisters Sophia G. Witherspoon of Alabama, Violet W. Alexander and Mary H. Morrison, now in the hands of my agent John Sharp who resides in Tipton County. My house and lot in Rutherfordton near 200 acres of land adjoining Col. Tanner's saw mill, about 200 acres adj. Mrs. Prather's mills on first Broad River, a little less than 100 acres on the Rock Mountain, also 2200 acres in Caldwell County and in addition to that all my lands in Catawba County supposed to be 100 acres, all those lands to be sold and the proceeds divided equally among the children, devisees and heirs at law of my three deceased brothers, that is John A. Graham, joseph Graham, & Dr. George F. Graham. The money that I deposited with the Revd. R. H. Morrison and a note I have one James W. Patton of Buncombe County, and I have on Alfred D. Kerr and Franklin Davison, then the two last notes are collected and cashed and from an aggregate sum, with money deposited with Mr. Morrison, to be equally divided among my three sisters. All my other notes & debts due to be divided among my brother William & my sisters Sophia, Violet and Mary which shall constitute one share, and the other among the children of my three deceased brothers. I appoint my brother William A. Graham, exr. I also give to him my gold watch, all my wearing apparel, a new buggy & harness which I bought in Philadelphia, and my saddle horse and saddle & bridle, 26 Oct 1848. James Graham (Seal), Wit: Joseph W. Calloway, L. B. Bryon, Jno. M. Craton. North Carolina, Lincoln County. Court of Pleas & Quarter Sessions, October Session, 1851. Will of James Graham produced for probate by William A. Graham and Dr. Joseph W. Calloway and L. B. Bryan of Rutherford being called as witnesses. Will was proved and executor qualified.

**York County Estates: Case 20, File 817** [SC Archives microfilm C2019]: Will of Thomas Grier of the county of Mecklinburg and State of North Carolina... To my beloved wife Susana Grier the management of the place I now live on (with the assistance of my executors and guardian hereinafter to be named), for the support of her and the family and it that should not be sufficient let what over additional support may be necessary be taken off the whole head or stock to keep, school, and clothe them until there are of age or until my said wife Susana marries. Should that event take place I will that an equal division take place between her and her two daughters Catharine and Susan of all my cupboard, dresser & kitchen furniture, looking glasses. Likewise my negroes Ben, Rhody, Silvy, Juliet, Esther, and Eliza and said negroes at her death to be disposed of among our children as she may think proper. To my daughter Margaret Neel the three negroes I gave to her when she married, also negro woman Rose which I lately gave to her, also a note that I hold on her husband Saml Neel worth at this time $185.60. To my son James Grier, that place he lived on that I paid for and negro man named Jack and negro woman Sally. To my son Thomas J. Grier all that tract of land he lives on following the older marked lines made for it except so much thereof sa was taken out by Porter claim, also negro man Jack. To my son Alexander Grier as much land in Wilson's or Alexanders districts agreeable to an article entered into between myself and the said Alexander Grier dated September 1821 and negro man Soloman and negro woman Jean, also 250 acres of land in Pery[?] County. To my son Andrew Grier all that tract of land on Paco Creek that he now lives on and negroes Stephen & Bill. To my son William M. Grier all that tract whereon Alex Hamilton lives near Armor's ford and consisting of several purchased, also that tract of land I purchased of my nephew Robt Bigham, also a small piece of land 18 or 20 acres cornering on the Rocky Branch and generally known by John Porters entry and my other purchase form John Pettus adj. Rice, and my negroes Luiza and Isaac, also $400 in cash to assist him in raising a house,one bed & furniture, a horse, saddle & Bridle. To my son Zenas Grier the place I now live on subject to the incumbrance of the family as heretofore stated, also the McMicking tract and the tract I purchased of Fares, also my negroes Frank, Leah & Manda, one bed and furniture, horse saddle & Bride, and $200 in cash. To my daughter

## YORK COUNTY SC WILLS (UNRECORDED)

Catharine Grier my negroes Phillis Jur., Adam, Bob, Letty, Rachel & Ather[?], one bed & furniture, one bureau & one table, one horse, saddle & bridle. To my daughter Susana Grier my negroes Reuben, Polly, Nelson, George, Edmund and Clary[?], one bed & furniture, one horse, saddle and bridle, one bureau, and one table, $200 in cash. All the children either among my immediate relations or acquaintances that have been named for me, 410 in cash. To my beloved wife Susana Grier and each one of my children, a Bible, a Westminster Confession of Faith, and Act and Testimony and the remainder of my books to b divided into ten lots as nearly as equal as may be and distributed to my wife and children each one a lott. To each subscriber in the Associate Congregation of Steel Creek of which I am a member, one pocket Bible and one act and testamony. I appoint my son Thomas J. Grier and Andrew Grier, exrs., and my wife Susana Grier and nephew Alexander Greer guardians of and for my family, 4 Feb 1825. Thos Grier, Wit: Ab Anderson, Martha Grier. Codicil... the frame of a house now stands for my son William M. Grier to be put up and raised in the site now chosen. Thos Grier, Wit: A. W. Alexander, Stephen McR--. Certified a true copy from Mecklenburg County in February term 1828.

**York County Estates: Case 27, File 1125** [SC Archives microfilm C2026]: The nuncupative will of James Latham. The last will of James Latham late of York District deceased declared by him by word of mouth the 9th day of February 1816. James Latham told Moses Latham the day that he died that he wishes him to see to the payment of his debts out of his estate and what then remained was to be given to Richard Latham, __ Feb 1816. Jacob Coonrod, Moses Latham (X), Richard Latham (X). Proven and subscribed to 23 Feb 1816. At same time qualified Moses Latham executor to the above nuncupative will.

**York County Estates: Case 36, File 1531** [SC Archives microfilm C2034]: State of Tennessee. At a court of Pleas & Quarter Sessions held for Montgomery County on Monday the 17th July 1815. The last will and testament of Isaac Rogers deceased was produce din open court and the signature to said instrument was proven in open court to be the hand writing of Isaac Rogers deceased and that it was found among his valuable papers after his decease by the oaths of William Lockert, Joseph Caldwell and John Neville and Charles Lockert, David Bird, Sarah Rogers came into court and were qualified as executors.

Will of Isaac Rogers of the State of Tennessee and County of Montgomery... To my beloved wife Sarah I bequeath my whole estate real and personal during her natural life or widowhood. It is believed that the use of the whole estate will be sufficient for the maintenance of her and children. At her death or marriage the estate be equally divided between my children Narcissa Rogers, Sally Rogers, William Rogers, Louisa Rogers and my youngest daughter not yet named. I request my friends Charles Lockert and David Bird with my wife Sarah to be executors. I. Rogers. Nov. 12th 1814. Certified to be a true copy from the minutes of the probate court, 18 May 1816.

## YORK COUNTY SC WILLS (UNRECORDED)

**York County Estates: Case 37, File 1563** [SC Archives microfilm C2035]: Will of John Roberts of York District.... wishing my wife and children all to be satisfied with the division I choose to make of my little estate... My wife to have my negro man John and my negro girl Sintha, my sorrel mare and young gray horse, three milk cows of her own choise, all my hogs and sheep, my household and kitchen furniture, one buro excepted, and the use of all of my land till my son Andrew J. arrives to the age of twenty one years, then to be divided equally between my two sons Andrew J. and Jesse M., and if my wife should bear a male child and it should live, it to share equal in the land, and if it cannot be divided my will is for it then to be sold and my son Andrew J. to make rights. My daughter Rachel E. to have my negro girl Dianna and one buro and $115 bearing interest from the first of March 1835 which was a present to her by an aunt and I put it to my use at that time. My son Andrew J. to have my negro boy Jerry and shork colt. My son Jesse M. to have my negro girl Enoriah. If my wife should bear a living child, my will is for it to have the child my negro girl Sintha is now with if it is living. I ordain James B. Good and my wife my executors, 21 March 1835. John Roberts (LS), Wit: John Good, Mathew Bankhead, Allen R. Jamerson. Proved 21 Dec 1835 by the oath of Matthew Bankhead. Jean Roberts (X) relinquished her executorship 5 Dec 1835, Wit: Andrew Nelson. James B. Good renounced his executorship.

**York County Estates: Case 38, File 1608** [SC Archives microfilm C2035]: Will of Mary Scott of Chester District, South Carolina... to my daughter Jane Hartness $50. To Katherine Martin one note due to me by Jas Martin her husband of $72. To my niece Jenny Fox all the remainder of my property both real & personal. I appoint James Scott & John Blair, exrs., 19 Dec 1815. Mary Scott (X) (LS), Wit: Leonard Strait, Saml Wherry, Sally Strait. Proved in York District by the oath of Leonard Straight 22 Sept 1817. At same time qualified James Scott & John Blair exrs.

**York County Estates: Case 39, File 1661** [SC Archives microfilm C2036]: State of North Carolina, Mecklenburg County. Will of Richard Springs... to my youngest son Richard C. Springs, 10 shares of the bank stock that I now own in the Commercial Bank in Columbia, South Carolina, and all the profits that may arise therefrom after my decease and eight negroes Jess, Need, Pleasant & her two children, Winney and her two children). The balance of my property with a lot of ground which I own in the town of Cheraw be sold and the neat proceeds & also my money, dues, dues, to be equally divided between my sons John & Andrew and my daughters Sophia Moore & Margaret Springs, and to the children of my son Eli, and the children of my daughter Cynthia Dinkins and Harriet Moore deceased, an equal share. To my daughter Margaret my carriage and to her daughter Margaret my two year old filley. I appoint my sons John and Andrew Springs, exrs., 25 Oct 1833. Rich'd Springs (Seal), Wit: Jos. H. Wilson, Wm. Carolan. Codicil dated 19 Dec 1833. Proved in Mecklenburg County, NC, Court of Pleas and quarter sessions, February term 1834. Certified to be a correct copy.

# YORK COUNTY SC WILLS (UNRECORDED)

**York County Estates: Case 54, File 2412** [SC Archives microfilm C2051]: Will of Nancy Chesney, widow lady, late of York District, South Carolina, deceased, declared by her by word of mouth the 15th day of September 1811, who said she will that John Wilson of the state and district aforesaid should have all the property she was then possessed of and also said it was not worth her while to mention the articles of property for she allowed him to have the whole. Signed 19 Sept 1811. John Ezell, Frances Ezell, Martha Ezell (X).

**York County Estates: Case 55, File 2440** [SC Archives microfilm C2051]: 17 May 1777. Will of Joseph Carrell of Allisons Creek in Craven County, state of South Carolina, planter... To my loving son Thomas Carrel the plantation whereon he now lives and my plantation on the north side of Little Cataba Creek joyning Robert Leeper. To my son John Carrel a horse of the value of £50 proc. money. To my daughter Mary wife to William Rachford a goun of her own choosing to be paid for out of my estate. To my daughter Elizabeth wife of Nathaniel Henderson my negro wench called Peg, said daughter Elizabeth paying to my daughter Jane £100 proc. money at the decease of her husband David Neel, but if my said daughter Jane dies before her husband David, then said Nathaniel Henderson to paid the said £100 to my daughter Jane's two eldest daughters. To my daughter Ann, wife of James Alexander, a goun such as she sees cause to choose to be paid for out of my estate. To my daughter Hannah wife of Richard Vanable my negro wench called Nann, and two gouns of her own choosing. My negro boy Cube be put up to sail and allow my sons and daughters to have notice thereof and the highest bidder of any of my children to be the purchaser of said negro boy and the said several gowns herein before bequeathed to be paid out of the price of said negro, and the residue of the price to be at my wife's disposal. To my sons Joseph Carrel and Samuel Carrel the plantations where they now live on, viz Joseph to have 400 acres on the lower end of said tract including his own house and spring and one half of the timber land on the south side of the creek and the meadow bottom that he has cleared, also a separate piece of 10 acres of meadow ground on the south fork of said creek where he sees cause to clear it exclusive of the aforesaid 400 acres. The remainder of the lands to Samuel Carrel with the negro boy called Adam, wagon, plows, gears, and allow my said son Samuel to take care of my wife Jane his mother. I do reserved out of my said personal estate just now bequeathed to my wife Jane, to my bound boy Matthew Carrel, to the amount of £25 proc. money in case or creatures to that amount and a decent suit of apparel from head to foot besides his ordinary wearing apparel at his arrival at 21 years of age. I appoint my son Samuel Carrel and Samuel Young of Rowan County, North Carolina, exrs. Joseph Carrell (Seal), Wit: Saml Young, William Young, Janet Young. "not to be recorded untill further orders"

**York County Estates: Case 58, File 2619** [SC Archives microfilm C2055]: Will of James Knox of the County of York and State of South Carolina... To my well beloved wife Elisabeth Knox one bed and furniture with her spinning wheel, one sorral horse, saddle and bridle. My lawful debts to be paid and my books accounts to be collected to discharge the same. I will that there be a sufficient maintenance given to my hon. father while he lives and if need require it sum hep to assist him if bodily weakness come upon him so that he is not able to help himself. To Ruth MisCaley[?] one horse and saddle valued to $50. I will that all my estate be kept together till the youngest be scooled and then need for a divide I will all my estate, lands, goods, and chattles be sold, 4 Sept 1795. Jas Knox (Seal), Wit: John Faris, James Nassey, David Knox.

**York County Estates: Case 58, File 2652** [SC Archives microfilm C2055]: February 20th 1814. Will of John Hood of the county of Bledsoe in and State of Tennessee... To my beloved wife Mary a sorrel mare and her saddle, also a large house Bible, an equal part of my estate with my children. To my daughter Elisabeth, my daughter Jane, my daughter Mary, my daughter Iby, my daughter Agnes, my daughter Martha, my daughter Permelia, my daughter Malinda Jean, an equal part of the balance of my estate except my working utensils, and those I give to my grandson John H. Marshall. I appoint my beloved wife my executrix. John Hood (X), Wit: Jas Hoge, Valentine Spring. Proved in Bledsoe County, Tennessee, May Session 1814 by the oath of Joseph Hoge and Valentine Spring, 2 May 1814. Certified to be a correct copy in Pikeville 2 Feb 1819, Samuel Terry, clerk.

**York County Estates: Case 60, File 2736** [SC Archives microfilm C2057]: 5 Oct 1778. Will of James Miskelly of Camden District... My wife Jane Miskelly do have her living off of the plantation whereon I now live, the use & service of a negro woman named Sann[?], four milk cows, any one of my horses, the disposal of my stock of wool amongst my present family, my best feather bed, half of my stock of sheep I allow to be exposed to sale & the remainder of my stock of sheep, an equal part of my dresser furniture. To my son James Miskelly the tract of land whereon I now live, 190 acres, and a negro child named Will. My negro woman Jane should not be sold out of my family, and if she has not children enough to be one to each of my three children James, William & Frances exclusive of the one already given to James, then the said wench & what children she shall have to be valued & the mount of the valuation be divided amongst my said three children and the wench to belong to my son James. To my daughter Frances a tract of land adj. James McNabb's land he now lives on, known by the name of the white oak bottom, 100 acres, also an equal part of my dresser furniture, cattle, etc. To my son William a tract of land of 100 acres known by the name of the Gardin, half of my plantation utensils. To my son in law Thomas Garvin a young bull to be his for ever. I appoint John Miller & Andrew Love, both of this district, exrs. James Miskelly (Seal), Wit: David Gorden, Alexander Clark, William Clark. Proved by the oath of all three witnesses 18 January 1780 before Wm. Bratton, J.P.

**York County Estates: Case 69, File 3394**: [SC Archives microfilm C2067]: Will of John McCaw of the Town of Yorkville... I give to my mother Mrs. Nancy McCaw all my estate both real & personal, 21 July 1835. John McCaw, Wit: Wm. Bratton, John S. Bratton, John B. McCaw. Probated 20 October 1842.

## YORK COUNTY SC WILLS (UNRECORDED)

**York County Estates: Case 74, File 3641** [SC Archives microfilm C2072]: South Carolina, York District. February 27th 1831. Will of Martha Peters Jun.... I allow all my just debts and funeral expences paid including a suitable head stone. I will to my brother James Peters the whole of the remainder of my estate. I appoint James Peters my brother, exr. Martha Peters (LS), Wit: Amsigh M'Clain, Benjn Chambers, Samuel Chambers, William Caldwell, G. Caldwell. Proved by the oath of William Caldwell 20 May 1843.

**York County Estates: Case 80, File 3888** [SC Archives microfilm C2078]: South Carolina, York District. Will of John A. McCarter of the district aforesaid... To my wife Elizabeth McCarter the tract of land which I now live on during her life or widow hood and in case she should marry, then I allow the land to go to my two youngest sons and be equally divided between them viz John and Robert. Also to my wife Elizabeth one negro woman named Milly, aged about 25 years, one stand of drawers, one cupboard and contents with the exception of which my daughter Sarah E. claims, also one bay horse named Star about 13 years old, and saddle, four head of cattle at her own choice, all the beds and furniture that she now claims, also two tables at her own choice, all the kitchen furniture. My daughter Hannah L. shall have her support off the plantation I now live on during my wife's life or widowhood, and I allow her one bed and stead and furniture which she now claims, and $50. To my daughter Sarah E. one negro girl named Juliann about six years old, one young bay horse named Ball about four years old, one stand of drawers, one bed and stead and furniture, also two head of cattle. To my son Christopher L. H., one negro boy named Steve about seven years old, one sorrel horse named Decater about 8 years old. To my son Jas L. the tract of land lying above where I now live joining lands with Robert McCarter and others, 120 acres, also one brown mare about five or six years old, my negro boy named Billy about 13 years old, and I allow my son Jas L. McCarter to pay my son David Z. McCarter $100, and I allow my son Jas all my black smith tools. To my son John C. $50 to be paid in case, and two head of cattle. To my son Robert M. one negro boy named Tom about four months old, one bay horse colt, about two years old, also two head of cattle. My waggon and geer and all the farming tools to be kept on the plantation for the use of the family, my hogs, sheep and ballance of all. I allow my block to stay int he house of the use of the family. I appoint my brother Robert McCarter, exr., 6 Oct 1835. Jas A. McCarter (X) (LS), Wit: Jas Bigger, George A. McCarter, Elias McCarter. Proved by the oath of George & Elias McCarter 16 Dec 1842.

**York County Estates Book F, pages 524-525** [SC Archives microfilm C1690]: Will of Jonathan Kuykendall of the District of York.... To my two children Isaac Kuykendall and Anna Carroll, tract of land on Fishing Creek and its waters, 300 acres at the mouth of Woods branch, the lower part to Isaac and the upper part of Anna. To my daughter Polly Smith my servant woman Eliza and all her family, also my servant man Tom. To my daughter Edy Davidson I give my negro girl Kitty. To my daughter Sally Kuykendall I give my negro girl Sintha. To the heirs of my daughter Elizabeth Davidson's body I give my two negroes Caty and Losson. To my daughter Anna Carrol my negro boy

Stephen and all my household furniture. To my son Isaac and daughters Edy & Sally and the heirs of my daughter Elizabeth and my daughter Anna, my negroes Dorea, Mike & Hester to be equally divided among them. I appoint my friend John L. Davis, exr., 27 Sept 1826. Jonathan Kuykendoll (LS), Wit: Robert Cooper, Henry Tipping Junr, Isaac D. Tipping.

**York County Estates Book F, pages 147-148** [SC Archives microfilm C1692]: South Carolina, York District. Sept 12th, 1827. Will of John McConnel Senr of the district aforesaid... To my children I leave what property is now in their possession of negroes &c and make no further provision for them during the life of their mother, one half or moiety of my land being the part my son Andrew lives on and marked off for him I leave to him and his heirs. The other half or moiety whereon I now live I leave my son John at the death of his mother or soon as the crop thereon growing is gathered. To my son John $100 and at the death of my wife Mary, I allow all the property then in her possession to be equally divided among my children born of her who may be living at the time of her death, the negroes to be divided if convenient and practicable without a sale particularly them I have had born in my lifetime and wishes an arrangement made by my children not to put them to public sale but to purchase among themselves. I appoint my son Andrew McConell exr. John McConnel (LS), Wit: William Little, Elizabeth Little[?], R. Sadler. Proved 17 Dec 1830 by the oath of William Little. At same time qualified And. McConnel, exr.

**York County Estates Book F, pages 148-150** [SC Archives microfilm C1692]: South Carolina, York District. Will of Mary Armstrong... To my son Jesse Kingsboro the bedroom bequeathed to me by my deceased husband, also one set of tea ware, and one set of plates, one bed and furniture, and one half of my share of the cattle, sheep and hogs, and also the balance of cash on hand after the other of my legatees have received their shares, in consideration of which he the said Jesse K. is to bear my funeral & other expences. To my daughter Sarah one cupboard and its contents except what is mentioned above for my son Jesse, also one tea table, all the remainder of beds and bedclothes, one chest and negro girl Hannah, Bucks on the new Testament, and the other half of all my share of the cattle, sheep and hoggs, also $100 in cash, and all my wearing apparel. To my granddaughter Mary Barnhill one negro woman named Lynn and in consideration of which she is to pay over to her brothers & sisters an equal divided of $66.33 1/3 in the space of two years after she comes in possession of said negro woman Lynn. This to be paid in room of my son Francis. To my son William the note of hand I hold against him in which he is to pay over to Francis my son $33.33 1/3. To my granddaughter Nancy Melissa my spinning wheel & $50 in cash. To my granddaughter Polly C. Armstrong, William's daughter,10 in cash. To my granddaughter Polly Armstrong (Frances daughter), $10 in cash. To my granddaughter Cynthia Barnhill $10 in cash. I appoint my son Jesse Kingsborough executor, 17 Oct 1830. Mary Armstrong (mark) (Seal), Wit: John B. Hunter, J. S. Campbell, Joseph A. Lawrence. Proved by the oath of J. A. Campbell 20 Dec 1830. At same time qualified Jesse K. Armstrong, exr.

## TESTATOR INDEX

Adams, Euxine 252
Adams, Francis 156
Adams, Jas. S. 248
Adams, Joseph 338
Adams, Margaret 148
Adams, Robert 23, 41, 321
Adams, William 36
Akin, William 113
Albright, John 271
Alexander, Catharine J. 258
Alexander, Hermon 162
Alexander, Hester 144
Alexander, Joseph 83
Alison, John 59
Allen, Andrew 95
Allen, George 310
Allison, Albert 128
Allison, Alexander 104
Allison, Hugh 32
Allison, Robert 164
Amberson, William 281
Anderson, Ann 273
Anderson, Eliza Ann 158
Anderson, John 106, 262
Anderson, William E. 316
Anderson, William Henry 250
Ardary, Wm 184
Armstrong, Arthur 170
Armstrong, James 150
Armstrong, Jesse K. 337
Armstrong, Mary 359
Armstrong, Robert L. 145
Armstrong, Sarah 232
Arnold, Josephus 50
Ash, John 1
Ash, William 141
Ashmore, Walter 12
Atkins, Samuel 47
Bailey, Elijah 80
Barnes, John 220
Barnet, Thomas 102
Barnett, Alexander 290
Barnett, John 78
Barnett, Rachel 329
Barnett, Richard 203
Barnett, Thomas 103, 167
Barnhill, Isabella 160
Barnwell, Cynthia E. 324
Barnwell, Mary C. 316
Barron, Frances 328
Barron, John 237
Barron, Thomas 151

Barron, William 238
Barronhill, Isabella 160
Barronhill, John 210
Barry, Jane 209
Barry, John 173
Barry, John H. 262
Barry, William 53
Barry, William A. 237
Bartlett, Daniel 143
Bates, Elizabeth 320
Bates, John 207
Bates, Robert 137
Baxter, Andrew 30
Baxter, Margaret 30
Baxter, Mary 211
Baxter, Wm 138
Beamgard, Godfrey 224
Beard, David 53
Beard, James 7
Beard, Jane 169
Beatty, Jonathan 131
Beatty, William 32
Beaty, Jesse 62
Bell, Robert 52
Bennett, James T. 324
Bennett, John 267
Benoist, James 48
Benson, Jacob 183
Berry, Catharine 6
Berry, Roger 154
Berry, Samuel 156
Bigger, Esther 337
Bigger, James 39, 296
Bigger, Joseph 2
Bigger, Matthew 8
Bigger, Moses 205
Bigger, Wm. M. 227
Birk, Francis 26
Black, Alexander 39, 94
Black, Jacob 241
Black, John 224, 294
Black, Joseph 296
Black, Martha 347
Black, Morrita 264
Black, Robert 11, 78
Black, Thomas 91
Blair, John 277
Blair, Nancy 340
Blair, Samuel 200
Blalock, Jeremiah 198
Bland, Edward 36
Boggs, Aaron 209

## TESTATOR INDEX

Boggs, Joseph 27
Boleyn, Button 295
Boyd, James 336
Boyd, Jane 284
Boyd, John 155, 255
Boyd, Joseph 139
Boyd, Thomas 217
Boyls, Mary 17
Bozwell, Robt 135
Bradley, Samuel 227
Brandon, John 35
Bratton, Jane (Sturges) 47
Bratton, Martha 167
Bratton, Robert 108
Bratton, William 107
Brian, Mary 243
Bridges, William 185, 289
Brown, John 276, 281
Brown, Joseph 195
Brown, Robert 206
Brown, William 43, 328
Brumfield, Charles 160
Brumfield, Elizabeth 200
Brumfield, John 312
Brumfield, Mary 309
Bryan, James 232
Buchanan, Saml 135
Burnett, James A. 341
Burns, Elizabeth 300
Burns, Laughlin 61
Burris, Elizabeth 254
Burris, Robert 316
Burris, William 92
Byers, David 20, 350
Byers, Martha 319
Byers, Sarah 72
Cairnes, Elizabeth 245
Caldwell, Robert 330
Calley, William 29
Camp, William 335
Campbell, Ann 332
Campbell, Elizabeth 149
Campbell, J. A. 305
Campbell, James 89, 98, 266
Campbell, Jane 335
Campbell, Robert 318
Carnahan, John 13
Carol, Joseph 54
Carothers, James 302
Carrel, Jeannett 25
Carrel, Joseph 21
Carrel, Thomas 188

Carrell, Joseph 356
Carrell, Thomas 178
Carroll, Elijah 285
Carroll, Henry 299
Carroll, John 218
Carroll, Joseph 218
Carrothers, William 246
Carruth, John 168
Carson, William 91
Caveny, John 299
Chambers, Elizabeth 184
Chambers, James 55
Chambers, John 150, 304
Chambers, Samuel 219
Chambers, William 133, 227
Champion, Richard 26
Champion, William 114
Cherry, Peter 221
Chesney, Nancy 356
Childers, Jacob 252
Choat, William 256
Clark, Ann 112
Clark, John 253
Clark, Joseph 87
Clendennan, Thomas 118
Clerk, Eli 250
Clerk, John 220
Conly, Patrick 126
Cooper, Isles 98
Cooper, John 151
Cooper, Margaret 187
Cooper, Robert 242
Coulter, Jedediah 292
Craig, Henry 74
Craig, James 6
Craig, Mary 133
Craig, William 40
Crawford, Agness 222
Crawford, Alexander 288
Crawford, Ann 269
Crawford, David C. 317
Crawford, James 123, 240, 344
Crawford, Jane 258
Crawford, Walter 71
Crawford, William 99, 318
Crow, James 45
Currance, Rebeckah 204
Currence, Hannah 345
Currence, Hugh 302
Currence, Susan 348
Currence, William 273
Curry, Charles 113

## TESTATOR INDEX

Cushman, Xerxes H. 167
Dale, Ann 105
Dale, William 31
Daniel, Holloway W. 289
Dannal, James 185
Darby, Zadock 152
Darwin, John 214
Darwin, John B. 303
Davidson, John 109
Davis, Thomas 137
Davis, Vincent 315
Davis, William 132
Davison, Elizabeth 247
Davison, Margeret 232
Deen, James 87
Dennis, John 286
Denton, Samuel 1
Dickey, John 2, 41
Dickey, Samuel R. 332
Dickson, William 189
Donahy, Eleanor 17
Donaldson, Tabitha 279
Donally, James 131
Donnally, Martha 205
Donnom, Isaac 233
Dowdle, Allen 107
Drennan, Thomas 76
Drennon, Mary 85
Dulen, James 248
Dunken, Mary 92
Dunlap, Benjamin 286
Dunlap, Susanna 236
Dunlap, William 173
Dunwoody, John 175
Durham, John 181
Dyson, Maddox 115
Eakin, Alexander 62, 65
Ellis, Benjamin 72
Ellis, John 186
Ellis, Robert 115
Ellis, Sarah Sumner 154
Ellwell, Hannah 299
Enloe, Isaac 186
Enlow, Isaac 125
Enlow, Mary 4
Erwin, William 104
Erwin, William R. 277
Evans, Rebecca 263
Faires, Alexander 149
Falls, John 212
Faris, James 48, 286
Faris, Robert 56

Faris, Thomas 331
Farris, Jane 334
Farris, Jean 79
Farris, Robert McLellan 254
Farris, Samuel 253
Farris, William 70, 243
Feemster, Edward 309
Feemster, James 202
Feemster, John 111, 118
Feemster, Joseph 64
Ferguson, James 16
Fewell, John 265
Floyd, Andrew 223
Floyd, James 277
Floyd, Mary J. 344
Forbes, John 178
Foreman, James 82
Foreman, Samuel 75
Fowler, James 49
Fulton, A. S. 289
Fulton, Daniel 249
Gallagher, Jane 191
Gallaspie, James R. 274
Gallimore, Edward 59
Galloway, William 222
Garvin, John 39
Gassaway, William 197
Gault, Elizabeth 151
Gay, Samuel 32
Gebbie, John 109
Gebbie, Joseph 156
Gibson, James 73
Gibson, Mathew 68
Gilham, Charles 48
Gill, Mary 172
Gillam, Ezekial 275
Gillespie, Margaret 144
Gillespie, Richard 311
Gillham, Thomas 44
Gilmore, Francis 90
Gilmore, John J. 349
Given, Samuel 291
Given, William 258
Givens, Mary 304
Givins, Daniel 105
Glass, Simpson 301
Glenn, James 247
Glenn, Wm. R. 350
Glover, James 51
Goforth, Johnson 347
Good, Ann 213
Good, James B. 291

## TESTATOR INDEX

Good, John 74
Good, John H. 329
Good, Thomas L. 315
Gorden, John 50
Gordon, Mansfield 297
Gordon, Nanny 15
Graham, James 352
Graham, Jane 15
Graham, Margaret 333
Green, Abraham 130
Greer, Agness 209
Greer, Henry M. 283
Greer, Mary 246
Greer, Robert 165
Greer, Susannah 222
Grier, Thomas 353
Guinn, Thomas 223
Gunning, Edward H. 300
Gwin, Richard 266
Gwinn, Elizabeth 250
Hacket, William 285
Haggins, Mary 79
Hagins, William 191
Hall, John 70
Hall, Major T. 319
Hall, William 166
Hambright, Frederick 117, 257
Hambright, Jefferson 275
Hambright, Josiah 160
Hamilton, David 45
Hamilton, Jean 106
Hamilton, Patrick 124
Hamilton, William 230
Hammel, Archibald 259
Hanna, Archibald C. 202
Hanna, James 28
Hannah, Rosannah/Rosy 144
Hannah, Sarah 162
Harbison, John 71
Harp, Thomas 60
Harper, Alexander 252
Harper, Matthew 234
Harris, Henry G. 289
Harris, Hugh 311
Harris, James 199
Harris, James M. 319
Harris, Mary 168
Harris, Nathaniel 165
Harris, Prudence 224
Harris, Robert 148
Harrison, Henry 183
Harshaw, Daniel 103

Hart, John 29, 148
Hart, William 110
Hart, Wm. T. 294
Hartness, Robert 30
Hays, Jesse 239
Hays, John 320
Hays, Robert 244
Heart, Priscilla 153
Hemingway, Wm 153
Hemphill, Alexander 5
Hemphill, James S. 321
Hemphill, John 230
Hemphill, Margaret 289
Hemphill, Mary 231
Hemphill, Samuel 136
Henderson, Esther 10
Henderson, James P. 267
Henderson, John 195
Henderson, Nathaniel 19, 192
Henry, Alexander 175
Henry, James 93
Henry, William 128
Hetherington, William 293
Hill, Solomon 157
Hill, William 34, 116
Hoff, Powel 114
Hogg, Thomas 140
Hogge, James 204
Hogge, John 209
Holloway, Alexander 193
Holt, Akilles 225
Hood, George 142
Hood, John 357
Hopper, Charles 345
Horsely, Susannah 293
How/e, Joseph 31
Howie, Robert 120
Howser, Christina 323
Howser, Henry 139
Howser, John 194
Hutcheson, Samuel 204
Hutchison, David 264
Irwin, Nathaniel 18
Jackson, David 123
Jackson, Elias M. 350
Jackson, Elizabeth 251
Jackson, John 198, 270
Jackson, Joseph 238
Jackson, Margaret A. 272
Jackson, William 90
Jackson, William B. 291
James, John 287

## TESTATOR INDEX

Jamieson, Joseph 299
Jenkins, Benjn 126
Johnston, David 21, 152, 239
Johnston, John 195
Johnston, Margaret 252
Johnston, Sarah 210
Johnston, William H. 332
Jordon, John 13
Julian, Jacob 38
Kell, John G. 307
Kendrick, William 149
Kenmure, James 58
Kennedy, John 338
Kennedy, William 31
Kerr, Jane 86
Kerr, William 64
Kidd, John 201
Kimbel, Solomon 322
Kimbrell, Nancy 226
Kindsey, Barbara 120
King, George 22
King, John 207
Knox, James 356
Knox, Samuel 37
Kolb, James 75
Kuykendal, Samuel 88
Kuykendal, Sarah 76
Kuykendall, Jonathan 358
Lambeth, Margaret 167
Laney, Joseph 6
Latham, James 354
Latham, Mary 180
Lattimore, Robert 4
Laughridge, Mary 304
Lawrance, Joseph 210
Lawrence, A. G. 338
Leathem, Andrew 12
Leathem, Richard 1
Leathem, Robert 317
Leech, James 110
Leech, Jerusha 336
Leech, William 14
Leeper, Robert 26
Lesly, Samuel 67
Lesslie, William D. 315
Lewis, James 13
Lindsay, John M. 274
Lindsey, John 119
Lipscomb, Wyatt 181
Little, William 147
Love, Alexander 10
Love, Andrew 64

Love, Margaret 73
Love, Robert 28, 166, 189
Love, William 161
Lowry, Samuel 184
Luck, Jane 133
Lusk, Elisabeth 29
Manion, Thomas 63
Manning, Joseph B. 349
Manning, Robert 308
Manning, Robert L. 349
Manning, Thomas 254
Mannon, Massey 189
Marley, Jameson 208
Martin, Michael 179
Martin, Thomas 316
Mason, James 152
McAdorry, Thomas 10
McAfee, Abner 275
McCall, Grizzell 266
McCance, John 86
McCants, James 305
McCarter, Andrew 342
McCarter, Christopher 146
McCarter, John A. 358
McCarter, Sarah 264, 282
McCarter, Walter 202
McCaw, John 157, 357
McCaw, Nancy 270
McCleland, Hugh 25
McCleland, Robert 46
McCleland, William 90
McClenaghan, Tenny 122
McClenahan, Jane 280
McClenahan, John S. 236
McConnel, John 359
McCord, James 18
McCorkle, Abraham 27
McCorkle, Joseph 267
McCully, James 296
McCully, Samuel 294
McCurdry, Robert 52
McDaniel, Thomas 159
McElmoile, John 94
McElwain, John 167
McElwee, J. R. 271
McElwee, John 246
McElwee, William 310
McFadden, Isaac 303
McFadden, Patrick 23
McFaddin, Sarah 339
McFarlan, John 158
McGarrity, Michael 5

## TESTATOR INDEX

McGill, John 343
McGowan, William Irwin 325
McGowen, William 125
McIlwain, Charles 315
McKee, James 288
McKee, Samuel 66
McKenzie, Joseph 134
McKiney, Neal 44
McKnight, John 3
McKoy, John 290
McLean, William 176
McMeans, James 182
McMurry, Nancy 93
McNeel, John 272
McNeely, Robert 242
McNeil, Mary 176
McNight, Margret 42
McPhilimey, James 68
McRight, Robert 174
McSwain, George 201
McSwain, John 77
McWhorter, Hugh 26
Meacheam, Bartlet 213
Meek, Adam 73
Meek, Ann 124
Meek, Jane 28
Meek, Moses 110
Mellon, George 37
Mesheau, Daniel 332
Milan, John 40
Miller, Abraham 163
Miller, David 114
Miller, Elvy 193
Miller, Francis 257
Miller, Hugh 158
Miller, John 49, 171, 271
Miller, Joseph 142, 196
Miller, Mary 309
Miller, Robert 44, 330
Miller, Samuel 218
Miller, Stephen 8
Miller, William 97
Milom, John 8
Minter, John 269
Minter, William 82
Miskelly, Frances 56
Miskelly, James 357
Miskelly, Jean 55
Mitchell, James 105
Mitchell, Robert 282
Molinax, Wm 132
Montgomery, Rebecca 88

Moore, Alexander 101, 102
Moore, Catharine 332
Moore, Ealeanor 104
Moore, Elizabeth 282
Moore, Gordon 228
Moore, James 272, 283
Moore, Jane 16
Moore, John 137, 187, 238
Moore, John S. 333
Moore, Nathan 180
Moore, Ruth 255
Moore, Saml 130
Moore, William 245, 334, 345, 346
Morgan, Peter 292
Morris, John 92
Moss, Gilley 256
Muldoon, David 42
Muldoon, John 157
Mullin, Mary Unity 240
Murphey, James 18
Nance, William 259
Nash, Lucy 82
Neeley, Elizabeth 184
Neely, David 112
Neely, Elizabeth 236
Neely, Gean 128
Neely, Jackson 4
Neely, John 266
Neely, Jonathan 138
Neely, Martha 101, 103
Neely, Samuel 235
Neely, William 215, 238
Nelson, William 86
Nickles, James 23
Nisbitt, Francis 176
Niven, John 287
Oldrage, Hannah 352
Orr, John H. 294
Packard, Zadoc 192
Pair, Mial 136
Parker, Thomas 70
Parks, William 295
Patrick, Elias 244
Patrick, Elizabeth 261
Patrick, Mary 342
Patrick, Robert 96, 188
Patrick, William 143, 323
Patrick, William H. 275
Patterson, Andrew 114
Patterson, Benjamin 256
Patterson, Elizabeth 313
Patterson, John 24, 101, 103

## TESTATOR INDEX

Patterson, Mary 167
Patterson, Robert 12
Patton, David S. 297
Patton, Joseph 108
Patton, Robert 79
Patton, William 25
Persley, James 125
Peters, James 247
Peters, John 130, 255
Peters, Martha 358
Pettus, George 117, 260
Pettus, John D. O. K. 138
Pettus, William 121
Plexico, James 284
Plexico, John T. 300
Poag, Nancy M. 330
Polk, Eleanor 56
Polk, John 54
Polk, William 148
Porter, David 42
Porter, Samuel 3
Powell, James 33, 55
Pugh, Jacob 324
Pursley, James 5
Pursley, Robert 212
Quinn, James 267
Rainey, William 171
Ramsay, Martha 276
Ramsey, Jane 84
Ramsey, John 142
Ramsey, Martha 252
Randall, Jacob 69
Ratchford, George 318
Ratchford, John 298
Ratchford, Mary 109
Ratchford, William 62
Ray, Henry 9
Rea, Francis 66
Rea, Henry 241
Rea, Mary 274
Rea, Sarah 113
Reeves, Cyntha 221
Reeves, Elizabeth 329
Renicks, Mary 58
Richardson, James 27
Riddel, George 178
Roberts, Andrew 196
Roberts, James 121
Roberts, Jesse 170, 171
Roberts, John 355
Robertson, John 207
Robertson, Rebecca 323

Robertson, Thomas 283
Robinson, James 19
Robinson, Mary 140
Robinson, Patrick 17
Robinson, William 134, 216
Robison, Joseph 324
Roddy, John 339
Rodgers, Michael 47
Rogers, Isaac 354
Rooker, Sarah 343
Ross, George 219
Ross, James 161
Ross, Rachael 11
Rowell, Mary A. 343
Rowell, William F. 197
Sadler, Jane 141
Sadler, Joseph 95
Sadler, Mary R. 241
Sadler, Richard 85, 117, 200
Sandefer, Elizabeth 199
Sandefur, Philip 119
Sandlin, Randal 143
Scott, Alexander 213
Scott, David 33, 34
Scott, John 311
Scott, Mary 355
Shane, John 122
Shearer, Hugh 16
Sherer, Thomas 225
Shirley, Elizabeth 269
Shurley, Philemon 307
Simeral, James B. W. 207
Simeral, Jean 77
Simral, James 292
Simril, Mary Emeline 309
Sinclair, Duncan 67
Sitgreaves, John 140
Smith, Edward 281
Smith, George 268
Smith, Henry 14, 182, 309
Smith, James 23, 136
Smith, John 19, 80, 99, 112, 203, 337
Smith, Josiah 124
Smith, Lillis 182
Smith, Nicholas 102
Smith, Rhoda 320
Smith, Robert 313
Smith, Saml D. 264
Smith, Sarah C. 295, 336
Smith, William 98, 260, 288
Smith, Wm. H. 129
Smith, Winefred 273

## TESTATOR INDEX

Spence, John 61
Spratt, Thomas 77
Springs, John 298
Springs, Richard 355
Sprott, Andrew 57
Sprott, James 249
Stanton, Eleanor 240
Stanton, William A. 204
Starns, Jacob 301
Starr, Arthur 28
Starr, John 250
Starr, Sarah 319
Steedman, Michael 205
Steel, Archibald 69
Steel, Joseph 24
Steel, William 174
Steele, Mary 218
Stephenson, Dorcas M. 280
Stephenson, James M. 242
Stephenson, William 120
Steward, Margret 12
Stewart, Alexander 159
Stewart, J. N. 345
Stewart, James 306
Stewart, Michael 81
Stewart, Nancy 322
Stewart, William T. 320
Story, Benjamin 251
Stuart, Archibald 188
Sturges, Jane (Bratton) 47
Sturgis, Daniel 7
Sturgis, Labon 22
Suggs, Laban 208
Summerford, William 262
Swan, John 175
Swann, Ann 263
Swann, John B. 342
Swann, Mary H. 329
Tate, James 165
Thomasson, James 280
Thomasson, James C. 306
Thomasson, Nathaniel 220
Thompson, Alexander 163
Thompson, Ann 107
Thompson, John 193
Thompson, Samuel 92
Thompson, Thomas 18
Thompson, William 31
Thomson, James 85
Thomson, William 145
Thorn, Hezekiah 265
Thrift, Abraham 72

Ticer, Clark 57
Ticer, Hugh 65
Tilghman, Joshua 194
Tipping, Henry 243
Tipping, James 15
Tolbert, Rezin 247
Turner, James 347
Turner, Robert 154
Turner, Thomas 129, 159
Venable, J. B. 349
Venable, Jane 155
Venable, John 36, 81
Venable, Richard 155
Venable, William 174
Vicars, Ralph 97
Waddel, David 127
Waddle, Joseph 2
Wagner, George 121
Walker, Elizabeth 178
Walker, Hugh 217
Walker, Thomas 25
Walker, Thompson 239
Wallace, James 323
Wallace, McCastland 349
Wallace, Oliver 9
Wallis, Martha 132
Wallis, Mary 259
Watson, David 226
Watson, David M. 307
Watson, Deborah 335
Watson, George 83
Watson, James 51
Watson, James Franklin 260
Watson, Samuel 89
Watson, Violet 134
Watson, William 30, 94, 301
Watson, William D. 347
Weathers, Edmund 265
Weathers, Isaac 108
Weathers, Randolph 263
Webb, Eleanor 308
Webb, James 102, 103
Wells, Hugh 158
Wherry, Dorcas 87
Wherry, William 285
Whisonant, Michael 314
White, Hugh 169
White, Janet 317
White, Jesse 234
White, Joseph 60
White, Margaret 183
White, Sarah 232

## TESTATOR INDEX

White, Wm 308
Whiteside, Hugh 162
Whitesides, Margaret 324
Whitley, Jonathan 20
Wilie, William 19
Wilkie, William 58
Wilkins, Smith 209
Williams, Charles 215
Willson, Richard 22
Wilson, Gazaway 322
Wilson, Hugh 51
Wilson, John 14, 271
Wilson, Robert 285
Wilson, Thomas 235
Wilson, William 34
Withers, Rufus J. 304
Withers, Sarah M. 268
Witherspoon, Isaac Donnom 331
Wood, Aaron 201
Wood, Dorothy 244
Wood, Foster H. 267
Wood, James 312
Workman, John 115, 129, 293
Workman, Robert 251
Wray, Henry 9
Wright, Mary 351
Wright, Samuel 257, 331
Wright, William 99, 100, 325
Wylie, Joseph 256
Wylie, Nancy 196
Wylie, William 260
Yarborough, Ann 294
Young, James 21, 84

## PERSONAL NAME INDEX

Abernatha, Jos H. 251
Abernathie, John J. 140
Abernathy, John 140
Abernathy, John J. 140
Abernetha, Margaret A. 273
Abernethey, Milton 273
Abernethey, Wm 273
Acock, Edmund 128
Adair-- see also Adare
Adair, Ann 112
Adair, James 112
Adair, Jane 112
Adair, Jean 79
Adair, John 19
Adair, Mary (Beard) 97
Adair, Mary 53, 54, 97
Adair, Poly 79
Adair, Thos Benjn. 97
Adam, Robert 148
Adams, Amanda 282
Adams, Amanda Caroline 338
Adams, Ann/a 23, 41
Adams, D. A. 321
Adams, David A. 321
Adams, Eliza 321, 325
Adams, Elizabeth 23, 36, 41
Adams, Emily 338
Adams, Erixene 248, 249
Adams, Erixene Susan 249
Adams, Euxine 253
Adams, Francis 10, 27, 36, 81, 84,
  114, 130, 156, 185
Adams, Hannah 41
Adams, Isabel 310
Adams, Izabella 41
Adams, J. B. 321
Adams, J. L. 332
Adams, J. Leander 305, 318, 338
Adams, J. M. H. 333
Adams, James 36, 252, 321
Adams, James H. 249
Adams, James L. M. 338
Adams, James S. 113, 148, 249
Adams, Jane 184
Adams, John 82, 123, 156, 185, 310
Adams, John G. 282
Adams, John H. 270, 279, 314,
  328, 338, 341, 351
Adams, Joseph 36, 123, 137, 148,
  176, 253, 321, 338
Adams, Leroy 270, 334
Adams, M. E. 321

Adams, Marg(a)ret 36, 148, 321
Adams, Martha 23, 41
Adams, Mary 41, 84, 114
Adams, Matty 123
Adams, Messina 161
Adams, Minerva 282
Adams, Neatey 123
Adams, Rebecca 295
Adams, Robert 23, 36, 41, 67, 123,
  137, 321
Adams, Robt E. 338
Adams, Rufus J. 249, 252, 253
Adams, Samuel L. 248, 249
Adams, Samuel LeRoy 253
Adams, Sarah 23, 41
Adams, Simpson 156
Adams, Susan 253
Adams, Thomas 249, 252
Adams, Thos H. 263
Adams, Watson 282
Adams, William 36, 84, 114, 123,
  131, 148, 156, 319, 321
Adams, Wm E. 338
Adare, Jean 49
Adare, John 49
Addison, Joseph 329
Adickes, Dorcas Antoinette 272
Adickes, H. F. 266
Adickes, Hennery F. 269
Adickes, Sarah 272
Adickes, Sarah R. 268
Adicks, E. J. 101
Adicks, H. F. 347
Adicks, Sarah 101
Adkins, Hartwell 125
Aiken, John 142
Aiken, Peter 1
Aikin, Alexander 205
Aikin, Margaret 205
Aker, Sarah 117
Akin, Alexander 73, 113
Akin, Elizabeth 113
Akin, George 73, 113
Akin, Joshua 73
Akin, Wm. 62
Akins, John 116
Akins, Nancy 55
Akins, Wm. 93
Albernon, Wm 179
Albright, Elizabeth 271
Albright, John 271
Alcorn, Jane 17

## PERSONAL NAME INDEX

Alderman, Jeremiah 108
Alderson, James 226
Alderson, Jeremiah 57, 108, 129
Alderson, Jerry 192
Alderson, John 295
Alderson, John S. 267
Alderson, Mary 108, 295
Alderson, William 108, 129, 192
Alexander, 222, 353
Alexander, A. W. 354
Alexander, Albert 162
Alexander, Albert Gallatin 162
Alexander, Alfred 162
Alexander, Alfred R. 258
Alexander, Alice 30, 178
Alexander, Ann 25, 356
Alexander, Catharine J. 258
Alexander, Eakins 66
Alexander, Eli 162
Alexander, Eli O. 258
Alexander, Eliza 240, 290
Alexander, Elizabeth 162
Alexander, Elizabeth C. 258
Alexander, Emeline 162
Alexander, Emily 206
Alexander, Esther (King) 83
Alexander, George Baldwin 83
Alexander, Harman[?] 151
Alexander, Harriet 220
Alexander, Hasting 162
Alexander, Henry 189
Alexander, Hermon 162
Alexander, Hester 144
Alexander, Isaac 153
Alexander, Isabella 278
Alexander, James 21, 258, 356
Alexander, James H. 200, 215, 230, 241, 278
Alexander, James T. 220
Alexander, Joseph 84, 106
Alexander, Lety 184
Alexander, Martha 83
Alexander, Mary 240
Alexander, Obadiah 112
Alexander, Oliver 162
Alexander, Saml B. 278
Alexander, Saml D. 106
Alexander, Samuel David 83
Alexander, Stephen H. J. 258
Alexander, Violet W. 352
Alexander, W. M. 177
Alexander, William 39, 63, 222

Alexander, Wm. R. 237
Alison, Albert 59
Alison, Elizabeth 59, 60
Alison, Hugh 104
Alison, James 104
Alison, John 59
Alison, Margaret Malvina 116
Alison, Richard 60
Alison, Robert 105
Alison, Thomas 104
Allen, Andrew 96
Allen, Betsy 96
Allen, George 310
Allen, James 96
Allen, Jenny 95, 96
Allen, Jno 96
Allen, Lucretia 114
Allen, Mary 310
Allen, Rebecca 310, 325
Allen, Samuel 96
Allen, Thomas 96
Allen, William 96
Allen, Wilson 96
Allison 21, 86, 208, 272, 280, 313, 337, 356
Allison, Adaline 128
Allison, Albert 128, 164
Allison, Alexander 32, 104, 105
Allison, Betsey Adaline Avalina 116
Allison, Caroline 164
Allison, Catharine 32
Allison, D. R. S. 314
Allison, Eliza 104, 164
Allison, Hugh 32, 105, 164, 165, 222
Allison, Hugh Parks 348
Allison, Jane 168
Allison, John 31, 60, 116
Allison, Lid 152
Allison, Margaret 32, 104
Allison, Martha 32
Allison, Mary 348
Allison, Mary A. 164
Allison, R. T. 350
Allison, Robert 32, 90, 129, 130, 164, 165, 222
Allison, Robert Alexander 104
Allison, Robert G. 145
Allison, Robert Rufus 348
Allison, Robt S. 275
Allison, Robt T. 171, 206, 213
Allison, Robt Y. 232, 276
Allison, Rosana 32

## PERSONAL NAME INDEX

Allison, Rt. 145
Allison, Sarah 164
Allison, Susan Jane Currence 348
Allison, Thos 164
Allison, Thos H. 164
Allison, Wm. B. 329, 348
Alston, Eliza M. 247
Alston, John A. 219, 247, 257, 293, 302
Alston, Mary Eliza 242
Amandah, Hannah Mary 138
Amberson, Mat(t)hew 23, 95
Amberson, William 23, 180, 281
Anderson, 352
Anderson, Ab 354
Anderson, Amelia D. 273
Anderson, Ann 273
Anderson, Ann E. 273
Anderson, Asbury H. 317
Anderson, Augustus F. 249
Anderson, Catharine 23
Anderson, David H. 316
Anderson, Eliza Ann 158, 159
Anderson, Isaac 273
Anderson, J. M. 262, 294, 309
Anderson, J. Monro/e 268, 309, 319
Anderson, Jane 106, 172
Anderson, Jas 158, 172
Anderson, John 106, 153, 185, 250, 262, 273
Anderson, John Monroe 250
Anderson, Margaret 74, 133
Anderson, Margaret Sarah 262
Anderson, Mary 273
Anderson, Mary Ann 316
Anderson, Mary J. E. 262
Anderson, Mary Jane Elizabeth 250
Anderson, Mary Rebecca 316
Anderson, Nancy 106
Anderson, Patrick 23
Anderson, R. F. 309
Anderson, Robt F. 273
Anderson, Samuel 24, 106
Anderson, Sarah Elizabeth 316
Anderson, Sarah S. 273
Anderson, Thomas Henry 315
Anderson, Violet A. 270
Anderson, William 23, 208, 256, 273, 331, 332
Anderson, William E. 316
Anderson, William Henry 106, 250
Anderson, William Jasper 316

Anthony, S. H. 345
Any (free), 329
Archer, Martha 336
Archery, Martha 320
Ardary, Alexander 184
Ardary, Jean 184
Ardary, John 184
Ardary, Joseph 184
Ardary, Nancy 184
Ardary, Robert 184
Ardary, Wm 184
Armstrong, Arthur 23, 170, 171
Armstrong, Elizabeth 76, 150
Armstrong, Frances 170
Armstrong, Francis 202, 212, 359
Armstrong, Isabella 337
Armstrong, J. K. 305
Armstrong, J. T. 332
Armstrong, James 150, 220
Armstrong, Jane 226
Armstrong, Jane W. 337
Armstrong, Jesse 170, 171
Armstrong, Jesse K. 145, 171, 206, 251, 337, 359
Armstrong, Jesse R. 232
Armstrong, John 150
Armstrong, M. C. 332
Armstrong, Martha 145
Armstrong, Mary 170, 171, 359
Armstrong, Mary Lalearin[?] 145
Armstrong, Nancy Malissa 232
Armstrong, Polly 359
Armstrong, Polly C. 359
Armstrong, Robert 337
Armstrong, Robert L. 145
Armstrong, Sarah 160, 170, 171, 232, 359
Armstrong, Sarah Jane 337
Armstrong, Thomas 150
Armstrong, William 126, 150, 170, 359
Arnderd[?], Kery 114
Arnold, Delphy 50
Arnold, James 131
Arnold, Jephus 19
Arnold, John 50, 62
Arnold, Josephus 50
Arnold, Polly 50
Arnold, William 50, 78
Arterberry, David 224
Arthur 45
Ash, Eleanor S. 304

## PERSONAL NAME INDEX

Ash, Elizabeth 1
Ash, Isbel 1
Ash, James 135, 141, 246, 291
Ash, John 1
Ash, Louisa Ann 304
Ash, Margaret 141
Ash, Mary 1, 141, 304
Ash, Mary M. 304
Ash, Polly 258, 291
Ash, Polly B. 141
Ash, Robert 1, 105, 141, 158, 304, 317
Ash, Samuel 141, 152, 291, 304
Ash, William 1, 73, 141, 169
Ash, William B. 113, 208
Ashcraft, Joel 175
Ashcraft, Saml 175
Ashford, William 12, 13
Ashmore, Cleranah 12
Ashmore, Ellenor 12
Ashmore, Margaret 12
Ashmore, Mary 12
Ashmore, Walter 12, 13
Ashmore, William 12
Atkins, John 47
Atkins, Rebecca/h 47, 48
Atkins, Samuel 47, 48
Atkins, Sarah 47
Attleberry, D. 266
Avery, E. 211
Avery, Edward 192
Ayres, David 215
Bailey, Bagwell 80
Bailey, Caleb 80
Bailey, Elijah 80
Bailey, Jean 80
Bailey, John 131, 142
Bailey, John H. 334
Bailey, Mary 80
Bailey, Polly 153
Bailey, William 80
Bailis, Jones 222
Baird, Ann Alvira 167
Bankhead 145
Bankhead, Betsy 52
Bankhead, Jane 296
Bankhead, Jean 52
Bankhead, John 52
Bankhead, Judah 83
Bankhead, Judith 106
Bankhead, Mary 52
Bankhead, Matthew 355

Bankhead, Robert McCurdry 52
Bankhead, Thomas 123
Barber, James 123
Barber, Robert G. 123
Barker, 314
Barklet, John 8
Barkley, Samuel 228
Barnes, Albertus 220
Barnes, Betsey 220
Barnes, Caroline 220
Barnes, John 220, 221
Barnes, Lucy 220, 221
Barnes, Polly 220
Barnes, Sally 220
Barnes, Samuel 220
Barnes, William 220
Barnet, Alexander 102
Barnet, Eliza A. 274
Barnet, Jane E. 262
Barnet, John 127, 147
Barnet, John B. 262
Barnet, John R. 262
Barnet, Margaret 262
Barnet, Martha Ann 262
Barnet, Rachal 148
Barnet, Richard 152
Barnet, Thomas 49, 102
Barnet, Violet A. 262
Barnet, William 102
Barnett, Abr'm 104
Barnett, Alexander 103, 115, 144, 190, 203, 206, 226, 245, 290
Barnett, Alex H. 330
Barnett, Ann 168, 335
Barnett, Catherine 290
Barnett, Eliza 345
Barnett, Elizabeth 78
Barnett, Emelia 335
Barnett, Emelina 305
Barnett, Fanny 78
Barnett, Frances Durham 203
Barnett, Frances P. 203
Barnett, George G. 143, 168
Barnett, Hamilton A. 290
Barnett, J. A. 323
Barnett, J. J. 203
Barnett, J. S. 260
Barnett, James A. 290, 329
Barnett, Joel 127
Barnett, Joel S. 203, 220
Barnett, John 78, 79, 116, 198
Barnett, John A. 316

## PERSONAL NAME INDEX

Barnett, John Allen 203
Barnett, Joseph 190
Barnett, Joseph Josiah 203
Barnett, Mary C. 330
Barnett, Mary Jane 305
Barnett, R. 196, 203
Barnett, Rachel 36, 290, 330
Barnett, Richard 127, 196, 201, 206
Barnett, Robert 37
Barnett, Sarah 83, 143
Barnett, Thomas 38, 39, 63, 108, 118, 143, 168, 171
Barnett, Wm. 60
Barnett, Wm. A. 205, 290, 329, 330
Barnhill, Cynthia 359
Barnhill, Isabella 160
Barnhill, John 160
Barnhill, Mary 359
Barnhill, Robert 160
Barnhill, Samuel 160
Barnhill, William 160
Barns, John 114
Barnwell, Cynthia E. 316, 324
Barnwell, James A. 316, 324
Barnwell, John 316, 324
Barnwell, Mary C. 316, 324
Barr, David 179
Barr, James 51
Barren, Wm. 66
Barron, A. 191
Barron, A. J. 237, 238, 259, 328, 329
Barron, Andrew 237
Barron, Archibald 227, 229, 237, 265, 329
Barron, Archibald G. 238
Barron, Catharine 6, 7
Barron, Elizabeth 151
Barron, Frances 329
Barron, James Barry 237
Barron, Jane 237
Barron, John 31, 151, 180, 193, 197, 237, 238, 328, 329
Barron, Lavinia[?] 265
Barron, M. E. 237, 260
Barron, Rebecca 238
Barron, S. D. 270
Barron, S. L. 238
Barron, Samuel 151, 265
Barron, T. C. 266
Barron, Thomas 82, 151, 238, 328, 329
Barron, Thomas G. 237

Barron, Thomas Y. 237
Barron, William 66, 151, 162, 197, 211, 220, 237, 238, 328, 329
Barron, William Y. 237
Barronhill, 170, 220
Barronhill, Isabella 160
Barronhill, John 210, 212
Barronhill, Mary Ann 210, 212
Barronwell, William 202
Barry, Alexander 211
Barry, Andrew L. 154
Barry, Catharine 53
Barry, Catty[?] Porter 53
Barry, E. A. G. 260
Barry, Eliz'a A. S. 237
Barry, Elizabeth 53, 237
Barry, G. E. 237
Barry, Issabella 173
Barry, J. D. 208
Barry, James D. 200
Barry, James H. 53, 262
Barry, James Hannah 53
Barry, Jane 209, 211, 237
Barry, Jane A. 209
Barry, Jean 7
Barry, John 53, 154, 173, 209, 237
Barry, John H. 262
Barry, John Henderson 53
Barry, Kate 53
Barry, Keatrin 7
Barry, Margaret 262
Barry, Margaret A. 209
Barry, Mary 156
Barry, Matilda 214
Barry, R. S. 289
Barry, Robert 173
Barry, Rodger 135
Barry, Roger 30, 92, 154
Barry, Sarah 173
Barry, Violet 262
Barry, William 53, 156, 173, 197, 214, 229
Barry, William A. 209, 211, 237
Barry, William Andres 53
Bartlett, Daniel 143, 148
Bartlett, Sophia 143
Bartlett, William 143, 192
Basdell/Basdill, Hannah 8
Bass 166
Bass, Amelia 161
Bates, Catharine 137
Bates, D. K. 324, 343

## PERSONAL NAME INDEX

Bates, David K. 254, 320
Bates, Elizabeth 320
Bates, Isis[?] 207
Bates, James 182
Bates, John 31, 46, 47, 72, 73, 106, 134, 136, 137, 207
Bates, Mary 31
Bates, Rebekeh 31
Bates, Robert 137
Bates, Sachariah 72, 73
Bates, Tennenas[?] 183
Bates, Thaddeus Kennedy 320
Bates, Thomas 137, 157, 183
Bates, Thomas A. 320
Bates, Zacheriah 224
Baxter, Andrew 27, 30, 208, 211, 237, 243
Baxter, Elizabeth 211, 221
Baxter, Fanny 211
Baxter, Henry 138
Baxter, James 30, 79, 138
Baxter, Jane 138
Baxter, Janet 30
Baxter, Jean 30
Baxter, John 27, 30, 138
Baxter, Margaret 30
Baxter, Mary 79, 208, 211
Baxter, Matilda 211
Baxter, Sarah 79
Baxter, Violet 211, 237
Baxter, William 138
Bayles, Jonas 48
Bayless, E. 106
Bayl(e)y, Elijah 80
Beaird, John 31
Beam, John 121
Beamgard, Adam 224, 225
Beamgard, Godfrey 225
Beamgard, Isaac 224
Beamgard, John 224
Beamgard, Joseph 224, 225
Beamgard, Samuel 224, 225
Beamgarde, Adam 226
Beamgarde, Godfrey 226
Beard, Adam 23, 41
Beard, Anny 101
Beard, Catharine 7
Beard, David 54, 97, 169
Beard, James 7
Beard, Jane 7, 97, 170
Beard, John 7, 19
Beard, Mary (Adair) 97

Beard, Mary 7
Beard, Permilla 143
Bearegarde, Samuel 255
Bears, Edward 33
Beatey, Rebekah 62
Beatey, William Jackson 62
Beatie, Jonathan 88
Beatty, 280
Beatty, Agnes 32
Beatty, Ann M. 341
Beatty, Eliza A. R. 190
Beatty, Eliza Ann 131
Beatty, Elizabeth 32
Beatty, Isabella 131
Beatty, Jane 131
Beatty, Jonathan 32, 131
Beatty, Margaret 131
Beatty, Nancy 131
Beatty, Robt R. 131
Beatty, Sarah 32, 131
Beatty, Sarah L. 131
Beatty, Susan 339
Beatty, W. C. 267, 271, 314, 341
Beatty, William 32, 131, 190, 339
Beatty, William C. 341
Beaty, Betsy 62
Beaty, Jesse 62
Beaty, John 62
Beaty, Joseph 26
Beaty, W. C. 318
Beaty, William 88
Beaty, William Jackson 62
Beauregard, Adam 255
Bell, 222, 299, 345
Bell, Christopher 173
Bell, Elizabeth 314
Bell, J. A. 344
Bell, James A. 277
Bell, John 52, 62, 265
Bell, Joshua D. 224
Bell, Margaret 183, 224
Bell, Mary 224
Bell, Nancy C. 277
Bell, Rebecca 173
Bell, Robert 52, 122, 138
Bell, Rosannah 16, 17
Bell, Samuel 173
Bell, Thomas J. 318
Bell, William 6
Bell, Y. J. 305
Belt, Stephen 242
Bennet, D. G. 297

## PERSONAL NAME INDEX

Bennet, John 352
Bennett 224
Bennett, Alsey F. 267
Bennett, Elizabeth 287, 324
Bennett, Hannah 352
Bennett, James S. 324
Bennett, John 192, 238, 267
Bennett, Jos. P. 267
Bennett, Joseph S. 287
Bennett, Lucinda 307
Bennett, Thomas C. 324
Bennett, Tirza M. 267
Bennett, W. C. 299
Bennett, William 352
Benoist, James 48
Benson, B. T. 202
Benson, Briget 183
Benson, Harriet 183
Benson, Jacob 183
Benson, John K. 167
Benson, Nancy 183
Benson, Walker 157, 211
Benton, Levin 139
Berrey, Jenney 53
Berry, Andrew 7
Berry, Cinthia 149
Berry, Hugh 5-7, 15, 30
Berry, James D. 154, 155, 157, 160
Berry, Jane 53
Berry, John 7, 41, 46, 53, 89, 109, 134, 135, 151, 155, 160
Berry, Kate 53
Berry, Margaret 135
Berry, Mary 97, 135, 252
Berry, Peggy 53
Berry, Richard 7
Berry, Rodger 109, 134
Berry, Roger 7, 151
Berry, Rosannah 135
Berry, Samuel 156
Berry, Samuel W. 157
Berry, Samuell Watson 89
Berry, William 7, 28, 142, 154, 181
Berry, Wm. A. 176
Betty, Jesse 46
Bigger, 37, 116
Bigger, Agnes 2
Bigger, Alexander 290
Bigger, Alexander B. 205, 313, 330
Bigger, Andrew 205, 290, 337
Bigger, Andrew J. 337
Bigger, Ann 8, 40, 290, 330

Bigger, Ann/e E. 205, 296, 313
Bigger, Eddy 39
Bigger, Eleanor 2
Bigger, Eli 182
Bigger, Esther (Patrick) 96
Bigger, Esther 337, 342
Bigger, James 8, 31, 40, 57, 102, 188, 205, 206, 229, 296, 358
Bigger, James A. 337
Bigger, James L. 313
Bigger, James Lysander 227
Bigger, James McKee 205
Bigger, Jane E. 313
Bigger, Joseph 2
Bigger, M. A. 260
Bigger, M. E. 307
Bigger, Margaret 2, 337, 342
Bigger, Margaret E. 313
Bigger, Maria 337
Bigger, Martha E. 205
Bigger, Mary 227
Bigger, Mary E. 229, 313
Bigger, Mary M. 274
Bigger, Mat(t)hew 2, 4, 8, 40, 205
Bigger, Moses 8, 40, 205, 206
Bigger, Moses A. 313, 330
Bigger, Robert 2
Bigger, Robt P. 337
Bigger, Sarah 2
Bigger, William 203, 205
Bigger, William M. 196, 205, 227, 313
Bigger, Wm McKee 178
Biggers 341
Biggers, Alexander B. 296
Biggers, James 186, 189, 216, 310
Biggers, Moses A. 296
Biggers, Wm. Mc. 206
Bigham, R. H. 256
Bigham, Robert 353
Bigham, Robert H. 239
Bigham, Wm. D. 256
Bird, Catharine 287
Bird, David 354
Bird, Edward 187, 228
Bird, Wm. Smith 287
Birk, Frances 26
Bishop, Dudley 100
Bishop, P. E. 262-264, 269
Bishop, Widow 43
Black, A. D. 330
Black, A. T. 281, 325
Black, Agnes 11

## PERSONAL NAME INDEX

Black, Alexander 39, 95
Black, Andrew 296
Black, Ann/a 39, 202
Black, Anne 95
Black, David 224
Black, David L. 264
Black, David Leroy 226
Black, Eleanor 85, 224
Black, Elisabeth 11, 78, 95, 296
Black, Ellen 141
Black, George 11
Black, H. C. 287
Black, Hamilton Wilson 95
Black, Hester 296
Black, Isabel 94, 95
Black, Jacob 11, 84, 106, 159, 160, 241
Black, James 92, 95, 117
Black, Jane 95, 119, 275
Black, Jefferson 305, 328
Black, John 11, 78, 82, 84, 92, 103, 105, 107, 117, 119, 141, 159, 180, 215, 224, 226, 347
Black, John B. 84, 106
Black, John G. 215
Black, Joseph 39, 78, 95, 202, 296, 299, 309, 310, 319, 320, 330
Black, Leroy 224
Black, Margaret L. 264
Black, Martha 78, 347
Black, Mary 17, 78, 91, 94
Black, Mary A. 330
Black, Mary Angelina 264
Black, Meribah 91
Black, Morrita 264
Black, Nancy 110, 117
Black, Pamela 296
Black, Robert 11, 72, 79, 139, 241, 296
Black, Robert A. 347
Black, Rus(s)el Washington 126, 187
Black, Samuel 78, 280, 347, 350
Black, Sarah Anne 95
Black, Templeton 95
Black, Thomas 91, 92, 228
Black, W. C. 292, 299
Black, William 78, 94, 95, 126, 187, 311, 347
Black, William B. 323
Black, William C. 234, 289, 323, 335, 346
Black, Woods 296

Blackney, John 4
Blackstock, William 47
Blackwood, J. J. 328
Blackwood, Jas 38
Blacstock, Wm. 47
Blair, 278, 321
Blair, Agness 99
Blair, Ann 341
Blair, Betsey 279
Blair, Cooper 183
Blair, David 279
Blair, Dorcas 183
Blair, Elva 200
Blair, Garrison 279
Blair, George D. 183
Blair, Irwin 340
Blair, Isabella 200
Blair, James 183, 279
Blair, James H. 183
Blair, James Harper 183
Blair, James P. 340
Blair, Jane 183
Blair, John 82, 83, 99, 103, 106, 131, 142, 179, 183, 245, 279, 340, 341, 355
Blair, John W. 279
Blair, Martha 341
Blair, Mary 200
Blair, Mary Margaret 341
Blair, Nancy 200, 277, 341
Blair, Samuel 131, 200, 215, 278, 341
Blair, Wm 279
Blake, Jane 294
Blake, John 294
Blalock, Betsey 221
Blalock, Edmond 198
Blalock, Jeremiah 132, 143, 198, 199
Blalock, John 157, 198
Blalock, Lucy 198
Blalock, William 198, 199
Bland, Dosha 36
Bland, Edward 36
Bland, Elizabeth 36
Bland, Frank(e)y 36
Bland, William 36
Blankenship, Isaac 108
Blankenship, Polly 108
Blankenship, Susanna 108
Blankenship, Thomas 13
Blankhead, James 11
Blanks, Richard 13
Blanton, Charles 276

## PERSONAL NAME INDEX

Blanton, Hester 179
Blanton, Jesse 313
Blanton, Malinda (Spencer) 179
Blanton, Richard 179
Blanton, Sarah 179
Boatright, Jas 263
Boatwright, Washington 312
Bobbett, Wm. 319
Bobbit, Jno 221
Bogan, 308
Boggs, Aaron 27, 209, 213
Boggs, Agness 27
Boggs, Caroline 266, 267
Boggs, Caroline G. 341
Boggs, Elizabeth 27
Boggs, Harvey 221
Boggs, James 27
Boggs, Jean 27
Boggs, John Renicks 27
Boggs, Joseph 27, 131, 209, 213
Boggs, Martha 134, 209, 319
Boggs, Mary 209
Boggs, Nancy 209
Boggs, Polly 27
Boggs, Thomas 27, 131, 209
Boggs, Thomas Gilleland 27
Boggs, William 213
Boggs, William Wallace 27
Bogs, Aaron 45
Bogs, Elizabeth 45, 59
Bogs, Jean 58, 59
Bogs, John Renicks 59
Bogs, Thomas 70, 71
Boid, Edmund 139
Boid, Edward 139
Boins, James 240
Boins, Susannah 240
Bolen, Britton 126
Bolen, Mary Ann 332
Bolen, Nancy Jane 332
Boleyn, Button 295
Boleyn, Elizabeth 295
Boleyn, G. R. 277, 295
Boleyn, George R. 296
Boleyn, Jane 295
Boleyn, John 295, 296
Boleyn, John A. 295
Boleyn, Joseph 295
Booker, J. 122
Boos, James G. 291
Borders, Hugh 186, 187, 228
Bostic, John 124

Bostick, Candace 201
Bostick, Floyd 52
Bostick, Francis 201
Boswell 201
Bowans, Nancy 170
Bowden, Margaret H. 281
Bowden, Margaret R. 281
Bowden, Samuel D. 281
Bowden, Wm. R. 281
Bowen, John M. 301
Bowen, Nancy (Roberts) 171
Bowen, Susannah 241
Bowen, W. J. 329
Bowen, Wm. J. 309
Boyce, E. E. 315
Boyce, William 312
Boyd, Andw 109
Boyd, Bennet Franklin 217
Boyd, Clarissa 155
Boyd, David 155, 206, 219
Boyd, David J. 210, 211, 234
Boyd, David Patton 255
Boyd, Elizabeth 139, 217, 219
Boyd, Elizabeth J. 281, 336
Boyd, Hannah 287
Boyd, James 217, 281, 312, 336
Boyd, James Lee 139, 140, 144
Boyd, Jane 155, 217, 284
Boyd, Jency 155
Boyd, Jincy 284
Boyd, John 134, 155, 217, 336
Boyd, John D. 219, 255
Boyd, Joseph 140
Boyd, Levin 139
Boyd, Louisa 217
Boyd, Margaret 109, 110, 155, 284
Boyd, Margt E. 336
Boyd, Martha Jane 255
Boyd, Mary 155, 217, 284
Boyd, Mary Margaret 255
Boyd, Nancy 255
Boyd, Nancy Clementine 255
Boyd, Peggy 87, 139
Boyd, Pemely 155
Boyd, Permelia 284
Boyd, Peter 87
Boyd, R. F. 336
Boyd, Rachel 217
Boyd, Rachel Louisa 255
Boyd, Robert 217
Boyd, Rufus 336
Boyd, Rufus J. 284

## PERSONAL NAME INDEX

Boyd, Sally 155
Boyd, Saml W. 309
Boyd, Sarah Elizabeth 255
Boyd, Sary 139, 140
Boyd, T. M. 204, 284
Boyd, Thomas 155, 217, 219, 234
Boyd, Thomas Jefferson 217, 255
Boyd, W. L. 287
Boyd, William 217
Boyd, Wm. J. L. 272
Boyers, D. 82
Boyes, Nancy 213
Boyes, William 273
Boyls, Ann 17
Boyls, Eleazer 17
Boyls, John 17
Boyls, Margaret 17
Boyls, Mary 17
Bozel, Robert 10
Bozwell, Margaret 135
Bozwell, Robt 135
Bradley, Albert 350
Bradley, Joseph 227
Bradley, Samuel 192, 227, 228
Bradley, Samuel A. 227
Bradshaw 352
Bradshaw, Thomas 261
Brandon, E. T. 296
Brandon, Francis 35
Brandon, George 35
Brandon, Irvine 35
Brandon, James 35, 36
Brandon, John 35, 36
Brandon, Joseph 35
Brandon, Mary (Lawson) 35, 36
Brandon, Pressillar 35
Brandon, Sarah A. 343
Brandon, Sussey 35
Brandon, Thomas 35
Brandon, Thomas L. 342
Bratten, John 95
Bratton, Agness 270
Bratton, Betsey Adaline 167
Bratton, Betsey E. 259
Bratton, Elizabeth 79, 108
Bratton, Hugh 83
Bratton, J. N. 343
Bratton, J. S. 166
Bratton, James 263, 329
Bratton, James C. 259
Bratton, James R. 286
Bratton, Jane (Sturges) 47

Bratton, Jane 32
Bratton, John 118, 130
Bratton, John S. 107, 158, 166, 226, 270, 357
Bratton, Martha 107, 167
Bratton, Mary 75, 107, 270
Bratton, Mary (Wallace) 108
Bratton, Robert 83, 108, 109, 259
Bratton, Ruthey 83
Bratton, Samuel 116
Bratton, Thomas 5, 118, 175
Bratton, William 30, 32, 74, 107, 108, 329, 357
Brattons, John 29
Bread, Mary 169
Breages, Thomas 234
Brem, J. 309
Brevard, Hugh 24, 31
Brevard, John 31
Brian-- see also Briant, Bryan, etc.
Brian, Aaron 243
Brian, J. M. 324
Brian, James 154, 243, 268, 286, 289, 349
Brian, Mary 243
Brian, Moses 243
Brian, Narcissa 289
Brian, Shff 277
Brian, Susan 243
Brian, Thos 243
Briant, Aaron 208
Briant, Augustus 189
Briant, James 103, 154, 160, 208
Bridge, Welborn 334
Bridges, Cecilia/Celia 289
Bridges, Edmund 185
Bridges, James 168
Bridges, John L. 289, 346
Bridges, Lucy 289
Bridges, Nancy 70
Bridges, Polly 289
Bridges, Robert 130, 185
Bridges, Scinthy 120
Bridges, Thomas 70, 182, 185, 186, 234
Bridges, William 185, 186, 289, 334
Briges, John L. 335
Briggs 299
Brison, Elizabeth 74
Broadwill, Elizabeth 51
Bromfield, Jesse 178
Browmfield, Charles 92

## PERSONAL NAME INDEX

Brown, Alexander 5, 112
Brown, Andrew 272
Brown, Archibald 43
Brown, Charles 43
Brown, Charlott 105
Brown, Daniel 180
Brown, Darcus 344
Brown, Dorcus 223
Brown, Elizabeth 282
Brown, Frances 31, 105
Brown, Hannah B. 206
Brown, Harriet A. 328
Brown, James 170
Brown, Jane 183
Brown, Jean 43
Brown, John 71, 72, 84, 124, 133, 188, 206, 215, 236, 260, 276, 282, 328
Brown, John A. 219, 328
Brown, John C. 206
Brown, John D. 307
Brown, John G. 207, 230, 275, 300
Brown, Joseph 42, 189, 195
Brown, Martha 245
Brown, Mary 5, 206, 344
Brown, Mary D. 328
Brown, Mary Elizabeth 276
Brown, Mary M. 350
Brown, Matthew 4
Brown, Polly 79
Brown, Prudence 202
Brown, Robert 186, 206, 207, 282, 291, 328
Brown, Robert Jackson 206
Brown, Rosannah 149
Brown, S. G. 350
Brown, Samuel 105, 219
Brown, Samuel G. 239, 243, 256
Brown, T. 193
Brown, Tabitha D. 328
Brown, Terza 276
Brown, Thomas 92
Brown, Usry D. 328
Brown, William 43, 118, 121, 156, 202, 207, 328
Brown, William C. 206
Brown, William L. 280, 328
Brumfield, Caroline 160
Brumfield, Charles 30, 160
Brumfield, Elizabeth 160, 200, 208
Brumfield, George 309
Brumfield, George M. 312
Brumfield, Isaac 160

Brumfield, James 77, 160
Brumfield, Jesse 112, 160, 207, 211, 220, 250, 263, 268, 269, 293
Brumfield, John 76-78, 160, 312
Brumfield, Mary 309
Bryan-- see also Brian, Bryant, etc.
Bryan, Aaron 233
Bryan, Augustus 233
Bryan, Benjamin 233
Bryan, Delilah 233
Bryan, James 233
Bryan, L. B. 353
Bryan, Margaret 111
Bryan, Mary 232, 233
Bryan, Moses 233
Bryan, Thomas 233
Bryan, William 233
Bryant, Augustus 189
Bryant, Margaret 111
Bryant, Mary 111
Bryon, L. B. 353
Bryson, Elizabeth 133
Bryson, John 171
Bryson, Margaret 134
Bryson, Rosanna 178
Buchanan, Barbara 135
Buchanan, James 135
Buchanan, John 135
Buchanan, John R. 189
Buchanan, Margaret 135
Buchanan, Samuel 135, 136
Buchanan, William 135, 136
Buffington, Jacob 110
Bullen[?], George 216
Bullinger, Margaret (Springs) 298
Bullock, 145, 314, 328
Bullock, Stephen 122
Bullons[?], George 216
Bulton, T. D. 257
Bunkhead, John 45
Buris, Easther 92
Burk 344
Burke, Francis 26
Burnes, Saml 136
Burnett, Adeline 341
Burnett, Alexander 341
Burnett, Eliza 341
Burnett, Hannah 341
Burnett, James A. 341
Burnett, James Josiah 341
Burnett, John 341
Burnett, Margaret 341

## PERSONAL NAME INDEX

Burnett, Mary 341
Burnett, Robert 341
Burnett, William A. 341
Burns, Amos 186
Burns, Daniel 61
Burns, Easter C. 207
Burns, Elizabeth 279, 300
Burns, Elvira 300
Burns, Henry 61
Burns, J. 191
Burns, J. F. 347
Burns, James 61
Burns, Jane 300
Burns, John 211
Burns, Laug(h)lin 61
Burns, Luke 61
Burns, Malichi 61
Burns, Peggy 61
Burns, Robert 61
Burns, Saml 125
Burns, Wm 186
Burres, Edw'd 117
Burris, Davis Z. 317
Burris, Elizabeth 254, 279
Burris, Esther 92
Burris, James 219
Burris, Jane 219
Burris, John 92, 217, 254, 255, 258, 317
Burris, Mary 92, 93, 317
Burris, R. Mc. 317
Burris, Reuben McConnell 317
Burris, Robert 317
Burris, Robert N. 317
Burris, Robert Walker 317
Burris, William 1, 92, 93, 135, 254
Burrow, Jno 142
Burton, Emily 256
Burton, Margaret 256
Burton, Mary (Pettus) 117, 118
Byers, Alamath 202
Byers, Alemith 350
Byers, Baldwin 83
Byers, Clement 157
Byers, David 21, 73, 108, 110, 124, 157, 350
Byers, David J. 350
Byers, David Theodore 350
Byers, E. G. 280
Byers, Edward 50, 51, 73, 85, 108, 110, 121, 124
Byers, Edward G. 260, 350

Byers, James 350
Byers, John 350
Byers, Joseph 83, 106
Byers, Marget 20
Byers, Martha 156, 319
Byers, Mary 157, 350
Byers, Samuel 20
Byers, Saml B. 106, 121
Byers, Saml Baldwin 124
Byers, Sarah 20, 72
Byers, Theodore 350
Byers, W. B. 333, 347, 349
Byers, William 3, 20, 72, 91, 108, 110
Byers, William B. 273
Byers, Williamson 63, 72, 126, 130, 131, 156, 187, 279
Bynum, Cynthia L. 284
Byrd, Ed. 195
Cain, Hugh 68, 126, 136, 157, 186, 206, 207
Cain, James M. 173
Cain, John 68, 85
Cain, Katherine G. 161
Cain, Martha 164
Cain, Robert A. 164
Cairnes, Elizabeth 245
Cairnes, Jane (Cunningham) 279
Cairnes, Jane 245
Cairnes, John 245, 340
Cairnes, Robert 245
Cairnes, Susan 245
Calcot, Elijah 217
Caldwell 315
Caldwell, Agness 69
Caldwell, Eleanor 69
Caldwell, G. 247, 338, 358
Caldwell, Gabraith 310
Caldwell, Galbreath 68, 69, 131, 157, 207, 330
Caldwell, Hugh G. 330
Caldwell, James 132, 199, 205, 264, 299, 323, 330, 336
Caldwell, Joseph 354
Caldwell, Margaret 68, 69
Caldwell, Margaret Ann 330
Caldwell, Martha 310
Caldwell, Robert 131, 199, 205, 264, 330
Caldwell, Robert A. 330, 336
Caldwell, S. M. 169
Caldwell, Sarah T. 264

## PERSONAL NAME INDEX

Caldwell, William 69, 114, 117, 119, 131, 132, 143, 247, 330, 358
Calhoone, Samuel 38
Calhoun, Charles 37
Callahan, John 171
Callender, Alaquil 225
Calley, Jacob 29
Calley, James 29
Calley, John 29
Calley, Mary 29
Calley, Pelick 29
Calley, Wm 29
Calloway, Joseph W. 353
Cally, George 13
Calton, Thos B. 227
Cambel, James 91
Camble, George 85
Camp, Adalissa 335
Camp, Joseph P. 335
Camp, Lawrence S. 335
Camp, Mary 292, 335
Camp, Susannah 121
Camp, Thos 292
Camp, William 210, 211, 335
Campbell 299
Campbell, A. P. C. 299, 305, 344
Campbell, Abigail 17
Campbell, Alexander 25, 149
Campbell, Andr P. C. 335
Campbell, Andrew 98
Campbell, Ann 89, 90, 154, 318, 332
Campbell, C. A. 305
Campbell, Capt. I. 190
Campbell, Captain 111
Campbell, D. M. 305
Campbell, David M. 302
Campbell, E. G. 337
Campbell, Elias 266
Campbell, Eliza A. 335
Campbell, Eliza M. 343
Campbell, Elizabeth 58, 149, 156, 232, 266, 305, 332, 335
Campbell, Elizabeth Jackson (Maclean) 177
Campbell, Elizabeth Jackson (McLane) 176
Campbell, Elizabeth Russell 169
Campbell, George 85, 177
Campbell, George W. 297
Campbell, Gincey 149
Campbell, Isaac 97, 98, 103, 115, 145, 157, 170, 189, 232

Campbell, Isaac A. 147, 204, 206, 211
Campbell, Isaac C. 145
Campbell, Isack 144
Campbell, J. A. 167, 171, 305, 359
Campbell, J. S. 359
Campbell, James 85, 90, 98, 23, 266
Campbell, James D. 90
Campbell, Jane 148, 149, 232, 266, 335
Campbell, Jane A. 284
Campbell, Jan(n)et 98
Campbell, Jean 36
Campbell, John 98, 149, 156, 190, 310
Campbell, Margaret 90
Campbell, Martha E. 335
Campbell, Peter 226
Campbell, Rachel 89, 318
Campbell, Rachel J. 90
Campbell, Robert 89, 90, 152, 155, 266, 318
Campbell, S. L. 296, 305, 341
Campbell, Samuel 98, 149, 305, 335
Campbell, Sarah 90
Campbell, Thomas 149, 266
Campbell, Violet 177
Campbell, W. E. 337
Campbell, William 89, 90, 149, 152, 177, 182, 186, 196, 201, 217, 245, 278, 280, 298, 305, 335
Campbell, Wm. E. A. 305
Campill, Wm. 270
Campiun, 305
Candlesh, Alexander 37
Candlesh, Mary 37
Candlish, Alexander 37
Candlish, Mary 37
Canseller, Phillip 177
Cantwell, James Smith 80
Cantwell, Katherine Gough 80
Cantwell, Sarah 80
Cantzons 233
Caps, James 33
Caps, Zack 281
Carell, Joseph 22
Carigan, Mary M. 321
Carlisle, Jane 186
Carlisle, Nancy Margaret 250
Carlisle, Robert 186
Carnahan, John 15
Carnahan, Mar(e)y 11, 13
Carnehen, John 13
Carnes, Eliza 278

## PERSONAL NAME INDEX

Carnes, John 278
Carnes, Robert 278
Carnes, Susan 278
Carol, Elias 54
Carol, Elizabeth 54
Carol, Hannah 54
Carol, Henry 54
Carol, Isbell 54
Carol, Jennet 54
Carol, John 54
Carol, Joseph 54
Carol, Martha 54
Carol, Samuel 54
Carol, Sarah 54
Carolan, Wm. 355
Carothers, James 35, 139, 150, 153, 206, 302
Carothers, James Franklin 302
Carothers, John Newton 302
Carothers, S. D. 288
Carothers, Samuel 150
Carothers, Samuel D. 302
Carothers, Thomas Milton 302
Carothers, William 150, 206, 207
Carothers, William N. 302
Carpenter, Charlotte 257
Carpenter, Isaac 308
Carpenter, Levina R. 308
Carr, Andrew 17
Carr, Catrin 17
Carr, Robert 184
Carrel, Ann 21
Carrel, Elizabeth 25
Carrel, Hannah 21
Carrel, Jane 356
Carrel, John 104, 256
Carrel, Joseph 21, 25, 57, 104, 148, 173, 193, 356
Carrel, Margaret 22
Carrel, Mary 21
Carrel, Mat(t)hew 142, 148, 356
Carrel, Rebecca 188
Carrel, Samuel 78, 79, 356, 173
Carrel, Thomas 25, 356
Carrell, Eave 200
Carrell, Elijah 208
Carrell, Elizabeth 200
Carrell, Esther 179
Carrell, Henry 160, 189, 200
Carrell, John 179, 180, 197
Carrell, Joseph 19, 178-180, 197
Carrell, Mat(t)hew 179, 196, 197

Carrell, Moses 25, 179
Carrell, Samuel 160, 197
Carrell, Thomas 19, 179m 180, 189
Carrenton, John 88
Carrenton, Lamuel 88
Carrigan, Cathrine 36
Carrigon, Catherine 148
Carrol 162
Carrol, Elizabeth 192
Carrol, Henry 299
Carrol, Mary 76
Carrol, Thomas 46
Carroll, Anna 358, 359
Carroll, Cynthia 285
Carroll, Elijah 274, 285
Carroll, Elizabeth 218
Carroll, Eve 299
Carroll, Henry 212, 226
Carroll, Isabella 299
Carroll, John 136, 218
Carroll, Joseph 191, 218
Carroll, Martha 299
Carroll, Mary 218
Carroll, Minor 197, 218
Carroll, Rufus Monroe 285
Carroll, Silas E. 285
Carroll, Thomas 188
Carroll, Zimri 299, 302
Carrols, Thomas 62
Carrothers, Dorcas 246
Carrothers, Hugh H. 248
Carrothers, James 193, 246, 293
Carrothers, Margaret E. 319
Carrothers, Rachel R. 254
Carrothers, Samuel 85
Carrothers, Samuel D. 193, 246
Carrothers, Thomas 246
Carrothers, William 229, 246
Carruth, Adam 169
Carruth, George 168, 169
Carruth, John 168, 169, 174, 186, 211
Carruth, Rufus K. 169
Carruth, Walter 169
Carsen, Matthew 91
Carsen, Susan 91
Carson, 78, 197
Carson, Andrew 1, 120
Carson, B. S. 279
Carson, Francis 91
Carson, Frank S. 279
Carson, Jean 91
Carson, John 20, 72, 90, 155

PERSONAL NAME INDEX

Carson, Joseph 72
Carson, Martha 276
Carson, Mary 81, 91
Carson, Robert 91
Carson, Samuel 1, 91
Carson, Shusanna 91
Carson, Thomas 32, 114
Carson, William 11, 91, 159, 279
Carter 61, 199
Carter, Henry 120
Carter, Polly 78
Caruth, George 130
Caruth, John 130
Caruthers, James 139
Caruthers, Saml 139
Caruthers, Wm 139
Caryl, Elizabeth 22
Caryl, Jennet 21
Caryl, Joseph 21, 22
Caryl, Margaret 22
Caryl, Mary 22
Caryl, Samuel 21, 22
Caryl, Thomas 21
Catey, David S. 188
Cathcart, Free Andy 329
Cathcart, H. I. 192
Cathcart, H. J. 157, 197, 203, 211
Cathcart, Wm 151
Cathey, George 132
Cathey, James 42
Cathey, John 132
Cathy, Geo 168
Cathy, John 186
Catton, D. S. 191
Cauble, Henry 177
Cauthen, John 185
Cavanah, Wm. 27
Cavany, Jno 143
Cavenny, Polley 99
Caveny, Isabella N. 299
Caveny, John 299
Caveny, Mary J. 299
Caveny, Nancy S. 299
Caveny, R. C. 299
Cawley, Martha 342
Chambers, 94, 285, 286
Chambers, A. H. 133, 189
Chambers, Alexander H. 304
Chambers, Alleson 219
Chambers, Barbara 299
Chambers, Benjamin 55, 62, 63, 78, 101, 124, 135, 141, 155, 161, 184, 185, 189, 198, 215, 219, 221, 230-238, 245, 247, 358
Chambers, Benjamin B. 219
Chambers, Benjamin W. 304
Chambers, Betty 124
Chambers, David 23, 39, 227
Chambers, Edmond 55
Chambers, Edmund 185
Chambers, Elisabeth 187
Chambers, Elizabeth 55, 133, 150, 185, 219
Chambers, Elizabeth J. 219
Chambers, Ellendor 129
Chambers, Emd R. 184
Chambers, Harriet 185
Chambers, Harriet A. 161
Chambers, J. S. 288
Chambers, James 55, 184
Chambers, James S. 304
Chambers, Jane[?] 185
Chambers, John 55, 86, 113, 150, 184, 185, 187, 189, 227, 228, 242, 304, 305
Chambers, John C. 219
Chambers, John J. 127, 185, 189
Chambers, Jon'a 124
Chambers, Lucretia 250
Chambers, Margaret 304
Chambers, Mary 150, 185
Chambers, Mary (Compton) 227
Chambers, Mary A. 189, 219
Chambers, Mary S. 188
Chambers, Mijamin 305
Chambers, Mijamin W. 304
Chambers, Pamela 314
Chambers, Polly 55
Chambers, Ptolemy P. 304
Chambers, Robert S. 350
Chambers, Samuel 124, 128, 131, 133, 167, 184, 185, 187, 219, 233, 247, 358
Chambers, Samuel C. C. 219
Chambers, Scena 227
Chambers, Serena L. 188
Chambers, Sylvanus 187, 219
Chambers, William 95, 124, 133, 150, 157, 185, 228
Chambers, William Maxwell 227
Chamblain, David A. 303
Champion, Delilah 114
Champion, George 27
Champion, John 27, 114

## PERSONAL NAME INDEX

Champion, Margaret 26, 27
Champion, Richard 27, 114, 276
Champion, William 27, 114, 132
Chandler, John 129
Cheery, Peter 221
Cherry, Margaret 183
Cheshire, Ann 105
Chester 269
Childers 303
Childers, Abraham 252
Childers, Jacob 142, 252
Childers, James 252
Childers, Janney 252
Childers, John 252
Childers, Lucy 252
Childers, Nancy 252
Childers, Rachel 252
Childers, Robert 252
Childers, Sary 252
Childers, William 252
Choat, A. L. 307
Choat, Augustine D. 256
Choat, James Simeral 256
Choat, Newton 256
Choat, Rachel 256
Choat, Rachel E. 256
Choat, W. 319
Choat, William 24, 256
Chriswell, 268
Clain[?], William 78
Clark 28, 50, 73, 104, 139, 164, 269, 310
Clark, Alexander 11, 39, 357
Clark, Ann 113
Clark, Eli Y. 253
Clark, Elizabeth 87
Clark, Henry 253
Clark, Jack 55
Clark, James 87
Clark, Jas A. 289
Clark, Jas H. 253
Clark, Jinsey 13
Clark, John 13, 80, 81, 215, 253
Clark, Joseph 87
Clark, Marg(a)ret 13, 87
Clark, Mary 87
Clark, Mary E. 343
Clark, Polly 81
Clark, Sarah 17, 87
Clark, Suzan 87
Clark, Thomas 87, 140
Clark, William 17, 357

Clarke, Sally Jinny 139
Clawson 226
Clawson, Ann D. (Pettus) 117, 118
Clawson, C. L. 297
Clawson, Jacob 128
Clawson, L. 295
Clawson, W. 247
Clawson, W. J. 257-259, 271, 280, 306
Clawson, William 295
Clawson, Wm. H. 192
Clawson, Wm. J. 277
Cleighton, Charles 23
Clendenan, Alexnader 119
Clendenan, James 118, 119
Clendenan, Margaret 118
Clendenan, Robert 116, 119
Clendenan, Thomas 119
Clendenan, William Hasler 119
Clendenin, K. 161
Clendinen, Robert 160
Clendinin, Robert 128
Clendining, Robert 81
Clerk, Allston 250
Clerk, Edmund 191
Clerk, Eli 250
Clerk, George R. 191
Clerk, Henry 198, 250
Clerk, James D. 220
Clerk, John 220
Clerk, Mary 158
Clerk, Mary Elizabeth 250
Clerk, Peggy 255
Clerk, Pinkney 220
Clerk, William 191, 220, 255
Clinton, James 19, 104
Clinton, Joseph 102, 104, 134, 145, 149, 180, 190, 206
Clinton, Mary 102, 104, 337
Clinton, Peter M. 245
Clinton, S. M. 321
Clinton, Thomas J. 206
Clinton, William 23
Clouney, Samuel 22
Clowney, Col. 303
Coal, N. N. 188
Cobb, Clesby 282
Cockerham, Henry Rufus 283
Cockerham, John 283
Cohran, John 148
Coker, Wm. 118
Coleman, R. W. 324
Collen, Starling 138

## PERSONAL NAME INDEX

Collers, T. B. 176
Collins, Barlow Thomson 145, 146
Collins, Caroline 145, 146
Collins, David 76
Collins, Nancy 145, 146, 316
Collins, Rhoda 316
Collins, T. B. 215
Collins, Thomas 179, 188
Colthorp, H. H. 298
Compton, Mary (Chambers) 227
Compton, Wm. 227
Conly, Alexander 126
Conly, Elisabeth 126
Conly, James 126
Conly, Patrick 126
Conly, Rachel 126
Conly, Robt. 126
Conly, William 126
Cook 242
Cook, Demsey 247
Cook, Hicksey 265
Cook, John 19
Cook, Polly 247
Cook, Silas C. 265
Cook, Thos J. 265
Coombes, John 241
Coombs, Catherine 274
Coombs, John 274
Coonrad, Jacob 120
Coonrod, Jacob 354
Coonrod, William 236
Cooper, Elizabeth 151, 308
Cooper, Hesl 98
Cooper, James 151, 188, 242
Cooper, James H. 154
Cooper, John 39, 70, 151, 187, 188, 242
Cooper, Margaret 151, 188, 189
Cooper, Mary 84, 242
Cooper, Nancy 98
Cooper, Nathan 28
Cooper, Robert 85, 131, 144, 151, 158, 159, 162, 173, 187-189, 202, 211, 242, 247, 359
Cooper, T. W. 308
Cooper, William 151, 187, 242
Coram, Margt 138
Correy, Nicholas 14
Corrie, John 167
Corry, Cynthia P. 310
Corry, James G. 328
Corry, Nancy 190

Corry, Nicholas 34, 87
Corry, Rebecca 328, 329
Corry, Wm. 328, 329
Corsin, Saml 120
Corsin, Thos 120
Cosper, Jacob 171
Costner, Sally 240
Couch, John 103
Coulter, Alexander A. 292
Coulter, Elkanah P. 292
Coulter, Jedediah 292
Coulter, Jno 292
Coulter, Julia L. 292
Coulter, Rachel 187, 292
Countryman, Wm 186
Cowan, Vincent 314
Coward, Jenney 102
Cowen, V. Y. 276
Craft, John 129
Crafts, Elizabeth 179
Crafts, Samuel 62, 179
Craig, Hannah 6
Craig, Henry 26, 74
Craig, James 6, 74, 133, 135, 245
Craig, Jane C. 335
Craig, Jean 6
Craig, John 6, 74, 133
Craig, Margaret 295
Craig, Martha 6
Craig, Mary 40, 74, 133, 135
Craig, Nancy 282
Craig, Polly 133
Craig, Robert 6, 74, 133
Craig, Samuel 6
Craig, Sarah 210
Craig, William 6, 40
Craton, Jno. M. 353
Crawford, Agness 99, 222
Crawford, Alexander 222, 288
Crawford, Alexander Lafayette 288
Crawford, Ann 123, 124, 258, 269
Crawford, David C. 317
Crawford, Edward 222
Crawford, Edward A. 317
Crawford, Edward Newton 288
Crawford, Elizabeth 124, 240, 258, 269, 318
Crawford, George 44, 45
Crawford, Issabella 99
Crawford, J. 324
Crawford, J. H. 283
Crawford, J. L. 311

## PERSONAL NAME INDEX

Crawford, James 71, 93, 99, 123, 124, 126, 164, 190, 240, 258, 269, 318,
Crawford, James (cont.) 319, 344
Crawford, James Harvey 288
Crawford, Jane 258, 318, 344
Crawford, Jean 123, 124
Crawford, John 318, 344
Crawford, Letty 71
Crawford, Marg(a)ret 99, 267
Crawford, Margaret Jane 288
Crawford, Martha 123, 124
Crawford, Martha A. 344
Crawford, Mary 99, 344
Crawford, Mary S. 317
Crawford, Robert 318
Crawford, Robert M. 240, 257
Crawford, Sarah 288
Crawford, Susan Isabella 288
Crawford, Walter 71
Crawford, William 71, 99, 124, 258, 269, 299, 310, 318, 319
Crawford, William N. 240, 344
Creek 320
Creige, John 9
Crenshaw, E. A. 273
Crenshaw, M. E. 333
Crenshaw, Margaret 252
Crenshaw, Mary 198
Cresswell, Elizabeth 154
Creswell, Henry 4
Creswell, Mary 205
Creswell, Samuel 53
Creswell, Wm 205
Crisp, John 163
Crocket, Ellen 265
Crocket, John 129, 191
Crocket, Robert 24
Crockett, E. F. 281
Crockett, E. T. 236
Crockett, John 75, 82
Croft, Samuel 199
Crosbay, Jesse 75
Crosby 300
Crosby, Allen 231
Crosby, Dennis 216
Crosby, Jesse 75
Crosby, John S. 307, 308
Crosby, William 259
Crow, James 46
Crow, Jason 45
Crow, Jenn(e)y 45, 52
Crow, John 45

Crow, Robert 45
Crow, Thomas 45
Crowder, 31, 66, 152, 188, 226, 296
Croxton, Benjamin 47, 48
Croxton, Lewis 47, 48
Cry, Mary 79
Cullender, Lawrance 205
Cunningham, H. B. 253
Cunningham, Jane 279
Cunningham, Jane (Cairnes) 279
Cunningham, Sally 273
Currance, Daniel 147, 189, 204, 211
Currance, David 188
Currance, Eleanor Stephenson 204
Currance, Eliza Parmela 251
Currance, Hugh 116, 121, 167, 181, 227
Currance, Hugh Ellas Davidson 204
Currance, J. D. P. 255
Currance, James D. P. 244
Currance, Jane 251
Currance, John 115, 116, 121, 145, 147, 211
Currance, Peter 204
Currance, Rebecka/h 204, 206
Currance, William 115, 145, 147, 167, 170, 188-190, 206
Currence, D. A. 345
Currence, Daniel 144, 154, 261, 274, 345
Currence, Daniel A. 273
Currence, E. M. 260
Currence, Hannah 143, 273, 345
Currence, Hugh 302
Currence, J. D. 259, 345
Currence, J. D. P. 316, 341
Currence, J. N. 274
Currence, James D. P. 261, 273, 274
Currence, John 24, 97, 98, 101, 103, 143, 144
Currence, John D. 302, 307, 348
Currence, M. H. 345
Currence, Margaret H. 274
Currence, Martha 274
Currence, Martha P. 290, 329
Currence, Milton H. 273
Currence, Nelson 345
Currence, R. F. 345
Currence, Rebecca 24
Currence, Robert F. 273
Currence, Susan 347-349
Currence, Susannah 302

## PERSONAL NAME INDEX

Currence, William 24, 143, 144, 204, 274
Currence, William A. 261, 273, 274
Currens, John 154
Currie, Youttaraih 23
Currien, James 229
Currier, Wm. 274
Curry, Charles 113
Curry, Elizabeth 113
Curry, Francis 42, 43
Curry, John 113, 114
Curry, John Mc. 283
Curry, M. C. Connell 209
Curry, M. C. McConnell? 209
Curry, Margaret H. M. 113
Curry, Mary T. 319
Curry, McConnel/l 113, 246, 283
Curry, Nicholas 34, 87
Curry, Prudence 113
Curry, Robert 113
Curry, Samuel 11, 42, 43, 328
Curry, Stafford 171
Curry, William 283
Cushman, Jane B. 167
Cushman, Xerxes H. 167
Dabney, Thomas 193
Dale, Anne/Anna 31, 105
Dale, Elizabeth 170
Dale, Frances 105
Dale, George 31, 32, 105, 158, 170, 180
Dale, James 31, 105, 158
Dale, Marian 105
Dale, Robert 31, 105, 119, 170
Dale, Widow 32
Dale, William 31
Danal, James 185
Daniel, C. C. 321
Daniel, Cornelius 204
Daniel, Cornelius O. 190
Daniel, D. 175
Daniel, David 42
Daniel, Harriet 309
Daniel, Holloway W. 289
Daniel, John 289
Daniel, Joseph J. 289
Daniel, William 289
Dannal, Cinthey 185
Dannal, Elizabeth 185
Dannal, Franklin 185
Dannal, Hannah 185
Dannal, John 185
Dannal, Sinthey 185
Dannal, Wm 185
Dantaff, George 24
Darby, Delilah (Jingles) 152
Darby, Jane (Smith) 152
Darby, Mary 152
Darby, Zado(c)k 35, 152
Dare, Thomas 168
Darnall, Elizabeth 273
Darnall, James 186
Darnall, Jos R. 168
Darnall, Jos Y. 168
Darwin, Elnathan D. 303
Darwin, Elsey/Elssly S. 303
Darwin, George 229
Darwin, Gilly 303
Darwin, James 214
Darwin, James M. 303
Darwin, John 214, 228, 229
Darwin, John B. 214, 303
Darwin, John W. 303
Darwin, Martin V. 303
Darwin, Pamela 214
Darwin, Payton B. 214, 228, 262, 279, 303
Darwin, Presley P. 303
Darwin, Robert G. 214
Darwin, Robert T. 303
Darwin, Ryton B. 309, 310
Darwin, William 214
David, George 113
Davidson, Charles 109, 110
Davidson, Edy 358
Davidson, Elias 109, 110
Davidson, Elizabeth 151, 242, 358, 359
Davidson, Franklin 195
Davidson, Hugh 109
Davidson, Hugh B. 160
Davidson, Isaac 109, 110
Davidson, Jacob 109, 110
Davidson, James 179
Davidson, Janet Starke 230
Davidson, Jenny 84
Davidson, John 106, 109, 110, 177
Davidson, John A. 305
Davidson, John G. 315, 316
Davidson, John S. 298
Davidson, Margaret 110, 305
Davidson, Mary L. 298
Davidson, Robert 80, 109, 113
Davidson, Samuel 45, 123, 142, 146

## PERSONAL NAME INDEX

Davidson, Sarah 48, 142
Davidson, Violet Wilson 177
Davidson, William 109, 110
Davie, Joseph 75, 86, 129
Davie, Lucinea 182
Davies, John L. 52
Davies, Jonathan 20
Davies, Walter 13
Davis  213, 344
Davis, Allen 120
Davis, Amos 228
Davis, Amy 104
Davis, Benjamin 315
Davis, Catherine 315
Davis, David 137, 148
Davis, David M. 155
Davis, Eb. 352
Davis, Elizabeth 52, 63, 64, 249, 252, 315
Davis, Frances 104
Davis, Francis 132
Davis, Francis C. 132
Davis, Franklin F. 232
Davis, G. 154
Davis, George 87, 92, 109, 113, 135, 154, 157, 160
Davis, J. 175
Davis, J. E. 210
Davis, J. Gist 347
Davis, Jacob 140
Davis, James 20, 52, 137, 148, 338
Davis, John 61, 132, 175, 188, 219
Davis, John B. 218
Davis, John L. 359
Davis, Jonathon 236
Davis, Joseph 93, 194
Davis, Joseph G. 315
Davis, Josiah 134, 137, 148
Davis, Larken 184
Davis, Larkin 120
Davis, Martha 132
Davis, Martha E. 132
Davis, Mary 140, 315
Davis, Polley 63
Davis, Sarah 315
Davis, Serena L. 304
Davis, Thomas 90, 97, 123, 132, 137, 138, 180, 188
Davis, Vincent 315
Davis, Walter 37
Davis, William 40, 47, 61, 116, 132, 134, 150

Davison, Elias 232, 268
Davison, Eliza Mary 188
Davison, Elizabeth 88, 89, 188, 247
Davison, Franklin 353
Davison, Franklin F. 232
Davison, Jacob 88, 89
Davison, James 17
Davison, James B. 232
Davison, James H. 232
Davison, Jane S. 242
Davison, Jno. 15
Davison, Margeret 232
Davison, R. J. 304
Davison, Robert 247
Davison, Wm. 10
Davison, Wm. B. 344
Dawkins, Elijah 146
Dawson, Isaac 120
Dawson, J. S. 347
Dawson, Joseph 87
Deal, Jacob 227
Deen, James 88
Delap 48
Delashmeet, Catherine 121
Denam, James 123
Denam, Peggy 123
Denham, James C. 122, 123
Denham, John C. 123
Denham, Peggy 122
Denis, John 74
Denkins[?], Robert 228
Dennis, John 120, 189, 286
Dennis, Mary 31, 286
Denny, Saml 17
Denton, Benjamin 1
Denton, Elisabeth 1
Denton, John 1
Denton, Joshua 1, 229
Denton, Samuel 1
Desant, Sarah 216
Dewit, Wm. 183
Dickey, 219
Dickey, Ann 332
Dickey, David 2, 3, 41
Dickey, Eleanor 3
Dickey, George 3
Dickey, James 3, 12, 41, 118
Dickey, Jane 3
Dickey, John 3, 41, 51, 278
Dickey, Martha 2, 3, 41
Dickey, Mary 3
Dickey, Mary Ann 51

## PERSONAL NAME INDEX

Dickey, Mathew 41
Dickey, Rebecca(kah) 41
Dickey, Robert 3
Dickey, Samuel R. 332
Dickey, Sarah 41
Dickey, Susannah 3
Dickey, William 3, 41
Dickson, Amanda Emeline 190
Dickson, David 22
Dickson, Isabella 175, 190
Dickson, James 87, 190
Dickson, James G. 271
Dickson, James Steel/e 190
Dickson, Jane 22
Dickson, Martha 189, 190
Dickson, Martha Jane 190
Dickson, Mary Levina 190
Dickson, Rachel 279
Dickson, Sarah 282
Dickson, Thomas 282
Dickson, Virgil Fernandes Erasmus 190
Dickson, W. M. 224, 258, 282
Dickson, William 190
Dickson, William M. 190
Dickson, William Warren Washington 190
Dickson, Wm. Warrant Washington 190
Dier, Sarah 308
Dill, John 145
Dillard, 118
Dillet, Mary 80
Dillingham, Sarah 257
Dinkens, S. H. 219
Dinkins, Cynthia 355
Dinsmore, Samuel 35
Dismukes, A. H. 167
Ditty 318
Dixon 142
Dixon, Gilbreth 139
Dixon, Lidia 323
Dixon, W. M. 150
Dixon, William 71, 175
Dobson, Huldah 186
Doby, Wm. C. 306
Donaghy, Andrew 65
Donahy, Andrew 17
Donahy, Elenor 17
Donahy, Isabella 17
Donahy, John 17
Donahy, Mary 17

Donahy, Samuel 17
Donahy, William 17
Donaldson, Tabitha 279
Donally, James 131, 132
Donally, Martha 131, 205
Donnom, Isaac 233
Donnom, Jane 233
Dorster, William 70
Doster, Enoch 70, 268
Doster, Mary 110
Doudle, Joseph 113, 144
Douglas, Robert 190
Douglass, Thos 207
Douglass, Thos H. 195
Dougless, Jesse 27
Dowdell, Margaret 222
Dowdle, Allen 103, 107, 193, 215
Dowdle, Benjamin 204, 215
Dowdle, David 107
Dowdle, Editha 107
Dowdle, Joseph 107, 193
Dowdle, Mary 107, 222
Dowdle, Nancy 107
Downes, Mary 105
Downey, Wm. 134
Downing, John 42
Downing, Wm. 141
Drenan, Hugh 43, 157, 185
Drenan, John 50
Drenan, Thos 50
Drenan, Wm. 157
Drennan, Ann 8
Drennan, David 76
Drennan, Harvey H. 285, 289, 320
Drennan, Henry H. 306
Drennan, Hugh 150
Drennan, John 2, 8, 12, 76
Drennan, Mary 76, 139
Drennan, Thomas 8, 76
Drennan, William 76, 134, 150
Drennon, Harvey H. 251
Drennon, Hugh 141, 222
Drennon, John 246
Drennon, Malinda 246
Drennon, Mary 85
Drennon, Thomas 26
Drennon, Wm. 141
Drinnin, Margaret 49
Duff, David C. 342
Duff, Eliza D. 328
Duff, George B. 167
Duff, Henry C. 248

## PERSONAL NAME INDEX

Duff, James 101, 103, 132, 133, 137, 149, 178, 180
Duff, Margaret 342
Duff, Mary 133
Duff, Polly 74, 133
Duffin, Adaline 292
Duffin, Noah 292
Duffy, Grover B. 167
Dulen 296
Dulen, Daniel 248
Dulen, Dolly 248
Dulen, Elizabeth 248
Dulen, Frances 181
Dulen, James 248
Dulen, John 248
Dulen, Margaret 248
Dulen, Nightwill 248
Dulen, Reuben 248
Dulen, Salina 248
Dulen, Sarah 248
Dulin, Reuben 245, 330
Dulin, Rubin 330
Duncan, Harvey H. 285
Duncan, Jas 166
Dunkin 45
Dunkin, Mary 92
Dunkin, Robert 109, 113
Dunkin, Thomas 92
Dunlap, Benjamin 287
Dunlap, David 173
Dunlap, Elizabeth S. 303
Dunlap, George 173
Dunlap, James 173, 192
Dunlap, James P. 236, 286
Dunlap, John 122, 163, 173
Dunlap, Joseph 286
Dunlap, Lurilla Sussanna Jane 236
Dunlap, Margaret Catherine Ann 236
Dunlap, Martha 236, 280, 281
Dunlap, Mary 173
Dunlap, Mary P. 236
Dunlap, Molsey 183
Dunlap, Nancy 236
Dunlap, Robt M. 182
Dunlap, Susanna/h 173, 236
Dunlap, Thomas 286
Dunlap, William 122, 149, 173, 192, 236
Dunlap, William B. 191, 236, 263, 287
Dunlap, William Benjamin 289
Dunlap, William Berry 286
Dunlap, William N. 173
Dunn, Jane 135
Dunwoody, Fanny 175
Dunwoody, Francis 98
Dunwoody, John 175
Dupont, Leah 80
Dupont, Peter Harris 76
Durham, Captain G. 142
Durham, Elizabeth 181
Durham, George 181
Durham, George G. 181
Durham, John 116, 181
Durham, William 181
Dyer, Sarah 322
Dyson, Aquilla 217
Dyson, Elizabeth 115
Dyson, Maddox 115
Eaken, Lemuel 245
Eakin, Alexander 62, 66, 73, 181
Eakin, Betcy 66
Eakin, Elizabeth 62
Eakin, Elphy 66
Eakin, Elvey 62
Eakin, Jean 62
Eakin, John 89
Eakin, Joseph 65, 66
Eakin, Joshua 73
Eakin, Nanc(e)y 62, 65, 66
Eakin, Peggy/Pegey 62, 66
Eakin, Thomas 62, 66
Eakin, William 27, 62, 66, 113
Eaking, Elizabeth 101
Earhardt 352
Eaton, Edward 329
Edmiston, Mary Ann 85, 92, 107, 108
Edmiston, Maryan 108
Edmiston, Samuel 108
Edwards, Edward 108
Edwards, Jesse 108
Edwards, Lucy 108
Edwards, Sar(r)ah 75, 108
Edwards, Stanton 126
Edwards, Stourton 98
Edwards, Stratton 194
Egger, Andrew 42
Egger, James 242
Egger, Nancy 102
Ekin, Alexander 62, 65
Ekin, Elizabeth 58
Ekin, Joseph 66
Ekin, Nancy 66
Ekin, Thomas 62

## PERSONAL NAME INDEX

Ekin, William 62
Ekins 53
Ekins, Elizabeth 93
Elder, Margaret 15
Eliot, William 60
Eliott, Wm. B. 60
Elison, Thomas 114
Elleson, William 219
Elliott, Andrew 46
Elliott, Dorcas 132
Elliott, Jane 135
Elliott, Saml 78, 132, 133
Elliott, Wm. 18, 60
Ellis 263
Ellis, Albird 186
Ellis, Benjamin 72, 73, 115, 116
Ellis, Betsey 119
Ellis, Dulcina 186
Ellis, Edmond/Edmund 186, 187
Ellis, Elizabeth 72, 154, 186
Ellis, Elizabeth Hall 72
Ellis, John 117, 119, 139, 140, 143, 186, 187
Ellis, Louisa 186
Ellis, Mary 72, 73, 115
Ellis, Neomy 186
Ellis, Priscilla 72
Ellis, Rebeckah 115
Ellis, Robert 72, 116, 154, 183
Ellis, Sally Sumner 115, 116, 154
Ellis, Sarah Sumner 155
Ellis, Stanford 186
Ellis, Thomas Sumner 72, 154, 155
Ellis, William 186
Ellison 5
Ellison, Robt 155
Elmore, John 58
Elms, C. 165
Elms, E. 265
Elms, W. W. 279
Elms[?], Malinda 265
Elsom, Sarah 167
Elwell, Hannah 299
Enes, John 106
England, Wm. 141
English, John 137
Enloe, Asahel 82, 186, 240
Enloe, Benjamin 67
Enloe, G. 206, 239, 240
Enloe, Gilbert 67, 93, 124-126, 136, 141, 186, 187, 207
Enloe, Isaac 126, 141, 187

Enloe, J. G. 348
Enloe, John G. 240, 315, 329, 331
Enloe, Louisa Ann 125, 186
Enloe, Nathaniel 125, 126, 141, 186, 187
Enloe, Vilet 186
Enlow, Asahil 125
Enlow, Christian 4
Enlow, Dillon 4
Enlow, Vilet 125, 126
Ephraim, 349
Eppis, Richard 140
Ervin, Arthur 77, 78
Ervin, Elizabeth 77
Ervin, Maria 273
Ervin, Thomas 273
Ervin, Thomas Spratt 77
Erwin, 250
Erwin, Alex 283
Erwin, Arthur 134, 219, 257
Erwin, Catherine 104
Erwin, Edwin 277
Erwin, F. Alexander 283
Erwin, Francis 105, 107, 109, 270, 277
Erwin, Francis A. 291
Erwin, Jane 257
Erwin, John 277
Erwin, John L. 336
Erwin, John S. B. 260
Erwin, Mary 93
Erwin, Nancy Adaline 302
Erwin, Sarah 104
Erwin, William 104, 113, 221, 277, 345, 346
Erwin, William B. 156
Erwin, William Edwin 260
Erwin, William G. 294
Erwin, William R. 277
Eskridge, James J. 289
Estes, Leonard 238
Etters, James H. 275
Etters, Phillip 314
Etters, Samuel 314
Evans, Allen Jones 263
Evans, Halcot 150
Evans, Halcut Clark 263
Evans, Haliot[?] 115
Evans, Hawket 155
Evans, J. J. 290
Evans, James Chancey 263
Evans, Thomas Howell 263
Evens, Rebecca 263

## PERSONAL NAME INDEX

Ewart, John 112
Ewing, Hannah 126, 187
Ewing, Jane 126, 187
Ewing, John 126, 141, 187
Ewing, Samuel 65
Ewing, William 126, 187
Ezell, Frances 356
Ezell, John 356
Ezell, Martha 356
Fair, Margaret 102
Fair, William 98
Fairs, John 54
Faires, Alexander 149, 150
Faires, D. W. 191
Faires, James 78, 127
Faires, Jennet 149, 150
Faires, Jesse 194
Faires, Jno 222
Faires, Miles A. 204
Faires, Robt M. 222
Faires, Samuel 149, 204, 205
Faires, William 149, 211
Fairis, Jno 121
Fairis, Wm 178
Falkener, Margaret 144
Falkener, Mary 144
Falkner, Isabella 205
Falkner, James 212, 215
Falkner, Nancy 205
Falkner, Thomas 192, 199
Fall, C. 212
Falls, Andrew 212
Falls, Drusilla 212
Falls, Elam 212
Falls, Elizabeth 212, 213
Falls, J. C. 212
Falls, James 212, 213
Falls, John 123, 155, 212, 213
Falls, Thomas 174, 212
Fallow, T. D. 228
Far, Sarah 236
Fares 353
Fares, James 116
Faries, Arthur 23
Faries, Jess/e 149, 150
Faries, John 57, 104
Faries, Nancy 70
Faries, Robert 5, 6, 15, 57
Faries, Robert B. K. 239
Faries, Samuel W. 239
Faries, Thomas 149, 150
Faries, William 70

Faris, Alexander 49, 79, 96
Faris, Ann/e 49, 56
Faris, Arthur 42
Faris, Catharine S. 286, 331
Faris, David 56
Faris, Elias 49
Faris, Elijah A. 286, 331, 332
Faris, Hanna/h 42, 45, 57
Faris, Harriet[?] 56
Faris, Harriet E. 331
Faris, James 48, 49, 79, 286
Faris, Jean 48, 49, 79
Faris, John 49, 297, 357
Faris, Mary 56, 286
Faris, Moses 56, 57
Faris, Richard 48, 49
Faris, Robert 41, 42, 44, 45, 54, 56
Faris, Robert Arthur 56
Faris, Robert M. 174
Faris, Saml 213
Faris, Sarah 56
Faris, Sarah G. 331
Faris, Susanna 49
Faris, Thomas 94, 286, 332
Faris, William 49, 211, 269
Faris, William G. 334
Faris, William J. 263, 311
Faris, Wm. N. 288
Farley, James 98
Farley, John 35
Farrar, John 288
Farrels, John 55
Farres, Moses T. 208
Farris, Alex W. 253
Farris, Ann 79
Farris, David 70
Farris, Edward T. 253
Farris, Eliz'a C. 254
Farris, Elvey C. D. 253
Farris, Hannah 56
Farris, Isaac 70
Farris, Isbel 76
Farris, James 70
Farris, Jane 243, 334
Farris, Jean 79
Farris, John 70
Farris, Johnathan 254
Farris, Joshua 70
Farris, Margaret 70, 243, 334
Farris, Mary 70, 243
Farris, Nancy 70, 243, 334
Farris, Polly 212

## PERSONAL NAME INDEX

Farris, R. B. W. 253, 254
Farris, Rachel 254
Farris, Robert McClellan 254
Farris, Samuel 253
Farris, Samuel W. 253
Farris, Sarah 70
Farris, Susanna 243
Farris, Thomas 76, 254
Farris, Urias 254
Farris, W. J. 334
Farris, William 70, 243, 254
Farris, Wm. J. 243, 334
Faulkner, 337
Faulkner, James 276
Faulkner, Thomas 126
Feari(e)s, John 26, 49, 98, 102, 104
Fearnell, Wm. 303
Featherston, E. P. 289
Feemster, Adaline 118
Feemster, Agnes 64, 111
Feemster, Anna 111, 309
Feemster, Anne 111
Feemster, B. E. 291, 329
Feemster, Bond E. 309
Feemster, Catherine 309
Feemster, Clarinda 64
Feemster, E. G. 309
Feemster, Edward 111, 112, 170, 196, 222, 227, 309
Feemster, Elizabeth 64, 118
Feemster, Ely/Eli 118
Feemster, James 64, 101, 106, 107, 110, 111, 172, 193, 200, 203
Feemster, James B. 202, 203
Feemster, John 64, 109, 111, 118, 160
Feemster, John Malinda 118
Feemster, Joseph 64, 85, 111, 191, 202, 203, 309
Feemster, Margaret 75, 118
Feemster, Martha 64, 111
Feemster, Mary 202, 203
Feemster, Melissa 118
Feemster, Minos 118
Feemster, Minos B. 118
Feemster, Nancy 202
Feemster, S. 204
Feemster, Samuel 111, 112, 118, 121, 170, 222
Feemster, Silas 118
Feemster, William 76, 118, 172, 202, 203
Feemsters, Jenny 64

Felchet, John 212, 215
Felchett, James 212, 332
Felchett, Jonathan 332
Felts, Allen 122
Felts, Silas 333
Felts, Wm. 333
Fendley, Robert M. 247
Fergesson, Susanna/h 236
Fergus, John 11
Ferguson, Andrew 8
Ferguson, Annaritta 16
Ferguson, Elizabeth 67, 68
Ferguson, Emmeline 307
Ferguson, G. F. 314
Ferguson, Hamblet 16
Ferguson, James 16
Ferguson, Jane 99, 242
Ferguson, Jona 68
Ferguson, Margaret 16
Ferguson, Mary 101
Ferguson, Moses 12, 116
Ferguson, Richard 16
Ferguson, Robert 99
Ferguson, Stewart 96
Ferguson, Thomas 16
Ferguson, William 38, 120, 136
Ferrell, Matthew 150
Ferry, James 213
Fewel, James 184
Fewel, Jane 184
Fewel, Jean 184
Fewel, John 192
Fewel, Wm. 104
Fewell, 256
Fewell, A. 328
Fewell, A. F. 266, 270
Fewell, A. S. 266
Fewell, Alexander 192, 221, 238, 265, 266, 269, 309, 329
Fewell, Amanda 265
Fewell, Asa 238
Fewell, Edmund 116
Fewell, Ezekiel 294, 311, 349
Fewell, Fanny 265
Fewell, James N. 294
Fewell, Jane 324
Fewell, John 197, 265, 266
Fewell, Margaret 238, 328
Fewell, Mary 197
Fewell, Patsey 61
Fewell, Rachel 248
Fewell, Robert 265, 266

## PERSONAL NAME INDEX

Fewell, Stanly 265
Fewell, Wm. 157
Fewell, Wm. B. 334
Fields, Mary 267
Find, Hugh 164
Findley, Elizabeth 52
Finely, Elizabeth 52
Finley, Isabella M. 245
Finley, Mary 114
Finley, Mary A. M. J. 343
Finley, Wm. G. 343
Finly, Peggy 86
Finly, Polly 86
Fitchet, James 255
Fitchet, John 125, 255, 256
Fitchett, Agnes 6
Flanagen, Paul 61
Fleming, Elijah 15, 21, 58, 59
Fleming, Jane Stuart 21
Fleming, Jean 84
Fleming, Mary 58
Fleming, Mary B. 59
Fleming, R. B. W. 180
Fleming, Young 84
Flemming, Betsy 244
Flemming, Eliga 27
Flemming, Elizabeth 221
Flemming, Polly 117
Flodin, Simon 348
Floid, Nanny 15
Flowers, Adaline (Springs) 298
Floyd, Andrew 190, 224, 277
Floyd, Betsey Caroline 282
Floyd, Betsy 349
Floyd, Elizabeth 277
Floyd, Elizabeth B. 344
Floyd, Elizabeth C. 344
Floyd, George 224
Floyd, George McWhorter 223
Floyd, Henry 223
Floyd, Izard 277
Floyd, Izzeral E. 344
Floyd, James 215, 223, 277, 282
Floyd, James N. 277
Floyd, John 202, 223, 344
Floyd, Margaret 344
Floyd, Margaret E. 328
Floyd, Mary 223, 224
Floyd, Mary A. 344
Floyd, Mary J. 223, 344
Floyd, Nathan 277
Floyd, Peggy 344

Floyd, Polly 337
Floyd, Robert 223
Floyd, Sarah 277
Floyd, Sarah Ann 277
Flynn, John 61
Fondren, Jesse 175
Fondren, Matthew 224
Forbes, Ann 178
Forbes, Archibald 178
Forbes, Arthur 178
Forbes, Elizabeth 178
Forbes, John 178
Forbes, Margaret 178, 320
Forbes, Rachel 178
Forbes, Rebecca 178
Forbes, Sarah 178
Forbes, Thomas 178
Forbes, Tobitha 178
Forbis, John 61
Forbis, Joseph 61
Forbus, Joseph 125
Foreman, Benjamin 75
Foreman, Bets(e)y 197
Foreman, Betsey F. 197
Foreman, Elijah/Elligah 75
Foreman, James 75, 82
Foreman, James L. 197
Foreman, James T. 250
Foreman, James Thomas 82
Foreman, Mary 82
Foreman, Mary A. 343
Foreman, Nancy 82
Foreman, Sally 82
Foreman, Sarah 82
Foreman, William 75, 82
Forman, Samuel 75
Forrester, 25
Foster, Anna 296
Foster, Catharine 48
Foster, Henry 48
Foster, J. J. 203
Foster, James H. 164
Foster, John 48
Foster, Mary 107
Fosters, Mary 48
Fowler, James 4, 8, 12, 16, 49, 50
Fowler, James Hinds 49
Fowler, Mary 49
Fowler, Robert 16, 49, 50
Fowler, S. 41
Fowler, Stephenson 49
Fowler, William 4, 49

## PERSONAL NAME INDEX

Fox  122
Fox, Jacob  154
Fox, Jenny  355
Fox, Priscilla  154
Freeland, Mary  327
Freeman, Margret McLelan  42
Freeman, Mary  347
French, Joseph  20
French, Judey  125
French, Sally  180
Fuglenwyden, John  148
Fuller, Alexander  282
Fuller, Alsey  150, 193
Fuller, Sarah D.  281
Fullton, James B.  77
Fulton, A. S.  289
Fulton, D. A.  227, 249, 289
Fulton, Daniel A.  199, 228
Fulton, Elizabeth  198, 249
Fulton, Horatio S.  289
Fulton, J. B.  257
Fulton, James B.  26, 31, 62, 77
Fulton, James W.  289
Fulton, S. D.  316
Fulton, T. D.  257, 289, 301
Fulton, Theodore  199
Fulwood, Robert H.  169, 288
Funches[?], James  179
Gabbie, Moses  109
Gabbie, Robert  11
Gabie, John  30
Gabie, Jos.  30
Gafney,  146
Gafney, Polly  203
Galbraith,  268
Galbraith, Amanda  331
Galbreath, Ann  188
Galbreath, George  16
Galimore, Pheby  59
Gallagher, Esther  191
Gallagher, Jane  191
Gallagher, Martha  191
Gallagher, Matilda  191
Gallaher, Jincey  179
Gallaher, John  179
Gallan, John  153
Galland  238
Gallant  268
Gallard, John  148
Gallaspie, Mary M.  274
Gallaway, Hugh D.  216
Gallegher, Jane  193

Gallemore, Edward  59
Gallespie, Jonathan  190
Gallimore, Edward  59
Gallimore, Ned  33
Gallimore, Pheby  59
Galloway,  310
Galloway, Alex'r  41
Galloway, Alexander  9, 41, 144, 193
Galloway, Daniel  120
Galloway, Elizabeth  230
Galloway, Hugh A.  203
Galloway, James  120, 142, 222
Galloway, James T.  222, 225, 227, 230
Galloway, Jane  222
Galloway, John  172, 193, 203
Galloway, Nancy  193
Galloway, William  112, 193, 222
Galloway, William W.  193
Gambol, John  215, 216
Gamelin, Eliza  323
Gardiner, James  145
Gardner,  33
Gardner, Editha  253
Gareson, David  18
Garetson, Josiah  206
Garetson, Polly  166
Garetson, William  167
Garison, Arthur  243
Garison, Austin  193, 207
Garison, Elias  195
Garison, Sarah W.  232
Garison, Valdaura Norris  232
Garresons, Isaac  62
Garrison, Agnes  49
Garrison, Ann  84
Garrison, Austin  293, 302
Garrison, Benjamin  49
Garrison, C. L.  319
Garrison, Fanny R.  336
Garrison, Helena  159
Garrison, Isaac  18, 77, 78
Garrison, John  302
Garrison, John F.  18
Garrison, Margaret  211
Garrison, Mark  18, 309
Garrison, Mary  319
Garrison, Mary B.  331
Garrison, Milton  159
Garrison, P. A.  309
Garrison, Pamela  284
Garrison, Peter  311, 319, 329

## PERSONAL NAME INDEX

Garrison, Thomas Spratt 77
Garvin, Benjamin 39, 56, 118, 151
Garvin, Hillariah 200
Garvin, James 39
Garvin, Jean 55, 56
Garvin, John 39, 56
Garvin, Margaret 39
Garvin, Mary 39
Garvin, Robin 39
Garvin, Sarah C. 334
Garvin, Thomas 56, 357
Garvin, Urcilla 156
Garvin, Violet 39
Garvin, William 39
Garvin, William W. 333
Gasaway, James 197
Gassaway, Caleb 197, 256
Gassaway, William 197
Gaston, Latitia 202
Gaston, Margaret 183
Gaston, William 83
Gault, Barborough 151
Gault, Eleanor Eliza 151
Gault, Elizabeth 152
Gault, George William 151
Gault, James 151
Gault, John 151
Gault, Joseph 151
Gay, James Hall 32
Gay, Jane 32
Gay, Mary 32
Gay, Samuel 32
Gay, William 32
Gebbie, Elizabeth 109, 156
Gebbie, Elizabeth B. 156
Gebbie, John 109
Gebbie, John A. 109
Gebbie, Joseph 109, 135, 156, 157
Gebbie, Lisa 109
Gebbie, Marget 156
Gebbie, Mary 109, 156
Gebbie, Matilda 109, 156
Gebbie, Narcilla 109
Gebbie, Rachel 109, 157
Gebbie, Robert 109
Gebbie, Robert M. 109
Gebbie, Robert W. 157
Gebbie, Selena 109
Gettys, James 149
Gettys, R. E. 304
Gibbin, Jon. G. 322
Gibbons, D. 322

Gibbons, William 312
Gibson, Catharine 68
Gibson, Elisabeth 68
Gibson, James 10, 73, 74
Gibson, Jean 74
Gibson, John 68
Gibson, John C. 78
Gibson, Joseph 74
Gibson, Margret 68, 74
Gibson, Martha 73, 74
Gibson, Mat(t)hew 59, 68
Gibson, Ramsey 68
Gibson, Reuben 115
Gibson, Thomas 68, 74, 109, 135, 141
Gibson, William 68, 74, 135, 141
Gil, James 83
Gilbert, Uriah 44, 45
Giles, A. 224
Giles, A. J. 295
Giles, Andrew 131, 133, 220
Giles, Laura 297
Giles, S. H. 295
Gilespie, John 112
Gilfellon, Robert 245
Gilfillan, Robert 341
Gilfillen, Robert 278
Gilfillin, Robert 220
Gilfilling, 217
Gilham, Elizabeth 48
Gilham, Ezekiel 72
Gilham, John 48
Gilham, Sarah 48
Gilham, Thomas 48
Gill, 158
Gill, Eliza 172
Gill, Elvira 172
Gill, George 126
Gill, James 82, 172
Gill, John 137, 158, 172, 173, 242
Gill, Mary 172, 173, 179
Gill, Nancy 172
Gill, Nancy H. 326
Gill, Robert 179
Gill, Thomas W. 172
Gill, Washington 172
Gill, William G. 172
Gill, Wm. R. 187
Gillam, Ezekiel 275
Gilland, Jenny 264
Gilland, Rebecca 264
Gillespie, E. E. 319
Gillespie, Elizabeth E. 311

## PERSONAL NAME INDEX

Gillespie, James R. 274
Gillespie, John 113
Gillespie, Johnston 144
Gillespie, Jonathan 144
Gillespie, Margaret 144
Gillespie, Richard 224, 307, 311, 336
Gillham, Charles 44, 48
Gillham, Elizabeth 17
Gillham, Ezekial 44, 124
Gillham, Ezekiel 275
Gillham, Isaac 2, 9
Gillham, Jane 44
Gillham, Thomas 2, 6, 9, 44
Gillham, William 44
Gillmore, Charles 12
Gillon, John 57
Gilmore, Charles M. 349
Gilmore, Danl 158
Gilmore, Enoch 90
Gilmore, Francis 90
Gilmore, J. J. 349
Gilmore, James 90
Gilmore, John 285
Gilmore, Joshua 90
Gilmore, William 134, 150, 185, 228
Gilmore, William C. 349
Gist, John 159
Gist, Joseph 106, 159
Given, Margaret 291
Given, Mary 291
Given, Samuel 291
Given, Samuel C. 291
Given, Samuel E. 258
Given, Samuel W. 291
Given, Solomon W. 291
Given, William 258
Givens, Agnes 79
Givens, Christiana 125, 187
Givens, Daniel 106
Givens, Elisa 126
Givens, Eliza 187
Givens, Leroy 193
Givens, Mary 130, 304
Givens, Nathaniel 79, 131
Givens, Ruth 126, 187
Givens, Saline 156
Givens, Samuel 109, 134, 158, 166
Givens, William 187, 314
Givins, Edward 106
Givins, Eleanor 105, 106
Givins, Lucy 105, 106
Givins, Samuel 105, 108, 135, 152

Givins, William 110, 126
Glass, A. 5, 339
Glass, Alexander 301, 337, 344, 349
Glass, Hannah 160
Glass, James 86, 87
Glass, Mary 87
Glass, Sarah 301
Glass, Simpson 301
Glen, David J. 350
Glen, Eliza 155
Glen, James 155
Glen, John 13, 155
Glen, John F. 155
Glenn, David J. 344
Glenn, Eliza 350
Glenn, Franklin 152
Glenn, James 74, 133, 135, 152, 247, 328
Glenn, James E. 247
Glenn, John 152, 206, 210, 211, 219, 247, 284
Glenn, John F. 220, 350
Glenn, Martha 74, 133
Glenn, Milton 210, 247
Glenn, Robert 247
Glenn, Sarah 210
Glenn, Sarah O. 350
Glenn, William 239, 247, 264
Glenn, Wm. R. 350
Glover, Benjamin 51
Glover, Berry 51
Glover, Betsey 221
Glover, James 51
Glover, James Barns 51
Glover, John 51, 221
Glover, Joseph 51, 260
Glover, Margaret 267
Glover, Mary 273
Glover, Mortler[?] 51
Glover, Patsy Cheek 265
Glover, Polly 51
Glover, William 51, 221, 183
Glovers, James 38
Goforth, Andrew 347
Goforth, Elizabeth 316, 347
Goforth, Hannah 347
Goforth, Johnson 347
Goforth, Preston 347
Goforth, Reuben 347
Goforth, William 347
Good, Ann/e 75, 214, 215
Good, David J. 316

## PERSONAL NAME INDEX

Good, Elizabeth M. 291
Good, George M. 291
Good, Henry 75, 107
Good, J. P. 291
Good, James 74, 106, 214
Good, James B. 74, 146, 167, 196, 213, 259, 300, 355
Good, James G. 74, 230
Good, James W. 291, 329
Good, John 74, 75, 86, 106, 121, 167, 213-215, 355
Good, John E. 315
Good, John H. 291, 300, 329
Good, Margaret J. 291
Good, Margaret L. 329
Good, Martha 75
Good, Mary A. 315
Good, Mary Ann 230
Good, Milton 291
Good, Thomas L. 315
Good, W. J. 264, 289
Good, Widow 145
Good, William J. 291, 300
Goodall, Richard 27
Goode, David J. 315
Goode, Margaret L. 309
Goode, Mary Ann 309
Goode, Sarah Ann 314
Goodrich, John 138, 148
Goodrich, Wm. 129, 138
Goore, Joshua 128
Gordan, Catharine 120
Gordan, Dorcus 161
Gordan, Mansfield 158
Gorden, David 55, 357
Gorden, Forbes 50
Gorden, James 51
Gorden, John 50, 51
Gorden, Jonathen 50
Gorden, Margret 50
Gordon 73
Gordon, Calvin 297
Gordon, Catherin/e 144, 162, 199
Gordon, Covin 297
Gordon, D'd 1
Gordon, David 1, 15, 16, 25, 29, 35, 56, 70, 71, 75, 76, 84, 85
Gordon, David A. 297
Gordon, Elizabeth A. 297
Gordon, Elizabeth Ann 199
Gordon, Green 276, 297, 330
Gordon, Hugh 15, 36

Gordon, Isabella 56
Gordon, James 15
Gordon, James J. 38
Gordon, John 15
Gordon, M. 202
Gordon, Mansfield 144, 162, 199, 297
Gordon, Mary 15
Gordon, Nanny 15
Gordon, Robert 15
Gordon, Samuel 15
Gordon, William 15
Gordon, William M. 297
Goudelock, Jas T. 288
Goza, John M. 336
Graham, Archibald 333
Graham, Daniel 137
Graham, Edward 77
Graham, Eleanor (McRight) 174
Graham, Elizabeth 136
Graham, George F. 352
Graham, James 353
Graham, James C. 255
Graham, Jean 15
Graham, John 54
Graham, John A. 352
Graham, Joseph 352
Graham, Margaret 333
Graham, Mary 54, 353
Graham, Nancy 15
Graham, S. 198
Graham, Sophia 352, 353
Graham, Violet 353
Graham, William 275, 353
Graham, William A. 352, 353
Gray, John 117
Gray, Margret 58
Gray, Thomas 173
Grayham, Polly 168
Green, Abraham 70, 130
Green, Allen J. 173
Green, Eliza (Jefferies) 182
Green, Eliza (Jeffreys) 181
Green, Elizabeth 130
Green, Emma 338
Green, Hannah 130
Green, Jacob 58
Green, Joseph R. 165
Green, Lewisa 130
Green, Louisa (Jefferies) 182
Green, Louisa (Jefferys) 181
Green, Nathaniel 13
Green, Robert 114

## PERSONAL NAME INDEX

Green, Samuel 13, 169
Greer, Agnes/s 209, 211, 222
Greer, Alexander 166, 354
Greer, Amelia 201
Greer, Anna Nercissa 165
Greer, Bets(e)y Hann/ah 85, 108
Greer, Catherine Malinda 165
Greer, Edward Henry 283
Greer, Emeline 281
Greer, Emily Elmenah 165
Greer, Henry 70, 71, 246, 283
Greer, Henry M. 246, 283
Greer, James 117
Greer, John 166, 201
Greer, John E. 165, 166
Greer, Joseph 166
Greer, Mary 209, 222, 223, 246, 283
Greer, Mary Margaret Jane 283
Greer, Polly Malise 165
Greer, Rebecka Clarissa 165
Greer, Robert 166, 209, 222
Greer, Susanna/h 209, 223, 225
Greer, Thos 270
Greer, Thos. P. 312
Greer, William 166, 283
Greer, William T. 165
Gregory, Nancy 233
Grey, Wm. 154, 190
Gribble, Polly 279
Grier, 164
Grier, Alexander 353
Grier, Andrew 353, 354
Grier, Betsy Hannah 92
Grier, Catharine 353, 354
Grier, James 353
Grier, Martha 354
Grier, Robert 92
Grier, Susan/a 353, 354
Grier, Thomas 354
Grier, Thomas J. 353, 354
Grier, William M. 353, 354
Grier, Zenas 353
Griffey, Thomas 6
Griffin, James M. 289
Griffin, Louisa 292
Griffin, Wm. 195, 292
Grimes, Daniel 137
Guignard, James S. 278
Guin, John 217
Guin, Mary 186
Guin, Richard 217
Guinn, Chesley 223

Guinn, Elizabeth 223, 224
Guinn, Jeptha 223
Guinn, Jesse 223
Guinn, Jesse T. 223
Guinn, John 223
Guinn, Littleton 223
Guinn, Mary 223
Guinn, Milley 223
Guinn, Nancy 223
Guinn, Richard 223, 224
Guinn, Sarah 223
Guinn, Solomon 222
Guinn, Thomas 223, 224
Guinn, Thompson 223
Guinn, William 216, 223
Guinn, Wm. W. 223
Guiton, Abraham 303
Guiton, Nancy M. 303
Gull, George 187
Gunning, E. H. 286, 350
Gunning, Edward H. 267, 300
Gunning, Joseph H. 300
Gunning, Pamelia 157
Gunter, Mary 274
Gurdin, Jane 236
Gut(t)ery, Frances 13
Gutridge, Jane (Pettus) 117, 118
Guy, William 113, 114, 158, 170, 201
Guyer, Isaac S. 281
Guyton, Aaron 52
Guyton, Elizabeth 52
Guyton, Hannah 52
Guyton, Isaac 140
Guyton, Margaret 52
Guyton, Nathan 14
Guyton, Robert McCurday 52
Gwin, Richard 266
Gwin, Mary 266
Gwinn, Elizabeth 250, 266
Gwinn, Jesse 269
Gwinn, Mary 266
Gwinn, Mary A. 269
Gwinn, Thomas T. 250, 266
Gwinn, William C. 250
Gwyn, Alex 279
Hacket, Hugh 285, 286
Hacket, James 286
Hacket, William 270, 286
Haco, M. T. 112
Hagans, Elizabeth 286
Haggins, Joseph 79
Haggins, Mary 79, 80

## PERSONAL NAME INDEX

Haggins, Mary Patten 79
Haggins, William 79
Hagin, C. 60
Hagins, Elizabeth 79, 236
Hagins, James 191
Hagins, Joicy 251
Hagins, Mary 191
Hagins, William 79, 191
Hagins, William J. 191
Hagins, William P. 191
Hagins, Wm. S. 251, 252
Hainsworth, 145
Hale, Thos. 19
Hall, A. N. 319
Hall, Ann 70, 71
Hall, Betsy 70, 71
Hall, D. 279
Hall, Daniel F. 243
Hall, Eliza 319
Hall, Elizabeth Ann (Watson) 301
Hall, James Temple 319
Hall, Jane 248
Hall, Jean 70
Hall, John 65, 70, 71, 166, 283, 293, 319, 337, 352
Hall, John B. 66
Hall, John R. 197, 224, 265, 311, 319, 336
Hall, M. T. 197, 211, 224, 265
Hall, Major T. 167, 243
Hall, Major Temple 319
Hall, Major Thomson 319
Hall, Margaret 70
Hall, Martha 70
Hall, Nancy 70, 71
Hall, R. F. 319
Hall, Robert McCaw 319
Hall, Saml B. 319
Hall, Sarah 70
Hall, Widow 116
Hall, William 12, 13, 61, 66, 70, 71, 139, 167, 319
Hall, William A. 166, 167
Ham, Jona'n 211
Hambleton, William 43
Hambrick, Elijah 201, 203
Hambrick, Elizabeth 201
Hambrick, H. N. 300
Hambright, 139
Hambright, Benjamin 117
Hambright, Charlotte 117
Hambright, David 117

Hambright, Elise 160
Hambright, Elizabeth 160, 161
Hambright, Frederick 117, 139, 161, 257
Hambright, Gilley 160
Hambright, Henry 117
Hambright, James 117, 257
Hambright, James Madison 275
Hambright, Jefferson 257, 275
Hambright, John 117, 161, 257
Hambright, Joseph 117
Hambright, Josiah 117, 161
Hambright, Liddia 257
Hambright, Madison 257, 275, 308
Hambright, Martain 160
Hambright, Mary 117
Hambright, Mary Amanda 275
Hambright, Michael A. 257
Hambright, Philip Boyd 275
Hambright, Sarah 275
Hambright, Susannah 117
Hambright, Terry 160
Hambright, Vina Catherine 275
Hamby, John 23
Hamill, Charles 67, 68
Hamille, Joseph 21
Hamilton, Alexander 45, 353
Hamilton, Catharine 45
Hamilton, Clouder 106
Hamilton, David 45, 214, 215, 230
Hamilton, James 45, 79, 80
Hamilton, Jean 45, 106
Hamilton, John 45
Hamilton, Lt. Col. 111
Hamilton, Martha 126
Hamilton, Patrick 124, 131
Hamilton, S. W. 176
Hamilton, Thomas 45
Hamilton, William 42, 43, 45, 86, 106, 230
Hamilton, William K. 230
Hammel, Archibald 259
Hammel, Rachel 259
Hamrick, George M. 303
Hamton, Elisabeth 125
Handerson, Ellanah 19
Haney, James 191
Hanna, 180
Hanna, Andrew M. 184
Hanna, Archibald C. 202
Hanna, Deborah 28
Hanna, Elizabeth 28

## PERSONAL NAME INDEX

Hanna, James 28
Hanna, Jane 28, 202
Hanna, Margaret 202
Hanna, Martha 28
Hanna, Robert 28, 84
Hanna, Rosanah Berry 28
Hanna, Sarah 28, 162
Hanna, William 28, 251
Hannah, Ann 144, 162
Hannah, Archibald 144, 145, 159, 162
Hannah, James 144, 162
Hannah, Jane 144, 162
Hannah, Margaret 144, 162
Hannah, Rosannah 144
Hannah, Sarah 144, 162
Hannah, William 144, 162, 317
Harbeson, John 50
Harbison, Esther 71
Harbison, James 71
Harbison, John 51, 71, 72
Harden, Abraham 189, 228
Harden, Harris B. 335
Harden, Lucy B. 314
Harden, Noah 335
Hardin, A. 257, 347
Hardin, Abraham 188, 195, 227, 234, 314, 316
Hardin, David D. 314
Hardin, Martin 234
Hardin, Noah 335
Hardister, John C. 304
Hare, Mary H. 334
Hare, Susan Jane 334
Hargrove, Thomson 38
Harp, Bawley 60
Harp, Cherubim 61
Harp, Cherybim 60
Harp, Elizabeth 60, 61
Harper 302
Harper, Alexander 252
Harper, Elizabeth 183, 234
Harper, Hugh 348
Harper, James 122, 149, 201, 211, 234
Harper, Jane 234, 252
Harper, John 206, 211, 234
Harper, John S. 252
Harper, John T. 201, 219, 343
Harper, Joseph 234
Harper, Margaret 234, 302, 348, 349
Harper, Martha M. C. 252
Harper, Matthew 21, 115, 155, 201, 234, 252

Harper, Robert 135, 234
Harper, Thos E. 343
Harriet, Nancy 111
Harrington, Nancy 214
Harris 173
Harris, Ann 20
Harris, Ausper 253
Harris, C. H. 199
Harris, Cervantas 199
Harris, Dupont Peter 77
Harris, Eleanor 148
Harris, Eleanor Jane 312
Harris, Eleazer 199, 200
Harris, Eliza Anne 290
Harris, Eliza C. 253
Harris, Eliza Isabella 312
Harris, Elizabeth 118
Harris, F. H. 319
Harris, Franklin H. 288
Harris, G. W. 258
Harris, H. G. 289, 290
Harris, Henry 199, 200, 326
Harris, Henry G. 165, 168
Harris, Hugh 38, 194, 200, 213, 312
Harris, Hugh C. 311, 312
Harris, Isaac 104, 136, 290
Harris, Isham W. 289
Harris, J. F. 308
Harris, J. H. 299
Harris, J. L. 326
Harris, James 60, 64, 122, 123, 168, 200
Harris, James L. 330
Harris, James M. 153, 193, 249, 293, 319
Harris, Jane 100, 199, 252
Harris, John 64, 118, 122, 165, 168, 200
Harris, John D. 200
Harris, John L. 311, 312, 328
Harris, John M. 200, 213, 249
Harris, Josiah 148
Harris, Margt M. 153
Harris, Martha 326
Harris, Martha Jane 200
Harris, Martha N. 302
Harris, Mary 168, 311, 326
Harris, Matilda R. S. 148
Harris, Nancy 165
Harris, Nathaniel 102, 165, 168, 267
Harris, Patience 289
Harris, Peter 76, 159, 242, 247

## PERSONAL NAME INDEX

Harris, Phebe 100
Harris, Prudence 224
Harris, Randolph C. 129
Harris, Rebecka/h 158
Harris, Robert 28, 56, 57, 65, 148, 213, 312
Harris, Robert H. 312
Harris, Robert Harvey 199, 200
Harris, Robert P. 288
Harris, Sammy 76, 77
Harris, W. L. 196, 211
Harris, Wiley/Wyley L. 131, 247
Harris, Wylie L. 199, 202, 218, 242, 258, 300
Harrison, Henry 183
Harrison, John 260
Harrison, Nancy 200
Harrison, Nathaniel 12
Harrison, William E. 183
Harshaw, Catherine 103
Harshaw, Cinthia 103
Harshaw, Daniel 103
Harshaw, Hugh 103, 121
Harshaw, James 103
Harshaw, Jephtha 103
Hart, Aloes 148
Hart, Andrew 80
Hart, C. M. 148
Hart, Capt. 38
Hart, Charles 110
Hart, Ebenezer 29, 30
Hart, Elizabeth 29, 111, 119, 148
Hart, H. H. 265
Hart, Harry 148
Hart, James 29, 148
Hart, Janey 111
Hart, John 27, 29, 30, 40, 110-112, 128, 138, 148, 192, 265, 293
Hart, Joseph 29, 112
Hart, Margaret 111
Hart, Mary 294
Hart, Polly 148
Hart, Priscilla 110, 111
Hart, Rebecah 148
Hart, Rebecka/h 148
Hart, Sally 111
Hart, Sampson 111
Hart, Samuel 29
Hart, William 29, 111, 148
Hart, Wm. T. 263, 294
Hartgrove, John 89
Harth, Andrew 80

Hartness, Hugh 156
Hartness, Jane 30, 53, 54, 355
Hartness, John 180
Hartness, Robert 19, 31
Hartt, Joseph 177
Harverson, Marget 76
Harverson, William 76
Harvey, Archibald 224
Harvey, William 287
Harvin[?], John B. 254
Hasket, Wm. 202
Hayne, William Edward 66, 116, 278
Haynes, Capt 89
Haynes, David 168
Hays, Adaline 253
Hays, Alison 320
Hays, Amelia 321
Hays, Ann 320
Hays, Emeline E. 274
Hays, Jesse 239
Hays, John 204, 222, 321
Hays, John J. 239
Hays, Mary 321
Hays, Mary C. 269
Hays, Robert 144, 156, 173, 200, 215, 227, 244, 269
Hays, Salley 244
Hays, Selena A. 239
Hays, Susan 321
Heart, Charles 153
Heart, Elizabeth 153
Heart, Harriet 153
Heart, Jane 153
Heart, John 153
Heart, Margaret 153
Heart, Priscilla 153
Heart, Sarah 153
Heflin, Fanny 114
Hemingway, Albert 153, 154
Hemingway, John 153, 154
Hemingway, William 153, 154
Hemmingway, Henrietta 246
Hemmingway, Mary 246
Hemmingway, William 246
Hemphill, 208
Hemphill, Alexander 5, 136
Hemphill, Alexander H. 231
Hemphill, Ann 52
Hemphill, David 136, 137
Hemphill, Eleanor 230
Hemphill, Emma K. 332
Hemphill, Esther 32

## PERSONAL NAME INDEX

Hemphill, J. 87
Hemphill, J. G. 322
Hemphill, J. H. 316, 324
Hemphill, Ja's 17
Hemphill, James 5, 17, 32, 137, 155, 212, 215, 231, 289, 322
Hemphill, James A. 231
Hemphill, James G. 231
Hemphill, James S. 146, 230, 231, 284, 285, 300, 307, 308, 321
Hemphill, James S. D. 321, 322
Hemphill, James V. 231
Hemphill, Jane 231
Hemphill, Janet 5
Hemphill, Jean 213
Hemphill, John 5, 106, 112, 121, 146, 164, 166, 167, 170, 180, 196, 230, 231
Hemphill, John G. 230, 231
Hemphill, Margaret 136, 289
Hemphill, Martha 230
Hemphill, Martha G. 321
Hemphill, Mary 5, 6, 231
Hemphill, Nancy 230, 231
Hemphill, Robert 5, 136, 231
Hemphill, Samuel 5, 54, 57, 136, 160, 231, 289
Hemphill, Samuel G. 230, 231, 321
Hemphill, Sarah 136, 137
Hemphill, W. G. 231
Hemphill, W. H. 231
Hemphill, William 136
Hemphill, William H. 230
Hempill, G. H. 324
Henderson, 229, 280
Henderson, Abiga(i)l 62, 109
Henderson, Christiana 96, 97
Henderson, Daniel 19
Henderson, Elizabeth 19, 62, 109, 168, 356
Henderson, Elizabeth Bowie 267
Henderson, Esther 10
Henderson, James 19, 36
Henderson, James Franklin 268
Henderson, James P. 195, 250, 268
Henderson, John 19, 23, 29, 53, 192, 195
Henderson, Mary 10, 195
Henderson, Mary Ann 268
Henderson, Nathaniel 19, 143, 192, 356
Henderson, Robert 10, 19

Henderson, Samuel 10, 19, 96, 97, 100
Henderson, Sarah 154, 192
Henderson, Thomas 19, 192
Henderson, Wm 195, 197
Hendrick, Mary 214
Henry, A. M. 330
Henry, Alexander 128, 175
Henry, Amanda S. 260
Henry, Andrew 175
Henry, Ann 175
Henry, Catherine 164
Henry, Charles 114, 143, 175, 199
Henry, Charles W. 114, 175
Henry, Cotesy 112
Henry, Cyrus L. 239
Henry, Eleanor 15
Henry, Elisabeth McKeam 128
Henry, Elizabeth 31, 105, 175
Henry, Esther 175
Henry, Frances 253
Henry, Francis 126, 128, 129, 155, 175
Henry, Isaac N. 273
Henry, Isabella 128, 175, 315
Henry, Jackson N. 128
Henry, James 4, 93, 105, 126, 128, 129
Henry, James J. 273
Henry, Jane 129, 310
Henry, John 67, 99, 112, 113, 123, 129, 137, 145
Henry, John A. 273
Henry, Josiah 129, 175, 182, 203
Henry, Malco(l)m 128, 130, 164
Henry, Margaret 72, 164, 190
Henry, Mary 93, 124, 128, 175, 258, 269
Henry, Melinda 175
Henry, Nelly 15
Henry, Palmer 105
Henry, Peggy 114
Henry, Robert 239
Henry, Robert A. 164
Henry, Thomas C. 190, 315
Henry, William 105, 128-130
Henry, William D. 128, 157, 185
Herdman, Elizabeth 234
Herman, John 282
Hermon, Margaret 282
Herndon, J. 349
Herndon, Joseph 341

## PERSONAL NAME INDEX

Heron, Andrew 169
Herrald, Jas 179
Herrald, Susannah 179
Herren, Andrew 148
Herrin, Andrew 103
Hetherington, James 293
Hetherington, Joseph 224, 293
Hetherington, Mary 62, 109
Hetherington, Rebecca 263
Hetherington, William 293
Hicklen, James C. 316
Hicklin, James C. 300, 311, 319
Higgens, Patrick 71
Higgins, Joseph S. 191
Higgins, Saml T. 191
Higgins, William S. 192
Highfill, Bennit 49
Hill 89
Hill, A. 115
Hill, Agness 34
Hill, Albert Potts[?] 157
Hill, Alexander 308
Hill, Amanda J. 240
Hill, Andrew 116, 152
Hill, Col. 5, 6
Hill, Elizabeth 34, 35, 121
Hill, Eugene 227
Hill, George 121
Hill, Hugh 34, 35
Hill, J. A. 307
Hill, James 36, 113
Hill, Jane 116
Hill, Jesse 30
Hill, John 55, 81
Hill, Kezia 34
Hill, Nancy 157
Hill, Pa. 78
Hill, R. 127, 157
Hill, Rachel 144
Hill, Reuben 61
Hill, Robert 116
Hill, Samuel B. 118
Hill, Sarah C. 308
Hill, Solomon 116, 121, 127, 157
Hill, W. 208
Hill, W. R. 181
Hill, William 34, 35, 60, 82, 116
Hill, Wm. M. 139
Hill, Wm. R. 127, 157, 167
Hill, Zenos S. 240
Hoff, Jane 114
Hoff, Powel 114

Hoff, Prudence 114
Hoge, George 1
Hoge, Jas 357
Hoge, Joseph 357
Hogg, 274
Hogg, Eli 140
Hogg, Elizabeth 140
Hogg, Elizabeth Anne 140
Hogg, Martha 140
Hogg, Sarah 241
Hogg, Thomas 103, 140, 241
Hogg, William S. 241
Hogge, Alexander 204
Hogge, Alexander C. 209
Hogge, Daniel M. 209
Hogge, Elizabeth 209
Hogge, Hannah 158
Hogge, Henry J. 209
Hogge, Isabella 204
Hogge, J. 209
Hogge, James 204
Hogge, James K. 209
Hogge, John 204
Hogge, Sarah 261
Hogge, Wm 133
Hogge, Wm. G. 209
Hogue, John P. 339
Hogue, Nancy E. 292
Holloway, Alexander 193
Holloway, Elizabeth 193
Holloway, Hugh A. 193
Holloway, James 193
Holloway, John 193
Holloway, Jonathan 193
Holloway, Margaret 193
Holloway, Mary 193
Holloway, Peter W. 193
Holloway, Robert Alexander 193
Holloway, Samuel 193
Holloway, William 193
Holsey, Margaret 121
Holt, Abraham 225
Holt, Akilles 225
Holt, Akillis 227
Holt, Allen Wylie 225
Holt, Catherine 225
Holt, Elizabeth 225
Holt, Hercules G. 225
Holt, James 225
Holt, Jane 225, 227
Holt, John 55, 225
Holt, Killis 225

**PERSONAL NAME INDEX**

Holt, Lucy 225
Holt, Thomas 225
Hood, Agnes 357
Hood, Elisabeth 357
Hood, G. D. 318
Hood, George 75, 142, 143
Hood, Henry 132, 142, 143, 236
Hood, Iby 357
Hood, J. P. 316
Hood, Jane 357
Hood, John 357
Hood, John P. 284, 318, 329
Hood, Malinda Jean 357
Hood, Martha 357
Hood, Mary 142, 357
Hood, Nancy R. 309
Hood, Permelia 357
Hoover, Mary 323
Hoover, Thomas 277
Hoover, Thomas B. 219
Hope, Allison 181
Hope, Amelia G. 303
Hope, Catren 32
Hope, Isaac 32, 164
Hope, J. M. 280, 347
Hope, James 29, 110
Hope, Jane 29
Hope, Jean 49
Hope, John 152, 154
Hope, R. H. 251, 281, 293, 294
Hope, R. S. 238
Hope, Robert 317
Hope, Robert H. 317
Hope, Robert S. 317
Hope, Samuel 29
Hopkins, John F. 143
Hopkins, John S. 131
Hopper, Anthony 345, 346
Hopper, Barbara 345, 346
Hopper, Charles 346
Hopper, Charles G. 346
Hopper, Humphrey 346
Hopper, Humphrey P. 346
Hopper, Jefferson S. 346
Hopper, John S. 346
Horn, Jesse 37
Horne 339
Hornly, Richard 36
Horry, C. H. 205
Horseley, Abram Roberts 293
Horseley, Nancy Amanda Jane 293
Horseley, Richard R. 293

Horsely, Richard 35
Horsely, Susannah 293
Horsely, Susannah Matilda 293
Horshaw, Catherine 103
Horshaw, Hugh 208
Horsley, Betsy 247
Horsley, Eleanor 247
Horsley, Nancy 247
Horsley, Rachel 247
Horsley, Rebeckah 247
Horsley, Richard 152
Houge, James Benjamin 293
Houlston 20
House, David 120
Houser, C(h)ristina 139, 323
Houser, David 139
Houser, Henry 139
Houser, John 139, 195, 323
Houser, Rebecca 277
Houston, David 28
Houston, James 171
Hovey[?], Samuel J. 230
How, Joseph 59
Howard, Amasa 233
Howe, 337
Howe, Ann 134
Howe, David 6
Howe, Hiram 66
Howe, Isabella 31
Howe, J. L. 258
Howe, Jane 10
Howe, Jo's 4
Howe, John 2, 10, 13, 31
Howe, Joseph 10, 31
Howe, Joseph R. 243
Howe, Mary 289
Howe, Mary Dunlap 31
Howe, Robert 32
Howe, Samuel D. 188
Howe, Thomas 31, 134
Howe, William 31, 115
Howel, Lucy 125
Howel, Williamson 214
Howell 228
Howell, Croker 275
Howell, Joseph 228, 347
Howell, Samuel 214
Howell, Sterling 180
Howell, Williamson 320
Howell, Wm. S. 303
Howell, Wmson 262
Howie, Alexander 120, 211, 225

## PERSONAL NAME INDEX

Howie, Margaret 120
Howie, Robert 7, 10, 120
Howie, Sarah 120
Howie, William 120
Howser, Doctor 323
Howser, Henry 117, 161, 195
Howser, Nancy 194, 195, 323
Howser, Polly 323
Hudson, Henry 209
Hudson, Henry C. 306
Hudson, Thomas 62
Huff, Jno'a 102
Huff, Margaret 130
Huggins, Alexander 277
Huggins, Joel 341, 351
Huggins, Joel A. 325
Huggins, John 325
Huggins, John Irwin 351
Hughs, Joseph 84
Hughs, R. W. 308
Hughs, W. R. 350
Hullender, Abm 189
Hunt, John A. 288
Hunter 305
Hunter, Amelia 338
Hunter, Benjamin 251
Hunter, David Wright 327
Hunter, Isabella 256
Hunter, J. B. 341
Hunter, J. Blair 305, 334, 344
Hunter, Jas. B. 339
Hunter, John 199, 200
Hunter, John B. 275, 279, 359
Hunter, Mary M. 270, 295
Hunter, Massey H. 226
Hurst, John 114
Husking, John 289
Husking, Nancy 289
Husky, Nancy 264
Huston, John 149
Hutcheson, David 32, 112, 116, 132, 133, 138, 185, 204, 206
Hutcheson, James 185, 207
Hutcheson, James P. 204
Hutcheson, John 204
Hutcheson, Leroy 185
Hutcheson, Margaret C. 204
Hutcheson, Polly 204
Hutcheson, Rhoda 204
Hutcheson, Samuel 112, 204, 206
Hutcheson, Samuel B. 204
Hutchinson, John 48

Hutchison, A. S. 266, 267
Hutchison, Adeline 264, 265
Hutchison, Agness 40
Hutchison, Ann 264, 265
Hutchison, David 40, 78, 265
Hutchison, Eugene 265
Hutchison, Hiram 96, 264, 265
Hutchison, John 47, 48, 79
Hutchison, Mary 264, 265
Hutton, Shusanah 49
Hynes, Alex'r 57
Iles, Sarah 165
Ingraham, Richard 103
Ingram, John 144, 217, 220, 285
Ingram, Richard 64, 102, 103
Ingram, William 217
Inman, Aaron 195
Inman, Hezekiah 195
Ireland, Mary 8
Irwin, Abigail 18
Irwin, Alexander 18
Irwin, Elizabeth 107
Irwin, Frances 105, 117
Irwin, Francis 144, 152, 175
Irwin, Henry 340
Irwin, James 18, 45, 277, 325
Irwin, John 328
Irwin, John F. 327, 341, 351
Irwin, Leah 18
Irwin, Mary 101
Irwin, Mary Frances 340
Irwin, Nancy 340, 341
Irwin, Nathaniel 18
Irwin, Suffia 18
Irwin, Susanna 18
Irwin, Thomas 119, 340
Irwin, William 18
Isom, James 221
Ison[?], Wm. 303
Jacks, Mary 168
Jackson 339
Jackson, A. M. 349
Jackson, Alexander 272
Jackson, Barbary 198
Jackson, Becky Maria 90
Jackson, Catherine P. 209
Jackson, Cresy 198
Jackson, D. F. 255, 256, 349
Jackson, David 66, 67, 123, 160, 212, 226, 231, 351
Jackson, E. J. 321
Jackson, Elias 123, 137, 148

## PERSONAL NAME INDEX

Jackson, Elias M. 271, 272, 275, 321, 351
Jackson, Elizabeth 90, 91, 198, 209, 238, 251
Jackson, Elizabeth J. 335
Jackson, Elvira 272
Jackson, Ephraim 198
Jackson, Erixana 351
Jackson, H. M. 351
Jackson, Hamilton 251
Jackson, Henry 198
Jackson, Hugh 123, 170
Jackson, Hugh M. 270, 171
Jackson, Isaac 198
Jackson, James 251, 272
Jackson, James B. 270, 271, 292, 323
Jackson, James Greenlee 198
Jackson, James L. 231
Jackson, Jane 198, 351
Jackson, Jane E. 349
Jackson, John 65, 122-124, 131, 136, 148, 157, 165, 171, 175, 176, 192, 198, 234, 249, 251, 271, 351
Jackson, John B. 270
Jackson, John C. 210
Jackson, John James 255
Jackson, John Newton 198
Jackson, Joseph 37, 238
Jackson, Katharine 349
Jackson, Keziah 198
Jackson, Lewis Elbert 90
Jackson, Louisa 198
Jackson, Margaret A. 272
Jackson, Mary 123, 291, 350, 351
Jackson, Mary E. 255
Jackson, Mary J. 305
Jackson, Mary M. 321
Jackson, Richard 102
Jackson, Robert 170, 351
Jackson, S. W. 317
Jackson, Sally 198
Jackson, Sampson 198
Jackson, Samuel 350, 351
Jackson, Samuel W. 270, 336
Jackson, Sarah 72, 255
Jackson, Susan 351
Jackson, W. J. 323
Jackson, W. T. 351
Jackson, William 62, 91, 123, 251, 272
Jackson, Willian B. 270, 292, 316, 324
Jackson, Zebulon 91
Jacobs, Ferdinand 249

Jameison, James 299
Jameison, John 299
Jameison, Milton 299
Jamerson, Allen R. 355
James, A. C. 289
James, Araminta 322
James, Daniel 219, 249, 254, 287, 323
James, Elizabeth 287
James, Jane 200
James, John 114, 119, 132, 143, 186, 216, 287
James, Lucy 195
James, Robert 322
James, Sarah 200
James, Shared/Sharid 195
James, Sherard 143
James, Sherid 186
James, Sherod 132
James, Sherud 187
James, Thomas 287
James, William 143, 203
Jameson, Elizabeth 170
Jameson, Helena 207
Jameson, James 13, 202
Jameson, William 103, 110, 158, 170, 200, 227
Jamieson, Allen 300
Jamieson, Allen Rowe 299
Jamieson, Eliza Ann 299
Jamieson, Helena 144
Jamieson, Jas 278
Jamieson, Joseph 112, 121, 278, 299
Jamieson, Milton 121
Jamieson, Nancy 299
Jamieson, Robert 296
Jamieson, William 82, 83, 111, 112, 121, 144, 158, 190, 275, 278, 279, 299
Jamison, Helena 173
Jamison, James 13, 173
Jamison, Jane 206
Jamison, Rachel 67, 113, 170
Jamison, W. 216
Jamison, William 156, 159, 173, 204, 207, 211, 214, 215, 225
Janes, John 215, 277
Jarrett, John 19
Jeans, Margaret B. 223
Jeans, Rachel 223
Jefferies, Eliza (Green) 182
Jefferies, James 182, 257
Jefferies, Louisa (Green) 182

## PERSONAL NAME INDEX

Jefferies, William 182
Jefferys, James 271, 328, 339
Jefferys, Louisa (Green) 181
Jefferys, T. S. 279
Jeffreys, Eliza (Green) 181
Jeffries, James 290
Jeffries, William 289
Jemison, James 43, 44
Jemison, Jeph 43
Jemison, Joseph 41, 44
Jenkins, Benjn 124, 126
Jenkins, David Mitchel 126
Jenkins, Elizabeth 117, 324
Jenkins, Jane 335
Jenkins, John 126
Jenkins, Lawson 236
Jenkins, Margaret 126
Jenkins, Mary 22, 126
Jenkins, Thomas 22
Jennings, D. Edmond[?] 197
Jennings, Doctor 277
Jennings, E. 131
Jennings, Ed 141, 148
Jewel, Jane 109
Jewell, Jean 62
Jingles, Delilah (Darby) 152
Johnson, Albert P. 315
Johnson, David 21
Johnson, James 120, 147, 191
Johnson, John 243, 262, 268
Johnson, Margaret 324
Johnson, Miles 289
Johnson, Saml 69
Johnson, Thomas 192
Johnson, William 150
Johnston, Alexander 39
Johnston, Amanda 239
Johnston, Anna Cora 333
Johnston, David 21, 152, 155, 239
Johnston, E. 196
Johnston, E. L. D. 320
Johnston, Eliza P. 245
Johnston, Elizabeth 21, 152, 239
Johnston, Emeline 239
Johnston, Evaline 152
Johnston, George 135
Johnston, George Augustin 333
Johnston, James 136, 159, 167, 193, 218, 239, 315
Johnston, Jean 21
Johnston, John 127, 152, 196, 252
Johnston, Joseph 39

Johnston, L. D. 320
Johnston, Margaret 195, 196, 252
Johnston, Margaret Dorcas 333
Johnston, Martha 252
Johnston, Martha Jane 239
Johnston, Marthew 129
Johnston, Mary 21, 239
Johnston, Mary Margaret 239
Johnston, Robert 21, 26, 32, 35, 37, 40, 135, 152, 196
Johnston, Samuel C. 252
Johnston, Sarah 21, 157, 210, 211, 239
Johnston, Sarah E. 210, 332, 333
Johnston, William 239, 304
Johnston, William F. 239
Johnston, William H. 245, 252, 284, 333
Johnston, Zeverah[?] 343
Jolly, Henry 14
Jones, Agnes 281
Jones, Clerk 190
Jones, Daniel 62, 76
Jones, Dudley 202, 244
Jones, Eliza J. 233
Jones, Genl 140
Jones, James 281
Jones, James S. 268, 281, 310, 324, 325
Jones, John 243
Jones, John J. 140
Jones, Thornton 243
Jonston, Moss 183
Jordan 212
Jordan, Mansfield 175
Jorden, Robert 81, 82
Jordon, Catharine 13
Jordon, Elizabeth 72
Jordon, Grizzle 72
Jordon, James 13
Jordon, Jane 13
Jordon, John 13, 72
Jordon, Margaret 13
Jordon, Robert 13, 72
Julia, George 63
Julian, George 38, 39
Julian, Hannah 38
Julian, Jacob 18, 38, 39, 63
Julian, James 38, 39
Julian, Margeret 38
Julian, Martha 38
Julian, Mary 38, 39

## PERSONAL NAME INDEX

Julian, Rachel 38
Julian, Susanna 38
Keenan/Keinan, James 61
Kell, Elizabeth S. 307
Kell, J. G. 300, 307
Kell, Joseph 113
Kelley, John 223
Kelly[?], Saml. L. 223
Kelough, Anne 140
Kelsey, James Lamar 209
Kelsey, John 209, 211
Kenady, Nathaniel P. 136
Kenan 151
Kenan, Rachel 197
Kendrick, Anthony 35
Kendrick, E'd 182
Kendrick, Edmund 273
Kendrick, John 122
Kendrick, John F. 169
Kendrick, John J. 191
Kendrick, Mary 214
Kendrick, Priscilla 149
Kendrick, R. G. 336
Kendrick, Salina 293
Kendrick, Sarah 35
Kendrick, Susan M. 301
Kenedy, John 119
Kenedy, Nathaniel P. 90, 202
Kenedy, Robert 33, 34, 90
Kenedy, William 34, 41, 121, 135
Kenmore, James 261
Kenmore, Jean 261
Kenmore, John 261
Kenmure, Elinor 58
Kenmure, Elizabeth 58
Kenmure, James 57, 58
Kenmure, John 58
Kenmure, Margret 58
Kennedy, Andrew 31, 32
Kennedy, Arthur 4
Kennedy, Caroline 313
Kennedy, Easter 175
Kennedy, James 4
Kennedy, James R. 338
Kennedy, Jane C. 308
Kennedy, John 308, 338, 350
Kennedy, N. P. 243, 256, 274, 314
Kennedy, Nancey 4
Kennedy, Naomi 310, 338
Kennedy, Nathaniel P. 239, 241
Kennedy, Rachel N. 338
Kennedy, Robert 3, 19

Kennedy, William 31, 32
Kennedy, Wm. M. 338
Keown, Jno 13
Ker, Peter K. 226
Kernon, Saml 195
Kerr, Alfred D. 353
Kerr, Andrew 86, 87, 160
Kerr, Catherine 160
Kerr, Daniel 118
Kerr, Elijah 202
Kerr, Henry 92
Kerr, Isabella 86, 87
Kerr, James 86, 157
Kerr, James K. 191
Kerr, Jane 86
Kerr, Jean 87
Kerr, Jo's 32
Kerr, John 49, 86, 87
Kerr, Joseph 33, 55, 68
Kerr, Joseph E. 86
Kerr, Margret 86, 87
Kerr, Mary 86, 87
Kerr, Mary E. 208
Kerr, Matilda 211
Kerr, Milley 243
Kerr, Polly 86
Kerr, Robert 86
Kerr, Robertson 167
Kerr, Sarah 167
Kerr, Sarah E. 202
Kerr, William 5, 8, 18, 32, 64, 86, 157
Kerr, Zenas 86
Kerr, Zenos D. 191
Kester, Eulisses 346
Kester, Henry K. 346
Kidd, Ann 92
Kidd, Easther 201
Kidd, Editha 201
Kidd, Elizabeth 201
Kidd, George 92, 154
Kidd, James 201
Kidd, Jane 201
Kidd, John 113, 114, 201, 202
Kidd, Martha 201
Kidd, Robert 201, 202
Kidd, Thos D. 157
Kidd, William 201, 202
Kilkelly, Mary 140
Kilpatrick, Hannah 87
Kilpatrick, Jane 29
Kilpatrick, Robert 88
Kimbel, Dicey 322

## PERSONAL NAME INDEX

Kimbel, Sargent Jasper 322
Kimbel, Solomon 322
Kimbell, George W. 295
Kimbell, Harris 322
Kimble, Spell 63
Kimble, Spill 57
Kimbrel, Thomas 213
Kimbrell, Jean 226
Kimbrell, Nancy 226
Kimbrell, Rebecca 267
Kimbrell, Rush 226
Kimbrell, William 226
Kimbrell, Wm. N. 243
Kincaid, Isabella 205
Kincaid, James 131, 132
Kincaid, John 2, 205
Kindrick, Joseph 149
Kindrick, William 132, 134, 135, 149
Kindsey, Barbara 120
King, Alfred J. 207
King, Benjamin 22
King, Elizabeth 207
King, Esther (Alexander) 83
King, Evander C. 207
King, George 22
King, Inglesby 207
King, James P. 207
King, John 22, 41, 99, 103, 107, 110, 113, 137, 144, 158, 173, 207, 211
King, Joseph A. 106, 207
King, Joseph Alexander 83
King, Legrand W. 207
King, Mary 22
King, Mary P. 227
King, Samuel 22, 107, 113, 137, 158, 173
King, Sarah L. 207
Kingsboro/ugh, Jesse 359
Kingsbury, Lawson 337
Kirk, Richard 236
Kirk, William 97, 169
Kirkpatrick, Andrew W. 172
Kirkpatrick, E. M. 333
Kirkpatrick, Elizabeth 241
Kirkpatrick, Isabella 204
Kirkpatrick, Janet 172
Kirkpatrick, Joseph 203, 241
Kirkpatrick, William 34
Kiser, Betsy 119
Knox, David 37, 38, 357
Knox, Elisabeth 356
Knox, George 71, 126

Knox, James 357
Knox, Jean 37
Knox, John 38
Knox, Joseph 38
Knox, Mary 37, 38
Knox, Mathew 38
Knox, Robert 38
Knox, Samuel 38
Knox, Sarah 37
Kolb, Abraham 130
Kolb, Betsey 76
Kolb, Catherine 75, 92
Kolb, Catty 76
Kolb, Elisabeth 76
Kolb, Elisabeth Louisa 75
Kolb, Elizabeth 75
Kolb, James 75, 76
Kolb, Jean 75
Kolb, Jeanny 76
Kolb, Joseph 75, 92
Kolb, Silas 75
Kuykendal, Elvina J. 305
Kuykendal, Elvira J. 304
Kuykendal, Isaac 242
Kuykendal, James 76, 88, 188, 258, 259, 271, 286
Kuykendal, Jesse 88
Kuykendal, John Coburn 88
Kuykendal, Jonathan 59, 76, 77, 89
Kuykendal, Robert Cooper 242
Kuykendal, S. J. 305, 349
Kuykendal, Samuel 76, 77, 89
Kuykendal, Samuel J. 305
Kuykendal, Sarah 77
Kuykendal, Susannah 89
Kuykendal, W. J. 258
Kuykendall, 329
Kuykendall, B. J. 318
Kuykendall, Edy 359
Kuykendall, Elizabeth 205
Kuykendall, Isaac 110, 208, 358, 359
Kuykendall, James 189, 235, 237, 242, 247
Kuykendall, John C. 131
Kuykendall, Jonathan 88, 110, 144, 159
Kuykendall, Jos 211
Kuykendall, Sally 110, 358, 359
Kuykendall, Samuel 88
Kuykendall, Sarah 76
Kuykendall, Susannah 88
Kuykendoll, Jonathan 359

## PERSONAL NAME INDEX

Lacey, D. 152
Lacey, Mary 120
Lackey, Ephrum 66
Lackey, Ester 66
Lackey, Wm. G. 320
Lacy, Mary 199
Lacy, Wm. 199
Lainey, Rettie Roper 112
Lambeth, Margaret 167
Lambeth, Mary 244
Lancer[?], Harbert 244
Laney, Isaac 18
Laney, J. A. 248
Laney, John A. 188, 196, 204, 206, 239, 240, 247, 284, 293, 330
Laney, Joseph 151
Langram, 131
Lanier, Buckner 183
Lanier, John L. 288
Lanier, Susanna 183
Lanos[?], Saml 114
Lany, Robert 119
Laree[?], James C. 303
Lassley, Agnes 104
Latcham[?], 13
Latham, Andrew 180, 203
Latham, James 354
Latham, Jane 300
Latham, John T. P. 300
Latham, Mary 180, 183
Latham, Moses 354
Latham, Richard 354
Latham, Robert 180, 274
Latham, Sarah 183
Lathan, Andrew 196
Lathem, Moses 77
Latimer, 285
Latimore, 157
Latimore, Robert 89, 232
Latimore, Sarah C. 232
Latta, Jane 134, 250
Latta, John 128, 141, 150, 179, 181, 228, 278, 340
Latta, Nancy 340
Latta, Robert 131, 343
Latta, William 340
Latta, William A. 128
Lattamer, Robert 116
Lattimore, 45, 59
Lattimore, Ann 4
Lattimore, Arthur 4
Lattimore, George 4

Lattimore, Robert 4
Laughlin, William 18
Laughridge, James 268, 304
Laughridge, Margaret L. 304
Laughridge, Mary 304
Laughridge, Samuel 268, 304
Laurence, 305
Lawrance, Allen 210, 211
Lawrance, Allen G. 225, 226, 255, 256
Lawrance, Amanda 255
Lawrance, Amelia 255
Lawrance, Clementine 210
Lawrance, Frances 210
Lawrance, Joseph 170, 211
Lawrance, Josiah 210, 211
Lawrance, Josiah A. 208
Lawrance, Martha 210, 255
Lawrance, Mary F. 255
Lawrance, Robert 210, 211
Lawrance, Sarah G. 255
Lawrance, William 210
Lawrence, A. G. 203, 339
Lawrence, Doctor 183, 204
Lawrence, Francis 338
Lawrence, Joseph A. 359
Lawrence, Margt 338
Lawrence, Martha 339
Lawson 145
Lawson, John 35
Lawson, Mary (Brandon) 35, 36
Lay, William B. 304
Leach, Edward 320
Leach, Joseph 143
Leaney, Joseph 6
Leaney, Wm. 6
Leany, Elizabeth 6
Leatham, And 196
Leathem, Andrew 12
Leathem, Andrew A. 317
Leathem, Ann 1
Leathem, Catharine 1
Leathem, Cath(e)rine 112, 113
Leathem, Elizabeth L. 317
Leathem, James G. 317
Leathem, Jean 12
Leathem, John W. 317, 318
Leathem, Moses 2, 6, 12, 77
Leathem, Purd(e)y 1, 12
Leathem, R. H. 322
Leathem, Ritchard 2
Leathem, Robert 2, 12, 317

411

## PERSONAL NAME INDEX

Leathem, Robert T. 317
Leathem, Ruth 1
Leathem, Sarah 1, 12
Leathum, Moses 296
Lee, Elizabeth 42
Lee, Henry 129
Leech, Catherine 110
Leech, David 6, 15, 41, 85, 110
Leech, Ealconer[?] 113
Leech, Ele(a)nor 75, 76, 110
Leech, James 110
Leech, Jane 108
Leech, Jerusha 336
Leech, John 8, 85, 106, 108, 110
Leech, Joseph 1, 205
Leech, Joseph 110
Leech, Margaret 14, 15
Leech, Martha 336
Leech, William 15, 110
Leeper, Blanch 26
Leeper, Catherine 26
Leeper, James 26
Leeper, John 26
Leeper, Robert 21, 26, 356
Leeth, Jane 202
Lefer 352
Lesley, Andrew 82
Lesley, David T. 340
Lesley, Rosanna 310
Lesley, Samuel 67, 164
Lesly 78
Lesly, Elenor 67
Lesly, Mary S. 67
Lesly, Samuel 67
Lessley, Margaret 104
Lessley, Samuel 105, 123
Lesslie, Eleanor Jane 315
Lesslie, Mary Elizabeth 315
Lesslie, Rachel Emmeline 315
Lesslie, Rosanna Jane 315
Lesslie, William D. 315
Letson, G. H. 298
Letta, Rachel 237
Letta, Rachel Miller 237
Lewis 271
Lewis, J. S. 271
Lewis, James 13, 76
Lewis, Jane 163
Lewis, John 13
Lewis, Joseph 163, 194
Lewis, Margaret 13
Lewis[?], Saml 126

Lier[?], Wm. 191
Liles, Martha 158
Linche, 123
Lindsay, Archibald 119
Lindsay, Eleanor 119
Lindsay, Elisha 119
Lindsay, Jacob 119
Lindsey, Catharine 274
Lindsey, Eliza C. 332
Lindsey, Henrietta E. 274
Lindsey, Isaac 119
Lindsey, James G. 274
Lindsey, John 119
Lindsey, John F. 274
Lindsey, John M. 215, 274
Lindsey, John McNight 42
Lindsey, Philip W. 274
Lindsey, Rachel 119
Lindsey, Robert 274
Lindsey, Robert M. 274
Linsey, Moses 274
Linsey, Violet W. (Maclean) 176
Lipscomb, Hannah 181, 182, 203
Lipscomb, Robert 181, 182
Lipscomb, Smith 146, 182
Lipscomb, Waddy 182
Lipscomb, William 146
Lipscomb, Wyatt 181, 182
Lister, Delilah 292
Lister, Saml 292
Little, Elizabeth 147, 148, 359
Little, Jane 147
Little, Margaret 147
Little, Polly 147
Little, William 115, 120, 136, 147, 148, 359
Little, Wylie 221
Little, Wylie L. 147
LittleJohn, John 146
Littleton, James 143
Livingston, 151
Livingston, Abraham 94
Lock, Len 307
Lock, Melinda 307
Lockard, 11
Lockert, Charles 86, 354
Lockert, William 354
Lockhart, John 51, 211, 216, 242
Logan, J. R. 276
Logan, J. S. 175
Logan, John R. 210, 276
Logan, Joseph 228

## PERSONAL NAME INDEX

Logan, Laben 316
Logan, Sarah C. 343
Logan, Thos 169
Logan, William 108, 166
Lohridge, James 187
Lohridge, Saml 187
Lominack, Susannah 294
Lominack, Thomas H. 261
Long, James 330
Long, James W. 283
Long, Rebecca 16
Long, Samfort 140
Love, Alexander 11, 73
Love, Andrew 4, 5, 9, 10, 11, 39, 42, 43, 55, 56, 64, 65, 73, 161, 357
Love, Andrew Franklin 166
Love, Ann 4
Love, Arthur 166
Love, Benjn. F. 222, 225
Love, Eales 241
Love, Ele(a)nor 28, 166
Love, Eli 241
Love, Elizabeth 10, 11, 28, 65, 264
Love, Francis 28
Love, Hugh 161
Love, Isabella 161
Love, J. A. 211
Love, J. M. 154
Love, James 4, 10, 11, 54
Love, James M. 105, 152, 166, 225
Love, Jane 189
Love, Janet 28
Love, Jenny 161
Love, John 28, 64, 65, 161
Love, Margaret 11, 73, 166
Love, Martha 161, 189, 341
Love, Mary 65, 75, 189, 206
Love, Mathew 65
Love, Mitchel 152
Love, Nancy 166
Love, R. M. 211
Love, Rachel 166
Love, Robert 4, 28, 32, 54, 57, 65, 105, 107-109, 117-120, 152, 154, 161, 166, 189
Love, Robert M. 105, 225
Love, Ruth 75
Love, S. L. 322
Love, Saml 65
Love, Sarrah 65
Love, William 5, 11, 17, 28, 33, 54,
 64, 65, 71, 73, 78, 87, 97, 98, 130, 136, 155, 159, 161, 162, 189, 192, 213, 215, 330, 336
Lovens, Rebeccah 50
Low, Wm. 130
Lowe, Emeline 258
Lowe, G. W. 290
Lowe, Robt 189
Lowrance, Jos 206
Lowrie, Jno M. 202
Lowrie, Samuel 120, 131, 144, 159
Lowry, Amanda 309
Lowry, Caroline 297
Lowry, Eleanor M. 310
Lowry, Elizabeth 309
Lowry, James 184
Lowry, John 184, 219
Lowry, John B. 278, 341
Lowry, Margaret 176
Lowry, Mary 49, 184
Lowry, Minerva 184
Lowry, Samuel 175, 184
Lowry, Susan 184
Lowry, William 184
Luck, Andrew 134
Luck, James 134
Luck, Margaret 133, 134
Luck, Martha 133, 134
Luck, Robt 134
Lusk, Elisabeth 29
Lusk, James 29
Lusk, Jane 133, 134
Lusk, Robert 20, 29, 43, 88
Lusk, Samuel 26, 29
Lynn, Robert 105
Lyon, Margaret 333
Lytle, William 100
M'Clain, Amsigh 358
Maclean, Alexander Augustus 176, 177
Maclean, Elizabeth Jackson (Campbell) 177
Maclean, John Davidson 176, 177
Maclean, Martha C. 296
Maclean, Mary Margaret 177
Maclean, Rebecca Isabella/h 176, 177
Maclean, Rebecca J. 177
Maclean, Richard Dobbs Spaight 176, 177
Maclean, Robert Hamilton Graham 177
Maclean, Thomas Brevard 177

## PERSONAL NAME INDEX

Maclean, Violet W. 177
Maclean, Violet W. (Linsey) 176
Maclean, William 21, 26, 177
Maclean, William Hayne 177
Maclean, Wm Mayne 176
Magh, Mary 205
Magh, William 205
Malissa, Nancy 170
Mallet, Jincy 286
Mallet, Martha 286
Mammon, Robt 140
Maning, Elizabeth 214
Manion, Catey 63
Manion, Elizabeth 63
Manion, Robert 63, 64
Manion, Thomas 63, 64
Manion, William 63
Mannin, Robert 252
Manning, Catherine 254
Manning, Commodore P. 308, 349
Manning, John 350
Manning, John M. 308, 349
Manning, Joseph 275
Manning, Joseph B. 308, 349, 350
Manning, Loson 254
Manning, Mary 308
Manning, Mary A. 349, 350
Manning, Mary Ann 308
Manning, Mary M. 308
Manning, Mijamin 254
Manning, Perry C. 350
Manning, Robert 254, 308
Manning, Robert L. 308, 349, 350
Manning, Thomas 254, 308
Manning, Thomas W. 308, 349, 350
Manning, William 179
Manning, William C. 308, 349, 350
Mannon, Mary Ann 139
Mannon, Massey 189
Mannon, Robert 140, 189
Mannon, Rodeck/Rodick 189
Mannon, Thos 189
Marable, Jemima 51
Marable, Natty 51
Marion, Jno Patrick 279
Marion, Peter 332
Marion, Robert 64
Marley, Jameson 208
Marley, John 144
Marshall, John H. 357
Martin 347
Martin, Abraham 316

Martin, Absalom 316
Martin, Alexandria 252
Martin, Andrew 316
Martin, Benjamin 316
Martin, Berry 234
Martin, Bird 313, 316
Martin, Catharine 53, 54
Martin, David Beard 53
Martin, E. C. 301
Martin, Elizabeth 316
Martin, Gabriel 316
Martin, Henderson 301, 316, 347
Martin, Hicks 316
Martin, J. M. 276
Martin, James 30, 40, 41, 53, 54, 97, 109, 133, 355
Martin, John 27, 29, 107, 159, 252
Martin, Jos 232
Martin, Jos G. 161, 232, 263
Martin, Josey 316
Martin, Katherine 355
Martin, Lakey 316
Martin, Mannon 179, 252
Martin, Margaret Lowrie 133
Martin, Martha 179
Martin, Mary 179, 316
Martin, Michael 179
Martin, Morgan 179, 252, 308, 350
Martin, Moses 350
Martin, Mourning 179
Martin, Perry 316
Martin, Shusanna 91
Martin, T. M. 316
Martin, Thomas 58, 119, 316
Martin, Thomas N. 195
Martin, William 58, 160, 316
Mason, Asa 176
Mason, Clayborn 153
Mason, David M. 153
Mason, G. W. 313
Mason, James 153, 201, 301, 314
Mason, John 152, 314
Mason, Martha 209
Mason, Mary 201
Mason, Nancy 152, 153
Mason, Richard 153, 219, 239
Mason, Thompson 152
Mason, William 127, 152, 153, 155, 157
Massey, Benjamin 183
Massey, L. H. 311
Massey, Mary 160

## PERSONAL NAME INDEX

Massey, Thomas 192
Masunan[?], Thos 165
Mathews, Elizabeth 35
Mathews, J. T. 309
Mathews, John 35
Matthews, Margaret 233
May, Arabella 265
May, Wm 229
May, Wm. S. 246
Mayner, Hiram 292
Mayner, Vina 292
Mayson, Wm. 152
Mc---, Jon 77
McAdorry, Ann 10
McAdorry, Elisabeth 10
McAdorry, James 10
McAdorry, Martha 10
McAdorry, Mary 10
McAdorry, Robert 10
McAdorry, Thomas 10
McAdory, Mary 99
McAdory, Robert 73
McAfee, Abner 276
McAfee, Amelia 275, 276
McAfee, Amzi 276
McAfee, C. E. 275
McAfee, Eliza 276
McAfee, Emily Jane 275, 276
McAfee, George Wellington 276
McAfee, Green T. 275
McAfee, Lawson A. 275
McAfee, Leroy 276
McAfee, Manda Elvira 276
McAfee, Pamelia 301
McAfee, Pinckney 275
McAfee, Tilman 275
McAlilly 269
McAlla, R. C. 293
McBee, Vardry 177
McBigger/s, William 201, 229
McBrayer, Saml 275
McBrier, Samuel 107
McCain, James 167, 222
McCain, Joseph 184
McCall 91
McCall, Alfred 266
McCall, Greze 13
McCall, Grizzel/l 134, 266
McCall, Hellanah 219
McCall, Hellienah 267
McCall, Hellinah 266
McCall, Hillary 116

McCall, John 2, 13, 59, 60, 266
McCall, Lucinda 266
McCall, Polly 30
McCall, Robt 270
McCall, Samuel 30
McCallen, James 13
McCallum, D. A. 318
McCallum, Duncan 302, 329
McCamon, James 97
McCance, David 86
McCance, John 86
McCannon, James 97
McCants, George M. 306
McCants, Henry Matthew 305
McCants, James 306
McCants, Jesse Franklin 305
McCants, Margaret Jane 305
McCants, Thomas 97
McCants, Thomas W. Sturgis 305
McCants, Tirzah 305
McCarra, Ann 63, 109
McCarter 195
McCarter, Andrew 186, 264, 343
McCarter, Andrew J. 342
McCarter, Andrew M. 343
McCarter, Anna 202
McCarter, Asenath 202
McCarter, C. L. H. 295
McCarter, Christopher 41, 147
McCarter, Christopher L. 296
McCarter, Christopher L. H. 358
McCarter, David 202
McCarter, David Byers 282
McCarter, David Z. 358
McCarter, E. 324
McCarter, Ebenezar 202
McCarter, Eleazer 202
McCarter, Eli Erwin 282
McCarter, Elias 146, 147, 274, 296, 305, 358
McCarter, Elizabeth 147, 282, 358
McCarter, Elizabeth C. 316
McCarter, Elizabeth Olivia 261
McCarter, G. A. 305
McCarter, George A. 147, 358
McCarter, George Alexander 146
McCarter, Hannah 202
McCarter, Hannah L. 358
McCarter, Ina[?] 202
McCarter, Isabella 202
McCarter, Isabella J. 343
McCarter, James 146, 147, 323

## PERSONAL NAME INDEX

McCarter, James A. 358
McCarter, James L. 295, 358
McCarter, Jane 264
McCarter, Jemima 322
McCarter, Joel 202, 343
McCarter, John 146, 147, 202, 344, 358
McCarter, John C. 358
McCarter, Kizziah 202
McCarter, Margaret 343
McCarter, Margery 264
McCarter, Mary 147, 342
McCarter, Mesinah 146
McCarter, Minor 282
McCarter, Nixency V. C. 343
McCarter, Oliver J. 343
McCarter, P. 212
McCarter, Robert 102, 103, 146, 147, 358
McCarter, Robert C. 323
McCarter, Rosanah 147
McCarter, Samuel 343
McCarter, Samuel W. 342, 343
McCarter, Sarah 202, 264, 282
McCarter, Sarah E. 358
McCarter, Sarah L. 342
McCarter, Scintha 102
McCarter, Simpson Hervey 282
McCarter, Thomas 282
McCarter, Walter 202
McCarter, William 146, 147
McCaula, R. C. 284
McCaw, Agness 107
McCaw, John 20, 78, 157, 270, 357
McCaw, John A. 132
McCaw, John B. 357
McCaw, Mary 157
McCaw, Nancy 270, 357
McCaw, R. G. 270
McCaw, Robert 116, 139, 157, 270, 277
McCaw, Robert G. 285, 286
McCaw, William 157
McCellan, Susannah 205
McCheney, James 215
McClain, Amziah 247
McClain, Andrew 121
McClain, Anne 121
McClain, John J. 220
McClain, Louse 121
McClain, Messina 121
McClain, Oliver 142

McClain, Rachel 121
McClain, Wm. 41, 63
McClanaghan, Tenney 108
McClaren, Robt 175
McClean, Jno D. 153
McClean, Moses 211
McClean, William 81, 96, 97
McClelan, Anne 46
McClelan, Elias Baxter 46
McClelan, Elisabeth 29
McClelan, Hugh 29
McClelan, Priscilla 46
McClelan, Robert 47
McClelan, Mary Anne 46
McCleland, Agness 26
McCleland, Elizabeth 25, 26
McCleland, Hugh 25, 26
McCleland, James 25, 26, 90
McCleland, Jane 26
McCleland, John 46, 90
McCleland, Jordan 90
McCleland, Margaret 90
McCleland, Mary Anne 46
McCleland, Polly 90
McCleland, Robert 25, 46
McCleland, Ruthey 90
McCleland, Samuel 46, 47, 90
McCleland, Sidney 90
McCleland, Susanna 90
McCleland, Thomas 46, 47
McCleland, William 25, 90
McClellan, Elias 205
McClellan, Elias B. 263
McClellan, John 149
McClellan, John D. 205
McClellan, Priscilla 190
McClellan, Robert 205, 254
McClelland, Ann 129
McClelland, Elizabeth 129
McClelland, Hugh 26
McClelland, Jinny 129
McClelland, Martha 129
McClelland, Mary 293
McClelland, Robt 126
McClelland, Thomas 129, 266
McClelland, William 26, 266
McClenachan, John 192
McClenaghan, James 122
McClenaghan, Jane 108
McClenaghan, John 108, 122
McClenaghan, Margaret 122
McClenaghan, Robert 122

## PERSONAL NAME INDEX

McClenaghan, Tenny 122
McClenahan, James 173
McClenahan, Jane 236, 281
McClenahan, John 24, 79, 80, 94, 111, 173
McClenahan, John L. 173
McClenahan, John S. 236
McClennan, John 305
McClintock, Polly 87
McCluney, James 230
McClure, Catherine E. 328
McClure, John 352
McClure, William 352
McColloch, Saml 132
McCollock 58
McColm, Duncan 181
McColm, Durnay 221
McColum[?], Duncan 176
McConnel, Andrew 167, 359
McConnel, James 187
McConnel, John 85, 106, 115, 359
McConnel, Mary 120, 359
McConnel, Reuben 135
McConnell, Andrew 196, 203, 218, 221, 252
McConnell, Emily 339
McConnell, Esther Serefina 317
McConnell, John 32, 317
McConnell, John R. 255
McConnell, R. 255, 291
McConnell, R. M. 304
McConnell, R(e)uben 29, 304
McConnell, Samuel 32
McConnell, Samuel G. 32
McCool, James 160
McCool, James A. 159
McCorckle, Jos 185
McCorckle, Wm 112, 114
McCord, Daniel 120
McCord, James 18
McCord, Jane 18
McCord, John 18, 120, 218
McCord, Sarah 120
McCord, William 18
McCorkel, Abraham 8
McCorkel, James 79
McCorkle, Abraham 27
McCorkle, Betsy 27
McCorkle, Elizabeth 27, 160
McCorkle, James 27, 30, 32
McCorkle, Jane B. 267
McCorkle, Joseph 27, 32, 267

McCorkle, Joseph W. 184, 221, 239, 267
McCorkle, Margaret 27
McCorkle, Mary 27
McCorkle, Robert R. 326, 328
McCorkle, Stephen 27, 178, 207
McCorkle, W. H. 279, 318, 326, 328, 348
McCorkle, W. R. 332
McCorkle, William 95
McCorkle, William H. 267, 341
McCormick, Robt 38
McCosh, Jas 196
McCosh, Joseph 225, 346
McCottry, John 216
McCown, Eleanor 6
McCown, Martha 10
McCoy, James 6
McCoy, John 258, 271, 277
McCraven, A. 81
McCraw, John 30
McCreedy, William 175
McCreight, Robert 175
McCreight, Wm. 94
McCrevan, Adam 80
McCuen, Joseph 184
McCulloch, James 132, 149
McCulloch, John 228
McCulloch, Samuel 45, 141, 149, 157
McCullock, Jas 134
McCullock, John 45
McCullock, Thos 175
McCulloh, David 344
McCullough, James 135
McCullough, Mary 86, 126
McCullough, Robert 81
McCullough, Samuel 86, 126, 135, 141
McCullough, Sarah 86
McCullough, Thomas 126
McCullum, D. A. 292
McCullum, Peter 292
McCully, Ervine 295
McCully, James 74, 175, 176, 271, 295, 296
McCully, James C. 296
McCully, James L. 295
McCully, James R. 295, 317
McCully, Jane 294-296, 335
McCully, Jennet 175
McCully, John 295
McCully, Mary 296, 335

## PERSONAL NAME INDEX

McCully, R. E. 317
McCully, Rebecca 296, 335
McCully, Samuel 104, 175, 176, 295
McCurdry, Mary 52
McCurdry, Robert 52
McDaniel, Anna Sims 159
McDaniel, Catherine Christmas 159
McDaniel, Eli 308
McDaniel, Mary 159
McDaniel, Sarah Gist 159
McDaniel, Thomas 159
McDow, Wm Thomas 233
McDowell, David 330
McElhaney, Thos J. 209, 223
McElhany, Eli 209, 213
McElhany, James 209, 213, 244
McElhany, John 223, 246
McElhany, Thos J. 201
McElhenny, Thomas J. 283, 352
McEllwee, Wm. 132
McElmoile, Daniel 94
McElmoile, James 94
McElmoile, John 94
McElmoile, Margret 94
McElmoile, Mary 94
McElmoyl, Daniel 305
McElmoyl, Mary S. 304, 305
McElmoyle, Daniel 187
McElwain, Charles 167, 193, 218
McElwain, David 167, 178
McElwain, Jane 167
McElwain, John 167, 224
McElwain, Robert 48, 116
McElwaine, Peggy 184
McElwee 139
McElwee, Agnes 310
McElwee, Catharine 326, 328
McElwee, Catherine 328
McElwee, Catherine E. 326
McElwee, Elizabeth 235-237
McElwee, George 246
McElwee, Gracy 247
McElwee, J. N. 260, 324
McElwee, J. R. 215, 271
McElwee, James 126, 132, 206, 211, 235, 246, 259, 271, 310, 311, 315, 344
McElwee, James L. 326, 328
McElwee, Jane 235
McElwee, Jane E. 271
McElwee, John 126, 129, 190, 247, 310, 311

McElwee, John N. 271
McElwee, John R. 246
McElwee, Jonathan N. 271, 310, 311
McElwee, Margaret 163, 246, 247, 258, 269
McElwee, Margaret A. 246
McElwee, Margaret W. 326, 328
McElwee, Martha 163
McElwee, Mary E. 326, 328
McElwee, N. 207
McElwee, Nancy 257
McElwee, Newman 315
McElwee, Rachel (McGill) 311
McElwee, Rachel D. 271
McElwee, Rebecca 271, 310
McElwee, Robertson 215
McElwee, Samuel A. 326
McElwee, William 131, 235, 246, 311
McElwee, William Meek 237, 311
McElwee, William W. 326
McEntire 275
McFadden 346
McFadden, A. H. 281
McFadden, Henry 339
McFadden, Isaac 94, 192, 236, 261, 281, 304
McFadden, James 339
McFadden, Jefferson V. 339
McFadden, John 23, 339
McFadden, Nancy 303
McFadden, Robert 213, 339
McFadden, Samuel 339
McFadden, Sarah 339
McFadden, Thomas 339
McFadden, W. P. 312, 349
McFadden, William 339
McFadden, William P. 245, 303, 304, 311, 339
McFaddin, Isaac 94
McFaden, Patrick 23
McFarlan, Josiah 158
McFarlan, Wm. 158
McFarlin 345
McFarlin, John 158
McFarlin, Paletha 158
McFarlin, Peter 158
McFarlin, Richard 158
McFarlin, Seala 158
McFarlin, Wylie 158
Mcfordsany, Mary 92
McGarraties, Michael 10
McGarrity, Elizabeth 5

## PERSONAL NAME INDEX

McGarrity, Michael 5, 10
McGee, Hall T. 233
McGee, John 310
McGee, Martha 233
McGee, Rachel (McGill) 310
McGill, A. J. 287, 345
McGill, Amanda C. 343, 344
McGill, Avelina M. 343
McGill, Betsy Bell 93
McGill, Clarissa H. 343, 344
McGill, Emmeline 310
McGill, H. 168
McGill, James 287
McGill, James H. 323
McGill, James Henry 93
McGill, Jane A. 343, 344
McGill, John 180, 190, 217, 310, 342, 344
McGill, Martha 93
McGill, Mary 344
McGill, Rachel (McElwee) 311
McGill, Rachel (McGee) 310
McGill, Sarah 210
McGill, Thomas 190, 254, 287, 323
McGill, William 93, 124, 126, 128, 129, 189, 190, 247, 295, 344
McGilliard, Martha H. 190
McGilvrey, Elizabeth 264
McGinis, Mary 160
McGinness, Hugh 261
McGowan, Catherine 257
McGowan, Eliz'a 257
McGowan, James Spratt 325
McGowan, John L. 325
McGowan, Mary Roberts 325
McGowan, Robert 325
McGowen, James 125
McGowen, Jane 125
McGowen, Joseph 125
McGowen, Mary 125
McGowen, Wm. 125
McHood, Saml 137
McIlwain, Alexander 304
McIlwain, Charles 315
McIlwain, David 315
McIlwain, Margaret 315
Mcintire, Faith 114
McJunkin, Joseph 84, 106
McJunkin, Marg(a)ret 84, 106
McKeal, Saml 105
McKee, James 40, 66, 72, 129, 138, 150, 169, 249, 288

McKee, James M. 204, 288
McKee, Louisa C. 288
McKee, Margaret 145, 146
McKee, Mary C. 288
McKee, Nancy 146
McKee, Samuel 66, 288
McKee, Thomas 137, 152
McKee, William 8, 28, 40, 66
McKelwee, John 124
McKelwee, Margaret 124
McKenney, 278
McKenney, John 75
McKenzie, Arthur A. 204
McKenzie, Daniel 120
McKenzie, Edward 132
McKenzie, Francis 132
McKenzie, Hezekiah 4, 134
McKenzie, J. E. 155
McKenzie, James 4, 132, 134, 205
McKenzie, Jona 205
McKenzie, Joseph 2, 4, 26, 60, 132, 134, 206
McKenzie, R. Eliza 330
McKenzie, Rebecca 4
McKenzie, Rebeckah 134
McKenzie, Robt 134
McKenzie, Saml 134
McKinney 41
McKinney, Augustus 256
McKinney, James 44, 182, 255
McKinney, Jean 44
McKinney, Joh'a 182
McKinney, John 75
McKinney, Neal 43, 44
McKinney, William 64
McKinzie, Eliza E. 240
McKinzie, Joseph 40, 59, 149
McKlewee, John 117
McKnight, Betsy 3
McKnight, Dixon 250
McKnight, Eleanor 3
McKnight, Elizabeth 250
McKnight, Isabella 3
McKnight, John 4, 201, 211, 224, 225, 250, 293, 324
McKnight, Mary 3, 339
McKnight, Robert 3, 4
McKnight, Sarah 3
McKnight, Thos. K. 203
McKnight, William 250
McKorkle, J. H. 200
McKorkle, James 136

419

## PERSONAL NAME INDEX

McKorkle, Margaret 183
McKoy, Elizabeth 290
McKoy, George Andrew 290
McKoy, Ira 290
McKoy, John 290
McKoy, Julia 290
McKoy, Mary 290
McKoy, Sarah 290
McKoy, William 290
McLain, John 217
McLane, Elizabeth Jackson (Campbell) 176
McLaw, Nancy 156
Mcldree, David 129
McLean-- see also M'Clain, Maclean, McClain, McClean
McLean, J. A. 314, 328, 341
McLean, Jane M. 338
McLean, John C. 342
McLean, John D. 342
McLean, Joseph A. 279, 338
McLean, Martha E. 313, 330
McLean, Mary D. 176
McLean, Mary Margaret 176
McLean, Wm. 48
McLeaven, Moses 42
McLellan, Elias 180
McLure 268
McLure, John 283
McLure, Robert 208, 283, 352
McLure, William 283
McMahan, Thos 125
McMakin, Martha 215
McMakin, Thomas 215
McMean, James 112, 128, 182
McMean, Mary 112
McMeans, Ameline 182
McMeans, Eliza 182
McMeans, Neely 182
McMican, David 37
McMicking, 353
McMorris, William 17
McMurry, Mary White 93
McMurry, Nancy 93
McMurry, William 93
McMurry, William Simpson 93
McNabb, James 357
McNabb, John 29
McNabbs, 1
McNair, Elizabeth 128
McNair, James 128
McNair, Jean 128

McNair, Rach(a)el 128
McNair, Saml 128
McNaught, William 21
McNeal, Jno 211
McNeal, Mary 180
McNeal, Patsy 78
McNeal, T. W. 128
McNeal, Thomas 46
McNeel, Daniel 32
McNeel, Esther 272
McNeel, John 225, 272
McNeel, Mary 176
McNeel, Mary Jane 325
McNeel, S. W. 282
McNeel, Samuel 95
McNeel, Wm R. 272
McNeely, Eliza Ann 243
McNeely, James 242
McNeely, Jane 243
McNeely, Jemima 242
McNeely, Margaret 243
McNeely, Mary 243
McNeely, Robert 200, 243
McNeil, Mary Jane 325
McNelly, Jno T. 200
McNelly, Robert 204
McNight 78
McNight, Elizabeth 42
McNight, Isabella 42
McNight, John 42
McNight, Margret 42
McNight, Mary 42
McNight, Robert 42
McNinch[?], Amanda 338
McPeke, Est(h)er 49
McPhilimey, James 68, 69
McPhilimey, John 68
McQuown, Wm. 6
McR--, Stephen 354
McRea, 38
McReight, James 175
McRight, Eleanor (Graham) 174
McRight, James 174, 175
McRight, Martha 174
McRight, Nancy 174, 175
McRight, Peggy (Williams) 174
McRight, Robert 174
McSwain, 296
McSwain, Catharine 77
McSwain, Catherine 201
McSwain, David 201, 203
McSwain, David J. 201, 203

## PERSONAL NAME INDEX

McSwain, Elisabeth 77
McSwain, George 201, 203
McSwain, Hanor 77
McSwain, James 201
McSwain, John 27, 77, 275
McSwain, Jon'a 170
McSwain, Mary 271
McSwain, Polly 201
McSwain, Sarah 77
McSwain, William 77
McWhorter, 184, 212, 280
McWhorter, Alexander 12, 26
McWhorter, Andrew 90, 124, 131, 135, 200, 208
McWhorter, Betsy 89
McWhorter, Delilah 212
McWhorter, Drusilla 185
McWhorter, Elisabeth 125, 187
McWhorter, George G. 43
McWhorter, Hance 88
McWhorter, Hugh 26, 90, 123, 129, 155, 156, 174
McWhorter, Jane C. 185
McWhorter, John 56
McWhorter, Margaret Ellen 304
McWhorter, Mary 304
McWhorter, Mary Laughridge 304
McWhorter, Moses 25, 26
McWhorter, Sally 26
McWhorter, Thomas 174, 212
McWilliams, Robert 211
McWoods 163
Meacham 250
Meacham, Bartlet/t 148, 192, 198
Meacham, Elizabeth 168
Meacham, Henry 129, 148, 168, 192, 198
Meacham, Henry Banks 129
Meacheam, 192
Meacheam, Bartlet 200, 213
Meacheam, Nancy 213
Means, H. F. 303
Meek, Adam 28, 29, 44, 48, 50, 51, 72, 73, 110, 124
Meek, Agness 73, 124, 241
Meek, Andrew 110
Meek, Ann 73, 124
Meek, Capt. 22
Meek, E. F. 341
Meek, Edward 241
Meek, Eli 157, 319, 333
Meek, Elizabeth 157, 314

Meek, J. M. 338
Meek, James 28, 29, 73, 110, 121, 124, 125, 146, 156, 170, 196, 203, 241, 244
Meek, James B. 229
Meek, Jane 29, 241
Meek, Jean 73
Meek, John 110
Meek, John H. 321
Meek, Mager Adam 33
Meek, Margaret 29, 73, 124
Meek, Martha 250
Meek, Martha K. 330
Meek, Mary 166
Meek, Moses 28, 29, 73, 110
Meek, Robert 110
Meek, Rufus Starr 251
Meek, Thomas 110
Meek, W. 216
Meek, William 73, 110, 124, 211, 217
Meek, Wm. B. 229
Megarrity 5
Meglamery, Elizabeth 58
Meglamery, William 58
Melissa, Nancy 359
Mellon, Elias 151
Mellon, George 37
Mellon, Jane 37
Mellon, John 37
Mellon, Jonathen 37
Mellon, S. 277
Mellon, Zanzas 37
Melton, George W. 350
Melton, S. 167, 271, 290
Melton, S. W. 184, 349
Melton, Samuel 116, 233
Melton, Samuel W. 331, 334, 339
Melton, W. G. 350
Melvaten, John S. 149
Mendenhall, B. J. 342
Meritt, Lucretia 267
Mesheau, Allison P. 332
Mesheau, Daniel 332
Mesheau, Nancy 332
Meshew, Daniel 125
Meshow, Daniel 231
Metts, Walter B. 347
Mickle, Thomas K. 294
Milan, Archibald 40
Milan, James 41
Milan, John 40, 41
Milan, Robert 40, 41

## PERSONAL NAME INDEX

Milan, William 40, 41
Milan, Zenos 151
Mildoon, Elias 141
Miles, Charles 73
Miles, Elizabeth 73
Miles, John 18
Miles, Mary 18
Millan, Ann 40
Millan, Archibald 41
Millan, James 40
Millar, Robert 44
Miller, 158, 268, 270
Miller, A. 174
Miller, Abraham 163, 192
Miller, Anna 114
Miller, Anne 8
Miller, Archy 104
Miller, Benjamin R. 197
Miller, Betsy 309
Miller, Calvin 271
Miller, Catherine 161
Miller, Charles 9
Miller, Charles Gerome 271
Miller, David 114, 330
Miller, David B. 284
Miller, Drusilla 142, 235
Miller, Elisabeth 8
Miller, Eliza Jane 326, 328
Miller, Elizabeth 49, 97, 237, 265
Miller, Elva 163
Miller, Elvy 194
Miller, Francis 187, 219, 257
Miller, Franklin 161
Miller, H. W. 111
Miller, Hannah 8, 9
Miller, Hend(r)y 49
Miller, Henry 49
Miller, Hugh 158, 242
Miller, Ibby 309
Miller, Isabella 114, 330
Miller, J. T. 192
Miller, James 8, 9, 49, 114, 242, 309, 330
Miller, James M. 197
Miller, Jane 9, 142, 171, 218, 222, 235
Miller, Jerome 163
Miller, Jerome C. 306
Miller, Jesse 9, 112, 148, 153
Miller, John 19, 49, 92, 142, 157, 158, 171, 197, 211, 235, 242, 271, 357
Miller, John L. 153
Miller, Jonathan 163, 193

Miller, Joseph 142, 197, 235, 237, 271, 306, 329
Miller, Mary 9, 97, 98, 104, 114, 142, 220, 309
Miller, Mildred 271
Miller, Nancy 196, 197
Miller, Nancy Warren (Neely) 235
Miller, Priscilla 9
Miller, Rachel 142, 197
Miller, Robert 45, 95, 114, 153, 274, 309, 330
Miller, Ruth 114
Miller, Sa. 243
Miller, Samuel 219, 222, 235
Miller, Samuel Neely 197
Miller, Sarah 97, 98
Miller, Sarah M. 192
Miller, Stephen 9
Miller, Thomas 271
Miller, W. P. 215
Miller, W. T. 210
Miller, William 9, 97, 98, 163, 174, 279
Millinder, Rachel 265
Mills, Hugh 118
Mills, John 80
Mills, R. G. 222
Mills, Robt G. 134
Millwee, John 37
Milom, Benjamin 8
Milom, John 8
Milom, Judith 8
Milom, Nancey 8
Milom, Thomas 8
Min, Mary 186
Ming, H. 133
Minges, Rebecca E. 325
Minter, Elizabeth 269
Minter, Ethalinda 269
Minter, Isaac 204, 222, 269
Minter, Jackson 269
Minter, Jacob 83
Minter, Jesse J. 269
Minter, John 82, 83, 101-103, 140, 193, 216, 223, 269
Minter, John L. 269
Minter, John T. 269
Minter, Jonathan 83
Minter, Josiah 83
Minter, Junius 269
Minter, Margaret 83
Minter, Martha 82, 83, 269

## PERSONAL NAME INDEX

Minter, Rebekah 269
Minter, Sarah 83
Minter, William 27, 82, 83, 217, 269
MisCaley[?], Ruth 357
Mishaw, Daniel 231
Misheal, Daniel 136
Miskelly, Frances 56, 357
Miskelly, James 55, 56, 357
Miskelly, Jane 357
Miskelly, Jean 55, 56
Miskelly, John 347
Miskelly, William 55, 56, 357
Misskelly, DeKalb 276
Misskelly, Elizabeth 276
Misskelly, Elizabeth Catharine 276
Misskelly, James 276
Misskelly, John 272
Misskelly, Lucian 276
Misskelly, Newton 276
Misskelly, Samuel 276
Misskelly, Sarah Jane 276
Misskelly, Thomas 276
Mitchel 229
Mitchel, Dawson N. 220
Mitchel, James 97, 105
Mitchel, Johnathan 20
Mitchel, Lilly 20
Mitchel, Thomas 214
Mitchell, 303
Mitchell, Catharine 282
Mitchell, Dawson N. 246, 282
Mitchell, Elizabeth R. R. 254
Mitchell, G. C. 322
Mitchell, H. 321
Mitchell, Henry 278
Mitchell, James 10, 29, 48, 54, 59, 60, 92, 93
Mitchell, Jean 124
Mitchell, John 20
Mitchell, Joseph 278, 340
Mitchell, M. O. 282
Mitchell, Mary Francis 278
Mitchell, Nancy C. W. 254
Mitchell, Rachel 105
Mitchell, Rebecca 278
Mitchell, Robert R. 282
Mitchell, Thomas 278
Mitchell, William 303
Mobley, Mary 121
Moffit, Wm. 191
Molinax, Thos 132
Molinax, Wm 132

Mongomery, John 48
Monks, Jean 90
Montgomery, Benjamin 88
Montgomery, Elizabeth 154
Montgomery, George 23
Montgomery, Hillery 88
Montgomery, James 67, 71, 352
Montgomery, John 126
Montgomery, Lucressey 88
Montgomery, Rebecca 88
Moody 352
Moon, John S. 249, 251
Mooney, Jonathan 22
Mooney, Nancy Minerva 312
Mooney, Rachel 22
Moor, James 138
Moor, Mary 83
Moor, Wm. 335
Moore 39, 71, 95, 145, 229
Moore, Alberta A. 283, 284
Moore, Alexander 23, 24, 28, 31, 33, 36, 40, 41, 44, 49, 59, 81, 101, 105, 167, 184
Moore, Alexander L. 284
Moore, Alfred 101, 105, 154, 158, 179, 188
Moore, Any [Amy?] 203
Moore, Brison 346
Moore, Casinda 282
Moore, Casindare 137
Moore, Catharine 332
Moore, Catherine 101
Moore, Charles 135
Moore, Clark 282, 340
Moore, Colvee[?] 229
Moore, Cyrus 282
Moore, Daniel 181
Moore, Darchus A. 101
Moore, Dianna 229
Moore, Doctor 78
Moore, Dorcus E. 346
Moore, Ealeanor 104
Moore, Edward 104, 245
Moore, Eli 107, 119, 130, 180, 213, 238
Moore, Eli P. 283, 284
Moore, Eliz. A. 332
Moore, Elizabeth 130, 137, 180-182, 346
Moore, Emeline 162
Moore, Francis E. 332
Moore, Francis J. 334, 335

## PERSONAL NAME INDEX

Moore, Frederic/k E. 345, 346
Moore, Gion 334
Moore, Gordan 214
Moore, Gordon 125, 170, 201, 229, 255
Moore, Goyen 228
Moore, H. Baxter 345, 346
Moore, Hannah 113
Moore, Harriet 355
Moore, Henry 137, 282
Moore, Isaac W. 334
Moore, J. M. 258
Moore, J. S. 294
Moore, Jack B. 228
Moore, Jacob A. 228, 229
Moore, Jacob Alexander 228, 229
Moore, Jacob B. 255
Moore, James 41, 59, 101, 102, 104, 117, 137, 170, 187, 202, 232, 244, 273, 284
Moore, James L. 244, 284
Moore, James O. 245, 290
Moore, Jane 16, 17, 209
Moore, Jesse 16, 17, 180
Moore, Jincy 181
Moore, Jno G. 229
Moore, John 16, 17, 101, 103-105, 130, 137, 144, 180, 187, 188, 214, 228, 238, 245, 255, 282, 318, 334, 335, 346, 347
Moore, John Alexr 187
Moore, John Gordon 228, 229
Moore, John M. 244
Moore, John S. 229, 238, 266, 270, 279, 319, 320, 333
Moore, John Starr 130
Moore, Jonas 58, 59
Moore, Jonathan 334
Moore, Joseph 17, 23, 100
Moore, Joseph P. 332
Moore, Josiah 49
Moore, M. A. 145, 187
Moore, Margaret 16
Moore, Martha 278, 340
Moore, Mary 59, 130, 135, 245, 272
Moore, Mary H. 325, 341
Moore, Mary Hall 351
Moore, Maurice A. 101, 284
Moore, Minerva 229
Moore, Nancy 137, 346
Moore, Nancy (Suggs) 245
Moore, Nathan 158, 176, 179, 181
Moore, Nathaniel 107
Moore, Orson 334
Moore, Peggy 181
Moore, Peter Marion 332
Moore, R. S. 272, 286, 299, 301
Moore, Rachel 101
Moore, Richard S. 284
Moore, Robert 16, 17, 180, 238
Moore, Robert J. 119
Moore, Ruth 255
Moore, Ruth B. 334, 335
Moore, S. E. 273, 348
Moore, S. R. 266, 279, 294, 319
Moore, Sally 146
Moore, Samuel 16, 17, 119, 130, 158, 179, 180, 181, 188, 215, 226, 238
Moore, Samuel R. 333
Moore, Sarah 146, 347
Moore, Sarah Alexander 144
Moore, Sophia 355
Moore, Stanhope 180, 181, 238
Moore, Susan Elizabeth 340
Moore, T. A 294
Moore, Temandia 229
Moore, Theodore A. 333
Moore, Thomas 104, 107, 130, 180, 238
Moore, W. A. 272
Moore, Walter W. 245
Moore, William 17, 37, 101, 102, 104, 107, 128, 133, 145, 190, 192, 196, 205, 211, 217, 219, 227, 245, 272, 273, 334, 335, 340, 347
Moore, William A. 284, 333
Moore, William S. 345, 346
Moore, William Thompson 228, 229
Moore, Zenas 180, 238
Moore, Zenos 181
Moore, Zenus L. 179
Moores, Guyen 33
More 278
Moreland, Alex 186
Moreland, James 185
Moreland, John 70
Moreland, Priscilla 316
Morgan, Ann Mary 130
Morgan, Anthony 292
Morgan, Caty 70
Morgan, Elias 292
Morgan, Elizabeth 70, 275
Morgan, George 192
Morgan, Gray 194

## PERSONAL NAME INDEX

Morgan, John 179, 292
Morgan, Louisa A. 292
Morgan, Peter 130, 292
Morgan, Robert 70
Morgan, Saml 292
Morgan, Spencer 292
Moris, Cyrus 112
Moris, Hannah 112
Morow, Richard 211
Morris, Ann Saile 92
Morris, Anne 144
Morris, Ezekial 75, 76, 92, 118, 144
Morris, John 22, 92, 289
Morris, Peter 196
Morris, Rebecah 92
Morris, Rebecca 15
Morris, Tabby 113
Morrison, 153, 353
Morrison, Alex 28
Morrison, Hannah 28, 316, 324
Morrison, James 28
Morrison, Mary H. 352
Morrison, R. H. 352
Morrison, William 28
Morrow, J. M. 306
Morrow, Jas 63
Morrow, Jas R. 202
Morrow, John 63
Morrow, Martha F. (Whisonant) 314
Morrows, James 56
Mosley, John 102, 121
Moss, Eliz'a 256
Moss, Ephraim 256
Moss, Fanny 256
Moss, Gil(l)ey 160, 161, 257
Moss, Henry 192
Moss, Howell 256
Moss, James 256
Moss, Jenny 320
Moss, Jeremiah 256, 257
Moss, Jerusha 336
Moss, John 256, 257
Moss, Joshua 139
Moss, Lewis 256
Moss, Martha 336
Moss, Molly 257
Moss, Nicholas 186
Moss, Patsey 257
Moss, Patty 256
Moss, Polly 256
Moss, Sarah 257
Moss, Willis 140
Moss, Wylie 256
Mtgomery, James 71
Muldoon, David 42
Muldoon, Elias 42
Muldoon, Elinor 42
Muldoon, Elizabeth 42
Muldoon, John 157
Muldoon, Lucinda 42
Muldoon, Mary 42
Muldoon, Rebecca 42
Muldoon, Sarah 42
Mulinax, Isaac 132
Mulinax, Sarah 131
Mulinax, Thos 140
Mullen, Mary Unity 240
Mullenax, Martin 228
Mullin, John 240
Mullinax, Frances 252
Mullinax, Joseph 252, 299
Mullinax, Thomas 252
Mullinax, Thomas H. 299
Mullinax, Wm 132
Murphey, Alex'r 18
Murphey, James 18, 19
Murphey, James L. 263
Murphey, John 18, 170
Murphey, Robert 18, 105
Murphy, Alexander 114, 120
Murphy, Charles T. 229
Murphy, Dorcas E. 284
Murphy, James A. 259, 263
Murphy, Jean 73
Murphy, John 7, 11, 19, 73, 114, 120, 154
Murphy, Margaret 99
Murphy, Rachael 11
Murphy, Robert 32
Myers, John S. 298
Myers, Sophia C. 298
Myers, Wm. R. 298
Myrick, Mathew 82
Nagle, Amelia 205
Nagle, William 205
Nance, Alexander 259
Nance, L. 292
Nance, Rebecca 259
Nance, Thomas 259
Nance, William 216, 259
Nash, F. M. 133
Nash, Lucy 82
Nash, Polley Turner 82
Nash, T. M. 131

## PERSONAL NAME INDEX

Nash, Travis Myrick 82
Nassey, James 357
Neagle, Amelia 313
Neagle, James 205, 313
Neagle, John 313
Neagle, Martha 313
Neagle, Mary Ann 313
Neagle, William 205
Neal, Jeptha 274
Neal, Margaret 26
Neal, Thos C. 294
Neal, W. H. 248, 312
Neel, A. H. 212
Neel, And'w 6
Neel, Benjn 277
Neel, David 356
Neel, James 81
Neel, Jane 356
Neel, Lucy 16
Neel, Margaret 353
Neel, Saml 353
Neel, T. W. L. M. 161
Neel, Thomas 6
Neel, W. H. 253
Neeland, A. 323
Neeland, R. 323
Neeland, Robert 205
Neele, Joseph 81
Neeley, 25
Neeley, Elizabeth 184
Neeley, Samuel 29
Neels, Widow 38
Neely, 78, 251, 260
Neely, Alexander 266
Neely, Amzi 101
Neely, Ann 4, 5
Neely, Benjamin 212, 213, 225, 226, 235, 237
Neely, Charity 160
Neely, Charles 134
Neely, Clarinda 101
Neely, Clarissa 101
Neely, Cynthia 215, 250
Neely, David 4, 27, 112, 215
Neely, Elizabeth 185, 227, 235, 237, 239
Neely, Frances 312
Neely, Hance 280, 328
Neely, Hannah 4
Neely, Hyde 266
Neely, Jackson 37, 112
Neely, James C. 138

Neely, James P. 228
Neely, Jane 5, 91, 165, 264
Neely, Jaxon 5
Neely, Jean 128
Neely, Job L. 288
Neely, John 37, 227, 228, 266
Neely, Jonathan 139
Neely, Jonathan M. 138
Neely, Margaret H. 302
Neely, Martha 102, 124
Neely, Mary 42, 138, 266
Neely, Matthew 5
Neely, Moses 31
Neely, Nancy Emaline[?] 138
Neely, Nancy Warren (Miller) 235
Neely, Peggy Eliz. 138
Neely, Robert 5, 24
Neely, Samuel 4, 5, 37, 38, 82, 109, 235, 352
Neely, Scinthia 218
Neely, Thomas 4, 86, 112, 114, 160
Neely, Thomas S. 250
Neely, Thomas M. 138, 220
Neely, Tillotson 267
Neely, Tillotson S. 238, 239
Neely, Tollotson 185
Neely, Tollotson S. 184
Neely, Violet 195, 309, 312
Neely, William 93, 106, 112, 141, 184, 186, 215, 218, 239, 302
Neely, Wm. H. 215
Neely, Zekiel 238
Neil 342
Neil, Martha 258, 301
Neill, A. H. 269
Neilson, T. S. 98
Nelson, 77, 291
Nelson, Andrew 86, 355
Nelson, Anne 86
Nelson, Jim 107
Nelson, Margaret 86
Nelson, Mary 320
Nelson, Mary C. 273
Nelson, Robert 86, 307
Nelson, W. N. 329
Nelson, William 86, 214, 215, 236, 321
Nelsons, William 74
Nesbit, Alexander 213
Nesbit, Margaret 213
Nesbit, Martha 173
Nesbitt, Samuel 18

## PERSONAL NAME INDEX

Nesmith, Jean 74
Nesmith, Jenny 133
Neville, John 354
Newman, Jonathan 310
Newton, Thomas 122
Nichells, Daniel 6
Nicholes, William 145, 146
Nichols, Betsy 265
Nichols, Daniel 313
Nichols, Mathew 324
Nickells, Margaret 6
Nickels, John 23
Nickes, James 6
Nickles, James 23
Nickles, Jane 23
Nickles, Matthew 23
Nickoles, William 145
Nickolls, Francis 219
Nickolls, Francis J. 218
Nickolls, Martha 219
Nickols, Edmund 294
Niell, Martha 269
Night, Mary 75
Nisbet, Alexander G. 215
Nisbett, Cathy 176
Nisbett, Francis 176
Nisbett, James 176
Nisbett, Jane 176
Nisbett, Nancy 176
Nisbett, Robert 176
Nisbett, William 176
Nisbit, William A. 255
Nisbitt, William 176
Niven, Daniel 287
Niven, James 287
Niven, Jesse 262, 287
Niven, John 288
Niven, Joseph Green 287
Niven, Patience 287
Niven, Pricilla 287
Niven, William Harvey 287
Nogan, Rachel 182
Nolen, Elizabeth 264
Norman 140
Norris, Melissa 146
Norwood, Susanah 125
Oats, Jane 246
Oats, Margaret A. 343
Oats, William 247, 344
Oldrage, Hannah 352
ONeal, Wm. 106
Orr, Augustus 294

Orr, James Harvey 294
Orr, John H. 294
Orr, Martha M. 312
Orr, Moses Manlius 294
Orr, Samuel Harris 312
Osborn, Emsley 310
Otterson, Narcissa 146
Ouneil, James 23
Ouneil, William 23
Owen, Virgil 252
Owens, James H. 157, 161
Packard, Leander 192
Packard, Margaret 192
Packard, Marthay 192
Packard, Mary 192
Packard, W. M. 295
Packard, William 192
Packard, Zad(d)ock 158, 192
Packard, Zedoc 192
Packherd, Zadock 186
Pair, Mial 136
Pair, Sally 136
Pair, Sarah 136
Palkard, Mary 192
Palkard, Zaddock 192
Palmer, 300
Palmer, Amanda F. 335
Palmer, Cynthia 274
Palmer, Henry 48
Palmer, Joshua 207, 274
Pane[?], Robert 123
Param, Sarah 211
Pardue, James M. 298
Parham, Elizabeth 237
Parham, James 237
Parham, Rhoda 18
Parish, Augustus 261
Parish, Isaac 108
Parker, Barton 254
Parker, Edy/Eda 119
Parker, Jess 87
Parker, John 228
Parker, John Lindsey 119
Parker, Robert 70
Parker, Susan 228
Parker, Thomas 70
Parks, Henry 295
Parks, Joseph 238, 295
Parks, Margaret T. (Watson) 301
Parks, Mary Adaline 294
Parks, Wm. 238
Parson, Benjamin 99, 168

## PERSONAL NAME INDEX

Parsons, Isaac 108
Partlow, D. P. 313
Partlow, Jane 262
Partlow, M. C. 313
Partlow, R. C. 313
Partlow, Robert C. 316
Partlow, William 62
Partton, Wm. 91
Patillow, Samuel 203
Patrick, Alexander 278
Patrick, An'd 180
Patrick, Anny 137
Patrick, Betsey 104
Patrick, Catharine 275
Patrick, Clinton 323
Patrick, Davey 143
Patrick, David 101, 143, 144, 188
Patrick, David Josiah Jesse 261
Patrick, E. 279
Patrick, Eleanor Paulina 261
Patrick, Elias 143, 244
Patrick, Elijah 279
Patrick, Elizabeth 143, 204, 261, 278
Patrick, Elizabeth Olivia 261
Patrick, Esther (Bigger) 96
Patrick, Franky Louise 244
Patrick, George A. 330
Patrick, George Anderson 244
Patrick, Isabella 96
Patrick, J. C. 317
Patrick, James 206
Patrick, James Duf 143
Patrick, James Reese 244
Patrick, Jesse 143
Patrick, John 278
Patrick, John A. 188, 189, 212
Patrick, John Allison 261
Patrick, John T. C. 275
Patrick, Joseph 278
Patrick, Joshua 31
Patrick, Josiah 143
Patrick, Josiah C. 317, 323
Patrick, Josiah Clinton 244
Patrick, Josius 143
Patrick, Lucinda 232
Patrick, Margrett 97
Patrick, Mary 96, 212, 342
Patrick, Mary Caroline 261
Patrick, Mary Elizabeth 244
Patrick, Mary H. 323
Patrick, Polly 212
Patrick, Rebecca Irrebella 261

Patrick, Robert 10, 31, 41, 66, 96, 97, 104, 115, 137, 143-145, 147, 154, 188, 189, 342
Patrick, Robert Vaughan 244
Patrick, Rosannah 96, 97
Patrick, Samuel 278
Patrick, Sarah 96, 97, 143
Patrick, Thomas 217, 245, 342
Patrick, Thomas J. Clinton 261
Patrick, William 41, 42, 101, 104, 115, 143, 188, 275, 323
Patrick, William D. 323
Patten, David 191
Patterson, Andrew 101, 103, 115
Patterson, Benjamin 63, 256
Patterson, Bobbit 256
Patterson, Elizabeth 12, 114, 115, 167, 205, 296, 313, 326
Patterson, Frances 294
Patterson, George 13, 63
Patterson, Hannah 167
Patterson, Isbel 1
Patterson, Jackson 256
Patterson, James 167
Patterson, John 1, 12, 24, 37, 101, 103, 139
Patterson, John Green 114
Patterson, Joseph 12
Patterson, Littleberry 136
Patterson, Littlebury 63
Patterson, Lydia 12
Patterson, Margaret J. 304
Patterson, Mary 101, 167
Patterson, Peter 12, 28
Patterson, Rebecca 24
Patterson, Rebeckah 120
Patterson, Richard 167
Patterson, Robert 12
Patterson, Sarah 12, 28
Patterson, Smith 256, 306, 322
Patterson, Susan 256
Patterson, Thomas 12
Patterson, William 12, 24
Patton, D. S. 293
Patton, David 79, 137, 200
Patton, David S. 192, 297, 300
Patton, Elizabeth 25
Patton, James 25, 79, 236
Patton, James W. 353
Patton, Jane 25
Patton, John 25, 79, 105, 200
Patton, Joseph 79, 108, 111

## PERSONAL NAME INDEX

Patton, Margaret 25, 308
Patton, Martha 136
Patton, Mary 79
Patton, Nelly 79
Patton, Robert 14, 79, 111, 252, 297
Patton, Sarah 79, 111
Patton, Thomas 25, 79, 116, 156
Patton, William 25, 91
Pattrick, William 103
Peeler, Anthony 63
Peeler, Daniel 63, 287
Peeler, Ruipheny 69
Peeler, Susan 287
Peler, Aaron 287
Peler, Elizabeth 287
Penic, 300
Penick, Elizabeth N. 350
Penick, Wm. C. 215
Perce, Mary 156
Perkins, H. 98
Perry, 306
Perry, C. R. 288
Perry, James 132, 206
Perry, Joseph W. Thomson 146
Perry, Rebecca A. 319
Persley, James 125
Persley, James McCord 125
Persley, Jane 125
Persley, Louisa 125
Persley, Rachael M. 125
Persley, Robert 125
Persley, Sarah 125
Person, B. 100
Person, Benjamin 143
Persons, Benjamin 108, 118, 122, 129, 138, 148
Peter, 281
Peter, John 103
Peters, Jacob 72, 125, 130
Peters, James 125, 130, 131, 247, 358
Peters, John 130, 155, 189, 224, 247, 255
Peters, Martha 130, 247, 358
Peters, Mary 255
Peters, Sarah 255
Peters, William 94, 130
Pettes, Agness 37
Pettes, John 37
Pettes, Stephen 37
Pettis, George 37, 38
Pettis, John 38
Pettis, Mary 37

Pettis, Rebecca 38
Pettis, Samuel Knox 38
Pettis, Stephen 38
Pettis, William 37, 38, 99, 100
Pettus, Ann D. (Clawson) 117, 118
Pettus, Benjamin Russ 260
Pettus, Eliza Ann 260
Pettus, Elizabeth 117
Pettus, George 38, 117, 118, 122, 192, 226, 260, 282
Pettus, Hannah Jane 260
Pettus, Jane 260
Pettus, Jane (Gutridge) 117, 118
Pettus, Jean 117, 118
Pettus, John 353
Pettus, John D. 138
Pettus, John D. O. K. 117
Pettus, Marria 122
Pettus, Mary (Burton) 117, 118
Pettus, Mary Elizabeth 260
Pettus, Rebecca W. 122
Pettus, Rebeckah W. 117, 118
Pettus, Samuel 138
Pettus, Samuel K. 121, 122
Pettus, Sarah 117, 118
Pettus, Saul 194
Pettus, Sintha/y 117, 118
Pettus, Stephen 117, 118, 138, 194, 200
Pettus, Stephen B. 122
Pettus, Stephen D. 260
Pettus, Stephen R. 122
Pettus, Susanna 117, 118
Pettus, Thomas N. 122, 260
Pettus, Violet 138
Pettus, William 91, 94, 118, 122
Pettus, William W. 122
Petty, Joshua 145
Phagan, James 229
Pierce, Cordelia 154, 155
Pilcher, John 110, 124, 156, 166, 179, 203
Pilcher, Robert 124, 179
Pinner, Robt 140
Plaxco, George 36, 125
Plaxco, Henry 20
Plaxco, James 20, 36, 125
Plaxco, Jane 20
Plaxico, W. S. 324
Plexco, G. W. 192
Plexco, George 106, 130, 169, 185, 186, 192

## PERSONAL NAME INDEX

Plexco, Henry G. 200
Plexco, James 228, 244
Plexco, John 125
Plexco, John J. 230
Plexco, John P. 244
Plexco, John T. 244
Plexco, Margaret 213
Plexco, Patsy 213
Plexco, Wm 192, 196
Plexico, Emeline 300
Plexico, Emeline N. 309
Plexico, Henry G. 284, 300
Plexico, J. Edward 300
Plexico, J. G. 291, 318
Plexico, J. S. 338
Plexico, James 284, 300
Plexico, James E. 300
Plexico, James G. 284, 300
Plexico, Jane 284
Plexico, John Ager 300
Plexico, John S. 284
Plexico, John T. 167, 284, 300
Plexico, Joseph 300
Plexico, Martha 300
Poag, Dorcas M. 330
Poag, Esther 258, 291, 304
Poag, James 157, 209, 330
Poag, Jane Elizabeth 304
Poag, John 71
Poag, Joseph 258
Poag, Louisa 291
Poag, Louisa J. 304
Poag, Mary Elizabeth 330
Poag, Mary H. 304
Poag, Mary Harriet 258
Poag, Mary J. 343
Poag, Matilda 221
Poag, Nancy 209
Poag, Nancy Adeline 330
Poag, Nancy M. 320, 322, 330
Poag, Samuel 71
Poag, Selena 330
Poag, William 258
Poag, William Barnet 117
Pog, Nancy M. 322
Polk, Charles 149
Polk, Eleanor 54, 56
Polk, Elizabeth 148, 149
Polk, John 54, 55, 122, 149, 191, 287
Polk, Mary 94
Polk, Taylor 56
Polk, William 149

Polkard, Mary 192
Polly, Rebeckah 112
Ponder, Jesse 132
Porter, 280, 353
Porter, Agnes 3
Porter, Ann 3
Porter, Betsy B. W. 99
Porter, Charles 1
Porter, David 3, 34, 42, 43
Porter, David H. 169
Porter, Elizabeth 99
Porter, Francis 43
Porter, Isabel 42
Porter, James 3, 38, 43, 154, 169, 170
Porter, Jane 231
Porter, Jeane 20
Porter, John 30, 34, 35, 43
Porter, Matthew 3
Porter, Nathaniel 3, 22
Porter, Peggy 43
Porter, Rebecca 3
Porter, Robert 113
Porter, Ruth 3
Porter, Samuel 3
Porter, Sarah 3
Porter, Violet 3
Porter, William 42, 43, 231
Potts, John 30
Potts, William 26, 30
Powel, Elizabeth 242
Powel, John 108
Powell, B. F. 319
Powell, Betsey 33
Powell, James 33, 55, 59
Powell, Jane 214
Powell, Jennet 33
Powell, John 33, 214
Powell, Nancy 33
Powell, Patsey 33
Powell, Rachel 214
Powell, Sarah 33
Powell, Sarah (Smith) 55
Powell, Thomas 33, 55
Powell, Volhonorous 33
Prather, 352
Prescot, Rebecca 279
Pressley, David M. 332
Pressley, Elias N. 246
Pressley, Elizabeth 328, 329
Pressley, James 112
Pressley, R. M 221, 328, 329
Pressley, Rebeckah 195

## PERSONAL NAME INDEX

Pressley, Richard M. 181
Pressley, Sarah 197
Pressley, Wm. 181, 209, 221, 227, 237, 247, 328
Pressly, Eliza 238
Pressly, Mary 238
Pressly, Wm. 238, 329
Price, Isaac 31, 152, 210
Price, John 38
Price, Mary 117
Price, Nancy 167, 210
Price, Thomas B. 248
Priestly, Betsey 184
Pugh, Edward C. 132
Pugh, Jacob 324
Pugh, John 324
Pugh, Rebecca 324
Pugh, Tomas 324
Punch 7
Purdy, Jane 173
Purley, Robert 212
Pursley, Catherine 212
Pursley, David 5, 6
Pursley, Elizabeth 289
Pursley, Ephraim 6
Pursley, J. E. 337
Pursley, James 5, 6, 189, 212, 215
Pursley, James M. 189
Pursley, Jane 5
Pursley, Jean 6
Pursley, John 5
Pursley, Mary 212
Pursley, Polly 212
Pursley, Robert 5, 6, 137, 212, 215, 344, 349
Pursley, William B. 212, 299
Pursly, Wm. B. 299
Putman, Hannah 119
Putman, Thomas 119
Putman, William 275
Quay, Aaron F. 327
Queen, Thomas 144
Quick, Nancy 269
Quin, James 71, 123
Quin, Jno 213
Quin, Sophia 117
Quin, Walter 71
Quin, Wm. 126, 161
Quinn 307
Quinn, Anderson 130
Quinn, Fanny 168
Quinn, Geo. W. 345

Quinn, James 155, 156, 267
Quinn, John 213, 222, 267
Quinn, Margaret 267
Quinn, Peter 168
Quinn, Richard 145
Quinn, Robt 269
Quinn, Solomon 174, 213, 267
Quinn, Walter 247, 267
Quinn, William 117
Quinton 63
Quinton, Mary 337
Rachford, Jennet 22
Rachford, Mary 356
Rachford, William 356
Rainey, James 180
Rainey, Jane 15
Rainey, John 172, 183, 203, 220, 222, 244, 285
Rainey, Julia B. 282
Rainey, Lilley Ann 172
Rainey, Rebecka 172
Rainey, Robert 171, 172, 274
Rainey, Rosanna/h 172
Rainey, Samuel 130, 158, 179, 180, 188, 238, 282, 292
Rainey, Sarah 285
Rainey, William 15, 56, 172, 183
Rainey, William G. 172
Rainy, Samuel 181
Ramsay, Martha 276
Ramsey 337
Ramsey, Abraham 142
Ramsey, Alexander 78, 142
Ramsey, David 142
Ramsey, Harvey 142
Ramsey, Henry 142
Ramsey, James 2, 22, 36, 40, 74, 84
Ramsey, Jean 78
Ramsey, Jenny 84, 142
Ramsey, John 34, 64, 142
Ramsey, Leny[?] 142
Ramsey, Martha 84, 179
Ramsey, Polly 252
Ramsey, Sarah 14, 142
Ramsey, Sary 252
Ramsey, Thomas 142
Ramsey, William 84
Ramsy, Martha 252
Ramsy, Thomas 175
Randal, John 139
Randall, Hanna/h 69
Randall, Jacob 69, 196

## PERSONAL NAME INDEX

Randall, James 196, 227
Randall, John 69, 117
Randall, Levi 69
Randall, Phebe 69
Randall, Silas 69
Randle, John 117
Randolph, Franklin 268
Raney, John 222
Rankers[?], Wm 279
Ratchford, Eliza 318
Ratchford, Eliza J. 318
Ratchford, Elizabeth 286
Ratchford, G. R. 257, 318, 348
Ratchford, George 62, 63, 109, 113, 189, 318
Ratchford, George R. 318
Ratchford, James A. 318
Ratchford, James W. 318
Ratchford, John 62, 80, 109, 298, 318
Ratchford, Joseph 62, 109
Ratchford, Margaret J. 318
Ratchford, Mary 25, 48, 63, 109
Ratchford, Moses 48, 62, 63, 109
Ratchford, Robert W. 318
Ratchford, Samuel 62, 63, 109
Ratchford, Sarah Catharine 298
Ratchford, William 21, 62, 63, 109
Rattree, Jas 253
Rattree, Thomas 253
Rawlinson, Franklin 346
Rawlinson, J. W. 262
Rawlinson, Jane C. 345, 346
Rawls, Shadrach 26
Rawls, Simpson 332
Rawls, William 332
Ray 337
Ray, Agness 9
Ray, Henry 9, 103
Ray, Isabell 9
Ray, Sarah 9
Rea, Alexander 67
Rea, Charlotte 113
Rea, Elizabeth 67, 113
Rea, Francis 66, 67
Rea, Henry 41, 241
Rea, John 122
Rea, Mary 67, 241, 274
Rea, Sarah 67, 113
Rea, Seah 66
Rea, William 67
Read, 48, 268
Read, Wm. 67

Redmond, James 40
Reed, Ewd. 189
Reed, George 85
Reed, Joseph 143, 160
Reed, Thos 163
Reeve, James 128
Reeves 296
Reeves, Allen 23, 100, 221
Reeves, Cynth(i)a 211, 221
Reeves, Elisabeth 18, 329
Reeves, Fredrick 23, 27
Reeves, Hiram 182
Reeves, James 147, 221
Reeves, James Allen 221
Reeves, James R. 149
Reeves, John 329
Reeves, Nancy 329
Reeves, Polly 221
Reeves, Rebecca 18
Reeves, Robinson 221
Reeves, Scintha 221
Reeves, Wiley 148
Reeves, Wm 115, 116, 152, 153
Regin 160
Reid, Joseph 279
Reid, Mary 150
Reid, Thomas 126, 133, 149, 150, 157, 162
Remey, John 217
Renicks, Elizabeth 59
Renicks, James 59
Renicks, Jean 59
Renicks, Mary 58, 59
Renix, Mary 27
Rennick, 109
Reynolds, Charlotte J. 299
Rhea, Archd 186
Rhea, Rebecca 323
Rice 353
Rice, D. S. 312
Rice, David J. 309
Rice, F. J. 312
Rice, W. J. 309
Richardson, James 28
Richardson, Jane 28
Richardson, Margaret 27
Richardson, Thomas 28
Richey, John 26
Riddel, Benjamin 178
Riddel, Genny 178
Riddel, George 178
Riddel, Hugh 178

## PERSONAL NAME INDEX

Riddel, John 178
Riddel, Peggy 178
Riddle, Benjamin P. 180
Riddle, Benjamin Peter 178
Riddle, George 26, 180
Riddle, Hugh 115, 127, 143, 152
Riddle, John 134, 149, 295
Riddle, Margaret 133, 178
Riddle, Martha 143
Ridley, Jane 6
Right, James L. 257
Riley, James 1
Rimmon, John 175
Rippy, Edward 346
Rippy, Mary 346
Rippy, Selina 346
Risk, James 46
Rite, Margaret 212
Roach, Abraham 18
Roach, Margaret 347
Roach, Margaret A. 348
Roach, Mary 18
Roach, S. M. 262
Roach, Samuel 148, 153
Roach, Sarah 293
Roach, Thomas 115, 120, 148
Roark, Reese M. 234
Robb, Joseph 28, 102
Robbisson, John 216
Roberson, Archibald 107
Roberson, Wm. 50
Roberts, Allen 266
Roberts, Andrew 170, 171, 196
Roberts, Andrew J. 355
Roberts, Celinda 121
Roberts, J. M. 316
Roberts, James 112, 121
Roberts, Jean 355
Roberts, Jess/e 73, 170, 171, 180
Roberts, Jesse M. 355
Roberts, John 121, 170, 171, 196, 355
Roberts, John J. 196
Roberts, Nancy 196
Roberts, Nancy (Bowen) 171
Roberts, Rachel E. 355
Roberts, Salinda 170
Roberts, Samuel 171
Roberts, Sarah 121
Robertson, Allan 323
Robertson, Allen 254, 266, 283, 323
Robertson, Benjamin 208
Robertson, Charity 207, 208

Robertson, Charles 62, 76, 78, 115, 116, 125, 139
Robertson, Charley 68
Robertson, Davis 125
Robertson, Elias 125
Robertson, Elihu 208
Robertson, James 208, 323
Robertson, John 116, 154, 208
Robertson, John H. 207, 208
Robertson, Jos O. 208
Robertson, Margaret 200
Robertson, Martha E. 283
Robertson, Nancy 112
Robertson, Rachel Dutathy 207, 208
Robertson, Rebecca 283
Robertson, Rebecka 323
Robertson, Rosinda R. 283
Robertson, S. 323
Robertson, Sally Minerva 207, 208
Robertson, Samuel 51
Robertson, Thomas 111, 115, 116, 137, 154, 174, 194, 208, 241, 283, 323
Robertson, William 49, 55, 112, 208
Robertson, Wm. L. 283, 294
Robeson, Arthur 137
Robeson, Mary 140
Robeson, Nancy 113
Robeson, William 113, 144
Robesson, Robert 216
Robinson, Agnes 17
Robinson, Allen 194, 219
Robinson, Archibald 113
Robinson, Arthur 113
Robinson, Catharine 20
Robinson, Cetura 17
Robinson, Charles 20
Robinson, Charleston 19
Robinson, Elijah 194
Robinson, Isabel/la 216, 301
Robinson, James 20, 217, 224
Robinson, James G. 166
Robinson, Jane 17, 134
Robinson, John 20
Robinson, Lucy 20
Robinson, Margaret 22, 183
Robinson, Martha 134
Robinson, Mary 140, 257
Robinson, Mary C. 224
Robinson, Melissa 216
Robinson, Nancy J. 241
Robinson, Patrick 18

## PERSONAL NAME INDEX

Robinson, Rebeckah 197
Robinson, Robert 134, 224
Robinson, Rocinda R. 241
Robinson, Samuel 18, 191
Robinson, Sarah 17, 20
Robinson, Thomas 106, 131, 155, 221, 251
Robinson, Washington 20
Robinson, William 20, 22, 107, 108, 110, 113, 134, 144
Robison, Andrew E. 324
Robison, Archibald 112, 137
Robison, Clark 112
Robison, Elizabeth 293
Robison, J. W. 334
Robison, Joseph 18, 324
Robison, Martha 113
Robison, Mary 293
Robison, Mary Catherine 113
Robison, Nancy 112
Robison, Richard 38
Robison, Thos 131
Robison, William 113, 216, 293, 324
Robisson, Clark 216
Robisson, Isabella 216
Robisson, James 216
Roddey, David 58
Roddey, John 236, 263, 287
Roddy, David 57, 58, 251, 273, 340
Roddy, David C. 339, 340
Roddy, John 261, 340
Roddy, Joseph W. 340
Roddy, Margaret J. 340
Roddy, Martha/n A. 340
Roddy, Mary G. 339, 340
Roddy, Mary J. 340
Roddy, Nancy G. 340
Roddy, Nancy Jane 340
Roddy, Sarah L. 340
Roddy, Thos. E. 339, 340
Roddy, Wm. L. 339, 340
Rodgers, Alice 47
Rodgers, Jonas 39, 47
Rodgers, Joseph 183
Rodgers, Michael 47
Rodgers, Ralph 44, 48
Rogers, Hugh 39
Rogers, Isaac 354
Rogers, J. 86
Rogers, James 161, 196
Rogers, James E. 280, 281
Rogers, Louisa 354

Rogers, Mary Jane 281
Rogers, Nancy 280, 281
Rogers, Narcissa 354
Rogers, Sally 354
Rogers, Sarah 354
Rogers, William 354
Rogers, Wm. D. 287
Rollins 120
Rooker, J. 153
Rooker, J. H. 213
Rooker, Jacob 167
Rooker, John 38, 39, 47
Rooker, Joseph D. 167
Rooker, Rebeckah 201
Rooker, Sarah 343
Rosborough, John 321
Rosborough, Nelly 321
Ross, Abigail T. 161
Ross, Alexander 11, 116
Ross, Andrew 161
Ross, Arthur 161
Ross, Charity 97
Ross, Deborah 171
Ross, Dorcas Ann 161
Ross, Eli A. 219, 257
Ross, Elizabeth Frances Elvaline 313
Ross, Francis 116
Ross, Frank 116
Ross, George 11, 119, 128, 161, 187, 208, 219
Ross, J. 288
Ross, J. M. 227, 252, 266, 270, 277, 284, 297, 300, 301, 331, 332, 352
Ross, J. W. 315
Ross, James 11, 156, 161
Ross, James Y. 161
Ross, Jane 338
Ross, John M. 171, 219, 254, 255, 257, 258, 279, 302
Ross, Margaret 161
Ross, Mary 219
Ross, Nancy 271
Ross, Nancy E. 338
Ross, Rachel 11
Ross, Robt A. 281
Ross, Samuel 338
Ross, William 11, 179
Rouche, Thos 147
Rouncipher, Sarah 69
Rouncival, Sarah 69
Rounscifer, Sarah 69
Rowel 346

## PERSONAL NAME INDEX

Rowel, Benjamin 82, 103, 137, 155
Rowel, Wm. 137
Rowell, Benjamin 198, 200, 207, 221
Rowell, Benjamin D. 197, 198, 343
Rowell, Betsey 197
Rowell, Catherine 198, 207
Rowell, Eliza 339
Rowell, Hannah J. 197
Rowell, Jane 339
Rowell, Mary 207
Rowell, Mary A. 197, 198, 343
Rowell, Mary Ann 250
Rowell, Mary E. 343
Rowell, Milley E. 197
Rowell, Nancy A. 197
Rowell, Nancy W. 197, 343
Rowell, Peggy C. 197
Rowell, Sally C. 197
Rowell, Thomas C. H. 197
Rowell, Thomas E. H. 197
Rowell, William 198
Rowell, William A. 197
Ruin, Nancy 250
Rush, James 142
Russel, John 297
Russell, Charles S. 254
Russell, Eli G. 254
Russell, Elizabeth B. 254
Russell, Isabella R. G. 254
Russell, James J. 254
Russell, John M. 254
Russell, Lucy 273
Russell, Mark C. 254
Russell, Mary Ann 254
Russell, Morrison 242
Russell, Robert M. D. 254
Russell, Robert Y. 334
Russell, Sarah M. 254
Russell, Wm. B. 254
Rutter, Edmund/Edmond 55
Saddler, Minor 193
Sadler, David 85, 95, 105, 107-109, 141
Sadler, Ealis 107
Sadler, Elizabeth 95, 141, 176, 180, 215
Sadler, Ethelwin 141
Sadler, G. S. 323
Sadler, Isaac 18, 19
Sadler, James 117
Sadler, James A. 221
Sadler, Jane 85, 141

Sadler, Jane Catharine 332
Sadler, Jean 141
Sadler, Joseph 17, 85, 95, 118, 141
Sadler, Lucien P. 276
Sadler, M. A. 323
Sadler, Margaret 258, 304
Sadler, Mary 19
Sadler, Mary R. 241
Sadler, Mary Robertson 200
Sadler, Minor 141, 159, 173, 180, 184, 191, 192, 200, 218, 221, 241, 263
Sadler, R. 120, 294, 359
Sadler, Rachel 18
Sadler, Richard 15, 19, 85, 92, 95, 106, 115-117, 136, 141, 148, 155, 200
Sadler, S. 323
Sadler, Sarah 147
Sadler, Sarah L. 158
Sadler, Stanhope 187, 219, 283, 318
Sadler, Susanna 18
Sadler, William 117, 141
Sale, Jno 39
Salmon, Hezekiah 16
Sandaland, Littleton 64
Sandaland, Randolph 64
Sandefer, Calvin 199
Sandefer, Caroline 199
Sandefer, Elizabeth 199
Sandefer, Elvira 199
Sandefer, Green 158, 199
Sandefer, Lowry 199
Sandefer, Margaret Elizabeth 199
Sandefer, O. 191
Sandefer, Philip 167, 192, 199, 218
Sandefer, Philip C. 158
Sandefer, William 199
Sandefur, Calvin P. 332
Sandefur, Elizabeth 119, 120
Sandefur, Green 120
Sandefur, Lowrie 120
Sandefur, N. Marion 276
Sandefur, Nathaniel M. 332
Sandefur, P. 147
Sandefur, Philip 120, 180
Sandefur, William 120
Sandefur, Wm. L. 332
Sanders, M. L. 345
Sanders, Wily 56
Sandifer, C. P. 251, 315
Sandifer, Calvin P. 315
Sandifer, James P. 137

## PERSONAL NAME INDEX

Sandifer, Philip 193
Sandifur, C. P. 317
Sandifur, G. 232
Sandiland, Littleton 63
Sandland, Anna 287
Sandland, James 287
Sandler, Morning 143
Sandlin, Jinny 143
Sandlin, Littleton 143
Sandlin, Mourning 143
Sandlin, Polly 143
Sandlin, Randal 143
Sandlin, Randolph 64, 143
Sandlin, Wm. 114
Sanlin, James 114
Sanlin, Littleton 142
Sanlin, Middleton 140
Sanlin, William 189
Saphe, Jacob 139
Sarratt, O. 345
Savall, Polly 165, 168
Saville, Austin 289
Saville, H. M. 290
Saville, J. B. 290
Saville, Nancy 322
Scholey, Franklin D. 307
Schooley, Elvira 307
Schooley, William 186
Schooley, William C. 307
Schooly, Samuel 215
Schooly, W. C. 215
Scoggans, Martha 175
Scoggins, Catherine 254
Scoggins, James 334
Scott, Alexander 57, 168, 200, 213, 215
Scott, Ana 132
Scott, Archibald 64
Scott, David 19, 31, 34, 63, 131
Scott, E. N. 248
Scott, Ebenezer 317
Scott, Elizabeth 317
Scott, James 33, 34, 102, 103, 107, 110, 113, 121, 178, 207, 355
Scott, James A. 305
Scott, James G. 213
Scott, John 19, 31, 63, 213, 311
Scott, Joseph 299
Scott, Margaret 34
Scott, Mary 34, 311, 355
Scott, Rebecca 29
Scott, Samuel 12, 31, 34,

Scott, Sarah 114
Scott, Sarah Jane 311
Scott, William 19, 44, 232, 311
Seahorn, John 34
Seapaugh, Peter 313
Sears, Jean 194
Seehorn, Daniel 131
Seismore, Saley 34
Semple, John 279
Shane, Frances 123
Shane, John 122, 123
Shane, Robert 122, 123
Shane, Samuel 123
Shannon, Catherine 109
Sharon 277
Sharp, John 352
Sharp, Turner 9
Shaw, Gilbert 294
Shaw, Wm. 151
Shearer, Hugh 16
Shearer, Lydia 16
Shearer, Thomas 16, 222, 227
Shearer, William 16
Sheerer, Thomas 111, 112
Sheilds, Robert 214, 241
Sherer, Ann/e 113, 225
Sherer, John M. 285
Sherer, Mary Ann 291
Sherer, Richard 225, 285
Sherer, Robert W. 285
Sherer, Thomas 225
Sherer, William 225, 269
Sherley, Eli Clawson 270
Sherley, Elizabeth 269, 270
Sherley, James 269
Sherley, Meredith 269
Sherley, Philaman 269
Sherrel, Richard A. 338
Sherrill, R. C. 253
Sherry, Andrew 87
Shew 136
Shields, Robert 215
Shillinglaw, Sarah 319
Shurley, Absalom 307
Shurley, Eli Washington 307
Shurley, Lucretia 307
Shurley, M. 267
Shurley, Philemon 307
Shurling, John 136
Shurling, Wm 136
Silleman, Mary 149
Simeral, Andrew B. J. 207

# PERSONAL NAME INDEX

Simeral, Francis H. 207
Simeral, Hugh 209
Simeral, James 195, 209
Simeral, Jean 77
Simeral, Miles G. 207
Simeral, Selena 207
Simeral, Sinthey 77
Simmons 180
Simmons, Daniel 221
Simmons, Holloway 156
Simmons, Jesse 149
Simmons, R. L. 341, 344
Simmons, Rachel 180
Simpson, Doctor 78
Simpson, Drusilla 237
Simpson, Elizabeth 24, 199
Simpson, Hugh 31, 103, 142
Simpson, James 25, 83, 107, 108
Simpson, Jean 107
Simpson, Jo 92
Simpson, Thomas 158, 180, 196, 199, 211, 218
Simral, Violet 7
Simril, Andrew B. 292, 293
Simril, F. H. 309
Simril, Franklin H. 293
Simril, James 85, 293
Simril, James Franklin 293
Simril, James P. 211
Simril, Jane 292
Simril, Jane Rosinda 292, 293, 309
Simril, Mary E. 309
Simril, Mary Emeline 292, 293
Simril, Mary J. 336
Simril, Miles G. 292, 293
Simril, Robert Eton 292
Simril, Synthy 85
Simril, Violet 6
Simril, Violet D. 293
Simril, W. N. 269
Simril, William D. 292, 293
Simril, Wm. N. 263
Sims, John 233
Sims, Rosinda 268, 269
Sims, Sarah 157
Sims, William 159, 160
Sims, William B. 307
Sinclair, Ann 68
Sinclair, Duncan 18, 20, 67, 68
Sinclair, Elias 68
Sinclair, Elijah 68
Sinclair, James 67

Sinclair, Jane 234
Sinclair, Jesse 68
Sinclair, John 68
Sinclair, Katharin 68
Sinclair, Mary 67, 68
Sinclair, Preshus 68
Sinclair, Robert 68, 116
Sitgreaves, Ann M. 161
Sitgreaves, John 140, 180
Sitgreaves, Martha 140
Sloan, Jane 334
Sloan, Margaret E. 343
Smarr, Jane 214
Smidday[?], Ann 108
Smith 263
Smith, A. F. 349
Smith, A. T. 335
Smith, Abraham 14, 142, 182
Smith, Abraham G. 182, 203, 334
Smith, Andrew N. 284
Smith, Ann 157
Smith, Avolina 288
Smith, Benjamin Felix 314
Smith, Carolina 314
Smith, Caroline 260
Smith, Cary 268
Smith, Charles 320
Smith, Charles W. 320
Smith, Coffey C. 296
Smith, Daniel 125, 130, 181, 182, 203, 229
Smith, Daniel W. 295
Smith, David 14, 182
Smith, E. W. 211
Smith, Ebenezer Walker 182, 183
Smith, Edward 198, 260, 281
Smith, Eli 176, 288
Smith, Eliza Jane 278, 320
Smith, Elizabeth 99, 136, 288
Smith, Fanny 281
Smith, George 102, 268
Smith, H. 273
Smith, H. H. 253, 254
Smith, H. R. 245
Smith, Henry 14, 130, 134, 142, 175, 176, 182, 205, 310, 320
Smith, Hugh/y 136
Smith, Isaac 125
Smith, Isabella 136
Smith, J. 260, 265
Smith, J. Bolton 267, 286, 349
Smith, J. J. 333

Smith, J. M. 331
Smith, J. William 288
Smith, James 24, 80, 102, 121, 136, 157, 182, 260, 288, 309
Smith, James A. 303
Smith, James M. 288, 334, 335
Smith, Jane 19, 99, 125, 264, 288, 309
Smith, Jane (Darby) 152
Smith, Jean 130
Smith, Jemima 125
Smith, Jesse 288
Smith, John 14, 16, 19, 47, 55, 80, 81, 91, 99, 100, 102, 112, 123, 136, 182, 186, 187, 203, 205, 206, 215, 232, 272, 288, 302, 309, 314, 335-337, 347, 349
Smith, John Cheek 100, 295, 333
Smith, John G. 334
Smith, John J. 203, 337, 341
Smith, John M. 260, 335
Smith, John P. 320
Smith, John R. 273, 281, 336
Smith, John T. 295
Smith, Jonathan 14
Smith, Joseph 19, 100, 129, 142, 273
Smith, Joseph G. 182, 203, 205, 206, 255
Smith, Joseph W. 335
Smith, Josiah 125, 320
Smith, Judge 230
Smith, Katherine 288
Smith, Lillis 23, 24, 182, 183
Smith, Luke 320
Smith, Margaret 128, 136, 203
Smith, Margaret Elizabeth 314
Smith, Martha E. 277
Smith, Martha S. 296
Smith, Mary 100, 102, 136, 260, 278, 313
Smith, Mary Jane 273
Smith, Matthew 5
Smith, Mihel 228
Smith, Mihill 125
Smith, Mijamin 136, 157, 161, 260
Smith, Mijamin Randolph 314
Smith, Miles 124, 125, 189, 215, 272
Smith, Myles 188, 212, 225, 226, 232, 251, 253-255, 277, 289, 299, 302, 305, 321, 335, 337, 339, 345, 349, 351
Smith, Nancy 136, 186, 217
Smith, Nathaniel 182

Smith, Neamiah 102
Smith, Netty 182
Smith, Nicholas 102
Smith, Polly 112, 136, 358
Smith, R. D. 232
Smith, Ralph 34
Smith, Rebecca 296
Smith, Rhoda 125, 228, 320
Smith, Robert 100, 136, 157, 186, 196, 281, 314, 320, 337
Smith, Robert Bailey 314
Smith, Robert C. 330, 336
Smith, Robert J. 320
Smith, Robert P. 337
Smith, Robert W. 281
Smith, Rodah 124, 125
Smith, Sally 153, 334
Smith, Samuel 94, 165, 217, 273
Smith, Samuel D. 264
Smith, Samuel H. 279
Smith, Sarah 80, 131, 182, 288, 330, 336
Smith, Sarah (Powell) 55
Smith, Sarah Ann 260
Smith, Sarah C. 295
Smith, Sarah E. 295
Smith, Sarah R. 303
Smith, Scynthia 182
Smith, Stephen 168
Smith, Thomas 102, 112
Smith, Thomas B. 129
Smith, Thomas H. 233
Smith, W. 217
Smith, W. G. 320
Smith, William 14, 24, 25, 29, 34, 59, 60, 81, 98, 102, 125, 129, 136, 179, 260, 273, 281, 288, 342
Smith, William B. 337
Smith, William H. 99, 100, 129, 347
Smith, William M. 260, 275, 296
Smith, Winefred 273
Smith, Zada D. 343
Smith, Zado(c)k D. 152, 264
Smitty, Jno 52
Snider, J. J. 329
Snoddy, Saml 202
Snyder, 352
Sorn[?], Wm. 125
Soward, John 85, 139, 151
Spain, Elizabeth Ann 304
Spears, 306
Spears, Richard 57

## PERSONAL NAME INDEX

Spence, Elizabeth 61
Spence, John 61
Spence, Patrick 71
Spencer, Jesse 254
Spencer, John 57, 58, 156, 179
Spencer, Malinda (Blanton) 179
Spott, Susannah 57
Spratt, James 77, 78, 103
Spratt, Margaret Jane 288
Spratt, Susannah 77
Spratt, T. D. 319
Spratt, Thomas 77, 78
Spratt, Thos. D. 288
Sprigs, And'w 101
Spring, Valentine 357
Springs, Adaline (Flowers) 298
Springs, Adam A. 298
Springs, Amanda J. 333
Springs, Andrew 355
Springs, Andrew B. 298
Springs, Buennet 333
Springs, Eli 355
Springs, Eli B. 298
Springs, John 60, 103, 108, 118, 122, 129, 138, 148, 168, 169, 192, 198, 221, 297, 298, 355
Springs, Julia Amanda 298
Springs, Lana B. 333
Springs, Leroy 298
Springs, Margaret 298, 355
Springs, Margaret (Bullinger) 298
Springs, R. A. 191, 297
Springs, Richard 38, 355
Springs, Richard A. 298
Springs, Richard C. 298, 355
Sprott, Andrew 57
Sprott, Charity 57
Sprott, David 57
Sprott, Eliza M. 249
Sprott, Elizabeth 57, 249
Sprott, James 57, 169, 249
Sprott, Jas M. 249
Sprott, Leonidas 249
Sprott, Margaret 169, 249
Sprott, Martha M. 249
Sprott, Polly 57
Sprott, Robert 249
Sprott, Susan 249
Sprott, Thomas D. 249
Stafford, Arthur 66
Stafford, James 66
Stafford, Samuel McKee 66

Stalings, Jacob 125
Standerd 37
Stanton, Eleanor 204, 240
Stanton, Eliza C. 204
Stanton, Isom G. 204, 206, 240
Stanton, Martha M. 343
Stanton, William 61
Stanton, William A. 204
Stanton, Wm. H. 206
Starling, Lidea 75
Starnes, Jacob 301
Starnes, John 335
Starnes, Joseph 331, 332
Starnes, Mary Caroline 335
Starnes, Robert T. 331
Starns, Green 301
Starns, J. G. 301
Starns, John 196, 301
Starns, Montgomery 301
Starns, Nancy 275, 301
Starns, Saml 169
Starr, A. S. 250
Starr, Arthur 14, 24, 28
Starr, Emery Stewart 251
Starr, Hannah 28
Starr, Hannah Emily 294
Starr, John 69, 85, 91, 130, 185, 250, 251
Starr, John Latta 251
Starr, Pamela Williams 28
Starr, Sarah 106, 319
Starr, Stewart 106
Stearn, Robert 209
Stedman, M. 47
Stedman, Michael 46, 213
Steedman, James 205
Steedman, John 305
Steedman, Mary 205
Steedman, Matilda 265
Steedman, Michael 205, 211
Steedman, William 205
Steel 37, 300
Steel, Abraham 174
Steel, Agness 69
Steel, Alexander 24, 185
Steel, Ammaline 174
Steel, Archibald 24, 69, 94
Steel, Betsy 163
Steel, Elizabeth 184
Steel, George 260
Steel, James 69
Steel, Jane 174

## PERSONAL NAME INDEX

Steel, Jenny 24
Steel, John 24, 69, 174
Steel, Jonathan 174
Steel, Joseph 14, 24, 69, 106, 117, 150
Steel, Martha 174
Steel, Mary 129, 219
Steel, Rachel 117
Steel, Rebecca 24
Steel, Rebecka 106
Steel, Robert 69, 106
Steel, Samuel 24, 174
Steel, William 24, 69, 163, 174
Steele 295
Steele, Alex'r 221, 219
Steele, Ann 218
Steele, Archibald 137, 183, 285, 320
Steele, David P. 297
Steele, Eliza A. 294
Steele, Elizabeth 293, 347, 348
Steele, Elizabeth R. 347
Steele, Francis M. 264
Steele, George 219, 300
Steele, Isabella 314
Steele, James 281
Steele, Jas. B. 281
Steele, John 97
Steele, John M. 320
Steele, John Newton 293
Steele, Joseph 218, 219
Steele, Margaret 209, 218, 281
Steele, Martha 293
Steele, Mary 218
Steele, N. A. 293
Steele, Newton A. 293
Steele, Samuel 219, 239, 293
Steele, Stourton E. 250
Steele, Susan 347, 348
Steele, Viney 218
Stephenson, Barbara 121
Stephenson, Dorcas M. 280
Stephenson, James 279
Stephenson, James G. 280
Stephenson, James M. 242
Stephenson, John 242
Stephenson, Mary 50, 242
Stephenson, Matthew 116, 120, 121
Stephenson, Polly 121, 242
Stephenson, William 120, 121
Stephon[sic], Wm. 13
Stern, Jacob 227
Stern[?], John 211
Sterns, Jacob 225

Stevens, Elizabeth 203
Stevenson, Elizabeth 6
Stevenson, Hugh 181
Stevenson, Jane 181
Stevenson, Jean 27
Stevenson, Martha 119
Stevenson, Mary 181
Stevenson, Matthew 26
Stevenson, William 13
Steward, Margret 12
Steward, Mary 12
Stewart, A. C. 322
Stewart, Alexander 81, 116, 159
Stewart, Alice E. 322
Stewart, Archibald 190
Stewart, Catherine 159
Stewart, E. K. 320
Stewart, E. L. 320, 322
Stewart, E. R. 322
Stewart, Eli 320
Stewart, Elizabeth 159
Stewart, I. J. 322
Stewart, J. A. 320
Stewart, J. J. 293
Stewart, J. M. 319
Stewart, J. N. 345
Stewart, J. S. 320
Stewart, James 64, 81, 159, 183, 306
Stewart, James H. 320
Stewart, James M. 240, 293
Stewart, John 132, 183, 189, 306
Stewart, Jonathan 195
Stewart, Joseph B. 190
Stewart, Josiah 306
Stewart, Lamuel 114
Stewart, Louisa 345
Stewart, M. M. 320
Stewart, Mary 159
Stewart, Mary M. 322
Stewart, Michael 81, 159
Stewart, Nancy 306, 307, 322
Stewart, O. G. 304
Stewart, R. 295
Stewart, Robert 295
Stewart, Rosanna/h 81, 159
Stewart, Sarah 81
Stewart, W. T. 322
Stewart, William 61, 88, 306
Stewart, Wm. T. 320
Stice, Charles 6
Still 242
Stillwell, A. 315

## PERSONAL NAME INDEX

Stilwell, Alfred 348
Stockton, Joseph W. 351
Stockton, Margaret 325
Stockton, Margaret B. 341
Stockton, Margaret Brevard 351
Stone, Charles 158
Story 339
Story, Benjamin 251
Story, Benjamin B. 251
Story, James 251
Stoup, Joseph 287
Stoup, Polly 287
Stow, Susan Elizabeth 334
Stowe, A. 338
Stowe, Abram 270
Stowe, Elizabeth J. 334
Stowe, Gaban 334
Stowe, Margaret 334
Straight, George 157
Straight, Leonard 355
Strain, David 49
Strain, Hetty 297
Strain, Jas 211
Strain, Joseph 85, 237
Strain, Margret 49
Strains, David 62
Strait, 329, 342
Strait, Dorcas 87
Strait, Leonard 87, 355
Strait, Mary 87
Strait, Peggy 87
Strait, Richard 324
Strait, Sally 355
Strait, Samuel 87
Streight, George 181
Streight, Leonard 134
Streight, Richard 175, 213, 224, 226
Strong, John R[?] 200
Strong, Nancy 200
Stroup, Alexdr 164
Stroup, Jacob 140
Stuart, Agness 188
Stuart, Ann 188
Stuart, Archibald 188
Stuart, J. P. 308
Stuart, James M. 188
Stuart, Jane 188
Stuart, Joseph B. 188
Stuart, Margaret 188
Stuart, Nancy 308
Stuart, Sarah 188
Stuart, William 188

Sturges, Barbara 307
Sturges, Daniel 47
Sturges, Geo 220
Sturges, George W. 307
Sturges, Jane (Bratton) 47
Sturges, John 47
Sturges, Joshua 47
Sturges, Mary (Wilson) 47
Sturges, Susan 185
Sturges, W. 215
Sturges, William 185, 186, 215
Sturges, Zaddock 186
Sturgis, Benjamin D. 270
Sturgis, Daniel 7, 8, 22, 23, 128, 138
Sturgis, David 7
Sturgis, George 22
Sturgis, James 8, 22
Sturgis, James Armstrong 7
Sturgis, Jane 7
Sturgis, Jean 22
Sturgis, Jean Bratton 22
Sturgis, John 7, 8, 22, 266
Sturgis, Joshua 7, 8, 22
Sturgis, Laban 7, 8, 23
Sturgis, Mary 7, 8, 22
Sturgis, Milat 137
Sturgis, Nancy 22
Sturgis, Thomas W. 289, 306
Sturgis, Zadock 138
Suggest, George W. 208
Suggs 271
Suggs, Andrew J. 208
Suggs, Catharine 348
Suggs, Catherine L. 208
Suggs, Eliza 348
Suggs, George W. 208
Suggs, Green M. 208
Suggs, Isaac 157
Suggs, Isaac F. 208
Suggs, Isaac T. 208
Suggs, Isaiah Leroy 208
Suggs, Jane 208
Suggs, Jane C. 208
Suggs, John W. 208
Suggs, Josiah L. 208
Suggs, Laban 208, 231
Suggs, Lelan 191
Suggs, Margaret E. T. 208
Suggs, Martha J. 208
Suggs, Nancy (Moore) 245
Suggs, Thornton 245
Suggs, Thos E. 278

## PERSONAL NAME INDEX

Suggs, Wm. G. 208
Sulivan, Samuel C. 123
Sumerford, Abraham 125
Sumerford, Isaac 125
Summerford, Abraham 262
Summerford, Crossey 262
Summerford, Edward 52, 262
Summerford, Elial 262
Summerford, Elizabeth Jane 262
Summerford, Elvirah 262
Summerford, Isaac 262
Summerford, John 262
Summerford, Loami 262
Summerford, Malinda 262
Summerford, Nancy 262
Summerford, Pamela 214
Summerford, Piety 262
Summerford, Polly 262
Summerford, Rueben Wilson 262
Summerford, Samuel 262
Summerford, William 262
Surges, Danl 148
Sutten, Jonathan 54
Sutton, James 121
Sutton, Jno'a 102
Sutton, John 114
Sutton, Jon'a 121
Sutton, Mary 121, 208, 266
Swan, Ann 175
Swan, Elizabeth 90
Swan, John 34, 35, 175
Swan, John B. 175
Swan, Joseph 34, 35, 175
Swan, Polly F. 175
Swan, Sarah 90
Swann, Ann 263
Swann, Eaton 342
Swann, Edward Eaton 329
Swann, H. L. 342
Swann, Jane A. 342
Swann, John 263, 329
Swann, John B. 329, 342
Swann, John M. 342
Swann, Joseph Addison 329
Swann, Mary H. 329
Swann, Moses B. 329
Swann, Moses Barnet 263
Sweazy, Wm. B. 212
Sweeney, Francis 140
Sweeney, James 140
Swinny, Eliza 140
Sylvanus, John 230

Tagart, Jas 118
Tagert, Jas 38
Talbert, Benjamin 289
Talbert, Rachel 99
Talbert, Resen 282
Talley, Henry 136
Talley, Honory 103
Tanner, Col. 352
Tate, Andrew 165, 302
Tate, Catherine 165, 221
Tate, Eleanor 165
Tate, Hugh 165
Tate, James 24, 88, 165
Tate, Jane 323
Tate, John 165
Tate, Luther 165
Tate, Marg(a)ret 62, 109
Tate, Martin L. 302
Tate, Nancy 165
Tate, Samuel 165
Tatem, Mary 18
Taylor, 115, 129, 163, 174, 251, 254
Taylor, Elizabeth 172
Taylor, Jane 251
Taylor, Thomas C. 172
Tecerd[?], Robert Clark 28
Templeton, George 15
Templeton, Jno 21
Templeton, Margaret 15
Templeton, William 15
Terry, Samuel 357
Tharp, Elizabeth 309
Thom, James 139
Thomas, John 272
Thomason, Jane 238
Thomason, Lemuel 112
Thomason, Nathaniel 100
Thomason, Polly 184
Thomason, Thos 207
Thomason, Wm 114
Thomason, Wm. P. 237
Thomasson, Alfred 280
Thomasson, D. H. 280, 306
Thomasson, Elizabeth 220
Thomasson, F. J. 329
Thomasson, G. L. 280
Thomasson, Hiram C. 280, 306
Thomasson, James 220, 280, 328
Thomasson, James C. 208, 280, 306
Thomasson, Jane 237, 329
Thomasson, Jane S. 306
Thomasson, Lemuel 220

## PERSONAL NAME INDEX

Thomasson, Nathaniel 100, 220
Thomasson, P. A. 280, 328
Thomasson, Polly 184
Thomasson, Simon B. 280
Thomasson, Thomas 220, 300
Thomasson, Thomas Jefferson 238
Thomasson, W. P. 293, 294
Thomasson, William 238, 280
Thomasson, Wm. B. 329
Thomasson, Wm. P. 219, 267, 280
Thompson, 228, 302
Thompson, A. 164
Thompson, A. W. 188
Thompson, Alexander 55, 92, 108, 124, 156
Thompson, Ann 108, 164
Thompson, Ann Ewing 108
Thompson, Ben. W. 122
Thompson, Cynthia 193
Thompson, Cynthia E. 193
Thompson, Elizabeth 163, 164
Thompson, Ephraim D. 264
Thompson, H. H. 320
Thompson, James 92
Thompson, John 18, 59, 92, 108, 110, 124, 156, 164
Thompson, John B. 164
Thompson, John Brown 108
Thompson, John L. 193, 204
Thompson, Joseph 164
Thompson, Joseph W. 164, 229
Thompson, Joseph Waddy 145
Thompson, Malinda Ann 193
Thompson, Martha 99
Thompson, Mary 101, 115
Thompson, Moses 92, 107, 108
Thompson, Nathaniel 92, 107, 108
Thompson, Phanney 18
Thompson, Samuel 92
Thompson, Sarah L. 193
Thompson, Sherid 26
Thompson, Thomas 18
Thompson, William 31, 124, 125, 160
Thompson, Youpheme 31
Thomson, Alexander 85, 146
Thomson, Ann 33
Thomson, Henry Hopson 145, 146
Thomson, J. W. 262
Thomson, James 85
Thomson, James M. 146
Thomson, James Maddison 145
Thomson, James Washington 145

Thomson, John 59, 85, 193
Thomson, Joseph W. 146
Thomson, Junius W. 146
Thomson, Moses 85
Thomson, Nancy Ragland 146
Thomson, Nathaniel 85
Thomson, Polly ___ 146
Thomson, Richard 145, 146
Thomson, Richard Franklin 145, 146
Thomson, Richard S. 146
Thomson, Samuel 51, 85
Thomson, Susan Ann 146
Thomson, William 146, 148
Thomson, William Hatten 145, 146
Thorn, Hezekiah 265
Thorn, James 194, 246, 282
Thorn, Sarah 324
Thornton, Robert C. 229
Thrift, Abraham 72
Thrift, Shadrock 72
Thrift, Spencer 72
Ticer, Ann 65
Ticer, Clark 57
Ticer, Henry 57
Ticer, Hugh 57, 65
Ticer, Jaen 57
Ticer, Mary 57
Ticer, Samuel 57
Ticer, Sarah 57
Tigleman[?], John 137
Tilghman, Eli 194
Tilghman, Elizabeth 194
Tilghman, Ivy 194
Tilghman, Jackson 194
Tilghman, John 194
Tilghman, John Newton 194
Tilghman, Joshua 194
Tilghman, Margaret 194
Tilghman, Mary 194
Tilghman, Nancy 194
Tilghman, Robert 194
Tilghman, Scintha 194
Tilghman, Sherwood 194
Tilghman, Stephen 194
Tilghman, Stephen H. 194
Tiller, Joseph 80
Tiller, Margaret 80
Timberlake, Cyntha 240
Timberlake, Richard 139
Tims, James 105
Tiping, Jno C. 202
Tippeng, J. C. 332

## PERSONAL NAME INDEX

Tippens, Mary 93
Tipping 109
Tipping, Elizabeth 15
Tipping, Henry 15, 110, 243, 244, 259, 359
Tipping, Isaac D. 243, 244, 359
Tipping, J. S. 330
Tipping, James 56
Tipping, John C. 158, 243, 244
Tipping, Margaret 243, 244
Tipping, Rosannah 15
Tipping, Rosey 244
Todd, Mary 10
Tolbert, Lewis 248
Tolbert, Rezin 208, 248
Tolbert, Thomas 248
Tom, William 43
Tomason, D. H. 324
Tommasson, Jeremiah 184
Tool 147, 154, 283
Torn[?], Thomas 20
Traddle, 60
Traves, John 222
Trimer, Catherine 143
Trimmier, Obadiah 179
Trimmier, Polly 179, 275
Turner 41
Turner, Barbery 347
Turner, Christopher 90, 143, 154
Turner, Daniel 129, 174
Turner, David 2
Turner, E. 182
Turner, Eaton 183
Turner, George 154, 204
Turner, Gordon 347
Turner, Isabella 129
Turner, James 47, 202, 345, 347
Turner, Jenny 101
Turner, Jenny Baxter 30
Turner, John 154, 210
Turner, Keziah 159
Turner, Martha 129
Turner, Mary 129, 143
Turner, Robert 154, 204
Turner, Rosanah 154
Turner, Samuel 105, 130, 136, 143, 165, 186
Turner, Thomas 130, 159
Turner, Thomas H. 344
Turner, Wm 154
Turnery, Daniel 189
Turretine, Editha Walker 83

Vanable, Hannah 356
Vanable, Richard 356
Veale, John 109
Veich, William 23
Venable 213
Venable, Agness 36
Venable, Andrew 36
Venable, Archibald 82
Venable, Bryson 36
Venable, Francis 36
Venable, Hannah 25, 101
Venable, J. B. 349
Venable, J. Brison 344
Venable, James 81, 36
Venable, Jane 81, 155
Venable, John 36, 81, 155
Venable, John Brison 223
Venable, Richard 21, 82, 155
Venable, Sarah 101
Venable, William 81, 155, 174
Venables, Archibald 81
Venables, James 82
Venables, Jane 82
Venables, John 13, 82
Venables, William 82
Vicalson, Catharine 92
Vicars, Ann 97
Vicars, John 97
Vicars, Ralph 97
Vicars, Theofillus 97
Vickers, Jane 175, 224
Vickers, John 175
Vickers, Wm 224
Viven, Jno 194
Waddel, David 127
Waddel, Elisabeth 127
Waddel, John 127
Waddle, Ann 2
Waddle, David 2, 116
Waddle, Elizabeth 2
Waddle, John 2
Waddle, Joseph 2, 116
Waddle, Lydia 2
Waddle, Margaret 2
Waddle, Sarah 2
Waddle, Susannah 2
Wade, Hampton 48
Wadkins[?], William 122
Wagner, George 121
Wagner, Isaac 121
Wagner, John 121
Wagoner, Isaac 121

## PERSONAL NAME INDEX

Wagoner, John 121
Wagoner, Mary 121
Walker, 43, 53
Walker, Andrew 217
Walker, Elizabeth 30, 178
Walker, F. 178
Walker, Felix 25, 30
Walker, Hugh 217, 220, 239
Walker, Isabella 258
Walker, J. H. 298
Walker, Jacob 178
Walker, James 25
Walker, Jane 239
Walker, John 178
Walker, Margaret 217
Walker, Martha 217
Walker, Mary 25
Walker, Mary Ann 217
Walker, Minerva 301
Walker, Peggie 25
Walker, Philip 142, 145
Walker, Rebecca 32
Walker, Robert B. 82, 112, 114
Walker, Samuel 304
Walker, Samuel J. 291
Walker, Sarah 217
Walker, Thomas 25, 160
Walker, Thompson 220, 239
Walker, Violet 30
Walker, Watson 30
Walker, Williamson, 180
Walker, Zenus A. 258, 259
Wallace 277
Wallace, A. L.[sic] 241
Wallace, A. S. 241, 274, 282, 285, 298, 304, 317
Wallace, Ad(d)eline 348
Wallace, Adeline 349
Wallace, Alexander S. 318, 333, 334, 349
Wallace, C. L. 305
Wallace, Clementine Virginia 348
Wallace, David 255
Wallace, Deborah 233
Wallace, Easther 200
Wallace, Elias 85, 120
Wallace, Eliza S. 331
Wallace, Elizabeth 166
Wallace, George Franklin 348, 349
Wallace, George T. 302
Wallace, H. A. 341
Wallace, Hugh 233

Wallace, Isaac M. 259
Wallace, Isabella 200
Wallace, J. M. 342
Wallace, James 10, 69, 120, 175, 203, 206, 302, 323
Wallace, James A. 290, 331
Wallace, James F. 192
Wallace, James Y. 151, 237
Wallace, Jo 63
Wallace, John 121, 200
Wallace, John R. 301
Wallace, Joseph 56, 62, 206, 348
Wallace, Judith 9
Wallace, Margaret 69, 181, 301
Wallace, Margaret C. 290
Wallace, Margaret E. 329
Wallace, Margret 323
Wallace, Mary (Bratton) 108
Wallace, Mary 151, 188, 213, 242, 259
Wallace, McCaslan/d 187, 192
Wallace, McCastland 349
Wallace, Milton 283
Wallace, Nancy 84, 237, 242
Wallace, Nancy L. 318
Wallace, Oliver 10
Wallace, Oliver Berry 9
Wallace, Rebeckah 165
Wallace, Robert 68, 69, 155, 191
Wallace, Robert M. 334
Wallace, S. Milton 283
Wallace, Simpson B. 286
Wallace, Susan E. 348
Wallace, Susan Elizabeth McDowell 348
Wallace, Thomas 9, 159
Wallace, William 154, 160, 200, 208
Wallace, William L. 179
Wallace, William Rufus 348
Waller 210
Waller, Samuel 90, 210
Wallis, Isaac M. 259
Wallis, James 132, 133
Wallis, Martha 132, 132
Wallis, Mary 259
Wallis, William 150
Walton, David 197
Ward, James 109, 131
Ward, Precillah 165
Ward, Prisclla 168
Ward, Sally 329
Ward, Sarah 329
Ward, Scarborough 80

## PERSONAL NAME INDEX

Ware, Mary 195
Ware, William 236
Warran, Hugh 237
Warran, Nancy 235
Warren, Hugh 218
Warren, Nancy 236, 237
Warren, Robert S. 281
Warren, Samuel 118, 235
Washington, Clarke 112
Wateres 101
Watson 53, 95, 224
Watson, A. L. 320
Watson, Albert 183, 336
Watson, Albert W. 260
Watson, Alberta 336
Watson, Andrew McWhorter 301
Watson, Ann 52
Watson, Aron 52
Watson, Catherine 89
Watson, Charlotte 226
Watson, Clark 174, 215
Watson, D. A. A. 338
Watson, D. M. 260, 290
Watson, Daniel M. 209
Watson, David 4, 18, 26, 51, 52, 69, 89, 94, 120, 121, 142, 151, 176, 181, 183, 209, 226, 227, 240, 260
Watson, David M. 237, 307, 336
Watson, Deborah 226, 336
Watson, E. 163
Watson, E. K. 260
Watson, Elizabeth 89, 174, 226, 302, 336
Watson, Elizabeth Ann (Hall) 301
Watson, Elizabeth M. 240
Watson, Emily 226, 307
Watson, Franklin 226
Watson, George 19, 83
Watson, Hugh 61, 89, 120, 121, 226
Watson, Hugh Parks 301
Watson, Isaac 1
Watson, J. C. 255
Watson, J. D. 323
Watson, J. J. 306, 322
Watson, James 52, 89, 94, 176, 226, 336
Watson, James Franklin 260
Watson, Jane 174, 226, 335, 336
Watson, Jane S. H. 176
Watson, Jeane 52
Watson, John 7, 21, 51, 52, 61, 88, 89, 121

Watson, John L. 260, 307, 336
Watson, John Lykin 301
Watson, Joseph 297
Watson, Joseph J. 252, 308
Watson, Katharine 52
Watson, M. A. 260
Watson, Margaret 148, 174, 226, 336
Watson, Margaret A. 253, 302
Watson, Margaret Adams 348
Watson, Margaret Jane 301
Watson, Margaret T. (Parks) 301
Watson, Margret 36
Watson, Mary 18, 83, 94, 155, 226
Watson, Mary Elizabeth 297
Watson, Mary Hopkins (Wilson) 301
Watson, Mary J. C. 307
Watson, Mathew 155
Watson, Melissa 174
Watson, R. J. 320
Watson, Robert 61, 89, 94, 103, 120, 121, 136, 168, 226, 260
Watson, Robt A. 260
Watson, S. L. 292, 337, 338
Watson, S. N. 338
Watson, Samuel 7, 16, 21, 24, 26, 51, 52, 61, 89, 176, 183, 226
Watson, Samuel Davis 301
Watson, Samuel L. 240, 241, 249, 251, 253, 260, 271, 295, 296, 337
Watson, Sarah 89, 308, 319
Watson, Sarah D. 322
Watson, Violet 30, 134, 135
Watson, W. L. 337
Watson, W. M. 260
Watson, Widow 118
Watson, William 30, 51, 82, 89, 90, 94, 124, 134, 155, 156, 174, 178, 191, 213, 226, 227, 301, 302, 336
Watson, William A. 176, 227, 240
Watson, William D. 260, 302
Watson, William David 348
Watson, William Marion 301
Watts, Margaret 121
Weathers, Amanda 263
Weathers, B. F. 263
Weathers, Benjamin 108
Weathers, Benjamin J. 265
Weathers, Benjamin P. 265
Weathers, Edmund 108, 168, 192, 200, 265
Weathers, Isaac 38, 108
Weathers, Isaac Newton 263

## PERSONAL NAME INDEX

Weathers, John B. 263
Weathers, John G. 265
Weathers, Nathaniel 51
Weathers, Pheby Jane 265
Weathers, Randall 211
Weathers, Randolph 263
Weathers, Sarah M. 263
Weathers, Thos J. 263
Weathers, William 57, 108
Weathers, Wm. R. 263
Webb, Eleanor 308, 322
Webb, Elender 102
Webb, Hannah 102
Webb, James 9, 102
Webb, Kesiah 102
Webb, Margaret 103
Webb, Mary 211
Webb, Nancy 102
Webb, Peggy 102
Webb, Priscilla E. 9
Webb, Samuel 102
Webb, Stephen 102, 103
Webb, Theoderick 9
Webb, Thomas 65, 102, 168
Webber, A. C. 301
Webber, Jno. G. 345
Weeks, John 192
Wells, Cintha 158
Wells, Eleanor 320
Wells, Hugh 105, 158
Wells, Ibby 158
Wells, Isabel 158
Wells, Larence[?] 158
Wells, Margaret 158
Wells, Mary 158
Wells, Thomas 158
Wells, William 158
Wenable, Hannah 25
West, Elizabeth 127
West, Harriett 224
West, Joseph 112
West, Martin 37
West, Mathew 91
West, Prudence 224
Westbrooks, Grey 194
Wethers, Pheby Jane 265
Wharey, Dorcas 29
Wheelan, Abraham 122
Wheeler, 298
Wheeler, B. T. 289
Wheeler, Rachel O. 289
Wherry, Andrew 87, 285

Wherry, Dorcas 87
Wherry, Elizabeth 106, 250, 285
Wherry, Hannah 87
Wherry, John 87, 126
Wherry, John A. 194
Wherry, Peggy 87
Wherry, Polly 87
Wherry, Samuel 87, 150, 355
Wherry, Sarah 150
Wherry, Thomas 87
Wherry, William 87, 106, 194, 250, 285
Wherry, Wm. C. 194
Whisenant, Eliza 188
Whisenant, Joseph 188
Whisenant, Nasa 188
Whisonant, Aaron W. 275
Whisonant, David W. 314
Whisonant, Henderson 336
Whisonant, J. M. 323
Whisonant, John 287
Whisonant, John N. 299, 323, 345
Whisonant, John V. 311
Whisonant, Margaret 314, 330, 336
Whisonant, Martha F. (Morrow) 314
Whisonant, Martha M. 336
Whisonant, Mary 330
Whisonant, Michael 314
Whisonant, Nancy 336
Whisonant, Nicholas 69
Whisonant, S. 323
Whisonant, Sarah 330
Whisonant, Susanna 69
Whisonant, T. P. 323
Whistenant, Aaron 195, 257
Whistenant, Anna 198
Whistenant, George 139, 161, 189, 195
Whistenant, Henry 132
Whistenant, John 139, 189, 199
Whistenant, Joseph 189, 195
Whistenant, Mary 198
Whistenant, Nicholas 195
Whitaker, Morison 160
Whitaker, Thomas 26
White, A. V. 308
White, Agnes 23
White, Derrel 201
White, Derrill 201
White, Dicy 185
White, Dorcas 183
White, Elizabeth 78, 201, 261

## PERSONAL NAME INDEX

White, Elizabeth Elvira 234
White, Elizabeth W. 234
White, F. L. 308
White, George 216, 265
White, George P. 169, 265
White, Henry F. 260, 261
White, Hugh 46, 60, 77, 78, 168, 169
White, Hugh M. 168, 169, 298
White, Isaac 317
White, J. A. 106
White, J. D. 308
White, J. F. 306
White, J. H. 308
White, J. J. 322
White, James 94, 169, 317
White, James Green Willis 234
White, James H. 308
White, Jane 8
White, Janet 317
White, Jesse 234
White, John 116, 189, 317
White, John J. 183, 306-308
White, John M. 322
White, Joseph 60
White, Joseph F. 169, 249, 256, 287, 290, 295, 320
White, Lawrence W. 234
White, Margaret 183, 191
White, Martha 60, 78
White, Mary 317
White, Mary Caroline 317
White, Moses 8
White, Nancy 201
White, R. P. 309
White, Robert 201, 236
White, Robert Logan 234
White, Sarah 169, 232
White, T. M. 292
White, Thomas 80, 81
White, Thomas M. 234
White, Thomas Spratt 77
White, W. E. 198, 322
White, William 46, 136, 183, 191, 308, 321
White, William E. 226, 288
White, Wm. Eliot 60
Whiteside, Abram 26
Whiteside, Betsy 162
Whiteside, Dorcas 64
Whiteside, Hugh 26, 29, 79, 80, 162
Whiteside, J. C. 312
Whiteside, James 25, 162

Whiteside, Margaret 25, 29, 162, 325
Whiteside, Mary Jean 64
Whiteside, Robert 162
Whiteside, Samuel 26
Whiteside, Susannah 162
Whiteside, Thomas 25
Whitesides, Austin 309
Whitesides, Austin S. 312
Whitesides, Hugh 179
Whitesides, J. B. 347
Whitesides, J. W. 323
Whitesides, James 179, 180, 309
Whitesides, John 309
Whitesides, John B. 312
Whitesides, Jonathan 122
Whitesides, Major 203
Whitesides, Margaret 179, 281
Whitesides, Margaret E. 312
Whitesides, Mary 108
Whitesides, Mary C. 312
Whitesides, Robert 179, 180, 244
Whitesides, Thomas 142, 236, 276, 309, 312
Whitley, Jonathan 20
Whitley, Sarah 20
Whyte, A. 264-266
Whyte, James 129
Whyte, James A. 106, 133, 135
Whyte, Mary C. 106
Whyte, Wm. E. 132
Wiggins, Eli 78
Wiley, James 345
Wiley, Nancy 144
Wiley, Samuel 108, 172
Wilie, Eliza 301
Wilie, John 19, 42, 43
Wilie, Martha 19
Wilie, William 19
Wilkenson, Charles E. 279
Wilkenson, James 279
Wilkenson, Nancy 279
Wilkenson, Thomas J. 279
Wilkerson, James W. 256
Wilkerson, T. J. 262
Wilkie, Ann 58
Wilkie, Catherine 234
Wilkie, Deborah 58
Wilkie, Elizabeth 58
Wilkie, George 58
Wilkie, Jesse 234
Wilkie, Joseph 234
Wilkie, Nancey 234

## PERSONAL NAME INDEX

Wilkie, Rebecca 58
Wilkie, Sabra 58
Wilkie, Sarah 58
Wilkie, William 58
Wilkins, Dan Quinn 209
Wilkins, Drury S. 209
Wilkins, Eliza 209
Wilkins, Franklin 210
Wilkins, John 209
Wilkins, Martha 209
Wilkins, N. S. 210
Wilkins, Peter P. 209
Wilkins, Robert 209
Wilkins, Sarah 209, 210, 212
Wilkins, Smith 192, 210, 211
Wilkinson, A. 25
Wilkinson, Nancy M. 303
Wilkinson, Wm. 304
Willey, Thomas 98
William, John 338
Williams 352
Williams, A. 164
Williams, Alexander 215, 216
Williams, Ann 215, 216
Williams, Benjamin Judge 216
Williams, Charles 216
Williams, Eliza Ann 216
Williams, G. W. 224, 235, 247, 257, 259, 262, 270, 271, 296, 304, 313, 318, 339, 341, 348-351
Williams, George W. 267, 327, 334
Williams, James M. 332
Williams, James R. 222
Williams, Jane 252
Williams, Jane A. 332
Williams, John 216
Williams, John H. 247
Williams, Katrine 5
Williams, Louisa 216
Williams, Mary 216
Williams, Mathew H. 285
Williams, Matthew 215, 216
Williams, Peggy (McRight) 174
Williams, Philip 134, 283, 352
Williams, Robert 251
Williams, Robert M. 174, 205
Williams, Robert McClellan 205
Williams, Thomas 134, 142, 156, 197, 216
Williams, Wulgave[?] 216
Williamson, Arthur S. 209
Williamson, Gregg 264

Williamson, James 10, 103, 117, 119, 130, 200, 215, 224, 226, 264
Williamson, Jane 249
Williamson, John 21, 226
Williamson, John N. 224
Williamson, Leroy 264
Williamson, Samuel 10, 24
Williamson, Silvanus 317, 343
Williamson, William 3
Willis, Mary 48
Willis, Robert 48
Willoughby, Margaret 339
Wills, James 216
Wills, Samuel 216
Wills, William 216
Willson, Elijah 22
Willson, James 15, 22, 66
Willson, Jean 66
Willson, Jemimey 66
Willson, John 22
Willson, Mary 22
Willson, Milley 22
Willson, Nancy 22
Willson, Rebeckah 113
Willson, Robert 22
Willson, Thomas 22
Willson, William 22
Wilson, 229, 321, 353
Wilson, A. B. 99
Wilson, Agness 180
Wilson, Catherine 99
Wilson, D. S. 314
Wilson, Daniel Sturges 47
Wilson, Drusilla 119
Wilson, Elijah 14, 187
Wilson, Elisabeth 14
Wilson, Eliza P. 322
Wilson, Elizabeth 69, 82, 83, 186, 289, 323
Wilson, Ezekiel 292
Wilson, Gassaway 206
Wilson, Gazaway 79, 227, 323
Wilson, Hezekiah 14
Wilson, Hugh 51
Wilson, J. F. 334
Wilson, James 48, 51, 65, 96, 162, 173, 236, 323
Wilson, Jane 183
Wilson, John 13, 14, 22, 99, 180, 235, 272, 322, 356
Wilson, John C. 301, 323
Wilson, John M. 342

## PERSONAL NAME INDEX

Wilson, Jonathan Beatty 131
Wilson, Joseph 14
Wilson, Joseph H. 355
Wilson, Jose 14
Wilson, Josiah 227, 322
Wilson, M. V. 345
Wilson, Marg(a)ret 322, 323
Wilson, Martha 51, 165
Wilson, Mary (Sturges) 47
Wilson, Mary 14, 22, 138, 289
Wilson, Mary Hopkins (Watson) 301
Wilson, Mathew 22
Wilson, R. M. 323
Wilson, Robert 14, 82, 83, 99, 110, 135, 141, 158, 173, 185, 204, 227, 285, 322, 334
Wilson, Robert M. 220, 342
Wilson, Robert W. 218, 322
Wilson, Sally 349
Wilson, Sarah 14, 272, 285, 322, 323
Wilson, Thomas 83, 220, 236
Wilson, Thomas M. 248
Wilson, W. M. 248
Wilson, William 34, 235, 236, 294, 322
Wilson, William B. 331, 332
Wilson, William J. 272
Wilsons, John 43
Windsor, Anna 110
Winget, Plannes 28
Winningham, Joseph 44
Wish, John 59
Wishart, Jane 175
Wisher, Agness 59
Wisher, James 59
Wisher, Jean 27
Wisher, Nancy 113
Wistenant, John 139
Wistenant, Nicholas 139
Withers, Amanda C. 268
Withers, B. F. 272
Withers, Benjamin F. 268
Withers, Elizabeth 47
Withers, Isaac N. 268
Withers, J. N. 347
Withers, John B. 268
Withers, John G. 265
Withers, John T. 256
Withers, Randolph 268
Withers, Rufus J. 304
Withers, Sarah M. 269
Withers, T. B. 298, 322

Withers, Walter C. 304
Withers, Wm 213
Withers, Wm. Randolph 268
Witherspoon, Andrew Jackson 233
Witherspoon, David 216
Witherspoon, Donnom 331
Witherspoon, George Mc. 331
Witherspoon, Isaac Donnam 233
Witherspoon, J. D. 187, 219, 233, 267, 319, 331
Witherspoon, J. H. 351
Witherspoon, J. R. 352
Witherspoon, James A. 216
Witherspoon, James H. 233
Witherspoon, John A. 347
Witherspoon, M. E. 351
Witherspoon, Nancy 331
Witherspoon, Sophia G. 352
Wood 358
Wood, Aaron 115, 155, 201, 206, 234
Wood, Achsah 201
Wood, Aron 66
Wood, Dorothy 245
Wood, Eliza C. 210
Wood, F. H. 247, 262
Wood, Foster H. 267
Wood, Isaac 201
Wood, Isabella R. 321
Wood, J. G. 301
Wood, Jacob Ferdinand 313
Wood, Jacob Pinckney 313
Wood, James 109, 182, 196, 200, 202, 227, 313, 316
Wood, James Madison 313
Wood, James Pinckney 313
Wood, John 234, 314, 316
Wood, John K. 201
Wood, John S. L. 313
Wood, Joseph 116, 160, 201
Wood, Joseph George Wellington 313
Wood, Katharine 267
Wood, Margaret 204
Wood, Martha 201
Wood, Mary 313
Wood, Mary Rippy 313
Wood, Matilda 201
Wood, Nancy F. Susannah Dill 313
Wood, Polly 182, 312, 313
Wood, Resin 201
Wood, Robert J. 244, 245
Wood, Sarah 210

## PERSONAL NAME INDEX

Wood, W. H. 271
Wood, William S. 243
Woods, 44, 45
Woods, Andrew 11
Woods, Edith 11
Woods, Nancy 152
Woods, Resin 152
Woods, Thomas 11, 51
Workman, Elizabeth 115
Workman, Isabella 251
Workman, James 115, 116, 129, 150, 155, 251
Workman, James S. 218, 219, 251
Workman, John 14, 115, 116, 129, 239, 293
Workman, John F. 218, 219
Workman, Margaret 115, 129, 251
Workman, Martha 29, 115, 251
Workman, Robert 115, 116, 251
Workman, Robert P. 293
Workman, Sarah 115
Wray, William 276
Wren, Elizabeth 273
Wren, Francis T. 273
Wren, Jeremiah L. 273
Wright 78, 131, 184, 280, 325
Wright, Andrew 92, 93, 99, 137
Wright, Andrew J. 327
Wright, Anna 18
Wright, Catherine 18
Wright, Charles 38
Wright, Cynthia Jane 193
Wright, Doctor 228
Wright, George 99, 134, 141, 216
Wright, Henry 93, 212
Wright, J. L. 219, 325, 326
Wright, James 167, 184, 326
Wright, James L. 207, 211, 257
Wright, James Spratt 325, 327
Wright, John 92, 93, 99, 100, 137, 201
Wright, John F. 327
Wright, Joseph 327
Wright, Lessley 206
Wright, Margaret 212
Wright, Margaret E. 325, 327
Wright, Mary 325, 351
Wright, Nancy 150
Wright, Nancy M. 193
Wright, Polly 100
Wright, Robert Newton 326, 327
Wright, Roderick 131
Wright, Ruth 269

Wright, S. 307
Wright, Sally 100
Wright, Samuel 142, 202, 230, 257, 320, 327, 331, 336
Wright, Sarah 18
Wright, Thomas 150
Wright, W. 270
Wright, William 18, 99, 100, 137, 187, 222, 245, 257, 270, 279, 328, 341, 351
Wright, William J. 326
Wright, Winslow 105
Wyley, Duncan 158
Wylie, Caroline 260, 339
Wylie, Eliza Jane 225
Wylie, Elizabeth 256, 261
Wylie, J. A. 193
Wylie, James 158, 196, 225, 227
Wylie, John J. 335
Wylie, Joseph 220, 256
Wylie, Joseph D. 256
Wylie, Lucinda 256
Wylie, Margaret 256
Wylie, Martha 225
Wylie, Mary 256
Wylie, Mary C. 301
Wylie, Nancy 196
Wylie, Polly 196
Wylie, Samuel 172, 193, 196, 225, 340
Wylie, Sarah C. 273
Wylie, Thomas 156, 311
Wylie, Thomas G. 256, 261, 300
Wylie, William 260, 261, 304, 339
Yarborough, Ann 88, 294
Yarborough, John 135, 154, 221
Yarborough, Minerva 294
Yates, D. 323
Young 279
Young, Agness 21
Young, James 12, 21, 69, 84, 85
Young, Janet 356
Young, John 12, 211, 212, 335
Young, Margaret 84, 85
Young, Mary 21, 300
Young, Robert 28
Young, Samuel 356
Young, William 204, 356
Youngblood, Eliza 286
Youngblood, Henry 286
Youngblood, Lucy 259
Youngblood, Mariann/e J. 331
Youngblood, S. C. 288

## PERSONAL NAME INDEX

Youngblood, Samuel 259
Youngblood, Samuel C. 259, 274
Youngblood, William 177, 189, 208

## SLAVE INDEX

Aaron 126, 128, 187, 198, 266
Abb 105
Abel 16, 179
Abner 134, 223
Abraham 47, 85, 116, 267, 322
Abram 33, 159, 181, 223, 236, 263
Absalom 172, 193, 268
Absolem 147
Adaline 226, 250, 255, 259, 276, 284, 292, 300, 305, 337, 345, 346
Adaline Jane 338
Adam 21, 109, 125, 179, 224, 255, 276, 286, 321, 351, 354, 356
Addaline 89
Addison 274
Adelaide 268
Adeline 168, 213, 341
Adeson 201
Adianda 331
Adolphus 314
Affy 250, 273
African Abel 179
Agg 203
Agga 236
Agge 103
Aggy 121, 127, 198, 242
Agner 130
Aim 87
Aimy 198
Albert 201, 267, 280, 303
Aleck 272, 294, 297
Alexander 262
Alfred 250, 297, 298, 310, 317, 338, 345, 346
Alice 120
Alick 232, 278
Alison 125
Allen 173, 195, 340
Allison 101, 168, 227, 235, 274, 280
Alsey 286, 304
Aly 285
Amaline 253, 302
Amanda 201, 217, 223, 272, 277, 284, 290, 295, 330, 337, 349, 350
Amanda Eliza 338
Ame/y 36, 56, 63, 226
Amos 96, 260, 273
Amy 30, 52, 54, 86, 164, 231, 262, 263, 282, 284, 305, 309, 321, 332, 344
Amzi 230, 232, 235, 300, 303, 338
Anaka 210

Anderson 237, 242, 276
Andrew 150, 192, 207, 223, 301, 337
Andrew Jackson 282
Andy 16, 201, 255, 338, 348
Aney 53
Angeline 315
Anica 191
Ann 102, 105, 147, 185, 227, 240, 243, 244, 252, 257, 264, 284, 287, 308, 310, 322, 337, 342, 344-346, 351
Anna 116, 159, 169, 288
Annica 75
Annie 349
Anny 135, 179, 184
Anson 128, 250
Anthony 63, 99, 223, 263, 296, 338, 344
Anton(e)y 53, 127, 183, 308, 321
Any 115, 218
Any (free), 329
April 172, 211
Araby 107
Arch(e)y 92, 107
Arma 54
Arnold 75, 242, 247
Aron 235
Arter 91
Arthur 121
Asburn 114
Ather[?], 354
Aude 191
Austin 115, 154, 301
Bacc(h)us 155, 217
Bachany 198
Bailey 237
Balaam 109
Barbe 276
Bartlet 117
Becca 261
Beck 8, 33, 63, 107, 108, 111
Becky 222, 288
Bed 259
Belfast 136
Belinda 120
Ben 6, 25, 33, 74, 79, 89, 107, 118, 120, 132, 139, 163, 166, 193, 198, 225, 233, 261, 270, 273-275, 286, 288, 290, 297, 301, 340, 344, 352, 353
Beny 328
Berry 276, 291

## SLAVE INDEX

Bet 37, 203, 239
Bets(e)y 125, 172, 260, 288
Bett/s 16, 64, 275
Betty 16, 79, 102, 107, 134, 168, 179, 218, 270, 288, 321, 328, 331, 342
Beverly 259
Bid 149
Big John 259
Big Peter 273
Bill 159, 180, 195, 198, 203, 213, 238, 244, 275, 293, 300, 340, 344, 353
Billy 87, 121, 253, 267, 270, 284, 337, 358
Bin 107
Black Bill 262
Black Smith Dick 233
Blacksmith Peter 297
Bob 29, 47, 63, 74, 94, 101, 118, 142, 169, 180, 181, 186, 203, 255, 260, 297, 316, 332, 344-346, 354
Bonapart 186
Bonnaparte 309
Booker 263
Boze 177
Bridget 153
Briena[?] 106
Brison 186
Brook 120
Bruce 346
Buenecid[?] 188
Buff 205
Bug 261
Burrell 265
Burwell 317
Butler 107
Caeser 263
Cagle 64
Calhoun 303
Calvin 244, 324, 338, 342
Cambridge 100
Candace 338
Candes 341
Candice 245
Candy 236
Carey 337
Carolina 205
Caroline 153, 159, 168, 202, 223, 230, 255, 258-260, 268, 271, 277, 284, 286, 301, 310, 338, 340
Carter 261, 352
Cass 237, 275
Cassy 241

Cate 18, 87, 117
Catharine 278
Catia 177
Cato 126, 187, 238, 351
Catto 79
Caty 166, 193, 244, 358
Ceasar 188
Celia 153, 209
Cenia 166
Chancy 163
Chandler 312
Chan(e)y 168, 184
Charity 264, 294, 302, 348
Charles 63, 77, 116, 126, 128, 169, 187, 194, 203, 209, 224, 236, 237, 244, 250, 262, 286, 294, 297, 298, 301, 308, 314, 349, 350
Charleston 285
Charlett 73
Charlotte 95, 121, 124, 130, 166, 191, 194, 244, 261, 297, 303, 310
Cherry 20, 72
Chess 266
Chisshire 66
Chloe 11, 190, 297, 346
Cia 255
Cinda 213, 275, 276, 294, 332, 338, 340
Cindah 266
Cintha 150
Cinthy 201
Clarissa 175, 181, 276, 284
Clary[?] 354
Clementine 338
Cloe 107, 174, 236
Coly 336
Condy 303
Corneli(o)us 133, 185
Courey 142
Creasy 169
Crecy 322
Creesa 305
Cresy 232
Cube 21, 356
Cubit 116, 290, 295
Cuffy 249, 337
Cur(r)y 36, 223, 234, 344
Cynthia 46, 85, 280, 302, 334, 348
Cyrus 128, 177, 204, 212, 223, 349
Dafney 255
Dallas 345, 346

## SLAVE INDEX

Dan 49, 117, 291, 308, 320, 321, 345, 346
Dana 297
Daniel 33, 35, 49, 86, 163, 182, 194, 198, 214, 235, 280, 293, 303, 308
Dapheny 176
Daphne 72
Darcus 46, 205
Dark 191
Darky 116, 244
Dave 1, 83, 117, 120, 147, 203, 225, 262, 346
David 76, 103, 163, 233, 267, 286, 298
Davy 133, 247
Dawson 346
Delhi 286
Delilah 101, 219
Delph 276
Delpha 184
Delphy 224
Derryman 29
Dian/a 28, 84, 251, 259
Dianah 53
Dianna 101, 118, 210, 355
Dick 19, 22, 26, 63, 64, 82, 120, 132, 153, 172, 184, 254, 286, 308, 332
Dick Perkins 282
Dico 35
Dilcy 168
Dilla 163
Dilsey 163, 278
Dim 138
Dinah 5, 8, 38, 60, 74, 100, 104, 139, 148, 226, 233, 250, 296, 297
Dine 48
Diner 79
Dise 186
Dizey 213
Doll 6, 26
Dolly 182
Dorcas 169, 263, 299, 321, 324, 349
Dorcus 116, 203
Dorea 359
Dovee[?] 175
Dovey 209
Dovve 28
Drucilla 336
Duff 37
Dulcina 275, 276
Dun 49
Ealse 101, 138
Easther 52, 150, 231

Ed 332
Edie 16
Edmond 184, 220, 281, 303
Edmund 98, 232, 354
Edom 102
Edward 278
Edwin 321
Edy 326
Ela 274
Eleanor 285
Eleck 138
Eli 221, 297, 340
Elias 33, 218
Elijah 109
Elim 294
Elisa 198
Elise[?] 237
Eliza 63, 147, 159, 166, 168, 201, 225, 233, 250, 252, 255, 264, 272, 275, 284, 299, 300, 308, 317, 329, 337, 343, 348, 353, 358
Elleck 118
Ellen 270, 301, 334, 335, 337
Ellick 140
Ellis 289
Ellison 276, 349
Elmiry[?] 203
Elon 186
Else 173
Elvira 153, 214, 235, 291
Elvy 135, 166
Emalene 282
Emaline 223, 247
Eme 148
Emeline 260, 305, 343, 348
Emeline Ann 346
Emily 302, 303, 347
Emily Ann 338
Emmy 332
Enoriah 355
Enos 148, 270
Ephraim 33, 201, 302, 337, 343
Esau 319
Esra 190
Est(h)er 30, 115, 154, 179, 212, 286, 288, 353
Ety 243, 244
Eunice 258
Eva 162, 275
Eve 37, 117, 321
Fab 91
Fabby 35

## SLAVE INDEX

Falley 242
Fan/n 35, 90, 124, 198, 263
Fann(e)y 20, 26, 75, 79, 152, 190, 220, 232, 267, 277, 294, 334
Fawn 226
Fayette 240
Feab 31, 195
Feb/e 86, 254
Fed 345, 346
Feeb 33
Feeby 291
Festus 116
Fib 183
Fir 120
Flora 16, 223, 233, 250, 282, 344, 349
Floro 15
Foster 291, 337
Francis 218
Francis Drake 116
Frank 26, 37, 117, 121, 127, 161, 201, 228, 241, 249, 250, 267, 294, 297, 315, 350, 353
Franky 139, 329
Frederick 30
Friday 131
Furrow 47
Gabe 276
Gace[?] 191
Garland 152
Gean 261
Geoffry 28
George 20, 24, 64, 69, 93, 106, 116, 122, 124, 150, 153, 181, 194, 201, 223-225, 231, 261, 278, 283, 285, 293, 295, 297, 301-303, 309, 321, 324, 331, 338, 344, 348, 349, 354
George Russell 338
Gilbert 171, 337
Giles 308, 321
Gilly 133
Gin 13
Ginny 87
Gladman 242
Golden 278
Gosia Miller 116
Grace 47, 295, 310
Graes 48
Granby 125
Grandison 274
Gran[?] 179
Green 201, 205, 218, 226, 231, 261, 277

Hal 150
Hamilton 267
Hampton 203, 277
Hannah 1, 27, 31, 35, 64, 86, 88, 104, 120, 130, 160, 165, 170, 175, 186, 193, 222, 232, 241, 263, 275, 276, 286, 291, 292, 297, 305, 337, 338, 344, 359
Hannah Mahela 282
Harding[?] 286
Hariet 346
Harmon 54
Harriet 107, 119, 147, 159, 185, 204, 250, 252, 255, 258, 260-262, 264, 267, 276, 280, 286, 287, 292, 297, 305, 315, 332, 338, 340
Harriot 111, 135, 166, 168, 199, 233, 243
Harry 15, 31, 35, 64, 77, 78, 107, 111, 117, 171, 182, 192, 207, 295
Harv(e)y 244, 317, 352
Henry 95, 155, 166, 174, 204, 214, 251, 252, 257, 272, 273, 278, 280, 291, 292, 294, 295, 297, 303, 321, 338, 343-346
Henry Griffin 276
Herriot 130
Hesse 33
Hester 243, 276, 359
Hicks 125, 186, 218, 275
Hiram 286, 340
Holly 223, 344, 349
Horah 66
Howard 275
Hugh 253, 299
Hulday 198
Humphrey 299
Ibby 339
Icey[?] 107
Isaac 30, 52, 66, 117, 123, 127, 153, 163, 165, 180, 194, 198, 203, 233, 236, 258, 270, 286, 290, 297, 301, 315, 321, 341, 343, 353
Isabel 188
Isabella 133, 180, 186, 187, 267, 278, 303, 346, 349
Isac/k 89, 191
Isam 133
Isbel 135, 151, 238
Isem 173
Isey 107
Isham 168

**SLAVE INDEX**

Isom 111, 166, 197, 213, 273, 280
Jack 8, 13, 37, 47, 60, 64, 102, 105, 107, 119, 121, 131, 150, 152, 172, 183, 194, 195, 199, 203, 225, 242, 253, 284, 288, 293, 297, 310, 324, 352, 353
Jack Williams 271
Jacke 64
Jackeah 191
Jackoles 308
Jackson 337
Jacob 64, 111, 117, 130, 135, 166, 169, 243, 267, 276, 291, 294, 319, 332, 341
Jag 118
Jake 117, 297, 298, 345, 346
James 28, 87, 130, 165, 250
Jamima 28
Jane 79, 120, 155, 165, 186, 193, 205, 223, 237, 244, 247, 250, 258, 276, 291, 303, 336-338, 343, 345-347
January 28, 37, 86
Jean 11, 191, 199, 297, 353
Jeff 111, 236, 344, 348
Jefferson 153
Jemima 205, 236
Jeneva 334
Jenkins 263
Jenn(e)y 63, 78, 96, 121, 254, 257, 275
Jep 139
Jerry 15, 125, 159, 174, 186, 228, 355
Jess 156, 255, 301, 355
Jesse 96, 275, 276, 281, 301
Jiles 291
Jill 1
Jim 24, 53, 54, 63, 107, 127, 139, 152, 179, 191, 193, 198, 237, 239, 243, 258, 276, 287, 288, 294, 301, 308, 310, 346, 352
Jim Williams 271
Jimmy 125, 317
Jin 91
Jincey 104, 297, 298
Jin(n)ey 194, 204
Jo 170, 345, 346
Joan 153
Joe 1, 8, 31, 47, 48, 52, 111, 122, 131, 146, 150, 184, 185, 213, 223, 255, 270, 286, 297, 298, 301, 310, 343

John 116, 130, 169, 223, 225, 226, 238, 239, 241, 259, 264, 266, 274, 276, 284, 286, 293, 297, 298, 303, 332, 338, 346, 349, 350, 355
Johnson 319
Jordan 57, 213, 276
Joseph 28, 53, 101, 181, 190, 250, 275, 289, 295, 301
Joshua 213
Juda/e 111, 173, 218
Jude 13, 25, 29, 60, 117, 134, 159, 173, 199, 203, 278, 286
Judy 86, 135, 179, 232, 238, 244
Jule 117
Julia 135, 263, 271, 301, 339
Juliann 358
Julie 345, 346
Juliet 267, 281, 353
Julius 177, 261
July 107
Juna 73
June 20, 107, 117, 130, 194
Kate 11, 106, 130, 173, 288, 336
Katena 183
Katharine 242
Keat 8
Kesiah 199, 237
Kiah 294
Kiney 185
Kit 13, 290
Kitten 294
Kitty 28, 107, 244, 358
Kiziah 286
Kizzy 287
Lancaster 184
Laray 180
Lark 313
Larkin 101
Laura 286, 290, 340, 343
Lavenia 133, 150
Lavina 102, 147, 185, 213
Lawson Henderson 339
Law[?] 199
Leah 353
Leander 232, 294, 309, 332, 337
Leane 177
Leca 349
Led 257
Lee 340
Leethe 89
Leggat 275
Legle[?] 226

## SLAVE INDEX

Lemon 152
Len 164
Lena 276
Leonard 150, 332
Leroy 211, 260
Lessey 153
Lett 142
Letta 280
Letty 136, 230, 262, 354
Levi 104, 149, 150, 263
Lewey 75
Lewis 63, 75, 101, 125, 166, 174, 179-181, 276, 287, 303, 308, 340
Lid 66
Lidia 105, 106, 169
Ligal 204
Lile 118
Lin 170
Lincoln 110
Linda 194, 218, 258
Lind(a)y 89, 203
Lindsay 293
Linus 107
Lisle 8
Lissa 276
Little 246
Little Bob 203
Little Charles 63
Little Jim 345, 346
Little Joe 184
Little John 259
Little Peter 273
Little Rose 272
Littleton 246
Liza 210, 255, 284
Lizzy(ie) 344, 349
Loe 273
Lond 95, 193
London 13, 191
Lonon 213
Loosy 205
Losson 358
Lot/t 226, 260, 293, 302, 348
Louisa 259, 277, 280, 286, 290, 332, 340, 343
Louise 259, 338
Lousana 186
Lovey 75, 273
Luce 25, 27, 47, 79, 107, 117, 180
Lucey 8, 165
Lucinda 101, 175, 301, 314, 324, 334
Lucretia 275

Lucy 11, 19, 60, 91, 98, 107, 162, 165, 192, 208, 213, 243, 244, 263, 270, 276, 286, 301, 345, 246
Luecy 53
Luiza 353
Luke 115
Lum 297
Luse 77
Lyd(i)a 104, 107, 166
Lydia 338
Lynn 359
Madison 116
Maida 198
Mal 276
Malinda/h 53, 199, 277, 291, 294
Mall 25
Manaway 131
Manda 353
Mander 286
Mansfield 232
March 51
Margaret 111, 199, 223, 225, 258, 276, 277, 280, 284, 286, 297, 298, 305, 308, 315, 316, 324, 332, 338, 345, 346, 350
Maria 64, 168, 242, 259, 344
Mariah 147, 149, 168, 172, 181, 198, 205, 232, 250, 251, 257, 258, 261, 262, 267, 275, 278, 300, 334, 342
Mark 305
Marry 134
Mars 233, 340
Martha 175, 251, 253, 261, 272, 290, 300, 302, 322, 329, 343, 348
Martha Ann 247
Martin 276
Mary 53, 66, 79, 138, 150, 168, 181, 186, 194, 198, 199, 205, 210, 218, 223, 232, 237, 238, 247, 251, 260, 262, 264, 267, 272, 275, 286, 287, 295, 316, 321, 329, 330, 337, 339, 345, 346, 349, 350, 352
Mary Ann 167, 252, 321, 351
Mary Jane 285, 339
Mary Susan 345, 346
Mary/Ma 235
Matilda 147, 167, 213, 259, 265, 337
Matt 250
May 108
McFadden 345
Melia 162
Melie 11

## SLAVE INDEX

Melinda 80, 217
Melissa 214, 297
Melitia 157
Mellon 338
Mender 63
Meriah 184
Merievoa 240
Micke 1
Mida 170, 232
Mike 359
Miles 305, 310
Miley 66
Mill/s 138, 230, 276
Milla 159
Mill(e)y 33, 57, 75, 77, 78, 115, 122, 156, 165, 169, 177, 181, 214, 245, 258, 266, 283, 295, 324, 332, 358
Mille 88
Miller 247, 254
Milton 253, 262, 270
Mima 181, 346
Mimay 62
Mime 166
Minerva 205, 223, 344
Miney 114
Mingo 170, 198, 337
Minny 313, 328, 348
Minor 144, 223, 226, 261, 343
Mint 324
Minta 40, 162, 163, 193
Minter 255
Minty 201
Mira 276
Miriah 135
Missy 173
Mitchel 217
Molly 250, 270, 343
Molly Esther 317
Monro/e 267, 329, 340
Montony 188
More 187
Moriah 159, 202, 239
Morris 29, 205, 337
Mose 118, 226
Moses 46, 80, 101, 107, 117, 119, 121, 125, 169, 172, 199, 251
Moss 38
Munday 31
Myles 335
Nan 8, 13, 31, 37, 105, 214, 321
Nance 47, 48, 58, 91, 114, 150

Nancy 23, 153, 172, 111, 192, 198, 207, 235, 243, 246, 250 277, 286, 297, 298, 303, 309, 315, 322, 330, 334
Nani 54
Nann 21, 24, 356
Naomi 338
Narcissa 126, 288, 291
Nat 9
Necessa 187
Ned 8, 31, 33, 35, 55, 92, 99, 105-109, 116, 139, 162, 166, 172, 173, 186, 198, 242, 244, 273, 276, 281, 284, 286, 301, 303
Need 355
Neel 345, 346
Nell 1, 31, 32, 86, 290
Nelly 213, 259, 310
Nelse 276
Nelson 107, 159, 182, 194, 205, 250, 316, 339, 346, 354
Nemo[?] 292
Neptune 78
Nercissa 344
Nero 276, 291
Netty 317
New 286
Newton 264, 297
Ninah 346
Nolen 305
Nonie[?] 120
Norris 297
Ochra 230
Old Adam 166
Old Ben 294
Old Jane 294
Old London 283
Old Sarah 286
Orseola 286
Osamy 276
Osborne 294
Osburn 251
Oscar 314
Paddy 120
Pad[?] 205
Pamela 196, 197
Pan[?] 117
Past 250
Pasty 258
Pat 119, 120, 179, 198, 276
Pate 55

## SLAVE INDEX

Patience 163, 201, 224, 236, 286, 302, 303, 346, 348
Patrick 291
Pats(e)y 155, 223, 260, 267, 332
Patt/s 35, 106, 107
Patty 169, 213, 242, 255, 343
Paulina 153
Peat 54
Peet 16
Peg/g 21, 86, 93, 97, 356
Peggy 133, 155, 181, 242, 252, 273, 286, 305, 309, 345, 346
Peggy Will 157
Pelina 159
Pen 109, 163
Penelope 297
Penny 199, 283, 346
Perlina 201
Perlinda 179
Pero 13, 123
Perry 278, 343
Pete 166
Peter 8, 24, 54, 85, 91-93, 95, 107, 120, 127, 131, 166, 172, 177, 181, 198, 213, 226, 259, 266, 270, 276, 286, 297, 330
Petre 101
Pettey 180
Pheb 37, 64
Phebe 24, 26, 63, 106, 126, 147, 155, 187, 200, 235, 241, 276, 337
Phebe Ann 338
Phebia 181
Pheby 125
Pheoba 19
Philes 275
Philip 30, 286
Philis 29, 290, 346
Phil/l 8, 182
Philles 1
Phillips 135, 177
Phillis 64, 148, 218, 283, 286, 297, 330, 354
Pickens 308
Pilly[?] 138
Pink 106
Pinky 179
Pinny 75
Pleasant 283, 355
Plent 297
Polina 218

Pol/l 12, 38, 139, 163, 233, 235-237, 251
Polly 107, 163, 209, 235, 252, 308, 354
Pompey 135
Pricilla 121
Primas 74, 193
Prime 128
Primus 107, 128, 155
Prince 20, 85, 93, 117
Priscilla 322
Pru 93
Puff 204
Pug 255
Rach 1, 138
Rach(a)el 16, 33, 74-76, 85-87, 105, 106, 124, 133, 167, 168, 174, 186, 225, 235, 260, 267, 270, 275, 294, 299, 345, 346, 354
Ralph 120, 173
Randal/l 197, 251, 275
Randolph 244, 297
Ransom 287
Rawley 163
Rebecca 172, 176, 185, 236, 294, 317
Rena/h 285, 332, 346
Rener 280
Reuben 259, 354
Rhena 252, 253, 274
Rhinah 253
Rhoda 270
Rhode 63
Rhody 261, 353
Ric 321
Rice 276
Richard 165, 209, 233
Richardson 124
Richmond 130
Riley 276
Rin 250
Rine 303
Ritta 166, 180, 183
Ritty 250
Roary 160
Robb 169
Robert 252
Rody 49
Rorey 13, 64
Rosa 223
Rose 7, 25, 30, 31, 14, 74, 117, 126, 128, 150, 157, 187, 191, 214, 226, 243, 297, 306, 313, 353
Roseline 348

## SLAVE INDEX

Rosetta 181
Rosinda 193
Ross 262, 310
Rosy 135
Rowel 345
Roxana 334
Rube 186
Rueben 276
Rufus 297, 298, 332, 337
Runy 104, 268
Russ 199
Ruth 46, 63, 147
Ruthy 280, 281
Sabina 46, 95
Sabrina 134
Sale 111
Saley 109
Sal/l 19, 28, 63, 64, 117, 120, 133, 173, 276
Sall(e)y 6, 131, 159, 173, 184, 209, 244, 266, 273, 353
Sam 9, 14, 26, 28, 36, 60, 63, 64, 66, 73, 74, 79, 91, 100, 101, 111, 116, 128, 141, 147, 148, 163, 168, 172, 187, 194, 198, 201, 213, 223, 224, 232, 236, 237, 244, 250, 251, 254, 260, 261, 272, 273, 275, 284, 291, 297, 310, 312, 315, 321, 322, 337, 338, 345, 346, 350
Sambo 136, 139, 233
Sampson 20, 53, 90, 149, 194, 198, 250, 273, 284
Samson 28
Samuel 172, 225
Sandy 16, 168, 297
Sank 49
Sann[?] 357
Sara 31
Sarah 11, 28, 53, 79, 101, 103, 105, 119, 128, 131, 152, 168, 172, 178, 179, 184, 205, 207, 210, 213, 225, 238, 243, 251, 273, 285, 291, 303, 308, 310, 338, 340, 341, 343, 347, 350
Sarah Julia 181
Sarah the Elder 168
Saraho 199
Savilla 332
Scicilly 159
Scipio 250
Sciss 294
Scylla 159

Sealy 286
Seaser 53
Sela 134
Selena 250, 260, 291
Selina 177, 204
Selline 79
Selvanus 237
Sendavella 275
Septima[?] 340
Serena 64
Shadrach 303
Shed 322
Shelton 349
Si 185
Siah 78, 344
Sias 179
Siby 261
Sigh 231
Sil 187
Silah 175
Silas 168, 178, 288
Sileah 288
Siley 261
Sill 185
Silla 163
Siller 276
Silt 125
Silva 54, 127, 159
Silv(e)y 74, 95, 198, 212, 234, 250, 263, 272, 353
Simeon 77, 98
Simmon 342
Simon 34, 104, 166, 169, 177, 193, 218, 225, 268, 284, 348
Simpson 278
Sinah 348
Sinak 201
Sinar 194
Sinda 134
Sintha 164, 355, 358
Sinthey 153
Smith 230, 286, 289, 291
Snow 9
Soloman 353
Solomon 16, 242, 311, 338
Sook 175
Sophia 147, 176, 181, 193
Sophy 277, 331
Squire 45
Stanford 346
Stanhope 268
Starky 237

## SLAVE INDEX

Step 38
Stephen 15, 88, 115, 154, 198, 201, 223-225, 252, 266, 309, 321, 328, 351, 353, 359
Steve 358
Steven 173
Su 27
Suck 135, 312
Suck(e)y 78, 198, 308
Sue 8, 15, 64, 109, 160, 223, 232, 263, 280
Suf/f 31, 96, 342
Suffy 346
Sukey 21
Sup 118
Surrenna 75
Susan 188, 236, 291, 294, 304, 315, 321, 338
Susanna/h 210, 276
Susy 308
Su[?] 243
Sye 64, 338
Sylla 99
Sylva 54
Sylvanus 267, 290
Sylvia 66, 131, 272, 276
Sylvy 343
Synthia 329
Tabitha 287
Tally 92
Tame[?] 186
Tann 106
Taylor 261, 306
Temay 282
Tena 183, 233, 334
Theresa 265
Tholly 166
Thom 329
Thomas 82, 187, 258, 301
Thompson 218
Tilda/h 79, 127
Tildey 165
Till 286
Tilla 340
Tim 346
Tina 293
Tinker 251
Tira 253
Tirie 29
Titus 346
Tober 8
Tob(e)y 106

Tom 1, 16, 37, 64, 75, 79, 89, 119, 131, 133, 138, 147, 160, 198, 203, 207, 225, 235, 237, 241, 242, 250, 261, 263, 273, 276, 286, 294, 297, 298, 301, 310, 338, 358
Tomson 89
Ton(e)y 53, 85, 101, 111, 119, 128, 169, 173, 199, 213, 243, 250, 267, 345, 346
Tony Miller 116
Torry 234
Turner 352
Van Buren 294
Vena 280
Venice 64
Vice 276
Vilet 66, 147
Vily 254
Vina 308
Vin(e)y 169, 235, 261, 284, 338
Violet 135, 155, 174, 239, 252, 261, 267, 273, 284, 290, 291, 297, 321, 343
Virgil 21, 217
Walker 96, 193, 342, 344
Warren 102, 337
Washington 159, 165, 182, 184, 195, 303, 324
Waties 337
Watson 135, 337
Watt 107
Wesley 315, 337
Wheeler 297
White 292
Wiley 198
Will 8, 19, 20, 31, 37, 80, 102, 130, 158, 159, 183, 272, 357
William 159, 183, 286, 297, 298, 321, 338
Willis 122, 213
Wills 54
Wilson 120, 285, 297, 323
Wiltha 80
Winna 159
Winne 63
Winn(e)y 84, 107, 120, 172, 179, 273, 302, 355
Winy 147
Wyona 286
Yellow Bill 262
Yogue 134
York 11

**SLAVE INDEX**

Young Adam 166
Young Ben 294
Young Charles 346
Young Jane 294
Young London 283
Young Sarah 286
Young Simon 346
Younger Nancy 345, 346
Youngue 305
Zacheriah 163
Zenah 150
Zimri 334

## PLACE INDEX

A. R. Church 279
Abbeville District 279
Aera Iron Works 59
Alabama 164, 172, 185, 198, 201, 242, 246, 268, 287, 352
Allison Creek 21, 86, 208, 313, 337, 356
American Tract Society 279
Amherst County, Virginia 146
Anderson's Creek 352
Anson County, NC 8, 9, 102
Antrim County, Ireland 53, 97, 286
Antrim Ireland 53
Antrim Parish Ireland 97
Arkansas 319, 330
Armor's ford 353
Ashville, NC 279
Associate Congregation of Steel Creek 354
Associate Reformed Congregation 149
Associate Reformed Presbyterian Church 326
Athens, Georgia 351
Babtist mission 216
Balleymaney, Ireland 286
Ballysavage Bern'd Lyndon 97
Baltimore, Bank Street, Water Street 80
Baltimore, Maryland 80, 119, 279, 341
Barnwell District 158
Beaver Dam Creek 59, 137, 145, 146, 157
Beaver Dam, Crowders Creek 245
Beaverdam 54, 223, 248
Becky's branch 329, 342
Bells Creek 222
Bersheba Church 330
Bethany Church 310
Bethel Church 216, 248
Bethel Congregation 23
Bethesda Congregation 53
Big Allisons Creek 116
Big Sugar Creek 183
Biggars Ferry on the Cataba 37
Black Jack field 270
Black Jack Grounds 31
Black Jack line 233
Blairsville 278, 341
Bledsoe Tennessee 357
Broad River 17, 146, 200, 206, 214, 228, 252, 308, 320, 334, 345, 352
Broad River Bridge Co. 278
Brown Creek NC 8
Buckhorn fork 51
Buffaloe Creek 145, 168, 225,
Buffaloe Mills 347
Buffaloe stump 229
Bullocks Creek 17, 19, 26, 28, 30, 34, 48, 50, 51, 53, 54, 71, 72, 73, 90, 104, 136, 164, 200, 276, 314, 328
Buncombe County NC 131, 353
Bunkham County NC 85
Burk road 344
Burmah mission 216
Butree[?] Creek NC 85
Buzzard Creek Tennessee 176
Cain Creek NC 139
Caldwell County 352
Camden 183
Camden Bank 278, 279, 326, 327
Camden District 3, 4, 6, 11, 12, 15, 21, 357
Cany fork Drowsy Creek NC 324
Catawba County 352
Catawba River 37, 39, 102, 122, 194, 292, 298, 306, 325, 345, 346, 352
Charleston & Cincinnati Rail Road Company 238
Charleston 66, 81, 279, 325, 326
Charleston District 347
Charleston road 329
Charlotte & South Carolina Rail Road, 274, 298
Charlotte NC 263, 298, 328
Charlotte Rail Road 306
Cheraw 277, 355
Cherokee Creek 33, 55
Chester 328
Chester Bank 325, 326, 328
Chester County 10, 71, 76
Chester District 43, 58, 82, 83, 134, 141, 241, 261, 269, 277, 349, 355
Chesterville 270
Chirah, Merchants Bank 277
Clark's Fork 28, 50, 71, 90, 258
Clems branch 38
Cleveland County, NC 275, 276
Columbia 119, 279
Commercial Bank, Columbia 277, 278, 325, 326, 355
County of Antrim, Ireland 97
Craven County 4, 12, 171, 356

## PLACE INDEX

Crowder's Creek 31, 66, 152, 188, 189, 226, 245, 296
Crowders Creek, NC 245
Currence Road 305
Dan River, Virginia 35
Darlington District 183
Davidson College NC 305, 321
Denegor, Ireland 53
Ditty Place 318
Drumahagles, Ireland 285
Duck River, Tennessee 128
Due West Corner 279
Dunagon 97
Dunagon, Ireland 97
Dunkins Creek 45
Dutchmans Creek 207
Ebenezar Church 112
Ebenezer Presbyterian Church 262
Ebet's Creek 17
Elbert County Georgia 19
Ellisons Creek 5
Erskine Seminary 279
Eutaw Springs 37
Fairfield District 122, 189
Farmer's & Planter's Bank 279, 341
Fishing Creek 7, 18, 30, 31, 95, 116, 118, 131, 134, 142, 154, 160, 207, 173, 250, 262, 272, 273, 283, 358
Florida 319
Four Mills Creek 47
Gallatin County Illinois 268
Gaston County NC 333, 334, 352
Georgetown road 215, 216
Georgia 19, 160, 227, 242, 289
Gilkey's Creek 17
Gion Moores Creek 334
Graniteville Manufacturing Co. 325
Guyen Moores Creek 33
Halifax County, NC 140
Halifax County, Virginia 35
Hamburg 328
Hamburg Bank 278, 325, 326, 340
Haywood County, Tennessee 352
Hibernian Society 279
Hickory Creek 275
Hills Iron Works 116
Hopewell 138
Houlston River 20
Illinois 172
Independent Presbyterian Church 285, 334
Indiana 312

Ireland 53, 71, 97, 286
Ireland, Drumahagles 285
John's Island 347
Jones Creek in 9
Kentucky 48, 59, 90, 242
Kilbride 97
King Creek 252
King Mountain Iron Company 311
Kings bottom 306
Kings Creek 33, 114, 194, 195, 308
Kings Mountain 195
Kings Mountain Rail Road Company 290, 310, 314, 318, 327, 330, 337
Kings Mountain, Battle Ground & the Crowbar 240
Lancaster District 60, 233, 298, 306
Langrams branch 131
Lick Creek NC 8
Linches Creek 123
Lincoln County, NC 26, 78, 176, 177, 245, 298, 352, 353
Lincoln Road 208, 321
Little Allison Creek 304
little Broad River 275
Little Catawba 21
Little Catawba Creek 177, 356
Little River 17
Livingston County, Kentucky 166
Locust Ridge place 201
Londonderry 279
Long Creek NC 78
Louisiana 103
Lower Steel Creek Church 312
Marion, Alabama 279
Maryland 80
Maury County, Tennessee 326
Mecklenburg County NC 4, 8, 37, 152, 194, 321, 353-355
Mill Creek 13, 96, 342
Millstone branch 38
Mississippi 229, 260, 310
Missouri 323
Mitchells Creek 303
Montgomery County, Tennessee 354
Moore's Branch 39
Moores Creek 71
Morrisons Creek 153
Nation Ford Road 312
Neds branch 252
Neely's Creek 25, 149, 251, 260
Neelys Creek Church 340
Neil Branch 342

465

## PLACE INDEX

New Acquisition District 10
New Acquisitions 11
New York 110, 279
Newberry Bank 326, 328
Ninety Six District 3
North Carolina 4, 8, 13, 25, 26, 29, 37, 60, 85, 102, 131, 139, 140, 152, 154, 167, 176-178, 194, 218, 245, 248, 275, 298, 304, 324, 333, 334, 351-356
North Carolina State Bank 277, 325
North County NC 78
Northampton County NC 154
Old Nation ford 47
Orangeburgh District 44
Packlot River 78
Paco Creek 353
Pacolet River 19, 145, 278
Pendleton District 171, 185
Pennsylvania 14, 21
Peoples Bank of Charleston 325, 326
Pery[?] County 353
Petesburg 279
Philadelphia 353
Pike County 323
Pikeville 357
Pinckney 331
Pinckney District 17, 22
Pinckney road 303
Pinckneyville SC, 172, 278
Quins Road 193
Richland District 80
Robinson County Tennessee
Rock Mountain 352
Rocky Allison Creek, 247, 256
Rocky Branch 353
Rowan County, NC 356
Rutherford County, NC 25, 178, 218
Rutherford, NC 139, 353
Rutherfordton 352
Rut[?] Road 275
Saluda Road 27
Saw Mill Place 268
SC Rail Road 278, 279, 326, 340
Schoolhouse branch 288
Scotland 97
Serats Creek 3
Sharon Congregation 278
Sharon Graveyard 277
Six Mile Creek 286
Smith ford road 321
Snyder's Creek 352

South Western Rail Road Bank 326
Southern Board of Foreign Missions 279
Spartanburgh County 33
Spartanburgh District 55, 78, 145, 146, 182, 313
St. John Parish 82
Statesville, NC 351
Steel Creek 37
Stone Graveyard 287
Stoney fork 31, 34, 116
Suder waters 275
Sugar Creek 38, 263, 298
Sumter District 215
Swann's bridge 329
Taylors Creek 115, 129, 163, 174, 251, 254
Ten mile creek 122
Tennessee 60, 62, 120, 177, 190, 201, 241, 242, 319
Texas 332, 347, 351
Theological Seminary 279
Thicketty Creek 145, 313
Thorn ferry road 199
Tipton County, Tennessee 352
Tools Fork Creek 283
Tryon County NC 29
Turkey Creek 15, 41, 94, 103, 172, 216, 242, 268, 278, 285, 318
Twelve mile Creek NC 8
Union District 145, 182, 228, 229, 303, 349
Union land 351
Unity Church 298, 320
Virginia 12, 35, 146, 182, 242
Washington DC 111
Washitaw River 275
White Oak Creek 23
Wild Cat waters 250
Wild Catt Creek 53
William's Creek 352
Williamsburg district 215, 216
Winston County, Mississippi 229
Wolf Creek 179, 252, 303
York County, Pennsylvania 151
York District NC 167
York Village 167, 242, 271
Yorkville Compiler 245
Yorkville Female Collegiate Institute 326

www.ingramcontent.com/pod-product-compliance
Lightning Source LLC
Chambersburg PA
CBHW072128220426
43664CB00013B/2175